BEHIND THE COUNSELOR'S DOOR

*Solutions to the
Most Common
Middle Schooler's
Problems*

BOBBI RISE

outskirts
press

The opinions expressed in this manuscript are solely the opinions of the author and do not represent the opinions or thoughts of the publisher. The author has represented and warranted full ownership and/or legal right to publish all the materials in this book.

Behind the Counselor's Door
Solutions to the Most Common Middle Schooler's Problems
All Rights Reserved.
Copyright © 2016 Bobbi Rise
v2.0

Cover Photo © 2016 thinkstockphotos.com. All rights reserved - used with permission.

This book may not be reproduced, transmitted, or stored in whole or in part by any means, including graphic, electronic, or mechanical without the express written consent of the publisher except in the case of brief quotations embodied in critical articles and reviews.

Outskirts Press, Inc.
http://www.outskirtspress.com

ISBN: 978-1-4787-7856-1

Library of Congress Control Number: 2016910636

Outskirts Press and the "OP" logo are trademarks belonging to Outskirts Press, Inc.

PRINTED IN THE UNITED STATES OF AMERICA

Dedication and Appreciation

My most humungous thank you to Patty W., whose idea this was. I am grateful for her as a trusted messenger, or angel, through whom the encouragement I needed came. This book would not be started or done if it weren't for her "guided" suggestion, followed by her gentle but constant push, cheering me on for years. She reminded me that I wasn't retired from my calling to help children, even after I retired as a school counselor. I hope I will achieve her vision.

To Yvonne D., my loving and inspirational source of spiritual guidance, I thank her for teaching me to challenge my self-doubts and help me to replace them with gratitude and positivity. She has helped me trust in the Universe and reach for that sunshine that could help me continue being an advocate for children. She has been in my life for almost forty years, nurturing me, my purpose, and my passion, and always, always offering help, however I needed it. She was my student, became my teacher, and is a wonderful reminder that angels walk the earth. She has my love and gratitude.

To my dear, dear friend Pam C., who understood the importance of this project and volunteered to support me as my first editor throughout the years – my sincerest thanks! She always seemed to be there right when life slowed me down, even though she was on the other side of the country. She was another angel sent to make this happen. I give my thanks to her from my very soul.

I also want to give my overwhelming appreciation to Sue D., the consummate editing professional, who brought these twenty chapters to the finish line. I have been blessed that she not only became a friend, but was also willing to spend many months working on my project. Angels arrived in many forms during the writing of this book, and she was certainly a timely one!

Thank you to all of my friends who offered to be a reader, editor, or support person. I guess, as my friend Mary always says, "I need a lot of people!" You all know who you are and can share in any positive difference this makes in the lives of others as it all ripples into the future.

And last, or first, and everywhere through and through, I give total gratitude for my husband of almost fifty years, Jack, who gave me an immediate thumbs-up on this project. Thanks to the man who provided me with quiet writing space for all the time I needed, and showed confidence in me all along the way.

Introduction

This series is a collection of real experiences of middle-school students, whose problems brought them to the school counselor. Their stories are told here. They represent twenty different typical problems that affect students most commonly in that highly emotional and socially unskilled environment. The experience of going through middle school is like nothing else a person will go through in his or her life. It not only offers a process of learning how to have friends and keep them, but also teaches lessons in social behavior that we carry with us as adults forevermore. It is a time full of bumps and bruises, and we either learn survival skills with integrity and character, or we don't--and that will make all the difference in our lives.

As we reach out to help middle-school students, it is so important that parents and professionals use these life lessons to show them how to become tolerant and accepting, compassionate and caring, fair and responsible. If we think of these experiences as bad, we lose the flavor of the gift. We are all here to learn, and we are all here to teach. Let's hope we do both with integrity. And if I can offer any wisdom from my own education, human understanding, and career in student growth and socialization, then that will be my pass-it-forward for the good of society.

I hope you are able to find as many clever ways to use these stories with their discussion notes and reflection questions as you can design. They are written to offer help to students who are shy, defensive, fearful, or ashamed, because they tell stories about other people. This avoids raising the defenses of the reader or listener. I truly wish I'd had someone who shared this collection of insightful experiences with me when I first started as a school counselor. I am happy now that this collection is in a form that can be used for students by their counselors, teachers, librarians, parents, and administrators of any middle-school family. Remember, every student is a potential neighbor, relative, co-worker, or president, so let's teach them well!

Table of Contents

Chapter 1: **Best Friends Forever?** (Close Friendships Changing) 1
Uh-Oh! 1
Timing Is Everything 3
Kind Truth 5
I Messages 9
Staying in the Moment 11
Discussion Points & Reflection Questions 13

Chapter 2: **Understanding Others Helps YOU!** (Leading Bullies to Feel Compassion for Sensitive People) 14
What's Wrong with Me? 14
Helping Bullies? 16
The Set-Up 18
Shift Number One – Jason's Mom 20
Shift Number Two 22
Jason's Back! 27
The Last Shift 28
Discussion Points & Reflection Questions 32

Chapter 3: **My Teacher Is Picking on Me!** (Students' Problems with Teachers and Failure Spirals) 33
Teddy's Defense 33
The Plan 36
Did "The Plan" Pass? 39
The Verdict 42
Discussion Points & Reflection Questions 45

Chapter 4: **Our Friends, Our Mirrors** (You Can Control Only Your Own Actions) 46
She's So Mean! 46
Plain Khaki or Grasshopper Green? 48
The Shock 50
The Twist 50
Discussion Points & Reflection Questions 54

Chapter 5: **I Feel So Lost and Alone** (Being New at School) 55
Orientation Panic 55
Butterflies in the Stomach 56
New This, New That, New Everything! 58
The Post-Tour Tour 61
First-Day Jitters 62
Discussion Points & Reflection Questions 64

Chapter 6:	**My Brain Feels Flooded and My Chest Is Pounding!** (Test Anxiety)	65
	What's Happening to Me?	65
	Phew!	67
	Hmmm	69
	The Monday Morning Voice-mail	72
	Discovering the Seed!	73
	Discussion Points & Reflection Questions	78
Chapter 7:	**But She Swore She Would Never, Ever Tell Anyone!** (Telling Secrets)	79
	Sleepover Invitations Hit the School	79
	Where Do I Run and Hide?	80
	Three O'clock	83
	From Five to Nine	84
	Silence	85
	The Monday Morning Post-Party "Buzz"	87
	Discussion Points & Reflection Questions	89
Chapter 8:	**Do I Save a Friend, Knowing It Will Cost Us Our Friendship?** (When to Call for Help for a Desperate Friend)	90
	Approach-Avoidance	90
	It's all in the Timing	93
	The Call	97
	In Just a Week	100
	Discussion Points & Reflection Questions	101
Chapter 9:	**He's Too Cool for Me at School** (Finding the Right Social Group)	102
	Fair-weather Friends	102
	A Two-Way Deal	105
	The Wall Ball Difference	108
	Colin's Lesson	109
	And Now…Damian's Lesson	111
	Discussion Points & Reflection Questions	114
Chapter 10:	**I'd Rather Die Than Get up in Front of the Class!** (Dealing With Fears)	
	I'm Not Strong Enough	115
	Time to Investigate	117
	Clearing the Path	122
	Anti-Panic Support	123
	Henry's Turn	128
	Another Morning Message	131
	Discussion Points & Reflection Questions	132
Chapter 11:	**My Friend Goes Ballistic Over Nothing!** (Anger Management)	133
	The School Nurse Stops In	133
	The Empty Hole	136
	Getting It!	138
	The Heart-to-Heart Talk	141
	Out-of-the Box Thinking	144
	A Plan with a Twist	147
	Discussion Points & Reflection Questions	150

Chapter 12:	**What Makes Her Want to Hurt Me?** (Rumors, Gossip, and Other Reputation Damage)	151
	A Little Birdie	151
	The Work	153
	Now…Greg	156
	Post Rumor Day	157
	Clean-Up	160
	Discussion Points & Reflection Questions	167
Chapter 13:	**He Puts Me Down Because I'm a Girl** (Sexual Harassment)	168
	When Meanness Begins	168
	The Lesson on Friendship	170
	Part Two of "The Lesson"	172
	Monday Morning	175
	The "Talk"	177
	The Hippo Birds	180
	Discussion Points & Reflection Questions	183
Chapter 14:	**When Does Being Special Go From Unique to Weird?** (How to Be Your Best Self)	184
	Charley's Tail	184
	Award-Worthiness	186
	The Boys' Meeting	188
	Charley's Choice	190
	Becoming Himself	193
	Breaking the Ice	197
	Discussion Points & Reflection Questions	199
Chapter 15:	**Everything at Home Feels Bad and Wrong** (Going Through Your Parents' Divorce)	200
	Letters to Parents in Transition	200
	Breaking Down the Walls	203
	John's Turn	205
	First Group Session	207
	And Then the Next Tuesday	210
	Hitting the Nitty-Gritty	213
	The Final Weeks	217
	Discussion Points & Reflection Questions	219
Chapter 16:	**I Will Suddenly Want to Cry Some More-- When Will It Stop?** (When Someone You Love Dies)	220
	See Me When You Get In	220
	Reactions Begin	223
	The Group Cry	227
	The Debriefing	229
	Helping Marilyn	232
	Discussion Points & Reflection Questions	236
Chapter 17:	**My Friends Are Smoking, and I Can't "Just Say No"** (Peer Pressure)	237
	The Basketball Game	237

	By Monday Morning	239
	Getting Down to the Truth	243
	The Verdict Is In	249
	Discussion Points & Reflection Questions	254
Chapter 18:	**They'll Like Me More if I'm Thinner** (Eating Disorders)	255
	The Referral	255
	The Confrontation	259
	The Hand-Over	262
	Eddie's Turn	265
	The Journey	271
	Discussion Points & Reflection Questions	273
Chapter 19:	**My Little Sister Is a Pain, and My Older Brother Beats Me Up!** (Coping With Siblings)	274
	The Middle Child's Dilemma	274
	The I&RS Meeting	277
	The Phone Calls Begin	280
	The Next Deal	281
	Tuesday Finally Comes	286
	The Deal Completed	289
	Discussion Points & Reflection Questions	292
Chapter 20:	**I Want to Run Away From Home!** (Teens and Their Parents)	293
	Larry's Suspension	293
	Larry's Story	298
	A Crisis Hits	301
	The Fix	306
	Finding Common Ground	309
	Discussion Points & Reflection Questions	313
	About the Author	314

CHAPTER 1:
Best Friends Forever?

Uh-Oh!

Tara always walked down the hall with different friends, none of which she ever called her BFF. Tara was cool. Everyone was her friend and she was friendly with everyone. Tara didn't care what other people were saying or thinking about her or anyone else. Her mom always told her, when she was little, that it was none of her business what everyone else thought. She'd remind her that it would probably all change in a heartbeat anyway. She told her that every time you'd find out how you were different from someone else, you might want to change to please them, and then who would be the real you? And how could you change fast enough to please everybody? Best not to know, she'd tell her. Be your *best* you, and you'll be happy.

Tara liked that thinking. It was quite freeing and definitely less complicated. It also made her the most admired among her classmates at Hillstown Middle School. Tara was actually respected *because* she didn't seem to need to be popular. And even though she often laughed at herself easily whenever she made mistakes, she never laughed at anyone else. She was always respectful of other people, their feelings, and their stuff. Tara's mom would also always say, "Tara, my dear, just be the kind of person you know feels best, deep down inside, and let everybody else learn in their own due time." And even when the school counselor talked about being "comfortable in your own skin" and respecting all others as equals, someone in the class would always look knowingly to another classmate and whisper, "like Tara Thompson." She truly was the only fifth-grader that everyone, including the boys, could go to comfortably with a problem. Today, it was Olivia who needed Tara's advice.

Olivia's voice sounded shaky and out-of-breath as she caught up to Tara in the hall, sprinting between science and math classes. Olivia started with a quick, "Hey Tara, how are you doing?" but she never paused for an answer.

Olivia's pain blurted out, "Missy is mad at me. I just know it! I can tell. She's suddenly barely talking to me and only about things that don't matter...way too casual-like and cold. I can feel the change--I know something's up. And those eyes of hers are so different when she's upset...I can always tell. She can't look directly at me, because she's talking about me behind my back...I just know it! You know how it's too uncomfortable to gossip about someone, and feel close at the same time? That's why her eyes can't meet mine for any longer than a quick glance, you know what I mean? I just know she's talking about me! Tara, what should I do? I'll just die if she's dumping me. We've been BFF's since we were in second grade!" Olivia wailed.

Tara immediately turned to Olivia and said, "Aw, Livy, are you sure? You two are so close. Maybe she's just having a bad day, like when her mom gets on her case about being on the computer too much. It may have nothing to do with you at all."

"Tara, I swear I can tell." Missy's voice quivered. "When she does look directly at me, it looks strange--like she's looking strongly into my eyes--like she's forcing herself *not* to keep looking away. It's nothing at all like when we're just hanging and she has her everyday, comfortable look. Her eyes are piercing!"

Olivia shared with Tara, "Missy always told me we would be best friends for life and even after. Whenever we slept over, she would always say that we were the 'real deal' in soul mates, now and forever, and now this?" Olivia cried. "And Missy's voice sounded really serious this morning in homeroom, Tara, I swear. It was really sharp, like darts. It's the kind that makes a dog's tail stop wagging and go down between its legs, you know?" Olivia continued, to prove she wasn't crazy. "She's also got that 'gotta-get-there-in-a-hurry' walk too, all business, like when she's avoiding someone. I know it well.

"Remember when Missy got mad at Jenna last week? I knew she was mad at her the night before, because she'd been online with me the whole night complaining to me about Jenna's annoying chatter, and about Jenna not listening to the teacher and getting Missy in trouble. So in homeroom the next morning, when Jenna followed her around the room to tell her about her new sweater for the class trip, Missy just stayed real busy sharpening her pencil, getting a drink of water, and doing things that didn't need to be done…just like with me this morning! She does that every time she gets annoyed with someone, and now me!" Olivia groaned. "Me? Her real-deal-forever soul mate?"

Tara started to comfort her when Olivia continued, "And who was Missy talking to last night about me? Who else knows that she's mad at me, and what did she say I did? I thought something was wrong last night when she didn't e-mail me back. I hate that. I pretended it didn't matter by not asking her about it this morning, and she didn't mention it either. That is so *not normal!*" Olivia sighed deeply. "I feel sick to my stomach and my chest feels so heavy. She's my BFF, and I've told her everything for three years…I mean everything…all my 'don't-tell-anybody-or-else' secrets. Oh my God, if she is telling someone, I am so dead! What is up? Was it something I said? Who else can't look at me? Oh my God, this could be so bad. We're supposed to pick partners for the class trip tomorrow, and I never once in a bazillion years thought we wouldn't be together! And what if…."

Tara quickly interrupted, "Liv, get a grip. Wow, girl, even if she is upset about something, you can always fix it. You guys talk about everything in the world. You don't have to assume the worst and panic. I'm sure you'll find the right time to ask her if something's wrong. Besides, you can't do anything about it till you see her at lunch, and we have this kicker of a math test coming up right now, so you just have to chill. We'll talk later, okay? Good luck, Liv."

Olivia knew Tara was right, and since they were a little late getting to class, they both had to quickly slide into their seats without looking at Mr. Smith and get started fast on their tests, which were already sitting on their desks.

As soon as the bell rang for third period, Olivia scooted right over to Tara as they were going into the hallway and heading for language arts class. "That really was a bear, wasn't it?" Tara complained. "Especially that last word problem! Will we ever run into those situations, ever, ever, ever in our whole lives?"

"I don't know. I only know I'm miserable and scared to even see Missy after language arts," Olivia interrupted. "It just feels all wrong and so cold, and I'm so scared she's dumping me. The thing is, when we get to the cafeteria today, what if she tells me the seat next to her, where I usually sit, is saved for someone else? Oh God, that will be so embarrassing! And then what do I do?"

"Stop, Liv. You're going psycho on me here again. You don't know that she would do any of that. And if she does, you can always just join me wherever I am."

"But Tar, everyone knows Missy and I sit together every single day--no offense," cried Olivia. "And thank you for being so nice to me, but I can't do that. You're different, all okay with yourself. You don't need to be part of the same group all the time, but not me. That would be okay for you. You can do that, be friendly with everybody and sit anywhere, and no one gets mad at you. You're friends with everyone. I'm not. I've never been away from Missy. I only have her. Even when she's not at recess, I just go see the nurse, or the counselor, or go to the library. I dread being alone. But at lunch, I really don't want to look like I lost my best friend when I go to another table. I always think the girls at the next table won't want me to sit with them. They'll think I'm only there because I don't have my first choice, and they'd be right. Then at night, everyone will talk about me like I'm a loser! Tara, I swear, I'm so scared!"

Tara's eyes lit up as she suddenly reacted. "Hey, Liv, why don't I join you at your table? There's always an extra seat, and I do that sometimes, so no one would notice anything really different. Then we could talk, and you won't feel alone or weird. What do you say?"

"Oh, Tara, you are a genius!" Missy shrieked. "That would so work! Are you sure you don't mind? Wait, I thought you were eating with Jenn and Dana these days."

"Oh I'm fine with it. In fact, I'd like that. I don't like that stuck feeling I get when I go to the same place all the time. After a while people think something's wrong when you do go to a different table, you know what I mean?" Tara smiled and continued. "Jenn actually calls me a 'free soul' because I just land wherever I feel comfortable. And Dana's happy as long as she has Jenn, so she could care less. So after language arts, we'll meet in homeroom and go to the cafeteria together, okay?"

"Oh, thank you, Tara, you are a lifesaver! And boy, do I know what you mean, obviously!" Olivia laughed and felt some relief that morning, for the first time.

As they turned the corner into class, Olivia looked back at Tara with a smile. "Thanks Tar, you're the best." Tara smiled back with a no-big-deal shrug and quickly slipped into her seat.

Timing Is Everything

Once again the bell rang, and language arts class was over. There was that din of hundreds of desk and chair legs simultaneously grinding into the dirty hardwood floors throughout the school, as students erupted from their seats and spilled into the hallways. It was always a zero-to-sixty sprint from those hungry, comatose-like dazes to lunchtime freedom.

Happy, animated conversations were in high, excited volume as everyone raced to homerooms. It was well known that everyone in that wing of the school would then need to drop off their backpacks and books in exchange for money, lunches, and jackets with automated smoothness and speed to get to the shortest lines in the cafeteria. Only Olivia was hesitating today, almost clinging to Tara as they made their way to the cafeteria. Missy always got to the table first, because she brought her lunch, milk box, and dessert and didn't have to stand in any line. That meant today, like always, Missy would already be seated when Olivia arrived at their table.

Olivia's brain was screaming, "Please let the seat next to hers be kept open for me like she always does, please?" Olivia's heart was racing in that old familiar panic attack. She was petrified of a public rejection and humiliation. She was convinced that everyone would see Missy was breaking up with her as her BFF. Her heart pounded and her throat burned, but she stuck close to Tara as they got into the milk line. Suddenly Olivia saw Missy come into the cafeteria with Ali, talking and laughing, and she headed right for their table. And then it happened.

"Oh, no," Olivia groaned heavily under her breath.

"What's wrong?" Tara asked.

"Look, Ali sat down right by her, right where I always sit. And they're laughing. I even saw Missy glance at me and look away too. I knew it! Tara, she's mad at me. What now? How do I handle this? Ali must know, and everyone will see!"

Tara turned around in line and looked squarely into Olivia's eyes with complete confidence. "Livy, you will be fine. We'll just get those two seats on the end, and we'll keep talking. You need to just act like nothing has changed, and we'll laugh, too. It will look like nothing's wrong…and you really don't know that anything is, anyway--not really, Liv, not really!"

Olivia's eyes had been filling up, but the confidence in Tara's strong voice shocked the tears away. "Okay, I can do this. But what should we talk about, Tara? Oh, I hope I can concentrate. How 'bout you keep talking in case I don't make sense, okay?" Olivia began to feel a little stronger as she gave the lunch lady her money for the milk, and followed Tara to the table as they had planned.

Tara still needed to talk about that math test, so she picked up where she had left off. "So, what's with those waste-of-time word problems, huh, Liv? Two airplanes flying at each other is such a dumb idea, don't you think? And what did you get for number three, the money problem?"

But Olivia wasn't really listening, just trying to smile, and hoping Tara didn't say anything she couldn't answer. And when she sat down at the very end by Pam, Pam looked confused, like, "What's with the change?" So Tara kept talking about the math test, and Olivia kept agreeing with her and looking as casual as she could, as if she didn't realize she wasn't sitting in the middle of the row of girls, alongside Missy. Pam waited a minute and then asked the burning question, right out loud: "Olivia, do you want us to all move down one seat so you can sit by Missy?"

Olivia shot a glance at Missy, who dropped her head and pretended not to hear it. And worse than that, Ali glanced at Missy to share a quick, knowing smile, but with her head held high, proud of her new chosen position at that table. Olivia began biting her lip to keep from bursting into tears, and her brain seemed to flood instead of thinking of words she could use to answer.

In a flash, Tara looked at Pam and then at Olivia and saved them all by asking, "Do you mind sitting here with me today, Liv? I want to pick your brain about that math test. I really think I bombed it, and it's so near the end of the marking period that I may never save my grade."

Olivia realized she had just been let off the hook. The diversion was perfect. Olivia appreciated Tara's quick and compassionate reaction, and knew she had just bought her some time, by filling the air when everyone else was silenced by this obvious Missy-Ali action. But she was still crushed. That confirmed that Missy was with Ali now, and everyone sitting there caught Missy and Ali's avoidance reactions and alliance. Olivia's worst nightmare…made real.

Tara watched Olivia carefully opening her chicken wrap without looking up and noticed a teardrop on her wrist, then another and another. Tara immediately tried to open the conversation up about the class trip the next day to divert the heavy discomfort at the table. She asked rather loudly what everyone was wearing, stealing the attention away from Olivia. Even before anyone answered, Olivia jumped up and bolted out the cafeteria door. Tara knew she was headed for the bathroom right outside the door, and no one at the table looked surprised or even willing to go after her. Missy's head was still down, and Ali stared at Missy's face for direction.

Pam blurted, "Is Liv okay? I think she was crying," but stopped short before she asked Missy if she wanted to go check on her. Tara grabbed both lunches and went right up to the cafeteria aide to ask if she could go to the girls' room to see if Olivia Martin was okay. She was certain she had gone there to let the dam break and the floodwaters pour.

Poor Livy, she thought as she threw open the girls' room door and began to look under the stalls for Olivia's clean, white sneakers, near where she could hear muffled sobs. "Are you okay?" she asked through the door under which she saw Olivia's sneakers. Tara wasn't comfortable with this feeling of urgency. She was afraid the lunch aide was going to follow her into the bathroom to make Olivia come back to the cafeteria, and that would be more than her friend could take. "I have your lunch here, do you want it?" she asked through the door, trying not to let the others hanging out in there know anything was wrong. But Olivia didn't answer. "Olivia, I think Mrs. Calvy is going to come in here in a little bit to ask you to get back to the cafeteria. Are you okay?" she pressed.

"I can't do it, Tara. I can't go out there. I'd rather die," Olivia whispered from behind the stall door. "I know I'm going to get in trouble, but I'd rather die than go back in there crying," she answered through her nose which was stuffy from sobbing. "Please don't tell anyone at the table I was in here crying, PLEASE?" Olivia begged.

"Oh, I would never do that, Liv. I'm here with you, but I know we'll both get in trouble if we stay. They'll tell the aides on the playground that you never came out, and they'll go looking for us, even if Mrs. Calvy forgets to come get us. Do you want to go see Mrs. Kaufmann? The aides never question us if we go to the school counselor, especially if you're crying, okay?"

Olivia was quiet for a minute. She knew Mrs. Kaufmann was always there for everyone, and she was kind. She'd been the school counselor for years, and even knew her mom from when she went to this school. Olivia also remembered Mrs. Kaufmann helped her in first grade. The bigger boys on the bus had laughed at her yellow boots with the ladybugs one rainy day, and she didn't ever want to take the bus again. Mrs. Kaufmann got the boys to understand why she was scared. She asked them to be kind and to watch out for her, as if she were their little sister. She remembered they were so nice after that, and she felt safe and special. Mrs. Kaufmann was also the one who always came in to talk with all the classes in the school about problems that would come up. Maybe she could help. Olivia knew, if nothing else, that Mrs. Kaufmann wouldn't tell anyone, and it might buy her some time to clear up her red, swollen eyes.

"Okay," Olivia answered softly. "Thanks, Tar."

Tara knew she had to get Olivia out of the bathroom and down the hall to the counselor's office before the cafeteria doors opened and all 137 students, especially Missy and the others from their lunch table, stampeded into the hall to get out onto the playground. And of course, that would be at the same time that all the older students would be coming in from recess to go eat. It would be hard to move, and even harder to hide. She coaxed Olivia out of the stall and handed her the barely eaten chicken wrap, all scrunched up in the brown lunch bag.

Tara put her hand on Olivia's shoulder and said, "Hurry up, Liv, our lunch is almost over, so it's about time for the switch." The two of them sped out of the girls' room and down the hall, like firefighters heading for a four-alarm blaze.

Kind Truth

Tara reached the school counselor's outer, hall door first, so she pushed it open fast so both of their bodies could scramble into her waiting room, just in the nick of time. They were safely tucked away from view of the crowds spilling into the hallway, as the school counselor's hall door clicked shut behind them. Tara knocked on Mrs. Kaufmann's inner-office door with a sense of urgency, while Olivia stood behind her, trying to dry her eyes and getting ready to try to explain why she felt so destroyed and sick to her stomach. Just as Tara turned around to Olivia to suggest that maybe they should take a seat and wait, the door opened, and two eighth-grade girls came out with Mrs. Kaufmann right behind them. All three were smiling, but were looking into Tara and Olivia's eyes, wondering what trouble brought them there that day as they switched places.

"Hi, ladies, how is everyone today?" Mrs. Kaufmann asked, as she looked right into Olivia's red eyes. It never took her long to figure out who was the "the one" hurting, even if the eyes didn't give it away.

Tara quickly answered, "Not so great. I'm really here to bring Olivia." Tara turned to Olivia and said, "Liv, do you want to tell it or should I?"

Then the girls moved to sit in the chairs facing the desk, with Mrs. Kaufmann taking her seat on the other side and facing them. There was always a big box of tissues and plenty of fidgety-type play items all around on the desk, in case anyone found it too hard to get started and needed a convenient diversion. Olivia grabbed the magnetic paper-clip man and began to contort the head and arms and legs, without even realizing what she was doing.

Olivia looked embarrassed to be there, but started to explain in a lowered voice, "It's about Missy and me. You know how we've been best friends since Mrs. Cornwell's class? Well…well…." And suddenly her voice cracked, and it was as if the dam broke again, and the floods gushed from her eyes into a heavy sobbing. "She's breaking up with me…I just know it," she blurted out between sobs.

Tara put her hand on Olivia's shoulder again and mumbled a soothing, "It's okay, Livy, it will be okay."

Mrs. Kaufmann looked at Tara first and smiled warmly. "Tara, you are such a good friend. Thank you so much for bringing Olivia to me. I just know there is absolutely nothing we can't make better, right, Olivia? We've fixed things before, and we can this time too. And Tara, you're right, it will be okay." She turned to Olivia and asked, "Is it okay if Tara waits outside for you in the waiting room now, so you and I can talk privately?"

Olivia hurriedly assured the counselor that Tara knew everything, anyway. She had no secrets and she was welcome to stay. Tara sat proudly near Olivia, feeling honored and trusted enough to be allowed to stay there, but Mrs. Kaufmann kept talking, "You see, ladies, I always make sure anyone who comes in with a problem has the complete freedom to say anything and everything on his or her mind, without having to worry if it will bother anyone. And maybe Tara might even like to go out on the playground for a bit before it's time to go back to class?"

Tara was actually thinking about the music quiz coming up after lunch, and how she would like to just sit in the waiting room and have this chance to study. "It's okay, Liv," she reassured her. "I'll wait right outside, right there," as she got up and went into the waiting area. "We can go back to class together when you're done. Is that okay, Mrs. Kaufmann?"

"Absolutely, Tara, that's a great idea!" Mrs. Kaufmann knew that guaranteeing Olivia's confidentiality would allow her to open up about any of the girls, without putting Tara on the spot for hearing it.

She also knew that sometimes these sessions went into many unexpected directions, such as about upsetting conditions at home, or other current fears or bad experiences from the past. And she had always felt Olivia had some past she needed to talk about, judging by her clinginess to Missy for the last couple of years, and her seriously red eyes today.

"Okay, Olivia," she quietly and caringly said, leaning forward at her desk as the door clicked behind Tara, "What happened with Missy, sweetie, that caused you to be so upset?"

"Nothing, but everything!" she exploded. "It's all what I just know is **going** to happen. I think Missy is breaking up with me as best friends by the way she's acting, and I just don't know what I'll do if she does. I don't have anyone else, and I've told her all my secrets for most of my life, and I will be so embarrassed to have nowhere to sit at lunch, and no one to hang out with on the playground. I will just die!" Olivia poured willingly.

Mrs. Kaufmann jumped in, "But even if you know Missy's signs, what makes you think she's not just mad about something explainable, perhaps just a misunderstanding? Or maybe someone told her you said or did something you didn't say or do? There might be something really small that will fix itself in a few minutes. Wouldn't it be worth at least knowing? I can help you. What do you say?"

Olivia got quiet. She knew all of these were possibilities, but her fear of being rejected felt like an explosion in her head, every time she pictured having that talk with Missy. The thing was, she also knew how Missy had acted for a couple of years, whenever she was mad at someone, and she knew Missy's determination when she was "done" with someone. "But how do I find out? I'm so scared to ask her. And what do I say, like why are you acting so strange? She'll just deny anything's wrong and keep talking and laughing with Ali. And all our friends can tell," Olivia said as her voice trailed off, and her head fell into her hands as she cried deeply.

Mrs. Kaufmann handed her some tissues and said, "Listen dear, my thinking is you need to know, so you can move forward. We could do that right now if you like. I can help you find out what's up, or you can do the asking with me here, right now. I can send for Missy from the playground, and I can just ask her honestly with you in the office, or I can go outside my door and just quietly ask Missy what she's feeling. What do you think? I'll tell her you're upset, thinking you've done something you need to apologize for, but didn't know how to start. Or, I can also ask her if she's dealing with something else, or if she just might be changing friendships. I'll assure her that the truth is a whole lot better and kinder than having to play a game that takes a long time, and gives out a lot of pain. I can't imagine you're doing your best work today with this on your mind, so why don't we just find out once and for all. What do you say?"

Olivia squirmed in her seat, feeling really scared to face Missy. She answered Mrs. Kaufmann, "But what would I say? And what if she just doesn't want to be friends anymore, or she just wants to be with Ali more than me?"

"Well, maybe that is the case. But how long can you go on avoiding her in school? Crying in the girls' bathroom in fear of this breakup can't keep happening either. You know, Olivia, sometimes people just need a little 'time-out' in their friendship, or maybe just some space, especially if they've done everything together for a long time. The thing is--you could both use more friends in addition to each other."

"But I don't want new friends. I'm comfortable being with Missy. I feel safe with her. I just don't know why she's not happy with me." Olivia started to cry again. "And how would I make new friends, anyway? Everyone thinks Mis and I are BFF's, so they'd leave me alone."

"Okay," Mrs. Kaufmann said with resolve, "I think what I'm hearing here is that you have a fear of having to make new friends in addition to feeling rejected, am I right?" Olivia nodded reluctantly. "I think you're afraid to come out of your safe and comfortable zone with Missy. I'm also guessing that it's been so long since you had to make new friends that you're not sure you can. Am I right?"

Olivia nodded again and dropped her eyes. She definitely had a fear of not being able to make new friends as her panic button on speed dial. "And just what makes you think you can't make new friends?" challenged Mrs. Kaufmann. "You are friendly and kind and happy--most of the time, that is." She smiled at Olivia, and Olivia smiled back. "In fact, I'll bet there are lots of girls you don't even know yet, not *really* know, you know?" They both laughed at how silly that sounded. "You don't have to be alone, Olivia, and new people in your life will add new and interesting things to talk about and do. This little, possible 'time-out' with Missy might be the best thing that could have happened to you. Making new friends around here is like playing musical chairs with changes every day, believe me. I see it all the time.

"It's actually quite healthy to make new friends, and very, very normal. For example, what about Tara? She's been there for you this time and seems to care. She's the perfect example of someone who enjoys being with lots of people, and they enjoy her. She's independent and friendly, and the perfect person to be with, while you add some new and interesting relationships to your life. And we can talk more about making that happen once we get past today. What do you say, Olivia. Shall we move forward?"

Olivia's resolve was weakening as she asked Mrs. Kaufmann, "But am I not good enough for Missy anymore? And what if she tells everyone why she doesn't want to be with me, like why I'm not fun to hang around, or…or what I do that has annoyed her for a long time, or…."

"Let me share something with you, my dear," Mrs. Kaufmann jumped in. "My husband and I have been married for thirty-eight years, and we love and care for each other very, very much. But even we need to have other friends, and we need to go out to do things with other people sometimes. And that doesn't mean there's anything wrong with either of us. We just need our time-outs too. I love to go shopping with a group of friends or go to a light movie, and he really doesn't. He likes to watch football, and I don't. So it works. When I come home from a shopping trip with my friends, I have all kinds of stories to tell him. And when he's had an afternoon shouting at the television with his friends, he's all refreshed and energized with his happy experience. And then we have new stuff to talk about together. See what I mean, Olivia?"

Olivia had a twinkle in her eye, as she smiled and asked with disbelief, "Thirty-eight years, really?"

Mrs. Kaufmann laughed. "I know. That's a really long time. But that's how we have stayed best friends, as well as husband and wife. Remember, Olivia, this is the time in your life to be learning about people. You should be discovering how they are all different, what you like about each of them, what makes you uncomfortable with some, and how to be a good friend, too. The idea is not for you to settle in with just one friend, so that you can be safe and comfortable. Olivia was really listening for the first time. You could see she was beginning to understand that it was not only **not** a bad thing that might happen, but actually a **good** one.

Mrs. Kaufmann continued, "The word 'Best' in 'BFF' makes a top or preferred spot that everyone else feels they can't compete with, so they leave you two alone. That's the only problem with girls naming one person as their 'BFF.' And let's face it…nothing really lasts forever. Change is the one thing you can count on, which is weird, huh? And that's what's making it hurt so much, now that your relationship has started the normal course of change. What is actually happening after almost three years is that you two need a time-out, or just some space, in order to be interesting to each other at a later time. And you both need to add friends... not lose each other, but to make life more interesting and help your friendship actually last."

Olivia seemed lighter. "I see what you mean, Mrs. Kaufmann, 'Best Friends Forever,' or BFF's, are really not 'forever.' Okay, I guess I could talk with Missy now. Can you call her in and stay here to help me get started?" she asked.

"Absolutely!" Mrs. Kaufmann assured her, as she quickly stood up and went toward her waiting-room door. But she turned back to say to Olivia, "You might want to eat your lunch right now while you have a chance."

As she went into the waiting room, she saw Tara had been sitting there studying, and she looked up with a smile. "Is Liv okay, Mrs. Kaufmann?"

"She's doing much better now, sweetie. Thanks for asking, and thanks for waiting, too. That was really thoughtful. Would you mind doing us one more favor right now? If I give you a note for Missy, would you run out on the playground and give it to her? I'd like her to come to my office right now so I can ask her a question before recess is over. Tell her I won't take more than a couple of minutes, and she's not in any trouble. Okay? And if you want, you can take your things with you and stay out there. It's a beautiful day and you need to get a little fresh air and sunshine yourself. And thanks again for being a really caring person."

Tara was happy to be able to run an errand, and happier still to feel like the problem had been turned over, and she could get a breath of fresh air before the music quiz. Mrs. Kaufmann always made her feel good inside about helping others, too. Tara skipped outside with the note Mrs. Kaufmann had scribbled and spotted Missy talking with Ali, not far from the door. She handed her the counselor's note as she delivered the message.

"Mrs. Kaufmann's waiting for you right now, and she only needs a couple of minutes; not to worry, nothing bad."

And she ran off to join Mara and Megan sitting on the swings, talking.

I Messages

Ali looked at Missy as she read the note from Mrs. Kaufmann. It read, "Missy, would you mind coming to my office right now? Sorry to interrupt playground time, and I won't keep you. I just have a question. Thanks."

"I'll bet it's about Olivia." Ali looked into Missy's eyes as she carefully spoke. They both knew Olivia tore out of the cafeteria, with Tara following close behind with their lunches. Ali knew Missy had been feeling guilty about how things were recently, and felt like she had made her cry. They both figured that neither one was on the playground, but had hoped it was because Liv and Tara were in the girls' bathroom, talking.

Missy looked worried as she grabbed her purple lunch sack from the pile of assorted lunch bags heaped by the door. She called back over her shoulder to Ali as she went inside, "I think you're right." As she hurried down the empty hall, Missy saw Mrs. Kaufmann right outside her waiting room door. *Maybe this will be just a quick nothing*, Missy hoped.

"Hi, Missy," Mrs. Kaufmann called to her as she approached. "I have a quick question for you, if you don't mind." Mrs. Kaufmann deliberately left the waiting room and office doors open so Olivia could hear the conversation that hopefully would lead up to a sharing and mending session. She wanted her to feel comfortable picking up from that point, if Missy decided to come in and talk. Mrs. Kaufmann continued ever so carefully to make sure Missy also felt comfortable. "I've been sitting in my office talking with Olivia about something that she's very afraid to ask you. She feels there's something not quite right between the two of you, and is scared she did something to make you angry. She had no idea how to ask you, but I've talked her into letting me help her clear the air. I know from many years' experience that everyone has their own way of looking at things, and they each have their version of 'the story,' and that they all deserve to be happy. That includes both of you.

"Do you think you would want to talk with her right now? I'm sure you saw how upset she was at lunch, so I hoped you'd both want to share your real feelings, and move forward to a solution if we need to. And if there's nothing wrong, at least she can ask you about things that she thought meant you were upset. The other thing is, if Olivia has done something wrong, then maybe she should know it so it doesn't happen to you again. What do you think? I'll ask you both to speak in 'I messages' from your hearts only and remember we're trying to communicate…not be right… and not hurt each other. I can help you too, okay? After all, your feelings need to be heard too, don't you think?"

Missy's eyes changed from looking fearful to looking relieved. She had been wishing she could just tell Olivia how she felt ever since the winter break, but it never seemed like the right time. Here it was, almost the end of the school year, and she wanted to ask Ali to be her partner on their class trip to the museum. Her mom kept reminding her to be kind whatever she did, but how do you be kind and honest at the same time with bad news? Telling Olivia that she was too clingy, or too needy, wasn't kind. Telling her that she wanted to hang out with other people, didn't feel kind either. But she didn't want to be "stuck" with Livy all summer again.

All she could think of was how much fun she and Ali had over winter break, when Olivia went to visit her grandmother in Florida. Missy kept thinking about how she and Ali giggled all through the mall, and how they fell in love with that one gorgeous boy they saw in the movie. Missy thought that Olivia never acted as silly as Ali did, like when she and Ali pretended to be his co-stars at their sleepover. Ali was so much more fun to be with. But Missy also felt like she had been dishonest with Olivia, by not telling her that she and Ali were chatting online at night now. Missy didn't know how she was going to say all that to Olivia, even with Mrs. Kaufmann's help, but she was willing to try.

"I'd like that, Mrs. Kaufmann, thanks."

Missy and Mrs. Kaufmann walked into the office and saw Olivia sitting there on the edge of her chair, wiping her mouth after choking down half of her chicken wrap and rolling up the rest nervously.

Mrs. Kaufmann knew to speak first. Staying upbeat, she began, "Well ladies, nothing makes me happier than to help two really kind people explain how they each feel to each other. And I know neither of you would ever want to hurt the other one, but you each need to explain what's going on inside of you. You two have been friends since the beginning of second grade, and friends do have their ups and downs. And I know it's hard to find the right words, but shall we try?" Both girls fixed their eyes on the school counselor because they couldn't look at each other. Seeing this, she happily took the lead. Mrs. Kaufmann prodded, "Okay, Olivia, did you want to ask Missy if you did something to upset her?"

Greatly relieved, Olivia finally looked sideways at Missy and carefully started. "Yeah, Mis, are you mad at me or something?"

"Oh, no, Liv, I'm not mad at all. I uh, see, uh, you know how Ali's mom and mine play tennis together? Well, when you were in Disney World over break, I went with my mom to her tournament and Ali was there, too. Anyway, we began to hang out and we had a really good time, so we started instant messaging at night. But I've been feeling really guilty, because I wasn't talking to you as much, and I didn't tell you about Ali and me, like I'm cheating on you or something. I didn't want to be with you because I felt like I was keeping a secret from you. I know we always promised not to keep any secrets from each other, and that made me feel really bad. I'm sorry."

Olivia was still for a minute, trying to collect her thoughts and get up her nerve to hear more of "Missy's truth," She had heard about Missy and Ali going to the mall from Jenna, but had thought their moms just went shopping together and brought them both along. So not hearing from Missy at night anymore now made sense. She was busy talking online with Ali instead of her.

"But Missy, you've been acting all mad at me, not like *you* did something wrong, but like *I* did something *to you*. Like in homeroom the other day, you kept avoiding me and acting all annoyed when I was trying to talk to you. You kept walking away from me, no matter how much I tried to follow you and tell you stuff."

"I know, Livy. I just felt like you were always next to me, always sitting by me, always picking me for your project partner, always following me around. I guess I was annoyed and I wanted some space. Don't take this personally, but sometimes I feel I can't breathe. I'm sorry. I didn't know how to say that to you. It's not like I don't want you for a friend anymore, but not BFF's, okay?" Missy looked at Olivia's eyes filling up and knew how terrible she must've felt, but there was no going back. The truth was out, and it hurt, the very thing she didn't want to do. "I mean it. It's not like I don't want to be with you, just not *all* the time. Can't we invite Ali along sometimes? And you can invite someone else too, like Jenna, okay?" Missy kept trying to make it better, but Olivia knew she was losing her best friend...forever.

Space for Ali, thought Olivia, as she was finding the strength to speak up. "But isn't that what best friends do? Pick each other and do stuff together?" Her voice began to be louder and more desperate. "What's so wrong with that? And you don't even like Jenna, remember? You told me she was annoying because she chatters so much."

The air thickened, and even with their beginning use of "I messages," Mrs. Kaufmann could hear Olivia's tone changing to more desperate. And Missy realized now that the truth was hurting Olivia, even when she tried to package it kindly, but she just couldn't stand to go back to that old, suffocating friendship any more. Suddenly she felt she absolutely could not be partners with Olivia on the trip the next day, and she had to speak up right now.

"Liv, I do need a break. I want some space, like tomorrow. I don't think we should be partners, okay?" Missy looked to Mrs. Kaufmann to understand and help.

For Olivia, the bomb had finally fallen. She had felt that same familiar feeling of terror in her chest three years before, when her dad told her he was divorcing her mom and moving away. That panicky feeling of abandonment was all too familiar. Olivia's filled eyes, quivering lips, and silence spoke volumes to Mrs. Kaufmann. The counselor jumped in and started talking to give Olivia time to digest this painful reality. "You both are doing a great job explaining what you feel. Let me see if I have this right…

"Missy, you want a break for a bit, like I do when I leave my husband at home to go out shopping with my girlfriends. And Olivia, this is uncomfortable for you, since you didn't know Missy felt this way. You feel embarrassed that the other girls will see the two of you aren't together, and that you need a partner for tomorrow's trip. Am I right, Olivia? I'm sure when I go away for a whole day, my husband would have planned to go golfing or something with a friend, if I had told him in advance I'd be gone so long, you know? Missy, I'm sure you can understand what Olivia is feeling at the moment about the trip tomorrow, right?

"So where do we go from here? I think I need to help Olivia deal with what is hurting her, and help her get her partner for tomorrow. I think she needs a little time to digest that you two are not going to hang out everywhere together right now. Missy, is there anything you need from me? Can I help you with how bad you must be feeling for Olivia, even though you must feel relief that you have finally spoken truthfully? I know you must feel a mixed bag of emotions, too."

Both girls were silent. That just seemed to sum it up. After a pause, Olivia reacted to Missy. "But you do that all the time at my house when you…" Olivia started, but the counselor reminded her gently to not to go back to old conflicts and stick with "I messages." Olivia stopped short and the silence was uncomfortable. She still had so much to say, but her throat burned, and she realized she really couldn't debate her way back into that old BFF relationship ever again.

Staying in the Moment

Mrs. Kaufmann then directed her next question to Missy, to give Olivia some time to get the flood of emotions out of her head. "Help me think through all the girls at your lunch table. Is there one you both like? Who would you both want to join you, if you were allowed to have a group of four tomorrow?"

The school counselor thought that if Missy could redeem herself by accepting Olivia as a friend within a group, she wouldn't feel so guilty. This would also help Olivia not feel so "dumped and humiliated," as she would say. Mrs. Kaufmann knew that no one would feel threatened with this group idea. They also needed to learn from this experience, and not to build up old resentments that would just contaminate any new relationship they could form. A group friendship was the way to go, a true win-win, for them both.

Missy got it immediately, and she lit up. Mrs. Kaufmann had thought of a way to help them transition from a tight pair, to a group of four--or maybe even more in the future. It was perfect, that is if Olivia would buy into it. Olivia was still hurting from being thought of as clingy. However, she knew this foursome idea would help make the possible news of their "BFF breakup" not so embarrassing. At least it would help Olivia appear to be still acceptable as a friend of Missy's, and not make her out to be the annoying dumped friend she feared she would seem. It was more like they were "opening up," and inviting more friends in.

"What a great idea!" Missy said as she looked at Olivia. "It would allow us to get to know new people, you know? And then we could still have time together too, on and off, but without hurting each other when we do. What do you think, Liv?" she asked excitedly.

Olivia listened as Missy told Mrs. Kaufmann that they had an odd number at their table, and that Sandy, Blair, or Tara often made a threesome. She suggested that one of them might want to join Ali and Liv and herself, because they were all even thinking about doing a funny song and dance routine for the variety show the last week of school.

Olivia gained her confidence and composure back by listening to how excited Missy was. The best part was that Missy seemed okay with her still being a "group friend," even if it wasn't a BFF anymore. Once she realized Missy wasn't that mad at her, she thought about this "friend group" idea and realized it wasn't bad at all. Besides, she knew she really needed to try not to be so clingy anymore. She remembered her older sister saying she was, too. So she had to admit, Missy might have been justified with feeling annoyed. She also realized there really wasn't such a thing as a "best friend *forever*" when it came to friends in school.

"I'd like to invite Tara into our foursome, Mrs. Kaufmann, is that okay?" Olivia offered. Missy smiled, relieved that things were definitely feeling better now. Olivia added, "And I think we should plan our song and dance routine on the trip tomorrow, Mis, don't you think? I have a new routine I'm learning in my tap class right now that I think would work."

Missy reacted enthusiastically, "Great! And I thought of the perfect end-of-year song that will make everyone laugh. I know Ali likes to sing, too. Do you think Tara would want to sing or dance?"

Olivia blurted out, "I know she would! She loves that kind of stuff. I think she's even taking an acting class right now, so she could be really good! Oh, this will be so much fun. I can't wait for tomorrow!"

Mrs. Kaufmann knew that recess was coming to an end, so she suggested to Olivia and Missy that they run out on the playground, while they still had a few minutes, and see if Ali and Tara would like to put an act together for that variety show. "See if they'd like to join you two to plan it tomorrow on the trip. I can let your homeroom teacher know that it would help if she could put the four of you in the same bus group tomorrow."

"Thanks, Mrs. Kaufmann. Come on, Liv!" Missy called, as she and Olivia grabbed their coats and lunch bags and took off out of the guidance office.

Olivia slowed up just for a second, making sure Mrs. Kaufmann's eyes caught hers. "Whew, thanks," Olivia said, knowing the school counselor felt the sincerity.

Mrs. Kaufmann did. She smiled and winked at Olivia. As she turned to go back into her office, she glanced at the sign she had just made for her waiting room. It read:

"The past is done and the future will happen however it unfolds ~ without my control.

But right now is my Present…my gift of lessons.

I only need to be the best me I can be, and only in this very moment.

The rest will take care of itself!"

She thought how well things turn out when everyone in conflict stays in the present moment and tries hard to be honest and kind. She also knew it wasn't easy to do!

Discussion Points:

- Being "in the now" removes the anger from the past and the fear of the future.

- Allowing change in relationships gives all people permission to be themselves.

- It is never okay to be in control of others or to allow others to control you.

- Giving ourselves and others room to grow shows acceptance and maturity. It shows an understanding that we all need to learn the lessons from our own journeys.

- New friendships provide new personal growth experiences--and the more the better.

Reflection Questions:

1. What advice did Tara's mother give her to be happy? Do you change who you are to be more liked by others? How often would you be willing to change before you would become tired or confused? Where do you spend time being your true, comfortable, and relaxed self?

2. What's wrong with having only one best friend at school? What are the advantages of having a group of friends? Is it really such a likely possibility to have one "best friend *forever*"?

3. What's the best way to let a friend know you are upset with what they said or did? Is it better to just let them know how you feel, or to tell them to change? How hard is it to accept someone telling you they didn't like what you did?

4. What's the best way to end a friendship? Under what circumstances would you do that?

CHAPTER 2:
Understanding Others Helps YOU!

What's Wrong with Me?

Mrs. Tanner, Emily Bauer's favorite playground aide, knocked on the school counselor's door, with Emily close by her side. Mrs. Tanner had also just sent Jason in from recess to the principal's office because he had been teasing Emily once again, and making her cry. They were all aware of the Zero-Tolerance Policy when it came to bullying in the Hillstown Middle School, and the aide had seen enough already during that Monday's recess to convince her something bigger than a warning was needed, again. Mrs. Tanner knew not to bring Jason and Emily in together. She also knew not to have Emily explain what happened to the principal, since that could look like she was in trouble which would make her feel embarrassed. Going to the guidance office was a safe place where she could get away from all the embarrassment. Mrs. Kaufmann, the school counselor, knew how to make her feel comfortable. She came right to the door and saw Emily with her very red eyes standing close to Mrs. Tanner, who was not her happy self, to say the least.

Without hesitation, Mrs. Tannner spoke to Mrs. Kaufmann as she moved quickly into the office. "Jason Abbott is up to his old tricks, and this time with Emily here. I sent him down to Mr. Gonzalez's office for discipline and brought Emily to you myself because she was so upset. I thought maybe you could help her if you have a minute?"

"Oh, I would love to help you, Emily, my dear. We can't have that kind of nonsense going on in my school! We need to get to the bottom of this for sure, so that you can be a happy camper out there on the playground every single day. And we have to find out what's going on with Jason. I wonder what on earth would make him think that it's okay to make you cry. Did he see you were crying, or was he doing that showing-off thing he does when he's not even paying attention to what he's causing?"

Mrs. Kaufmann knew to jump right into the troubleshooting for Emily, but she was also worried about Jason, who was right now in very hot water with the principal. Jason would probably hold Emily responsible for getting him in trouble now, in addition to whatever he was teasing her about. The counselor knew these bullying cases needed very careful handling, so they didn't go "underground," where teasers would just get even off school grounds and make their victims even more miserable. Jason had some anger issues in addition to his need for attention, and both would get him into daily trouble.

Mrs. Tanner turned around to leave the office, saying, "I'm leaving you in good hands, Emily. You and Mrs. Kaufmann can get to the bottom of this whole mess, I'm sure. I have to get back out on the playground. Feel better, Emily."

"Thank you, Mrs. Tanner," the school counselor answered. "I love knowing you are my eyes on playground. I feel so good knowing you're looking out for all our 'chickens' out there. Even our 'teasing chickens' need to learn how to behave, right Emily? So today let's start with Jason, and you can help me show him what is playful, okay-teasing and what is not. I'd really love to see him grow up to be a fine young man that you would be happy to have as a neighbor one day, okay?" she said to Emily with a big smile.

Emily smiled back, feeling more comfortable and a bit amused by the thought of Jason as a grown-up man--and nice, no less! But then her face fell, and she began to panic. "But will he know I've told on him?" she urgently asked. "I don't even know what he thinks is so wrong with me that he has to pick on me all the time. I've never done anything to him."

"Oh, heavens no, Emily, there's absolutely nothing wrong with you. You are exactly who you are meant to be, and you are the most perfect you there is!" Mrs. Kaufmann reacted immediately. "And we'll be very careful not to give Jason anything to be angry about, I promise. Besides, you may not have done a thing, my dear. Sometimes people get picked on just because they're too nice to say anything back, making them a safe target for the bully, you know? And let's say you did do something accidentally that he thought you did to him on purpose--wouldn't it be great to find that out and we can let him know it was a misunderstanding? That would clear the air and maybe defuse him. I promise I won't make a move without your permission, okay?"

Mrs. Kaufmann was quite convincing and very positive. She was an old hand at these situations and always said these were all her chickens, and that they were all just learning here at *her* school. She believed all children only wanted to be accepted and loved deep down inside, just like grown-ups. She also knew that there were plenty of children out there who had not been made to feel worthy of being loved, so they ended up showing off to get attention, like Jason. And others felt overly sensitive when getting attention and always tried to hide in the background to feel safe, like Emily did. It was when the Jasons and the Emilys needed to work together to resolve their bully-victim problems that it got tricky.

"Okay," Emily hesitantly answered, knowing that Jason regularly teased everyone, and he would certainly not find change easy. The teaser was who he was, and how he was, all the time. She was definitely afraid of him and how he embarrassed everyone so easily and at the drop of a hat. The worst part was that he always seemed to get away with it. Most of the people who were standing around watching would laugh along with him, forcing his victims not to want to seem like bad sports. And because most of the kids were laughing, it just encouraged him to continue, as if he were a comedian entertaining his audience… but not Emily. Her face would flush, and the lump in her throat burned when she swallowed. She hated attention, and she never knew how to evaporate fast enough after he'd throw his verbal dart at her in front of everyone. Jason's loud put-downs made her tears flood so easily that it made the embarrassment turn to complete and utter humiliation. She would go home at the end of each day it happened wondering what was wrong with her that would make Jason pick on her so easily, and even worse, why everyone else would laugh along. She couldn't look at it from Jason's needy point of view, since the thought of being his target automatically flashed that memory of terror.

Remembering these nightmarish times that he had teased her, Emily knew how badly she wanted it all to end. She sat up straight, deciding she was ready to help Mrs. Kaufmann "fix" Jason--that is, as long as she didn't have to confront him herself!

"I will see Jason when Mr. Gonzalez is done with him, and he'll never know we even spoke, okay? I'll just talk with him to see what's going on, why you, and we'll see how we can get started making some changes," Mrs. Kaufmann assured her. "In the meantime, you, my dear, can go back to homeroom along with everyone else coming back from recess, especially knowing Jason is right now being 'held captive' in the principal's office." Mrs. Kaufmann gave Emily a big warm smile. "And your eyes aren't red anymore, so no one will even know you were here, including Jason. The best part is that you have art class next, which I know you love!"

As Emily was gathering her coat and lunch bag, Mrs. Kaufmann reminded her, "I'll connect with you later so no one will notice, but not until after I've had a chance to work with Jason. And if you need me before that, just slip a note under my door, or let your mom or teacher know to give me a call. When I send for you, I'll write a confidential note to your teacher to send you on an errand to my office with a book that I supposedly need, okay?" And when you get here, we'll just use that time to talk. Your teacher will know what I'm doing, and the kids in your class know how much I love to talk with all my children, so they won't be surprised you didn't come back right away." She gave Emily a knowing wink, assuring her once again that she and her secrets were safe.

Emily definitely perked up with what she thought was an excellent plan and thanked Mrs. Kaufmann. She slipped out of the office, scurrying happily to put her coat away and get to art class to get to finish up the bowl she was working on for her World Hunger Day project. At the same time, Mrs. Kaufmann grabbed her keys, locked up the guidance office, and headed for the principal's office to see if Mr. Gonzalez was done meeting with Jason. If he was, Jason would then be hers.

Helping Bullies?

When the principal's door suddenly opened, Mrs. Kaufmann could see a room full of upset faces coming toward her as she sat facing that door in the waiting area. First was Jason coming through the doorway, reluctantly, with his head drooped so no one could see his bright-red cheeks, and with shoulders so far down that there was no question he was in big trouble. Following him were his parents, Mr. and Mrs. Abbott. Mr. Abbott appeared as if he were ready to explode, but in complete silence, as he trailed behind Jason. Mr. Abbott's jaw was squared, with his teeth clenched, looking down at the back of Jason's head piercingly. Mrs. Abbott was next, with her eyes immediately lowered so as not to meet those of anyone in the waiting area, including Mrs. Kaufmann's.

"Please wait here while I get the form for you to sign," Mr. Gonzalez said firmly, as he hurried past them to the office filing cabinet to grab the *Out-of-School Suspension Form*. The last person in the room had stayed seated in one of the half-moon circle of chairs facing the principal's desk. It was the school psychologist, Mrs. White, who had been working with the Abbott family for a year and a half on anger management, and was called to the meeting today to help determine what punishment would be best for Jason for this next case of bullying. The Zero-Tolerance Policy at the Hillstown Middle School was no laughing matter, and that was pretty evident by all of the serious faces so far.

Mrs. Kaufmann gave a quiet hello to all the Abbotts as they all took their seats in the waiting area with her. Both parents acknowledged her with a nod, while Jason gave her a long, pleading look for help in his silence. "Hi, Jason," Mrs. Kaufmann broke the silence, answering his look, but was interrupted by Mr. Gonzalez returning very businesslike with a form in his hand.

"I need one of you to sign this form indicating you are aware of Jason's out-of-school suspension for Tuesday, tomorrow, and what his responsibilities are as far as making up his work for the day. I will need to meet with all three of you on Wednesday morning at 8:30 sharp, and I am suggesting that Jason meet with Mrs. Kaufmann to come up with a behavior improvement plan during his recess time once he has returned. Is that okay with you, Mrs. Kaufmann?"

Mrs. Kaufmann gave a small appropriate smile and warmly responded to Mr. Gonzalez while still looking at Jason. "I would be delighted to." She was sharing her answer with everyone as she continued, "You know, everything that seems like a bad thing that happens to us is actually teaching us a lesson in life, as long as we learn from it and don't just repeat it. I'll be happy to help Jason figure out what great gift of a lesson in life he will get from this experience."

After her words, the emotion in the room seemed to soften with Jason and his mom. The little shift to positive thinking broke the tension for them, but Mr. Abbott signed the form aggressively and shook the principal's hand as if he had to go along with an unfavorable business deal that had been struck. In the meantime, Mrs. Abbott turned to Mrs. Kaufmann, and with all sincerity, thanked her for helping Jason again, lowering her voice to ask if she could call her later for help. Mrs. Kaufmann lowered her voice as well, assuring Mrs. Abbott she would call her in the morning. She told her she would be happy to help and looked forward to the call. Mr. Abbott nodded at Mrs. Kaufmann briefly as he shook her hand quite firmly. With his face still strained, he thanked her in a lowered voice, but turned immediately to leave without looking to see if his wife and son were coming. He marched out the door, mumbling something over his shoulder as he did, and he appeared not to care who knew he was angry.

Mrs. Abbott looked embarrassed at first, and then turned to Jason and whispered, "Don't worry, dear, we'll have a good time tomorrow," as they both scurried like two bad kids after Jason's angry dad.

Mrs. Kaufmann went into the principal's office to talk with him and the school psychologist to see if her suspicions were right. She knew that something in the parenting styles definitely needed an adjustment! Jason had to deal with his dad's anger for this inconvenience, something that would tell Jason that his dad saw him as a problem. Jason was certainly able to witness that his dad was angry with the principal and the school policy, and to have to take time off from his busy schedule to deal with things so unimportant as this silly teasing he did on the playground. This was the wrong lesson for Jason to be getting, for sure. His dad said his son was doing "what boys do" and this crying girl was just an "oversensitive crybaby." Certainly Jason needed a role model who saw that his meanness on playground was unacceptable. Now he knew his dad wouldn't speak to him and his mom because his day was disturbed for what he called "nonsense." Mrs. Kaufmann knew that what Jason really needed was for his dad to make this event important for Jason. While giving Jason the feeling of acceptance and love, he needed to make clear that meanness was never okay. He needed to have Jason understand that teasing people to make them cry or feel embarrassed was the sign of someone who didn't have enough character to do the right thing. It was also a sign of neediness. It showed that Jason was trying too hard to be the center of attention, too hard to show everyone he could make them laugh, and not trying at all to be careful with the feelings of those around him. If he knew he was important to his dad, and not just an inconvenience in his work day, maybe Jason wouldn't try so hard to feel important or powerful at school. This would have been a perfect opportunity for his dad to give Jason the lesson he needed to be learning. Now, it appeared that his dad needed to be learning his lessons first.

Mrs. Kaufmann also noticed that Jason's mom went completely in another direction with her reactions to Jason getting in trouble. It almost appeared as if she tried to balance out the dad's angry reaction and her son's fear with a whispered promise of a happy day. She was downplaying the seriousness of the suspension so that Jason wouldn't learn his lesson about bullying at school. Jason needed to have that unpleasant punishment for upsetting people so he could remember it the next time he started the teasing. Instead, his mom gave him the opposite message--that what he did was okay, that she would protect him from the unpleasantness, that she and his dad didn't agree as a parenting team, and that his dad's anger should be feared. She was acting as peacemaker in a secretive way, joining Jason as if she were on his level, instead of acting in a parental position. That combination certainly wasn't going to teach Jason anything except that his mom would enable him to continue being the bully, because it was okay by her.

Mrs. Kaufmann could see that Jason was a child reacting to a lot of wrong messages at home. He wasn't feeling worthy of his dad's time, and he needed a mom who was strong enough to be his loving parent and not his friend. And when Mrs. Kaufmann expressed that in the meeting that followed with Mr. Gonzalez and Mrs. White, they both agreed. Mr. and Mrs. Abbott definitely needed some family counseling to find out what part they both played in helping Jason learn how to change his bullying behavior. Mrs. Kaufmann asked Mrs. White if she was able to convince Jason's mom and dad to go to counseling.

"Not yet, but I'm not giving up," she answered. "The dad feels it's not that big of a problem and doesn't have the time. The mom appears to be afraid of upsetting the dad, so she just plays peacemaker and agrees with whatever he says. I've required meetings with them about anger management whenever Jason gets suspended for bullying, but the dad usually cancels. It's very frustrating."

Mr. Gonzalez turned to Mrs. Kaufmann and asked if she would work with Jason in the meantime, and he asked how little Emily Bauer was doing.

"I would be happy to. I think of both of them as victims in this case. Emily is okay if she doesn't have to be with him." Then Mrs. Kaufmann smiled. "Actually, Emily will get the happy day tomorrow when she realizes Jason is absent. We also have plans to meet again, so I can help her with some coping skills and maybe to understand what makes people tease in the first place. And as for Mrs. Abbott, I'm giving her a call tomorrow morning, because she asked me to. I think she's feeling out of control too, and about ready to make some changes in her own life. She might be realizing that Jason's getting in more and more trouble, and what she and her husband are doing is not working. This might be my perfect opportunity to help turn around that negative parenting pattern. We'll see."

The others agreed and stood up feeling they at least had a plan, but that it would not be a fast or easy one. Mrs. Kaufmann left the principal's office quickly. She needed to talk with Emily's and Jason's teachers, and Mrs. Tanner. They all needed to know to look out for Emily while they tried to help Jason change. She also planned to call Mrs. Bauer, Emily's mom, to let her know they had met that day and that they could meet again anytime. Mrs. Kaufmann knew it would be no easy task to have all of these people shift their somewhat legitimate thinking of "Jason the Bully" to one that understood he was also learning from his personal experiences and pressures. The hardest part would be to do this without sharing the confidential details of his home life…no easy task, for sure.

The Set-Up

On her way through the hall back to her office that Monday afternoon, Mrs. Kaufmann spotted Emily coming out of art class, talking with Tara excitedly about their projects being chosen for the World Hunger Day display. Mrs. Kaufmann winked at Emily, who smiled back and quickly turned her head away to look straight ahead, so no other students would see her making eye contact with the school counselor. Tara, on the other hand, called out to Mrs. Kaufmann with a cheery hello and ran over to her to tell her the good news about their beautiful bowls being chosen. Mrs. Kaufmann stopped to praise them, and Emily relaxed, joining in the socially acceptable conversation that was not about her problem.

Tara then inserted, "I'm so happy for Emily, since Jason upset her at recess today, so this makes up for it—right, Emily?"

Emily's face turned white as a ghost at first, since no one had mentioned it since she went back to class. "Uh, yeah, a little," Emily quietly answered, not wanting anyone else to overhear.

Mrs. Kaufmann quickly answered both girls, "I think this is wonderful and so deserved. You both have done a beautiful job on the bowls. She then took the cue and lowered her voice as well, "And yes, you both deserve to be happy today!" Emily looked relieved and grateful that she didn't have to talk about that embarrassing moment again today, out loud there in the hall, and she beamed with pride for feeling special and being honored. Mrs. Kaufmann gave a knowing wink to Tara, as if to say *Thank you for helping Emily.* And Tara had her usual knowing smile for Mrs. Kaufmann. She always felt so good when she was appreciated for her kindness.

As Emily and Tara turned to head for their next class, Tara lowered her voice and put her hand over her mouth sideways to speak into Emily's ear so no one else could hear. "By the way, Em, I'll watch out for you from now on whenever I see you-know-who get into one of his you-know-what moods," she said as she gave a gentle elbow to Emily's side. "And if I can't stop him, I'll let Mrs. Tanner know right away whenever anything starts up in the future," she assured Emily as they skipped off to their next class. Mrs. Kaufmann caught Emily's beaming smile stretch even wider across her whole face. She was thrilled to have Tara as her protector, since she was so popular with everyone. And Mrs. Kaufmann knew Tara would be the perfect ally.

She then turned to go toward her office, to call Emily's mom. *Tara and Emily, what a great match right now*, she thought. Just at that second and out of the corner of her eye, Mrs. Kaufmann spotted Mrs. Tanner and stopped short to catch her as she was about to pass her office. "Thank you again," she called to Mrs. Tanner. "You are one terrific lady, and you handled that so well!"

Mrs. Tanner gave a proud "thank you" back to Mrs. Kaufmann and also thanked her for being there for all the "little Emilys" in the school. "I'm always so grateful for having a safe place to bring kids who need a little privacy. We're a good team."

Mrs. Kaufmann gave her a smile and a thumbs-up and went right inside her office to make her call on the phone. "Mrs. Bauer?" she asked, as Emily's mom answered. "This is Mrs. Kaufmann, Emily's school counselor. I wanted to let you know that Emily had some tears today from an uncomfortable moment during recess. It seems one of the more outspoken boys in her class was entertaining everyone as he and a small group of boys were teasing the girls trying to learn to jump rope…Double Dutch style. He pointed and laughed at Emily right when she tripped on a rope and yelled out, 'Way to go, Grace! Take any coordination lessons recently?' This really embarrassed her, and her eyes filled up. It was a good thing that Mrs. Tanner, the playground aide, was near enough to witness the whole thing. She sent the boy to the principal's office and brought Emily to me. She was fine in just a bit, and is aware that I will be working with this young man to see if we can make sure this doesn't happen again. I just wanted to call and let you know what happened today."

With her voice cracking, Mrs. Bauer immediately and quite emotionally thanked Mrs. Kaufmann over and over and began to tell her how Emily inherited her high sensitivity from her. She explained how she herself had always cried so easily as a child and still "floods in a flash" when she's embarrassed. Mrs. Kaufmann admitted, "I was one of those highly sensitive little girls at one time, too, and I'd be delighted to help Emily to develop some coping skills. And if you'd like some tips I've learned, I'd be delighted to share them with you, anytime."

Mrs. Bauer sniffed a little, said she'd really like that like, and admitted she had never really known what to tell Emily that would work. She thanked Mrs. Kaufmann again for her call and for all her help. She also let Mrs. Kaufmann know that Emily would be petrified if she thought anyone could see her go into the guidance office for fear they'd ask her why she was there.

"Oh, we have a process, not to worry. Once Emily lets me know she wants to see me, I contact the teacher of the class that she could leave most easily. Then I ask that teacher to pretend to randomly select her to run an errand and write on her pass to go to my office. That way, the other students have no idea she's meeting with me. We have to get rather tricky to make sure all confidentiality is kept around here," Mrs. Kaufmann laughed.

"That's very clever!" Mrs. Bauer declared in great relief. "May I also sneak into your office to talk sometime? I'd have to make sure no one sees me, or they'll ask Emily why I was there."

"Oh, absolutely, but we'd need to schedule a time I'm not planning to see students. We can even meet before or after school, or we could always just talk on the phone. Whatever makes it work best," Mrs. Kaufmann assured her, and they exchanged their goodbyes.

Mrs. Kaufmann then zipped down to Mr. Gardener, Emily and Jason's homeroom teacher, to let him know what happened on the playground that day. She caught him in the hall and told him that Jason was sent home with his parents and would be serving an out-of-school suspension the next day. She asked him to put together some work for Jason to do at home. She also said to expect Jason to come to him for the work he missed while he was out. Mr. Gardener replied to Mrs. Kaufmann, "I'd be glad to. I sure hope you can do something to convince him that bullying everybody isn't going to win him a popularity contest around here! What a shame he made Emily cry!"

Mrs. Kaufmann answered, "It was a bad day for both of them. I've spoken to both parents and they will both be meeting with me in the future, but separately. In fact, Jason will be having some counseling with me during his recess time for a bit. I also suspect there are some issues in Jason's home life that might explain why he does the teasing and bullying. That would make him a bit of a victim, too. We'll see." As Mrs. Kaufmann started to walk away, she finished up with a hopeful comment, "Maybe we can turn things around this time, you know? It certainly would make Jason's life better, as well as all the rest of the students who are his victims."

"Good luck with that!" Mr. Gardener called after her, as he went back into his classroom.

Shift Number One — Jason's Mom

The next morning, Mrs. Kaufmann came to work early and saw Jason's name printed at the top of the Out-of-School Suspension list. She took those morning announcements and hurried down to speak with Mr. Gardener again, before the students would be coming in. She needed to pick up the work for Jason to do that day while he was to be home, *not* having fun. Mrs. Kaufmann also asked Mr. Gardener to keep an eye on Emily and Jason the next morning, when Jason would be coming back. Emily would not only lose that feeling of "freedom" from humiliation, but, instead, she might be highly anxious that Jason would want to get even. Certainly no one could predict Jason's behavior these days, and Mrs. Kaufmann figured any corrected parenting from home was a long way off. She also figured her best strategy was to strengthen little Emily and help her with her with shifting her thinking about herself, but not until she made that call to Mrs. Abbott.

Not wasting any time, Mrs. Kaufmann placed the call. "Good morning, Jason," she said as she heard Jason answer the phone. "This is Mrs. Kaufmann calling to let you know what work you'll be doing today while you're at home. I'll need to talk with your mom, too, but first I want to make sure you know it will be important for you to understand why you're not here today, and that it isn't a free day off from school, you know?"

"I know," Jason answered her with a lowered voice--quite different from the upbeat one he used to answer the phone. "My dad told me that if it weren't for Emily puttin' on the crybaby act, this whole thing wouldn't have cost him a day's work yesterday. He also told me Mr. Gardener will be giving me extra work to do today, but my mom said this morning I don't have to do it."

Mrs. Kaufmann reacted quickly. "Oh, yes, it does have to be done, Jason. That's actually your ticket back into school on Wednesday when you go to Mr. Gonzalez's office first thing in the morning. That's what makes out-of-school suspensions unpleasant. Otherwise, it would be just a day off--hardly a punishment, right? I'll let your mom know that, too, so you won't be in any trouble when you come back. And you and I will spend some time together during playground time for a while making sure this won't happen to you anymore, okay?"

Jason's voice lowered once more. "Okay," he answered with a defeated tone. "I'll go get my mom."

Mrs. Abbott picked up immediately, and Mrs. Kaufmann explained the suspension work and why it was important to make sure it was done, that he didn't celebrate the day off. "You know, Mrs. Abbott, I sense there's a difference of opinion between you and your husband about Jason's behavior. Am I right?" Mrs. Kaufmann started off. "I have to tell you that he's getting mixed messages about having to do the punishment work, and mixed messages about the teasing he's doing at school. The reason why it is called bullying and not teasing, just so you know, is because it has such an emotional effect on those he teases, and because he does it so often, making his victims feel helpless over and over and afraid of him. And none of those who come to me when they are crying think they have done anything to him. The worst part is that Jason thinks he's getting respect from all his friends, when in fact, they have actually been laughing with him when he's teasing, just so he won't turn on them. He's losing respect and eventually, he'll have no friends. They will soon feel too uncomfortable to be around him because they won't want to risk embarrassment themselves. Jason could end up very lonely and become more and more angry."

Mrs. Abbott immediately reacted with alarm. "Did you say he has made more kids than Emily Bauer cry? And he did it over and over? Oh, my, gosh! I just thought he liked Emily and that was how he gave her attention, or at least why he was trying to get her attention. Oh, I feel terrible. You know, my husband is a lot like Jason. He always says that kids who cry when you tease them are just too sensitive and that something is wrong with them, and they just need to toughen up. He tells Jason all the time that he has to be tough in order to make it in this world, and I must admit that his dad is pretty tough on him. I try to lighten things a bit so Jason has at least one easy parent and one hard one, you know? I guess I try to balance things out when his dad gets scary angry. I know Jason gets afraid of his dad, so I'm the good guy.

"Gosh, I never thought he was doing anything more than just doing kid teasing. My husband and I both thought the school was being ridiculous calling my Jason a bully. He really has a big heart, you know? I think he just wants his dad to be proud of him, and he really needs his dad's attention since his dad is such a workaholic. He's almost never home. Oh, I feel so bad now. I never knew. What can I do?"

Mrs. Kaufmann was thrilled that Jason's mom was getting it. She asked, "Does Jason understand that when he's afraid of his dad, how uncomfortable and powerless it feels? If so, maybe talking with him about it today can help him understand what Emily and the others feel. When he's teasing the other kids, they get so embarrassed and feel so powerless. Then they dare not cry or they know they'd be called a bad sport, or worse – a crybaby. It's just a thought. And, in reality, learning to be more sensitive to others' needs is called *emotional intelligence,* and it's really important if you want to succeed in the workplace. It's what gives you the edge and makes people feel more comfortable around you, knowing you won't hurt them or anyone around them, using humiliation in public. Respectful treatment of others is important, and so is a sense of humor. Both are important to win in today's competitive world. And, I will tell you that it will make a lot of difference in the way the other students and teachers see Jason around here. I've heard the kids are beginning to call him 'mean' behind his back, while they still laugh at his jokes. That is so sad, because he really does have a good heart, and he doesn't see what's happening. He believes being tough is what he's supposed to try to be. I hate to see that downward spiral happen to any of my little chickens here, as I tell the kids. The turnaround will come if your husband understands this, too. Let your husband know that spending time with Jason and approving of him being a strong, funny, kind, and respectful person is what will make you both proud and give him the best rewards in life. The other kids would actually admire him if he was strong enough to resist hurting others. It's easy to tease. It takes more effort to stop before you speak and think of the consequences--a lot more effort. And if you and your husband agree in your parenting, Jason will not be confused as to how to be the best Jason that he can be. What a relief for him, too. I know I couldn't have pleased both my parents if their thoughts were opposite. Maybe that will take some of the pressure off of him. What do you think?"

Mrs. Abbott answered with a lighter and happier voice, "Thank you so much. That really makes sense, and I never thought we have been giving our poor little guy an impossible task and, even worse, that it would end up hurting him. I will come by to pick up his work, and when I get home, Jason and I will sit down to talk about what he admires in his friends. And I will tell my husband what you said. I don't think he'll agree right away, because he can be pretty stubborn at times, always thinking he is right, especially after spending his whole life believing it. But, I do know he loves Jason and will listen, eventually. Maybe I can have him call you?"

"Sure, I'd like that." Mrs. Kaufmann said enthusiastically, realizing this was the shift of thinking she was hoping for with Jason's mom, and now there was the opportunity to maybe make it happen with his dad. "And I have some resources the two of you can use with Jason, which might help show him the difference between 'okay teasing' with friends and bullying. You can have them whenever you'd like them."

At that moment, a blaring fire alarm started sounding throughout the school. "Mrs. Abbott, I have to run. It's a fire drill, as I'm sure you can hear. Are we okay, then?"

"Oh sure, you go, and I'll be by in a little while to get Jason's papers. Talk to you soon, and I don't know how to thank you enough."

"No problem," Mrs. Kaufmann barely finished saying as she hung up the phone, grabbed her bag and keys, and merged into the swarming crowd moving through the deafening hallway to get to the outside door. She spotted Emily and Tara scurrying and giggling together down the hall just ahead of her. This day without Jason was a nice day for Emily, because she had nothing to fear. *I think it will be even better for Emily once she understands why he does what he does. Then she'll begin to see that it will be better for her, too, real soon…I can feel the change coming in my bones*, Mrs. Kaufmann thought.

She smiled at all the students and emerged outside into the bright sunshine. She saw Mr. Gardener lining up his students outside and handed him a note. It asked him to pretend to send Emily Bauer to the main office right after recess. She signed it with a big smiley face, which was her code for when she needed them to "play along." She would just wait around the corner from the main office and "happen" to run into Emily as she went by. And she knew Emily would understand what was happening as soon as she saw her. *Good plan*, she thought, *and now, for shift number two!*

Shift Number Two

A whole day had now gone by after Jason was sent home. Emily Bauer was having her "Jason vacation." She and her best friend Sarah kept trying to conquer Double Dutch jump rope with giggles and laughter and without fear of any loud, embarrassing put-downs. It was marvelously freeing for both of them, because they were two timid peas in a pod. They heard Mrs. Tanner's playground whistle announcing that recess time was over. Then they ran to where Mr. Gardener's classroom was lined up by the outside door. Mr. Gardener was standing before them and very casually he asked, "Hey, Emily, would you mind taking this to the main office for me?"

Of course Emily felt proud to be picked, and she took the item from his hand and went down the hall and around the corner to the main office. There, right as she turned the corner, was Mrs. Kaufmann standing near her office door, alone with a big smile and a little wave. Emily immediately knew. She took a quick look behind her, saw no one in the hallway, and then turned around to smile back with a really big, toothy smile. She slipped into the office knowing it was finally her special time to get to talk about Jason while he was gone. She also remembered her mom saying something about tips for when she was trying to hold back the tears. She was also happy to get out of the geography map work that the other kids would start doing while she was in the guidance office. She dreaded having to go up in front of the class to point out places on the map.

"Hello, my dear Emily!" Mrs. Kaufmann spoke with her most positive, upbeat voice as she closed the door behind them. "Are you having a wonderful day?!"

"It's really been fun," Emily beamed. We had a party in Spanish, and a fire drill, and Jason is absent, and I finally can do Double Dutch, so he can't make fun of me anymore!"

"Oh sweetie, that's wonderful. I don't think I ever did get the hang of that Double Dutch stuff, not really. I used to just be the rope-turner and was happy with that. Anyway, I thought this would be a good time to slip you out of class for a little talk. Is it a good time for you, or do you think you'll miss something you need?" Mrs. Kaufmann asked, knowing the answer but waiting to see if Emily really wanted to be there.

"Yes, thank you for taking me! I hate having to go up to the board in front of everyone in map-work class!" she answered with great relief.

"Great. I thought we could talk a little bit about fear and how the body handles it, okay?" Emily looked eager to hear and adjusted her tiny body on the big office chair to get comfortable.

"Some of us feel it a little more," Mrs. Kaufmann started. "We have these neurotransmitters in the brain, and we have all that dendrite activity going, which are the fancy words for when we have what I call 'juicy brains.' We are what they call 'highly sensitive people,' and that's okay if we can keep it all in check and not let it flood and embarrass us. I have learned a lot about fear since I grew up afraid of my own shadow, you know what I mean? I would feel fine, and then something little would feel like a threat and whoa, Nellie! Immediately, my throat would burn, my eyes would fill up, and I wanted to crawl into a hole so no one could see me start to cry. And holding it off was almost impossible. It was so embarrassing, and I couldn't seem to talk myself out of it happening. Then my eyelids would start to overflow, that warm stream of tears would trickle down over my cheeks, and I knew it was all over, you know?"

"Yeah, I know." Emily's happy face got a bit more serious, as it was obvious she could feel that uncontrollable panic all over again. The good thing was that she knew she was safe in that office, and that Mrs. Kaufmann seemed to know exactly what she experienced. She had Emily's complete attention.

"Since then, as a school counselor," Mrs. Kaufmann continued, "I have read some great books and talked to a lot of psychologists who have given me a gazillion tips for my students. I really wished I had known these helpful ideas way back when I was your age, and a boy named Eddie made fun of everybody in gym class. Anyway, I did learn about the brain. Did you know there are a couple of different places in the brain that get active when you see something that makes you feel unsafe? One part is the logical, thinking part called the neo cortex, up in the top or front. It's the logical, rational part that tells you not to panic when it feels the adrenalin rush. It's reasonable, but it's just a teeny bit slower than the other part of the brain, the limbic part. The limbic part reacts emotionally and is the part that sends a terrorized lizard scurrying away when it sees a snake coming. The lizard just does that fight or flight thing when he feels he's in danger, and you don't mess with a snake when you're a lizard. So, the little lizard has no logic, and he doesn't talk to himself to calm down or think about what he should do. He just doesn't have one of those logical parts to his brain. Instead, he just feels the fear and instinctively takes off like a little green bullet with legs.

"Oh, and the other thing about fear is the whole sequence of physical things that happens once the fear triggers it. That's when they all go off. The adrenaline immediately has a rush, which affects a whole lot of other systems and parts of our bodies. You can get red in the face, you can cry, your throat can burn, your knees can get very weak, and your heart can pound – all in an instant, and all before you can say anything sensible to yourself. So, Emily, you can't blame yourself for having an active sensitivity. You were born with it. It proves you are more aware than most other people, like having longer antennae, and more of them. You pick up more information. The down side is that when the emotional part of your brain goes on automatic pilot, you have to wait it out a bit.

"The extra brain activity can really be a good thing because you see and notice more than other people. Take Jason, for example, maybe his brain can't pick up on the fact that you were embarrassed, or that, when you turned to walk away, you might've started to cry. The only problem is that the fear thing or panic can seem to take off without your permission. So what do you think so far?"

Mrs. Kaufmann had been watching Emily ease her tightened face and shoulder muscles and relax into her seat as she was talking. She knew Emily was listening but was curious what she was thinking.

Emily blurted out, "That's so cool. I never knew why it all happened so fast, and I kind of feel better that I'm not bad or weird or something. And I've tried to tell myself to calm down like my mom says, but it never works so I thought I was going out of control. This makes me feel a lot better, but I also feel like I don't know how to make it stop." Emily hated the panic and would give anything to never feel out of control again.

"Well that's where *the shift* comes in, as I call it. You see, if it all begins with something happening that makes you feel you are in danger, and your emotions get all aroused, then that sets off even more adrenalin in the body's chain reaction. So, what do you think would be the place to make the whole panic attack cycle to stop? How about at the very beginning with what you think is a threat?"

Mrs. Kaufmann looked too excited and too confident to make Emily think it couldn't be controlled, though she had no idea what the school counselor was talking about.

"Okay," Mrs. Kaufmann continued. "You see, if the triggering event, like Jason nearing your Double Dutch game, or a snake, or your turn at the map skills board, was something you thought couldn't hurt you, then the whole panic reaction wouldn't start in the first place. It would be as if Mrs. Tanner was walking by instead of Jason. You like her a lot and she's kind to all children, so she wouldn't be a perceived threat – or something you thought would hurt you.

"Another thought… if you were to gain more confidence in yourself being able to handle scary things better, Jason and being in front of the class wouldn't seem like a problem, even though you may have high sensitivities. You'd be confident that you were fine, like a giant with a pesky mosquito buzzing around. The truth is, everyone understands how tripping over a rope is normal when you're learning something new like Double Dutch. And you know people like you a lot, because you are such a kind person and you are never mean to anyone. You also know that Jason shows everyone standing around just how unkind he can be by picking on a sweet girl minding her own business. With all of that firmly in your head, you'd think of Jason as making a big mistake in front of everyone and maybe it wouldn't be embarrassing to you at all anymore.

"If you actually saw Jason as someone with a problem, maybe you'd wonder what on earth drives him to keep making that mistake and makes him lose more and more of his friends. Having that shift of thought can stop the panic altogether! Oh, and here's another shift of thought. What if you realized Jason was actually teasing you, in the only way he knows to get your attention, because he likes you? Wouldn't you think of it so differently?" Mrs. Kaufmann giggled. "You'd think he has a lot to learn about making girls like him!"

Emily laughed right out loud instantly. "That's crazy!" She paused, thought about it again, and giggled sheepishly with a twinkle in her eye.

"I'm just saying, what if? Or, what if you thought he thought that's the tough guy he was supposed to be. What if the adults in his life put pressure on him to be like that? Maybe he's trying hard to be someone he isn't, and he can't seem to be that, either. Wouldn't that change him from the bully to a bit of a victim? I can't help but notice the kids who need to control things more than others, or need to have more power or need more attention. I assume they feel out-of-control or forgotten about, and I feel sorry for them, you know? I feel like everyone will eventually get annoyed with those kids, and someday they will have no friends. It's kinda sad.

"Maybe Jason doesn't get to have a juicy brain like yours, so he doesn't get it, or he can't get it. Maybe he doesn't have the antennae long enough to pick up on the signals and cues from other people. You can almost feel bad for some bullies who may have a sad story and can't feel good enough just being themselves. So that's what I think when someone is doing that kind of thing to other people, and I feel sorry for them. I've shifted my thinking from them as bad, to them as having to learn a hard lesson."

"I get it," Emily suddenly spoke up. "It's as if Jason is the victim of something else, and he doesn't know how to fix it. The only thing is, when I tripped and fell the other day, why did everyone laugh with him when he made fun of me? Don't they get it? And why didn't they feel bad for me since they knew I was crying?" Emily's eyes started to fill up. This was the part that hurt her the most.

"Oh, that's easy. Those onlookers will automatically react to that uncomfortable moment with Jason in power with a nervous laugh. I'll bet you dollars to donuts that if I were to ask all of them what they thought about what Jason said and did to you, they'd say it was mean, but they felt like they couldn't do anything against him or for you at the time. They respond with a little laugh, because he's laughing and he's controlling the crowd. And they aren't against you at all. They just don't have the power or the fearlessness to stand up to Jason. Next time he teases someone else, notice how you feel sorry for that person being teased, but you absolutely know 100% that you are not calling Jason on it in front of everyone. No way. And notice the other sympathetic people standing around who don't laugh, and don't stand up to him, and don't tell on him. They are afraid. And that, my dear, is the reason it seems like all the good people in the crowd seem to have agreed with the bully, even though they haven't – maybe all of them don't agree, but no one stands up for you because they have fear, too. Make sense?" Mrs. Kaufmann leaned back and waited to hear from Emily.

"So everybody's afraid of him? And maybe he's afraid of something that makes him be that way? That means everybody has some fear?" Emily asked, a little saddened.

"Yes, but it's not bad, it's just what human beings feel as they are learning or remembering they are fine being just who they are. In school, everybody tries to be accepted and liked, and sometimes they do the craziest things, thinking that will do it. Sadly enough, we could be the best at being ourselves, and we forget that. We keep thinking we aren't good enough, and yet we're each perfect. I'm the most perfect Mrs. Kaufmann there is! And you are the most perfect Emily Bauer there will ever, ever be in all of time! No one can be you better than you. And the best part is that you are always learning and getting even better at being you every minute of every day!"

Emily's face had the strangest smile. She was really thinking about what Mrs. Kaufmann was saying, and it made her feel so good inside. She even thought, for just a second, that all Jason had to do was relax and maybe he would be a better Jason. "Cool," she softly mumbled.

Mrs. Kaufmann seemed to pick up on what Emily was thinking. "Even Jason will learn in the near future, we hope, that he doesn't have to try so hard to be cool and tough. If only he had a juicier brain to be able to see how much embarrassment and fear he causes. If he could just see how his fear rules his brain, and how easy it is to let his thinking shift to be more understanding. So, all you have to do is feel sorry for him and his victim when he starts teasing someone. You don't need to laugh along, and no one expects you to stand up to him. You only need to have on your face what you are feeling for the whole thing, like sorry or sad or worried.

"If enough people could have the confidence to just be what they are and feel what they feel, then the reactions might be noticeable for Jason to see the effect he's having. It would be like a natural lesson. He'd no longer see all the onlookers as his approving audience. Instead, he'd realize they were all just a lot of individuals each looking at him with disapproval. The day that happens, he may just finally get it."

"I get it now. I do feel better when I feel sorry for him instead of me," Emily admitted. "I didn't think he was losing his friends, because I thought everyone was on his side because they laughed. I didn't realize they were just followers and afraid of him. That helps. The only thing is, Mrs. Kaufmann, what about when he teases me the next time, and my 'lizard brain' makes me cry?" Emily challenged her.

"Well, that's where the tips and tricks come in!" Mrs. Kaufmann was pleased to offer. "First of all, once the brain does its flooding and the adrenalin does its number on your body, you need to relax, breathe deeply, and let the brain and body have some time to run its adrenaline course. Even if your 'lizard brain' wants to panic because it thinks it's supposed to be in control, now you know it will just take a few minutes for the body's physical reactions to finish, and you will get yourself back to what feels like normal. You aren't out-of-control. You are just feeling real physical reactions. That sequence of events will run its course, and normal will come back, I assure you. Just accept that this is the feeling of fear, it is real and you don't have to be afraid of it. It's a real and natural feeling."

Mrs. Kaufmann continued. "As for what you do while you're waiting right there in the moment, here are some choices. First, you actually can cry. Since you now know that everyone in the crowd is not as tough as Jason, then most, if not all, will see what he did and they will know it was wrong. It's as if you get to make a statement without having to do anything other than be yourself. The consequences will be the perfect after-effect. Remember Tara felt bad for you yesterday? I'll bet a lot of other people felt bad for you, too, or at least were happy they weren't you! Allow him to learn his lesson. He needs to learn it.

"On the other hand, if you feel stronger and don't cry, you can just look at him as if he doesn't get it. Remember that it's not about you not being okay. It's about him *needing* control or attention. Try to stay with that thought to feel in control. Then the attention of the others around you will go back on him, and they will witness that *he's* not okay. Don't tangle with him. He's had a lot of practice, and being insulting is not you. Don't get down to that level. Stay Emily. We all love her! And you and I will help him find the good Jason in there and bring him up a level. I need to help all my chickens, remember? And lastly, if you're lucky enough to have a friend near you who would make you feel not alone, that's great. Sometimes it only takes one ally or friend to make an actual *force* of two people, and that may be enough to make the bully less confident."

"I have Tara!" shrieked Emily. "She told me she'd be there for me!"

"I thought so. And Tara has no problem being who she is. I'm very impressed with that, because not too many people your age have that sense of being comfortable or being worthy. It's special, and she's lucky. Notice how she accepts all people as they are and never insults anyone, never judges anyone as wrong or bad, and never blames anyone. She is just who she is, and all other people have the right to be who they are. I love that about her, don't you?"

Emily was quiet for a minute. She had never given that any thought. Right now she couldn't even think of another person in her whole grade like that. In fact, she didn't know many adults like that, either. "That really is special. I wish I could feel that comfortable being whatever it is I'm supposed to be. I'm just not sure what that is."

"I can tell you. Think about this. Who are you when you play with your new puppy? Are you sensitive to his needs? Do you have a sense of humor when he's funny? Are you caring to make sure he doesn't get hurt? Are you clever finding ways to keep him active? Do you nurture him and cuddle with him to make him feel loved? So you are all those things and more, right? Wow, you are really special. And truly, Emily, doesn't everyone like you because you are kind and respectful of them? I won't embarrass you by making you answer that, but a lot of people know what a great person you are. I would definitely invite you over to my house if I were in your class. I would enjoy having fun with you, for sure!"

"Thanks," Emily shyly mumbled. "My mom always tells me to 'do good things unto others no matter what they do unto you' and I try."

"Well, my dear, we have to stop for today. Geography is almost over, so I have to slip you out to the next class."

"Oh, that's okay, Mrs. Kaufmann. I don't mind if anyone sees me. I can just tell them we were talking about lizards' brains!" she laughed and stood up. She walked out of the office with a peppier walk than the scared little shuffle she had coming in.

Mrs. Kaufmann smiled to herself. She saw that Emily grew a little today, and she felt good that she seemed ready for tomorrow! She also knew tomorrow would hopefully be shift number three – Jason!

Jason's Back!

Sarah ran to tell Emily that she just saw Jason coming in the front door of the school with his parents, and that they looked all serious. Mr. Gardener was in the hall to get his homeroom students to come into the classroom before the late bell rang. He heard Sarah calling out to Emily, but he quickly interrupted with a cheery, "Good morning, Emily Bauer. And how are you today?"

Emily had just made it before the bell, and smiled back. "Good morning! I'm fine, thanks," as she went into her classroom. Mr. Gardener was happy he interrupted Sarah so that Emily wouldn't hear the news even though she would soon enough. Jason might make it to homeroom, but he doubted it. Re-entry after a suspension took a little time. Hopefully he would be back a little calmer, but he doubted that, too. Knowing Jason, he would be angrier than ever, so Mr. Gardener was happy Emily was having a happy morning…so far.

Mrs. Kaufmann left her office to go down to greet Jason and his parents. What happened at that re-entry meeting would say a lot about whether Jason had changed his thinking. She hoped he finally could see that his teasing caused embarrassment. She also hoped his parents were both more aware of his unusual need for attention and for approval.

"Good morning," Mrs. Kaufmann said to Jason and his parents when she saw them sitting in the waiting room outside of Mr. Gonzalez's office.

"Good morning, Mrs. Kaufmann," Mr. Abbot responded as he stood up to shake her hand. Jason smiled, and his mom looked up at her, also smiling. "Thank you for your time and your advice," Mr. Abbott added. "You just never know what kids are thinking, but my wife told me about your conversation, and I realized we needed to have a talk with Jason. We've explained why he has to think before he teases others. I think he understood that he's been going too far to get the approval of his peers. Anyway, Jason has promised me that there won't be another incident of bullying."

"I'm really happy to hear that. I'm sure Jason just needed to connect what he was doing to how it has affected others. He has a kind heart and I'd hate to think he was turning his friends against himself while he's trying to impress them," Mrs. Kaufmann assured them. She also reminded them that she would meet with Jason during his recess to give him some help dealing with how to make that change. She shook their hands, told Jason to come to her office after lunch, and left to check on Emily.

As she left the main office, she was feeling relieved that Jason's parents had talked and had helped Jason understand that he needed to watch what he said. Better yet, Jason was now aware he had made his classmates uncomfortable, and he even seemed to be really embarrassed. This was actually great news. She saw a different Jason with a calmer, more humble look on his face. She also noticed Mr. Abbott looked not only less angry, but also somehow more quiet and cooperative. Jason's mom looked relieved that the tension was gone and a turnaround was started. Mrs. Kaufmann told all three how proud she was of them turning what seemed like a bad thing into a great lesson. She said she couldn't wait to chat with Jason during recess, to hear how he planned to make things better. She stood up and added, "Mr. Gonzalez will also be very happy to hear Jason is a new young man!" Just then, Mr. Gonzalez's office door opened, the Abbotts stood up, and they disappeared into the room.

Mrs. Kaufmann was heading back to her office when she saw Emily and Tara walking toward her, smiling and waving hi. Feeling Emily's boost in confidence right then, she took that as permission to speak to her in public. She wanted to give her the good news that Jason seemed like a changed man. "Hi, Tara! Hi, Emily! How are you two? How's the World Hunger Day display coming along?" She thought that was the perfect comment to make out loud, getting them to come over and talk with her more privately.

"Oh, you should see it--it's beautiful, even if we do say so ourselves," bragged Emily with a cute little smile on her face.

"In fact the whole display has been chosen to go to the county library!" Tara chimed in happily. "Hey, Mrs. Kaufmann, when does you-know-who come back from suspension?" she asked for Emily's sake.

"Well, I'm happy to tell you that I think he has understood what he was doing and has promised not to do it anymore. Isn't that the best news ever?" Mrs. Kaufmann was showing her joy.

"Really, really?" Emily jumped in.

"Really, really," she answered. Mrs. Kaufmann knew there were no guarantees when it came to people wanting to change and then actually doing it, so she added, "Or at least I believe he's really, really going to try."

"Cool," Tara said as she and Emily turned to take off happily for their next class.

The Last Shift

It was time for recess and Jason promptly arrived at Mrs. Kaufmann's door. He came in with much more energy than what he had that morning at the principal's meeting. "Hi, Mrs. Kaufmann," he said, as he sat down on one of the big chairs facing her desk.

"Hi, Jason," Mrs. Kaufmann answered back with an upbeat energy to her voice. "So you survived the suspension?"

"Yes, but just barely," he grinned. "My father was so mad at me when we got home on Monday that even my mom looked afraid. I figured I was going to get grounded for the rest of my life for making him leave work and come to the school for me. After we got home, he wasn't speaking to anyone. He just slammed the door when he took off for work. I didn't see him again that day. The next day, it was so weird. He got home from work early. He and my mom did a lot of talking, and I mean a lot!"

Mrs. Kaufmann jumped in, "Do you think it was about you?"

"Oh, it was about me all right, and it was about what you said to my mom, too, because I heard your name a couple of times. I couldn't hear it all, but whatever my mom said to him calmed him way down, and she usually can't do that. Anyway, instead of my dad going to work this morning, we all had to sit down at the table and talk some more. He said you said that everyone's beginning not to like me. Is that true?" Jason was looking into Mrs. Kaufmann's eyes as his were filling up with tears. He took his sleeve and wiped them away roughly to pretend his eyes just had something get in them.

"Well, my dear, I do know that kids don't like to be afraid of their friends. I've heard from some that when you tease people that aren't your friends, like Emily, they see that as mean behavior. I do know that your friends like a lot of things about you and would probably feel more comfortable being with you if they didn't have to worry about the kids you tease. I know you aren't a mean person, but I think you and I have to talk about teasing and when it's okay," Mrs. Kaufmann assured him.

"When is it okay?" he asked.

"When you and a friend are together and you are enjoying a feeling of trust and closeness and you say something that brings you closer with laughter. It's when the two of you trust that neither one is trying to hurt each other. It's fun and it doesn't embarrass or humiliate or out-power the friend."

"So I like Emily, and I was just trying to be funny. Why'd she have to go and cry and make people think I'm mean or something?" he asked with sincerity.

"Jason, have you ever cried in public? Like right in front of other kids when you didn't want to?" Mrs. Kaufmann asked.

"Yeah, when I saw my neighbor's dog get hit by a car. I couldn't help it. I thought he was dead, and I always took him for walks. It was so embarrassing because I couldn't stop. I just ran to the bathroom to hide."

"I remember that day, "Mrs. Kaufmann nodded. "That must've been awful. I've had tears come down my face, too, and right when I don't want them to! Well, that's what happens to Emily when she's afraid. It's automatic and she is so, so, so embarrassed that she usually doesn't want to come to school the next day. She wants to hide out at home."

"She's afraid of me?" Jason asked with complete shock. "Me?" he said again. "Why? I was just joking! All I said was something like 'How was charm school, Grace?' My father always says that to me, and I don't cry," he insisted.

Mrs. Kaufmann knew this was hard to take because Jason really wasn't mean. He was copying the kind of teasing his dad had taught him. And he thought he was making his friends laugh so they'd like him. "Well, Jason, here's the deal. Whenever we speak in front of a crowd of people, what we say has much more power, or shock, or ability to embarrass the person you're talking about. Notice that you're not talking to Emily, and you two aren't close friends who trust each other. To her, you are unpredictable and scary. And she knows she can't do comebacks because she isn't like that. She isn't a teaser. So she has to stand there with everyone appearing to laugh at her, and feel all humiliated until someone can help her go hide. Understand?"

"I guess so," Jason answered weakly. He was definitely beginning to relate to that instant crying thing, and the awful embarrassment thing. He wasn't sure about the power thing, but it made sense. "So what do I do about Emily if she's afraid of me now? And how do I fix things with my friends if they don't trust me?"

"Well, Jason, how do you feel about getting Emily to trust that you won't tease her anymore? Are you really ready to change? You know, once you start treating people with respect, they'll start to notice you're acting differently than when you made fun of them. It may take some time before they'll realize that and trust that you won't hurt them. However, you really can't out-power or embarrass them in front of the other kids from now on. If you do, they won't trust that you've really changed. Maybe a short apology to Emily might help her think you care about her feelings. How do you feel about doing that?" Mrs. Kaufmann put out a lot of tough questions to him to see if he was serious about changing his behavior.

"I guess. That will be weird. I don't know how to do that," Jason said looking shyer than he had ever looked before.

"What if I let Emily know you'd like to say you were sorry? I'm not sure I can get her to come face-to-face with you, but I could try. I could let her know she'd be safe with you and me in this office, and that you weren't intending to hurt her anymore. But, this is only if you want to, and only if she's willing. I could even call her in from the playground right now and meet her outside this door so she doesn't have to talk to you if she's too scared. What do you think?" Mrs. Kaufmann was quite convincing, and Jason trusted that she would keep her word. Plus, he figured she could help if anything felt too weird or went wrong with Emily, like crying or something.

"Okay," he spoke firmly, probably to convince himself he could do this.

Immediately, Mrs. Kaufmann scribbled a note to Mrs. Tanner and went into the hallway outside her office. She asked a student who was passing by on the way to recess to please deliver it. The note requested that Mrs. Tanner please ask Emily to please go see Mrs. Kaufmann for a minute or two, because she had a question. In less than five minutes, she heard Emily huffing and puffing, out-of-breath from running across the field to come inside to see her. As soon as she heard Emily's knock, she got up and went out into the hallway to talk to her.

"Emily my dear, I have the best gift for you right now, but you have to tell me if you are brave enough to receive it," Mrs. Kaufmann announced, holding her breath.

"Sure, I guess, what do I have to do?" Emily answered with a question and looked confused by not being invited into the office.

"Guess who is inside my office right now and is sorry for the way he teased you, and wants you to know that? And all you have to do is step inside, with me there, and let him apologize. Can you do that? Can you remember to make the shift in your thinking to remind yourself that he's been a bit of a victim, too, that he wants to change his ways, and that he really wants people to like him again? What do you say, sweetie? Can we do this together?" Mrs. Kaufmann knew Emily just needed to feel safe, and this was a pretty good set-up for that.

"Can I leave if I want to?" she checked.

"Absolutely, the instant you feel uncomfortable. I think, though, that you realize now that he doesn't want to hurt you. He wants you not to be afraid of him. And you get to practice your courage right here and now. The new and improved Emily Bauer! Are you ready?" Mrs. Kaufmann gleamed with a huge smile as she opened the door to her office for Emily to follow her in. "Jason, I let Emily know how you feel so she would be willing to come in and hear what you have to say. Would you like to tell her something?" she coaxed.

"Yeah, Em, I'm sorry. I was just joking around with my friends. I wasn't aimin' at you. And it just struck me funny when you guys were trying to jump in between two messed-up ropes goin' all over the place. Besides, my father says that to my mom all the time, and she never got upset. I didn't think you'd cry to get me in trouble. I even thought you'd laugh. Sorry," Jason repeated. He was so sincere that you could see Emily's anxiety just melt.

"That's okay. And when I cry, it just happens when I get embarrassed. Like, whenever you make fun of me in front of everybody, and then they all laugh, that makes me feel like there's something wrong with me. Tears just roll out and I don't know how to get away so everyone won't see. Mrs. Kaufmann says I have that kind of brain. My mother thinks she does, too." Emily tried to make sure Jason didn't think she was trying to get him in trouble.

Jason realized how the two of them were so different. "I was just teasing, not trying to hurt you. Don't you tease Sarah or your other friends sometimes, too?" he challenged her.

Holding her ground for the first time, she answered him firmly, for Emily, "I tease with them so we can laugh together. I never do it to make them feel uncomfortable, and I never say anything embarrassing about them out loud in front of a bunch of other people. That would make them not want to hang out with me. Plus, it would make me feel like I was being a mean person, and I don't like that feeling."

Emily had given Jason an easy lesson in friendly teasing versus mean teasing and, seeing Mrs. Kaufmann's approving face, went a little further. "And if I kept doing that kind of teasing to Sarah all the time until she was afraid of me, then they'd call me a bully."

"I'm not a bully!" Jason snapped back and Emily got quiet. Mrs. Kaufmann quickly jumped in, "Not anymore, I am thrilled to say! Right, Jason? You're a whole new person, and I am so proud of you for being willing to apologize to Emily. And Emily, I am so happy you were courageous enough to talk with Jason and let him know how you feel. You both did an excellent job explaining how you see things differently. Jason, you have helped Emily see today that she doesn't have to be afraid of you anymore, right Emily?"

"Uh," Emily paused, "I guess so."

Mrs. Kaufmann asked Emily, "What can Jason do to assure you he's not going to scare you anymore?"

"I don't know," she said quietly. "Just before when Jason said he wasn't a bully, he said it kinda strong and it made me feel a little bit scared," she admitted.

"Really? Oh my God, I just got excited. That's just my excited voice. I can't help it!" Jason exclaimed.

Mrs. Kaufmann announced quickly, "Now, look at that. You both have something about yourselves that you can't help. Emily reacts to fear easily, and Jason reacts to blame easily. Fears and tears for Emily, excitement and a louder voice from Jason, and neither one of you feels you can control it. They are great areas to work on for both of you. But they are also great areas to forgive of each other as well. Emily, can you understand that when Jason gets excited, he's just being him – nothing to fear? And Jason, can you understand that Emily doesn't cry to get you in trouble, but because she's embarrassed and she's just being herself, too?"

Both Jason and Emily happened to answer with a yes at exactly the same time at which point they both looked at each other and laughed. Mrs. Kaufmann laughed, too.

"You know what I love about all my little chickens here at my school? It's when they learn to understand each other. My guess is you both feel a lot better about each other now that you don't have to take anything personally from now on. Emily gets to grow up to be the best Emily she can be, and Jason gets to grow up to be the best Jason he can be. And what if someday you ended up being neighbors? Wouldn't that be a hoot?" Mrs. Kaufmann leaned back in her chair happily, knowing the final shift was made.

And, once again Emily and Jason looked at each other and laughed, having no idea what "a hoot" was!

Discussion Points:

- All people have their own lessons to learn, different from all others.
- The way people behave can cause different reactions in different people.
- Sensitivity varies from person to person. Some have a lot, and some don't, and nobody is wrong because of it.
- If you have learned something about treating people fairly, it doesn't mean all others have learned it, too. Be patient with them.

Reflection Questions:

1. Have you ever thought some people were mean or bad and then changed your mind when you got to know them?

2. Do you think all people act the way they do for a reason they think is right? What causes some people to make fun of others? What do you do when you see someone do that?

3. Are all people the same when it comes to being shy or sensitive? Are there people more sensitive than you? Are there some less sensitive than you? Is it something you think can be controlled easily?

CHAPTER 3:
My Teacher Is Picking on Me!

Teddy's Defense

"I couldn't find my homework, but I did it, honest! You can even call my mom. Mr. Moonie is so mean. He should be called Mr. Meanie! He wouldn't believe me, and he gave me a zero and a lunch detention today. And my dad is going to have a fit!"

Teddy was almost in tears, he was so angry, as he paced back and forth in front of the school counselor's desk. Instead of taking off with his friends after the last Hillstown Middle School bell rang for the day, he had raced to the guidance office to get help. He didn't want to go home with that homework detention slip his teacher, Mr. Moonie, had given him. He was so angry and so scared that he didn't even mind getting his language arts teacher in trouble by telling on him. After all, to Teddy, it really wasn't fair at all. And he always felt safe with the school counselor, Mrs. Kaufmann, because she at least always listened to what he had to say… unlike Mr. Moonie.

Teddy continued ranting desperately. "And he's done that to me before. I know he doesn't like me, because he keeps picking on me. Last week I had to stay in from recess because he said I didn't do the composition we had for homework, but I did. When I handed it to him, he handed it back to me saying it wasn't long enough, and I was getting a zero. How come he gets to make up stuff like that? He just did that because he wants to pick on me. Sarah Dempsey's composition was just as short and he accepted hers. That is so, so, so not fair!"

As Teddy finished his explosion, he stopped pacing, collapsing into the chair in front of the big office desk. He looked into Mrs. Kaufmann's eyes through his tears, hoping she could save him from going home with that slip that was to be signed and returned to the teacher the next day. Mrs. Kaufmann knew Teddy got upset easily and was behind in homework every now and then, but today he seemed really at his limit.

"Oh, Teddy, I'm sorry you're feeling so upset. I can understand why you don't want to get into trouble with your parents again. Are you still grounded from the D you got in that class on your report card last week?"

"Yes! And my father went crazy and unplugged the TV in my room, too. Now he's going to be even madder! I'm afraid he's going to take away my computer this time. This is so not fair--I did the work!" Teddy announced loudly as he got more agitated. His eyes filled again as he sprung out of his chair and went back to pacing.

"Okay, my dear, can you wait a few minutes while I call Mr. Moonie, or do you have to go right home?"

Before her last words were uttered, Teddy exploded. "Please, no, don't call him. He'll get even madder at me and pick on me more, for telling on him, to you!"

"I don't have to, but I actually think if I call him, just the opposite would happen. See, once he knows you were so upset and came to me to try to fix things, maybe he'll see how much you care and want things to be better. It might help your parents feel better, too, if they thought you were this upset. The important thing, though, is that you would be willing to do what needs to be done, to make everyone happy. My guess is that you don't know what that is. Am I right?"

"You're going to call my parents, too?" Teddy gasped. "Not them, oh no, please don't call them. I'm already in enough trouble!"

Quickly, Mrs. Kaufmann assured Teddy of her usual procedure. "Teddy, what I normally do, and I won't if you don't want me to, is to first call the teacher and tell him you'd like to make things better between you both, and wonder what you can do to make that happen. And we know what he's going to say. He'll probably complain that your homework is not coming in on time, or you don't complete it, or something like that. He will give us his entire list of things that are bothering him, so you and I will know it all. Then you and I come up with a homework plan that you think will really work, and one that takes care of all the problems. We'll make sure it will make him happy.

"And then, the next part is when I call your mom and explain how upset you are. I'll tell her we've put together a plan to improve things between you and Mr. Moonie, and I'll assure her it should improve your grade, too. We'll ask for her help making this plan work. What do you think your mom would say to me if I called her with that?"

Mrs. Kaufmann gave a big smile. She then told him she didn't have to do any of that, but usually kids didn't get in as much trouble if they were sincere about accepting the responsibility for changing. She assured him that if he was honest about making things better, his parents might even be relieved. "And the bonus is typically that the adults become supportive and help their kids, rather than become angry, frustrated, and punishing. And then the last part is presenting a plan we are all excited about, including your parents. How could everyone not be happy about that?"

Mrs. Kaufmann continued, while Teddy seemed to look really interested and sat down facing her again. "See, Teddy, parents get upset when they feel their kids won't do what they need to do to succeed in life. They feel responsible, and they get all emotional when they feel so helpless. Then they figure if they punish their kids, then the kids will start to do what needs to be done because they don't want to be grounded, or they want to get their televisions back, or whatever. But now, think about this, my dear--if their kids actually offer to do that themselves, and even ask for their help, well…that can make all the difference in going from fear and anger, to loving support. Can you see how that works? You can take the load off of them if you really want to make things better. And, as for teachers, they feel responsible for teaching. They have a certain amount they must cover in a school year, and then the students are tested on it all. Every teacher feels that the student test results are really their results – showing how well they taught. So, you see, Mr. Moonie cares about you learning, but he also feels your test scores are really his report card. Does that make sense?"

Teddy had been positive that any phone call would just blow things up worse. But as he listened, he could see the logic in the plan that was being offered. "Oh," he said, as he figured maybe there was hope with this way out. He didn't have another idea, and maybe he could trust this had worked for the school counselor in the past. What did he have to lose? "Okay, you can call Mr. Moonie, but please don't tell him I'm here. I don't want him to come and yell at me some more."

"I won't if you don't want me to. I'll let him know I'm just looking for information so I can help you to help yourself." She smiled, and Teddy smiled a weak smile back. He leaned forward on the big desk between them, biting his nails while bracing for that call. "Oh, and did you say you needed to get right home? I don't want your mom to worry that you're not home as fast as she thought you would be." Mrs. Kaufmann knew she'd need a little time for this call.

"Oh, no, that's okay," Teddy assured her. "I told my mom this morning I was going to stop by the music room after school again today, to get some sheet music to practice for the play try-outs. My mom knows I take a while there, since Mr. Maurice has a whole lot of choices, and he sometimes teaches me stuff on his electric guitar. We even jam together! He is so cool, and he helps me a lot. He really likes me."

Teddy had just made it obvious to Mrs. Kaufmann how he was excited to do a lot of extra work for a teacher he liked and thought liked him. "That's really great. I hope you get music that shows how talented you are on that guitar, because I'd love to see you make the play. I also can picture you getting a solo for the holiday concert if Mr. Maurice thinks you're ready. You've been such a fast learner!"

"That would be awesome!" Teddy lit up at just the thought. He loved playing the guitar and would forget all else whenever he got into it. It even took away his worry at the moment, just imagining playing a song like a rock star with a microphone on stage.

"Okay, let's make that call to Mr. Moonie. Are you ready?"

"I guess it's okay if you tell him I'm here, Mrs. Kaufmann." Teddy sat up, bravely getting ready for whatever was going to happen.

She winked at him and said, "You're very courageous. Thank you. That will impress him, I'm sure. And did you know how bravery is defined? It's when you face your fears rather than avoid them, and that's what you are doing. I am very proud of you, Teddy." She picked up the phone and dialed Mr. Moonie's extension. He answered very quickly and seemed to be annoyed.

"Hi, Mr. Moonie, I'm here with Teddy Cambria. He knows he hasn't been giving you his best work recently and wants to start doing better in your class. What can I tell him you'd like him to work on to improve his grade in language arts?"

"Oh, he knows," Mr. Moonie snapped back loudly. In fact, Teddy could hear his voice over the phone across the desk, and his eyes got wider. Mrs. Kaufmann signaled him with an assuring nod and motioned with her hand to relax and just be patient, letting her handle it. He sat back, squirming in his seat, but was staring at her with his heart pounding through his throat.

"Oh, I'm sure you've told him," Mrs. Kaufmann answered in her most calming voice, "but I'd like to write it all down so we can work on an improvement plan together. Just give me the list so it covers everything that has typically gone wrong. He says he really does want to start doing better, and I believe he means it. I'll even call his parents to see if they can support his plan from home. After all, that's what we all want, right?" Mrs. Kaufmann felt she needed to soothe the moment with Teddy's teacher, so she didn't stir the pot and set him off again.

"If you can make this student want to work, it will be a miracle!" Mr. Moonie continued his rant. "He is so lazy, and he cuts corners on everything he does. If I ask him to write ten sentences using the new vocabulary words, he writes three- or four-word sentences showing me he never looked them up. That's why he's getting a D in my class. He can't pass a test. And he doesn't read. I assign thirty minutes a night, and he hasn't finished a book yet, one month into the new marking period. I even let them pick the books! And when I ask for a paragraph every night in his writing journal, he'll just string three or four sentences together instead of a paragraph. I get the same or better work from the kids with learning disabilities, and Teddy is actually very smart. In fact, today he used that old excuse that he did his homework, but didn't have it. Why should I believe him? No homework, no credit is my policy. How else can they learn what I'm teaching, if they don't practice? I can't wait to see how he does on the achievement tests at the end of the year! It will look like I didn't teach him a blessed thing!" Mr. Moonie had taken one long breath and spewed out all his anger at once, and ended with a sarcastic comment.

"I can see where that would be upsetting. Teddy and I certainly have our work cut out for us, but we will come up with a plan that should show improvement starting tomorrow. By the way, do you need for him to read only books, or can magazine articles count sometimes, too? And if Teddy needs help learning the parts of a good paragraph, where should he go for help?"

"Oh, I would show him whatever he needs, if he'd just show a little interest. I'm here after school on Tuesdays, Wednesdays, and Thursdays. And I don't care what reading he does, I just want him reading at his level, thirty minutes a night. And sorry I went off about him just now. I just get so frustrated with students who are so smart and yet so lazy. They learn they can get by with so little effort because they are so smart. They don't even mind failing language arts, because they can't see the consequence down the road. We both know how important reading and writing are in our lives, and that it can really make or break us all through school. Teddy has so much potential and he's throwing away his career options. He doesn't even seem to care, and that just frustrates me so much." Mr. Moonie finally opened up to Mrs. Kaufmann about his serious concerns when it came to students in general.

"I know. Is it okay if I tell him all you said, so he can see where you're coming from? I think he thinks you don't like him, but if he knew how much you want him to do well in life, then he may realize just how much you do care for him. Would that be okay?" Mrs. Kaufmann knew Mr. Moonie also needed to see the situation from Teddy's point of view, too, though Teddy looked quite uncomfortable when she said that. Again, she winked at Teddy as if to say it would be all right, trust me.

"Sure!" Mr. Moonie reacted with gusto. "Really, anything you need to help turn this student around. And for the record, I really do like him. He has such a great personality and is really talented. I feel bad when I have to give him a recess detention for no homework, since I know how much he loves to play soccer at recess. He is a good kid, and I want him to work up to his ability. I just get frustrated, and that may be why he thinks I'm not happy with him. Please let him know that it's only about his lack of performance that I get on his case. I am really sorry if he thought otherwise. Please tell him, okay?"

"I will be more than happy to tell him. Thanks so much for all your help, and I'll have him let you know if he is able to go for extra help after school to get what he needs on paragraphing, okay? I'll see if his mom will let him stay after school with you for that." Seeing Teddy look relieved and totally relax in his seat made Mrs. Kaufmann feel good about the first part of her deal. *Now for part two*, she thought.

The Plan

"Okay, Teddy," Mrs. Kaufmann said with renewed energy, almost like she was shifting gears from being very calm and careful with Mr. Moonie's anger, back to being upbeat and helpful with Teddy. "Now I think I have enough information from Mr. Moonie to help you. Oh, and by the way, he does like you. You'll never guess why he gets on your case. He thinks you're a great kid who is really smart but wastes his ability being lazy. How about that?" she announced to him triumphantly. Of course Teddy smiled really big. He was like a puppy dog that truly just needed people to like him and give him a little pat once in a while. And Teddy knew he messed up with homework here and there, so he felt like he was just always in trouble and no one liked him.

"So what do we have to do now?" he asked Mrs. Kaufmann. "Are you calling my mom next?"

"Not, yet, my dear. We have a plan to design. *Then* we can call your mother. Are you ready to work on one with me now? I mean are you really ready?" Mrs. Kaufmann was energetic and as positive as she could be, hoping for a lot of the same from Teddy. And it seemed to be working as Teddy sat straight up in his chair, looking ready.

"Yup!" he said, finally feeling like his night might not be so bad after all.

"Okay, first we have to figure out a very usable schedule for you to do your homework every night, and what homework you'll do when. Then, we'll troubleshoot where things go wrong in the process. We have to look at each step, from getting an assignment in the classroom, all the way to bringing it back, done. There really are a lot of steps along the way, and you might have your homework done perfectly and on your desk at home, but you know his policy!"

"I know," Teddy moaned. "No homework, no credit," he mimicked Mr. Moonie.

"That's right," Mrs. Kaufmann agreed. "And you know what? It really is a good policy. Most people will have that same grading policy no matter where you go in life. Besides, if you were the teacher, how would you grade something that's not there?" She winked at Teddy, and he smiled with an acceptance of this new truth in his life. He had to admit, his teacher was actually right.

"And lastly, we'll start a system you can use to make absolutely sure your homework is done the way Mr. Moonie wants it done, so he thinks you didn't do a lazy, shortened version. Does that sound like a plan?" Mrs. Kaufmann was getting a brand-new small notebook for Teddy. She wanted to make it look official and to make sure that Teddy, his parents, and Mr. Moonie could all read what the new deal was.

"Let's start with homework time. How do you like to work? Do you prefer doing the quick, easy assignments first to get them out of the way? Or do you like to tackle the hardest ones first, and then finish off with the easier ones? And where do the language arts assignments fit in?" she asked.

"Well, I usually save language arts for last because I don't like writing or reading. I like doing my math and science homework right after dinner, since it always seems easy to me. The problem is, the longer into the night I wait to do language arts stuff, the more tired I get. Then, I *really* don't want to do it. Plus, my favorite TV shows come on at 8:00, and I also want to play games on the computer. So then I rush through the language arts stuff, so my mom will see that I did them, and then I can watch TV. The only thing is, she asks me if I did my reading, and we argue about that, so I don't always get to watch TV in the end anyway." Teddy was being completely honest and sounded frustrated with what must've been his nightly torture.

"I have an idea." Mrs. Kaufmann perked up. She suggested a totally different approach. "Why not come home from school and do the written part of your language arts homework right away, while you're having your snack? That would make it really nice with the snack and all, and it would get it out of the way for the night. And it might not seem so hard if you weren't so tired by then. Your brain would not feel drained from all the other homework, and there would be no computer game or TV show that would be calling to you, you know? What do you think? Would that work?"

"I guess so, except on Tuesdays when I go to karate. We have to leave by 4:00 for my class, and since I ride my bike to school, I don't get home until 3:30. But, maybe my mom wouldn't mind picking me up from school on Tuesdays. She picks me up whenever I ask her to, so that might work. When she does get me on Tuesdays, I usually have extra time before we leave for karate. Can you write that down in the notebook to ask her?"

"Great idea, Teddy, and here's another thought. What if she can't get you after school on Tuesdays? Can you use some of your last-period spelling practice time to do your written language arts homework instead? Maybe Mr. Moonie would let you use that time if you promise to practice the spelling words with your mom, like maybe when you're going back and forth to karate? And I'm sure your spelling test grades would have to stay up to cut that deal, don't you think?"

"That would work. My mom never minds quizzing me, and Mr. Moonie has always told us that as long as we use that last period wisely, he doesn't care which we do." Teddy then looked a little embarrassed as he admitted that he and his friends usually just wanted to talk. He said that they pretended to be practicing spelling with a partner, but it really let everyone get away with just talking with friends.

"Okay, so we've found a good time for the written language arts. Now, how about the reading you need to do each week, and the journaling afterward? How many pages, and when do you read?" Mrs. Kaufmann continued as she wrote down what Teddy had agreed to do right after school.

"Well, I have a book I picked out to read, but when I go to bed and find my page, I fall asleep so fast because it's boring."

"And maybe you're too tired by then, too?" Mrs. Kaufmann thought he might have to really change up the reading part, by the sound of his daily schedule. "Does the reading have to be done on school nights? And did you know Mr. Moonie said magazine articles are acceptable, too?" she asked.

"They are?!" Teddy asked with great excitement. "Even my sports, and car racing, and guitar magazines? I read them on the weekends all the time! I love them!" Teddy was totally renewed. He found the perfect answer on his own. "So if I just read an hour on Saturday morning, and an hour on Sunday morning, and, of course, write about it in my journal, I can be done with my whole week's worth of reading homework? Really, that is so cool! I can do this!"

Mrs. Kaufmann was thrilled that Teddy was so excited. "And if you do the reading on the weekend before that next school week, instead of playing catch-up on the weekend that follows it, you will really be ahead of the game! It will be as if you were turning in a week's worth of homework before it's even due! Won't that knock Mr. Moonie's socks off?"

Teddy's eyes lit up. He was feeling he could honestly do this plan now, and the burden had lifted. "You got it, my friend!" said the school counselor. "You have a great plan so far. Let's just finish out with the troubleshooting, and then we'll call your mom, okay?" Mrs. Kaufmann knew Teddy was definitely on a roll.

"Sure!" Teddy was totally fine now.

"All right, the last part of the plan is to look at each step along the way. Ready?" Teddy couldn't sit up straighter or be more positive. "Do you always write down the homework assignments?"

"Yes, Mr. Moonie makes us copy them from the board first thing in the morning when we come in."

"Do you understand what you are to do for each one?" she continued.

"Not really, because he doesn't explain it till we get to the end of the day."

"When does he explain it?" Mrs. Kaufmann pushed.

"Usually just as we are packing up to go home. I am sorta listening, but it's sometimes too noisy, and I'm rushing and thinking about what books I need to take home," Teddy explained. "I'm also really happy to just be getting out of there," he admitted.

"Would it help if Mr. Moonie explained it before the last few minutes of the day?" Mrs. Kaufmann offered. "I'll bet if he realized what's happening to you, he might realize it could be happening to others, too. Okay, let's keep going. Who do you ask for help when you get home, and you realize you don't understand what you're supposed to do?" Mrs. Kaufmann figured this could be one of the reasons his work had been unacceptable.

"I ask my mom, but my mom doesn't know what he wants, and she tells me it's my job, so I just do what I think he said." Teddy was realizing right then that not understanding some of the assignments was definitely causing him a problem. Up to then he had been only guessing at what Mr. Moonie wanted them to do, and getting that right had been hit or miss.

"You know, Teddy, you actually might have a legitimate problem that could be fixed by your teacher. I could let Mr. Moonie know about his timing, and maybe he can explain the homework directions after lunch or something. However, just in case he plans to continue what he's been doing, have you ever thought about calling someone at night, just to make sure it's clear what you are to do? And hopefully you know someone who is a good student in his classroom. Also, maybe after school on the days you get a ride from your mom and he offers extra help, you could stay for just a few minutes to say you couldn't hear him, and would he please repeat it. I don't know any teachers that would not want to do that for their students," Mrs. Kaufmann assured Teddy.

"I could do that. Bethany Thompson is my next-door neighbor and gets 100's in language arts. I can ask her when we're walking home any day, because she's nice and she never minds, either. I just have to catch up with my friends after talking to Bethany, because I'll get teased. Denny Pritchard always laughs at all the guys whenever they talk to girls. He points at them, and he yells out that we love them!" Teddy told Mrs. Kaufmann.

"What if you start out walking with Denny first and then tell him you have to run and ask Bethany a quick question about the homework, and you'll be right back? Do you think that would let him know what it's really about, so it wouldn't be so much fun to tease you?" she asked Teddy.

"Nah, I bet he'll tease me anyway. I think that's how he gets the girls to get all upset, and he seems to like that. But I can try it, just to see if it works. Otherwise, I'll tell Bethany to ignore him, and I'll remind Denny she's just my neighbor. That might do it." Teddy was into the problem-solving swing of things, for sure.

"That just might work," Mrs. Kaufmann said, showing Teddy she liked his idea. "Okay, a couple more troubleshooting questions and we're done. If you have the correct homework, and you get it all done, where do you put it to take back to school?"

"Oh, on my desk, but I think that's not working because that's where it is today," Teddy replied, with a mischievous smile across his face.

Mrs. Kaufmann laughed. "Well, I guess not. Where else could your homework go so that you know for sure it goes with you to school the next day? And I suggest it goes there as soon as it's done, so you don't have to remember it in the morning when you're not thinking yet," she said, leading him right to the logical answer.

"I guess if I put it in my backpack as soon as I finish it, I can't forget it," Teddy concluded. "And Mr. Moonie always lets us go to our backpacks to get our homework when he comes around to collect it, because that's my homeroom, too, so the backpack is right there in the closet."

"Perfect! Teddy Cambria, you have now officially completed your homework plan! Congratulations! Oh, I almost forgot, I think you needed some help writing paragraphs, too. Remember, Mr. Moonie might be quite impressed if you go see him after school this week. Besides Tuesdays, which don't work for you, he offered Wednesdays and Thursdays, too. This could really prove to him you are sincere about making things right. I also can't help but think your grade is going to come way up now, and this should make your parents ecstatic! You must be feeling pretty good right about now, too, huh?" Mrs. Kaufmann was thrilled for Teddy. She liked him a lot and knew he was just not very organized. And it seemed such a shame that he really believed his teacher was picking on him.

"Call my mom!" Teddy demanded. "She will love this!" he exclaimed, as he jumped up out of his chair. This time his pacing was from excitement.

What a different place Teddy is in now, in just a handful of minutes, thought Mrs. Kaufmann as she dialed his mother's number. A woman answered who sounded like Teddy's mom. "Mrs. Cambria? It's Mrs. Kaufmann, and I have some really good news!"

Did "The Plan" Pass?

"Hi, Mrs. Kaufmann, you have good news? And it's about Teddy?" Mrs. Cambria answered, almost with disbelief.

"Yes! He's actually here with me now, and we have spent a good deal of time working on a master plan for changes he's willing to make to improve his grade in language arts class," Mrs. Kaufmann announced proudly, while looking at Teddy's proud face as well.

"Oh, for heaven's sake, that is amazing news. What brought this about?" Mrs. Cambria questioned her.

"Well, you know how you bottom out when things get really bad? That's usually when you realize something has to change, because you're so miserable, right? Well, I think today was Teddy's turning point. He had forgotten to bring his homework to school today for Mr. Moonie, and ...."

"What? Again? Oh, no!" Mrs. Cambria interrupted Mrs. Kaufmann, sounding more frustrated than angry. "His father told him if that happened one more time...."

"Wait, please let me tell you the whole story, okay?" Mrs. Kaufmann jumped in, so Teddy's mom would not get all worked up. "I promise, you will hear you have a changed boy." Mrs. Kaufmann saw some fear on Teddy's face but continued in her positive manner, smiling at Teddy to help calm his fears.

"So, anyway," continued Mrs. Kaufmann, "your young man, as sensitive and kind as he is, was so upset with everyone being angry with him, and feeling unable to please anybody, that he came to me to get help. So he bravely let me call Mr. Moonie to ask him for specifics on everything he needed to change. Then Teddy took the list, and very honestly and sincerely worked with me to construct a new homework plan, taking everything into consideration. He's really been troubleshooting like a pro, and I think he has done an excellent job. Now all we need is your support. Would you like to hear the plan?" Mrs. Kaufmann hoped her enthusiasm would be contagious.

"That sounds wonderful! And thank you so much for helping him," Mrs. Cambria declared with the very enthusiasm Mrs. Kaufmann wanted to hear. Mrs. Cambria continued, "When Teddy and I talk about homework, the conversation always ends up with me hollering at him, and then he ends up crying. We never get anything accomplished."

"Okay, well for starters, I'm going to put my phone on speaker so we can all hear each other, okay?"

"Hi, Teddy," Mrs. Cambria said, to see if he could hear her.

"Hi, Mom," Teddy answered, letting everyone know they were connected.

"Let's get started," Mrs. Kaufmann began. "How do you feel about helping Teddy begin his language arts homework right when he gets home from school, by making sure he eats his snack with it? Teddy figured he wouldn't be too tired yet, and he usually doesn't have any other plans for that soon after he gets home, because he wants to sit down and eat, anyway."

"Sure, that sounds like a really good, efficient idea if he's willing. What do I do if he doesn't want to do that work?" she asked.

Teddy heard the question, and Mrs. Kaufmann let him answer it. "I guess I won't go out to play until it's done?" he asked his mom, as if to agree to his own unpleasant punishment. "I'll also make sure the rest of the homework is done right after dinner, so I can have enough time to play some computer games before TV. Is that okay, Mom?"

"Thank you, Teddy," Mrs. Kaufmann praised him. "That is a great built-in consequence. I think you will really appreciate having it to motivate you on the days you really don't like the assignment."

"I like it, too, Teddy. It shows me you really mean to stick to this plan." Mrs. Cambria followed Mrs. Kaufmann's positive lead.

"Let's continue." Mrs. Kaufmann then reported to Teddy's mom more of the plan. "Teddy offered to do all his reading and journaling on the weekend actually *before* the reading is due. He will be turning in his journal entries on Monday mornings, and they won't be due until Fridays. Mr. Moonie even agreed to let him read age-appropriate magazine articles. Isn't that great?" Mrs. Kaufmann kept up her cheerleading approach, feeling as if the old frustrating feelings on both sides were slowly slipping away, and were being replaced by a hopeful and refreshing change for their evenings. "Also, Teddy said he will put each piece of his homework into his backpack immediately as he completes it, so he can't possibly forget his homework anymore."

"Wow, this is so great, Teddy! I can't wait to share this with your father when he comes home tonight. I even think maybe we can consider giving you back the games you had taken away, if you can follow this plan the rest of this week," Mrs. Cambria offered.

"Thank you, thank you, Mom!" Teddy was really excited and happy.

"Of course," Mrs. Kaufmann broke in, "we do have to make sure Mr. Moonie thinks this will take care of everything that concerns him. And Teddy, if you really try to do a good job on your assignments, and not rush through them, I'm sure he will be astounded by the new you!"

"Oh, I will. And, Mom, can I stay after school for some extra help from Mr. Moonie on Thursday this week? I don't get paragraphs," Teddy offered.

"Music to my ears," Mrs. Cambria laughed. "Oh, but what about your language arts homework on Tuesdays, when you have karate?"

"Oh, yes, Teddy said he can do the language arts homework during that last-period class when the students are supposed to be studying their spelling words with a partner," she said as she winked at Teddy, and he responded with a smile. "Of course, we will check this out with Mr. Moonie, too. Plus we have to let him know that at the end of the day, when he tells the class how he wants the homework done, there's always a lot of hustle and bustle in the classroom, and Teddy doesn't always hear or remember, because he's packing up and hurrying to leave with the rest of the students. I thought he might be able to move that to another time, but we'll see."

"Mom, you know how you like to quiz me when I have a test?" Would you mind doing the spelling words with me when you drive me to karate on Tuesdays?" Teddy jumped in.

"Certainly, that would make sense. Boy, this is an excellent plan, Teddy Bear. You really can do such great things when you put your mind to it," Teddy's mom praised him. "Unless something comes up, I'll try to pick you up on Tuesdays so you can have a little time to change and have your snack at home before your class," she offered.

Teddy knew everything would be fine now, and that he had done something his dad should be proud of, too. He added, "And any day I don't understand something, maybe you can call Bethany Thompson for me?"

"Sure, honey. Actually, I can just call her mom because we're friends, and she can put her on the phone for you to talk to really quickly. I know calling her yourself would feel weird," Mrs. Cambria suggested, trying to give Teddy a full opportunity to make sure it was all very clear.

"Well, Teddy, it sounds like Mom likes your plan, and I'm sure Mr. Moonie will, too. I'm sure he's already gone for the day, so we'll talk to him tomorrow. Maybe we can meet with him in morning homeroom? The best thing you can do is call Bethany today when you get home, to make sure your first assignment turned into him is done really well. We don't want him thinking you are lazy, so tonight's homework for tomorrow is really important, okay?" Mrs. Kaufmann wanted to set the stage for the teacher's supportive reaction to Teddy the next morning.

"Okay, Mom, I'm not going to Mr. Maurice's today, so I'm coming home, okay?" Teddy was talking happily and comfortably with his mom now.

"Sure Teddy, and I'll sign your homework slip, and we'll get you started on your plan before your dad gets home. I'm going to let you share your whole story with him, and I'm sure things will be fine. I love you--see you soon." Mrs. Cambria was also sounding happy and relieved by all she heard. "And thank you, Mrs. Kaufmann. I can't tell you how much I appreciate your doing this."

"You are so welcome. I think he could use some praise and any other positive reinforcement you can think of to get this commitment to continue, if you know what I mean," Mrs. Kaufmann added.

"I do, and I'll talk to my husband tonight. I think we'll be fine. Have a good evening." And with that, Mrs. Cambria hung up the phone.

"Thank you, Mrs. Kaufmann," Teddy chimed in immediately. "Bye!" He grabbed his backpack and tore out the door for home.

Mrs. Kaufmann jumped up and went out of her office, calling to Teddy down the hallway, "Don't forget to come to school a little early tomorrow so we can talk to Mr. Moonie in homeroom. And by the way, good job, kiddo. I am really proud of you!"

"I will, and thanks again," he called back, with a voice fading as he ran through the school doorway and headed for the bike rack.

Mrs. Kaufmann knew that the supported plan was now in place at home. All that she now needed to do was to turn the tide of Mr. Moonie's frustration into one of pride. That might be no easy task. It depended on Teddy and his willingness to make the hard changes. As she picked up the phone to leave a message on Mr. Moonie's extension, she was still thinking about Teddy and his evening. She was hoping that Teddy's excitement would be praised by his dad that night, and that Teddy had what it took to make sure his language arts assignment was done really well. *I can only help get it started*, she thought. *After all, everybody has free will and makes their own choices on their personal journeys.*

"Hey, Mr. Moonie," Mrs. Kaufmann started her voice message. "Good news. Teddy and I created a very workable plan for him to improve his grades, and his mom supports it completely. I think you will see a new Teddy tomorrow, if all goes well. Call me when you get in tomorrow morning if you have the chance, okay? I'd love to share what Teddy and I eventually put together, and with his mom's blessing. I also hope Teddy will be in early, too, so maybe he can explain it to you. He's extremely proud. I hope you will be, too." Mrs. Kaufmann felt she had planted the seed and could go home now feeling good that "The Plan" passed…so far.

The Verdict

Mrs. Kaufmann could see her voice-mail button was red as she walked into her office early the next morning. She hoped Mr. Moonie had already arrived at school and left a message. She figured Teddy might show up any minute and wanted to talk with Mr. Moonie before they were all together. She picked up the phone to listen to the message before she even put her purse down.

"Good morning, Mrs. Kaufmann. I got your message from yesterday after school, and I am happy to hear Teddy may be doing a turnaround. I am, however, a little skeptical. I guess I need to see it to believe it. You know lazy kids. They are full of promises until they get lazy again. Anyway, stop down or call me when you get in. I have to put up a lot of board work, so I'll be here in my room," Mr. Moonie said with his usual business-like tone.

Mrs. Kaufmann quickly put her bags down and took off for his classroom, closing her door with a "Be Right Back" sign just under her Welcome sign. She arrived at his door within minutes and gave him a cheery "Good morning!" hoping to start the conversation off on a positive note.

"Good morning," Mr. Moonie responded. "So I hear Teddy is a 'new man'?" he said, with a twist of sarcasm in his voice.

"Oh, I have my fingers crossed!" Mrs. Kaufmann said, with a twinkle in her eye. "I know you'll believe it when it happens, but I really think he's willing to own his plan this time. He was so sincerely honest with me about what goes wrong. For example, as the admittedly disorganized person that he is, he doesn't hear your homework requirements at the end of the day, no less write them down when he's packing up. Would there be any way or a better time he could get those specifics, when he's paying more attention and not so rushed? He also said sometimes it's hard to hear because everyone else is moving around and stacking their chairs at the end of the day, too."

"That's true," Mr. Moonie conceded. "Maybe I can spend more time in homeroom in the morning when they are all writing down the assignments from the board. Or, better yet, I can also write down the requirements with more detail. And I've started thinking about putting the daily homework information on my website. This is actually giving me some ideas to help all the students, as well as their parents."

"That would be excellent. I'll bet you would really cut down on missing work and get a lot better results on their test scores, too," Mrs. Kaufmann jumped in. "Also, I'll let Teddy tell you more, but he's going to take you up on your offer to read magazine articles instead of books. I figure his high interest is there, which will get him to enjoy reading and into a schedule that may work. Once he has that in place, maybe some really short exciting books will be the next transition step. What do you think?"

"That does sound good, and I will be thrilled if he actually does start reading. As for the journaling, do you think he'll come by for paragraphing help?" Mr. Moonie asked, as his voice began to sound less cynical and more willing to be supportive.

"Yes, he and his mom would be happy if you would help him, and I think they were planning to do that this week. Also, he really wants to start his language arts homework in your end-of-day spelling practice time on Tuesdays, because he has to go to a class after school, which will take up his homework time. He promised to study his words with his mom that day in the car going to and from the class." Mrs. Kaufmann felt his cooperation and thought she'd take care of that little bit of negotiating before Teddy came in, so the stage was set for success.

"Sure, that works even better because he can come up to me for help on his homework right then. That's as long as he can concentrate with all the students talking and quizzing each other. He is easily distracted, but I have seen him really focus, too." Mr. Moonie had just finished as he and Mrs. Kaufmann felt the chilly air come down the hall, along with Teddy Cambria. He was walking more confidently this morning, and Mrs. Kaufmann hoped it was because he had done a great job on the homework.

"Good morning, Teddy!" both Mr. Moonie and Mrs. Kaufmann called out to him at the same time.

"Good morning," Teddy answered with a continued confidence. He just knew Mrs. Kaufmann was telling Mr. Moonie about the phone call he and his mom had had with her the day before.

"How did it go with your dad last night?" Mrs. Kaufmann asked Teddy right away.

"Fine. He wasn't mad. In fact he really liked our plan, but he wants to wait until this weekend to give me my games back, to see if I will keep it up all week."

"That's good news, Teddy. And remember, it's really your plan. How did it work out last night? Oh, and please share with Mr. Moonie, too. I've been telling him you'll read magazine articles, and you'll do your Tuesday night homework in that last period study time instead of spelling, and he's okay with that—right, Mr. Moonie?" Mrs. Kaufmann was trying very hard to make the smooth transition from where Mr. Moonie and Teddy had left off yesterday, and it seemed to be working. She knew so much about success being the result of setting the right intentions and working from an "I can do it" attitude.

"Yes, Teddy. And I'll be interested in hearing how your homework and reading will be done from now on. Why don't you come in and show me what you did last night and tell me all about it? Oh, and I hear you are a really good musician! Is that right?" The positive tone of Mr. Moonie's voice spoke wonders. Mrs. Kaufmann could hear him put out every effort to make things feel changed and positive between him and Teddy. And when Teddy began to brag about all he did last night, and all he intended to do, and his love of guitars and soccer, Mrs. Kaufmann knew Teddy was going to be just fine. His plan had passed, and the verdict was a big "thumbs up"!

Mrs. Kaufmann went back to her office and called Mrs. Cambria to let her know how well it had gone with Mr. Moonie. Mrs. Cambria confided in Mrs. Kaufmann, "You know, last night was the first time in a long time Teddy had all his work done, and done well. There was no homework fighting, and he snuggled up so happily between his father and me on the couch. I felt like our Teddy Bear was back."

Mrs. Kaufmann knew then the shift had happened with all of them. She also knew how powerful a force it is once you decide to make a positive change with the confidence that you can do it. That's when it happens!

Discussion Points:

- People who show strong emotions against you may really be acting from their fears.

- When you are in a bad cycle of things going wrong over and over, you can break that cycle with your own positive actions first.

- Sometimes you need to take a good, honest look at what you're doing to contribute to the problem in order to find a way to fix it.

- People who give you constructive criticism might be doing it to help you. Listen to it first, to see if it might be true.

Reflection Questions:

1. What made Teddy change his mind about how Mr. Moonie felt about him? When someone disapproves of something you do, does it seem like they don't like you in general? Do you dislike some qualities or behaviors of some people but like other qualities or behaviors about them?

2. What was Mr. Moonie really upset about?

3. Why was it easier for Teddy to work for Mr. Maurice, the music teacher, than for Mr. Moonie, the language arts teacher? Do you see people respond to you better when you show them you like them?

4. What was it about Teddy and Mrs. Kaufmann that helped them design a successful plan?

CHAPTER 4:
Our Friends, Our Mirrors

She's So Mean!

Cassie rolled her eyes and cupped her hand around her mouth as she whispered something into Jenn Tritter's ear. Jenn's head tilted back immediately with loud, exaggerated laughter, and they both looked behind them down the hall at Ashley. "Ashley's pants are the ugliest green I've ever seen, like grasshopper green," Cassie squealed to Jenn so everyone around them could hear. Jenn followed that remark again with her dramatic, attention-getting laugh, to make sure everyone knew she agreed with Cassie and found whatever she said to be wildly entertaining.

"I hate them!" Ashley whispered to Beth, as they were just ahead of them heading for math class. "They are so mean!" Ashley mumbled as she kept her head down.

Beth glared back at both Cassie and Jenn to declare her loyalty to her friend. Ashley flew toward the girls' room they were about to pass without even feeling her feet, and Beth kept up by her side as they both pushed through the door to get safely inside. Ashley's face was beet red, and she could hear the dreaded horrible laughter of Cassie and Jenn echoing in the hallway as they passed by outside the bathroom door. Ashley was more mortified than angry and felt there was no place to hide to make those mean girls leave her alone. And Beth knew Ashley was right. Once Cassie and Jenn got on a roll, they would continue the taunting for the rest of the day in and out of all the classes.

Ashley fumbled through her purse to grab her cell phone and call her mom. Once her mom answered, she cried, "Mom, would you please, please, please drop off my khaki crop pants at school for me before you leave for work?" And with that, the late bell rang through the halls, making Beth check her watch immediately.

"Why, honey, what's the matter? Are you okay? Did something happen to your new green ones?" her mom reacted with concern. She knew that sound of her daughter's voice crackling into tears very well.

"Uh, no, I mean yeah, I'll tell you tonight, Mom. I'm okay, I just can't wear them," she answered, hurriedly clearing her throat so as not to alarm her mother. "Thanks, Mom," Ashley said as she turned off her cell phone and dropped it back in her purse. She then wiped the tears off her cheeks and turned to Beth, speaking urgently. "Beth, you have to get to class! You can't be late again to Mr. Garfield's class. He'll lose it all over you because of the last time. Thanks for sticking by me. I'll go down to Mrs. Kaufmann's office right as class begins and see if she can call Mr. Garfield to excuse me, and maybe she'll let me wait there for my mom. I'd rather die than to go to class with everyone laughing at my 'grasshopper-green' pants! Just go!" Ashley insisted.

Beth looked relieved and gave her a quick, "Are you sure?" And with Ashley's nod she called out, "Thanks!" over her shoulder as she gathered her things and bolted out the door to algebra.

Ashley went to the big mirror on the bathroom wall to see if her eyes still looked red and waited until the hall fell silent. She then slipped out the door and scampered like a mouse just down the hall to the Hillstown Middle School's guidance office door and pushed her way in to the waiting area, knocking impatiently on Mrs. Kaufmann's inner office door.

"Hi, Ashley," Mrs. Kaufmann answered with concern as she opened the door. "Are you all right?" Ashley's anxious face was telling her the answer.

Ashley answered quickly, "Can I please come in, Mrs. Kaufmann? I didn't know where else to go. It's Cassie. She's doing it again. She started making fun of me as loudly as she could to Jenn Tritter in the hallway so Jenn would laugh and everyone else could hear. Now they're all looking at my new pants, and everyone's laughing at them and me. I just called my mom and she's bringing me my plain khaki-colored pair of pants when she goes to work. Can I stay with you until she comes?"

"I like those pants, Ashley. I really do. Is there something wrong with them, like a rip or stain or something I don't see? I think they are really cute!" she assured her.

"I did, too, until they started laughing and pointing and calling them 'grasshopper green.' Now I don't ever want to put them on again."

"Tell me when your mom goes to work. Is she leaving right now? And I thought you and Cassie had different math classes. Aren't you scheduled for algebra right now? You wouldn't even be with her."

"I know, but I didn't want to be in the hallway at the same time, because she could start it all over again. And my mom will leave for work in about thirty minutes, so she should be here right about when algebra's over. Oh, and would you please tell Mr. Garfield that I'm here with you, so he doesn't think I skipped class? Please?" Ashley begged.

"First of all, my dear, I really can't let you sit out of an algebra class that you need because you want to avoid Cassie, but I can send you to class with a note to Mr. Garfield saying you had been talking with me at the beginning of class, and would need to return to me right before the end of algebra." Mrs. Kaufmann's offer to Ashley appeared to raise no objection. "That way you'll get your lesson in, I'll meet with the parents that have an appointment with me in a few minutes, and you can still avoid Cassie in the hallway as you come to get your new pants. I have to say again, I really like your pants. They are cute as a button!" Mrs. Kaufmann insisted with a smile. "I don't get what's wrong with grasshopper green or lizard green, or turtle green, or any other green for that matter. When they are cute, green is just a color. Besides, I happen to like grasshoppers, anyway." And she smiled again.

"But what if everyone laughs at me in algebra?" Ashley challenged her.

"No one fools around in Mr. Garfield's class, ever, right? You'll be entering when everyone is working, and you'll leave before it breaks up at the end, so you should be safe. May I ask, what was the reaction to your pants this morning when you got to homeroom?" Mrs. Kaufmann challenged back. "I'll bet you got a lot of compliments from your friends, right? And do you really want to send the message to Cassie that she can control you? You need to be the one who has the power over what you do. What if she does that with your khaki-colored pants? Would you call your mom to change them, too?

"Maybe we have to plan for a different strategy after algebra. Personally, I would have announced how much I really liked my new pants right out loud if she was trying to make me feel bad about something I liked, but that's me. I know you wouldn't be comfortable doing that. It's just that no one has the right to treat another person with such little respect for their feelings, but we don't have to let them control us, you know? Anyway, what do you say? Let's not let her comments rob you of an algebra lesson, too, okay?"

Mrs. Kaufmann then wrote out the two passes, one for arriving late, and one for leaving early, with a brief note to Mr. Garfield saying she would explain why later.

"I guess that would work, thank you, Mrs. Kaufmann," Ashley answered quietly. She realized it all made sense, but she could still feel the embarrassment as that echo of their laughter played over and over in her mind. She left the guidance office, holding the outer door politely for a man and woman who were just coming in. She looked both ways in the hallway and, seeing no one but the custodian sweeping, she arrived at the algebra class door in no time. She handed the passes to Mr. Garfield and quickly landed in her seat. He never missed a beat with what he was describing on the board, so the students held their gaze on that instead of Ashley. She was relieved and caught his approving nod toward her as he waited for a student to answer a question. She was home free – for now.

Plain Khaki or Grasshopper Green?

As algebra class was nearing the end, and the homework was noisily being turned in, Mr. Garfield nodded again to Ashley without calling attention to it. Ashley knew this meant she was allowed to leave, and was grateful no one else noticed. She gathered her books smoothly and went out the door without any disturbance. She went back to Mrs. Kaufmann's guidance office waiting room and sat down. She could hear people talking in the inner office, so she decided not to knock but just sit there safely, out of sight and with no chance she could run into Cassie and Jenn.

Within just a minute, the office door opened, and the school counselor emerged with someone's mom and dad saying their "thank yous" and "goodbyes." Mrs. Kaufmann looked to Ashley to let her know to scoot right on into the office while she finished up her parent conference confidentially. And within another couple of minutes, Ashley heard Mrs. Kaufmann re-enter the office with a robust greeting. "Well, I'm delighted you're back, Ashley, my dear, and with those adorable pants of yours! Did you have any problems going in and out of Mr. Garfield's class? And did you get your algebra lesson and homework assignment for today?"

Ashley smiled. "Thanks, Mrs. K, I don't think Beth would've been able to explain 'functions' to me on the phone tonight so I could do my homework, and I know my mom can't. It's a good thing I went, after all. And Mr. Garfield didn't say anything for anyone to hear, so that was good, too. Thanks again."

"You're welcome, sweetie. By the way, I never got a call from the office that your mom dropped off your pants. Do you want to run down to the office and see if maybe she did? Or are you okay with your adorable green ones for the day?" Mrs. Kaufmann gave Ashley a knowing smile and was hoping she was feeling a bit stronger after algebra. She waited through a long pause.

"I'm not sure I can. I'd like to try, but what if Cassie really gets to me? Maybe I can just run down to the office and check. Then, if they're there, I can take them with me for just in case?" Ashley knew she shouldn't bow down to the pressure, since she wouldn't be able to keep it up anytime Cassie was out to get her, but just this time she needed to test her ability to ignore her.

"I have a better idea," Mrs. Kaufmann interrupted. "How about you and I talk for a few minutes to get to a better solution, and I'll just call down to the office to find out, okay?" She picked up the phone, asking Ashley if she knew why Cassie was doing what she was doing. She was interrupted by the office telling her that Ashley's mom had just dropped the pants off. "That's good to know. I have Ashley with me now, and she will come by sometime this afternoon to pick them up off the counter. Thanks." Mrs. Kaufmann hung up the phone, noticing Ashley looking a little surprised, since she expected to go right down to the office to get them.

"Shouldn't I just go now?" she reacted.

"I wanted to see if we can come up with a different plan first. You can't wear plain clothes forever, and maybe there's something that can be done to make Cassie treat you better. Can I help you be done with this whole problem?" Mrs. Kaufmann suggested. "I'm not trying to hold the khaki pants hostage, Ashley; you can go get them when we're done if you feel you still need them, okay?" Mrs. Kaufmann joked. "Remember though, that really will only fix it until she thinks of the next thing to tease you about – like khaki pants! Now, let's do some troubleshooting. It sounds like she's angry, or jealous, or hurt, or something. Do you have any idea what may have happened right before the teasing began?"

Ashley hesitated before she finally began to shed some light on recent events. "I, I, well, last weekend, we were all at Jake's birthday party, and I think she likes him, but he asked me to go out and not her. I'm thinking it might be about that, but I'm not sure. I didn't make him like me, so why should she be mad at me? I didn't try to take him away from her, because they weren't going together. He never actually asked her to go out. And Jake and I already broke up yesterday anyway, so I don't get it."

"I have an idea," Mrs. Kaufmann perked up. "I need to work with a few girls in your class on a Peer Leadership project again this afternoon. If they end up talking about the party and they share anything with me about this, would you like to know?" Mrs. Kaufmann knew the girls loved to talk while they prepared for their classroom outreaches, and this would be the perfect opportunity to ask about how great Jake's party turned out, since they had all been excited about it the week before.

She continued appealing to Ashley. "Sometimes we don't even know what we do that impacts other people. And sometimes people get all wrapped in themselves and can't see the bigger picture. We automatically assume the other guy is to blame, even if it's all a matter of what we think we see, or how we interpret what appears to be happening around us. Want me to see what 'the word on the street' is? Of course I won't be telling you who said what. That would be private. But I can ask if it's okay that I share with you. Most of the girls coming are very kind and would hope to help you clear things up. That's why they were chosen as Peer Leaders in the first place. They really care about others."

"Yes! Absolutely!" Ashley answered with enthusiasm. "That's what I need. Thank you."

"That's great. I meet with the Peer Leaders during seventh period, and I don't want you to lose any more class time, so how about you swing by my office on your way out of school at the end of the day? Sound good? Now let's get you back to class. What do you have next, music? And you can stop by the main office and grab the khaki pants for 'just in case you need them' on your way to class, but I don't think you really need them any more do you? Besides, grasshopper green is so much more 'the hot color' this spring than khaki, don't you think?"

Ashley smiled and agreed. "I guess so. It just made me feel safe. I won't be near Cassie much this afternoon anyway, since we have specials pretty far apart and different homerooms. I'll come right here on my way home. Thanks, Mrs. K!" And she quickly took her pass to get into music class late and gathered her books.

"Oh, one more thing, Ashley--I'd like to suggest that you put some thought tonight into whether you would be willing to talk to Cassie yourself in my office with my help, or let me talk to Cassie for you, especially if the Peer Leaders don't end up talking about the party. It's just a thought and may seem scary at first. I can promise you that I'd focus on making it a very safe problem-solving chat, if you know what I mean. And you could get a lesson on how to do that type of mediation talk. You'll learn 'I messages' for yourself in case this ever happens to you in the future with Cassie…or with anyone, for that matter. I can't promise you that it will all stay relaxed and unemotional the whole time, but I've never had two people not resolve a conflict if they were both willing. And I won't let you both leave until you're both ready. Just give it some thought, all right? Okay, see you after school!"

"Uh, okay, I'll think about it." That was all Ashley could promise just then, as her head was suddenly flooded with visions of that possible meeting. She walked down the hall feeling relieved, at least for that day.

The Shock

At the end of the day, Ashley promptly arrived at Mrs. Kaufmann's door with great hope that the Peer Leaders had given Mrs. Kaufmann the answer to why Cassie had been mean to her. She really didn't want to have to meet her face-to-face, because Cassie always seemed so popular and always talked so loudly about everyone she wasn't close to. She seemed to be able to influence everyone, and Ashley never understood why. She just knew to keep her distance.

"Hi, Mrs. Kaufmann!" she called in to her open office door. "Did they say anything about me or the party?"

"Oh, Ashley, yes, as a matter of fact, they did. Come in, and let's close the door in case anyone else comes to see me." She continued excitedly. "It seems they were all talking about the 'party picture room' that Jake made on the internet inviting people to download their pictures. Do you know what I'm talking about?"

"Yes, I even put my pictures on there, but what does that have to do with Cassie and me?" Ashley asked, confused where this was going.

"Well, it turns out that one of the pictures of Cassie was really embarrassing to her. The Peer Leaders said it was one of your pictures, and that everyone has been making fun of her all day. They said she was in the background of a picture doing something not okay, and I have no idea what. They didn't say. They were just feeling bad for her because of it, and I didn't want to pry. Do you think that might've been on one of your pictures? Remember I said you might not even know that you did something, but she could be blaming you?"

"Oh, my gosh. I didn't think so, but I'll have to check it out tonight. I just downloaded them last night really quickly before I went to bed as soon as I saw the invitation for the picture room. Uh-oh. What if I did put something bad on there and I didn't mean it? I can delete it, but only after everyone saw it. I'd better go, Mrs. Kaufmann. I have to get home and try to see what she would be upset about. There might be a lot of people who didn't go online yet today, so maybe I can still delete it before they get home from school. Gotta run! Thank you so much!" Ashley threw on her jacket and headed out the office door.

"Good luck, my dear. I hope you find it. You can send an e-mail to me tonight or let me know tomorrow morning how you made out." Mrs. Kaufmann called after her. "Please think about talking with her tomorrow, okay?"

"I will," she called back, but was thoroughly focused on her mission at hand, with her heart pounding in her throat.

The Twist

As Mrs. Kaufmann walked into her office the next morning, she saw the usual red message light blinking on the phone. She hit the button to hear the messages while she put away her coat and turned on the computer. The first message was from a student from the evening before.

"Can I please meet with you, Mrs. Kaufmann? This is Cassie Birnkrandt. I have a problem, and I don't know what to do about it. I can come in early to talk, if you have the time. You can call my cell phone in the morning, since I plan to come over early for extra help in math. I can wait outside for a while first, in case you can call me in. I just really don't want anyone to see me waiting near your office door. No offense, but I'm dealing with something really embarrassing, and I don't want everyone knowing I needed to see you. Thanks, Mrs. K. Bye."

While Mrs. Kaufmann was listening to Cassie, her e-mail messages had come up and there was one from Ashley that read, "OMG! I did put a bad picture on Jake's party room page. I deleted it, but I have to ask you what to do. How do I apologize and convince Cassie I'm really sorry? The thing is, she posted one of her and me in our bathing suits from last spring, acting all sexy. It's an awful picture of me and really embarrassing, so now she may think I'm apologizing just to make her take it off. Can she do that? Can she put any picture of me she wants anywhere on social media without my permission? I can't believe it! She did that on purpose! See you tomorrow morning."

Mrs. Kaufmann now realized they were both coming in before homeroom this morning and could be running in to each other even then. Before she could act, there was a knock at her door. "Did you get my e-mail?" Ashley asked as she appeared in the office doorway. "I can't believe she did that. She posted it last night, and it's so bad of me. I look like a jerk, and she looks great. Now what do I do?"

"Did you think about what I asked you to? Would you be willing to talk to Cassie if we did it right now?" Mrs. Kaufmann asked.

"Right *now*?" Ashley choked on her words.

"Yes, we can, if Cassie would be willing to talk with you. She might be too upset, I don't know. But I do know I can call her and ask. She's actually coming in early this morning for math help, but has to wait at the front door until the teacher gets here. What do you say? This is the fastest way to resolve it all, and wouldn't that be so wonderful to put this all behind you?"

"Okay, I guess it would," Ashley agreed.

Mrs. Kaufmann picked up her phone and called Cassie's cell phone right away. "Cassie, this is Mrs. Kaufmann. I was wondering if you would like to come in to my office and talk with Ashley, who is here right now. Just so you're aware, she didn't know you were in the background of one of the pictures she posted on the party room page, and she felt really bad about it when she found out you were embarrassed. She wants to talk with you, if you are willing. What do you say? It really might be a good thing if you both could make peace with this, don't you think? She deleted the one she thinks upset you and hopes you could do the same. Good idea?"

Cassie was surprised Mrs. Kaufmann had Ashley with her, and that she knew all about what was going on. Now she felt bad for the picture she posted, but she also realized that Ashley must've really been upset if she actually went to see the school counselor. "Okay, I can come in right now," Cassie said quickly, "but will they stop me at the main office if I come in before the bell?"

"I'll call them and tell them you're coming to see me. Just come on in. And don't worry about a thing." Mrs. Kaufmann knew she was really speaking to both of them at the same time, with Ashley listening to what she was saying on the phone to Cassie. "You and Ashley are both kind people, and I believe this all started by accident. I also believe that what upset you is for the same reason it upset her. You both don't like to feel embarrassed. I totally understand how it happened, but now we can make it better very easily. See you in a minute."

"Okay, thanks, Mrs. Kaufmann. I'll be right there." Cassie sounded relieved, now that she heard Ashley was sorry and that Mrs. Kaufmann understood why she did what she did. She also knew she had to apologize to Ashley for the horrible picture of her that she posted on the internet to get even, but she was willing to do that now. As she went by the main office window, they saw her and waved her on so she sped down to the school counselor's office. She was just a little bit nervous about how it was going to go, face-to-face with Ashley.

"Are you okay, Ashley?" Mrs. Kaufmann asked before Cassie arrived. Mrs. Kaufmann needed Ashley to know she was safe, and Cassie was in a good place and willing to listen. "I believe Cassie is ready to hear what you have to say. I might suggest you apologize first, now that you can understand why she was so upset. I figure it will help if we start off at least owning responsibility for what we've done and move toward more understanding. I just always ask everyone to start with an 'I message,' okay? It makes everyone feel less defensive than when we start off with the word 'you.' That makes it sound like an accusation.

"Starting with the words 'I feel…' lets you understand what the other person is feeling and no blame is assigned. Usually, you can relate to that so you can feel some empathy and, eventually, some forgiveness. You don't have to defend yourself, but you do need to explain yourself. That really helps the other person understand you. After all, we are all just good people feeling like we want to be accepted and safe with each other. You and Cassie may be very different people, but neither one of you likes the feeling you get inside when you know you're being hurtful to someone else. You'd both rather be the kind, caring girls that you really are. I know that in my heart." Mrs. Kaufmann had a good feeling about this meeting and thought she'd continue laying the groundwork.

"Good morning, Mrs. Kaufmann." Cassie spoke quickly as she walked through the office doorway in a very businesslike manner. She plopped herself down in the office chair alongside Ashley, but without looking at her. She kept her eyes focused on Mrs. Kaufmann's eyes as best she could.

"Good morning, my dear Cassie. I'm so glad you're here. We don't have much time before the morning bell, so let's talk about this unfortunate misunderstanding so it can be cleared out and you both can have a great day, okay?" Mrs. Kaufmann spoke comfortably in front of both the girls to put them at ease. "Ashley, did you discover something yesterday that you did by accident that you'd like to explain to Cassie?"

Ashley looked right at Cassie and started pouring out her words. "Cassie, I'm so sorry. That picture of you with your arms around Cheryl's neck looked really bad, but I swear, I didn't even notice it in the background when I posted the pictures. I had been laughing and focusing on Matt and John making faces at each other for my camera. They were trying to look like geeks when I took the picture, so I was just looking at them. Then yesterday I found out everyone was talking about that picture, but about you and Cheryl behind them, not Matt and John. Then, when I got home and saw it, I deleted it right away. I'm really sorry. It was an accident." Ashley spoke quickly, holding back the tears and thinking Cassie was going to get mad again and stop her from finishing what she had to say before she lost her nerve.

Seeing that Ashley was really sorry, Cassie interrupted her, "That's okay, Ash. I thought you meant to post it on purpose. I didn't know it was an accident. I thought you were being really mean. And after Jake asked you out and you knew I really like him, I was so hurt. I was called so many names yesterday that I wanted to just die. So I guess I tried to get the attention off of me and put it on you. I couldn't think of anything else to tease you about, so I used your new outfit, and figured I'd make fun of the color. I know it was lame, and I'm sorry. I just thought you were being really mean to me." Cassie was so sincere in her pain that Ashley realized Cassie was feeling everything she would have felt, too, had things been reversed.

"I'm really sorry. I didn't know that. Is that why you posted that bathing suit picture of me?" Ashley was realizing that she and Cassie were more alike than she had ever thought before.

"Yeah, I'm sorry, too." Cassie truly felt bad about what she did. She realized she had tried to defend herself and yet had done something that was just as "mean" as what she was defending herself against. And she was definitely realizing the same thing about the two of them mirroring each other's reactions in the same way.

"Do you really think my green pants look bad, Cassie?" Ashley asked.

"No. I actually was jealous. I saw them when my mom and I went shopping, and she said we couldn't get them. When I saw you wearing them, and I thought you had been so mean to me, that was the only thing I could think of saying about them to make you not wear them. Sorry. And I was really angry that Jake wanted to go out with you and not me. I couldn't make him like me no matter how hard I tried, and you didn't even have to try. That made me even more upset."

"Funny how we can't control other people's behavior, huh? Well, not funny, but true." Mrs. Kaufmann wanted the girls to see the great lessons that were being given to them from this experience. "Also, I think we've realized that anything you do where there are cell phones or cameras around, and that's pretty much everywhere nowadays, is a possible picture posting for all to see. So that means all you do can now be seen by the world," Mrs. Kaufmann reminded them.

Cassie jumped in the conversation right then, "Oh, yeah, Ash, I'm sorry about that bathing suit picture, too. I was really mad. I'll get rid of that right away."

"That's great," Mrs. Kaufmann added. "And Ashley, you said you deleted that embarrassing one of Cassie after school yesterday, right?"

"I did. And thanks, Cassie. That one of me was really bad. You picked a good one to get even, that's for sure," Ashley laughed as she forgave Cassie.

Mrs. Kaufmann gave her last bit of a lesson for them before she stood up to send them off. "I know you two realize this now… that we also own our own feelings about whatever happens, and we need to allow others to own theirs. Ashley, you could have decided you were okay with your cute new pants, even if Cassie felt that jealousy or anger and teased you about them. I know you didn't want her to be upset, but you didn't have to be controlled by her, either, because you can only control your own behavior, not hers. And Cassie, Ashley knew she hadn't done anything to take Jake away from you, so that was something that hurt you, but she didn't have to feel responsible for it. We all follow our own paths or journeys in life. We just have to remember to also allow all of the seven and a half billion other people on this earth to follow theirs. I know it's hard to do, but it is good to remember when you're faced with a problem like this one, right?"

Mrs. Kaufmann saw that the girls were agreeing with her, and that the air had totally cleared. The school bell sounded with perfect timing, allowing all of the other students inside to start their day. Cassie and Ashley immediately jumped up out of their chairs, grabbed their backpacks, and began chatting happily. They were obviously feeling connected again. "Are you two okay now?" Mrs. Kaufmann asked, so that they could hear each other's comfort in their answers.

"We're fine," they both answered in perfect unison, almost in a singing harmony, causing them to giggle together too.

As they all walked to the office door, Mrs. Kaufmann asked, "Now wasn't it so much better that you two talked it out instead of letting all the anger and fear get bigger and bigger? Who knows how long it could've lasted? And, by the way, can you both see how you are so much the same? You actually show each other what it feels like to be on the other side – like mirrors. If something happens like this again, talk to each other. You really don't need me. Being honest with your feelings is all you need. You are both really good people and deserve to give each other at least that, okay? Oh, and don't forget to let Beth and Jenn and maybe Cheryl, too, know that the misunderstanding is over and the pictures are deleted, to give them some relief from the tension, too. Have a great day, ladies!"

Once again the girls answered at the same time. They giggled again as they started down the hall almost shoulder to shoulder. "Thanks, Mrs. Kaufmann," they said together as they headed to homeroom, with no worries that anyone would see them now.

"You're welcome," Mrs. Kaufmann answered, knowing they were in their own little happy world and not really listening anymore. She was thinking, *All my little chickens*, as she would lovingly call them, *stir up the same kind of fears in each other, and yet have the same needs. They are all mirrors, just little mirrors. What a great way for them to learn all the lessons they need to understand themselves.*

Discussion Points:

- All people are different, but we have similar feelings.

- We should not try to control other people, their decisions, or choices. We only need to control our own behavior.

- All of our decisions and choices have consequences…some good…some not so good…and some unexpected.

- We need to remember to treat people the way we would like to be treated.

Reflection Questions:

1. Do you think that everything you think is true? How hard is it to admit you didn't know something that you swore you did?

2. Are you able to think of someone you don't like as just a person like you? Are you able to imagine yourself feeling like they do if you switched places with them? Do you believe that all people just want to be accepted and safe?

3. When you are upset by something someone did to you, are you able to think back to what you may have done to them before that? Do you believe all arguments have two sides?

4. What are the hard parts about having an argument with another person? What is good about making up with a friend after an argument? Why are we so tempted to get even with someone for what they did to us? How do you feel about it after it's over?

CHAPTER 5:
I Feel So Lost and Alone

Orientation Panic

"I don't know what to wear," screamed Josie from her bedroom. "I don't know what they will all be wearing today, or what they'll think is geeky if it's too new or too dressed up, or whether they'll think I'm trying to be too cool by not dressing up, or...."

"Stop!" interrupted her mother from the kitchen, calling out loudly to end this next panic. "Just put on your new white pants and that cute top we got yesterday, Josie. None of those other new kids know what anybody else is wearing either. Did you forget that this is a new-student orientation we're going to? This is for everyone who is new, so none of them will be certain what the regular kids who already go there wear."

"But what if they have their *old* students there, too, you know, those kids that are like the leaders of their classes who help the teachers? They will be getting their first impressions today when all of us new kids come in. They'll be deciding right away who they think is cool, who's nerdy, and who's a loser, just by looking at us. All kids do that. I know. I always looked at the new kids at our old school to decide who I wanted to know and who I didn't. What I wear is really, really important, you know?" Josie called back, almost in tears as she stood in front of her closet door in her pajamas.

She knew this was going to be a scary morning for her, with all the new information about where she was to go for the first day in this middle school. She was so afraid of getting lost, not being able to open a locker, missing the bus home, forgetting a rule and getting into trouble, and walking everywhere alone with no friends. It was all like a nightmare. Why couldn't her dad have just kept his old job and let them all stay in their old home, in their old town where she could just be comfortable like it always had been? Why did she have to be "the new kid?"

"Okay, Josie," her mom spoke comfortingly, drying her hands with the kitchen dish towel, as she came into her bedroom and sat down on the edge of her bed. "Honey, let's sit down a minute and talk about today. I know we can make it more of an exciting experience rather than such a frightening one if we try, all right?"

"But it is scary. I won't know anyone, and they'll all be looking at my clothes and shoes, and telling me stuff I'm supposed to remember. What if I'm not pretty enough, or cool enough, or smart enough for this new place? Plus, this is my only chance to make a good first impression and I just can't blow it!" Josie broke into tears as she collapsed into her giant lime-green bean bag chair on the floor across from her mom.

"Oh, my dear, you can't see yourself, and I know you won't believe me, but you are perfect just as you are! You are Josie Wyatt, the only Josie Wyatt there is. You come packaged with all your uniqueness – your personal tastes, your style, the things you like and those that you don't. No one else could be as good at being you as you can be, and you can't be *not you*, anyway, even if you tried. You'd just be phony, or you'd look needy, you know? Those are the kids that keep trying to impress everyone, and they end up annoying everyone instead. Trying to make sure you are what they want just won't work. You just need to be the best you that you can be, that's all, and that's easy because it *is* how you're most comfortable being and behaving, anyway," her mom explained.

"Look, honey, I've been the new guy a lot in my life, and I've learned a few things from changing schools. That's how I found out that I couldn't be anyone else but me, anyway. I also found out that the people who were most like me were the ones who would like me most, and that they would end up being my absolute best friends because we'd be so comfortable together. Those are the people you hope you can make friends with early on, the ones you laugh with easily. So all this fuss about what kind of person you'll look like by the clothes you pick isn't worth your time. Pick out the outfit *you* like, one that says, "Hey, world, this is me, the perfect Josie Wyatt! This is my new outfit, and I like it!" Her mom's upbeat coach-like voice ended her little talk. "How 'bout we get a move-on so we won't be late? Now *that* would be a bad start! See you downstairs in ten minutes."

With that, Josie jumped up realizing the time, feeling a little better and grabbing her brand-new outfit, throwing a reluctant "okay" toward her mom.

Her mother then hurriedly went from Josie's room to get herself ready and make sure her younger brother Ben was dressed for his orientation as well. "Ben, are you ready? What are you doing? We're leaving in ten minutes," she yelled across the house.

"I've been sitting here watching TV waiting for everybody," Josie's six-year-old brother announced, never blinking from his zombie-like stare at the TV screen of cartoons. Ben was so unlike his twelve-year-old sister. He was happy about making new friends at his new school and not the least bit worried about a thing. Josie, on the other hand, could not get rid of the anxiety looming around her head and chest over every thought about how it would be. Their mom knew it would all be over in just a few days when the newness would start to grow old, but today might just be the hardest of all for Josie.

Ten minutes later, all three of them piled into the car. Their mom started the engine while Josie got into the front seat and began to bite her nails. Ben fell into the back seat happily playing with his new red racing car and humming a tune that went with the fantasy he was enjoying in his head. They backed out of the driveway and were finally headed for this event that they had talked about even before they had moved just a few days ago.

Butterflies in the Stomach

As their car pulled up to her school, Josie looked up and saw the words Hillstown Middle School across the front-door entrance. "Is this my school?" Ben asked as he looked out the window.

"No, this is Josie's school. Your elementary school is called Duncan Elementary and it's behind Josie's, on the other side of the playground. Your new-student orientation will be after hers. And by the way, Ben, that means you will have to sit quietly and patiently while Josie hears what she needs to hear. You have to be patient just like all the other younger sisters and brothers of the new kids for this orientation, until it's time for us to go to yours. Okay?"

"Okay," Ben answered like a robot, because he was barely listening as soon as he knew it wasn't his school.

"I think I'm going to throw up," Josie said quietly, as her mom brought the car to a halt.

"No, you're not. You will be fine. In fact, you might end up meeting a girl today from the new students that you could pal around with on the first day. Why don't you concentrate on that? Listen for someone who lives near us and maybe takes the same bus, or who is in your same homeroom, or just anything that you might have in common. And if you want, you can invite that person over for lunch after these new-student orientations, or maybe for just a visit this afternoon to get to know each other. Who knows, maybe that person might end up being your friend? That will give that little busy brain of yours something to do, other than creating these scary what-ifs that you are so good at doing."

Josie's mom was good at diverting Josie's attention to something positive, and it worked this time, too.

All three of them followed the signs to the office, where the office secretary quickly directed them to the cafeteria, because the orientation was about to begin. As they approached that room, the noise spilling out into the hallway became louder and louder. When they arrived at the big double doors, they could see a room filled with many new families in rows of chairs, talking amongst themselves nervously, as well as teachers just back from summer vacation huddled and sharing vacation stories in the back of the room. There was a group of administrators dressed more formally all talking together at the big table in the front, getting ready to be introduced. Josie's wide eyes scanned the room looking for any girls who might be her age, but her mom was moving too fast in order to get seated before the man turning on the microphone at the podium could start speaking.

"Good morning," his voice from the podium boomed out cheerfully over the crowd. "How is everyone this wonderful morning?"

Small mumbles from the adults were quite a subdued contrast to that robust voice starting the program. "Oh, we can do better than that," he laughed and declared loudly throughout the cafeteria. "Good morning!" he boomed again, inviting a response from the crowd.

"Good morning," the audience responded at much greater volume, and almost in unison, showing the school principal that he had everyone's full attention, and with even some smiles and giggles this time.

"That's much better," he complimented the crowd. I am Mr. Gonzalez, the principal of Hillstown Middle School, and I welcome you all to our school. I'd like to begin with a short PowerPoint presentation about the school, and introduce some of the teachers who happen to be here today getting their rooms ready. Then I will send the new students with Mrs. Kaufmann, the school counselor, to the library, so she can talk with them. While they're with her, I can talk to just the parents about your responsibilities for the year, until they return. Mrs. Kaufmann will end her portion in about thirty minutes, and will pair off our student leaders at each grade level to tour your children around the school for about fifteen more minutes, ending up back here. After you're reunited with your children, feel free to let them show you around the school one more time, or as often as you need to in order to feel comfortable for the first day. Then, those of you with younger children entering our K-3 school, Duncan Elementary, can go across the playground, along the walkway behind us to make it in time for their orientation.

"Okay, let's begin. First, let me introduce you to a few people." And with that, the principal presented many key people in their school system: the superintendent, the vice-principal, the school psychologist, the school board secretary, the school nurse, the PTA president, and finally, the school counselor, Mrs. Kaufmann. Josie had been sitting straight up, rather stiffly. She listened to each person speak, almost as if she had to memorize every word. In the meantime, Ben kept fidgeting and looking all around the room at the murals on the cafeteria walls. He could care less who all the people were and was just trying to sit still.

"Relax, Josie," her mom said quietly, knowing the butterflies in her stomach were certainly fluttering at this point. "You will be fine. Remember to see if you can connect with someone you feel comfortable being with, and get her name and phone number if you can, too." Josie didn't answer. Her attention was riveted on the school counselor as she stood up to speak.

"Good morning everyone, it's so good to see you all here today," Mrs. Kaufmann smiled fully and spoke in a quiet but welcoming voice over the microphone. "I always get excited to meet all my new students this time every year," she bubbled over with enthusiasm. "And my job today will be to have some nice, quiet time for us all to get to know each other. Just so you are warned, though, I plan to brag about our school," she said, smiling even bigger. "And to make sure we get rid of the butterflies this morning, I will be giving each of the students our new handbook, as well as their homeroom assignment, their class schedule, and a map of the school.

"Once everyone is comfortable with that information, I have two of our student government officers assigned to take each small group of new students by grade level for a tour around the school. I'll also make sure each student gets the names and phone numbers of the other students in their group, if that's okay with all of you. I'll also let them exchange e-mail addresses if they have them, and I encourage you all as parents to write down the names and numbers of anyone you connect with here today, too. That way, by the end of the program, all of the new students will have made new friends, found their homerooms, and walked through their class schedules. I figure that should help put those butterflies to rest, don't you think?"

Mrs. Kaufmann continued talking in her upbeat manner a little more to the parents, to let them know in what ways she could help them and how to contact her. Then, she finally invited all her new students to stand up and join her, as she would lead them to the library to get started.

Josie almost popped up out of her chair as if she were on a spring, stumbling across her mother's feet to get out of the row of chairs and up to the front of the room with the school counselor. She was so nervous and so ready to do whatever she was told. Besides, she didn't want to be left behind, or miss a word, or look like she didn't care. Josie's mom had given her a pat on the back as she passed over her and promised she would be right there waiting for her when she was done.

"Be your perfect self, Josie!" she whispered as Josie took off, hoping her daughter could even hear her, with her head so full of emotion.

Josie's mom noticed the tension in Josie's face relax a little once she joined the group, and knew she was in the right place and safe with the school counselor. Then Josie's mom tried to relax, too, as she watched the unusually quiet group of about thirty-five new students follow Mrs. Kaufmann out of sight, with Josie right in the middle. Her mom prayed she would be fine, and looked back up at the principal, Mr. Gonzalez, who was back at the podium, jokingly waving goodbye to the students as they left the room and starting his "just-for-parents" presentation.

New This, New That, New Everything!

"Okay, guys, it's just us," Mrs. Kaufmann laughed, as they got out of sight of the big cafeteria doors. "We can all relax now. No more boring speeches…just us, and I promise to take care of all of you as if you were my very own personal children, like a mother hen in a chicken coop with all her little chickens! I just can't wait to get to know all of you, and I want to make you all as comfortable getting to know me as I can, so you can come to me at any time you ever have a problem. My job is to make sure everyone is happy here. Isn't that just the best job in the world?" She spoke with so much enthusiasm and sincerity that as the students followed her into the library, they all appeared to have changed from scared to death to enthused and ready to begin. "Okay, who would like to help me hand out some of this 'stuff'?"

Within minutes, everyone was scurrying around, passing out handbooks and bus schedules and class schedules, while Mrs. Kaufmann chatted comfortably to the big group, telling them she would explain it all once everyone had what they needed. Students began to say things to each other as the tension in the room disappeared. Everyone was into what was going on, and they all felt together--bonding in their newness, which was evident in the smiles all around the room. Once they all had their new materials and were back in their seats looking them over, Mrs. Kaufmann began to talk about how the schedules worked. She told them about what the first day would be like. She told them how and where to get their buses and where to go if they got lost. She explained that new kids would be given a buddy to make sure that didn't happen anyway, and then she laughed, saying that the butterflies would be wasting their time in their stomachs. She also introduced each helping student, who said a few words about their own first days at the school, and handed out "Hello my name is" stickers for everyone to fill out – blue ones for the new students, and red ones for the helpers. She asked that they all write their grade numbers under their names, to help everyone know who their classmates would be.

At this point, she asked for all students to sit at the big round table assigned to their grade level, and she had the helpers put a standing card on each round table with a number on it. The students all got up and began to crisscross each other all over the room in an excited but controlled chaos, for just a minute or two. Then, as it quieted down, Mrs. Kaufmann asked the helpers to go to their assigned tables – one boy and one girl with red name tags at each table. These students were older by one grade, and had just completed the grade that those newly grouped students were about to enter. They knew everything that the new students needed to find out about. They knew what the work was like, and what each teacher was like, and what was expected. It was a perfect pairing. There was no need for the new students to worry about whether the helpers would be their friends. They were their personal mentors now, and the new students felt safe. The girls huddled together, and the boys did as well. In fact, Josie was already feeling so much better. Just moving around and hearing the counselor sound helpful and approachable relieved some of her anxiety already. And she would now be able to see some names of the other new students in her grade. Best of all, the two helping students for her table gave everyone a card with their names, e-mail addresses, and phone numbers. Erin was the girl mentor and Joey was the boy, and they were both going to be with her table of students as their tour guides. They both seemed so friendly and helpful, too.

Then Mrs. Kaufmann had everyone pick up a pencil from the center of the table and open their handbooks to the inside front cover. She then started an exercise that made the room as wonderfully noisy as could be, helping to get rid of the remainder of the anxiety. She simply asked everyone to write down the names of everyone at their table, some identifying information they could use to remember each of them, and get their phone numbers and e-mail addresses if they had them.

And then the buzzing began! Josie was immediately connecting with the girl seated next to her with the enthusiasm of a drowning person suddenly grabbing onto a life raft. It became comical as they were all eventually helping each other with personal descriptions, so that each new student had the completed list before the talk was to continue. They mostly spent time explaining how they came up with their e-mail addresses, and enjoyed the free time of not being "talked at" for a little while. They all shared their nervousness with one another, and it was clear that none of them felt alone anymore.

"Is everyone done?" Mrs. Kaufmann interrupted with a big enthusiastic smile, after a good amount of time had passed. Most of the students were just chatting and not writing anymore, so she felt safe she hadn't rushed the process. In fact, Josie was talking with the girl next to her, Dee Ballister, who she described in her handbook with a phrase "tall, blonde hair pulled back, and more nervous than me." They were talking about what to wear on the first day and giggling quietly about how cute their mentor, Joey, was, when they were suddenly interrupted by Mrs. Kaufmann's raised voice.

"Okay, then. I want you all to promise me you will call or e-mail each other tonight or tomorrow just to chat, okay?" Mrs. Kaufmann called across the room, convincing them they could make the first day exciting rather than scary, since they'd all feel like they already had made a friend. Several of the boys at the table sat looking straight ahead, as if they had no intention of getting on the phone, but the majority of the girls looked at one another with an enthusiastic smile.

She continued, "Help each other feel connected here. You can always send me an e-mail if you have a question, and I promise to answer it before the first day. My e-mail address is in the handbook with my office phone number. You or your parents can always feel free to connect with me, because that's what I'm here for, remember? My job is to make sure all my 'little chickens in my chicken coop' are happily solving problems and learning lots of new 'stuff' every single day!

"And keep something in mind," Mrs. Kaufmann pointed out with a new enthusiasm. "Just because you are new to the school, doesn't make you the only new students to the grade. All the other 'old' students from here are just as nervous coming in on the first day to all their new classes and new teachers and new schedules. If anything, you guys are getting a real jump on the first day. You will have had 'the inside scoop on the coop' from your tour guides and a complete tour of the school. You might even be meeting some of the teachers as you go into the classrooms today, if they are there getting everything ready for you. Plus, all the teachers will be getting class lists with the new students starred for the first day, so they know to really watch out for you. They will pair you up with helpful students who are in your classes, so you'll have personal guides that the rest of the 'old' students won't have! Cool, huh?"

Mrs. Kaufmann's cheerleader approach was working. The new students all looked at each other after that, like they were the lucky ones who had even more information than all the others. Now she had their full attention!

Mrs. Kaufmann then asked the students to look up at the big screen with a huge sample schedule on it. As she began to explain something called the "six-day cycle" and "specials rotations," Josie began to feel a little bit anxious again. She couldn't follow the explanation at first, and, the more she began to flood with the fear of getting lost, the harder it was for her to even hear what was being said. Within a couple of minutes, she could hear Mrs. Kaufmann's voice calmly ask if the helpers at each table would explain it a little better on the actual schedules each student had just received. Josie was immediately relieved when several students at her grade-level table all nodded and looked like she felt and feared--lost and confused.

Joey, the helper nearest her, immediately stood up and leaned over Dee and Josie and another boy, Dave, and started to explain how the first day of school was called "Day 1," and the day that followed would be called Day 2, and the days that followed in order were 3, 4, 5, and 6. Then the numbering would start again: 1, 2, 3, and so on, cycling around and around all year. If there was a vacation or a bad-weather day that closed the school, everyone would just pick up where they all left off. He pointed out on each of their schedules how it simply was a rotation. He showed them how to see patterns in their special classes, and how to read the codes for the rooms. After a couple of minutes, the students were comparing their schedules with delight, noticing who had what classes together and when, and who they had for homeroom teachers. It wasn't hard, it was just new. All new and now rather exciting!

"Are we all okay with our schedules? Will you be able to explain them to your parents when you get home?" The previous quiet of confusion and fear was now gone. In fact, it was hard to break up the little conversations going on between the students, and the room had definitely become noisy, but in a most satisfying way. Mrs. Kaufmann saw it as her report card. She knew it was now the turning point from the unknown to the known, and that made all the difference in their emotions. Now they were ready for their tour. All barriers were down, and they wanted to get out there and see their rooms, and the lockers, and how close they'd be to one another in the hallways.

She organized the groups so that each helper had between three and five new students. The mini groups were small enough for them to hear each other, and close enough for even the shyest to ask questions. The helpers had their lists of topics to cover, such as gym-class routines, grading, homework, field trips, late bells, etc., and a map of the school for each student to follow and mark their own classrooms. She reminded them that the new students' parents would be waiting for them in the cafeteria when they were done, and may need them to tour their parents around again. The helpers were anxious to take over and quickly took off. Josie and the other new students kept very near one another in happy, chatting huddles. They were all sticking very close to their tour guides as well, to hear every single word they spoke.

Mrs. Kaufmann called after them at the library door, "Have fun discovering your new home away from home! You will love our school! And tour guides, hang on to everyone in your group – don't lose any one of my new little chickens!" She could hear them all giggle at her silliness as they scurried away, and she loved that they did.

The Post-Tour Tour

Back in the cafeteria, Mr. Gonzalez was just finishing up talking with the parents. He was funny and had put them at ease, even though he had to inform them about school policies and procedures. He had given them information on such concerns as supply lists, lunch money, room parents, drop-off and pick-up routines, school rules on drugs and harassment, the discipline system, and so forth. Once they were done, they all meandered to the refreshment table to talk amongst themselves as new neighbors. There the parents made new friends, too, and waited for their touring children to come back to them. Josie's mom was a little worried about Josie, since she always created her own "what-ifs," scaring herself more than any reality she experienced.

As she started to introduce herself to a woman she had sat near during the principal's talk, Ben immediately started to lunge toward the cookies and juice he spotted on the table. "Whoa there, Benny," his mom quickly reacted. "Let's just slow down. How about we just take one or two, leaving the rest for all these other people, okay?" Looking disappointed, Ben let his mom help steer him by the shoulders into the line that had formed, while he stared at the cookies with the sprinkles on top.

Josie's mom wanted to make new friends as well, so she started the ball rolling with that introduction. "Hi, my name is Oriana Wyatt," she said to the woman behind her in line. "My daughter is in the sixth grade. I think you were sitting in front of me during the talk. Are you here today with your daughter, too?"

"Oh, so pleased to meet you. I'm Linda Blaisdell. My daughter Monica Richards is in the sixth grade, too. We have different last names, because I use my maiden name and she has her father's last name. We've just moved here this week, and I am feeling overwhelmed. Oh, that's right, we've all just moved here. After all, this is a new-student orientation." She laughed at herself. "Was your daughter as nervous as mine was this morning? Oh, my goodness. I've never seen Monica so emotional!"

"Yes, Josie was too. It was a complete and total meltdown just ten minutes before we left. Thank goodness Ben couldn't care less. Sixth grade is a lot harder because of the whole social thing. I understand that being new is hard, because, heaven forbid you don't fit right in! And they know they have a lot of new information to learn. Typically, my Josie sees everything new as scary first, and huge. We never moved before, so she doesn't have the confidence that she'll be just fine as she learns what she needs to know and do. The big thing for the girls right now is to make friends. That's 'do or die' level of importance at this age."

Monica's mom shared quietly to Josie's mom, "I know. I'm just hoping that this talk and tour time went well for them. I know Monica will be fine once she feels settled in, too, but those first few impressions can make her become unglued at any moment she doubts herself. If she could just feel excited about the whole new-beginning thing, she could radiate that joyful person she is inside most of the time. My fingers are crossed on this experience."

"Hi, Mom," Oriana Wyatt suddenly heard from behind her, coming from her now-perky Josie, answering her prayers that it went well.

"Guess what?" Monica also popped up beside her mom with her newly enthused voice. "I can take you all around the school and show you my classrooms. And my homeroom teacher, Mr. Donard was there and I met him. He was so, so, so nice! And he was in his shorts, working on a ladder!"

"And I met mine, too. Her name is Mrs. Kindeya," Josie chimed in. "She had her own little kids there helping her get the room ready. She's a mom like you!"

Both moms looked at each other with great relief. The butterflies were gone for now. Josie's mom quickly decided there was just time enough to walk around the school once more before they had to cross the playground to get to Ben's new-student orientation. He had already gobbled up his cookie and asked to have another "one for the road," as his mom always said.

"Sure, Benny, just one, and after we walk around Hillstown for a bit with Josie, we get to see your Duncan Elementary School. Are you excited?" his mom asked.

"Yup," Ben mumbled with his mouth full of cookie, happy with just that.

First-Day Jitters

Even though Josie had had a great time at the orientation meeting Monica and Dee, and they had e-mailed each other back and forth all weekend, she still had some fears for this official first day of school. They all did. They began to wonder about things they didn't know yet and the handbook couldn't tell them – like what to wear. She knew her teacher seemed human enough, and that she would live through this day, but what if she ended up alone somewhere? Monica and Dee weren't in her homeroom, so what if her assigned buddy didn't have exactly the same classes? What if she missed the bus to come home?

"What's going on in that little head of yours, Josie? I see the wheels spinning as you're pushing your breakfast around on your plate. I also see your feet wagging back and forth, like they do when you're anxious about something. I thought you were okay with today?" Josie's mom questioned her at the breakfast table before she and her brother were to finally start their first day of school.

"I'm fine. I'm just a little scared. Like, what if I miss my bus?" she challenged her mom.

"Call me from the office and I'll come get you! You may have to wait a little bit, but they have chairs, and they will never close a school with a student still inside!" she answered matter-of-factly. "That's just not a problem, and neither is anything else that could happen to you today. Why don't you look at your first day at Hillstown as a 'free ticket' – like a gift? You're allowed to *not* know anything today, and you are completely excused. No one expects you to know a thing, and yet you already do know a whole lot! This is your free day to make all kinds of mistakes and laugh at it all, and know you will be taken care of. It will show all the other kids that you have a sense of humor, you are human, and not perfect, just like them, and you're okay with yourself.

"Now, could you have a better opportunity to tell all your classmates what a great friend you could be? It's the best chance you could get to tell them how great you are and let them feel comfortable with you. We all make the mistakes we need to teach us our lessons, after all, and we love to be around people who get that that's how it works. It makes you real, honestly you, and someone I'd be comfortable to hang around with any day of the week!" Josie's mom encouragingly answered her, hoping meltdown number two was not on the way.

It worked. Josie realized it really was a "free ticket" day. And she planned to sit by Dee and Monica in the cafeteria at lunchtime, so that was no longer a worry. She had gym that day, but no one had gym clothes, so she didn't have to change for gym either – another thing to not worry about. Actually, between her new outfit and her new friends, she was beginning to feel excited, and not in the "jitters" sort of way anymore.

As Josie, Ben, and her mom got into the car for the real first day of school, emotions were high, but happy this time. Josie and Ben repeated back to their mom where they were to get off the bus, and what their pick-up routine at the bus stop would be. This morning, they were going in by car and not by bus, so they could get there a little early. Josie was happy to be dropped off in front of the school, to wait outside with Dee and Monica until the bell rang to come in. She had her map, her handbook, her schedule, all of her new supplies, and best of all, her confidence. She realized that it was all her thinking that had given her such panic, nothing that actually happened. When she decided to just be okay, she was.

Ben was more interested in seeing the side of his new sneakers that flashed when he walked, which had his full attention. As he was dropped off, he ran into the crowd showing off his flashy feet. Instantly, a boy from his classroom area noticed his sneakers and showed off his own, and they began running in circles to impress themselves and each other. Ben just didn't do any what-if thinking. He almost always liked where he was, doing what he was doing, Ben as himself, right now.

When the bus pulled up at the bus stop at 3:30 that afternoon, Josie and Ben got off, and they both ran up to their mom's car. She had been waiting for them at the end of their street as promised. "So, how was it?" she asked them both.

"Fine," Ben answered, as he was pulling out his artwork and other first-day-of-school forms from his new backpack to hand to his mom.

"Cool," Josie reacted right away, too. "Can Monica come over after school tomorrow? Guess what? She lives right around the corner, just one bus stop away. She got off right before we did! I think we can ride bikes to each other's house. Can I, Mom?"

"Sounds good, I can call her mom tonight to see if it works for them. And Ben, hang on to those papers till we get home okay? So you both seem happy to have had a good day. Josie, did anything you worried about happen?"

"I lost my way a couple of times, but even the old kids didn't know where any of their classes were, so we all just laughed and walked around looking for them together. And the teachers were really cool about it. They stood out in the hall between classes saying things like, 'Any lost souls? Anyone out there need help?' Even the principal and Mrs. Kaufmann were out in the halls helping people with their lockers and their schedules. It was kind of fun, actually."

Josie's mom knew she would be fine. The best part was that Josie learned she would be okay in the future whenever she would be new again, like in high school, in college, in her first job, and forever. "How did you handle all the new rules, and teachers, and everything?"

Josie sighed, "Yeah, I have a lot to remember, but I realized that everything I have to do is really for sixth-graders, so I should be able to do it. I don't think the teachers would expect me to do seventh-grade work or memorize everything in one night, right? And I don't believe I can really get lost now, either. And even if I did, I'd still be okay."

"That's so good to hear, honey. I am really happy for all the learning you had in just this one day!"

Then from the back seat of the car Ben announced, "Josie, the teachers aren't allowed to lose you! That's why they went to teacher school!"

Josie rolled her eyes and her mom laughed. Ben was right. The teachers did know what they are doing, and because of that, it had been a really great first day of school.

Discussion Points:

- Fear takes away your happiness. Excitement brings it back.

- Being your natural, comfortable self allows you to make friends who are looking to be natural and comfortable, too.

- Making mistakes is human, normal, and expected as part of the learning process.

- Trying hard to impress people tells them you don't think you are good enough as you are. That may make them feel uncomfortable or even annoyed.

Reflection Questions:

1. Who enjoyed getting ready for the new-student orientations more, Josie or Ben? Being new to a situation can stir our fears, so what should we remember to calm ourselves down?

2. Having something in common can bring people together to become friends, so why is it good to be different, too?

3. What are those qualities about each of us that make us different from others? Do you believe it makes us special? What takes the least amount of effort to be…the comfortable, real you or the one that you think will make you popular?

4. How can you tell who is popular and who is not? Do popular students always keep their popularity year after year? Are the popular students the ones everyone feels most comfortable with? What's the difference between a person you think is popular, and a person you most admire?

CHAPTER 6:
My Brain Feels Flooded and My Chest Is Pounding!

What's Happening to Me?

"Mrs. Kaufmann, I just called to see if I could talk to you tomorrow morning at school. I wasn't sure if I should call your office and leave a message tonight, but my mom said I could. I've been studying really hard since after dinner, but now I'm getting so scared I'm going to panic again when I take my science test tomorrow. Can I see you tomorrow morning if you have some time for me? My test is not until sixth period. Maybe you could leave a pass for me with my homeroom teacher in the morning when you hear this message? Oh, yeah, this is Susanna Morris. Sorry, I forgot, and thanks, I really appreciate it!"

As Mrs. Kaufmann listened that morning to the other messages left on her voice mail overnight, she took off her coat, put her purse away, and quickly took out a blank pass to fill out for Susanna's homeroom teacher. She knew that test anxiety isn't something that can be fixed with one appointment, but she remembered well her own panic attacks even in graduate school. She wanted to offer Susanna some of the tricks she knew worked for her.

She listened to the remaining messages to make sure none were emergencies, and then she ran Susanna's pass down to her homeroom teacher's classroom. "Mr. Hudson," she said as she knocked on his door coming into his classroom. "Good morning! I have a favor to ask of you this morning. Would you mind sending Susanna Morris down to see me once she comes in and gets settled? She may be sensitive about anyone knowing she's coming to see me, but she did call last night asking to see me this morning. Would you mind?"

"Susanna? She's an outstanding student. Is there anything wrong that I should know about?" Mr. Hudson asked with surprise.

"Nothing we can't fix!" Mrs. Kaufmann answered positively, but without really answering him. She knew she couldn't share Susanna's problem without her permission, but she didn't want Mr. Hudson worrying that it was about him, or something he should know about. She added, "It's just something she's dealing with, and I'll ask her if it's all right if I share. If there is something you can do to help her, I will definitely let you know. Thanks for asking. Okay, I have to run and get these other passes out to some other teachers. Have a great day!"

Mrs. Kaufmann smiled and zipped out the door and down the hall to deliver a few more passes. She then went right back toward her office to get there before Susanna could beat her there.

"Hi, Mrs. Kaufmann, thank you so much for sending for me!" Susanna called out to Mrs. Kaufmann, as they both ran into each other heading to the guidance office.

"Hello, my dear. I did get your message, and I have so much to share with you. Come in, come in!" Mrs. Kaufmann said excitedly. "There are so many things you can do to help deal with this test anxiety, and I can't wait to give you a whole list of things I've learned from when I was in your grade. Have a seat, and get ready for me to talk really fast. We only have homeroom time, because your first-period teacher doesn't want you to miss her class. I can have you back later today, but let's see what we can get done right now, okay?"

"Okay, I'm ready," Susanna answered enthusiastically. "I hate what happens when I take tests. I can't even think when I get started, and nothing I look at even feels like I have ever heard of it before. And I study really hard!"

"Oh, I know," Mrs. Kaufmann assured her. "You're not the only one, and plenty of people have that happen even as adults. Back when I was in school, I used to be able to answer everything perfectly when my friend and I would quiz each other the night before an exam. But then, during the test, it was like there was nothing in my brain. I would look at the first question, draw a blank, and then I suddenly couldn't think," Mrs. Kaufmann shared. "But, I must tell you that because of that, I ended up learning a lot about the brain and the way anxiety affects it. So let's sit down and get started, okay?"

"Yes, thank you so, so, so much!" Susanna said happily, as she slid into the big chair across from Mrs. Kaufmann's office desk.

"Well first of all, the good news is, it can be controlled, but at first you may have to deal with the cycle of reactions differently than you will later," Mrs. Kaufmann assured her. "The truth of it all is the *underlying* fear that you might not do well, and why you have that fear. We'll eventually try to get to the bottom of why it's so important to succeed, what will happen if you don't, and what goes on in the brain and body when the fear thought enters your head and sets off the physical chain reaction that you're actually *feeling*."

"Oh, that's so good to know. I was wondering what was wrong with me," Susanna said in relief, and sitting expectantly for this new understanding.

Mrs. Kaufmann continued, "There are different parts of the brain that do different jobs. One of them is the neo-cortex, or the analytical, logical part of the brain. When doctors do those brain scans to see what part is working when we are thinking and problem-solving, like when we are taking tests, that's the part where the blood is flowing and it's nice and red and busy. Then another part of the brain is the emotional part. When the scanner shows that part of the brain all red and busy, it's when a person has a lot of emotion, like fear, going on. And when that's happening, that's when the logical part of the brain is more blue, or less active."

"Oh, I get it," interrupted Susanna. "So when I'm panicking, the emotional brain takes over mostly, and my thinking part isn't working as much?"

"That's right. And guess which part of the brain reacts the fastest?"

"Is it the emotional part?" Susanna asked.

"You guessed it!" Mrs. Kaufmann exclaimed. "The emotional part of the brain gets in the driver's seat as the fear takes over, so that it's actually hard to think, using the thinking part of the brain or the neo-cortex. However, the good news is, if you can practice a little breathing trick and relax, the fear will pass, and your neo-cortex will become more in control again."

"Phew," whispered Susanna.

Mrs. Kaufmann continued, "Here's what you'll need to do when you're going into your tests to try to keep the panic from happening in the first place. Just quietly at your desk, breathe deeply, taking in a full lung's worth of oxygen, hold it, and let it out slowly. I do it to the count of four going in, holding it to the count of four, and letting it out to the count of four. By doing this, you've also distracted your mind from the thinking that causes that brain chemistry to shift over to that emotional part of the brain. Do this four times and you will have replaced that carbon dioxide building up in your lungs with fresh oxygen. This can help delay or even stop the panic before it can even start."

"Oh, that would be so great! Does that always work?" Susanna asked hopefully.

"No, not always," Mrs. Kaufmann admitted, "but it does sometimes, and that makes it worth the try. And even if it doesn't stop the flood, now you know that part is temporary. The emotional part of the brain will allow your thinking part to get back in charge once you relax and take nice, deep, slow and even breaths. And you may need to try some positive self-talk, too."

"We can't talk during a test, Mrs. Kaufmann," Susanna interrupted.

"Not out loud, my dear," she assured Susanna. "It's just having some sentences you say to yourself in your head that makes you see things differently, and takes the fear away. We'll come up with them the next time we meet. But now, I'd better get you out of here and headed for first period." Mrs. Kaufmann stood up and walked with Susanna to her door. "I know you can do this, sweetie. If you relax, study again at lunchtime to keep the information fresh in your memory, and go into science working at being calm, knowing you have a new way to control the brain, you'll be just fine!"

"Okay, Mrs. Kaufmann. When should I come back?" Susanna asked as she headed for the hallway.

"Are you able to come down eighth period? Is that when you have your library time for your research paper? Why don't you ask your teacher ahead of time if you can spend the first half of that class time with me? If she thinks your research is in good shape, I can meet with you then," Mrs. Kaufmann offered.

"Thanks, Mrs. K," Susanna called over her shoulder as she disappeared into the sea of bodies flowing in opposite directions, filling the hall like rush-hour traffic on a busy highway.

Phew!

A sudden knocking on her office door brought Mrs. Kaufmann out of her intense focus on the paperwork she was filling out and onto Susanna's happy face as she came bursting into the room. It was eighth period, and she was right on time for their talk. "I did it! I did exactly what you said. Susanna spoke without any pauses. "The test papers were being handed out right as I was coming into the room, so I started my old usual instant panic and I got all choked up. Then, I did the breathing thing as I waited it out. I told myself that this would be done in just a couple of minutes and I'd have my thinking brain back. And it worked! Plus, I had gone over the review sheet again and again during lunch at our table, so I knew everything we were told would be on it. I think I did great!"

"Fantastic, kiddo," Mrs. Kaufmann answered just as fast. "I knew you would be fine. And I think that going back over the material once more is really important for your confidence, too. Did you know that when you memorize rather meaningless information, you can lose up to half of it within twenty-four hours after you study it the first time, if you don't study it again?"

"You're kidding!" Susanna was surprised.

"Your brain can hold on to new material that has no great meaning to you for just so long. Say you study a list of facts for a history quiz on a Sunday afternoon, and then never look at it again until the test arrives on your desk Monday afternoon. About half of that material will be getting hazy, or might even be gone from your memory. That's why it's good to go back over it the next day."

"I never knew that!" Susanna exclaimed. "Sometimes I make up a gimmick to remember a list of things in order, and I admit I'm not too good at remembering it later."

"That's because the gimmick has no real meaning. The new information that sticks to your memory the best is the 'stuff' that has meaning to you. It's the material that adds to something else you already know, so that you can get a visual image of it altogether. And if you study to make it make sense, then that will last in the memory a whole lot longer."

"That does make sense. Last Sunday, my mom and I made chocolate chip cookies, and now I think I will remember the recipe forever, because I was actually making it," Susanna added.

"And the more ways you put information into your head, the better it will stick. If you write it, draw it, say it out loud, and even have some kind of hands-on activity, then your brain uses different places to store it at the same time, like a hologram. And if you attach the fact to some emotional experience, the emotional memory lasts the longest! So, if you study with someone, and something you're studying makes you laugh and connect it with another real event, then your emotional memory will also hang on to that information in that storage area. Isn't that cool?" Mrs. Kaufmann laughed.

"That really is. I didn't know that. That will help me study things I don't like and can't concentrate on."

"Okay, and now, Susanna, I have to ask you what would happen if you actually failed the science test?" Mrs. Kaufmann directed her question like a spear to the target. Finding out what made Susanna afraid in the first place would be so helpful, if Susanna could face that fear.

Susanna's face grew immediately pale. "I can't imagine what would happen. I think my parents would really go ballistic. I'd probably be grounded and lose my cellphone. I don't even want to think about it!"

"Okay, but you didn't, so let's not worry about that. You actually never really do fail anything, even though you're afraid you will. You probably cost yourself some time, though, and that may be lowering your grade some, don't you think?" Mrs. Kaufmann suggested.

"Oh, I'm sure I mess myself up every time I think the test is really important!" Susanna answered.

"And what makes it seem so important?" Mrs. Kaufmann pried a little further.

"Like… if it could mess up my report card grade. That would be so bad," Susanna answered.

"Would it be bad for you, or bad for you to show your parents?" Mrs. Kaufmann continued.

"Uh," Susanna hesitated. "I'm not sure. I guess both," she admitted uneasily.

"That's an interesting question to ask yourself, don't you think?" Mrs. Kaufmann pointed out. "I'm just trying to help you find out why failing a test feels like such a catastrophe. I mean, I know it always seemed that way to me, too, but I had to do my own work in my head as to why I was so fearful. You know there are plenty of kids who don't like failing, but they don't have a huge fear of it," Mrs. Kaufmann told Susanna.

"You're kidding! They aren't afraid of failing?" Susanna asked in total disbelief.

"No, they just take the test and hope for the best. I guess they figure they'll cross that bridge when they come to it," Mrs. Kaufmann said with a bit of lightness in her voice, amused that Susanna found that so hard to believe.

"Oh, I have to go!" Susanna blurted out. "I was only supposed to be out for half this period, and I have to get back to get the homework. Can we talk more about this sometime, Mrs. K?"

"Sure. I'd be happy to. I'm also hoping you'll think more about what I asked you. Maybe you can talk about it with your mom when you get home today, unless you'd like this to be just between us. And would it be okay if I talked to your teachers to see how they think you're doing this marking period?"

"Sure, you can talk to my teachers. And I'll talk to my mom, but maybe not today. I have choir practice after school and piano lessons after that, and a bunch of friends coming over for a sleepover tonight," Susanna said. Maybe I can talk with her over the weekend." After taking the hall pass Mrs. Kaufmann had just filled out, she popped up to leave.

"You know, Susanna, you might want to try some of your new tricks and studying methods for the social studies test tomorrow, you know? Pick the ones you like and try them out, and we can talk next week, just to see what kind of progress you're making, okay?"

"I will, and thanks again, Mrs. K," Susanna answered as she headed out the door and back to her library class.

Mrs. Kaufmann realized Susanna had not responded to her comment about it being "just between the two of them," and yet she did say she *might* bring it up to her mom – sometime. At least she gave permission for her to talk to her teachers. After all, she really was a good student. That left this discussion still floating in the "confidential" category, and Mrs. Kaufmann needed to honor that when it came to Susanna's parents. *Maybe next week we'll see if Susanna was able to talk to her mother*, she thought, as she made some notes to herself. She needed to talk to her teachers to see how she was doing, what kind of student she was, if she lacked confidence, if she had other fears, and whether she ever expressed concern over telling her parents bad news. Then she needed to go to her file to check her report card and her ability and achievement test scores. That would tell her whether Susanna really had a reason to worry about failing a test.

I love this detective work, she thought, as she turned on her computer to get to Susanna's records. *I'm beginning to get a hunch about what might be happening in Susanna's head. It is such a common pattern for very good students to identify with being just that – very good students, as though that was who they were and not just a part of how they perform. The fear comes at the thought of losing that! They then don't know who they would be. Definitely a scary thought.*

Hmmm

Straight A's on every report card in Susanna's record, and a very good set of test scores was what Mrs. Kaufmann found in Susanna's personal file. "That's what I thought," Mrs. Kaufmann mumbled to herself, as she scrolled through the many pages of her history on the computer screen. There were High Honor Roll Certificates and teacher observations checking off such behaviors as "extremely responsible and cooperative" for all her years at school. *I see that she really has no reason to have this fear of failing*, thought Mrs. Kaufmann. *I can't wait to meet with her this week to see if she brought it up to her mom last weekend, and what her teachers would say about her anxiety.*

"Hey there, Mrs. Kaufmann," the deep voice boomed over her shoulder. It was Mr. Hudson, Susanna's homeroom teacher, poking his head into her office door. "Would you be able to come to our Team Meeting this afternoon?" he asked. "A few of us have some questions to ask about some of our students."

"Sure, I'd be happy to. And I have a couple of questions for all of you as well. It's at 2:15 as usual?" Mrs. Kaufmann asked just, to be sure.

"More like 2:30. Everyone wants to get a few things done before we start, okay? Oh, and we have been talking about having you come in to do some classes on some social issues. Would you have some time for that in the next couple of weeks?" Mr. Hudson asked.

"I would love to. Actually, I was just thinking it was time for me to come into classes to talk about character development, so this will work out nicely. They do fit together, after all!" Mrs. Kaufmann answered with enthusiasm.

"Great, see you at 2:30 in my room," Mr. Hudson replied.

Mrs. Kaufmann closed down the computer and headed down the hall to the gym and into Mrs. Campbell's office where she was recording physical fitness scores. "Hi, there, my favorite gym teacher," Mrs. Kaufmann said, as she approached Mrs. Campbell with a big smile. "May I borrow your brain for a few minutes, or is this a bad time?" she laughed.

"There's never a bad time for you, but the brain may already be gone. I've been recording all of these scores so long, I'm going cross-eyed! And what can I do for my favorite school counselor?" she laughed back.

"The *only* school counselor," Mrs. Kaufmann chuckled. "Listen, I stopped in to ask about Susanna Morris. I was wondering what sort of pressure she puts on herself in gym class to get an A on her report card?"

"Funny you should mention that. Last week we were doing the physical fitness tests, and she got pretty upset over a couple of them. She's not a great athlete, but she really tries so hard. That's why she gets good grades, but that doesn't make her running speed or broad jump scores any higher. The physical fitness test scores are just what they are, and hers are not at the top, compared to others in her class. She's not used to that!" Mrs. Campbell told Mrs. Kaufmann. "In fact, one day just after we began the testing, she came to me almost in tears asking how much these scores were going to count on her report card grade. I actually had to assure her a couple of times that they didn't affect the grade, before the tears in her eyes went away. It was really sad."

"That makes sense," Mrs. Kaufmann added. "Her worry about grades is definitely eating her up inside, and I have to find out why. I don't know if it's pressure from her parents, her identification with being a smart student, or just a low self-esteem. Whatever it is, she's really feeling the negative effects."

"What a shame," Mrs. Campbell joined in. "She is naturally very bright and could be truly enjoying school instead of having to suffer from all that anxiety. When I see her playing ball on the playground with her friends at recess, she seems so much freer and lighter than when she feels she's performing for a grade in gym class. When she comes to the gym, she immediately seems to tighten up, to make sure she doesn't make any mistakes. I hope you can help her."

"I think if I can just help her shift her thinking in the right direction, the rest will take care of itself. We'll see. And thanks for sharing," Mrs. Kaufmann answered her as she headed toward the gym door.

"I'd be happy to anytime. By the way, I am so glad we finally made it to Friday! Enjoy your weekend, my favorite school counselor!" Mrs. Campbell called after her cheerfully.

"You have a great weekend, too, my favorite gym teacher!" Mrs. Kaufmann joked back and headed down the hall to the Team Meeting about to start.

"Hello, everyone," Mrs. Kaufmann said as she entered the doorway, just as the other teachers were taking their places with their clipboards, coffee cups, and water bottles around a large round table in the back of the classroom.

Mr. Hudson spoke first. "I'm so glad you could make it. We have a couple of students we'd like to refer to you, but we'll need to run it by their parents before we do. One of them is Brad Jennings. He just teases people something awful. He has no idea how annoying he is to them, and the other kids just don't respect him. He has no friends anymore, and that makes him try even harder, but all in the wrong directions. He teases in order to be funny – and it isn't funny. Last week, our team decided we would call him on it whenever he did it in the middle of our lessons, but it hasn't seemed to make a difference. I mentioned it to his mother at Open House, but she just agreed it's what he does to his little sister at home, and it makes her crazy, too. Do you think you could talk to him?"

"Sure," said Mrs. Kaufmann. "I've known Brad since he was a little guy just starting school in kindergarten. He was always so silly and thought he was the class clown back then, too. His peers are so much more mature and the difference has become even greater. So now he's not only annoying, but not cool, and that's the kiss of death at this age! Just let me know if his mom is okay with my talking with him. My guess is she'll welcome it."

"Good to know, and I'll let you know as soon as I reach Mrs. Jennings," Mr. Hudson replied. "Oh, and we have one more, Susanna Morris. She seems to be upset a lot recently. Mrs. Weil, you have her for

English. Would you tell Mrs. Kaufmann what happened last Monday with her homework?"

"Sure." Mrs. Weil took it from there. "I was collecting the homework from over the weekend, and Susanna couldn't seem to find hers in her English notebook. She seemed absolutely panicked, frantically rummaging through all of her books and notebooks. She then ran up to my desk to ask me if she could go back to her homeroom to look in her backpack. When I reminded her of the rule that no one could go back to their homerooms because classes were going on, she started to cry. I quietly told her that because she had never forgotten her homework before, I would be happy not to mark it as late this one time, and she could drop it off on my desk before the end of the day. Believe it or not, even that didn't settle her nerves. You could see she was preoccupied by that thought for the remainder of class. Such stress for a little girl!"

"I'm not surprised," Mrs. Kaufmann said quietly to the group. "She has her anxiety level way up, and we're working on it. Has anyone else witnessed anything like this?"

With that, every teacher around the table nodded in agreement, so Mrs. Kaufmann continued. "Have any of you talked with her parents about this, or has either of them mentioned it to you?"

"Actually I did hear from the office staff of an experience with her father one day," Susanna's math teacher chimed in. "They said he had brought her to school second period during my math class, because she had had a morning doctor's appointment. I gather that while Susanna was on her way down to my classroom, Mr. Morris, her father, was still signing her in at the main office. He told them that she had complained to him all the way over here, because she thought this made her late for school. It seemed that nothing he said would make a difference since the kids know if you have three unexcused 'lates,' you get a detention."

Her math teacher continued, "So the father asked at the main office if this was going to be counted as a tardy on her report card. When they said it would be counted as an excused late, not a tardy, he then asked them to please call down to me to make sure Susanna was assured it was an excused late. Mr. Morris said to them that she gets so worked up about these things, and was sure it was going to ruin her day if no one told her. He also said that nothing he had already told her helped because…" and Mrs. Weil laughed, "he said that he was 'only her father and what could he know,' and that made the secretary laugh, too, just as she called down to ask me to tell her."

"That just helped me a lot," Mrs. Kaufmann told the teachers at the table. "And I have already started working with her when she asked to see me. I knew her mom had encouraged her to call me, so I asked her to tell her mom how we made out. I'll be interested to see if she does over the weekend."

"I also hear from Mr. Hudson that we have some social problems among the students in general for this grade level," Mrs. Kaufmann spoke with a gleam in her eye. "Let me guess, playground time has offered some *opportunity* for some lessons to be learned? It always seems to happen after the newness of the new school year wears off, and some natural conflict begins to run its course. And I was just thinking about starting my character education classes, so the timing is perfect. Will it be okay if I schedule to come in to do a class with each of you during your health classes next week or the week after? You can e-mail me what works best for you, and I'll try to keep all those classes free."

"That would work really well into our schedules, since we're all about ready to start the unit on how the emotions affect the body. And thanks so much for coming, Mrs. Kaufmann," Mr. Hudson said as they were all getting up to beat the last-period bell, to get back to their homerooms for the end-of-the-day dismissal.

"Have an excellent weekend, everyone," Mrs. Kaufmann said, as she got up and quickly left, going around the corner toward her office in case there were any students waiting. It was the end of the school week, and she was thinking about Susanna's weekend, too, wishing she could relax and just be a carefree little girl. Hopefully she'd find out on Monday.

The Monday Morning Voice-mail

"Good morning, Mrs. Kaufmann. This is Mrs. Morris, Susanna's mother. I know I'm calling before you're even in this morning, but I wanted to catch you early enough so maybe you could see Susanna again? She had another meltdown this morning on the way out of the house, something about thinking she got the wrong cover for her social studies report. Anyway, I thought I'd better call you to see if you could help her one more time. Would you please give me a call when you get a chance? I'd love to fill you in. And thank you for all your help."

Mrs. Kaufmann heard the words "see Susanna again" and immediately knew Susanna had talked with her mom and told her she'd been in to see her on Friday. She didn't know what exactly she had shared, but she now knew the dialogue was definitely all opened up. Mrs. Kaufmann called her right back. "Good morning, Mrs. Morris. I'm so happy you called. I was hoping we could talk, but I wanted to see if Susanna would talk with you first."

"Oh we did, and we have, and we will probably continue, Mrs. Kaufmann. As I'm sure you know our Suzie has always been a high performer all through school. She always got her straight A's very easily--that is, up to now. It seems she is struggling this year to keep that up, and she has become really upset over even a B, no matter what we tell her. I really don't believe her father and I have put any pressure on her to get straight A's. In fact, we make a really big deal about them all the time, always celebrating her outstanding report card and telling her she's so smart. We really try to encourage her positively. And now it seems like she has a meltdown every time she has trouble doing anything at all, just like the panic she feels when she takes tests."

"Has she talked to you about some of the strategies I suggested on Friday about studying and about controlling the brain? I'm just curious about how much she shares with you," Mrs. Kaufmann asked.

"She tells me most everything, I think. I'm noticing, though, she has started to leave out things she doesn't want me to know, like about her friends. It's as if she's getting more and more selective with her sharing, you know?" Mrs. Morris continued. "I'm not sure what to do anymore. I'm afraid of adding more pressure, but I want to help her. And I definitely don't want her to feel guarded with what she feels safe to tell me. Would you have some time today to talk with her?"

"Sure, I would be really happy to. I have an all-morning meeting at the high school, but I will call for her when I get back. I'm hoping I'll be back by lunchtime, so I can use her playground time for our chat. That way she won't miss any class time, which I know would set her into a tailspin for sure!" Mrs. Kaufmann laughed. "Not to worry, Mrs. Morris. We'll get to the bottom of her anxiety. We just all need to really listen to what she's afraid of when she does share. I will encourage her to allow me to tell you what her fears are as I learn them, but we start out confidentially, so I may not be calling you back right away. I have to allow her some safe space to vent, just so you know," Mrs. Kaufmann warned her.

"That's fine. I'll just wait to hear back, and I'll leave you messages as to anything that goes on at my end," Mrs. Morris offered.

"That would be really helpful, thanks. And I have to run. Talk to you later, and not to worry. All things do work out here at Hillstown Middle School. It's really where they're supposed to learn this stuff!" Mrs. Kaufmann assured her as they said their goodbyes, even as Mrs. Kaufmann was grabbing her purse and turning off her computer to leave for her meeting.

Discovering the Seed!

"Hi, girls!" Mrs. Kaufmann called cheerfully to three girls as they were coming out to the playground for recess. She was just getting back from her meeting at the high school and noticed that Susanna was one of them. She thought this might be the perfect time to chat, but didn't want anyone to know they were meeting. "Could I please borrow three of you to help me bring in some small boxes of forms from my car, and bring them to my office with me? I just don't have enough hands. And would one of you just run over to Mrs. Tanner, the playground aide, to tell her that the three of you are coming in with me?"

"Sure!" they all responded quite cheerfully. One of the girls ran over to Mrs. Tanner, who waved; Mrs. Kaufmann waved back, and the girl ran back to join them. Then the four of them went toward Mrs. Kaufmann's car. The counselor walked briskly, so as not to waste time that she needed with Susanna alone, later. The three girls were skipping and laughing as they felt privileged to be chosen to do something special. Each girl grabbed a small box of pre-printed forms and walked behind Mrs. Kaufmann, almost giggling without reason, and in a line like ducklings after their mother.

When they got to Mrs. Kaufmann's office door, she unlocked it, and they went in to put the boxes down. Susanna caught Mrs. Kaufmann's wink when the other two had their backs to her, and Mrs. Kaufmann quickly asked, "Would any one of you be willing to help me staple some of these forms for a little bit? I don't think I would need more than one helper."

Susanna instantly said, "I will!" before either of the other girls had a second to think. *That was perfect*, thought Mrs. Kaufmann, and she winked one more time at Susanna as the other two darted out the door for the playground, with Mrs. Kaufmann calling out, "You ladies are the best! Thank you!"

"Good play, Susanna. That was well done. I wasn't sure you knew what I *wasn't* saying," Mrs. Kaufmann laughed. "I just wanted a chance to catch up with you and see how things were going, but I couldn't say anything out loud. So let me ask you, would you like to talk right now, or would you prefer to be outside with your friends?" This was Mrs. Kaufmann's way of seeing whether students really wanted help or not. Those who did would always stay and welcome the chance to end whatever pain was in their lives. It usually turned out that *their* answer was *her* answer as to how they felt.

"Thanks, and yes!" Susanna declared quickly and then rolled right into her story. "So I talked with my mom over the weekend, and I told her all you told me. I did my report yesterday and tried to make sense out of what I was writing, and it worked. I remember what I wrote about so much better than when I didn't really pay attention to what I was actually saying in the report. The only thing is, I got a little scared this morning when I looked at my report cover and wasn't sure if I got the kind the teacher didn't like, so I panicked. My fear goes so crazy and so fast, it seems."

"It's that emotional part of the brain I told you about. It can beat the rational part any day! That's why you have to be willing to wait out the adrenalin fallout," Mrs. Kaufmann reminded her.

"What's adrenalin fallout?" Susanna asked, looking for more of an explanation.

"Yes, that's what I wanted to share with you today. When the fear part of the brain, the limbic area, sets off the adrenalin in the body, it's like a lizard discovering a snake is ready to attack and the little guy just flees instantly. No thought, no reasoning, just run! That's where that comes from, the 'flight or fight reflex,' with no need for the neo-cortex to give you a logical and reasonable course of action. Then the adrenalin shoots out into the body all the revved-up energy it can, so the lizard can do a real high-speed bolt. When the heart pounds, the blood flows faster, and the breathing picks up, his senses become extremely alert, and he's so much more capable physically than he was when he was just napping in the sun on a rock. Then again, lizards don't have an advanced neo-cortex like humans do. When that limbic part of our brain sets off that whole adrenalin reaction, the neo-cortex of our brain is not the primary part working, and that's why you feel flooded with more emotion than with the ability to reason," Mrs. Kaufmann explained.

She continued, "That's also why your body is so weakened when the adrenalin rush is all over. Some people are known to have had super energy when faced with a very dangerous situation, and they end up being able to lift the front of cars, or boulders, or whatever. Then, afterwards, there's a physical drain. Sometimes the knees feel weak and shake, or you feel like crying. That whole process takes place rather quickly, but it can be upsetting. Fighting it, by being alarmed by it, keeps the adrenalin pumping, which is not what you want, believe me," Mrs. Kaufmann explained.

"So that's why I always want to cry right after I have one of those brain freezes when I start my tests!" Susanna exclaimed. "I never knew that. So I *am* normal?" she asked Mrs. Kaufmann, somewhere between asking for confirmation and wanting to shout for joy. It was a true "aha" moment for Susanna and a very interesting lead for Mrs. Kaufmann.

"Oh, my dear, did you think you weren't normal because of these fear reactions?" Mrs. Kaufmann asked her compassionately. "They are so common around here. You have no idea how common that is!"

Susanna's eyes filled up right to the edge of her eyelids as she nodded with a lip quivering and throat burning so badly that she couldn't speak. "Oh, I'm so sorry, Susanna. I wish I had known that that was troubling you. I also wanted you to question yourself about what would go wrong if you did really fail an exam, and not just a B, but an F. Did you have a chance to do that?"

Then the tears ran down her cheeks freely and Susanna tried to talk through it with her broken voice. "I don't know. I just know I can't. I would disappoint my parents so badly, because they are so proud of me being their smart daughter. They tell everyone about my good grades. I just *can't fail*!!" She started to sob and collapse into herself on the big office chair.

"Here, sweetie," Mrs. Kaufmann said in a soft voice, sliding the box of tissues close to her on the desk. "I know it's a scary thought when you feel you will disappoint someone, especially people you love and want to impress. But here's a thought that might surprise you. Your parents want you to be happy and healthy more than they want you to be smart, did you know that? Moms and dads want all good things for their children, and they love when they get good grades, go to good colleges, get great jobs, and earn great money, so that they will have what they need in life to keep them happy and healthy!" Mrs. Kaufmann said in her low and encouraging voice.

Susanna's tears began to stop, and she reached for a handful of tissues, blew her nose, and sat up, listening attentively. "Really?" she asked, looking into Mrs. Kaufmann's eyes through her own teary red ones.

"Oh, my goodness, yes, they do get excited when you do anything well, but above all they want to see you happy in life. Giving yourself panicky experiences and having anxiety until it brings you to meltdowns is not what they want for you, believe me. If you just studied your best and went into every test with confidence that you will give it all you have, and then answer all questions the best you could…that would be all they could ask for. Then they'd have their happy 'Little Suzie' back…who they miss very much, I'm sure."

Susanna perked up when she heard her mom's endearing name "Little Suzie." She loved when her parents called her that when she was little and carefree, something she now remembered fondly. Her eyes filled up again as she thought about how much she missed that time of her life, without all the pressures of performing well.

Mrs. Kaufmann continued digging, knowing she and Susanna were right at the source of her anxiety. They were right where the seed of fear started blooming into this nightmare for Susanna. "When was the first time you realized how important it was for you to get those A's?" Mrs. Kaufmann asked.

Susanna paused and looked off to the side for a few very long minutes, or so it seemed to Mrs.

Kaufmann. "I remember Mom telling Dad one day how so very proud she was of me for being so smart and getting such good grades, and Dad said he was, too. I felt like that was so important to them. Then I remember when my friend Julie was talking to Amanda, and I could hear her at our table in the cafeteria. She said I was so smart, and she wished she had half my brain. I remember feeling like I was special for that. Then Mrs. Dougherty, my teacher in second grade, told my mother I was going to go to a great college someday, because I was able to get such great grades. It all seemed to happen all at once, and I've always worked to be that smart person. Everyone expects it now, and I can't imagine failing a test. The thought of it really just seems so scary. Who or what would I be then, if that's what I am to everyone?"

"Oh, that's not *all* you are to them. You are so much more. But do you think that that may be why you have so much anxiety when it comes to grades?" Mrs. Kaufmann asked.

"Maybe, uh, yeah I guess so," Susanna said quietly, as if she was surrendering to that awful thought as it held her hostage.

"Okay, now we're getting somewhere," Mrs. Kaufmann spoke with confidence. "You, my dearest Susanna, are so much more than your brains or your study habits. That's just what's standing out and getting the attention of others right now during your school day. Do you belong to any other groups, or do other things that aren't about your brains? Weren't you accepted into choir? That means you can sing, and I believe you take piano, too, so you are quite musical. And I know for a fact you are a very caring person by the way you love and take care of animals. I also know you must be a compassionate person, because of all the friends you have. They wouldn't like you if you weren't kind. And you told me you love to have fun with your friends, so you must be fun to be with. And if you're laughing with them, you must have a sense of humor. This is beginning to sound like you have a lot of wonderful attributes and talents. You are so much more than your study habits!"

Susanna started sitting up straighter and higher as Mrs. Kaufmann listed all of her attributes. She was getting the idea. "But if I fail anything ever, or even if I get a B, everyone will talk about it. It will be a big deal and so embarrassing."

"I almost wish you would get a giant B so that the talk could happen, but just for the day. Then it would be old news after that, and the burden of having to get straight A's would be over. Then you'd join the ranks of the rest of your friends, and they'd probably even like you more, because they wouldn't dislike feeling inferior to you. You would be closer to them, and your report card could still be straight A's, because a B on a test usually doesn't cause the whole marking period's average to come down a whole grade until you're in college. There! Now how would that feel? Like a catastrophe?" Mrs. Kaufmann joked.

Susanna let loose a huge giggle. She wasn't expecting that. And Mrs. Kaufmann just had to giggle back. Mrs. Kaufmann continued to create the visual picture of Susanna getting that giant B on her test and waving it in the air as if to declare, "I'm normal and I'm okay and I got a B, so there!" Susanna giggled again. Mrs. Kaufmann had her practice this scenario as they did a little rehearsal. "Okay, let's imagine you getting a paper back now with a C on it – and don't panic, this is just practice to desensitize you. It's a C, not the end of the earth, not outside the realm of possibility, nothing to jump off a roof over, just a C. Of course, no one really wants one if they hope to be on the Honor Roll, but you would live and find out it really wasn't a catastrophe. Earthquakes can cause a catastrophe, not a C on a test. See what I mean?"

"What about my parents?" Susanna challenged. "They wouldn't be very happy with that."

"All right, imagine me being Susanna, and you're Mom, okay?"

"Okay." Susanna let out another amused giggle.

"Hi. Mom, I'm home. You won't believe what I got on my science test...a C! I am so disappointed. I studied so hard, and you know I knew everything when we practiced last night. I'm going to meet with my teacher during playground tomorrow to see what I did wrong," Mrs. Kaufmann said, imitating Susanna.

"Okay, Susanna, what do you feel like saying to me, as if you were your mom?"

Susanna spoke with a huge smile on her face, feeling kind of silly and lowering her voice to sound like a mom. "Oh, you poor little Suzie. I know you really did work hard. I'm sorry you're disappointed. Do you want some cookies?"

Mrs. Kaufmann laughed out loud. She wasn't expecting Susanna to get into the role so well. "You've got it! No catastrophe, just love and support… and cookies. Your parents were kids once too, and they know you can't be perfect all the time if you're human. It's just too much to expect."

"I see what you mean," Susanna admitted.

"So you're okay being Susanna, the great singer, piano player, compassionate pet sitter, and really 'fun friend' with or without straight A's?" Mrs. Kaufmann asked.

"I am right now. I just hope the fear thing doesn't happen all of a sudden," Susanna answered, a little reluctantly.

"It might, out of the old habit of thinking. Now that's where those little sentences to you come in," Mrs. Kaufmann reminded her.

"Like what should I say?" asked Susanna.

"Right when you feel the adrenalin reaction in your chest and throat and heart, you'll need to say something to yourself, to remind yourself this is just one test and only a test – not the end of the world. I've already done my best studying I can do. No matter what happens on this paper, I am still a great, loving, and talented person. My parents will love me no matter what grade I get, and my friends really don't care if I get A's or B's. Little affirmations like that, okay?"

"Oh, okay. Will they help make the emotional part of the brain slow down?" Susanna asked.

"It will help you change the insecure thinking that starts the emotional part of the brain taking over. If you're fine knowing you've done everything you could to get ready, that your parents accept you exactly as you are as their daughter, and your friends and teachers also think you are such a responsible and caring person no matter how you do on your test, then what else would matter? Who else do you perform for?" Mrs. Kaufmann assured her. "Would it be okay with you if I called your mother and told her what we've talked about?"

"Yes, I'd like that, because I'm not sure I can remember all that we did talk about!" Susanna answered quickly.

"That's great. And I'll let your mom know about the breathing, and the self-talk, and the need to keep you reminded that you are loved for all you are, not just your study habits. Your fears were based on what you thought everyone thought, if you know what I mean. Don't believe everything you think," Mrs. Kaufmann said with her usual little giggle.

Susanna smiled at how absurd that sounded. "I think I have to think about that," she answered back, proud that she was able to keep up with their little word game.

"You are very funny, too, Susanna! Let's get you off to class. And if you ever start to forget what a cool person you are, stop in and we'll practice some of that thinking again. I always enjoy your company," Mrs. Kaufmann said very sincerely, making out a pass and handing it to her.

"Thanks, Mrs. K. I will," Susanna replied with a huge sigh. She walked out of the office without her usual worrisome fumbling, rushing, and scurrying. She seemed to be moving at a comfortable pace for the first time.

Mrs. Kaufmann had just witnessed a new Susanna. She appeared to be safe in her own skin…without the old frantic worry. She had stood up and walked out of the door at a comfortable speed, with her back upright, instead of lurching forward. It was a nice change to see, and all from a shift of thinking. Mrs. Kaufmann then called Mrs. Morris to share it all with her. She reminded her to be just as proud of *all* the delightful aspects, virtues, and behaviors Susanna had, so she could feel equal pride from her parents. Mrs. Morris realized then that she had over-emphasized Susanna's whole academic performance, and only that, and needed to spread her compliments and praise around. Mrs. Morris thanked Mrs. Kaufmann, and Mrs. Kaufmann in turn thanked Mrs. Morris.

"It really does take a village to raise our children," Mrs. Kaufmann added as they said their goodbyes.

Mrs. Kaufmann smiled to herself as she began to open her e-mail to schedule those character education classes with the teachers. "Building great character in our kids is really the important part of all of our jobs together here at our school, and I do love my part!"

Discussion Points:

- Fear may seem like just an emotion of the mind, but it can really affect your body.
- We can control the triggers of our fears if we can find the source.
- We sometimes feel like we need to please others, but we can hurt ourselves while trying.
- Making mistakes and not being perfect is what all people do. It's what makes us human.

Reflection Questions:

1. How does fear feel in your body? Does it ever seem to be so strong that you can't think clearly? How long does it usually last until you can focus easily on what you need to do?

2. What do you think you don't do well enough? Who is it that you think you need to please? What is the worst thing that would happen if you failed at it?

3. Where do you go for help with things that scare you at school? What do you do when you need help with things that scare you at home? What advice do people give others to help them when they are afraid?

4. When you are confident in what you are doing, do you have any fears? What sentences can you use to make you feel more confident when you do have fear? Does breathing deeply help you relax?

CHAPTER 7:
But She Swore She Would Never, Ever Tell Anyone!

Sleepover Invitations Hit the School

"Did you get invited to Kim's sleepover?" Karen asked Anita, while moving at warp speed toward the cafeteria to see who all got invited to the big upcoming sleepover birthday party. It was the big buzz, happening everywhere you could find any two girls standing together at Hillstown Middle School that day. All the girls in the grade knew Kim's mom made the best food and bought the best favors and made up the best games, so this would be the party of the year. But the really best part was the great basement game room they would get to have all to themselves, all night, for those never-ending spooky games and girl-talk cliques.

"No," said Anita, "did you?"

Karen immediately felt terrible that she even brought it up, and didn't know what to say next. She did get the invitation tucked in her desk that morning in homeroom and almost squealed in delight. "Yeah, I did, but it's on the same night as our parents' movie night, so I don't know if I'll be going to the party, or coming to your house that night," Karen answered, trying to sound casual, like it was no big deal.

"Lucky!" Anita snapped back at her best friend with great envy. "I'm actually happy you did, so at least you can tell me all about it. Last year neither of us was invited, and we were both dying to know what happened. And sorry I snapped, Karen. Don't mind me. I'm just jealous because Kim's parties are the best, ever. You are so lucky!"

"I know. I am really lucky, because I didn't even think Kim liked me. I really wish you were coming too. That would be so cool, and I'd have someone to talk to in the middle of all of her friends. I will tell you every detail, I pinky swear!"

Karen smiled and winked as she and Anita hooked their pinky fingers around each other's to seal the deal! They then both scurried into the cafeteria through the big double doors, and headed right toward the big table in the back near the snack machines. Anita slid all the way over on the bench to her usual place, with Karen sliding into her usual spot in the middle. The rest of the eight other girls soon filled in the spaces on either side of the long table.

Immediately the squealing began, as most of the girls started sharing their good news with one another. All but Anita and one other girl, Austen, had been invited, and the two of them became noticeably quiet. Seeing them looking uncomfortable, Karen immediately nudged the girls to her left and right and used her eyes to point out Anita and Austen, with their heads, down eating their lunches without engaging in the conversation. It worked. Within a minute or two, the message was sent to change the subject, and one of the others immediately threw out a comment on the cute new guy they saw in the office getting registered that morning.

"I hope he's in my homeroom," Karen quickly said with a big smile.

"I hope he lives on my block!" Anita topped Karen's wish joyfully and felt relief that she and Austen didn't have to try to pretend they weren't really there anymore. All the others felt relief too. They liked Anita as the nice, quiet one. They didn't want her to feel bad that she wasn't invited to the best party of the year, but they knew Kim always invited the popular or lively friends, and Anita was neither. They didn't want Austen to feel uncomfortable, either. Austen seemed nice enough, but they didn't really know her, since she was new this year. She just always seemed to join their table of seven for lunch, making it a full table of eight, and that was fine with everyone. Whenever the lunch aides had to separate the naughty boys acting up at a boy table, they'd put each one at a different girl table wherever there was an extra seat, so Austen actually saved the girls by filling up their empty one.

At that point, it got very quiet as the girls were eating their lunches and taking turns getting up and down to get milk or ice cream. "Wasn't that vocabulary quiz hard?" Karen threw out the question to the table. "I studied those words really hard last night, but her definitions seemed different from what we had in our notes."

"I know. Mrs. Glass always does that. I think she doesn't want anyone to get a 100," Anita chimed in, as she crumpled up her brown bag and the other garbage, getting up to toss her trash. Right behind her was Karen, with her garbage as well. "Thanks," Anita said to Karen as they caught up together at the recycle can. "You saved me from squirming in my seat. I hate feeling left out of that party, but it's even worse to feel left out at our lunch table too."

"No problem. You can do it for me some time when I want to crawl into a hole," she answered matter-of-factly, trying not to sound too sympathetic so Anita wouldn't feel bad again. They were really good friends and had learned how to watch out for each other's feelings. Both girls went back to pick up their books and head out the door for recess, feeling connected once again.

"I'll be glad when today is over and the whole 'party talk' dies down," Anita added. "Of course it will pick back up again the end of next week, right before that Friday night, but by then, hopefully, everyone will know who is going and who isn't. Maybe they can be a little more tactful when they bring it up."

"I don't know, Anita, so many people are so thoughtless. They just feel like they need to brag that they made the cut, like it's all about them. I think they forget about everyone else. They just have to prove they are cool or wanted or worth inviting. I can always hope they'll be more considerate, but I'll have your back in case they don't," Karen offered as they both walked to the equipment basket at recess to find the extra-long jump rope.

"Thanks, Karen," Anita repeated. "You really are a great friend!"

Exactly twenty minutes later, what Anita feared most happened.

Where Do I Run and Hide?

The end-of-recess whistle blew, and all one hundred thirty-five students ran from every corner of the playground area to converge into one long line by the outside door, to go back inside. It was there in line that Anita heard Tommy call out to Kim, "I heard you didn't invite Anita from your lunch table to your sleepover party next weekend, how come?"

Kim called back to him into the now-much-quieter area of students in the front of the line, "Because she's so boring. I hate to say it, but she never has much to say, and it's supposed to be a p-a-r-t-y!" She spelled out the word with emphasis on every, single letter, thinking she was impressing Tommy with her own energy.

Anita heard it loud and clear. In fact, everyone heard it loud and clear. It was so humiliating, as all eyes begin to search for her in the crowd, and all of them, except Anita, were so relieved it wasn't them. Karen did too, and she whipped her head around to find Anita, just in time to see her break out of the line with her head down, and push her way through the crowd at the door to get to the playground aide standing guard. She took one look at Anita, whose eyes were brimming with tears.

The compassionate woman leaned over to comfort Anita, saying, "Honey, why don't you head in to see Mrs. Kaufmann. I just saw her go into her office a minute ago, so she should be there. I'll let your teacher know where you are, okay?"

Anita couldn't answer. Her throat burned, and she could barely see through the welled-up tears in her eyes. She was alone in the hallway, thank goodness, as she headed to the school counselor." She pushed open the outer door passing through the empty waiting room to get to the interior office doorway. Seeing Mrs. Kaufmann at her desk, she just came right into the safe harbor she had always known before. She sat down heavily on the chair across from Mrs. Kaufmann's desk, breaking into heaving sobs. "I am so embarrassed I want to die!" Anita cried, as she dropped her face heavily into her cupped hands, with her shoulders heaving up and down.

"Oh, honey, what happened?" Mrs. Kaufmann asked, surprised to see Anita look so broken. "Here are some tissues," she offered as she slid the box over to the edge of the desk near Anita. Anita started pulling tissues one after the other very quickly, creating a huge wad of white tissues to absorb her sea of tears.

"Thanks, Mrs. Kaufmann. It's just so embarrassing," Anita continued, still heaving with deep sobs. "It was bad enough I wasn't invited to **the** party of the year, and that all my friends were, and they all knew it at the lunch table. But just now, as I was lining up to come inside from recess, everyone was saying how I was boring and they didn't want me there. They said it was supposed to be fun and I wasn't, and that's why I wasn't invited." Anita sobbed into her hands again, and would have continued for hours if Mrs. Kaufmann hadn't asked her to start telling the story from the beginning.

As Anita recited scattered details of her morning as best she could remember, Mrs. Kaufmann listened intently, and Anita's sobs lessened to sniffles. She seemed to have reached the end of her emotional flooding. "Who actually said you were boring, my dear?" Mrs. Kaufmann asked. "And remember that it always just seems like everyone's agreeing, just because they all stay quiet, but no one likes to challenge the person who is calling out the hurtful or show-off-like comments. Sometimes they just don't even know what to do. So who made that comment?"

"Kim said I was boring and I never have much to say. She called it out to answer Tommy when he asked her why I wasn't invited. She said it right when everyone in line was getting quiet to go inside, so everybody heard it." With that, Anita's eyes filled up and the tears streamed down her cheeks once again.

"Anita," Mrs. Kaufmann interrupted softly. "I know that felt so embarrassing. You, my dear, actually are a very kind, caring, and quiet girl – but in no way boring. Your abilities and activities are all so interesting. You're just not loud. You would never call out something negative about someone else in front of a lot of people. You would never want to embarrass anyone, not ever, and everyone knows that about you. That makes you a very special person. In fact, if I were your age and in your class, I would want you to be my friend. And someday, I hope you grow up and move in next door to my house so you could be my neighbor!" Mrs. Kaufmann smiled and watched Anita's tears stop, and a shy little smile open up across her face.

Anita asked Mrs. Kaufmann, "But why would Kim want to do that to me?'

"Well, I could be wrong, but whenever I see Kim in the middle of a group of people, it always appears she is working hard to get attention, and she always speaks loudly, as if she wants to get their approval. It may be that she was just calling to Tommy to please him, and didn't even think about anybody else who might be listening, even less you. I would also guess by now that someone has told her you were right there and went inside crying. She might be feeling terrible right about now. No one dislikes you, Anita--you're just too kind--and I'm sure Kim doesn't, either. It was just really bad timing, and she wasn't thinking. And I'm not saying I wouldn't have been embarrassed too, at that moment, with everyone looking and listening, but think about it now. You were the nice person who had something bad happen to you, and they must have all felt compassion for you. I'll make one more guess, and that is that a lot of the people who heard it think less of Kim for doing that. Being loud is not as admirable as she thinks it is, is it? I'm hoping she'll think before she speaks from now on. I believe we all learn our lessons one way or another, don't we?"

Anita had been listening, and she was sitting up taller in her seat as she thought about what Mrs. Kaufmann was saying. It made sense that others may have had more sympathy for her than she thought at first, and she knew she never did anything to hurt anyone, even Kim. She was accepting that it may have just happened, and not on purpose. Of course, Anita knew that she still wasn't going to the party and Karen was, and now she had to get back into class, and was scared everyone would look at her as she came into the room. "Do I have to go back to class now?" Anita asked Mrs. Kaufmann, hoping she wouldn't have to. "Everyone is going to stare at me, and besides, we're just working on our research projects with our partner. Karen and I actually have it almost done ahead of time."

"I'll call your teacher right now and see what he thinks about your waiting till the end of class to go back. If he wants you to stop by at the end of the day just to connect, can you do that?"

"Yes, thanks, Mrs. Kaufmann," she happily replied.

"And actually, going back to class at the end of this period, when everyone is packing up and not paying attention to the door, might be a good idea. Karen can let you know how people reacted to it all after you left the playground and went inside. Knowing no one is making fun of you should make you feel much better about the whole thing. Who knows, Kim might even apologize between classes, and then everyone else will see it and know that things are mended. If they are confident that you two are okay now, they won't need to try to make you feel better and keep bringing it up. Want to try that instead?"

Anita hesitated as she tried to visualize it happening. Talking to Kim felt a little scary, since she didn't know if she might cry. However, it did seem better than everyone coming up to her, which might be worse, because it could last all afternoon. "Okay, I'll go back now and slide into my seat near Karen, and I'll just start working right away. Would you call Mr. Howard to let him know why I was here? I'd like to just go right to my seat when I get to the room, if that's okay with him."

"Absolutely," Mrs. Kaufmann said as she lifted the receiver. "Hello, Mr. Howard. As you know, I have Anita here with me now, and she's coming back to class hoping to slide in without being noticed. Would you help her with that? She was so embarrassed outside by a loud, hurtful comment, and now that she's feeling better, she doesn't want to stir that pot again, okay?" After a minute or two of apparently listening to the teacher, she gave a quick thanks and hung up. "Anita, Mr. Howard said he would do anything to help out such a kind young lady!"

Anita blushed. She gathered her backpack, lunch bag, and coat, but stopped in her tracks. "Uh-oh, if I walk into class with all my lunch and playground stuff, everyone will know I never went back to homeroom to put it away."

"Oh, feel free to leave it here in my office, and then just remember to stop by after school to get it, or you will have one very chilly walk home, my dear!"

"Thanks, Mrs. Kaufmann," Anita said, relieved as she left the office and scurried down the hall to class. Mrs. Kaufmann took the lunch bag and coat and placed them neatly on a chair by the office door, so she wouldn't forget them either. She began to think about some of the rather recent changes in Kim's behavior, based on the stories the students had been telling her. She made a note to talk with Kim's teachers that afternoon when they had their team planning period. Something was up with that little chicken in her chicken coop, for sure!

Three O'clock

Later that afternoon, Mrs. Kaufmann saw Mr. Howard on his way to the teachers' team planning meeting. She caught up to him and asked, "How did it go with Anita? Was she able to avoid stirring any looks and chatter in the room?"

"Oh, she was fine. The kids were all talking and working with their partners on their projects, and the room was so busy that no one even noticed her come in. I did notice, however, that Kim McNulty made a lunge for her as everyone was leaving, and Anita looked quite uncomfortable. I assumed Kim may have had something to do with the playground incident, or was just being a busybody, since I've watched her become the center of attention recently," Mr. Howard said, sounding disturbed by Kim's new unlikeable behavior. "She seems to want to be Miss Popularity or something these days, and getting into everyone's business – a bit out of control, if you ask me."

"I thought her name had come up a few times in my office, too. Do you think your team would mind if I stopped in before your meeting, just to ask the other teachers if anyone else has noticed her change of behavior, or if they know of anything going on at home?" Mrs. Kaufmann asked.

"We'd actually like that. Maybe you can shed some light for us too," Mr. Howard answered with enthusiasm. "In fact, we have her on our list of students to discuss today, for that very reason."

They arrived at the classroom with the other four teachers, and Mrs. Kaufmann explained she wanted to sit in on the meeting to see if anyone was observing some changed behavior in Kim McNulty. No sooner had she spoken her name than the conversation immediately flared up. They were taking turns sharing recent events they had witnessed before they had even taken their places around the big, round conference table. "I've been watching her call out in class and do nonstop talking to the point I had to contact her mom," one of the teachers offered. "And her mother said she was acting out at home too, which was especially hard with the newborn twins."

With that very comment, everyone suddenly understood the recent behavior and became more or less relaxed. This was not anything new to teachers, to see the older sibling get all out of sorts and need attention when there was a new baby that had arrived into the family and house, not to mention two new babies. "I think we may have our answer. But let me ask, has she done anything mean, or is she just a bit out of control?" Mrs. Kaufmann checked.

The quick responses from all around confirmed that she just seemed to need attention, but that her good-natured character was still there. "And I'm sure you heard she's having the annual big birthday bash again this year, and the invitations are out and stirring quite a buzz. I'm sure this may have something to do with her being even more out of control."

The meeting continued, and several more mysteries were solved or assigned to various members of the team. Mrs. Kaufmann knew she still needed to reconnect with Anita, to see if she was okay when she came by for her coat and lunch bag right after the dismissal bell. She hurried back to her office to check the voice mail for any end-of-day emergencies, before Anita would be there.

The three o'clock bell rang, signaling the end of the school day, and it was no surprise that Anita was at Mrs. Kaufmann's door within a couple of minutes. What was a surprise was that Kim McNulty was by her side, and the two of them appeared really happy. "Guess what, Mrs. Kaufmann. Kim invited me to her birthday party on Friday night. I am so excited!"

Kim looked a little embarrassed at first, knowing Mrs. Kaufmann had spent some time with Anita, helping her deal with a mean comment she made on playground that day. She suspected the school counselor saw the invitation as an apology – which it was. "That's wonderful, Anita! What are you planning to do at the party this year, Kim? I remember last year was a clown and a pony, like a fair, wasn't it?"

"How do you remember that stuff?" Kim asked, somewhat surprised.

"Well, it was the party of the year, and the talk was happening everywhere, even in my office," Mrs. Kaufmann explained. "I guess the only problem," she continued, "is that once it becomes 'the best party ever,' everyone wants to be invited, like to a royal wedding. Then, of course, those who thought they had a chance and didn't get an invitation are very hurt or disappointed, or both. But I understand. After all, how could you really invite everyone?" Mrs. Kaufmann laughed.

Kim quickly agreed and said, "This year, my mom said she just wanted to make an all-night movie marathon with a small group of close friends, with popcorn animals and all sorts of other movie-themed games. She even got a whole trunk full of costumes for party favors, so we could act out some scenes from our favorite movies. She's been so busy with the twins that she felt bad for me, I guess. And I've been grounded, forever, for talking back to her a lot recently. I said I hated her a few weeks ago and felt so bad later. Then when she told me last week I could still have a birthday party, I was shocked. I didn't think I'd have a party at all this year. I can't wait! Oh, and Anita, promise me you won't tell anyone ever, about my mom and me, okay?"

"I promise," Anita answered happily, with a smile that spread ear to ear across her little face. Anita's eyes were huge. She looked like she wanted to explode with joy and pride, because she had never been one of the "chosen few" before. She had always just been the nice, quiet girl, and today she was one of the envied.

"Okay ladies, you'd better get moving or you'll miss your bus." Anita and Kim spun around and went out the door, waving an over-the-head goodbye. "Anita, your coat!" called Mrs. Kaufmann, as she handed the coat and lunch bag to Anita, who rolled her eyes, but was still smiling her giant smile. Mrs. Kaufmann gave her a wink, and a big knowing smile right back.

From Five to Nine

Mrs. Kaufmann was putting a few folders to look over that evening into her briefcase when the phone rang. She was really tired from a very busy day and almost didn't pick up the receiver. She was thinking that if she had left her office a little earlier, the message would just be there in the morning. The problem was, there was a little voice in her head that reminded her that she was there to help children, and this could be an emergency. She knew she needed to pick up the phone, and, when she did, she heard a sobbing girl's voice. It was Kim's.

"Oh, Mrs. Kaufmann, can I talk to you right now? My mom is at the doctor's with the twins, and I just can't wait until morning. Please?"

"Sure, Kim. Are the twins okay?" Mrs. Kaufmann answered with concern.

"They're fine, just a check-up. It's *my* emergency. You know how I told you about all the surprises my mom planned for my party, when Anita and I were in your office after school? Well, I think Anita told Karen, who told everyone else, and now all our plans are ruined. Everyone, everywhere, knows exactly what we're doing Friday night. There are no more surprises, and that messes everything up! How could Anita do that? I wasn't going to invite her, but I did to be nice, and now she's ruined everything!!"

"Have you talked to Anita or Karen yet?" Mrs. Kaufmann asked. "I would think that neither of them would want to hurt you or ruin your party on purpose, so there might be a simple explanation."

"I don't know what to say to Anita. I'm so mad at her and Karen that I don't want to speak to either of them. In fact, I want to tell them not to come to my party at all now," Kim cried into the phone.

"I think you might want to find out what happened before you do that. You need to know what you're dealing with, don't you think?" Mrs. Kaufmann asked, and then suggested she e-mail Anita and Karen directly, to ask them if they told anyone about her surprise party plans. "See what they say, and try to wait before you respond, okay? That way you'll have some space between when you get the answers and when you have to say something back. I'll be here in the morning if you want to come in to talk. Just leave a voice message for me, and I'll let the office know to let you in before the bell. And Kim, I have to tell you that if I were going to your party knowing all the great things that were going to happen, I wouldn't need them to be surprises. I would be even happier anticipating all the fun I was going to have. Nothing is ruined but a little shock value. The fun will still make your party the best ever!"

"Okay, thanks Mrs. Kaufmann. I will call your voice mail tonight and let you know what happened. I do feel a little better now," Kim said, with a quieter and calmer tone.

"You're welcome, Kim. Please remember that Anita and Karen are good people, just like you. I've never known them to do mean things to anyone, so try to think what you would want them to do to you, if you happened to tell one of their secrets, okay?" Mrs. Kaufmann offered.

"Okay, I'll try," Kim answered and hung up.

Mrs. Kaufmann wrote a pass to allow Kim to come see her at nine o'clock the next morning just in case, and tore it off the message pad to take to the main office on her way out of school. She hoped Kim would soften, and that Anita and Karen would be honest with her, though that was a lot to ask when there was so much at stake. A lot could happen between five o'clock today and nine o'clock tomorrow morning.

Silence

The next morning, Mrs. Kaufmann came into her office and checked to see if there was a red blinking light on her office phone, telling her she had voice mail. There was one, and it was from Kim. She listened to the message, hearing a different tone in Kim's voice…one that was less sad, and with more of the deeper sound of anger. "Mrs. Kaufmann, I e-mailed Anita last night and I didn't hear back from her. My computer just went silent, no dings to tell me I had mail. I think she knows what she did, and she won't admit it. I'm sure she e-mailed Karen, because she didn't answer me either. I am so mad and don't know what to do. I hope it's okay if I come in to see you this morning." And then there was a click. No goodbye, just a firm-sounding voice ending in the air.

Before Mrs. Kaufmann could put her things away, there was knock on her door. "Mrs. Kaufmann, can I come in?" It was Anita. She stood in the doorway looking scared to death, and Mrs. Kaufmann could guess what she was about to say.

"Sure, my dear--what's up?" Mrs. Kaufmann asked, protecting the confidentiality of the conversation she had had with Kim the afternoon before.

"I did something terrible last night, and I don't know what to do now."

"What did you do, Anita, and are you sure it was terrible?" Mrs. Kaufmann asked in a soft and understanding voice.

"Remember yesterday when Kim was talking about how she had gotten in trouble with her mom and asked me not to tell anyone? Well, when Karen called me last night, I was so excited that I was going to Kim's party that I kept talking and told Kim what the party plans were. Then Karen told Donna, and Donna told Sandy, and now everyone knows about the movie theme. I found out that the party plans were a secret *after* I had already told Karen, and she had already told Donna. I didn't e-mail her back last night because I felt so bad. But I honestly thought the secret was about her and her mom not getting along, not about the party plans."

"Well, that makes perfect sense to me, Anita, and I can tell you that Kim may be coming here any second. Would you be willing to stay to explain to her what happened, the same way you just explained it to me?" Mrs. Kaufmann asked. "I don't think she would be upset with you if she realized you didn't understand what she meant when she asked you to promise. I do think she'd be really angry if she thought you ruined her surprise on purpose. What do you say? I'll be here to help if you need me," Mrs. Kaufmann assured her, "but your honesty would be best if it came from you."

Before Anita could even answer, Kim appeared in the doorway. Kim immediately looked at Mrs. Kaufmann with a questioning look, as if to ask why Anita was there. Mrs. Kaufmann took the lead right away. "Good morning, Kim. Guess who stopped in to see me about something that was worrying her?"

Anita looked fearfully at Kim, and Kim became quiet.

Mrs. Kaufmann broke the silence by saying, "Anita, do you want to explain to Kim what happened last night, or do you want me to? I think it would be best if it was in your own words."

Anita hesitated, as if to get her nerve up, and then she spoke quickly. "Kim, I am so sorry. I didn't mean to tell Karen what I did. I don't even think I knew that you wanted that part kept a secret. And I'm sorry I didn't answer you last night. I was scared you would be so mad at me that we couldn't be friends anymore. I'm sorry."

Kim reacted just as fast and angrily. "But you told me you would never, ever tell. What I told you about my mother and me was not for anyone to hear!"

"I didn't tell that part, I swear, Kim," Anita defended herself. "I only told Karen about all the stuff you said we were going to do at the party, that's all, really. I didn't tell her anything about you and your mom."

"But I meant the party stuff was a secret, too. Now everyone knows all about it, and there's no surprise."

Mrs. Kaufmann jumped in right when she felt Anita didn't know how else to apologize. "Girls, I can see exactly how this miscommunication happened. It's so clear now that it actually wasn't so clear yesterday. I think Anita is now realizing you wanted everything you said to be a secret – the part about her and her mom, as well as all the information about the party. And Kim, I think now you can see that Anita feels terrible that she didn't understand what you meant and didn't even think she was doing anything wrong. And Anita, I'm sure you can see why Kim is upset that her secrets about the party were told. But you know how I always ask everyone to get into the other guy's shoes?"

Both girls were silenced as they began to hear the truth about what happened. And they did know Mrs. Kaufmann had a "thing" about trying to see things from the other guy's perspective. They said "yes" in quiet harmony.

"So then there was no crime here. Not really." Mrs. Kaufmann continued, "Everyone was just doing what they thought was okay. Kim thought Anita betrayed her promise, which she didn't. Her promise was not to talk about any personal problems at your home, and she kept that promise. And Anita didn't answer Kim last night because she was scared, and didn't know what to say. Can you both see how this happened? Kim, what if you shared something with Karen that you thought was okay to share, and Anita, what if Kim let all the secrets out of the bag that you wanted to use to surprise everyone at a party of yours? This all came from a misunderstanding yesterday, right here."

Anita looked at Kim and said, "I am really sorry, Kim. I was so excited that you wanted to have me come to your party, after I heard you thought I was so boring. I didn't mean to ruin everything for you."

Kim answered, "And I'm really sorry I said that yesterday, Anita. I don't know why I said it so loud either, except that I kind of like Tommy."

Anita giggled and Mrs. Kaufmann smiled at Kim's honesty.

Kim continued, "That must've been so embarrassing. You really aren't boring at all, you're just quiet. I thought that having to act out all the movie skits at my party would make you uncomfortable, and that's why I didn't invite you. And now I do understand what went wrong with the promise."

"Thanks, Kim. That means a lot to me, because I thought you didn't like me in general, and I didn't know what I did to make you think I wasn't worth being your friend. Then last night, I thought you wouldn't want to speak to me anymore."

"I didn't," Kim laughed, "but Mrs. Kaufmann told me to put myself in your shoes, so I tried."

"Okay girls, I think you two need to get to homeroom before the late bell. I'm really glad you were both so honest. I knew two great people couldn't stay upset with each other for very long," Mrs. Kaufmann teased.

Both girls quickly grabbed their backpacks and coats and started for the door. Mrs. Kaufmann called after them, "Just think, now you two can talk between yourselves all about the party for the next two days, because neither of you has to keep it a secret--right, ladies?"

"Oh, that's right! I can plan stuff now, thanks Mrs. Kaufmann!" Kim quickly answered, as the girls hustled through the doorway and into the crowd of students pouring into school and heading for their classrooms.

Good kids, Mrs. Kaufmann thought to herself as she finished unpacking her briefcase for the day. *They just need to speak honestly and kindly to one another and walk in the other guy's shoes whenever they don't know what to do.*

The Monday Morning Post-Party "Buzz"

"Good morning, Mrs. Kaufmann! Guess what?" Kim called out to the school counselor in the hallway, outside her office door, as they both happened to be heading for the main office.

"Hi there, Kim, tell me, I can never guess. Oh, wait, maybe I can! Does it have to do with your party? Was it spectacular? Did everyone have fun, and did you girls stay up all night?" Mrs. Kaufmann guessed.

Kim laughed and said, "Yes, yes, and yes, except for one little problem."

"And what was that?" asked Mrs. Kaufmann.

"You won't believe this! Donna and Sandy happened to roll out their sleeping bags near each other after we were done with all the games and snacks for the evening. They started whispering about Karen's parents always fighting, and how Karen told Donna confidentially that she was afraid that they were getting a divorce," Kim said lowering her voice. "Of course Donna made Sandy a promise that she'd never, ever tell anyone. Then, Sandy was chatting live with Deanna on Saturday night, and happened to tell her that Karen's parents were probably getting a divorce, but for her not to tell anyone, either. Anyway, by the time Sunday night came, Anita got an e-mail about Karen's parents getting a divorce, as if it was common knowledge and everyone knew. Then I heard Karen's mom got a call from someone's mom, who is her friend, and found out that everyone thought she and her husband were getting a divorce. It was such a mess, and Karen got into so much trouble."

"Uh-oh," Mrs. Kaufmann said. "How are things this morning?"

"Oh, it's the buzz all right. What a coincidence that this type of situation had just happened between Anita and Karen and me last week. What a mess it is when people tell each other's secrets. Now Karen isn't speaking to Donna, and Sandy got in trouble with the person she told."

"I think if we didn't tell our secrets to others in the first place, there wouldn't be so many broken promises," Mrs. Kaufmann said with a sigh. "Kids feel that when someone trusts them with a secret, it's like a prized gift, you know? The person receiving the gift feels special, but then, as time goes on, the secret begins to be a burden. They no longer feel free to just say whatever's on their mind anymore, and, from that point on, they have the burden of watching what they say and holding the secret inside. Anyway, after a while they can't keep the secret anymore, because it's too hard, so they decide to be 'the giver' of that prized gift to someone else. That way, the load is shared, and therefore lighter."

"Wow, I never thought of a secret that way before. It's almost like giving someone a problem!" Kim said with a surprised tone.

Mrs. Kaufmann continued, "And of course everyone thinks the person they tell will keep it inside them forever, forgetting that they themselves couldn't even do that."

As Mrs. Kaufmann and Kim finished up their walk together down the hall, Mrs. Kaufmann asked Kim, "Do you think I need to be braced for some aftermath from the weekend in school today? What do you think?"

"I think the biggest storm is over, but there are a lot of bad feelings out there between lots of my friends. I'm not sure who to talk to today, or if everyone thinks my party caused it all," Kim admitted.

"Your party was a happy gift to all of those girls, don't forget that. And keep in mind, you can't control other people, or cause them to make the choices they make. We all have free will to make our own decisions, and then we learn from our own mistakes. This time, I think there was a lot of learning going on outside of school this weekend!"

"No kidding, Mrs. Kaufmann, and thanks!" Kim answered enthusiastically, as they arrived at the main office and started to go their separate ways.

"You're welcome, Kim. Have a great Monday. Oh, yes, and Happy Birthday, Birthday Girl!" Mrs. Kaufmann called to her, seeing her beam her big famous, beautiful smile and knowing her lesson had already been learned!

Discussion Points:

- When someone tells you a secret, it's a sign of trust between friends and feels like a gift. After that, it's a burden to have to keep.

- When you try to understand other people, just imagine being them in the same circumstances. That's when you'll truly understand their feelings.

- Bragging often makes people feel bad. They wish they had what is being bragged about. That can make others dislike the person who is bragging.

Reflection Questions:

1. When someone tells your secret, do you feel like they did it on purpose? Do you get hurt or angry because they didn't keep their word? Can you keep all secrets?

2. When you are given a party invitation, do you keep it quiet so the "non-invited" don't feel hurt? When you give out invitations, do you do it so that others don't have to feel bad about not being invited? Have you ever had limits on who to invite or how many?

3. When someone says something about you out loud, and everyone there laughs along, does that mean they were thinking about you being there and deliberately wanted to embarrass you? If someone says something unkind in front of others, and they don't say anything, does that mean they agree?

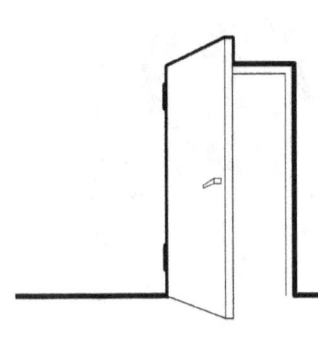

CHAPTER 8:
Do I Save a Friend, Knowing It Will Cost Us Our Friendship?

Approach-Avoidance

Sam walked nervously into the waiting room outside the school counselor's office and started to knock on Mrs. Kaufmann's half-opened inner office door. "Hi, Sam," Mrs. Kaufmann said cheerfully when she saw him appear. "How come I'm so lucky as to have you visit me today?" She got up from her desk and walked toward him, opening the door wider.

Sam brushed by her as he rushed into her office, apparently happy to be out of the waiting room and into the room where confidentiality was the understanding. He went right over toward her big desk, plopped down on one of her big black office chairs, and grabbed one of the gel hourglass toys she had on her desk for students to fidget with whenever they felt anxious. Pausing at first and looking only at the toy, he finally started speaking with reluctance and uncertainty, "Uh, I'm not really sure how to begin, or even if I should be here, or if I should tell. This is really weird."

Mrs. Kaufmann asked Sam, "Are you afraid to tell me something because you're not sure what will happen if you do?"

"Yes, and for a lot of reasons," he answered reluctantly.

"Well, what if you just talk about the problem or dilemma and describe the situation without telling me who's involved? We'll treat it as if we were saying 'just pretend' or 'what if someone else did this?' Then I'll understand what you're worrying about, and maybe I can put your mind at ease by letting you know what I would do. How does that sound?" Mrs. Kaufmann offered.

"Uh, okay, I guess I can do that, thanks, Mrs. Kaufmann." Sam answered with noticeable relief in his long, deep exhale. He continued, "Okay… okay… well, what would you do if you had a friend who told you a secret that you swore you'd keep… then it turned out that the secret was about her wanting to hurt herself – I mean really hurt herself. Also, your parents are friends with her parents and you are all on the same street, and you'd have a lot to lose if anyone found out you told. The only thing is, she might really hurt herself seriously, and she's your friend and you don't want her to do that. So what do you do?"

"Okay, I get why you're in such a dilemma – I mean, not that it's about you," she said, smiling as if she slipped. "There's a big price to pay for telling, but an even bigger price possible for this friend and neighbor if you don't, right?"

"Yes," Sam blurted out, knowing he was admitting it wasn't anyone else and that it was him, and he knew he was right on the edge of telling Mrs. Kaufmann who the girl was. He just really didn't want to hold on to this secret any longer, and he needed only a little nudge from Mrs. Kaufmann to relieve him of this worry and fear.

Mrs. Kaufmann reassured him that he would be fine. "I can definitely help you sort this one out, because it's happened many times before, believe me! And your heart is in the right place, Sam. You are a kind, caring, and compassionate person, one of the reasons this girl most likely shared her pain with you. You are a safe friend, and she trusts you. But now, you have the burden of knowing that if this trust was broken, she would get upset with you. However, at the same time, you are worried that she really might hurt herself and maybe seriously. I can't imagine how I would feel if she did anything really serious, especially if I could have saved her but decided to keep it a secret." Mrs. Kaufmann spoke with strong emotion – no longer keeping it light, and also validating Sam's decision, to make sure he felt right about doing what he was doing.

"Okay, first things first," Mrs. Kaufmann continued. "We'll need a little time right now for sorting it all through, so that you're comfortable with our decision. Does your teacher know you're here with me?" Mrs. Kaufmann asked Sam, not wanting to alarm him, but letting him know that he wasn't going back to class right now. She knew she couldn't postpone this conversation, being fully aware that there was a girl out there at risk right then. The seriousness spoke for itself to her, and now to Sam.

"Not really. I just said I needed to go to the bathroom, and I slipped in here as I was going by, because no one was in the hall. The only thing is, she's in my class right now, and she'll get suspicious if I go back after being out too long," Sam said. "She just told me this morning at the bus stop, and I've been thinking about it all day."

"What a tough day you had, knowing it didn't feel like either decision was a good one. I hope you didn't have any major tests today," she said to make some non-emergency-sounding small talk. "Sam, take a breather while I e-mail your teacher that you're with me right now and that we'll need a few more confidential minutes to get something done." She then quickly e-mailed Sam's teacher, Mr. Gentry, to make sure he didn't bring Sam's absence to anyone's attention. She then began to slip through some schedules on her computer screen. She matched up that class roster with his bus route and saw the girl who lived two doors down. Good news…she was the girl in his class. It was Aleeshia David, and Mrs. Kaufmann was not surprised. Aleeshia was always perfect…perfect grades, perfect appearance, and perfectly controlled – too much so.

"Doesn't Aleeshia David live two doors down from you, Sam? Is Aleeshia the girl you're worried about?" Mrs. Kaufmann asked directly deciding to cut through the part where Sam would have to tell. She figured if she guessed who the girl was, he didn't have to actually give her name, and maybe that would help reduce some of the consequences down the road.

Sam's face flushed instantly anyway, turning deep red down through his neck. He realized he had said too much and wished he could get back to history class this minute. He wanted to just tell Mrs. Kaufmann he changed his mind, but it was too late. "What will you do now?" he answered instead of a yes, since she now knew. "I just don't want her to be mad at me."

"Oh my dear, not to worry. I am so happy you did the right thing. I promise to take it from here, and I will do what needs to be done to keep her safe in the most caring way possible. I also promise to make sure she understands what a painful decision you had to make choosing the option that was good *for her* and *not* the one good for you. You've taken a risk at the loss of her friendship, which you value, to save her. That is such a sacrifice and so selfless. I am very impressed with your maturity and character."

"Thank you," Sam mumbled, feeling almost embarrassed by all the compliments, and relieved that what he did seemed suddenly so right.

"Right now what I need to know is how serious she is in her thinking about hurting herself. What did she say this morning that she wanted to do to herself, and if you can, try to remember her exact words if possible, okay?" Mrs. Kaufmann coaxed carefully.

"Oh, I won't ever forget them, believe me," Sam answered readily. "She told me how she had brought home a bad grade the night before, and her parents flipped out. She had been stressed out recently, too, trying to get enough practice time in to make the girls' basketball team as well as the school play. She said she just wanted all the pressure to end, and then Aleeshia said, 'Maybe I should just kill myself, then everyone will have to find someone else to push on.' I couldn't believe she said that, so I immediately tried to make a joke to try to lighten things up because she seemed so serious. The thing is, she said it like under her breath, so no one else could hear her at the bus stop. So anyway, I told her if she did that, I'd be left alone on our street having to put up with all the other jerks that lived there, and I'd have no one to talk to in the morning while I waited for the bus. She didn't even react, and that's what scared me. She always laughs at what I say. It was weird, and it felt wrong for some reason."

"I'm glad you trusted your instincts. A gut reaction or intuition can really mean a lot to us even if we don't know why. It's *how* she *didn't* say something rather than what she *did* say that had the most impact on you. So then what happened?" Mrs. Kaufmann continued, listening very intently.

"Nothing happened, because the bus came right then. We both got on, and she sat in the middle of the bus with her friends, and I kept on going to the back to be with mine. I've seen her all day in and out of classes and lunch, but she's always with her friends, so we usually don't talk until after school walking home from the bus stop again," Sam recounted. "I just couldn't wait any longer."

"We'll be fine, and again, you did the right thing, and I'm very proud of you, because it was a difficult decision, I know. Now I need to tell you what I'd like to say to Aleeshia when I call her down to see me…" Mrs. Kaufmann started to explain but was interrupted abruptly by Sam's reaction.

"You're calling her down now…with me here? What am I supposed to say when she walks in, that I told on her?" Sam sounded panicked.

"No, no, Sam. What I was going to ask is if you did want me to explain to her what you went through today worrying about her, or if you didn't want me to mention you at all," Mrs. Kaufmann answered quickly.

"But I think I'm the only one she told, so she'll know I'm the only one who could've told!" Sam challenged.

"Well, I usually call students I'm worried about to my office for a different reason to get started. Then I get into a conversation with them that I hope will cause her to be self-disclosing, which means she tells me about the stress she's feeling. You don't have to be involved at all," Mrs. Kaufmann explained.

"But won't she know I was just here?" Sam continued.

"No, I'll let you go to the library to return a book for me while I ask Mr. Gentry to send Aleesha down to me with a book I want to borrow from him. That way, she won't know you've been here, and she'll think she's been sent on an errand. By the time you've gone to the library and then all the way back to class, Aleeshia will already be in my office," Mrs. Kaufmann confided in him.

Sam paused, and then his worried face suddenly relaxed. "That's pretty cool, Mrs. K, thanks. So she'll never know it was me who told?" Sam asked, just to be sure.

"Not necessarily. I'm sorry I can't promise you anything except that I will keep our conversation confidential. See, if she pretends nothing is wrong at all, as she might possibly do, I still have to confront her with her words, because I can't just let her go home, knowing she could hurt herself. So that means I will have to eventually let her know why she's really here, and that someone heard her say that she wanted to kill herself. We both know she's smart enough to figure out it had to be you, and that's why I'm asking you this. If it goes that way, and she asks me if you came in and told me, do you want me to continue to say that I can't disclose who did? Or would you rather I explain that it was you who came in struggling with a problem and I guessed it was her? That way I can explain how hard it was for you to possibly end your friendship in order to save her life. What do you think? I can easily go either way," Mrs. Kaufmann offered.

"Oh boy, I don't know." Sam paused. "I think I might as well go with the way where you explain it was me and all the rest, because she may never want to talk to me again. I guess. Yeah, that way," Sam decided.

"Sam, I promise to try to have her offer it up to me first, to leave you out of it. Then if ever you want to tell her what you did at some later time, you can whenever you're ready. Otherwise, we both have to do what's right for Aleeshia, don't you agree?" Mrs. Kaufmann said, as she stood up to end the conversation and get Sam off to the library. She gave a book to him randomly from her desk to take to the librarian and to get him out of sight.

"Oh, and what do I say to my teacher when I get back to my classroom?" Sam checked as he was about to leave her office.

"You don't have to say anything at all. Just try not to call any attention to your coming in and sitting down. I will have explained to Mr. Gentry that you were helping me with another student, so you'll just need to catch up on what you missed while you were gone, okay?" Mrs. Kaufmann added. "Mr. Gentry will know to ignore you coming into the room so no one else will pay attention."

"Okay, thanks," Sam said as he started to leave her office.

"Thank *you*, Sam. You are a really good person! And I will take good care of Aleeshia so you don't have to worry anymore," Mrs. Kaufmann assured him.

As Sam closed the outer door behind himself, Mrs. Kaufmann picked up the phone right away to call Mr. Gentry. She quickly explained to him that Sam was on his way back via the route to the library, and that he needed to slip into class without being noticed. Then she also needed to see Aleeshia, but supposedly chosen randomly to run an errand for him. Without asking what was up and knowing Mrs. Kaufmann really couldn't break confidentiality, he said he'd send her down immediately with the manual she supposedly wanted to borrow. After Mrs. Kaufmann thanked him and hung up, she then thought, *Oh boy is right. I definitely need to handle this very carefully or Aleeshia will deny anything that sounds the least bit **imperfect**!* She then checked Aleesha's afternoon schedule on the computer to see what classes she had next that afternoon in case she needed to inform her teachers that Aleeshia was with her. And then she made one more call to Mrs. White, the school psychologist, telling her about the situation. She asked if she would mind stopping in to her office in about fifteen minutes to sit with Aleeshia David and her, just in case there was something more worrisome involved than an idle comment at the bus stop. Mrs. Kaufmann was laying the groundwork for what might be the worst-case scenario, but hoped for the best.

"Hi, Mrs. Kaufmann," a voice called into her office from the doorway. "I have a book for you from Mr. Gentry." It was Aleeshia sounding in a rush, not wanting to miss one second of class time.

It's all in the Timing

"Hi Aleeshia, it's so good to see you," Mrs. Kaufmann called out and jumped up to greet her. "Come in, come in, I'd love to chat a bit, if you have a couple of minutes. I can always write a pass, so that shouldn't be a worry."

"Oh, okay," Aleeshia answered a little reluctantly and came into the office, wondering what they were going to talk about.

"Have a seat. I have a couple of ideas about what I'd like to do for your class and I want your opinion, okay?" she asked casually, just to get Aleeshia comfortable.

"Okay," Aleeshia answered as she sat down across from Mrs. Kaufmann at the big desk.

"Well, here's what I've been thinking about. You know how students in your grade start feeling the stress of grades and sports and clubs and other things after school? And just to add more stress, the state testing is about to begin. I started wondering if they might like to form a discussion group, just to talk about how they all deal with it. I've also thought of whether we should offer tutors after school to help anyone who would like extra help. What do you think? Think anyone would sign up for either of those offerings?"

Aleeshia thought for a minute and politely said she didn't think so. "I think a lot of kids would want it, but I'm not sure they'd want everyone to see they've signed up for it."

"Good call, Aleeshia. You're right…too embarrassing. Okay, what if we set up the group to meet before school, when no one was around to know why any students are going in early? And, the sign-up would be confidential through a note, or e-mail or voice mail," Mrs. Kaufmann suggested.

"Well, I would do that if I wasn't too tired from staying up late studying the night before. Those state tests are scary for everyone, I must admit, but I wouldn't be able to stay after school because of all my after-school activities," Aleeshia admitted.

"This is really helpful, my dear," Mrs. Kaufmann continued. "What kinds of things do you think other students would want to talk about? If I made a list of things that stress everyone out, maybe there would be a lot of interest."

"Well, definitely the testing, and then the homework, and then finding time to be with friends--oh, and parents expecting too much," Aleeshia added with a little more emphasis on the last item.

"Yeah, parental pressures, that's a good one," Mrs. Kaufmann said casually, to encourage more conversation with Aleeshia. "I remember wanting to talk about my parents when I was in school, and I was so tired of hearing them say that it was all in my best interest."

"I know!" Aleeshia agreed with enthusiasm. "My mom and dad think I have to be perfect all the time. I always get A's, but I got a C on my history quiz yesterday, and when I showed it to my mom last night, she told my dad and they both went ballistic. I was crying and couldn't concentrate on my English essay after that, so that will probably be a bad grade now too. And they said I couldn't keep spending so much time after school in the gym anymore practicing basketball, but they still expect me to make the team. Don't they get that I have to practice? And I have piano lessons and a math tutor and acting lessons after school, too. I'm afraid I will forget something every day I leave for school, and pray I don't get too much homework every night to do after all my lessons 'cause I'm so tired."

Mrs. Kaufmann was relieved that Aleeshia was just pouring her heart out and wanted to continue to encourage the flood of feelings. "I'm sorry this is all happening, Aleeshia. What do you do with all that stress?" she asked to see if Aleeshia would keep going with her pent-up feelings.

"Oh, I'm all right," she quickly detoured with an instinct about where this was going. "I'll just study harder tonight," she answered quickly as if it was getting too uncomfortable. She then stood straight up with a sudden need to leave. Now Mrs. Kaufmann knew her hand was forced, and she had to confront her with that comment she made.

"Aleeshia, I need for you to sit down, my dear, because I have another question for you. This may feel a little uncomfortable, but I need for you to be honest with me. Have you ever said to anyone that you wanted to end all this stress by ending your life?" Mrs. Kaufmann asked her directly, but softly, so as not to cause her to deny and withdraw.

Aleeshia paused, and with her head dropped down and her eyes looking into her lap, she lowered her voice and answered reluctantly, "Yes, I did. I said that this morning. She then looked up. How did you… I mean did someone tell you…like Sam?" she slowly realized what had happened.

"No, Sam didn't give me your name, but he did come in to see me with a serious problem and a horrible dilemma. See, he has this friend that he was really scared was going to hurt herself, but he had promised to not repeat what she told him. He was too loyal to get her help for fear she would get mad at him, and he didn't want to lose her friendship more than anything. But, he was even more scared she would hurt herself, and he couldn't have that on his conscience, plus he couldn't imagine her being hurt. He was willing to sacrifice your friendship and lose you in order to save you. Isn't he a really good person?" Mrs. Kaufmann kept defending Sam. "I just eventually guessed it was you, because you're the only girl I ever see him talk to, and I know you two are neighbors and stand at the same bus stop. So I actually saved Sam from having to break his promise."

Aleeshia gave a weak smile as Mrs. Kaufmann was talking. "He is a good friend," she finally said. "I was very upset this morning, but I didn't really mean *kill myself.* That's just an expression. I just still felt like crying from last night. I felt better as soon as I got into homeroom and saw all my friends, really, Mrs. Kaufmann."

"Hi there, Mrs. Kaufmann, how's my favorite school counselor?" a woman said enthusiastically as she just came into the office, seeing Mrs. Kaufmann and Aleeshia talking at the desk.

"Hi, Mrs. White, I'm glad you stopped by. Do you know my friend Aleeshia David? She is such a great student and so talented, too! We were just talking about all of the extracurricular activities she's doing right now," Mrs. Kaufmann added, giving the school psychologist an opening for some directed conversation.

"Well, I'm delighted to meet you, Aleeshia," Mrs. White said happily, as she joined the two of them, pulling a chair up next to Aleeshia. "What kinds of things are you doing right now?"

Aleeshia perked up and proudly listed all of the classes and lessons she was taking after school, and then threw in all the things she planned to try out for, coming up soon, as well as the following fall.

"Wow, I have to hand it to you. How do you balance all of that and get good grades, too? I think I would be pretty stressed out trying to find the time for everything. How do you do it?" Mrs. White went right to the heart of the problem.

"Well that's what we've been talking about," Mrs. Kaufmann jumped in. "Aleeshia, is it okay if I share what you told me about the other pressure you feel? You, know, the feelings you've been having because of the need to do well in everything?"

"It's okay." Aleeshia agreed, realizing Mrs. White was there to help, too.

"Well, actually, maybe *you* should tell Mrs. White about what you were feeling this morning and what you told a friend before you came to school," Mrs. Kaufmann encouraged. "See, Mrs. White is also someone that kids talk to here at Hillstown Middle School, especially when the stresses get to be too much. She really helps relieve the pressure for a lot of students. Maybe she can help you, if you're willing to share."

Aleeshia looked like she really didn't want to tell it again, but she also knew if she did, there might be something to make the stresses not so bad. "Well, I've been feeling like I'm on a roller coaster and I can't get off. There's always something that I think I'd better do, but I can't seem to get it done because I have to do other things, you know? So, sometimes I get depressed and sad and all that. And when my parents ask me what's wrong and I tell them, I know they don't understand, and I just want to cry. So last night when I got in trouble for getting a C on a quiz, I started to cry…really cry, and this morning I didn't feel any better."

Mrs. Kaufmann prodded just a little more to get Aleeshia's actual words, for Mrs. White to hear. "Did you want to tell Mrs. White what you said this morning at the bus stop, or would you rather I share that with her for you?" Mrs. Kaufmann gave her a choice as to *who* would tell, but not *if* it was told.

"I just said I wanted to kill myself, but I didn't mean really kill myself. I just wanted the stress and the sadness to end, that's all," Aleeshia admitted.

Mrs. White quickly and kindly reacted, "And do you still feel that way now?"

"Oh, no--well, I do wish I didn't always have so much to do, and that my parents understood how hard it is to please them all the time, but I don't want to die, okay? I just want things to not be so hard, that's all," Aleeshia explained.

Mrs. White pursued. "Have you ever felt those same feelings before?" she asked.

"Well, yes, whenever all the tryouts come, and the state testing talk starts, you know, like all the parents and teachers keep telling us it's coming and that we have to do really well? That's when I start to freak out, and then something else gets thrown on the pile, and it makes it all too hard. I usually have a meltdown with my parents, or I talk back or something, and then I get punished. I just can't take that. I'll cry myself to sleep, and then I get depressed for a while." Aleeshia once again shared freely once she got on a roll.

"And do you ever tell your parents all of this?" Mrs. White asked.

"I did once, and my mom told me that if everyone else was handling it, then I could too and not to be so dramatic. She called me a 'drama queen,' and I hate that. Last time I slammed my bedroom door when my mom said that, so she punished me by taking away my computer for the night, and I needed it to do homework. She wouldn't listen. She just said that I should go to bed early and then get up early to do it. That way I wouldn't be chatting online with my friends, wasting time. She has no idea how little I really do compared to everyone else." Aleesha's anger was building, and she reached a point of beginning to cry.

Mrs. Kaufmann made a quick suggestion. "Mrs. White, I have an idea that might really help Aleeshia. Aleeshia, remember I said I was considering running a group for students to get some extra support from teachers before and after school? And, before anyone could come, I would need to get his or her parents' permission to attend, right? So, what if I was to call your parents to let them know I was inviting you to join this group and explain why our students may want to come to it--that is, because of the stresses they feel at this testing time of year. Then that would explain and validate what you feel to your parents. What do you think?"

Mrs. White jumped in with an enthusiastic reply. "Great idea, and I'm wondering if maybe there should be a parent workshop on the stress students feel in general, at this age. Maybe even a PTA presentation would go hand in hand while the student group is running. I'd be happy to help you with that, Mrs. Kaufmann. Maybe we could do that together?"

Aleeshia looked from Mrs. White over to Mrs. Kaufmann to see her reaction. She didn't really know Mrs. White, but she had known Mrs. Kaufmann for all the years she had gone to this school. Everyone said Mrs. K would always be willing to help you deal with anything, even your parents, and she thought this might be one of those times.

Mrs. Kaufmann lit up. "Oh, Aleeshia, wouldn't that be perfect? During that first conversation, I would get to explain to your mom and dad how much pressure is on you so they'll realize you're not a drama queen after all. Then I could tell them about the workshop Mrs. White and I are running to help students manage their feelings, structure their time, and not create expectations of being perfect all the time. I would like to also let all the parents know that when they see the pressure becoming as great as it has been on you, it might be good for parents to talk to a counselor, to learn some ways to help their children deal with it all. Like the idea?"

The whole time Mrs. Kaufmann was talking, Aleesha was imagining what her parents' reactions would be. She hesitated at first, thinking nothing would work with her parents, but after a few minutes, she said with a smile, "Maybe it could work, because it's coming from you. At least they'd probably stop calling me a drama queen!"

Mrs. Kaufmann and Mrs. White laughed with Aleeshia. "And I have to ask you another question. How do *you* feel about talking with an outside counselor if our school talks don't work with your parents? I keep thinking that they might have some good ideas to help you get off that roller coaster ride! The big thing is you'd feel supported, and the counselor would help your parents, too. How do you feel about that if we need to do it?"

Aleeshia looked uncomfortable. She knew her parents were busy people and she was already asking a lot of them when it came to taking her to her activities every day after school. "I don't know if they'll want to do that," she answered honestly.

"Even if they thought you were as overwhelmed and as sad as you've been?" Mrs. White asked. I mean, if your parents were to know how bad you felt this morning, do you think they'd want to help you?"

"Yes, I guess so. I'd like to see how Mrs. Kaufmann's call goes about the group and the parent talk first, just to see how they react. Then I guess that will tell me if they still think I'm 'full of bologna,' as my dad says."

"I like this idea!" Mrs. Kaufmann was so enthused that Aleeshia began to look really positive for the first time since she came into the room.

Mrs. White stood up and announced, "I like it, too. Listen, I really need to run. I have a meeting I need to go to. Let me know if I can help you anytime, Aleeshia. That's what Mrs. Kaufmann and I are here for. Please remember that, okay?"

"I will," Aleeshia answered, giving Mrs. White a big smile.

"And Aleeshia, I want you to think about going to counseling with your parents, if they are willing. The counselor could really make life easier after just talking a few times with each of you, you know?" Mrs. White coaxed one more time.

"Okay, I will. Thanks," Aleeshia said, as Mrs. White walked to the doorway.

Aleeshia looked relieved, even happy. Someone was willing to talk to her parents and make them understand her stress, her depression, and her occasional feelings of hopelessness.

Mrs. Kaufmann walked Mrs. White out, as they quietly said a couple of words to one another about following up with Aleeshia's parents. Mrs. Kaufmann walked back over to her desk and picked up the phone to call Aleeshia's mom. "Aleeshia, I'll call your mom right now so you can be comfortable hearing what I've said, okay?"

Aleeshia was so surprised. "You're going to call her right now, while I'm here?"

Mrs. Kaufmann smiled, "Sure, why not? That way we'll both know how your mom reacts, okay?" Mrs. Kaufmann knew that if her mom reacted badly, it would be a huge disappointment to Aleeshia, which could make things worse than they were that morning. Mrs. Kaufmann needed to know it would be okay before she let Aleeshia leave her office.

Aleeshia's eyes opened wide. She was really uncertain which way her mom would react, but Mrs. Kaufmann was dialing the phone, and there was no turning back now.

The Call

"Hello, Mrs. David? This is Mrs. Kaufmann, the school counselor at Hillstown Middle School, and I'm calling to let you know about a group I'm forming for Aleeshia's class later this month. She's with me now helping me plan it out, and I wanted your opinion also, from a parent's point of view. Because I know it's such a stressful time for our students at this testing time of year, Mrs. White, the school psychologist, and I thought it would be helpful if we could work with interested students on time management, de-stressing methods, organizational skills, test-taking skills, etc. I know Aleeshia is one of our top-performing students, so I assumed she might want some of these test-taking tips. She also may sometimes feel overwhelmed managing all she does in addition to getting great grades. Is that something you're willing to give permission for her to do?"

"Uh, sure, that would be great. Sounds like a really good idea. As a matter of fact, just between us, she's been having meltdowns at home recently, and her father and I try to not give it any attention. I would actually like some ideas on how to handle her over-reactions. She does have mood swings, but I figured it was just the age. I'm really grateful for any help you can offer," Aleeshia's mom admitted.

Mrs. Kaufmann was happy Mrs. David was so receptive, which would make the process run so much more easily for all concerned. "Well, what a coincidence, because I was also considering giving a workshop for parents, too, so you're welcome to come to that as well."

"That really sounds great. When and where will the group and the workshop be?" Aleeshia's mom asked.

"I actually haven't created the schedule yet, since I've just started the planning process. So let me ask you, do mornings work for you, and would a student group meeting before school work for Aleeshia?" Mrs. Kaufmann asked, hoping to almost design them around Aleeshia's and her mom's schedules. Then Mrs. Kaufmann decided to introduce one more idea. "I can also suggest a couple of counselors who are excellent in their help for adolescents and their parents, but they work outside the school, if you feel you might want to get help sooner or privately, just a thought."

Aleeshia had been listening quietly as Mrs. Kaufmann spoke to her mom, but with these last words, she looked up wide-eyed. Mrs. Kaufmann knew she had stepped one step beyond what Aleeshia expected on this call, so Mrs. Kaufmann gestured with a thumbs-up and a big smile to Aleeshia to show her the confidence she was feeling.

"Oh, I hadn't thought of that," Aleeshia's mom answered. "Uh, I'm not sure her dad will want to go that far, unless you think Aleeshia is experiencing more than the usual stress all kids feel. Do you think that's the case?" Mrs. David asked directly.

Mrs. Kaufmann now had to make a decision between the implied confidence she held with Aleeshia or speaking on her behalf, and she knew there really was no decision. Just like she talked about with Sam, saving someone's life is more important than the good feelings between the two of you. However, she did want to keep the trust and the line of communication open with Aleeshia for the future. "Mrs. David, can I put you on hold for just a second? I just need to ask someone something."

"Sure," Aleeshia's mom answered.

"Aleeshia," Mrs. Kaufmann said seriously, "I need to let your mom know that what you've been feeling isn't just the average experience for kids around here, and that it really reached a point where you could use some help. I will need to tell her what you said this morning in order for her to understand that counseling is what would work best. How do you feel about that?"

Aleeshia sat upright immediately. "Are you really sure you have to? Will I get into trouble? Maybe you could just tell her…."

Mrs. Kaufmann interrupted. "Aleeshia, my dear, it really is the best way to go here, and you will not get into trouble because you could really use some help. Parents don't like it when their kids carry on about things to get their way, but this isn't the case here. What you said this morning wasn't for their benefit…it was you wanting things to change. I'd like to see a happy Aleeshia walking through the halls of my school, not someone who can't take it anymore, wouldn't you?"

Aleeshia relaxed back into her chair as if the momentum of what would happen next was no longer in her control. "I guess so," she said softly and almost in defeat.

"Trust me, my dear. This is the turning point that will make all the difference for you. It's actually a good thing, you'll see," Mrs. Kaufmann said, with sympathy for what Aleeshia was feeling, and yet with complete confidence in the process at this point.

"Yes, Mrs. David? Sorry to keep you waiting," Mrs. Kaufmann said, as she resumed the conversation with Aleeshia's mom. She continued, "You asked if I thought Aleeshia was experiencing more stress than most and I would have to say I do. She puts a lot of pressure on herself to be perfect and to take on so many activities, but she can't always keep all those saucers spinning perfectly, if you know what I mean."

"Oh, I do!" Aleeshia's mom said with a great deal of emphasis. And come to think of it, she has been acting out quite a bit recently and having regular meltdowns. Last night's was the worst ever, and she wasn't her usual happy self even when she left for school this morning. Has she done that at school, too?"

"Oh, no," Mrs. Kaufmann assured Aleeshia's mom immediately. Then she continued, watching Aleeshia's face and body language. "I only came to realize it today when I had heard from a worried friend that she made a comment this morning about wanting to just kill herself. I've since been talking with her and realized she just threw the comment out there, and she swore she didn't really mean it literally. The only thing is that's a sign of feeling overwhelmed and not knowing how else to fix it all. You don't need to be alarmed, but you can't take it lightly. So, that's where we come in. Our jobs as parents and school counselors include helping our kids learn how to deal with stress. And since it will take me a little time getting the group and the workshop organized, my suggestion would be that you and your husband look into some outside counseling now to give you some guidance and to give Aleeshia some peace of mind temporarily. What do you think?"

"Oh! Definitely! Aleeshia's mom said with great energy. "I had no idea it had reached that level. And if you can give me the names of any counselors you'd recommend, I will call one today and get things moving along."

Mrs. Kaufmann, still studying Aleeshia, said to her mom, "That would be great, Mrs. David. In fact, I can just send you our referral list now if you'll give me your e-mail address. I am so happy you're willing to act on this so quickly, too. I will continue to talk with Aleeshia about this now as well, so she understands how the process works, okay?" Mrs. Kaufmann said, as she winked at Aleeshia.

Aleeshia smiled, looked relieved, and sat back more comfortably in her chair. "Thank you so much for your help, Mrs. Kaufmann," Aleeshia's mom said gratefully. "I really appreciate your acting on it so quickly as well. And yes, I would love it if you explained it to Aleeshia, and I will call her dad right now. Thanks again!"

"No problem, and it was good talking with you. Please let me know how things are going at some point in time, and I'll keep you posted on the group and the workshop, okay? My guess is you and Aleeshia will be able to run them once you've had a chance to pick up some strategies." Mrs. Kaufmann laughed.

"I hope so." Aleeshia's mom laughed, too, as they both said their goodbyes and hung up.

Aleeshia was now smiling. Mrs. Kaufmann sat back in her seat and simply said, "So, how'd we do?"

"It was good," Aleeshia answered, showing a sense of relief as well as one of hope. "And it sounded like my mom was really okay with it all?"

"My dear, Aleeshia, she loves you! She will always be okay taking care of you. She may not always know how to help you with your anxiety, but she will always want to. The best part is now the counselor can help you and your parents learn how to talk about things more comfortably, so you won't have to keep things all bottled up inside anymore. And, the counselor can help you all decide how much you should try to do at once, and that trying to be perfect is not only not necessary, but not healthy! Won't that be a relief?!"

Aleeshia just sat there for a minute, imagining all of that. She then quietly said, "Cool."

"Okay, let's get you back to class. It's right at the end of the period, so stop back into Mr. Gentry's class just to 'catch up' with him and get your homework. Then you can scoot to the locker room for gym class without anyone really noticing. And remember, your parents love you! You are one great kid and deserve to be happy," Mrs. Kaufmann assured her once again as she handed Aleeshia the hall pass as she went out the door.

"Thanks so much, Mrs. K!" Aleeshia said, as she took off down the hall.

Mrs. Kaufmann smiled, grabbed her calendar, and headed for Mrs. White's office to tell her the good news and set a date for the parent workshop. The change-of-class bell rang, and the students poured out into the hallways. Mrs. Kaufmann and Sam spotted each other at the same instant. Sam wanted to say something to her, but stayed with his friends not to draw attention. Mrs. Kaufmann smiled at him with a wink and a small, thumbs-up gesture.

Sam smiled back and mouthed the words "Thank you."

Mrs. Kaufmann mouthed the words back to him. "Thank *you*!"

In Just a Week

On the way down to the gym for the spring talent show that Friday afternoon, Mrs. Kaufmann ran into Mrs. David coming in the door to see the show. "Hi, Mrs. Kaufmann, do you have a minute?" she called to her.

"Sure, Mrs. David, and how is everything going?" she asked, as she came a little closer.

"Oh, I just have to thank you so much for directing us to a counselor," Aleeshia's mom said with great appreciation. "It has worked so well. First of all, we had no idea Aleeshia was that stressed, and it was a good call on your part. And why she would not want to tell us also became very clear. We kept calling her a drama queen, which makes me feel so bad now, but we just thought she was trying to manipulate us. The counselor also suggested my husband and I pull back on the expectations. We always thought we should set the standard high, expect a lot and she'll strive to meet it. We found out that she set them high enough for herself, so we had just added to that."

Aleeshia's mom continued, "Also, the counselor helped Aleeshia pull back on all she's trying out for at once. He suggested a more reasonable schedule and to choose her favorite activities rather than try out for, or sign up for, everything. Boy, just those three things have made all the difference in the world. Plus, we know how to talk about it together now. Oh, and Aleeshia called Sam and thanked him for being such a good friend. Thanks to you, Mrs. Kaufmann, Sam was encouraged to do the right thing and now he feels really good about it. They are thicker than thieves, those two, and I'm really glad they are such good friends. I really can't thank you enough," Mrs. David repeated as she reached out to give Mrs. Kaufmann a hug.

"Oh, I'm so happy it's all working out. You're so welcome. It really is my pleasure to help our students out – especially when they just don't know what to do next."

Just then Aleeshia's mom saw Aleeshia walking with her friends toward the gym and toward them. "Uh-oh, I'd better run. Heaven forbid Aleeshia's friends see me talking with you in the hallway. It's nothing personal, Mrs. Kaufmann." Aleeshia's mom laughed as she turned quickly and headed for the gym.

Aleeshia's glance suddenly caught the sight of them talking, as well as her mom then turning and heading for the show. Aleeshia's eyes then caught Mrs. Kaufmann's, who once again, did her famous hallway wink.

Aleeshia smiled her biggest smile ever, gave Mrs. Kaufmann a little happy wave from the hip, and skipped off with her friends.

And that was all Mrs. Kaufmann needed to know.

Discussion Points:

- Trying to be perfect is unhealthy.

- There is never a good reason to keep a secret when a person wants to hurt themselves or others. Finding the trusted adult to talk to is making the right decision.

- We all have to accept that we have limitations. And sometimes, we have to accept that we need to ask for help, and that is a perfectly healthy thing to do.

- Trust your intuition when you think something doesn't feel normal, and pay attention.

Reflection Questions:

1. How long would you have waited before you told a trusted adult that a friend said she wanted to kill herself? Would it be wise to try to figure out yourself if she was serious or not? Do you think anyone ever really knows what another person is thinking? Do you understand Sam's problem in deciding to tell?

2. Do parents sometimes push their children too hard to do better? Do they sometimes not push hard enough? How can parents know how their children really feel?

3. Do you ever feel overwhelmed? Do you ever feel like you're not able to keep up, or you've taken on too much? How do you back off, or drop something, or balance what you have when there is too much to do? Do you ever talk to your parents to let them know what you're feeling?

CHAPTER 9:
He's Too Cool for Me at School

Fair-weather Friends

Directly under the "Welcome" sign on her office door was the taped-up, crooked piece of notebook paper that read: *Out on playground. Be back in 10 minutes. Mrs. K.*

Mrs. Kaufmann knew that as the school counselor, she needed to go outside to the playground at the beginning of the school year to watch the dynamics of the students at recess. She needed to know if there were any students appearing to be left out of the social groups and looking alone, especially the new students. There was only one lonely boy. He was not new, nor was being alone something new for him.

"Hi Damian, how's it going?" Mrs. Kaufmann asked Damian Markus, who was sitting by himself, leaned over, and aimlessly scribbling with a stick in the dirt with his head down. He was on a bench near the door, and, in stark contrast way behind him, there were 234 other students in his grade happily running around, playing games, or standing in groups excitedly talking.

"Nothing much," he answered, coming out of his thoughtful quietness and looking up. He then appeared relieved to be talking to someone, even if it was just the school counselor.

"So, what did you do over the summer, other than grow taller?" Mrs. Kaufmann remarked.

Damian smiled really big. "I know. I'm actually almost as tall as my mom now," he bragged proudly.

"I'll bet you are," Mrs. Kaufmann replied. "So what did you do last summer?" she persisted.

"It was good. I went with my family on a vacation to California to see my grandma for a week, and we took Colin Harwood with us. Then I hung out with him every day when we got back. We rode bikes, played basketball, played my computer games, swam in my pool, and my mom took us to the movies a lot!"

"Well, that sounds like fun. Are you and Colin in the same class this year?" Mrs. Kaufmann asked, to start fishing for why Damian was not playing with him then. She could see Colin shooting hoops on the basketball court with a few friends, so she knew he was in school.

"Yes, we are, and we take the same bus, too," he answered, but then he seemed to get quiet.

"Don't you guys hang out during recess this year when you're in school?"

"No." Damian didn't offer anything more.

"Hey, would you be willing to help me back in my office right now? I could really use your opinions for some activities for my New Student Groups, and I have to get back there and get started." Mrs. Kaufmann used this as a somewhat legitimate reason to bring Damian back to her office to talk. She didn't want to make him feel like he had done something wrong, but she did want to see why he didn't seem to have any friends. She knew he had had a tough time making friends the year before when he was new, but she remembered he finally connected with another new student, Colin, at the end of the year. And yet now, even after being with him all summer, Damian seemed to be disconnected from him, too. "You interested?"

"Sure!" Damian said, jumping up at the chance to go inside and not have to continue sitting there alone. He hated that everyone could see him all by himself for the whole recess time, which only proved to the world that he had no friends.

Once Mrs. Kaufmann came into the quiet hallway with Damian and they started heading to her office, she quietly asked the big question. "So why were you sitting all by yourself out there, Damian? I thought you and Colin struck up a friendship last year, and it sounds like it was pretty good all summer, too."

"I don't know. He doesn't want to hang out with me when we're at school, just at home," Damian admitted, and showed he was really hurt.

"Did anything happen last summer that caused your friendship to be strained?" Mrs. Kaufmann asked. "And do you want to talk about this a little bit before we do the other 'stuff' I was going to do with you?"

"Yeah, I guess so," Damian agreed, as he and Mrs. Kaufmann entered the guidance office together.

"So tell me why you aren't playing basketball with him today instead of being alone. I know you like basketball, and you two played last summer," she pursued.

"I don't know. We even have a lot of fun hanging out after school and on the weekends, but he just acts like he doesn't know me when we're at school. We stand at the bus stop together in the morning, and then, when we get on the bus, he goes right to the last seat, where he has his whole group of friends waiting for him and saving him a seat. I'm not part of that group. They even all yell at me to move when I try to sit in Colin's seat when he's absent. They all think they're so cool!" Damian said angrily, but still showing the hurt in his voice.

"Does Colin ever try to invite you into his group of friends, like at recess?" Mrs. Kaufmann went a little further.

"No, he never does. It's as if I'm not good enough for him when he's with his cool friends, so I should know not to try to join him, either. It really stinks, because he is my only friend, so I have no one else to hang around with at school, and he doesn't care. My mom says that he's what's called a fair-weather friend," Damian said, getting a little choked up.

"Do you know what that means?" Mrs. Kaufmann asked.

"I think a fair-weather friend is someone who likes you when it's good for him, and then he doesn't like you when it's not good for him, or when he has something better to do. My mom noticed that he liked me at my house last year when he had no friends, and especially when she took us places. But, since school started and he's in the cool group, he didn't want to even be seen talking with me in school, even though he'd come over to swim in our pool after school at our house."

"I'm sorry, Damian. That really must have upset you when you started school this year," Mrs. Kaufmann said quietly. "Have you mentioned it to him when you hang out after school?"

"No, and I don't want to," Damian answered firmly.

"I'm just thinking that maybe he doesn't realize how that must hurt you when he does that," suggested Mrs. Kaufmann.

"I don't think I want to hear what he has to say," Damian said strongly. "It would be too embarrassing that I'm just not cool enough, and it would just make us both feel bad, and then that would end everything for us. At least, for right now, we do have a good time outside of school...as long as his friends aren't around."

"But Colin wouldn't have hung out with you all summer if you weren't fun, so what makes you think you're not cool enough to be with him?"

"I guess because his friends think so when we're here at school. Those are the guys that always made fun of me last year, remember? It's the same group that called me a loser last year. And they really think Colin is cool because he's so good at basketball," Damian explained.

"But you're good at basketball, too. I've seen you play!" Mrs. Kaufmann challenged him.

"Yeah, I guess, but I'm not really like them, and I know it. I'm just different, that's all," Damian said as he dropped his head and lowered his eyes.

"In what ways, like, what would they do that you wouldn't, or what do you do that they don't?" Mrs. Kaufmann kept pushing, knowing Damian was allowing her to get to the heart of the problem, and this would be her best opportunity to help him. Then she reminded him of what that group of boys had done last year, and that he wasn't a loser at all. "Remember that last year they only called you a loser after you got embarrassed up in front of the class, forgetting something. Remember we talked about everybody forgetting things, even them?"

"I remember," Damian said, and then he got quiet for a minute. "I guess I just don't jump into things. I don't feel right yelling out funny comments to people, and I don't like to take chances doing things. I'm not comfortable showing off. I'm more comfortable being quiet, but I do like basketball. I'm just…well… not somebody needing everyone's attention or trying to be all cool."

"Boy, you sure just hit on something so smart, and you don't even realize it," Mrs. Kaufmann said, raising her voice. "Those boys are all *needing* attention. They *are* different, but, unfortunately, kids label that behavior as cool, and they see you as quiet or shy. Okay, I'm getting a clearer picture of what you're thinking now. Tell me if I have this right. You're thinking that kids are cool and have confidence because they feel free to call out comments about others, show off, and get a lot of attention, right?" she checked.

"Right," Damian answered.

"Well, guess what? That's really their way of trying to be in control so they feel safe themselves. It's like they are on a stage trying to prove they are funny, or prove they are witty. Why? Because something inside of them thinks they *need* to prove it to others. If they were okay being who they were, they wouldn't have to work so hard showing off, you know? It is how they have learned to be okay themselves, and then, that becomes who they are. It's their form of power, which they only feel they need because they *believe* they *don't* have it. Does that make sense?"

"I'm not sure," Damian said reluctantly. He was truly unable to see these cool kids as feeling like they really *needed* anything.

"All right, let me ask you a question. When you hang out with Colin at home, does he call out unkind things to you?"

"No, we're both nice to each other. He never shows off there, because, I think, he knows he doesn't have to with me. And he doesn't actually try to hurt me when we're here at school, either. He acts up and gets louder like his friends do on the bus and at school, though, just not at me," Damian admitted.

"Okay, then. Can you see he's actually working harder when he's being what everybody calls 'cool'? It sounds like he's really himself when he's with you--happy, comfortable, safe, and easy company. Then when he has to crank up the level of 'output' to stay safe in that cool group, he has to work harder for their approval. And since they made fun of you last year and decided that you wouldn't be in their closed, safe, cool group, then Colin can't be seen hanging out with you in front of them, or he wouldn't remain safe in their group. Make sense now?"

Damian's eyes lit up for the first time. "Yes!" he exclaimed. "So they really are *needing* to stay cool in order to stay in their group! Wow, that's a lot of work. Now I'm really happy *not* to be invited into it!"

"You're exactly right! Plus, if one of the so-called *cool* kids ever did want to let go of that required show-off behavior just to return to the ranks of the regular folks like us, people would remember how he made fun of them. They couldn't trust that he wouldn't do it again, so he's kind of stuck there. Once we're embarrassed by someone, our memories don't like to let go of the frightening memory. It's a safety feature of our brains."

"Makes sense, because I wouldn't play basketball with that group even if Colin did invite me. I just know I would be made fun of eventually."

"See? Colin was new at the end of last year, and he tried so hard to make friends. He went for the cool factor and thought he needed to try to be like them, instead of just being himself. I guess he didn't think he was good enough. He's the only one that can be him, and you're the only one that can be you. You're both perfectly who you are!" Mrs. Kaufmann exclaimed. "The best part for you is that you're staying you and becoming better and better at that. You have a good, kind, fun, and funny person to share with others, and it's not getting appreciated here at school as long as you sit alone."

Damian smiled but didn't say anything. He wasn't feeling all that perfect at the moment.

Mrs. Kaufmann continued. "What I think…no, what I *know* you need to do is make new friends. Colin can be an at-home friend. You can respect his need to try really hard to stay cool at school, and then enjoy the 'nice Colin' at home when you hang out and truly enjoy each other's company there. And, the kids on the playground have already seen you sitting alone last year and now on several occasions this year, which makes them wonder why you're all alone, and so they'll keep their distance. What we can so easily do is think about the new boys in your class and see if there's a personality match for you with any one or more of them. That's where your help for me comes in!" Now Mrs. Kaufmann was grinning ear to ear.

Damian enthusiastically answered, "Sure, what can I do?"

Mrs. Kaufmann said with a huge smile, "I have a plan, but right now I have to get you back outside so you can slip into the crowd as they're about to line up and come in from recess. I don't want to have your whole class see you coming from my office, or they'll really think you do have a problem. Believe me, you don't. You are fine, and you are going to make new friends. I can help you without anyone knowing what we're up to, and you will show the world what a fantastic kid you are," Mrs. Kaufmann said excitedly, as she stood up to get Damian back out to recess.

"I will send passes to your teacher for you to bring the new boys down to my office for lunch tomorrow, which is easy because it's pizza day." Mrs. Kaufmann stood up, and looking directly at Damian declared, "I've decided that Damian Markus has just been appointed the New-Student Ambassador from your class, and I really need your assistance, Mr. Ambassador. I need you to help me help the new boys from your class get adjusted to our school! What do you think? Okay, now you have to hurry up and get going, because you only have one minute before the end-of-recess bell rings."

"That's so cool, Mrs. Kaufmann, thanks!" Damian declared, jumping up from his seat, grabbing his lunch bag, and tearing down the hall toward the playground exit door. He called back over his shoulder, "I can't wait for tomorrow!"

"Me too, Mr. Ambassador," Mrs. Kaufmann called back. "Me too!"

A Two-Way Deal

Mrs. Kaufmann got in early the next day and wrote out passes for Damian and the three new boys so they could come to the guidance office for lunch. She put them in their teachers' mailboxes and then went down to the cafeteria. She asked the cafeteria aide if she would set aside five pieces of pizza for those four students and her for their lunch meeting together.

She went back to her office and picked up the phone to call the parent of one of the new students. She left a voice mail message, since there was no answer. "Mrs. Stein, this is Mrs. Kaufmann, the school counselor from the Hillstown Middle School. I just wanted you to know that I've invited Jason to join me for lunch with some other new students from his class. I wanted to make sure he's getting acclimated and making friends. Also I didn't want you thinking there was anything wrong because he was invited to my office. I try very hard, like a mother hen, to get to know all my little 'chickens.' I use any excuse to be able to chat a little and make sure they are making healthy relationships and having a good academic experience here. When they're doing well and are happy, then I'm doing my job and I'm happy. If you have any questions, please don't hesitate to call me."

Mrs. Kaufmann then called and left messages for the other two parents of the new boys and then heard the start-of-school bell ring. She headed for the front door of the school to give a happy good morning to the students pouring into the building. She also liked to look at them all as they passed by her…their faces, their body language, and the way they walked in talking with others or alone. It helped her feel like she was doing her homework by watching out for the students in general.

"Hi, Mrs. K," a voice called to her. As she saw Damian's happy face in the crowd, she knew the excitement was still there.

"Can I still count on you to help me out at lunchtime, Mr. Ambassador?" she called to him with a wink.

Damian's positive disposition said it all. "Yup, I'll be there!" he answered, moving toward his classroom with confidence, a sense of self-importance and speaking loudly enough for others to hear all around him.

"I knew I could count on you! Thanks, Damian," Mrs. Kaufmann called to him as he rounded the corner and went out of sight.

The morning was filled with appointments and meetings and phone calls, but it was almost lunch time, and Mrs. Kaufmann had to head out to pick up the pizzas from the cafeteria. She also grabbed some milks and napkins and flew back to her office just in time as she saw the three new boys headed toward her, proudly led by Damian.

"Hey guys," she called, "perfect timing. Come on down!"

All four boys hustled in enthusiastically through her office door and headed for the couch and chairs in the sitting area. It always struck Mrs. Kaufmann funny that when boys in a group entered into her office, they always turned it into a contest to see who could get to the best chair first. Some thought the swivel chair was the prize, others thought the couch, and still others wanted the single thickly cushioned seats. They all raced to what they wanted and looked happy so it was always a good start.

"Hi, guys!" Mrs. Kaufmann started cheerily. "Are you all okay giving up time in the cafeteria for just one day?"

A chorus of yeses came from the group.

"Okay, we have Jason, Kyle, and Stefan as my new students, and Damian as my ambassador to help me today." Mrs. Kaufmann did the introductions quickly while distributing a slice of pizza on a paper plate with a napkin and milk to each of the boys. The boys happily began devouring the pizza like they hadn't eaten in a week, occasionally slurping their drinks in between. Mrs. Kaufmann knew that an eating fest would bring the party atmosphere to this gathering, making the boys feel a little closer and more open to talking.

"So, what do you think of this school so far, guys? I haven't had a chance to do my little 'new student check-up' these past two weeks since school started, but I've seen you all happily hanging out with other students on the playground." She made sure she didn't make eye contact with Damian, to let him relax so he knew that this meeting wasn't to target his problem openly.

Stefan answered first. "I love it, especially the rock-climbing wall in the gym!"

"Yeah, me, too," Jason chimed in.

Stefan said, "My mom wants to have a Halloween party to help me get to know more kids, and she wanted me to make sure I especially invited you guys since we're all new," he said as he looked at Kyle and Stefan. "Oh, and you're invited, too, Damian," he said quickly as he realized he had left him out.

"Thanks!" Damian said, as he lit up.

Mrs. Kaufmann noticed Kyle was smiling and agreeing, but was not as talkative as the others. "So, Kyle, are you liking this school and getting to know people here?"

"Yeah, I like it here. I do miss my friends from my old school, though. On the playground, I've been allowed to join in the soccer game on that far field, and I really like soccer, so that's good."

"I do, too," Damian heartily agreed. "When I was in my old school two years ago, all the boys played soccer every single day at recess. I miss that, too, but I love the cafeteria here better. The food is so good, and the teachers are mostly really nice," he added.

"How does that work?" Mrs. Kaufmann interrupted. "If someone wants to play, can they just run out on the field and join a side, or is there someone they need to ask? How does anybody get to play soccer, new or not?" Mrs. Kaufmann saw a perfect opening for Damian and Kyle to have a common interest, and a perfect activity for Damian to join in during playground. It seemed like a win-win, but she knew there could be some bad history for Damian if he loved soccer but wasn't playing, so she needed to tread carefully.

"Oh, I just asked David, the kid that grabbed the soccer ball from the playground aide's equipment cart, right as we went out on recess the first day," Kyle explained, as if it was no big deal. "David just told me to go to the other side when we got to the field to make the teams have the same number of kids, that's all."

Mrs. Kaufmann noticed Damian was quiet and wasn't jumping on this opportunity to connect with Kyle, so she respected his lead and just continued with the same line of discussion. "And Stefan and Jason, do you guys play soccer, too?"

Stefan jumped in, "No, Jason and I have been playing Wall Ball with a whole bunch of guys, and it's a lot of fun. I never did that before in our old school, because all of the outside walls near the playground had windows and we weren't allowed."

Jason agreed. "It is fun. I used to play with a couple of kids in our old neighborhood after school. I lived in a condo with my mom, and we had a community house with a plain brick wall that was perfect. It was just low and we'd shoot over the roof sometimes, but we never minded."

"I have no idea how to play Wall Ball. I see all the students out there having a great time, but I don't think the kids in my neighborhood ever played that. Does everyone play it nowadays?" Mrs. Kaufmann asked all of the boys.

"I never played it at my old school," Kyle said, "but I'd like to learn how."

Mrs. Kaufmann looked at Damian and asked if he had ever played it at his old school. Damian looked relieved that she didn't simply ask him if he knew the rules. The truth was he had never played it before and had already been going to Hillstown Middle School for a year. "No," he answered, "I never did back in California."

"Well, we have the perfect match here. We have two teachers and three willing learners matched up for a quick review of the rules before it's time to go outside. Jason and Stefan, would you two mind teaching the three of us how it's played? I won't be joining you at the wall, but at least I can watch and know what's going on from now on! Do you mind?" she laughed as she asked for their help. She thought, *This is really working out for Damian just as I hoped. The ambassador came to help the new kids, and it worked the other way around, too. It was a good two-way deal.*

Immediately Jason and Stefan began to excitedly explain the game to the others, making it seem pretty simple. Mrs. Kaufmann interrupted with a quick comment, "I don't mean to interrupt, and I want to hear all the rules, but let's start to clean-up while we're talking. That way you guys can go out to recess ahead of all the other kids waiting to be excused in the cafeteria." The boys kept talking and explaining while they tossed all their garbage into the trash can. When they were done, Mrs. Kaufmann announced, "Perfect timing! Now I think I get it. Kyle and Damian, do you think you could play it now?"

Damian and Kyle were then all excited to try and asked if they could all leave for recess right then so they could get the ball from the equipment cart before anyone else did.

"Oh my goodness, yes, you guys are new or newish and deserve a few breaks here and there! I'll be out to watch you all soon," Mrs. Kaufmann said as they all got up and headed for her office door. "Just please don't run in the hall, and wait at the outside door until that bell rings so none of my new little chickens in my chicken coop gets hurt or in trouble. Most of all, have fun!" she said with a big wide smile.

She watched as they competed in a fast walk/slow run toward the outside playground door. Mrs. Kaufmann laughed to herself, because the boys all looked so happy, including Damian. His problem with Colin was not solved, but at least he now had some potential new friends.

The Wall Ball Difference

The next morning, Mrs. Kaufmann headed down the hall toward the classroom, and she ran right into Kyle and Damian just coming into the school. "Good morning, guys. How was Wall Ball yesterday?" she asked them.

"It was a lot of fun," Damian said happily. "Stefan is really good at it, and I'm just learning. In fact, Kyle offered to come over to my house after school so we could practice. We went over to the big white church around the corner from my house, where we played against the back wall in the parking area," Damian bragged. He was a different person now that he had made a new friend.

"He got pretty good yesterday," Kyle added. "I really like that game." As they approached their classroom door, Kyle went right in. Damian stayed back a little so he could speak to Mrs. Kaufmann.

Mrs. Kaufmann knew he wanted a minute to tell her how it went. "So, did our plan work? Do you and Kyle feel like a good match, and how about Stefan and Jason? Do they seem like potential friends, too?"

"They're all fun to be with, but Stefan was a little more like Colin when we were playing. He liked to laugh when people messed up. He wasn't mean or anything, just loud and needed attention. Maybe he was trying too hard, but it felt uncomfortable to me. Jason's really quiet, like he doesn't say much of anything, so it's harder to hang out with him, but he seems nice. I think Kyle is the easiest for me to be with, since he doesn't try to embarrass anyone, and he's funny." Damian had obviously been thinking about what made a good friend for him this time. "I am still uncomfortable with Colin, though, and I'm not sure how to handle after school, since I'm not there for him when I'm with Kyle. What should I do?"

"I think we should talk one more time, but not now. The late bell is going to ring, and you need to get into your classroom and get settled. I don't want to have you stop in from lunch or recess because now you need to establish that friendship you've started. You need to sit at Kyle's table at lunch, and then go outside with him as fast as you can to get to the wall or the soccer field before the others fill up the spots. That will help establish what your routine will be."

"Yeah, I was going to ask if I could come down to your office from my study hall," Damian offered. "I'm in the media center today last period, and I've finished my project, so I don't really have anything to do."

"Perfect," Mrs. Kaufmann answered. "I'll ask the librarian to send you to me once the class gets started." Damian then darted into his classroom just as the late bell rang.

Perfect again! Mrs. Kaufmann thought.

Colin's Lesson

Mrs. Kaufmann had no one in her office, so she decided to head outside with the students leaving the cafeteria and heading to the playground. She really wanted to see Damian happily enjoying recess. As she went through the door to go outside, she ran into Colin. "Hi there, Mr. Harwood, how are you doing this year?" Mrs. Kaufmann figured this might be a good opportunity to learn a little more about him. "And how was your summer?"

"I like it here a lot this year, now that I'm not 'the new boy' anymore! And last summer was good. I hung out with Damian Markus. We found out we live on the same street," Colin told her. "And this year I have a lot of new friends, too."

"That's great news. I knew you would make more friends. You know, I'm wondering if you could help me with some of our new boys this year. I've noticed the girls have all invited the new girls to their homes and have great friendships starting up, but the boys don't seem to be hanging out after school with anyone. Maybe you can help me learn how you were able to do that?" Mrs. Kaufmann was fishing for a way to invite Colin into her office to chat about friendships without making him feel uncomfortable. "I always do 'new-student check-ups' and I think you might give me some advice, since you've made so many friends."

"Sure!" Colin seemed flattered. "Do you want to talk now?"

"That would be great, if you don't mind giving up shooting hoops today." Mrs. Kaufmann needed to make sure he was okay with that.

"I don't mind at all," he answered enthusiastically.

"Great!" Mrs. Kaufmann said. "Let's go back to my office, where I can write things down at my desk, okay?"

"Okay," Colin said, and then continued, "Did you want to know how I make friends?"

"Yes, I want to suggest some successful strategies for boys that feel too shy to just invite someone to come to their house to hang out," Mrs. Kaufmann suggested.

They walked back toward the guidance office together, with Colin explaining what he did when he first moved here. "Remember I came the last month of the school year? You suggested that I really try to make at least one friend before the school year ended so I wouldn't have a real lonely summer. You told me to look around at the different lunch tables to see where everyone seemed happy and talking rather than the tables where kids were just sitting and eating and not happy. You also told me to see who was at my bus stop that might also be in my class," Colin explained.

"The most crowded table in the cafeteria seemed to be the really popular kids. Then there was another table where I saw Damian and recognized him from our bus. I just sat down with him, and we started to exchange some of our lunches that we didn't like. Then we hung out on playground till the end of the year and saw each other riding bikes on our street. That made it easy for us to get together over the summer."

Mrs. Kaufmann went to the heart of the matter. "Do you and Damian hang out together now?"

"Only at home, because that popular table of boys wasn't full on the first day this year so I finally got to sit down with them. I had a lot of extra food, so I gave it all away and they liked me. So now I play basketball with them at recess, too. I'm really lucky they let me into their group," Colin bragged.

"Do you feel comfortable with them?" Mrs. Kaufmann asked. "And does Damian join you with them at school?"

"Well, uh, some of the kids in that group really don't like him. One of them, who seems like the leader, calls him a loser, which makes me really uncomfortable, because then everybody laughs, and I don't want to. But they call everybody everything and, a lot of the time, they are really funny," Colin confessed honestly.

Mrs. Kaufmann agreed. "That would make me uncomfortable too, especially knowing he's a friend. Is there a way you can stand up for him by letting them know he's really a good person, or are you too new to the group to start challenging the leader?" Mrs. Kaufmann decided to give Colin a bit of a challenge of character. "And who are we talking about here, is it Steve or Raoul?"

"It's Steve, and everyone sort of follows what he says. I am new to the group, so I have to go along with them right now, I think. Maybe I will later on," Colin offered.

"That would be really great, if you could be so cool as to be the leader type, but in a good way. I never thought of you as someone who would be comfortable making fun of people. And you know what? If the group sees you as strong enough to have an opinion and voice it, they may respect you more than Steve eventually. I wonder how many kids in the group also feel uncomfortable being mean. Maybe Steve just thinks he's performing to an approving audience because they all laugh. He is getting a positive reaction, so of course he will continue. If the laughter stopped, but not in a put-down kind of way, you know, but just in non-agreement, maybe he'd stop cutting on other kids. You could be the strong, cool person that could turn things around, because you really know Damian personally, and they don't. That would only be when you're ready, that is."

Colin sat listening. He heard a strong message coming from Mrs. Kaufmann, who was very clear that Steve's put-downs were in fact mean, not funny. He was reminded that Damian didn't deserve to be laughed at and called a loser, which his conscience was also telling him. He knew this was a challenge to rise above the group, instead of going along with behavior that didn't make him proud of himself. But he also knew it could cost him this whole group of friends if they were too used to following Steve's lead. Colin explained his fear to Mrs. Kaufmann.

"But, if I tell everyone Damian is really nice, the group might turn on me, and then *I* would be called a loser." He could picture toppling from the popular group--and rightly so. He had only been there since the previous June, and he didn't think he should challenge the leader just yet.

"I actually agree with you, Colin. It would be a real sign of daring on your part, and you are so smart to be able to understand how all this social stuff works! I could suggest a way to be courageous with much less risk, if you want to hear it." Mrs. Kaufmann offered.

"Sure, I could use it," Colin answered with interest.

"Well, are there some boys in the group that seem more like you, uncomfortable with the put-downs that Steve calls out into the crowd?" she asked.

"Yes, I think there are three of them who never cut on anyone, and two I'm not sure about. Then there are Steve and Raoul, who do most of the making fun of everyone. Those are the eight of us at the lunch table, and then we go outside to recess every day and go right to the basketball court with a few guys from another table," Colin answered.

"Do any of the three kinder guys ride your bus and therefore live around you?" she asked.

"Yes, two of them live within a street or two away, and I see them riding bikes with a couple other kids that play basketball with us at school," Colin answered.

"That works well into my plan," Mrs. Kaufmann smiled. "Would you feel comfortable joining them bike-riding sometime, or finding a basketball hoop around where you live?"

"Sure, I even rode around yesterday after school with one of them, because Damian had a friend over and couldn't hang out with me."

"Well, here's my plan. Over a gradual period of time, I suggest you start hanging out more and more with those kinder guys with whom you feel most comfortable. Ride bikes, play Wall Ball, and maybe even get a basketball game going somewhere locally, where there's a court or even just a net. Then, invite Damian over to join your local group in a game of basketball, and let him prove to those other kids that are your new, kind friends, that he is a good person, a good basketball player, and just a little shy. Soon, those kids will see what you see in him, and they'll learn he's not a loser. Then, when Steve calls him that at school, the group of you won't find it funny, and Steve won't have a laughing audience anymore. What do you think?" Mrs. Kaufmann figured she gave Colin a way to redeem himself with Damian, stay kind himself, and maybe teach Steve a lesson in kindness along the way.

"Yes, that would so work!" Colin exclaimed. Then I wouldn't have to challenge Steve. I could just show him instead. Good idea, Mrs. K!"

"And you've learned something today, too. It's a stronger power when you lead by example, than when you tell someone how to behave. Besides, it should feel good to be true to yourself, and not to follow the lead of someone doing less than honorable deeds, just to get his approval. Having the safety of a group does feel good in middle school, I must admit, but not at the sacrifice of your character, don't you agree?" Mrs. Kaufmann wanted Colin to see the lesson in it all. He was good in his heart, and she wanted to keep it that way! "You know what?" she continued. "I think there's still a few minutes left of recess time if you want to get back out on the playground," she offered.

"Oh, okay. Oh, wait. Didn't you want me to help you with the new students?" he questioned.

"You just did. Look at all you're doing to help Damian. Look at the example you're setting for the 'old' kids," she giggled. "And, by doing the courageous thing, I can tell your story, without any names of course, to all the other new kids that ever come to this school. Are you amazing, or what?" Mrs. Kaufmann spoke triumphantly with a huge smile as she stood up from her chair.

"Cool." Colin smiled a huge smile as well, getting up from his chair. He felt a little embarrassed by all the fuss at first, but, at the same time, Mrs. Kaufmann knew he would turn that into pride once he was able to make things right. He headed for the door. "Thanks, Mrs. Kaufmann," he said as he scooted down the hall, pushed open the door, and bolted out into the playground, like a bird freed from a cage.

Ah, yes, we have our 'nice Colin' back! she thought, as she headed back out onto the playground. Now she would see how Damian was doing with Kyle, hoping in her heart that they both enjoyed each other's company and it was a match.

And Now... Damian's Lesson

Mrs. Kaufmann turned the corner on the playground and saw the big block wall that was the outside of the gymnasium. It had no windows and was perfect for Wall Ball. She walked up to the area, keeping her distance so she wasn't in the way of the game, but she could watch all the boys hustling for position and interacting. Watching students play sports always gave her so much information as to what kind of character each student had. Some showed they had to win at all costs, including breaking rules and being poor sports, and others just enjoyed the competition without grudges or expectations.

Stefan grabbed the ball away from Jason, who didn't grab back. Damian and Kyle were out there, trying really hard, and laughing when they missed. They truly enjoyed the game and each other. Damian caught sight of Mrs. Kaufmann, and she gave him her wink. He smiled back and turned right back to the game. He fit in nicely, and it was such a pleasure to see. She turned and walked back inside to talk with some upset girls collecting in her waiting room. She was now really looking forward to talking with Damian at the end of the day.

Several counseling sessions and two meetings later, the last period of the day finally arrived. Mrs. Kaufmann was waiting at her desk when Damian's head poked around the corner as he came into her office. "Hi! Damian. It's good to see you, my dear," Mrs. Kaufmann cheerfully said.

"Hi, Mrs. K," he answered, also quite cheerfully.

"So, how's Kyle and how's Wall Ball working out? You looked quite good at it when I saw you out there today. I was impressed!" Mrs. Kaufmann complimented him.

"Thanks. Kyle and I are good. And guess what? Colin came out late for playground today and said hi to me as he ran by. He almost seemed like he was normal, and it was a real shock. Did you say anything to him, Mrs. Kaufmann?"

"You know I can't talk about what I talk about," she said, smiling at Damian, "but I can assure you that I couldn't bring him into my office to tell him what you told me, either. I just talk with each person as to what he or she is dealing with, and help each of my students see what needs to be done to be a good person."

She continued, "It's never really hard. We simply just need to see the world of seven billion people, each one experiencing his or her own journey of lessons. Then, every time we see someone doing something different from us, instead of judging it badly, we try to understand it. And whenever we don't know how to act, we try to do something that will be for the good of that person, or for the good of the situation. Just add good, not bad. It's like we are all in a big boat floating along, and when we add water, or good acts of kindness, the water level gets higher. That helps raise us all up. And, if we're selfish, we take out from the water, and it lowers the whole boat. I just remember to respect other people and respect myself, and to always remember we are all in this together."

"That's a neat way to look at all people. So our boat is Hillstown Middle School, right? And Colin is in the boat with me even if he doesn't like me, right?"

"Remember we talked about Colin wanting to impress the boys in his new group? I want you think back as to whether Colin himself ever called you a name, or was it someone else in his group?" Mrs. Kaufmann asked Damian.

"Uhhh, I can't remember him saying anything to me. I think it was always Steve or Raoul that made fun of me. Steve was the one that called me a loser in class last year, and Mr. McWilliams sent him down to the office, so I think that's why he doesn't like me," Damian answered.

"Then what makes you think Colin doesn't like you, if he comes to your house all the time to hang out? Is it just because he doesn't talk to you when he's with Steve and his group?"

Damian reluctantly answered, "Yes, I guess that's what I thought."

"Could you be wrong? Remember, he was trying to make a bunch of new friends and fell into a group of kids that accepted him. The problem for him was that he had to choose between you or that whole group. That whole group played basketball every day and welcomed him in. They play aggressively and Colin likes that; you don't. They make fun of each other and like that, but you don't. So it looked like Colin was a better match with them at school, and a match with you at home. Does that make sense?" Mrs. Kaufmann asked Damian. "I also know how comfortable you are with Kyle, who plays at your energy level and is thoughtful. I can see where Stefan's behavior isn't like yours. So it's really about making a match, you know?"

"That's true. I watched Stefan today, and he was grabbing the ball away from everyone. And poor Jason said nothing, ever, but Kyle was just like me."

"See? We all just like to have fun and be comfortable if we can. Sometimes, though, a person, and especially a new person, will try extra hard to get into a group, and he then takes on the same behavior as the members of the group. If he gets their approval, he stays. If he doesn't, he could be out, and then the group could turn against him, remember?" Mrs. Kaufmann reminded Damian. "And then there are the Damians and Jasons who are quiet and don't do that. That group would make them feel too uncomfortable. After having those bad experiences, they would prefer to be alone rather than with a group with whom they don't match."

"That's right, I remember. I guess I'm not really mad at Colin. I just don't know how to act around him when he acts too cool to be with me, when he's with them. What do I do after school?" he asked Mrs. Kaufmann.

"Well, the way I see it is you have a choice. You can try to understand Colin and yet still respect yourself, or you can get angry with him and separate from him. My guess is you'd like it to simply work it out for the best, right?" Mrs. Kaufmann had Damian's attention.

"Right," he answered.

"You enjoy his company at your home. You don't enjoy his company at school, but you both have other people to be with at recess anyway. You really don't have anything to change. Would you imagine Kyle to be okay with having Colin join you two after school?" she asked.

"Yeah, Kyle's really nice. He wouldn't mind. Besides, three people playing Wall Ball is better than two." Damian laughed. "So if I just include everyone, it will be okay. But what if Colin starts that embarrassing thing Steve does. What then?"

"If that should happen, then Kyle won't like it and neither will you. No approval for Colin will be a real sign for him to stop doing what he's doing. Then the cutting comments will gradually stop and will be replaced with a less-cutting form of friendly teasing. If he was to be comfortable with the two of you, he'd have to do what kind people do that brings them together, not tears them apart. You and Kyle would end up being his teacher, but I think that won't even be the case here," Mrs. Kaufmann suggested. "Colin seems like a good kid to me. I'd give him a chance at home to be the person he was all summer, but that's up to you."

"I like that idea. I'll let Colin decide. If he's nice, he stays, if not, I don't invite him again. It now just seems pretty simple," Damian concluded.

"Yes, it usually is pretty simple," Mrs. Kaufmann repeated. "And now, let's get you back to the library. I'm really proud that you got your project done early. You must be relieved."

Mrs. Kaufmann wrote up a pass for Damian and handed it to him. Damian answered, "I am relieved, about the project and about Colin, too." He grabbed his backpack, took a couple candies out of the candy dish, and went toward the door. "Thanks, Mrs. K."

"You're welcome, my dear. It is truly my pleasure!" Mrs. Kaufmann said, with a good feeling inside. She thought, *It is pretty simple, after all. All we need to remember is to just add good.*

Discussion Points:

- A fair-weather friend is someone who only wants your friendship when it's convenient for them. A real friend is with you through good and bad times.

- When people want to impress new friends, they might behave in a way they normally wouldn't, just to get accepted. People make friends based on similarities and differences and should make comfort and fun the most important goals.

- Teasing someone to embarrass them is never okay. Close friends doing friendly, bonding teasing of each other will feel closer. Not laughing at a person being mean helps take away their audience and sends a message that it's not acceptable.

Reflection Questions:

1. What do you do when you know one friend doesn't fit in with your other friends? Is it okay to have different friends in different places? Should you exclude people from hanging out, or should you include them and allow them to decide if they want to join you or not?

2. Why do you think Steve called Damian "a loser" in front of everyone? What made the people standing around him, and hearing the put-down, not speak up for Damian? Would you?

3. What's the best way to help someone when they are being embarrassed without being aggressive with the teaser or bully? Would you ever be willing to go to the victim later to show him or her support?

CHAPTER 10:
I'd Rather Die Than Get up in Front of the Class!

I'm Not Strong Enough

The red light on the phone was flashing as Mrs. Kaufmann came into her office at the Hillstown Middle School one morning. After hitting her message button and punching in her passcode, she set it on "speaker" and listened as she put away her briefcase and turned on her computer. The school counselor played them to the end to make sure there weren't any emergencies. However, the last one sounded more urgent than the others.

"Mrs. Kaufmann, I'm a little desperate this morning. We had a bad night with Melanie, and this morning she's throwing up for fear of giving her book report today in front of the class. Would you please call me? I'm not strong enough to physically make her get into the car against her will, and she is so upset. I'm not even sure it's right to force her." Mrs. Addison sounded at wits' end.

Mrs. Kaufmann knew this was a time-sensitive call, so she picked up the phone without hesitation and dialed her number. "Mrs. Addison? This is Mrs. Kaufmann. I got your message and I'm wondering how Melanie is doing now."

"She's watching television in her room trying to settle her stomach, and I honestly have no idea what to do. She's never been so scared, and I can't just pick her up and make her to go to school against her will as if she was a toddler. What do I do?" Mrs. Addison's voice cracked as she began to cry.

"May I talk to Melanie? I'd like to see if I can find out what her fear is, and you can feel free to listen in on an extension," Mrs. Kaufmann offered.

"Sure, anything, thank you," Mrs. Addison said gratefully. Then she went to Melanie's room and handed a remote phone to Melanie, saying, "It's Mrs. Kaufmann, Melanie. She wants to see if she can help you this morning. Here, please take the phone."

"Good morning, my dear. I understand you're really afraid of doing your book report today at school. Can you tell me what it is that you are imagining will be the scary part?" Mrs. Kaufmann asked Melanie. "Maybe I can help a little."

"Uh, I don't know. I'm just really scared." Melanie sounded panicked.

"Okay, well I'm thinking we certainly could do a little detective work if you want to feel better. I'd like to sit and talk with you in person, though, because it's easier and more comfortable than if we try to problem-solve on the phone. How about you and your mom just come on over to my office, and we'll figure out what makes it seem so scary, okay?" Mrs. Kaufmann coaxed.

"Are you going to make me go to my classroom first?" Melanie asked, sounding as if that would have made all the difference in her answer.

"No, my dear, you can just come to be with me now, a little before school starts, so no one sees you.

Just come directly to my office. Have you had breakfast yet? I have some juice and some breakfast bars here. We can just relax, and chat, and see if we can figure out what will make you feel less frightened. Does that sound okay? The big thing is we don't want you to be absent or late, because that goes on your record. At least you'll be here at school, and even though you're in my office, that counts as you being present in school. And you know you don't have to be scared with me, so just come on over, okay?"

"Okay, I guess I can do that." Melanie sounded less reluctant and quietly accepted the help. She then handed the phone back to her mother, and stood up to finish getting ready for school.

Mrs. Kaufmann heard Melanie's mom say hello again. "Mrs. Addison? Will you be able to come right over with Melanie? I will call down to the main office that I'm expecting you both, so there's no hold-up when you come in the front door. They will buzz you in, and you just head back to my office," Mrs. Kaufmann assured her.

"Yes, yes, oh, thank you!" Mrs. Addison blurted out in a grateful but rushed tone. "Melanie and I will come right over." Mrs. Kaufmann could also hear Melanie's mom continue speaking for a bit as she trailed off with "Melanie, put on your shoes and jacket…." and then the click.

Mrs. Kaufmann called the main-office extension and gave the receptionist the heads-up that Melanie Addison and her mom were coming over in a few minutes and needed to be buzzed in quickly. She explained that she wanted them to go right to the guidance office as unnoticed as possible. She then left a voice message for Mr. Markum, Melanie's teacher, to let him know that Melanie was coming in to her office before school this morning and therefore should not be marked late or absent.

Mrs. Kaufmann then checked on Melanie's background. She pulled up her records on the computer to see if there were any indications of her having had such immobilizing fear in the past, either with other teachers, or earlier in this school year. There was nothing indicated, though she noticed she hadn't joined any activities, clubs, or sports that would require her to perform in front of a crowd. She then called Mr. Markum back and left another voice mail.

"Sorry to leave another message before you've even arrived to school this morning. I meant to ask you when I called before if you know of any reason Melanie should be so scared of doing her book report today. I'm not sure what the new situation is, or if she almost always reacts to public speaking with such fear. Maybe you can just tell me what part fear plays in her life in general? If you could call me back later to shed some light on this, I would so appreciate it. You can just leave me a message in case I don't answer when you call. I don't always interrupt the counseling session if I'm lucky enough to be breaking through at that moment to some emotional insight! Thanks." Mrs. Kaufmann spoke hurriedly and hung up just in time.

"Good morning," Mrs. Kaufmann heard at her office door. She looked up and saw Mrs. Addison standing right at the inner office door in the waiting room. Melanie was standing behind her mom with very red, swollen eyes. She looked embarrassed, with her head down, trying not to look directly at Mrs. Kaufmann.

"Oh, please come on in," she said as she stood up in a hurry to greet them and bring them into her office, closing the door quickly behind them. "Hi, Melanie, not to worry, we will get through this together. I've never ever seen a problem that couldn't be fixed. It's what life is all about, experiencing new situations, learning how to handle them, and growing into a wiser and stronger person every day of our lives. The last thing I want to see is such fear, making you feel so uncomfortable."

The school counselor led them to her little couch and chair sitting area. She continued, "Just so you know, the majority of people feel nervous when they have to get up in front of their peers. It's been listed at the very top of surveys, asking people what their most feared activity was. What's stranger still, on those same lists, the fear of dying comes lower on the list. So, the joke is, people would rather die than get up in front of the class!" Mrs. Kaufmann said while laughing at the absurdity. "Of course they don't want to die, really, but that's how common your fear is," she assured Melanie, trying to make her a little more comfortable and less embarrassed. Melanie looked up at the school counselor and giggled, so she seemed to be relaxing already.

Mrs. Addison jumped in, "That's exactly what Melanie said this morning! I just don't know how to help her face this, so I can't thank you enough for seeing us this morning. I've honestly never seen Melanie so scared before. I know she doesn't like to give book reports, but this is the first time I've seen her have such a meltdown."

"You know, this is not as uncommon as you may think. It's just the first time it seemed un-doable to Melanie, that's all. So let's find out why it appeared to be so scary this time, okay Melanie?" Mrs. Kaufmann assured them both, as she dove right in to start the repair work. She still had hope that Melanie would end up giving the report that day on time, proving to herself it was not as bad as her thinking made it seem.

Melanie answered quietly, "I'm not sure, but I just can't do it, Mrs. Kaufmann. I just really can't," she said as her big brown eyes filled to the brim, and then a stream of tears rolled down her cheeks.

"I believe you, Melanie, and I have to tell you that I've experienced the same thing in my life. I used to think I couldn't do things because I really believed I was going to mess up if I tried, you know?" Mrs. Kaufmann asked.

"I know. That happens to me all the time now, and I don't know why," Melanie answered.

"Well, that's something we certainly can do a little detective work about right now, if you like," Mrs. Kaufmann offered.

"Okay," Melanie answered with a little more energy than before, and with a little hope in her voice.

Taking that cue, Mrs. Kaufmann looked at Mrs. Addison and said, "Well, Mom, this would be a good time for you to get on with your day so Melanie and I can get to work. What do you say?"

She didn't look at Melanie on purpose. She wanted her mom to leave so Melanie could finally be detached from her and speak freely. She wanted to avoid Melanie getting spooked and starting to cry or clinging to her mom, so she kept the positive energy up, moving her mom along toward the door as quickly as possible.

"Yes, I do have to get to work because I'm running a little late. Will you two be okay?" she asked, making sure she was showing she wasn't abandoning her daughter.

Mrs. Kaufmann gave a robust response to keep everything positive and jumped in before Mrs. Addison could turn the energy backward. "Oh, we'll be just fine. I love to play detective work with my students! It's actually fun, and it really works to solve problems. Melanie will be so much smarter when we're done, I can assure you." Mrs. Kaufmann kept trying to "cut the cord," as she would say, and get Melanie's mother out of the door, while keeping Melanie in a positive frame of mind.

Mrs. Addison finally caught on, and she quickly grabbed her purse, told Melanie she'd be home to take her to karate after school, thanked Mrs. Kaufmann, and scurried out the door.

"Have a great day, Mrs. Addison. Melanie and I certainly will!" she called after Melanie's mom, as she turned the sign on her inner office door that had said "Welcome!" to the back side that read, "Busily Problem Solving -- Please Leave Me a Message. :)" She closed the door, turned to Melanie, and said with a big smile, "Okay, now where were we, my dear?"

Time to Investigate

Melanie's eyes widened as her mom left and the door closed behind her. "Mrs. Kaufmann, am I going to have to go back to class now?"

"Oh, heavens no!" Mrs. Kaufmann answered her, trying to keep the session upbeat. "We have work to do to find out what triggers that fear buried in your head somewhere. Too bad we can't just open up the brain, like the battery compartment on a remote control, and just replace the parts not working right! But that would be too easy, and would take all the fun out of our mission, right?" Mrs. Kaufmann chuckled.

Melanie smiled at that image. "I really wish I could. This year has been the worst ever, and I've started getting stomachaches, too," she offered.

"I'm not surprised. Nervous stomachs go along with anxiety or fear, since the stomach acid fills up in there. Are you feeling sick to your stomach right now? I have some crackers, and they often absorb some of that acid and help make you feel better right away," Mrs. Kaufmann offered as she stood up to get some crackers and a bottle of water.

"I think I'd just like the water right now," Melanie answered. "Thanks, Mrs. K."

Mrs. Kaufmann brought the water bottle over to her big desk and said, "Come on over, and let's sit at my desk, okay? You can play with the 'fidget toys' while we talk."

Mrs. Kaufmann had a few interesting items on her desk, on the side where the students would come to sit across from her. She had a magnetic paper-clip paperweight so the students could build little paper-clip structures on the magnet block. It seemed to help distract them from looking directly at her, if they were uncomfortable saying what they wanted to say. She also had a four-inc- high glass cylinder paperweight that had a very thick and colorful substance inside, that would ooze around very slowly as the students rotated and revolved the container. Then there was a three-inch hourglass, a rubbery stress ball, and a spongy ball with strings. These were the favorites and were the best facilitators of the heaviest conversations in her room.

As Melanie was moving over to the desk, Mrs. Kaufmann filled in the conversation space with a change of topic. "I love this office, don't you? We can sit in this little office part of the room, or my living room part of the room where we were, or get a cold drink from the little kitchen with the refrigerator and little cabinet in that corner of the room. It's like we're just hanging out at home, right?" Mrs. Kaufmann was making light and happy conversation to keep Melanie's attitude upbeat. They had to transition from the safe connection with her mom to the serious fear of giving the book report. *A little space or a change of pace, a couple of giggles, and a cold bottle of water should make that happen*, she thought.

"This one is cool," Melanie laughed, as she turned the glass cylinder around, watching the purple sparkly goop ooze around inside.

Perfect, thought Mrs. Kaufmann. "Okay, Melanie, let's start figuring out this fear thing your head has going on. When was the first time you began to feel uncomfortable talking in front of the class or a group of people?"

"I think I've always been scared," Melanie answered. "I just like to stay in my seat. I'm never sure if what I'm going to say is right, and I don't want to be embarrassed, and I don't want people to laugh at me."

"When was the first time you felt as scared as you were this morning? You know, like you really can't make yourself do it?" Mrs. Kaufmann asked.

"This morning was the worst. I've never felt so scared! I mean, I just can't imagine getting up in front of that class."

"Okay, I heard you say *that class*. My guess is there's something about that class that is more frightening than other classes. What do you think?" Mrs. Kaufmann continued.

"Uh, yeah, I guess so. Mr. Markum is nice and everything, but I just feel really uncomfortable when he calls on me…so to do a whole report in front of everyone…" Melanie's voice cracked, and then the tears began to pour, as she covered her whole face, sobbing into her hands, hunched over in her chair. "I'm sorry," she whimpered.

"That's okay, my dear. You can let the tears come out," Mrs. Kaufmann said encouragingly as she pushed the box of tissues over to her. "Tears are natural, and I am very used to seeing them flow, so don't even think about having to apologize to me. I'm going to keep going with this, okay? I can just see how that image is really upsetting you, but we can learn more about your feelings now than we could if you didn't just connect with them." She continued validating Melanie's tears. "So, last year, who was your teacher?"

"Mrs. Post," she answered.

"And the year before?" Mrs. Kaufmann continued.

"Miss Winkowski," Melanie answered with a weak smile through her tears. "She was my favorite teacher ever."

"What if you were to give your report today in front of Miss Winkowski instead of Mr. Markum? Would you feel the same fear?" Mrs. Kaufmann questioned.

"No, she was funny and he's more… more… like…not funny, just serious," Melanie answered, as she began to see where her school counselor was going with this.

Mrs. Kaufmann then asked, "When the students did book reports for Miss Winkowski, or even Mrs. Post, what was it like for them, do you remember?"

"Well, it wasn't scary at all, because Miss Winkowski made it fun. She would say we were all trying to sell our books so we had to make it like a commercial, but we couldn't tell the ending. It was just fun, because when I was talking, I was thinking that they weren't thinking about me, just whether they liked the sound of the book. While I'd be talking, the rest of the kids talked a little, so it wasn't all silent or anything. That made it easier. Plus, I don't even remember anything about grades, so I wasn't thinking about that, either. Besides, all of the kids in my class were nice."

"Are all the kids in Mr. Markum's class nice?" Mrs. Kaufmann asked.

"Well, it has to be really quiet, because Mr. Markum is so strict. Plus we have Henry, who makes Mr. Markum all mad and everything. He's always fooling around and calling out in class to make everyone laugh. No teacher can stop him, so it makes it a little scarier to talk in front of him, too," Melanie admitted.

"It's beginning to make a lot of sense to me why it's harder to do a book report now than it was before. Do you see what makes you feel fear? You have a shyness that makes it uncomfortable in the first place. You believe you might mess up and that would be horrible. Then you have a teacher who keeps things rather serious, so it's all quiet with everyone's attention focused on you. In addition, there's an unpredictable student in the room who makes fun of students just to get attention. I totally understand your fears, and I would not like that situation either. Does that make sense to you?" Mrs. Kaufmann summed it up for Melanie.

"I know. I just can't go up in front of that class," Melanie said with dread and determination.

Mrs. Kaufmann finally said the words that Melanie didn't want to hear. "And yet you know you will eventually have to do this. So now we have to figure out why the other kids in the room can, and for you it feels undoable." Mrs. Kaufmann just put the reality out there. "Let's go in that direction for a bit, shall we?" she asked. "What do you fear might happen?"

Melanie's eyes filled up again. She knew eventually she was going to have to speak in front of that class, but just not now. "Well, I feel choked up, and it's hard to breathe because I'm so afraid. I even start to yawn a lot, and my eyes tear up and I can't stop it. I also forget what I wanted to say, so all of that will make my grade bad, and then Henry might make fun of me, and then everyone will laugh at me, and I would be so embarrassed I'd want to die. Even thinking about it makes it seem real and makes me want to cry."

"I totally understand, and so would Mr. Markum if he ever knew. I'm thinking of a lot of temporary solutions here to make you feel comfortable for today, but the big thing is giving you some strategies for handling things if they ever do go badly," Mrs. Kaufmann suggested. "Okay, so let's see what we can do to make this better just for today, and get past this one. How about we try out some possibilities to see if any of them make it sound easier to do?" Mrs. Kaufmann tried to keep it light.

Melanie said nothing, because the fear was rising again, and it was feeling like everything was closing in on her.

Mrs. Kaufmann knew this was critical timing. "Melanie, what if we spoke to Mr. Markum before the book report today to ask him if there could be another way we can do this just for today?"

Melanie relaxed her breathing. "That would be great," she said instantly.

"No promises, Melanie. I'm just thinking that talking with Mr. Markum may help. He also may not be able to let you off the hook, since he knows speaking in front of a group is a skill you need for when you grow up. However, maybe he can allow us some more time to deal with this fear and then have you give the report. Would you be willing to talk with him about this?" Mrs. Kaufmann asked.

Melanie went white as a ghost. "Do I have to talk with him?" she asked immediately with her eyes bigger than ever.

"Oh, no, I will talk with him at lunchtime, if that's okay with you. I just have to see how he feels about this assignment. I'm hoping he'll see that you need to get set up with some public speaking strategies, as well as some anxiety-reducing or relaxation ones, too. You are certainly welcome to sit in on our talk, but you don't have to. That's up to you," she assured Melanie.

"Oh, good, thank you!" Melanie exhaled in great relief.

"By the way, what period do you have language arts this afternoon, when you're supposed to do this book report?" Mrs. Kaufmann asked.

"Sixth period," Melanie answered.

"Okay, so I need to talk with Mr. Markum at lunch and then get back with you fifth period. And you need to get off to first period today before you miss any more time from math. Will you be able to catch up with the lesson in that class well enough once you get in there?" Mrs. Kaufmann checked.

"I'm good at math, and we just check homework at the board for the whole beginning of class, anyway. I understood it last night, so I'm fine," Melanie assured Mrs. Kaufmann.

"Do you mind going up to the board, writing up the homework problems in front of the math class?"

"No, I don't, because there are five of us up at the board at any one time. That's when the class is kind of noisy anyway, so I don't think anyone's actually looking at me. Besides, once we all correct our homework and I know I got it right, I'm up there with the others just showing how I got that right answer," Melanie explained. "I'm not being graded."

"Do you feel as much confidence when giving a book report as you do when you're in front of the math class?" Mrs. Kaufmann asked her.

"Not really. In math, there's a right answer. There we all make mistakes and it's okay if I do, too. In language arts, the whole room is completely quiet, and all their eyes are on me. The teacher is grading my words as I'm talking, and I don't know what he thinks is an A. Then there's always Henry. I'm so glad he's not in my math class!" Melanie exclaimed.

"Do you think you aren't going to do well when you speak?" Mrs. Kaufmann double-checked.

"I'm never sure what's supposed to be in a book report," Melanie admitted. "I just read the book and then I write my thoughts down, but I might not be saying what Mr. Markum wants. I just don't know."

"That's so helpful for me." Mrs. Kaufmann smiled, as if this last comment was the breakthrough.

"What's helpful?" Melanie asked, somewhat surprised by the reaction and that the school counselor's questions seemed to have come to an end.

"I have a great idea! While you're at lunch, I will speak with Mr. Markum about how scary this is for you, and what we've been through this morning with your mom. I have a feeling he'll still want you to do it today, and he's actually right, so I needed a way to have him help you through it. So, here's my plan. What if he was to hear or read your report before class, and let you know if he thought it was worth an A, or what else you needed to cover it in order to make sure it was an A? Then you would have his approval before you were to even get up to speak. That way you could feel confident about your content and only focus on the speaking part.

"We could also find out, once and for all, how much that one grade really matters toward the whole report card grade. We could do the math. Once you feel confidence in your actual report like you do in your math homework, the fear wouldn't get so big as to make you forget what you have to say. You'd know your talk would be fine, so you could forget about Henry making a negative comment. How does that sound?" Mrs. Kaufmann asked excitedly.

Melanie thought about it for a bit from behind her wall of fear, and then she finally spoke. "I think that would be good, but can we talk again fifth period, just in case? I think I'll start to get that fear thing again by then." Melanie was checking to make sure.

"Sure, we can do that. I know you will have a little bit of fear, and that's okay. Fear is a normal emotion for all of the billions of people in the world. Just remember those surveys! Fear of public speaking makes it to the number one spot on the list, so you are not alone. In fact, fear of anything tells you when you don't think you're good enough, or that you're feeling you're not safe, or that something will happen that you think you won't be able to handle. What *you're* experiencing today is not an 'everyday thing,' or an 'everybody thing,' and is called panic. That much anxiety sets off a whole chain of events that the body feels, and it isn't a great feeling, as you well know. We'll talk about how to deal with that later. Our work together will help you to discover you are just fine, and safe, and that you can learn ways to deal with anything. I promise to help you, starting with this book report!" Mrs. Kaufmann spoke with complete confidence. "Does all of this make sense to you, my dear?"

"Yes, I guess it does. I just never thought about it that way. Thanks, Mrs. K," Melanie said, as she looked somewhat relieved. "Do I go to homeroom first and then to math?"

"Yes, I'm going to give you a pass for your homeroom teacher that explains you were here with me since before school. You'll need to go there to check in and get your morning books. Then I'll give you a pass to get to math class from there. Make sure you get your homework, okay?" Mrs. Kaufmann coached.

"Okay, thanks, Mrs. K. Can you give me a pass to come back fifth period to make sure Mr. Markum is okay with my report?" Melanie questioned.

"Oh, right. Let me give you three passes. But what do you have fifth period, specials? I really don't want you to miss any more time from your classes today."

"It's okay. Yes, I have art today, and I'm ahead on my silkscreen project," Melanie responded.

"That's excellent. Okay, we have a plan, and you will be just fine today. Here are your passes, and you are not to spend any more time thinking about that book report today, okay? Every class can be happy, and your day can be really nice if you want it to be. We will save fifth period as our time to put your mind at ease," Mrs. Kaufmann promised her.

Melanie smiled. "Okay, thanks, Mrs. K, I'll try."

"Before you leave, may I have your book report to show Mr. Markum?" Mrs. Kaufmann reminded her.

"Oh, that's right," Melanie said, as she stood up to get it from her backpack. She pulled it from her homework folder, handed it to Mrs. Kaufmann, zipped up the bag, and went to get her jacket, knowing all was set and she needed to start this school day.

"Thanks, my dear, and now let's get you off to class," Mrs. Kaufmann said, as she handed the three passes to her. Melanie took them, thanked her, and quickly slipped out of the office and toward her homeroom down the hall.

Mrs. Kaufmann then picked up her phone and dialed Mr. Markum's extension.

Clearing the Path

"Mr. Markum, this is Mrs. Kaufmann," she said, after the call went to his voice mail. "I just want you to know about a meeting I had with Mrs. Addison and Melanie this morning, and I need to ask you for some help. Would you please call me this morning when you get a minute, or even stop by? Thanks."

Mrs. Kaufmann spoke quickly while checking her e-mail messages on her computer for the morning. She then looked on her computer for the schedule of Henry Marquis, suddenly deciding she needed to speak with him today. She and Henry had become old buddies after all of the times he had been sent to her office straight from the vice-principal's office, or for a mini-counseling session following his out-of-school suspensions. Henry seemed to get himself into trouble quite a bit with his lack of self-control. His need to have attention and be the class clown made him call out comments that he thought were funny. It looked like he was back to his old tricks again this year. Finding out that he was in his social studies class at that time, she called his teacher to see if he could be sent to her office for a little chat.

"Hello, Mr. Alvarez? Would this be a good or bad time for me to have a little chat with Henry Marquis?"

"I'd be delighted to send him!" Mr. Alvarez exclaimed with a chuckle indicating he, too, was having some difficulty with Henry. "But I can't unless it's an emergency. They are taking a quiz right now."

"Okay, thanks. I'll just grab him at some other point today."

Mrs. Kaufmann looked back at his schedule, seeing Henry had his special education classes at the times of the day she couldn't meet with him, or at least not until sixth period. She knew he was going to have to sit and listen quietly to oral book reports that period, because he was in Melanie's class then. That's when it dawned on her. *What a perfect time for me to have our chat*, she thought. *It would serve to be a present for Melanie, as well helping to give her a successful experience in public speaking*. Mrs. Kaufmann then wrote out a pass for Henry to be sent down sixth period out of Mr. Markum's class, and then she headed down to the main office to slip it into Mr. Markum's mailbox. She clipped a note to it to let the teacher know she needed to speak with him that morning about Melanie Addison, in case he didn't have a chance to get his voice mail, since that was the critical piece of her plan. While she was there, she double-checked on the attendance card to make sure Melanie was not marked absent or tardy for that day. Once that was verified, she felt all was going well again.

Sitting at her desk, Mrs. Kaufmann was checking over the report card grades for the school, looking to see who she needed to put on her "Academic Check-up" list. "Hello in there," a voice called into her office from the waiting room. "You needed to see me?" Mr. Markum asked.

"Oh, yes! Thank you so much for stopping by. I won't keep you but five minutes, because I know you're on your way to lunch," Mrs. Kaufmann assured him. She quickly recapped the morning's events from the mom's desperate phone call to "the plan." She had to make sure Mr. Markum understood that what Melanie had was a panic attack, not just the average fear of doing an oral book report in front of a class.

"So how can I help her? I don't want to let her off the hook," he responded.

"Oh, no, we can't do that. That would enable her fear to continue, for sure. The best gift we can give Melanie is to reduce the fearful images she has, in order for her to do this report this time. Most importantly, she needs to have success with it instead of the trauma she's dreading. We all know that success builds confidence, and that's what she's lacking here," Mrs. Kaufmann assured him and then continued, "I would like you to help her understand what she needs to do to get an A for the content of the report, and then what weight that grade has in the overall average for her grade for the marking period. In fact, I even have her book report with me, if you want to scan it to see if it's what you want to hear this afternoon," Mrs. Kaufmann added.

"I wouldn't ask this of you if it wasn't such a critical time in Melanie's escalating fear. Panic isn't pretty and can become a habit, especially if her phobia becomes the phobia itself after a while, you know, the fear of the fear? I just think we have a chance of turning this around right now if we can work to make this one oral report successful today, and then I can follow up with some strategies for her to use in the future."

"Funny thing," Mr. Markum answered. "Melanie always does well on her written reports, putting in all the required parts. It's just that public speaking piece that needs to be improved. I'll grade her written report during lunch anyway, and I'll drop it back off on my way back to class. Maybe, before the oral reports start in my class today, I'll privately remind her that this written report is only equal to one of five quizzes this marking period, which, all together only equal one-fourth of her grade. She'll realize then that this written report is simply one-twentieth of the final marking period grade. I don't want my underachievers to know that, though, if you know what I mean! You can remind Melanie how I come up with the students' final grades. Like I said, the quiz average is a fourth, the unit test average is a fourth, the homework average is a fourth, and then the big project is the last fourth. Participation only averages in when a decision or a borderline grade comes into question. You can do the math with her, and that should reduce the importance of this oral part of her report. Does that help?"

"That definitely helps a lot. Thank you. I'll be meeting with her fifth period to let her know all that you're doing for her this time. I'll also give her some self-calming strategies, like deep breathing. Hopefully we will remove the conditions that take away her confidence, and then hope for the best!" Mrs. Kaufmann asserted. "One more thing, I just remembered," she continued. "Is it okay if I borrow Henry Marquis to have one of our little reminder chats during that book report class? I understand he's not handling his impulses to be the class clown very well recently."

"You're right about that. I was just about to make another phone call home. That's something else we can tag-team," Mr. Markum offered gladly.

"I know his unpredictable comments cause her yet another fear during her oral reports. She thinks if she falters on the book report, Henry is sure to make fun of her. We both know her shyness and insecurities can't handle that sort of public humiliation," Mrs. Kaufmann threw in. "Anyway, if that works for you, I've already put a pass in your mailbox. Thanks again, and you'd better get going to lunch."

"Okay, then. I like our plan. I'll make sure to be reassuring to Melanie as well. Have a great afternoon, and good luck with Henry!" Mr. Markum laughed as he moved through the doorway and down the hall, quickly checking his watch to see what he had left of his fourth- period lunch break.

Anti-Panic Support

Mrs. Kaufmann passed Mr. Markum in the hall at the end of fourth period, and he quickly handed her Melanie's book report with a giant, red A+ on it. "She'll be fine if she even just reads this report and looks up once in a while," he assured Mrs. Kaufmann. "And I'll send Mr. Marquis down to you at the beginning of sixth period, once I've reminded the whole class about the grading of these reports."

"Great," she answered. "I'll tell Melanie that you've graded her report in advance, so she'll know it's what you want. That way she'll know she has your approval when she does speak. That might just make this oral report happen without any panic after all. Thanks so much for your help." She was relieved that everything was going so well for Melanie. She had had a feeling that Melanie was an over-achiever and put a lot of pressure on herself to perform.

"No problem. I'm glad I could help, and I will also set the stage for some serious respectful listening, with consequences clearly spelled out for anyone who makes a speaker feel the least bit uncomfortable," Mr. Markum assured her, as he turned to leave for class.

"That would be great. Have a good afternoon," Mrs. Kaufmann said, as she began to look at the list of students, getting a little backed up from her busy morning and with time running out in the school day. *At least I have Melanie in school, not crying, and planning to go ahead with her most frightening experience ever. I feel really good about that!* she thought.

Mrs. Kaufmann had three students come by with some issues to be resolved, and as the last one stood up to gather her things, Melanie appeared in the doorway. "Am I too early?" she asked the school counselor, seeing that she was writing out a pass for that student to get to fifth- period class.

"Hi, Melanie. No, as a matter of fact, your timing is exquisite, and I have the best news ever!" Mrs. Kaufmann exclaimed. Melanie smiled and sat down across from her at the big desk. "I spoke with Mr. Markum about how he grades the reports, and I found out how that all works. It turns out this written report is equal to one quiz grade, and all your quiz grades together only equal one-fourth of your total marking-period grade. Since you have about five quizzes to average, this one oral book report is only worth about five percent of your grade, so it's not that big at all. Plus, and with a drum roll please," Mrs. Kaufmann joked, to pick up Melanie's excitement, "Mr. Markum read your book report during his lunchtime and gave it an A+. He said it has everything in it that was required, so all you have to do is read it looking up once in a while! How great is that? He understands your fear and wants you to relax and feel good about this." Mrs. Kaufmann gleamed.

"Oh my gosh," Melanie whimpered in relief and disbelief. "That is so great to hear, thank you so much."

"Okay, now we have to run through the checklist of your fears to see if the big ones are in a good enough place now. First, do you have confidence now in *what* you're going to say?" Mrs. Kaufmann continued.

"I guess so, if I got an A+," Melanie smiled almost guiltily.

"So now do you think you can read it, and look up once in a while so it looks like you are talking to the class?"

"I'm not sure about that one," Melanie admitted. "That's the part that's really scary to do, look at all those faces looking at just you."

"I understand," Mrs. Kaufmann said. "And what is it that makes that scary for you, my dear?"

"I don't know, exactly, it just is," Melanie said, appearing to squirm a little more in her seat.

Knowing she was bringing her to the edge of her comfort level, she asked Melanie, "What is it that you imagine could happen?"

"Uh, I just see myself losing my place, or stuttering, or something like that. I guess I don't know how I'll do and just think something might go wrong," she answered.

"Okay, then what? Because the things you mentioned that could go wrong are all perfectly normal things that do go wrong all the time when people are nervous and speaking in front of the room. What do you envision being the problem with making a mistake like that?" Mrs. Kaufmann continued.

"That's what I'm scared of…I just don't know what will happen." Melanie's voice was getting shaky.

"Nothing can happen that you can't handle is what I know, but you don't have that confidence. I feel like you think something bad will happen, like you'll collapse onto the floor?" Mrs. Kaufmann challenged

Melanie to go there mentally with a bit of an exaggeration.

"Oh, I don't think I'd ever do that," she defended herself quite strongly.

"Okay, but what exactly do you think would be your worst thing to happen?" Mrs. Kaufmann pushed.

"Uh… uh… I guess I picture Henry Marquis laughing really loud when I lose my place, and then my eyes fill up and I feel like I want to cry," Melanie admitted.

"And then what?" The push continued.

"I don't know what would happen then."

"Let's picture this. Your eyes get a little teary, Mr. Markum scolds Henry, all the other students feel terrible watching you feel so uncomfortable, and then they all feel sorry for you. Am I right so far?"

"Yes, I guess they would," Melanie answered.

"So you continue on with your report anyway, feeling that little bit of a choked-up burn in the throat, which has to go away in a couple of minutes. Plus, Henry has been quieted and given his lesson about calling out, and, because of that, the others will now be saved from his remarks during their own oral reports. When you sit back down in your seat after you're done, all your friends will think of you as saving them and being very brave. You also now have completed this A+ for a quiz grade, Henry's learned another social lesson, and it's all a huge win-win. You're the hero for the day, and all because you faced your fears!" Mrs. Kaufmann enthusiastically announced.

She continued, "And that's only if all of the things go wrong that you could think of! Now, think of this--what if you made a mistake and no one even gave it a second thought? What if Henry knew better than to embarrass you, someone who is shy, because he's becoming more compassionate or because you don't ever hurt him?"

Mrs. Kaufmann then made Melanie go through some more helpful imagery. "I want you to picture some of the students that you know in that class that seem pretty confident. Think of kids that act more like leaders than followers, or even Henry, the class clown. Picture how they change when they have to stand up in front of the class and give their oral presentations. Imagine how you've seen them get uncomfortable up in front of the room in the past. Can you picture the times they've gone from confident to nervous? I'll bet you can, because it's perfectly normal to feel that way when you think you're in the spotlight to be judged."

Melanie was very quiet the whole time Mrs. Kaufmann was making her picture all of these images. She stayed quiet for a while after that, too.

"What are you thinking now?" Mrs. Kaufmann asked.

"I guess I'm still picturing myself making a mistake when I'm talking," she repeated.

"Let's practice the report, and I'll time it to see how long you're actually speaking, okay?" Mrs. Kaufmann offered.

"Good idea," Melanie said, as she took her report out. "Should I just start reading now?"

Mrs. Kaufmann said, "Let's try to make this similar to what it will be like when you actually give it. Why don't you stand over there by the couch as if you were in the front of the classroom, and I'll stay at my desk and time you? This could be a good practice for you."

Melanie agreed as she moved across the room. She faced Mrs. Kaufmann, they both looked at the clock, and she began to speak with only a tiny hint of discomfort. When she was done, Mrs. Kaufmann gave her a huge smile and clapped her hands. "That was a really good book report, Melanie! I didn't even know that stuff about the author, which made it all so much more interesting. No wonder you got an A+ for the written part. And you spoke for a little less than three minutes, so you really aren't up there for very long at all. I also like the way you look up every so often. How did you manage to hold your place on the paper?"

"I put my thumb on the line where I was reading from so I didn't lose my place," she said proudly.

"Good idea. When I speak now, and this is what I've learned after many years of being in school and learning some tricks, I write out the report on numbered notecards, so the parts I read are in chunks, one chunk per card. That way I actually plan where I'll look up." Then Mrs. Kaufmann asked Melanie the big question. "How do you feel about doing this report now?"

"A lot better," Melanie said without hesitation and without showing any anxiety.

"Excellent! Any fears left?" she double-checked.

Melanie thought for a moment. "Yes," she said. "Henry Marquis. I just don't think he'll feel sorry about anyone and keep quiet."

"Well, just between us, Mr. Markum told me he will watch out for anyone who might want to call out anything during these oral reports. He's going to make sure all the students in the class know to sit up, listen quietly, look interested, and are warned about the punishment if they make anyone feel uncomfortable in any way. Cool, right?" Mrs. Kaufmann smiled again. "See, I told you we could work through a plan," she boasted. "Does that help, too?"

Melanie reacted by sitting up straight as an arrow with a huge grin on her face. "Cool!" She sat there envisioning that as well.

"Okay, then," Mrs. Kaufmann said. "I want to give you a chance to listen to this last little thought. I will ask you to concentrate on this next image as I give it to you. It's called guided imagery. It's part of a positive thinking effort you need to do to replace the old one of scary 'what-if's' that you create out of self-doubt. Ready?" she asked.

Melanie said she was ready, with complete trust and enthusiasm.

"Here we go. You can close your eyes if you want to, but whether you do or not, just imagine this vision of you," Mrs. Kaufmann suggested. Melanie sat back in her chair, and her eyes willingly shut. Then Mrs. Kaufmann softened and lowered her voice into a flowing series of statements. "Let us both picture Melanie being called on to come up to the front of the room to do her report. She doesn't want to feel her heart pick up its beat, so she reminds herself to relax and take nice deep breaths in and out on her way up, knowing she will do an excellent A+ report.

"She gets to the front of the room and pictures herself as an actress whose three-minute performance of reading a prepared script is one she will perform with enthusiasm. She focuses on making the class learn something new. She is there to make three minutes of their lives go from boring to interesting, from just waiting through another report, to reliving her happy book-reading experience through her excitement. You are this Melanie. This is you, feeling your enjoyment of your book, and you will see in their faces that your performance is really enjoyable. They all look interested; they look positive – even Henry. They feel like it was a better class because of your performance. That will relax you and make you want to entertain them even more. You aren't just Melanie, now. You are a talented actress performing a review of a book you really liked. You are convincing them all to get that book so they can enjoy it, too. You are successful, and they are happy, and they clap as you finish your performance.

"Your teacher smiles, knowing you have just shown all the other students how to give a really, really great oral book report. You are happy too, and you can't wait for another opportunity to perform. so you can get that wonderful feeling of affecting an entire room full of people. You want to relive that power to affect people and their emotions in a positive way. You look forward to another experience of seeing it on their faces, watching you with great attention for **what** you have to say, and not just how you are doing. You sit down feeling very successful, and you see the look of admiration from the faces of all of your classmates. The teacher also looks very pleased. You *have* been very successful today, and you can't wait to go home and share the whole wonderful experience with your mom." Mrs. Kaufmann finished the guided imagery. "You can open your eyes whenever you are ready," she said quietly, and then remained so.

Melanie sat silently, opening her eyes slowly like waking up in the morning to a sunlit room. She grinned and said, "That was awesome."

"I know you're ready now, my dear. Let's get you back to class, okay?"

"Okay," Melanie said, with a sound of peaceful calm in her voice.

"Break a leg!" Mrs. Kaufmann said to her, as she laughed and handed Melanie the pass back to art class. "That's what they say to an actress before she goes on stage. Believe it or not, it's supposed to be a wish for good luck!" Mrs. Kaufmann giggled. "You will be excellent, my dear. I feel it in my bones."

Melanie took the pass, put her book report in her backpack, and headed for the office door. "Thanks, Mrs. K," she said, sounding confident as she headed out the door to go back to class.

She's ready, I'm sure, Mrs. Kaufmann thought. *In fact, right now, I should give Mrs. Addison a quick call and put her mind at ease.* She looked up Melanie's home phone number.

"Mrs. Addison?" she asked as the woman at the other end of the phone answered. "This is Mrs. Kaufmann. I wanted to give you a call to let you know Melanie and I worked together a couple of times today, and I even got Mr. Markum's help to assure her that her written report was excellent. She will be giving her report next period, and I can predict she will be fine."

"Oh, thank you so much for letting me know. I have been worried all day, and now I feel so relieved!" Mrs. Addison exclaimed.

"You're so welcome. I actually have to run. I'd be happy to hear how it went if you think Melanie would like to call my voice mail tonight. I'm hoping she might want to brag! Have a great rest of the day!" Mrs. Kaufmann said quickly.

And after Mrs. Addison also said goodbye, Mrs. Kaufmann went back to her list of students to see, and called for the first one to be sent to her. She needed to see a few before Henry Marquis came at the beginning of sixth period. She knew Henry's session would require some creativity. This time she needed to effect a change in his attitude about being the class clown, without repeating any of her old strategies. That would take some thought, since she knew why he felt he really needed attention – even if it was negative.

There were no more students in Mrs. Kaufmann's waiting room, and she could hear the din of chatter out in the hallways finally ending as classes finished changing. That would mean Melanie was now in Mr. Markum's language arts class and about to do her oral book report. It also meant that in a few minutes, Henry would be arriving at her door. She looked up his recent report card grades and saw that they had gone down in almost every subject. She saw his grades were low even in his special education classes, where grades were more aligned with an individual's ability than based on the normal curve against the general population. Clearly something was going on in these past few weeks.

Mrs. Kaufmann called his math teacher in the resource room. "Mrs. Keltner? It's Mrs. Kaufmann. I'm about to meet with Henry Marquis about his lack of discipline recently. Are you aware of any changes in his home or at school that could shed some light on the drop in his grades?"

"Hi. Yes, his parents have recently separated, and he's been acting out everywhere. I was actually about to call you about it. His grades have been steadily going downhill, because he's not doing any homework. I hate to punish him by taking away his playground time, but he needs to do the work, and that's the only time I can help him with it. Would you like me to send him down last period today?" Mrs. Keltner asked.

"Thanks for asking, but he should be on his way here even as we speak. Thanks for the update. That will really help me help him. Talk to you later," Mrs. Kaufmann answered.

Henry's Turn

Mrs. Kaufmann thought she heard someone in her waiting room. When she went to check, Henry was sitting there, hoping not to be noticed so he wouldn't have to get back to class anytime soon. "Hi, Henry, I'm glad you came. We haven't talked in a long time, so I sent for you. I'm doing my academic check-ups. Come on into my office, and let's see what we can do to help you get your grades up, okay?" Mrs. Kaufmann tried to keep it upbeat and sound casual, so Henry wouldn't feel like he had to defend himself. "I also have to ask how things are going at home, because when things change there, usually grades change at school, you know."

"Yeah, I know. I know my grades aren't good," Henry admitted with his head down and his eyes lowered.

"So what's new at home, Henry?" Mrs. Kaufmann went right to the heart of the problem.

"Well, my dad moved out, and my mom is crying a lot," he answered, with his eyes still lowered.

"I'm sorry, Henry. That must make things difficult. How do you get help with your homework at night?" she pursued.

"I don't," he answered.

"I know your grades are calculated using the test results, but I also know that test results depend on how well you do your homework and study for tests at home. Would you want some homework help after school for a while?" she asked.

"I have to go home to babysit my brother after school. That's okay. I'll just do better," Henry offered.

"How about coming in for academic help before school, or with your classroom teacher during playground time?" Mrs. Kaufmann asked.

"I really don't want to give up my time on playground, and I really, really don't want to get up early!" Henry declared.

"I don't blame you," Mrs. Kaufmann agreed. "But if you don't keep your grades up, you'll be off the basketball team. That means you need a C or better, and you definitely don't have that right now in your math class. I think you need to do something, and I'm happy to help you make that happen. Do you think a homework buddy would help if you run into trouble with it at home at night?" she suggested.

"I really like that idea, but who do I call without it being embarrassing?" he questioned.

"Well, I'm starting up a Peer Tutoring Program in which students in all grades can sign up to help other students of their grade or from a lower grade. They pick the subject they do well in, and they promise to be available for one person that signs up for him or her for homework help. You can sign up to be a tutor for music since you're very good at it. Then, when all the tutors have signed up, I copy the final list of willing volunteers and post it in all the classrooms. That way each student can select his or her best match. Once you see someone you feel comfortable with, you can ask if it's okay if you call them for help in math sometimes. And that's how the whole program works. Does that sound better than early morning or no playground?" she asked, knowing the answer.

"Sure, I'd do that!" Henry announced, smiling in relief from having not to make his life even worse.

"Excellent!" Mrs. Kaufmann said, as she turned her chair to face her computer, went to her e-mail, and then read along with what she was typing to all the teachers in the middle school so Henry could hear.

"To all staff: Re: Peer Tutoring Program. Please encourage your students to complete the volunteer sign-ups by the end of the week so I can post the names of the willing and send a letter home to their parents. Make sure they indicate their grade level and the subject in which they feel comfortable helping others. Thanks, Mrs. Kaufmann."

She finished her e-mail, turned back to Henry, and smiled. "There. If you have a question that stops you from doing your homework at night starting next week, all you'll have to do is call the homework tutor that you get paired up with, and I'll help with the pairing…not to worry. In the meantime, if you have a question at night for the next couple of days and can't get any help, I will let your mom know she can drop you off for the academic help time before school." Mrs. Kaufmann grinned at Henry. "There. Now you don't have any excuse not to do your homework." "And," she continued, "if you don't do your homework at night, and you don't come in to do it before school, your teacher will be keeping you in from playground to help you until it's done, because that isn't one of those negotiable items! We insist you grow up smart and ready for that big world you'll have to navigate on your own one day," Mrs. Kaufmann said, with a soft firmness.

Henry did his usual moan of resistance, but with a smile. It was as if he had to keep up his reputation for not liking to work, but didn't want to offend Mrs. Kaufmann. They had an understanding, and he knew she was not trying to hurt him. This was the help he needed right now.

"Also, my dear, I have to share with you something I've become aware of recently. Teachers and students have mentioned you've been acting out in class and calling out comments about other kids. They agree you're not trying to be mean, just trying to be the class clown. I assume it's because things aren't exactly comfortable for you right now at home, so you're looking for attention here. Do you think that might be a possibility? See, I always think of you as well-behaved and calm when everything is normal and calm in your life, but not so much in control when your home life is not so much in control. What do you think?" Mrs. Kaufmann asked point blank.

Henry looked surprised and uncomfortable. "I didn't think I was hurting anyone. I was just joking around," he said in his own defense.

"I do understand that things are tough for you right now. You know, when you feel fear deep inside, sometimes you act differently because of the overall discomfort or lack of balance. The problem is, your classmates are feeling embarrassed by your saying things about them in front of everyone. My guess is that now they just feel uncomfortable in general, not knowing when you'll laugh at something they say out loud, or make fun of something they do. Being the class clown won't win you any friends, for a good reason. They are embarrassed. What you say may not seem that bad to you, but the fact that you want to make fun of them, and in front of a lot of people, is what will make them think you're mean and unpredictable. Have you noticed that the other students aren't choosing to play with you recently? That must be making things even a little harder."

Mrs. Kaufmann tried to appeal to Henry's good heart. "Henry, you can choose to stop doing this and get your friends back. This one you can do if you want to. What do you think?"

Mrs. Kaufmann didn't stop between questions because she wanted to complete the whole picture of what Henry needed to do, not what he would likely deny. She appealed to his heart, showing an understanding of his misbehavior, but also making the unwanted consequences more glaring.

Henry sat quietly. The little homework problem and discussion they had just had seemed pale compared to this news. It was sinking in as he listened to Mrs. Kaufmann. He couldn't believe his friends and his teachers were complaining about him. And they were thinking he was mean? He wasn't sure what to say or where to begin. "They think I'm mean?" he finally asked with noticeable disappointment.

Mrs. Kaufmann was relieved to see that it mattered to Henry. It was a good sign, and she hoped it would motivate him to change his behavior to, at the least, keep friends, and at the most, not to embarrass people. "I'm sorry to be the one who delivers this news, but I'd rather it be me so I can help you, rather than one of your teachers who would have to call your parents and discipline you. Do you think stopping yourself from calling out comments in class will be hard to do? I would think that if you could remember that the students think of that behavior as attention-getting and not funny, that would be a real turn-off to help you stop, right?" Mrs. Kaufmann suggested encouragingly.

"It might be hard sometimes, when something makes me laugh," he reacted.

"I know. That's a tough thing to do, hold back laughter. It's one of the skills you learn in life as you get older. Imagine grown-ups laughing at each other's errors? It would be so immature. Maybe if you could keep in mind how awful you feel when someone laughs at you in front of other people? It's just so embarrassing, isn't it? Henry, I know you are just trying to be funny, and things aren't easy at home right now, but I want you to understand that being funny at the expense of someone's humiliation isn't really funny.

"In fact, everyone in the class can feel really uncomfortable watching it happen to someone they care about. And when your classmates feel they have to watch out for you embarrassing them, they will gradually not want to hang out with you at all. You'll start to lose friends, and you really don't want that, I know. You are a good kid, you have a caring heart, and you're really funny. Can you use your sense of humor without using it against anyone?"

Mrs. Kaufmann could see Henry was past the shock and openly listening. It was just what she hoped for, but she also knew his impulsivity would make that self-control a challenge. "I'll be happy to help you anytime you'd like to talk about it or want to find ways to stick to this decision. And, don't forget, you'll have your own homework hotline buddy next week.

"One more thought I'm having, Henry. I have always observed that shortly after a parent moves out of the home, the kids feel a little ungrounded for a bit. Do you?" she asked directly.

"Well, a little," he admitted. "I didn't know your dad could just stop being your dad and just move away. I had a dream that my mom decided not to be my mom anymore, either," he said, with tears filling his eyes.

"Henry, that's perfectly normal for you to think that, and from a kid's point of view, it's logical. But here's the reality. Your father will always be your father, and your mother will always be your mother. They love you and you love them, and none of that is a part of what's going on between them. They may not want to live together, but they will always be your parents. You don't have to worry about who will take care of you, because you can be guaranteed that they will work that out, even if it means they have to share time with you in separate places. That will be taken care of for you. Besides, the law requires that children are always protected. So that fear doesn't have to exist in your head anymore. Just try to make sure you take care of *your* jobs in life, and let them figure out all the rest. Does that sound okay?"

"Yeah, I guess," he answered thoughtfully.

"Listen, my dear. I'm very proud of you right now. You're willing to try to learn to do your homework on your own and be responsible for that and your behavior all at once. I will call you down next week to see how everything's going, and by then, the tutoring program should be all set up and you can pick one of the volunteers, okay?" She ended their talk on a positive note.

"Okay Mrs. K, thanks," Henry answered, appearing to be ready to go back to class.

"How 'bout we get you back to language arts before you miss all the book reports?" she said, as she wrote out the pass for Henry to go back to class.

Henry took the pass and darted out of the office. "I'm sure he's glad to get back to class, and I believe he should be able to turn things around in the classroom with this shift of thinking," Mrs. Kaufmann said to herself. "At least Melanie should have his best behavior for today when he gets back, if she hasn't already finished."

Another Morning Message

Walking over to the red flashing light on her phone, Mrs. Kaufmann put down her purse on the desk the next morning and immediately started checking her overnight messages. She was really hoping she would hear back from Melanie or her mom as to how it had gone. Instead, she had a voice mail from Mr. Markum.

"Mrs. Kaufmann, I just had to tell you that Melanie did just fine with her oral book report. She seemed a little nervous when she started, but as she went on, her reading was smooth and she looked up every so often. You could tell that she was really pleased. I also have to tell you that Henry came back to class rather subdued. I don't know what you said, but he sat quietly for the rest of class. Thank you!" Mrs. Kaufmann couldn't help but feel great relief.

She listened to the rest of the messages and then decided to go down to the main office to pick up the Peer Tutor Volunteer lists in her mailbox. She passed Henry coming in the front door. "Hey, my friend, are you here early to get some help with your math homework?" she asked excitedly.

Henry proudly answered, "Yup, I only have the word problems to go!"

"I am so, so proud of you! That means you will be out running around on playground today. Good for you! Oh, and Mr. Markum left a message for me that you were so well-behaved yesterday during the book reports. I'm doubly proud of you, my dear! Don't forget that next week we'll let you look at the tutor lists and see if there's a student that you might know from your neighborhood, or bus, or not. You can pick your own tutor, okay?" Mrs. Kaufmann was truly happy for Henry's efforts and wanted him to feel the reward.

"Okay," he said, grinning ear to ear, and headed down to his math teacher's room for his morning extra help.

Mrs. Kaufmann made a decision not to mention her Changing Families Group meetings to Henry right then. Those students, whose parents were in transition, were currently meeting before school, and she knew Henry would not be receptive to that at all. She figured she'd just wait a while and offer that to him when he would be more ready.

The school counselor continued down the hall in the other direction and went into the main office. In her mailbox were some of the tutor lists and a piece of white lined paper folded in half and in half again. On the front was her name written in pencil in large script. She opened it, and on the inside were the words: "Thank you! From Melanie." Mrs. Kaufmann couldn't wait to see her in the hallway sometime that morning. If she didn't see her by lunchtime, Mrs. Kaufmann hoped her waiting room would be empty during Melanie's recess so she could go out onto the playground and "just happen to run into her" out there. She knew this wasn't the end of Melanie's fears, and they would be working together on this for a while, but it was a really good beginning of the end.

Discussion Points:

- Worrying about not making a mistake could bring on paralyzing fear. Expecting that you won't make mistakes is unrealistic. We aren't born all mature, wise, educated, experienced, talented, and strong. That's what we grow into by practice.

- The process of learning is the process of trial and error. That means you will have to find out what is right by trying other choices until you finally discover the right way or the right solution, or fine-tune the skill. It isn't failure…it is the "practice part" of the learning process.

- All teachers are as different as all people everywhere. Students need to simply do their best as they adapt to their teachers' unique styles and expectations.

Reflection Questions:

1. What's the best way to get over a fear of something? What baby steps can you take to face your own fears? What people can you count on to help you at those times when it seems like it's too scary to face alone?

2. What statements can you make in your head to remind yourself that you'll be okay when you're afraid? Do you feel courageous when you face a fear and conquer it?

3. What are some causes that make a person doubt whether they will be okay? Do old experiences of failure replay in your memory? Do you sometimes tune into made-up "what-if thinking" that gives you more to worry about? Can you change that channel?

CHAPTER 11:
My Friend Goes Ballistic Over Nothing!

The School Nurse Stops In

"Knock, knock," said a woman's voice at Mrs. Kaufmann's door. "Is anybody home?"

Mrs. Kaufmann got up and went to the office door just as the school nurse appeared in her doorway with a student whose eyes were noticeably red. "Mrs. Cain! Come in. I see our friend Ray Shanley is with you. Come on in, both of you. To what do I owe this nice surprise today?" Mrs. Kaufmann said with delight, but at the same time noticing a scratched and reddened cheek on Ray's face.

"Well, Ray was sent in from recess to see me with a bruise on his face. I was told that while they were playing soccer, Anthony Barrows and Ray Shanley got into a little scuffle, and Ray's cheek suffered the damage. Anthony ended up in the vice-principal's office to see Mr. Stein for starting the fight, and Raymond was sent to me for repair. Anyway, Ray and I were talking about Anthony and how he has a tendency to really lose it sometimes. He's his friend, and yet he just seems to go ballistic over nothing and occasionally gets way too aggressive. I'm wondering if you might have some time to talk with Ray about how to handle Anthony. Do you have any time right now?" Mrs. Cain checked with the school counselor before she left Ray to get back to the health office.

"I sure do! Come on in Raymond Shanley, and thank you, Mrs. Cain, for letting me have a chance to chat with him." Mrs. Kaufmann assured Mrs. Cain that she would take it from there.

"Thanks, Mrs. Kaufmann. I'm sure you can help Ray deal with this Anthony and all the other 'Anthonys' he's going to know in his life! And I'll give Ray's mom a call so she knows what happened today. I'll let Mrs. Shanley know he's having a chance to talk with you about it, also," Mrs. Cain said, as she left the guidance office and went back across the hall to her office, which was filled with students coming in from playground.

"Boy, that cheek looks like it hurts. How did it all happen, Ray?" Mrs. Kaufmann led the questioning as they both took their seats across from each other at her big desk.

"Well, I went out to the soccer field with Anthony when we went out for recess, like we always do. We usually play hard and have a good time. Anthony is really good at it, and I'm not, but I play okay. Anyway, today we were on opposite teams, and when he was kicking the ball down the field and running toward me, I tried to get the ball, and he tripped over my foot. He thought I tried to trip him, and then he immediately just lost it and punched me in my face. I went to push him away before he hit me again, and we both fell over.

"That's right when the playground aide, Mrs. Tanner, came over and told us both to get up off the ground and follow her inside. She dropped me off at the health office to see Mrs. Cain, and she took Anthony to Mr. Stein's office. I don't even know if I'm going to be in trouble, too. And Anthony's my friend! He never even gave me a chance to explain that I was just trying to get the ball away from him." Ray couldn't believe that Anthony seemed like a loose cannon.

Mrs. Kaufmann questioned Ray a little further. "Has he done this before?"

"Yes, three times just recently, and they were all such a shock," Ray answered.

"Have you ever seen him react so dramatically with other kids?" she pursued.

"Oh, yeah, but they were kids who teased him, or made fun of him, or tried to fight with him, but not me until this year," Ray said, still not believing the change in his friend.

"How long have you been friends?" continued Mrs. Kaufmann. "And have you had any arguments recently?"

"We've played together since we were little, because we live near each other and our parents are friends, too. And we always hung out riding bikes and stuff without any arguments until last summer. Anthony seemed to get really mad at everyone over the summer, even me, over nothing!" Ray repeated, because he just didn't understand what was going on.

"Did you ask him about it last summer, or this year so far?" Mrs. Kaufmann asked.

"No, I just kept thinking he was crazy and didn't want to set him off again," Ray explained.

"I understand. I think I wouldn't have wanted to start trouble either. But, what made you hang out with him again after each seemingly crazy blow-up?" she went a little further.

"I don't know." Ray said. "I guess it was just easier to keep doing what we always did. We always wait at the bus stop together, we always go out to the soccer field after lunch, and we always get off the bus at the end of the day, expecting we'll meet up later at the park down at the end of our street. It's just what we do. I've tried to be really careful not to tease him or joke too much so I don't set him off. A couple of days last week I didn't even go back outside after I got home after school. I guess he just figured my mom didn't let me go back out, or that we had something else we had to do. Actually, I don't know what to do anymore because I do want to go out after school." Ray sounded very frustrated.

"Well, I'm really curious, too, as to why he's suddenly having such anger management problems. I will definitely be seeing him now that he was brought in to Mr. Stein's office for fighting on playground. I also have to talk with Mrs. Tanner to see if she thinks you were part of the fighting or just the victim of an angry explosion. I'm thinking I can't take you down to the office to find out, because we need to avoid Anthony seeing you with me. I wouldn't want him to resent that he ended up being in trouble and you didn't. Maybe I should go outside to ask Mrs. Tanner what she saw and what she figured you were to do after the nurse checked out your injury. How about you go back to the health office now and stay there until I come back in from the playground, okay?" Mrs. Kaufmann suggested.

"Okay," Ray answered.

"I'll walk over with you so I can explain to Mrs. Cain what our plan is," she said, as she reached for her sweater and her office-door keys.

"Hi, Mrs. Cain. May I have a word with you out here in the hallway for a second?" Mrs. Kaufmann asked, so the nurse would be able to hear her privately and away from the students that filled her health office. As the nurse came out to meet her, Mrs. Kaufmann quietly said, "Would you mind letting Raymond stay with you until I get back from talking with the playground aide? I just need to know what she saw out there with Anthony Barrows, and whether she felt Ray had to be disciplined for fighting on playground."

"Sure, he can stay with me," Mrs. Cain answered willingly. She turned to go back into her office and, seeing Ray standing just inside her health office door, said, "Hey, Raymond, why don't you join me until Mrs. Kaufmann comes back? We still have about ten minutes left of playground time, and then you can go back to class."

"Thanks," Mrs. Kaufmann said to the nurse as she threw her sweater over her shoulders, headed down the hallway, and went out the door to the playground.

Mrs. Kaufmann got outside in the bright sunshine and the cool breeze and looked for Mrs. Tanner. She saw her way over by the swings, so she started walking briskly in that direction. Three girls ran up to her to say hi and walked with her, making happy conversation, until Janey, one of the girls, asked her, "Did you hear what Anthony Barrows did again, Mrs. K?"

"What's that?" she responded, acting like she knew nothing so she could hear it from the students' point of view.

"He got in another fight and had to go inside to get detention, we think," Janey said. "He hit Raymond right in the face."

"Oh, dear, and what happened then?" she asked.

"Raymond pushed him away, and Anthony fell down for a second. He was really mad and was trying to get up just when Mrs. Tanner got there and took him inside to the office," Samantha chimed in. "And Raymond's face looked really red," she finished.

"Thanks for sharing with me. I hope they'll both be okay," she said to the girls as she approached Mrs. Tanner.

"You hope they're **both** okay?" Samantha questioned. "You hope Anthony's okay, too? He was the one who hit Ray. He didn't even get hurt," she protested.

"Well, I figure, when people are in a good place and not upset about anything, they treat others respectfully. If something's wrong, then they react to what they think is wrong, or what they fear. That means Anthony is probably upset by something, and then he did what *he thought* he had to do. Now, on top of it all, he's probably in trouble down at the office, and therefore with his parents, too. That's why I hope he's okay. He's dealing with a lot right now," she said rather matter-of-factly. "You are all my little chickens in my chicken coop," she added, "and I want you all to grow up to be good people, happy people, and good neighbors!" she added.

The three girls all mumbled something like "I guess so," as they realized she had a point, but they were not really wanting to feel sorry for Anthony, since he seemed like the "angry bad boy." As Mrs. Kaufmann reached Mrs. Tanner, the girls all said goodbye and ran off to play.

Mrs. Tanner saw them coming toward her and was looking forward to a chance to tell Mrs. Kaufmann what she had seen. "Hi, how's Raymond?" she called out to Mrs. Kaufmann.

"He's fine," she answered. "He's in the nurse's office waiting to find out if he's been reported for fighting," she answered.

"Oh, heavens no. What I saw was Anthony hitting Ray right in the face. Then, when he was about ready to hit him again, Ray pushed him away. Anthony lost his balance, thankfully, he fell down, and I had a chance to get to them before Anthony could get back up and hit Ray again. You know, I think Anthony has a problem. He gets so angry so fast recently. And yet, he's a good kid most of the time," Mrs. Tanner observed.

"That's good to know. Yes, I have that same feeling. He is too quick to flare up, and with his friend, no less. Have you ever seen this much anger before this school year?" Mrs. Kaufmann asked her.

"No, that's why I think something's really wrong. He used to be so easygoing, but now he's ready to fly off the handle over nothing. One of the boys on the field told me, when I came back outside from bringing the boys in to the offices, what had happened. He said that Ray was trying to get the soccer ball from Anthony during a play, and Anthony tripped over Ray's foot and fell down. They figured Anthony thought Ray tripped him. Ray… his good, kind, cooperative friend, Ray!" Mrs. Tanner noted.

"Yes, I think something's up. I just need to do a little checking around to see what else has changed. Thanks so much for letting me know what you've seen. I'm lucky to have you out here as my eyes on the playground." Mrs. Kaufmann turned around to go back inside and let Raymond know he wasn't in any trouble. She also knew she had to get right down to the vice-principal's office to find out Anthony's fate.

The Empty Hole

Mrs. Kaufmann went directly to the health office and saw Ray sitting quietly on a chair in the nurse's waiting area near Tim, an older boy who rode his bus. Tim was giving himself his insulin injection before going to lunch. "Does it hurt?" Ray had just asked him. Mrs. Kaufmann waited a minute to let Tim answer.

"Yeah, I guess a little, but it's just a pinch that saves my life, as my doctor reminds me. Besides, you can get used to most anything, and then it becomes just what you do," Tim answered casually, as if he was used to being asked that question.

"Boy, that's the truth!" Mrs. Kaufmann interjected. "To me, life just is what it is, and we can be happy if we can accept what we're given, instead of mad about what we don't have. It's the old 'glass half full' thinking. Oh, and Ray, guess what? You're not in any trouble. You can go back outside, because everyone pretty much figured out what happened out there. I'll let Mrs. Cain know, too, okay? Have fun."

Ray got right up out of his seat, turned to Tim and wanted to say something, but he didn't know what, so he just nodded to him and said, "Later."

Tim gave Ray a "later" back. They both felt some kind of connection that they would each tuck away for some other time…maybe on the bus.

Ray went out the door, and Mrs. Kaufmann gave the all-clear signal to Mrs. Cain while she was taking students' blood pressures, and she nodded back and smiled. Immediately, Mrs. Kaufmann headed to the vice-principal's office to get some more past and present information about Anthony.

As she arrived there, she could see Mr. Stein welcoming Mrs. Barrows and inviting her into his office. Mrs. Kaufmann could also see Anthony on a chair facing the doorway. Mrs. Kaufmann saw Anthony look up, see his mother entering the room, and drop his eyes. Anthony mumbled, "I'm sorry, Mom," without lifting his head.

Mr. Stein saw Mrs. Kaufmann in the hallway and immediately said, "Would you like to join us, Mrs. Kaufmann?"

"Yes, I would." She walked right up to Mrs. Barrows, extending her hand and saying, "I'm Mrs. Kaufmann, the school counselor, Mrs. Barrows, and I know Anthony, here. I hope I can be of some help for you all."

"Thanks, yes, I'm not sure what's going on. I understand from Mr. Stein that Anthony was fighting? I am so sorry, and I'd sure like to know the reason this time!" she declared, looking at Anthony and showing him she was annoyed. It was a real problem that she had to be called away from her busy day at the office for the second time and so early in this school year. She looked back at Mr. Stein and asked, "Is the other student hurt?"

"He did have to go to the health office, but I understand it was a bruise on his cheek from Anthony punching him in the face," Mr. Stein answered.

Her head immediately turned back to Anthony in surprise. "Why did you hit him? I've never known you to just haul off and punch someone before. What has gotten into you?"

"I'm sorry, Mom, but he tripped me and made me fall down while I was going down the field with the soccer ball. I had to do something to show everyone I won't take that and do nothing."

Mr. Stein interrupted immediately to take charge of this meeting. "First of all, Anthony, the other students saw what happened, and they said that boy was trying to get the ball away from you, since he was on the other team. You fell because you tripped over his foot, which is part of the game. He didn't try to trip you at all. The problem was that you *wanted* to hit him, and that's why you're here in this office right now. I will not tolerate any violence in my school, young man."

Mrs. Barrows agreed right away and said, "I have never allowed my boys to resort to fighting. Their father and I have always taught them to use their words when something hot comes up between them and any other kids. I am really sorry. Anthony and I will have that talk when we get home, I can assure you, Mr. Stein. His father is in the hospital right now dealing with some health issues, but I will make sure he is informed. I'll also let his big brother have a little talk with him, too, since he should be home from college this coming weekend for the Freshman Break."

Mr. Stein then said, "Mrs. Kaufmann, I'd like you to meet with Anthony sometime tomorrow when he's serving an in-school suspension to talk about anger-management." He then looked at Anthony's mom and said, "Mrs. Barrows, he'll be going home from school right now with you, but he will have to go to his locker to get his books first. He'll have to make up whatever classwork he'll be missing this afternoon and tomorrow while on in-school suspension. He'll also need to do his homework tonight and tomorrow night as well. That will be Anthony's job to make sure he has it all completed, and he can turn that in to me first thing when he returns. I will let him know then where he will be all day tomorrow doing his work. As for tomorrow, Mrs. Barrows, you'll need to meet with me for a debriefing at the end of the day before Anthony can go home," he concluded.

"I will be very happy to meet with Anthony tomorrow, Mr. Stein." Mrs. Kaufmann answered him, but was looking in Anthony's eyes. "I'm sure we will get to the bottom of these feelings you're having recently, because they really aren't who you are. I don't ever remember the 'old Anthony' being so unsettled as to act out physically, so we'll just figure it all out tomorrow, okay, Anthony?"

Mrs. Kaufmann wanted to plant some seeds into everyone's thinking about the real issue or issues that were causing this change in Anthony. As soon as she heard that his dad was in the hospital, and his big brother had left for college, she knew those changes may well have left an emptiness in him. This dark hole in him could easily be at the bottom of his acting out.

"Okay," Anthony answered quietly. He looked at Mrs. Kaufmann with those "please help me" eyes she often got when a student was in big trouble between the school and the parents. It was always a crying-out for someone who would just listen rather than just punish. After all, that was what Mrs. Kaufmann did: she listened.

Mr. Stein stood up to shake hands and thank everyone, and then led them out to the main office to the student sign-out sheet. "Thank you, Mrs. Kaufmann," Mrs. Barrows said, shaking her hand as well. "Yes, I can see we have a lot to talk about tonight," she added, sternly looking at Anthony, whose head went back down.

Mrs. Kaufmann walked back to her office hoping that she may have pointed out to Mrs. Barrows the need to do a little understanding of the causes of his anger, if she wanted to have a productive dialogue. *I wonder what the health issues are that the father is experiencing right now*, she thought. It all seemed clear to her that it was such bad timing for Anthony, emotionally, with his brother just moving out at the same time as his dad was in the hospital. She guessed that his mother probably hadn't been able to devote enough time for Anthony recently with all that had been on her plate. She figured Anthony's reaction to these losses was probably coming out of him as anger. The next day's talk would be interesting.

The next morning, Mrs. Kaufmann came to school and saw Anthony sitting in the main office waiting for Mr. Stein to take him to his in-school suspension room. "Good morning, Anthony," she said caringly. "Do you have all the books and work you'll need for today, or would you like some help getting it from any of your teachers?"

"I'm okay," he answered. "I think I got it all. When do we meet today, Mrs. K? Do I need a pass?"

Mrs. Kaufmann was getting the mail out of her mailbox and said, "I have no idea. I will come find you, not to worry. You'll just need to concentrate on getting all your work done today, you know? You don't need to get into any more trouble," she said, to show him her compassion for the mess he was in.

"I will," he answered and then added, "My mom and I had a long talk after she got home from the hospital yesterday, and I'm grounded for a week. She said my dad said I should be allowed to play computer games, even if I'm grounded. That means I can't go out after school to play, but I can play on the computer at least."

"I know you prefer to be playing outdoors in the fresh air and exercising after school, rather than sitting inside, but those are your consequences, I guess. All right, I have to get to my office for now. I'll come find you later, my friend." She then turned around to leave the office.

"Thanks, Mrs. K." Anthony answered, and then with a more positive energy he added, "Can I ask you something?"

Mrs. Kaufmann stopped and faced Anthony. "Sure, what's on your mind, my dear?"

"How's Ray?" he asked uncomfortably.

"His face or his feelings?" she answered honestly and then smiled.

"Both, I guess," he said, getting her message.

"Ray will be fine, and we'll talk about that later. Be thinking about whether you would like to be able to speak with him yourself today… if he's willing, that is, and I'll be there to help. See you later," she said as she took off for her office. She knew that a conflict resolution session would help them both to see what happened from the other guy's point of view.

Getting It!

Mrs. Kaufmann got to her office the next morning and put the mail she had just retrieved onto her desk. She bent down to pick up two little handwritten notes on the carpet that had been shoved under her door. Both were from students who wanted to see her when she had a chance, but neither one said it was an emergency. She then turned on her computer to pull up her e-mail and picked up her phone to hear her voice messages while the computer was loading up. After all of the contacts were read and prioritized, she began to write passes for students to see her and added one more. She wrote out a pass for Raymond and then walked it down to his homeroom teacher. When she saw the teacher was not there, she just left it on his desk and continued delivering the other passes for students she needed to see that morning. Right as she finished, the school bell rang and the students came pouring in from all the doors with a whole day's worth of energy.

She went back to her office and made a call to Mrs. Shanley to see how Ray was doing. "Good morning, Mrs. Shanley. It's Mrs. Kaufmann, the school counselor. How are you, and how is Ray this morning?"

"Oh, I'm fine and so glad you called. Last night Ray talked a lot about whether he should stay friends with Anthony after today's event. He just doesn't trust him anymore. His cheekbone really bothered him because the punch was so hard, and this morning he actually has a black eye. I'm not sure what to tell him. I really don't want my Raymond hurt again, but my husband and I don't know if Anthony's anger will cause some other retaliation out of school in the neighborhood if Ray does decide not to be friends with him," Mrs. Shanley explained.

"Well, my honest guess is that it might just work itself out between the two of them today if I can get them both talking and really listening to each other. I should be seeing Raymond any minute now, so I can ask him if he would be comfortable doing that, or not. If not, I'll see if it's because he's in this 'friend-break-up' dilemma and really doesn't want to fix anything between them. Does that sound like something you think he may want to do, talk to Anthony?" Mrs. Kaufmann asked her.

"Oh, I know he wishes he had the 'old Anthony' back, as he says. The two of them always had such a good time. Anthony does tend to be a little bossy sometimes, almost the same as the way he was treated by his older brother, but nothing aggressive or mean. And my Raymond has always been such a good-natured kid, so he doesn't mind being a follower, most of the time." Then Mrs. Shanley expressed her true concern. "That's why I hope you don't encourage a friendship that will be bad for Ray. I'd like him to learn to be an equal with his friends and take turns being a leader."

"Oh, I will definitely make sure we empty all stored-up issues. Then I will work with them to obtain either a mutual and equal place of respect for each other, or a comfortable parting of ways. I will let the boys lead me into what naturally needs to take place for both of them at this time in their lives. Thank you for the insight you've given me to be able to understand where Ray stands right now. That will help me a lot, especially if he goes into his quiet and agreeable place he usually finds most comfortable," Mrs. Kaufmann said gratefully.

"You're so welcome. Thank you for all your help, and have a great day," Mrs. Shanley responded.

"You, too, and don't worry. We have two good kids here. They really are," Mrs. Kaufmann said confidently.

No sooner had Mrs. Kaufmann put the phone down than there was a little knock on her office door from the waiting room. She hoped it was Ray, since there were no other passes given out for the homeroom time this morning. She opened her office door, and there was Raymond Shanley with a truly dark black eye right above a pink bruised cheek.

"Did you want to see me?" Raymond asked, handing his pass to her.

"Yes, yes, please come in. What a beautiful shiner you have there. It looks like it really hurts. Does it feel as bad as it looks?" Mrs. Kaufmann asked, as she gestured for Ray to come into the room and sit down across the desk from her.

"Not that bad now, but last night it kept me awake, so we put some ice on it this morning. My mom and dad weren't happy last night. I'm not even sure if I want to hang out with Anthony at lunch today, but I hate to give up soccer. I really love playing that during recess."

"I'm sure you do. And just so you know, Anthony won't be in classes or on playground today, so feel free to enjoy your soccer. I do have a couple of questions for you about Anthony, though. What do you feel about your friendship with him in general? Are you happy with your relationship?" she asked.

"I was, but I'm not anymore…I don't think. I can't tell if he's going to get mad at me, or even how mad. I don't hang out with anyone else, though, so I'm not sure…like…what to do after school," Ray said honestly.

"What if Anthony's behavior was like it used to be?" she challenged him. "Does he ever talk about his anger with you, or has he been talking about his family at all?"

"No. Not really. We just play soccer at recess, and then we shoot some hoops after school, and we're not really talking much when we're playing. Though, he told me last year right before school let out that his grandmother had just died. He didn't talk much after that. Maybe he was quiet because he was sad. Then this summer he told me his brother was going to move out to go to college. He sounded the same as he did when his grandmother died. I felt bad for him until he began to get mad about everything. After that, I couldn't feel bad for him anymore," Ray explained to Mrs. Kaufmann.

"Did he ever mention his father?" Mrs. Kaufmann pried a little more.

"Yeah, his dad is sick right now. He had to go to the hospital on our first day of school," Ray remembered.

"Boy, he's had a lot of unhappy events happen to him in just the past few months, huh?" Mrs. Kaufmann said, hoping Ray would see the connection. "So when he gets home from school, is his mom there?" she pushed.

"No. Anthony's mom goes to the hospital to see his dad right after she gets off of work. Anthony has to go right home and call her so she knows he's made it home and is having a snack. After that he's allowed out to play basketball for an hour, because he comes out to play about a half hour after he gets home. That's when I go out, when I see him," Ray told Mrs. Kaufmann.

"I was wondering if you'd be willing to talk with Anthony sometime today about what happened yesterday. Maybe he can explain why he got so mad. He also might be able to let us know what's been bugging him," Mrs. Kaufmann offered Ray.

"Not really," Ray answered, feeling uncomfortable with having to face him. "I think that he still wanted to fight me again yesterday when he was taken inside. Then he got a suspension and I didn't, so that has to have made him even madder. I don't think he wants to talk with me, either."

"What if I start it off with a question for Anthony about what he was mad about yesterday, when you guys were playing soccer? I will keep it positive, so he understands I'm trying to make things right between you two and clear the air. You'll need to listen to him so you hear what angered him. Then you'll have a chance to explain that you were just playing the game and trying to get the ball away from him, being on the opposite team. Once you tell him you didn't intend for him to trip over your foot, I think he'll be able to see how fast he's getting angry. He may have already realized that after he thought about it last night. Then we can talk about what's been going on in his life, and the events that are making things hard for him right now. What do you think?" Mrs. Kaufmann coaxed.

"I guess so. Will I come here first or after he's already here?" Ray asked.

"Which would you prefer?" she asked.

"Do you think I should be here first, like it was an accident that we just happened to bump into one another?" Ray asked her.

"I like to be as honest as I can. I would be happy to talk with him first to make sure he's in a good place and willing to talk with you in a positive way. Then, when you stop by the office going out to recess, I can go out into the waiting room and let you know where he stands. If it works out that Anthony's not angry any more, you can feel safe coming into the office and sitting down to talk with him. And if you do, he'll know you're willing to clear the air with him. Right there the set-up is perfect…two willing people attempting to understand one another. I feel very positive about the outcome, and I would like you to feel more comfortable around him, whether you end up staying friends or not. What do you think?" she checked to see if Ray was getting comfortable with the idea.

"It does sound okay, now, and I would like to be friends with him if he wasn't so angry," he offered. "He was always a lot of fun before."

Mrs. Kaufmann looked right into Ray's eyes and said, "Do you know what Anthony needs to know in order to understand that he has to change?"

"What's that?" Ray answered.

"If he knew that he would lose friends when they get too uncomfortable or feel too unsafe hanging out with him, it might make all the difference. You might be the only one he could hear that from and get it, because you have enjoyed his company up to now, and his anger is the only thing that's changed," Mrs. Kaufmann explained.

"I don't think I can say that, Mrs. Kaufmann," Ray said recoiling in his seat.

"What if I suggested it, and asked if you were feeling that discomfort because of his unpredictable anger? You would only need to nod in agreement, if you felt it rang true. If not, you could shrug your shoulders or just say no. It would be your call," she assured him. "I'll be happy to put it out there so we can address the possibility. It will also lay the groundwork if you decide you really don't want to hang out with him anymore. Sound okay?"

"Oh, yes, I could do that," Ray answered more confidently.

"That's wonderful. Ray, you know you are a really great person. I'm so proud of you to have the courage to face Anthony, knowing you still have a little reserved fear."

Ray smiled shyly. "Thanks," he quietly answered.

"Okay, let's get you back to class," Mrs. Kaufmann said, trying to wrap things up and get going on her day. "Okay, so you're going to just stop in on your way from lunch when it's time to go to recess today, right? I'll bring Anthony in during lunchtime first, so he'll be here when you get here. Anthony and I will talk about how he's doing before you come in. I don't want you to have to give up class time for a friendship issue. That wouldn't be fair to you. You're a good student and you don't deserve to miss anything you'll need. Raymond, don't worry about our talk. You really won't have to say much of anything. Just showing up will make all the difference for both of you, okay?"

"Okay," Ray said, looking relieved and taking the pass Mrs. Kaufmann had just written out for him. "Thanks, Mrs. Kaufmann. See you later."

"Have a great morning, Ray," she said, as he opened the office door and looked into the waiting room filled with students.

"Who's next?" Mrs. Kaufmann asked the students waiting there, while thinking about getting them all off to class as quickly as their problems could be resolved. She thought, *I sure hope I can help Anthony see the need to reach out for help right now. It's all so clear that he could use someone to talk to.*

The Heart-to-Heart Talk

It was almost Anthony's lunch period, so Mrs. Kaufmann headed down to the in-school suspension room so she could invite Anthony to her office to have lunch with her. She knew he was probably so tired of sitting alone, doing work with no one else there but the supervising teacher, that he would be happy for the change of scenery. She also knew his punishment really was a good lesson for him, to make him think twice about fighting on playground.

"Hi, Anthony," she said as she entered the classroom. She saw the suspension teacher, who was quietly working in the far corner of the empty room.

"Is it time for Anthony's lunch?" the teacher asked.

"Yes, and I can keep him with me if you'd like to get some lunch yourself," she offered.

"Absolutely!" she answered. "Thanks. I'll see you back here when this period is over?"

"Sounds good," Mrs. Kaufmann answered. The teacher stood up, grabbed her purse, and left the room. "How are you doing, Anthony? Was your morning kind of long?"

"Boy, was it! I really wished I was in class, believe it or not," he answered.

"I believe it," she answered. "If you're ready for lunch, let's go. I'm sure hungry."

"I am too," Anthony answered, grabbing his lunch bag and heading out the door toward the cafeteria.

Mrs. Kaufmann followed him, saying, "Anthony, once you get your milk and whatever food you need, come right back here to the cafeteria door and meet me. I'll be waiting for you. Then we'll go have lunch together in my office."

"Okay," he said, as he hurried into the cafeteria to get into the milk line. He was feeling temporarily like a free man.

The two met after a few minutes, walked back to Mrs. Kaufmann's office, and set up their food on either side of her desk. They focused on eating and casual conversation at first. Then Mrs. Kaufmann asked Anthony, "How did the morning go for you? Did you get a lot of work done?"

"Yeah, I think I have the whole day's work done and most of my homework for tonight, too. I can't believe I got so much done!" he exclaimed as he ate through his peanut butter and jelly sandwich in a flash.

Mrs. Kaufmann asked Anthony very casually while she nibbled away on her salad, "So what happened yesterday for you to get this suspension?"

"I punched Ray Shanley in the face. I got so mad at him because I thought he deliberately tripped me. I couldn't believe he would do that to me, because we're friends," he said in between sips of his milk.

"You *thought* he tripped you?" Mrs. Kaufmann asked, still eating her salad.

"Yeah, at least I thought that at first. Last night on e-mail, Sean said I was out of line hitting Ray, since he was just playing the game. It made me feel really bad, because I figured Ray wouldn't really try to stop me from getting a goal by tripping me," Anthony admitted.

"Well, that's a good thing that you're able to see it from that angle. Most guys would just stick to their guns and swear they were right. You're a really good person, Anthony, and you are able to admit when you might not be right. That's hard to do. Do you wish you could talk with Ray Shanley, because I've invited him to stop by today during recess to see if he'd like to talk with you," she admitted.

"Yeah, I would like to fix things. I feel bad that I punched him. He's a friend, and I really shouldn't have done that," Anthony told Mrs. Kaufmann.

"That would be good for both of you. I know he would feel better if he knew how you felt," Mrs. Kaufmann suggested. They continued with their lunch and some small talk about school and soccer and basketball. At the end of the lunch period, Mrs. Kaufmann heard a quiet knock at her door. It was Ray Shanley, who looked into her office and saw Anthony cleaning up after his lunch. He waited to see Mrs. Kaufmann's reaction to his being there in order to know whether Anthony was in a good place to talk.

"Oh, come in and join us, Raymond. Anthony and I were just talking about the misunderstanding he had yesterday on the soccer field. I'm sure Anthony could tell you the same thing." Mrs. Kaufmann started up the mediation.

Anthony looked up at Raymond and reacted with surprise. "Oh. Raymond! You have a black eye! Did I do that?" he asked, sounding very apologetic.

"Well, yes, when you punched me," Ray answered evenly, trying not to provoke him.

"Ray, I'm really sorry, man. I thought you had tried to trip me, and I just went crazy because I thought you were my friend," Anthony admitted.

"I *was* your friend," Ray said in his most quiet manner.

Mrs. Kaufmann jumped in, hearing what mmight have been a new problem emerging… the threat of the friendship ending. "You know, you guys are both good people and are friends, too. We all know you two had a misunderstanding. Thank you, Anthony, for apologizing. And thank you, Ray, for coming down to see if you could work this out. I was thinking we need to talk about Anthony's reaction, okay?"

"What do you mean?" Anthony asked.

"Well," Mrs. Kaufmann answered, "I was wondering what made you so angry so fast yesterday? You never used to react like this. And Ray is a friend you enjoy. You don't usually think of him as someone who would want to hurt you, right? What made you jump to that conclusion when it shouldn't have even occurred to you?"

Ray jumped in. "Anthony, I was just trying to get the soccer ball, like just playing the game, you know?"

"I know. Sorry, Ray," Anthony said with embarrassment.

"It's okay. I just don't know why you get so mad at me. You never used to," Ray said.

"I don't know why I've been getting so mad recently, either. I just lose it and can't help it," Anthony confessed.

Mrs. Kaufmann interrupted, "Anthony, I was thinking about that too, and I have some thoughts. Whenever kids are dealing with a lot of 'stuff' that makes life a little harder, they feel uncomfortable and a little angrier. Do you have some things that seem hard in your life right now? And if you'd like Ray to leave, I can let him go out to the playground."

"No, it's okay that he stays, because he knows what's going on for me," Anthony answered.

"So what's going on for you?" Mrs. Kaufmann repeated.

"Well, my dad's in the hospital with cancer, and my mom is always with him. Sometimes she doesn't get home until I'm ready to go to bed. They both say he'll be fine, but it still seems a little scary. I used to talk about it with Danny, my brother, but he's in college now, so I can't," Anthony shared with them both.

"I'm so sorry to hear that, my dear. I'm sure those are changes that make life a lot harder for you this year. Maybe I can help you in some way? I can ask your mom, okay?" Mrs. Kaufmann volunteered.

"I'm fine, Mrs. Kaufmann, but thanks," Anthony answered.

"You can hang out with me at my house when we get home after school, you know?" Ray offered. "I didn't know your mom didn't get home until late. You can have dinner with me and my mom and dad if you want."

"That would be nice, thanks, Ray, but I'm okay at home, really," Anthony said, feeling really grateful.

Mrs. Kaufmann saw the friendship was back, with a whole new understanding. The last change that was needed was for Anthony to see that his anger could cost him friendships. He could actually make people feel too uncomfortable to be with him. "Anthony, I have to ask you something. Last night, when you realized that Ray didn't want to hurt you, did you feel bad about hitting him?"

"Yeah, last night my mom said I'd be lucky if Ray still wanted to be friends with me, and that I was losing my temper enough recently to make everyone not want to be near me. Sorry again, Ray," he added.

"And Ray, do you believe that Anthony realizes now that his anger isn't about you, really?" she asked.

"I can see why now. Sorry, Anthony. I didn't know you had so much going on," Ray spoke sincerely to Anthony.

"And sorry about that shiner," Anthony added.

Ray smiled unexpectedly and laughed. "That's okay. I actually got a whole lot of sympathy today. The bad thing for you is that everyone's saying you go crazy when you get mad. You do, you know."

"Uh, I guess I do. I don't even feel like it's me who's doing it when I lose it. It just happens so fast," Anthony admitted.

Mrs. Kaufmann saw that this was the opportunity to talk to Anthony about going to counseling for a few sessions to deal with this out-of-control anger. She also knew that he had a right to have this discussion privately...without Ray. "Well, guys, I do feel like we're in a good place right now. I also should be letting Ray get out on playground for a little bit of time before he's got to go back to class. Anthony, I know you can't go out on playground today, but maybe you can just stay here with me a while before you have to go back to the suspension room. Sound good?"

Both boys agreed. As Ray got up to leave he said, "See you on the bus, Anthony, and thanks, Mrs. Kaufmann."

"My pleasure!" she answered. "Ray, please close the door as you leave so we don't have anyone listening to us from the waiting room."

Out-of-the Box Thinking

With the click of the door, Mrs. Kaufmann turned to Anthony and said, "I have something to share with you that I didn't want Ray to hear. My feeling is that your anger is more like a rage reaction that feels out of control for you, and I don't want to see it happen anymore. You really could lose your friends, lose your privileges, and lose respect from your parents and teachers. No one wants to be around people who are out of control because they are scary and unpredictable, you know?"

"I know. I got some e-mail from two girls in my class who like Ray. They said I was a really mean bully now." Anthony's voice sounded like it was breaking.

Mrs. Kaufmann quickly jumped in. "Listen, Anthony, there is something you can do to get help. I want to recommend to your mom that you speak to a counselor a few times to talk about the changes in your life, the losses, and your feelings about it all. It would be good for her, too, because she's going through all of these changes, also. I would guess she isn't the same person she was before, either?"

"She's been crying a lot and gets mad at me for everything I do, it seems. She was really mad last night, and I got grounded for a week. Ever since Grandma died, she's been so sad to have lost her mom. Then Danny went to college and Dad got sick, so I don't think she'll have time to take me anywhere."

"Well, I can suggest it, and we'll see what she can do, okay? Are you willing to go?" she asked.

"What does this person do?" Anthony asked, looking anxious.

"Well, the counselor will sit with you, like we are now, and talk with you so you can understand and manage your feelings. Once you can manage them, those uncontrolled outbursts should stop. You'll be back in control and back to the great Anthony we all know and love," she said as she smiled kindly so he wouldn't feel like this idea was a punishment.

"Are those people nice?" Anthony checked.

"They wouldn't have decided to work with kids if they didn't enjoy helping them. They also know if you're uncomfortable, you would have a hard time talking with them, and that would make their jobs harder. So, yes, they are nice people," Mrs. Kaufmann answered confidently.

"I don't think my mom has any time to go anywhere, though. She's with my dad every day on her way home from work, so she doesn't get home till late," Anthony claimed.

"Some counselors might have appointments on Saturdays, or your mom and dad might be willing to give up one visit one night a week. Maybe your mom and you could go to an appointment after she comes home from work, and then from there you can go with her to the hospital. If you can't go upstairs in the hospital to see your dad, she can go up to see him while you do your homework in the waiting room. I'm sure you can all figure it out. I just know counseling will help you and your mom so much that it will be really worth it," Mrs. Kaufmann assured him.

"Will you tell my mom?" Anthony asked.

"Yes, I'll call her this afternoon while you're in the suspension room. Can she take calls at work?" Mrs. Kaufmann checked.

"Yes, she has her own phone at her desk in her own office, and I call her all the time," he answered.

"Great. As for you, you need to wash up after lunch, so I'll give you a pass to the bathroom and then come back here. I want to walk with you back to your suspension classroom so I can make sure your teacher is back from lunch, too."

Anthony was back in no time, and the two of them walked to the suspension room. Once Mrs. Kaufmann saw the teacher was there and ready for the afternoon, she turned to Anthony and said, "They will call for you from the main office at the end of the school day. That's when you'll meet with Mr. Stein and your mom and me. We'll all know more about the counseling at that time."

"Okay, thanks." Anthony went into the room, and the door closed behind him. Mrs. Kaufmann then went back to her office and called his mother's work phone number.

"Hello, Mrs. Barrows?" Mrs. Kaufmann asked when she heard a woman answer.

"Yes, it is. Who is this?" she asked.

"It's Mrs. Kaufmann, Anthony's school counselor."

"Oh, yes. I'm glad you called. Did you have a chance to speak with him today yet?" Mrs. Barrows asked quickly and then continued, "I do want you to know that he was punished at home, too. I am so sorry he seems to be losing it recently. I just don't know what's gotten into him. I can understand he's not dealing well with his dad in the hospital, but to be hitting his best friend just doesn't make sense to me."

Mrs. Kaufmann assured her she had spoken with Anthony. "We not only talked about his behavior, but I was also able to have him talk with Ray. That worked out well, and they understand each other now. The only problem is that Anthony has realized that when he loses it, he really isn't himself. This is upsetting to him now, because he not only dislikes being out of control, but he also realizes he's losing friends and respect because of it."

"I know. Last night I was really angry with him, and when I started to ask him to tell me why he hit Ray, he just shut down. He's never done that before. I'm not sure what to do anymore, and my plate is full, so I don't have a lot of patience. I just grounded him for a week, and I don't really believe that's going to help him with his anger either," Mrs. Barrows admitted.

"Well, I know you both could use some help with all the changes and losses you've both dealt with recently. Anthony doesn't know how to handle these emotions with the loss of his grandmother, his brother leaving for college, his dad in the hospital, and you needing to be with your husband after work. He didn't even realize his anger could be coming from all this. One suggestion is that he gets some help through counseling, and I've already told Anthony I was going to call you and let you know that. Do you think this is something you can do right now?" Mrs. Kaufmann asked.

"Oh, I don't know. I would have to check my insurance plan to see what they cover, but I will find out. I'm also not sure when I would find the time with my husband in the hospital, but I'll figure that out, too."

"That would be the perfect help for him right now, since it's the most direct and quickest way to turn things around. You might also want an opportunity to talk with someone, too, just to help you deal with all the feelings you must have as well…just a thought," Mrs. Kaufmann added.

"Oh, I know I need something!" Mrs. Barrows agreed immediately. "I'll see what I can do, and thank you for seeing Anthony today and helping the boys save their friendship. Oh, and by the way, do you think I should be grounding him?"

"Well, just so you know, his day here has been pretty uncomfortable so far. We don't make suspension fun at all, so I'm sure by the end of the day of sitting with one teacher alone in a room, and working for six hours with no play should be punishment enough. The only person he talked to today was me and a little bit with Ray, so that's really bad," she added sympathetically.

Mrs. Kaufmann continued, "I also think Anthony really needs the exercise and the happy connection with other kids by playing outside after school. The problem is, once you give a punishment, it's generally not good to go back on your word unless the circumstances are really unusual. So, if you can make a counseling appointment, it would validate that this is not your everyday situation. Then, you can tell him you've decided not to ground him after all, because things have been so challenging for both of you, and you've learned that today's punishment was hard enough. That way, he'll see that you are fair in your decisions, but that you are still in control, not him. With that said, he shouldn't expect you'd take a punishment back next time in a normal situation. Does that sound reasonable to you?"

"Yes, and I'm relieved. I didn't know how I was going to monitor his after-school grounding anyway, with my being gone and all," Mrs. Barrows admitted. "As it is, I just have my next-door neighbor 'keeping an eye out' for him. He used to go to my mother's house a couple blocks away after school, but after she passed last spring, my neighbor found out and offered to just be available. She's a grandma who doesn't drive much anymore, so she's usually home. She has always really liked Anthony, too. She doesn't have any grandchildren locally, so she says she's happy to help us out. We're really lucky to have her."

"Does he go there to check in every day when he gets home and for dinner?" Mrs. Kaufmann asked. "I'm just thinking that Anthony has lost four available connections after school and throughout that dinnertime part of the day…his grandmother, his brother, his dad, and you. Is it possible to arrange it for him to go check in with that neighbor after school every day? He could play outside from there and feel like someone is looking out for him, just in case he gets hurt or anything. Then, if you supplied his dinners, do you think she would mind enjoying time with him until you get home at night? I don't know, maybe this is a crazy idea for your circumstances, but I'm trying to think out of the box. My guess is that you would feel better about his safety, and he would have someone to talk to. That way, your attention to your husband in the hospital would be spent knowing Anthony was well taken care of," Mrs. Kaufmann suggested. "Being free on the streets after school until dark is the worst time of day for kids. And to have a lack of accountability…well, that's when the risk-taking opportunities are the highest, so that trouble can easily find them."

Mrs. Barrows quickly reacted, "You know, I have been terribly worried. I kept saying to myself that because he was old enough to babysit now, he should be old enough to be by himself. The thought of him getting hurt and having to get to Mrs. Paolini's house felt like a stretch, but I also knew he played basketball with Raymond Shanley and figured his mom was also always home at dinnertime. It's just so hard when I have to be at the hospital every day after work," Mrs. Barrows explained.

"I can just imagine how draining that worry can be with all the rest that you are juggling. Do you think Mrs. Paolini would be a willing temporary 'substitute grandma' for Anthony?" Mrs. Kaufmann asked.

"You know, she always asks us to come in for some iced tea because she's lonely, and I'm always too busy. She also could use the extra money for sure, because she lives on a pretty tight budget since her husband died. That might be really good for all of us. Plus my husband has been worried about his 'little man,' and he doesn't need that while he's dealing with chemotherapy." Mrs. Barrows' energy was definitely picking up.

"Sounds like a good plan. Do you think Anthony will like the idea?" Mrs. Kaufmann asked.

"I don't think he'll want his new-found freedom taken away at first, but he does like her, and he knows she likes him. You're right, with all the missing people in his life, he does need to feel a sense of caring and protection when he gets home from school these days. Up to now I've just had him making that call to me from the house, to check in as soon as he got home, so I would know he made it home okay. He does need more than that, at least while his dad is in the hospital," Mrs. Barrows answered, thinking about how comforting that idea was.

"I must also tell you that we offer a district-wide, after-school program for our students, but it's mostly for the younger kids. Our middle-school students sometimes feel embarrassed going there unless we set something up where he would be the older, volunteer-type student-helper. I just don't think he needs to add more responsibility to his plate," Mrs. Kaufmann told her.

"Well, I have to get going. I'm so glad you called, and I feel better about Anthony. I'll check on the insurance coverage for outside counseling, and I'll stop in to talk with Mrs. Paolini when I pick up Anthony from his in-school suspension. I understand we need to talk with Mr. Stein before he can be released today.

It's a type of 'debriefing' with you and the school psychologist, I understand? Oh, boy. I'd better get moving if I'm going to leave early, too. Okay, let me talk to you later, Mrs. Kaufmann, and thanks for your help," Mrs. Barrows said with a sudden stirring of motivation now to get on with her phone calls coming in and her time running out.

"You're so welcome. Good luck with all of the arrangements. If you need any recommendations, I can help you with that. And I'll definitely try to talk with Mr. Stein this afternoon, so he knows about all that you're doing for Anthony. That may make the post-suspension conference move along a little faster, too. Have a great day," Mrs. Kaufmann said quickly to get off the phone and let Mrs. Barrows get back to work.

Good plan, she thought. *I sure hope she can get Anthony and herself into counseling.*

A Plan with a Twist

The afternoon proceeded to fly by with a sixth-grade teachers' team meeting, a fourth-grade Peer Leadership Outreach program, and an eighth-grade assembly, at which Mrs. Kaufmann did her annual explanation of the required community service volunteer hours. It was suddenly the end of the day, and she had to race down to the vice-principal's office to let Mr. Stein know what she and Anthony's mother had discussed.

Just as she hurriedly approached the main office door, she saw Mrs. Barrows being buzzed in through the main front doors of the school. "Hi, Mrs. Barrows, looks like we're both heading to the same place. I never got a chance to talk with Mr. Stein this afternoon after all. How did you make out with the insurance company?" she asked.

"Oh, I didn't have much luck. Their acceptable amount leaves us with a lot to cover on our own. I did call my husband, who is a little concerned about the cost with all of our medical expenses right now, so I didn't pursue it. I don't want to worry him. Plus I want to pay Mrs. Paolini for her time, too, so we'll have to see what we can do," Mrs. Barrows answered, sounding rather stressed and disappointed.

As they sat down in the office waiting area for the meeting with Mr. Stein, the school psychologist, Mrs. White, walked into the waiting area as well. Mrs. Kaufmann introduced Mrs. White to Mrs. Barrows. In less than a minute, Mr. Stein's office door opened, and he appeared in the doorway.

"Oh, good, we have everyone here, so we can get started. I'll have my secretary call for Anthony to gather his belongings and come to the waiting area while we have our chance to talk first. Then we will include him in the second part of our discussion and go from there. Has everyone met one another?"

"Yes," Mrs. Kaufmann replied, "I just introduced them. Mrs. Barrows and I had a chance to talk today as well, right after I spoke with Anthony, and that was right after we had a little conflict resolution with Raymond."

"How did that go?" Mr. Stein jumped in.

"It went very well, actually. I was working with two great kids who really didn't want to be angry with each other. They have an understanding now, which makes it better than before."

As they all sat down, Mrs. White asked to be filled in. "I'm just wondering what exactly happened yesterday, Mrs. Kaufmann. What was the suspension for?"

"Well, Anthony Barrows thought his friend, Raymond Shanley, tripped him on purpose while playing soccer. Ray was just trying to get the ball and said Anthony tripped over his extended foot, and then Anthony hit him in the face. As he was about to hit him again, Ray pushed him away, hard, and Anthony fell down. That was when Mrs. Tanner spotted the scuffle and brought Ray to the nurse and Anthony here."

Mr. Stein then asked Mrs. Kaufmann, "Did Anthony understand what he did and apologize to Ray?"

"Yes, he realized it at night when a couple of girls e-mailed him and called him a mean bully. That hurt, and my guess is that's when he shut down on you, Mrs. Barrows. He was digesting all of this and was feeling bad for what he had done, and to his friend," Mrs. Kaufmann explained.

Mrs. Barrows reacted quickly. "That makes perfect sense now when I think about it. He was so not himself last night. I wasn't either, though, and I interpreted him as being angry and uncooperative, so of course I grounded him for a week. I guess I just couldn't take any more after the day I had, either."

Mrs. Kaufmann spoke next to get right to where she and Mrs. Barrows left off earlier. She needed to shorten all the time it would take for the vice-principal, the school psychologist, and Anthony's mom to cover all the ground they already covered.

"Mrs. Barrows' husband is in the hospital right now, and he's in the middle of receiving chemotherapy. Her mom, Anthony's grandmother, who lived locally and was active in their lives, died suddenly last spring, and Anthony's older brother Danny moved out of the home in August to start college. So, needless to say, Anthony's anger comes from an understandable place. He admits he doesn't even know what's happening when the rage takes over and he feels out of control. I've suggested counseling and Mrs. Barrows is looking into her insurance plans, but is dealing with large medical bills and a new expense for child care after school. I also hoped Mrs. Barrows could have some sessions herself, just because she is being torn between her job, visiting her husband in the hospital, and being home for Anthony, which is all very stressful."

There was silence for a few seconds while Mrs. White and Mr. Stein absorbed all that information. Mr. Stein spoke first. "Well, that does take a bit of a turn in my thinking about Anthony. I wasn't aware of all he had on his plate. The in-school suspension had to happen because it's the school policy for fighting, but I have a whole lot more compassion for your situation right now."

Mrs. White then offered her help. "Mrs. Barrows, I would be happy to meet with Anthony here before school on Tuesday mornings, if you can bring him in then. That way he'd get to know me, and he'll have Mrs. Kaufmann and me to turn to if he needs to talk with someone during the school day."

"Oh, that would be so great. Thank you. I would be happy to drop him off before school on my way to work. I hate leaving him at home in the morning half awake and hoping he gets off okay. I know he's old enough, but it's still difficult for both of us right now."

"No problem," Mrs. White said with a warm smile.

Mr. Stein asked, "Are you home when Anthony gets home from school?"

"No, I have been going to the hospital after work, so he just checks in with me by phone and plays outside. He can't have friends in, and he has a neighbor lady he can go to, but that's not a good situation, either. Mrs. Kaufmann suggested I ask an elderly neighbor, who is right next door, if she would be responsible for Anthony, from when he gets to her house after school to when I come home. I'm going to ask her when we leave here today."

Mrs. White broke into the conversation with support for the idea. "I think that idea is much better for him than being left on his own, even if he's not too thrilled with the idea. Freedom after school is an invitation for whatever presents itself, including risk-taking behavior."

Mrs. Barrows immediately replied, "Anthony really likes her. It's like she's a 'substitute grandma' right now, as Mrs. Kaufmann called her. I think my husband and I will feel a lot better about him, too."

Mr. Stein then concluded, "I think we have a great plan. Mrs. Kaufmann, did you say you had a chat with him today about anger management?"

"I did, and he's even willing to go to counseling to feel more in control of his emotions," she answered, "so Mrs. White, Anthony should be very cooperative for your appointments."

"Yes, that will be really helpful for us. Thank you again," Mrs. Barrows said to Mrs. White.

Mr. Stein then stood up to open his office door and said, "I'll go get Anthony and bring him in now."

As Mr. Stein returned, Anthony walked through the door with him and looked quite uncomfortable seeing his mom, the school psychologist, and the school counselor all looking at him. He sat down quietly by his mother, and Mr. Stein addressed everyone. "Well, we all know why we're here. Anthony's in-school suspension was the requirement for anyone who fights on playground, and that's what happened with you, young man. Do you think you will be doing that again?" he said sternly, looking at Anthony, who was looking at him as respectfully as he could.

"No, I won't," he answered.

"Okay, then. Your punishment is done, and that's in the past now. Tomorrow we start a new day, okay?" Mr. Stein wanted Anthony to feel closure on this event. "I also understand you made it right with Raymond, and I'm proud of you for that."

"Thank you," Anthony said with a small smile. He was feeling a little better with the way this was going now.

"Anthony, Mrs. White has offered to help you feel more comfortable with your emotions one morning a week, and Mrs. Kaufmann will be available during the school day if you have anything you want to talk about with her. Does that sound it will work for you?" Mr. Stein asked.

"Yes, thank you," he said to Mr. Stein. Anthony then turned to his mother. "I'm sorry, Mom."

Mrs. Barrows immediately took his hand and said, "It's okay, honey. We'll get some help, and we'll get through this just fine. You know how Mrs. Paolini always asks for us to stop in and visit? Well, when we leave here we're going there. I'm going to ask her if she would want to be your grandma-type person for when I'm not home after school. I'd like you to be able to go to a warm, safe house with someone happy to see you, instead of our empty house. What do you think?" she asked Anthony.

He lit up. "Really? She always offers me cookies and is so nice."

"I'm so glad you like her," Mrs. Barrows said with relief, "and that will make things much easier on me now that your father and I know that you are cared for and happy." She then looked at Mr. Stein to see what else needed to be done.

He immediately responded with his conclusion. "I think we've all had a good meeting today with some plans that will certainly help everyone, don't you think so, Anthony?"

"I do," he answered, sitting up straight in his chair.

"I also wish you good luck today with your neighbor, Mrs. Barrows. She sounds like the perfect caregiver," Mr. Stein continued. "And Mrs. White, you and Mrs. Barrows will need to connect in order to plan Anthony's first appointment." Mr. Stein then ended the meeting, saying, "Mrs. Barrows, and Anthony, tomorrow is a new day, and it can be a really good one!"

Mrs. Kaufmann threw in one more comment for Anthony's benefit as they were all getting up to leave the office. "The most important thing is that Anthony feels like the old Anthony again – just wiser. Ray will be happy when he's back, too," she said with a wink at Anthony, who then gave a big smile.

Mrs. Barrows thanked everyone, and quickly left the school, with Anthony behind her, moving at a happy gait. The others also all moved toward their offices. Mrs. Kaufmann was happy they would now have Mrs. White to talk to, and at a much more convenient time than they had talked about, with no added expense. Plus, the fact that Anthony might be going home to someone after school sounded so right for him now. He needed to feel connected and important to someone who cared for him when his family was not available. The plan was different than what was discussed before the meeting, but it was now even better. Mrs. Kaufmann knew to trust the process!

Discussion Points:

- Stored-up anger often emerges in different places under stressful conditions.

- When someone becomes very angry with you over what seems to be nothing, it may be nothing you did wrong, or just a misunderstanding. Try to have a talk to clear the air.

- When you feel any extreme emotion in a way that feels out of control, reach out to a trusted adult to let them know. Allow help from professionals, because you haven't had the professional training to understand the causes or the solutions for yourself.

Reflection Questions:

1. Were you expecting Anthony to realize and admit he was wrong about being tripped? Would you have been willing to do that?

2. What do you expect from a close friendship that's different from your other relationships? Does that mean it would hurt more if you didn't get what you expect from a friend?

3. When someone hurts you, is it hard to listen to that person explain why? What kind of thinking do you have to do to really hear them with understanding?

4. What did you feel for Anthony when the girls thought of him as a mean bully?

5. Do you ever get so angry that you feel out of control? How would you feel about going to talk to a counselor outside of your school?

6. Do you ever pretend to be friends with people you don't want as friends just because it's hard to separate from them? Would you have stayed friends with Anthony?

CHAPTER 12:
What Makes Her Want to Hurt Me?

A Little Birdie

"You have to go to class, Sheila! Playground time is almost over. What are you going to do, stay sitting on the girls' room floor for the rest of the day crying?" Janet pleaded with her crying friend. "We've been in here almost all playground period, and they have to be looking for us. We could get into so much trouble! Here's a tissue; dry your eyes and let's slip outside before the recess bell rings."

Sheila cried a little harder at the thought of going "out there." "I'm so embarrassed. I just want to crawl into a hole and disappear – forever! Why did someone want to hurt me like that?" she sobbed. "That is so mean!"

"I don't know, but we have to go," Janet persisted.

"You go, I'm staying. I can't face everyone who thinks I kissed Greg at your party on Saturday. That was so mean for someone to say that to everyone. And Greg, oh, I can't even imagine how embarrassed or even angry he must be. He probably thought I was the one who made that up. Oh, God, I don't know how I can ever face him again!" Sheila's voice trailed off, groaning as she began to cry again, but even harder than before.

"I have to go, Sheila. I can't get into any more trouble. My mom's mad at me already for staying up past bedtime last night. Why don't you go to Mrs. Kaufmann's guidance office? She'll let you finish crying there, and she'll even call Mr. Jackson to tell him she's got you," Janet suggested as she gathered her lunch bag and jacket.

"I can't do that either. What if, when Mrs. Kaufmann calls Mr. Jackson, he insists I come to class and she has to send me with these red eyes and red face? I would have to walk into a room with everyone looking at me and thinking I was kissing Greg at your party, or that I made that up and started that rumor. I am too, too, too embarrassed!" Sheila said, with no intention of leaving.

"There's the playground bell! I have to go. If you stay here all afternoon and don't get caught, I'll see you after school and we'll walk home together, okay?" Janet offered.

"Okay, thanks, Janet. You are such a great friend," Sheila called after her, as she left the girls' room in a hurry. She headed straight for Mrs. Kaufmann's office and knocked at her door. "Mrs. Kaufmann?" she called through the door. "Can I talk to you for a second, really fast?"

The door opened, and Mrs. Kaufmann was on the phone. She saw Janet looked troubled, so she asked the person she had just called if she minded being put on hold for a minute. The person was agreeable, and Mrs. Kaufmann pressed the "hold" button and looked at Janet. "What's wrong, my dear?"

"It's not me, Mrs. Kaufmann. It's Sheila Trentacosta. She's in the bathroom crying and is too embarrassed to come out. I stayed with her all recess, but now I'm afraid I'll get in trouble, and I know she will. She's just too petrified to be seen, and she thinks if she comes here, Mr. Jackson will insist she come to class."

Mrs. Kaufmann got back on the phone, taking it off hold and asking, "Do you mind if I call you back? I have a situation I really need to take care of right now." There were a few more comments and then she hung up, writing a reminder down on her "to-do" list.

"Okay, now what happened to make Sheila so upset?" Mrs. Kaufmann asked as she quickly turned back to Janet.

"Well, there was a rumor about her kissing someone at my party this past weekend. Nothing like that happened at all, but I guess some kids who didn't come to my party are spreading the rumor, and now it's all over the school. Sheila would never ever do that, plus the party was called Birthday Olympics with a lot of games and prizes, and all outside with parents all around. It just wasn't like what everybody's saying. I know you've helped me before, and I hope you can help her now. I just feel terrible for her," Janet explained.

"Thank you so much for being a good friend. I will take it from here, and not to worry. I don't send students back to class before they're ready. I do have to ask you to do something for me, though. Every time you hear someone pass that rumor, make sure you say that it's not true. In fact, I suggest that you spread the word that you know for a fact that this is a made-up rumor that is not true, and if you feel comfortable, add that it's unkind to want to hurt her reputation. Would you be willing to do that for her?" Mrs. Kaufmann asked.

"Sure, I can do that for her. I can talk to people when we change classes in the halls, and then I can use social media tonight. The only problem is that we're really good friends, and people may not believe me. They'll think I'm just sticking up for her, so they won't spread my message around. Anyway, I'll try. Now I'd better go so I'm not too late for Mr. Jackson's class," Janet said as she looked at the clock.

"You are a really good person, Janet. Thank you again. Would you please get Sheila's missed work and homework for her and bring it here after school?" Mrs. Kaufmann said to her. Janet agreed and then left the office, doing a sprint down the hall to class.

Mrs. Kaufmann grabbed her keys and left her office, locking the door behind her. She went down to the girls' room and went in, finding Sheila sitting on the floor in the back corner of the room.

Sheila looked startled and jumped to her feet saying, "Uh, hi, Mrs. Kaufmann, uh, I was just…."

"It's okay, Sheila. A little birdie told me you were here and crying. I've come to bring you back to my office so we can talk and fix this problem. Everything can be fixed, you know?" Mrs. Kaufmann assured her. She spoke fast in order to save Sheila from making up an excuse that she'd later have to admit making up.

Mrs. Kaufmann waited for her to grab her jacket and lunch bag, while she chatted to ease her discomfort and break the silence. "I heard there was another one of those embarrassing kissing or boyfriend rumors again today, and I know how awful it can be to be the victim of one of them. When I was about your age, they said I liked a boy in my class that no one liked. His name was Harry and I will never forget him. He always annoyed the girls during recess. I had a crush on another boy, Tommy, who I thought was so nice and funny and cool, and who my friends said liked me back. But there was a girl who had a crush on Tommy too, so she didn't like me. Anyway, she told everyone I liked Harry. The girls laughed really hard or gave a big cringing 'ewww' when they were told. I felt bad for Harry because of all the 'ewwwing,' if you know what I mean." Mrs. Kaufmann gave a giggle as she relayed the story of her horrible day.

Sheila actually giggled back, mostly because the thought of Mrs. Kaufmann being a little girl and liking a boy struck her funny. "Did that Tommy stop liking you?" she asked as they walked back to the guidance office.

"No--well, I don't know. The first week or so he couldn't look at me at all, and I couldn't look at him.

It was really uncomfortable, and I figured he thought there was something wrong with me if I liked Harry. I wasn't old enough to date or hang on the phone with a boy, so I had no way to know for sure. It just seemed like he didn't like me anymore, because he was avoiding me so much. Then, later on that summer, we happened to be in the same summer camp, and we ended up talking and then having a good laugh about it. He admitted he was embarrassed whenever he heard his name used as the boy I really did like. He said he just didn't know how to act or what to say. Then he also admitted how embarrassed he was for me. He figured it wasn't true because Harry upset everyone with his dirty clothes and no manners. That one mean comment made it seem like there was a huge elephant standing right between us for the whole rest of the year, and we just couldn't even talk about it," Mrs. Kaufmann shared with Sheila, who now was all wrapped up in the story.

"Okay, we're here. You can put your things down while I call Mr. Jackson and let him know you're with me," Mrs. Kaufmann told Sheila as she punched in that teacher's extension on the key pad.

"I won't have to go back, yet, right?" Sheila instantly checked, with raised anxiety.

"Oh. No. Not yet. We have some work to do to get to the bottom of this rumor-telling and gossip-spreading," Mrs. Kaufmann assured her.

"Phew, thank you. I just can't face them, and I know Janet will get all my work for me. I keep thinking about what they're thinking about me, and my face gets really hot instantly. In fact, it feels like it's on fire," Sheila said very seriously. The happy "walk-'n'-talk" with her counselor was suddenly gone, and now she felt right back in her terrible embarrassment.

"Mr. Jackson? It's Mrs. Kaufmann. I have Sheila Trentacosta with me right now. There was an incident on the playground, and some problems have resulted from it that we're going to have to work on together now. At the end of your class, would you mind giving Janet Merlotta any classwork and homework that Sheila missed? I'll have Janet give it to Sheila after school. I'll be happy to go over it with Sheila if she needs any instruction."

Mrs. Kaufmann didn't really ask if this was okay with him. She knew she wasn't about to have Sheila go back to that humiliation, and Sheila could hear that clearly. Sheila then settled into her seat as the two adults finished up the call.

"Okay then. It's time to get to the bottom of this rumor-telling nonsense!" Mrs. Kaufmann spoke in a rather business-like way. Sheila could tell the school counselor took her embarrassment seriously. She continued, "I have such a problem with a student, or anybody for that matter, who thinks it will be fun to embarrass someone else. In all my years of paying attention to how teasing affects people, I have discovered one basic rule. If you tease *with* someone because he or she is your friend and it brings you closer together, then it's okay. But if you're not friends, and the teasing isn't meant to help you bond or enjoy each other's company, then it's most definitely not okay! Kids think if it makes people laugh, then they are funny, but that is very selfish thinking. In those cases, it's all about the teasers trying to appear clever or witty at the expense of others. That is clearly self-serving and unkind. And, if the teasers actually *try* to embarrass others, then that is definitely mean-spirited. So tell me what happened and we'll begin to fix things for you."

The Work

"Well, I came to school all happy this morning because the weekend was so much fun and Janet's party was, too," Sheila relayed. "It was a Birthday Olympics party with a lot of games, and she invited a lot of people from school from our class, but not that many people from other classes. When we went to gym class right before lunch today, everybody in the locker room was talking about the party. When I got changed and went into the gym for class, I noticed a lot of people looking at me and laughing. There were some people actually staring at me during class, and I kept looking at my clothes, thinking I didn't zip or button something. Then, when I went back to class to get my lunch and line up to go to the cafeteria, I felt like it was still happening in the hall. No one was walking *with* me, just looking *at* me. It was so weird."

"That must've been really uncomfortable," Mrs. Kaufmann commented.

"You have no idea. Then, when we got outside, Janet ran up to me and told me that everyone was saying I kissed Greg at the party, and she asked me if I was all right." Sheila's voice broke into sobs and she moaned, "I just can't face any of those kids again. I just want to go home!"

Mrs. Kaufmann immediately jumped in, "I really understand, Sheila. That sounds like a nightmare, so I don't blame you for wanting to just run away. But the thing is, you can't. We need to face the problem. Everyone knows that not handling it is not the best way to handle it, if you know what I mean. For rumors and gossip, we need to get the truth out there, and I've actually talked with Janet and know she's willing to do that this afternoon and on the internet tonight."

"Oh, good!" Sheila reacted immediately. "Do you think everyone will know it wasn't true by tomorrow?"

"I don't know about that, but there's a good chance most people will know what Janet is saying about it by tomorrow, just by social media and talking on the phone. I always say that starting a rumor among students your age is like taking one big match and lighting a dry prairie. You get an almost instant prairie fire in only one recess. But once the fire burns out and the newness of the telling is over, there isn't that much you can do. I just hope the truth or correction is as interesting to pass along as the rumor was."

"Me, too," Sheila mumbled, with a bit of hopelessness in her voice.

"Oh, don't get me wrong. There are other things we can do, my dear," Mrs. Kaufmann offered in response to Sheila's saddened tone. "First of all, you and Janet should easily get your friends who went to the party to pass along their comments that this rumor was really not true. They just need to find out that all the guests were busy outside together and mixed in with all the parents. They only need to picture it all out in the open, and then that rumor just wouldn't make sense. Plus the fact that you became so embarrassed at the very thought of it says how unlikely it was to happen. Then add the fact that Greg is out there telling his friends that it never happened, too. Once their friends tell their friends, then that should about do it."

"Yeah, that's true," Sheila admitted, and her voice had a hint of relief.

"The other thing you can do is to trace it all backward, though that is a bit more challenging. Most people are afraid of getting their friends into trouble, so they may not want to tell you who told them. It has to be done with the intent to find who really thought it was true in the first place. When you ask each person, you tell them that you want the one who started the rumor to realize that you aren't like that," Mrs. Kaufmann suggested.

Sheila asked, "So, if Janet was to go to the person who told her and asked who she heard it from, and continue with the detective work, she might find out the name of the 'rumor- starter'?"

"Hopefully the whisper-down-the-line chain isn't too long. You never know. Maybe there just was a misunderstanding of what one person said to another, ending up in a series of changes all along the way. Maybe no one wanted to hurt you. What if everyone was just passing it along with innocent changes? That's always another possibility, but unfortunately, it still has the same embarrassing result."

"That's true," Sheila perked up. "I mean about it not being on purpose. That makes me feel a little better. I was thinking that there was someone out there who wanted to hurt me."

Mrs. Kaufmann continued with the possibility that it wasn't on purpose. "Actually, when kids make up rumors about who likes whom, or who kissed whom, they do it because it's kind of a thrill for them to do the matchmaking. It's as if just imagining it with another person makes them both have a good time, never even thinking about the embarrassment that could result. They don't see it as mean or bad, because it's about a good thing…kissing represents *liking* someone. To many kids, that's just an innocent attempt for a shared giggle."

"I guess so," Sheila said thoughtfully.

"And here's the truth. All students really love to talk about everybody and what they're doing at one time or another, because they are all doing interesting things, right? Like anyone kissing someone is definitely an interesting topic, don't you think?" Mrs. Kaufmann giggled.

Sheila giggled back. She seemed to be feeling much better about it all now.

"Okay, here's my question to you. Were most of the kids in your class at that party and therefore would know it's not true?" Mrs. Kaufmann asked Sheila.

"The class I'm in this afternoon, yes. Most of them were there. Just a couple of boys in my class weren't invited, because Janet told her mom they weren't nice to her. It was mostly kids in the other class that we have gym with in the morning who were giggling at me." Sheila explained.

"So, if you go back to class this afternoon, everyone there will know in their hearts that it was not at all likely that the rumor is true, right?"

"Uh, I guess so," Sheila admitted reluctantly.

"And we know that Janet was going back to your class after lunch to tell everyone that the rumor was definitely not true, and that whoever was making it up was being unkind or misheard what happened. That means you're safe to go back there today, at least. Then after the buzz spreads through social media tonight, the rest of your grade should have the news of you being innocent, right?" Mrs. Kaufmann smiled.

"I hope so," Sheila answered, sounding quite a bit more positive.

"Then do you think you can get back to class this afternoon?" Mrs. Kaufmann asked.

"Yes, and I'm supposed to have a quiz on the fifty states of the US in my next class today. My mom quizzed me last night and I remembered all fifty of them then, but I just don't know if I still know them anymore after all this today," Sheila explained.

"Why don't I do a little practice with you here, so you can see if you're ready? I know you don't have your afternoon books with you, but I have a map of the US, and I can hold it far away so you can't see the words as I point at each state, okay?"

"Okay." Sheila perked up. She was a good student, and Mrs. Kaufmann knew she just needed her confidence back, a change of topic, and motivation to get back to class. The two of them went through the whole map without one error. "I can do it!" Sheila exclaimed when she was done.

"Are you ready to get back to class and get that 100% you've worked for?" Mrs. Kaufmann asked with a big grin.

"Yes, I'm ready. Thanks, Mrs. Kaufmann."

"I'm giving you a hall pass, and I'd also like to add a private note to Mr. Jackson. I want him to know that you were dealing with a rumor and to make sure you're okay this afternoon. Is that all right with you?" Mrs. Kaufmann checked.

"Yes, thanks, I'd appreciate that." Sheila agreed.

"I was going to let him know that Greg needs watching-out-for too, since he was also a victim of a rumor. I'd hate to think he was as embarrassed as you were, but was too uncomfortable to do anything about it but suffer through it," Mrs. Kaufmann offered.

"Me, too," Sheila said quietly. "What do I do about Greg and me in the same class today?"

"You don't have to do anything. Let's face it. You will have some discomfort in life occasionally, but this time you didn't do anything wrong, and you don't have to apologize for what others thought was funny.

It's like standing on the edge of a beach. Sometimes a big wave suddenly washes over you. You weren't prepared for it, and you're a little shook up if it knocks you over and tumbles you around, leaving you a little salty. But in the end, it was just a wave, and you're fine. You shower off the salt later, and go on living a little smarter and a little stronger. Just think of all you learned today!" Mrs. Kaufmann said in an upbeat way, handing Sheila the pass for her to get back to class.

"Thanks, Mrs. Kaufmann," Sheila said. She then took the note, gathered her lunch bag and jacket, and walked out of the room feeling much better than when she had walked in.

Now...Greg

Shortly after Sheila's repair session was over, Mrs. Kaufmann was checking her message board outside her office in the waiting room. She also checked her e-mail and voice mail to see if there was anyone else waiting to see her. After all, Mrs. Kaufmann knew this was now playground time for the next two grade levels, and all of the playground shifts always had great potential for some excellent social and emotional lessons. There was one e-mail that caught her eye and sounded more urgent than the rest. It was from Mr. Jackson. His e-mail message simply said, "Got your note. Please call me when you get a chance. Thanks."

Mrs. Kaufmann immediately picked up the phone and called him. Sitting at his desk and seeing her office number come up on his phone, Mr. Jackson answered quickly. "Hi. Mrs. Kaufmann, I have to speak softly since I've just started the students on their geography quiz. I can't say a whole lot because the room is so quiet they might hear, but I need you to know something."

"Yes, you can code whatever you need to tell me or ask, and I'll decipher with you," Mrs. Kaufmann offered.

"Good, thanks," Mr. Jackson said, relieved that she understood his dilemma.

"Is it about the rumor?" Mrs. Kaufmann offered.

"Yes," he answered.

"About Sheila or Greg?" she continued.

"Yes, the second name," he said in a whisper.

Mrs. Kaufmann continued with the prompting. "Is Greg upset?"

"Yes, thank you!" Mr. Jackson said as if the guessing game had arrived at the finish line earlier than he expected.

"Should we wait for after the quiz so the others don't suspect, and he isn't even more traumatized?" Mrs. Kaufmann suggested.

"Perfect timing," Mr. Jackson answered cryptically. "How or when do you suggest?"

"Wait until the quiz is over and the students stand up to take their break. What special do they go to after the quiz?" Mrs. Kaufmann asked.

"Art," he answered.

"Perfect. Just hand him a book or whatever to drop off at my office on his way there, since my office is on the way. Then, when he stops in, I'll strike up a conversation with him and give him a chance to talk about it if he wants to. If he's worked it through and doesn't want to talk about it, then he can keep going to art with no one even noticing. Sound good?" Mrs. Kaufmann asked. "Oh, and I just have to tell you that Janet was Sheila's dear friend who came to me for help even though she knew it might make her late for class. No need to say anything, but I'd hate to see her get in any trouble."

"Good to know, thanks, and no, she won't," he quietly said, and hung up.

Mrs. Kaufmann called Mrs. Trentacosta, Sheila's mother, at her office. A message said she was out to lunch, so she left a voice mail just to make sure that she knew Sheila had worked through the rumor problem. She also assured her that she was given an opportunity to make sure it didn't affect her geography grade.

Mrs. Kaufmann took a few bites from her sandwich and a sip of tea just as Greg Boulton appeared in her doorway.

"Come on in, Greg," she said encouragingly, since she knew he was shy.

"Mr. Jackson said you wanted this book?" Greg asked Mrs. Kaufmann.

"Yes, thank you, Greg. And how have you been doing this year?" Mrs. Kaufmann asked casually.

"Uh, fine," he said, turning in a hurry to go out the door to get to art.

"Greg, I heard about the whole Janet's party rumor-thing today, and I was wondering if you're okay. I know it can be so embarrassing when kids make stuff like that up."

"Yeah," he said, looking a bit embarrassed. "No big deal," he offered.

"I'm sorry that happened, and I know Janet is working to undo the rumor and set the record straight. If you do want to talk about it, I am happy to help. My guess is, after any rumor runs through a group, and then the correction goes out, then the interest is no longer there. The next day will offer new news about someone else, and you won't be of any interest anymore, which means by tomorrow this will all be over. Oh, yes, one more thing. Mr. Jackson knew something was upsetting you from playground, and if your grade on the quiz wasn't good, I'm sure he'd let you take it again," Mrs. Kaufmann said reassuringly.

"Thanks," Greg said, looking relieved and grateful, and then looked like he just wanted to get to class.

"Thank you for bringing me the book, and have fun in art!" she said letting the discomfort end for him.

At least Greg knows I know, and I'm working on it in case he does need to come back, Mrs. Kaufmann thought. *I don't need to call his mom since he didn't come on his own to see me, and he wasn't noticeably upset. He actually was dealing with it fairly well, and he was just obviously hoping it would all just go away.* Mrs. Kaufmann picked up the rest of her sandwich and made a note to herself to see Mr. Jackson and to check on Sheila, Janet, and Greg the next morning.

Post Rumor Day

"Good morning, Mr. Jackson!" Mrs. Kaufmann said happily as she ran into him the next day at the staff mailboxes, just as they both arrived at school. "I was hoping to see you this morning to catch you up on what was going on with Sheila, Greg, and Janet. I figured we needed a chance for a real conversation."

"Good, morning, yes, I would like that. And thank you for helping me in code on the phone yesterday. I know there are 'little ears' right near my desk listening in, and they usually are a lot more informed than I am as to what just went down on the playground," he answered smiling.

"Boy, that's the truth!" Mrs. Kaufmann agreed. "Well, the background is simply this… yesterday there was a rumor that shy little Sheila kissed Greg at Janet's outdoor Birthday Olympics party over the weekend. Janet tried to help Sheila cope with the horrible embarrassment by going with her to the girls' bathroom while Sheila cried, but recess time ran out, and Janet knew she had to get back to class. Sheila couldn't stop crying to go with her, so Janet stopped in my office to ask me to go help her, and then ran to your class fearing she might be late."

"Oh no! Not Sheila, of all kids!" Mr. Jackson exclaimed as he got the impact of how difficult it must've been on her. "What happened when you met with Greg? I noticed when he came back to class after playground yesterday, he was in his seat with his head down before any of the rest of students had settled in. He must've been embarrassed, too. I'm glad you gave me a way to get him to you without anyone noticing."

"Oh, yes, I have to get that book back to you. Thanks for reminding me," Mrs. Kaufmann added and then continued, "When Greg stopped in, I could tell he really didn't want to relive that embarrassment all over again with me. I just referenced it so he knew we didn't have to discuss it then, but that if he did want to talk about it later, I already knew what happened and would be willing to help. I also let him know that Janet was working to undo the rumor, so at least he had peace knowing it might be put to rest on the internet last night. Actually, maybe you can send Janet to my office during homeroom this morning? I can find out where we are in the rumor-control process."

"Sure," Mr. Jackson agreed. "What a shame these kids don't realize just how much damage they actually do to one another. I still can remember the time when I was in fourth grade, and someone announced out loud in the cafeteria that I liked a certain girl. My face was so hot and I just wanted to crawl into a hole and disappear. I don't think I thought about anything else for the next day or so, and my grades definitely suffered."

"I think we all have at least one of those memories, if not more. I know that learning to deal with embarrassment can only happen if you're embarrassed, but that doesn't make it any easier," Mrs. Kaufmann agreed. "Okay, let me get to my office and see if any of their parents called and left messages. I'll look for Janet during homeroom. Thanks," Mrs. Kaufmann added.

"You got it," Mr. Jackson said, as he got his mail and headed for his classroom. Mrs. Kaufmann also got hers and went directly to her office. Once she unlocked the door and went in, she put down her briefcase and headed right for the blinking red light on her telephone.

The first message was from Sheila's mom. "Hello, Mrs. Kaufmann, this is Mrs. Trentacosta. I wanted to thank you for your call yesterday. It's always so nice to get a heads-up before the kids get home from school. I have to thank you for helping her feel better and get back to class, too. She thinks she did really well on her United States quiz, and I just wanted you to know that I think the girls went back and forth on the internet last night enough to have solved the world's problems, as well as figuring out what may have happened. There are a few guilty parties, but I won't name any names. Just know that Sheila is fine today. In fact, she seems happier than normal as she ran out the door for school just now. I think that so many of her little friends gave her so much sympathy and attention that she felt really good about herself." Mrs. Trentacosta laughed. "This little incident may have even helped with her self-esteem. We'll see. Anyway, I have to get to the office. Thanks again for all you do over there at Hillstown Middle School."

Mrs. Kaufmann smiled, as she then listened to the next voice mail. "Mrs. Kaufmann, I'm Janet Merlotta's mother. I understand she came in to see you yesterday. Would you please call me when you get in?"

Short and to the point, Mrs. Kaufmann thought as she called Janet's mom back. "Hello, Mrs. Merlotta?" she said as the woman answered. "This is Mrs. Kaufmann, Janet's school counselor, just returning your call."

"Oh, thank you for calling me back so fast. I just wanted to make sure my daughter isn't in any trouble. She told me she was a little late for class because she was in your office talking with you about Sheila. Did she get into trouble for being in the bathroom during the whole playground period?" Mrs. Merlotta asked.

"She's not in any trouble at all. I've explained her lateness, or actually kindness, to her teacher. In fact, I think of her as having really gone out on a limb for a friend. She's a very good student, as well as a truly good person. You've done a great job raising such a thoughtful and responsible young lady," Mrs. Kaufmann assured her.

"Oh…thank you. That's so nice to hear. My husband and I are very proud of her. In fact, last night we allowed her to stay on the computer a little longer than normal because she said she wanted to help Sheila tell everyone that the rumor about her and Greg wasn't true," Mrs. Merlotta added.

"That's what I mean. You must be very proud of her. I've asked her teacher to send her to me for a book this morning, and I will tell her I'm proud of her, too," Mrs. Kaufmann promised, as she heard someone come into the outer waiting room. "I think this may be her coming now, so let me go, and feel free to call me if you have any other questions."

"Thanks, I will," Mrs. Merlotta replied as she hung up.

Just as Mrs. Kaufmann also hung up the phone, Janet appeared in the doorway of her office. "Hi. Mrs. Kaufmann. Mr. Jackson sent me down to you for a book for him?"

"Good morning, my dear. How are you? Yes, let me go get that for you. Come on in. While I'm looking for it, let me ask you how Sheila's doing today?"

"Oh, she's fine this morning," Janet assured Mrs. Kaufmann. "Sheila and I even think we know who started it all in the locker room yesterday. We found out that Karen Hitchings was talking about Greg and saying stuff, like she liked him and was wishing she was at the party, so we figured she might be the one. Anyway, everybody was connecting with everybody else last night, and then Sheila and I noticed that Karen suddenly stopped. Everybody, except Karen, was telling Sheila how bad they felt for her yesterday. That made Sheila feel really good last night, and she seemed really happy this morning."

"I'm so happy for Sheila!" Mrs. Kaufmann exclaimed. "Do you know how Greg's doing today so far?" she continued.

"Well, he wasn't on the internet last night, but if he read any of the comments, he'd know that a lot of girls like him, so he shouldn't feel too bad about it all," Janet said, "just maybe embarrassed by all the attention. He seemed fine when he came into class just now."

"Yes, I'm sure he was embarrassed. He is a bit of a shy person, too. I just hope that all the talk about all of this ends today. Sometimes students just want to keep the talk up because it's the news and they like the fantasy of the rumor. Also, kids often feel flattered when a friend tells them a rumor or secret, as if they are chosen to get a gift from them. Then, they feel like they are *giving* a gift when they share it with someone else. It makes everyone feel special, forgetting entirely about what it's doing to the victims of the rumor!"

"I know!" Janet said excitedly. "You wouldn't have believed all the kids who really got into it last night…like who likes who, and who told who, and all that. At least I got to tell a whole bunch of people that Sheila definitely didn't do what they said she did. And most everybody said they figured she didn't anyway. That's what made Sheila feel so much better."

"You know, Janet, you are a really good friend. Taking care of and standing up for your friend yesterday was so kind. Then you even took a chance to come to me to get her help while running late for class. That was also a brave thing to do. And to top it all off, you also worked at helping to clear up the rumor yesterday and last night, and that has really made all the difference here. I am so proud of you. Thank you, Janet Merlotta. You are a really good person!" Mrs. Kaufmann said with enthusiasm. "Oops, and look at this. Mr. Jackson's book was right on the top of my desk all this time while I've been looking for it. Here you go, my dear."

Janet was grinning from ear to ear. She appeared to be feeling appreciated for her helpfulness, and she took the book from Mrs. Kaufmann. She gave a quick thank you and left the office with a little bit of a hop in her step.

Mrs. Kaufmann smiled. She knew what a difference it makes when someone appreciates you. She then checked the rest of her voice mail messages and turned on her computer to get her e-mail. She had her list of names of students and teachers that she needed to see for the day. She took her pen and crossed four of the names off the list: Mr. Jackson, Sheila, Janet, and Greg. Then she wrote down, "Karen Hitchings?"

Clean-Up

Mrs. Kaufmann knew there would be a few more students suffering from the emotions stirred by the rumor yesterday, but she wasn't sure which students would reach out for help. With all that online chatter last night, there was sure to be some ripple effect in school today, she thought, and she was right. By second period she received an e-mail about this very rumor from another teacher, Mrs. Keiland.

It read: Mrs. Kaufmann, Can you help me? I'm not sure what's going on with my girls, but there is something hot happening. They came in this morning and were all in little groups talking about one another. I've seen some tears and a lot of notes. I just told them to leave all their issues outside the door, because we had too much work to do today to let that interfere. The only thing is, I know I don't really have their attention. There are too many dirty looks going around. Help!

Mrs. Kaufmann wrote back: Send the one with tears down to the main office in such a way that she thinks she was randomly chosen to run a note down there for you. Write "To Mrs. Kaufmann" on the inside of the note. I will just intercept her on the way and bring her to my office to talk. I'm here now and I have some time.

Mrs. Keiland's next e-mail popped right up: I'm sending Karen Hitchings right now. Thanks!

Mrs. Kaufmann went out into the hallway between Mrs. Keiland's classroom and the main office to wait for Karen. It was no surprise that she was the one. She figured that Karen was being punished by the girls who may have been ganging up against her for starting a rumor. Whether it was meant to be mean or not would soon be found out. Whatever the deal was, Mrs. Kaufmann knew there'd be a new lesson learned today, if not more than one.

"Hey, Karen," Mrs. Kaufmann called out, as she saw her come into sight from around the bend of the hall.

"Hi, Mrs. Kaufmann," Karen called back.

"Read the inside of the note Mrs. Keiland sent with you," Mrs. Kaufmann said, as she winked at Karen with a smile.

Karen unfolded the note looking a little confused, read the words "To Mrs. Kaufmann," and then she looked up and smiled. By then she had arrived at the guidance office.

"Come on in, sweetie. I have the feeling you're hurting today. Mrs. Keiland said you had some tears this morning? I'm also aware of most everything having to do with yesterday's rumor. Can you tell me if that has anything to do with your tears?" Mrs. Kaufmann asked Karen, as they both quickly walked into her office and closed the door. She could see Karen's eyes filling up and knew they'd better get inside to talk privately as fast as they could.

"I think I started it," Karen blurted out as the tears rolled down her cheeks. "I'm so sorry, I didn't mean it to hurt anyone, and now everyone is so mad at me."

"I'm sure that is very hard for you to deal with today. How do you know they are all mad at you? Could they all be thinking you were just passing the news, like they all thought they were doing yesterday?" Mrs. Kaufmann asked.

"No, they're mad. Even Claudia, who was my best friend, isn't speaking to me. She said that I was so mean to Sheila that she didn't want to be my friend anymore." With that, Karen sobbed openly.

Mrs. Kaufmann slid the box of tissues over to her on the desk. "Can you tell me how it all happened, like what did you say and what was on your mind when you said it?"

Karen blew her nose and wiped her eyes to get herself back to talking. "I was in the locker room and I heard the girls from Janet's party talking about how much fun they all had over the weekend. I was feeling jealous, I guess, but I knew I was in the other class and none of us were invited, so I wasn't mad. Anyway, when I asked Dee to tell me who was there, she started naming everyone including Sheila and Greg. So I was picturing a party like my older sister's, where a couple of the kids going together ended up kissing. I just said something about imagining Sheila and Greg together kissing, and that was all. I even like Greg, and I think Sheila's really nice too, so I just imagined them together as a couple, that's all. I didn't even think it was a bad thing, just like a fun thought."

"I completely understand," Mrs. Kaufmann said, and continued. "I guess that's when the prairie fire was lit."

"What?" Karen asked, confused.

"Oh, it's a little image I have of how fast a rumor takes off in a school. It's like striking a match in the corner of a dry field of prairie grass, and the whole fire just immediately takes off, burning every last blade of grass in no time at all. You were the match. You put an image out there of something they found funny or surprising, or both, and everyone had to tell as many people as possible. Between the locker room during fourth period, and the playground, there probably wasn't anyone left who didn't hear it, or some form of it," Mrs. Kaufmann explained. "That's how fast these rumor fires burn!"

"But I didn't say it to hurt them, and I didn't say it to be passed on. I just had a thought and said it out loud," Karen protested in her defense.

"I know you didn't, but the thought of kissing at this grade level is shocking for those kids who don't have college-age brothers and sisters like you do. Plus, you created an image of two specific shy people they all knew, which got into everyone's heads as pretty surprising, too. The tough thing for Sheila and Greg is that it was such an embarrassing thought, and they knew everyone around them had a picture of them kissing in their heads. I think you can see why it didn't end up so well."

"Oh, I didn't even think of that," Karen admitted. Now I feel more terrible for Sheila and Greg. I even understand why my closest friends are mad at me, but now what do I do?"

Mrs. Kaufmann looked straight at her and said, "Do you want to apologize?"

"Yes, but to Sheila or Greg, or Claudia, my closest friend?" Karen asked.

"Yes," Mrs. Kaufmann said, surprising Karen at first. "I'm just saying yes to all of them. Once they tell others you made it right, gradually you will be forgiven."

"But they aren't speaking to me. What if they don't listen or let me?" Karen asked tearfully.

"Would you like my help?" Mrs. Kaufmann asked.

"I don't know. What will you do?" Karen asked quickly.

"Well, I can send for them to come here, like one or two at a time if you think you can face them. I'll let them know you have something you want to tell them, and then it will be up to you to apologize. I don't believe any of those girls would act badly in front of me, but there's no guarantee they'll forgive you. They just may be upset enough to want to be angry with you. I think, though, if they heard your version of what you were originally thinking, they might understand you weren't trying to be mean. From all my years helping students talk to each other, I've learned that if a person can understand you, then they can relate to what you've done from their own experience. And once they relate to your feelings, then they can forgive you. They may see you as human just like them. What do you think?" Mrs. Kaufmann coaxed.

"Okay. Can we start with Sheila?" Karen asked.

"Sure. That was my thinking, too. I might also suggest we add Janet, since it was her party and she has been trying to undo the rumor for Sheila since yesterday. Besides, I have to make sure Sheila wants to do this. She may be too shy, or too uncomfortable without Janet."

Karen got quiet for a bit and then said, "Do I have to talk to them both at the same time?"

"You don't have to, but you stand a better chance getting it done if we do," Mrs. Kaufmann suggested.

"Okay, I'll try," she answered reluctantly.

Mrs. Kaufmann picked up the phone and called Mr. Jackson. "Mr. Jackson, would you be able to send Sheila and Janet to me right now, or am I interrupting something they need to be doing and can't easily make up?"

Karen listened quietly and nervously. She wasn't even sure what she was going to say when they both got here. She just hoped Mrs. Kaufmann would help somehow.

"Great, thanks. Tell them privately that I just have a question for them, and I will meet them in my waiting room when they get here, okay? Thanks again." Mrs. Kaufmann finished her call with Mr. Jackson, hung up, and told Karen not to worry because she would help her. Mrs. Kaufmann went to her waiting room and within two minutes, Karen could hear her say, "Hi, ladies! I'm so glad to see you. I have some really good news for you both. I found out how the whole rumor-thing started! And the best part is the person who started it never meant to be mean. She just had a funny thought and said it out loud. The sad news is, she's feeling really bad about it and doesn't know how to apologize. Would you both be willing to hear this from her?"

Both girls said yes right away and looked relieved. Mrs. Kaufmann then said, "Karen is actually inside my office, and she wanted to apologize now if you're okay with it. I don't want to push you into it. If either of you is uncomfortable with this idea, you certainly can go back to class and decide what you want to do about it later. You tell me, okay? I just wanted to help you put this all to rest so we can move on and have a normal happy day today."

"Sure, I'd like this to be done too," Sheila spoke first.

Janet then agreed as well. "That would be good."

Mrs. Kaufmann led the girls from the waiting room back into her office, where Karen was sitting looking very, very nervous. They all took their seats around the big office desk, and Mrs. Kaufmann broke the intense silence. "Karen, my dear, this is your chance to explain to Sheila and Janet how this all happened, just the way you did to me, okay?"

"Okay, well…uh…I'm really sorry. I was in the locker room asking about the party and who was there, and I was imagining my sister's pool party last summer, when she was home from college and was kissing her boyfriend by the pool. Then I, uh, just pictured two people who were at your party being a couple, like my sister and her boyfriend, and I just said it. I was imagining you, Sheila, like going with Greg, like a nice couple. I am so, so, so sorry. I can't believe everyone thought I meant it really happened. I was saying like what if, and then this all went out of control. I'm really, really sorry," Karen apologized, getting choked up with tears pouring down her face once again.

Sheila spoke first. "Oh, that's okay, Karen. I totally understand. Now I'm thinking that all that happened wasn't even your fault. It was a little like that telephone game where each person adds to what the last one said, and then the message gets all messed up."

"Yeah, Karen, I get it now, too." Janet admitted. "I thought yesterday that someone was really trying to be mean to Sheila. Thanks for apologizing. I can tell the other girls what really happened if you want. I mean, I can tell them about this meeting. Maybe that will help?" Janet asked.

Mrs. Kaufmann jumped in. "Actually, that would be really helpful, don't you think, Karen?"

Immediately Karen started to cry again, but in relief. "Thanks, Janet. That really would be so great." She spoke into the tissue as she blew her nose and tried to stop crying. "I wasn't sure how to apologize to everyone, since no one was talking to me."

"Sure, I can do that. I was telling everyone yesterday and last night that Sheila didn't kiss Greg at my party, and that the person who said that was mean. Now I think I was starting my own rumor in a way." Janet laughed a little in discomfort. She looked at Karen and continued, "I'll be happy now to tell everyone what really happened, and that you weren't being mean. I'll do that today."

Sheila quietly said, "I will try to do that, too, but I still feel a little embarrassed bringing it up."

"Sheila, you really shouldn't feel like you have to be talking about this anymore today. Yesterday was hard enough, and even today the uncomfortable image is still being talked about. I think you need to just get through today, knowing it will all soon be done." Mrs. Kaufmann assured her. She continued, "And, Janet, that is so kind of you to offer to help Karen today. You are a really nice person to be so understanding and forgiving and helpful, too!"

Just then, Karen, who was sitting by Janet, reached over and patted Janet on the back of her shoulder. "Thanks," Karen said softly, which made Sheila and Janet both smile.

Mrs. Kaufmann continued, "You know, ladies, I think the most important thing now is to make sure everyone knows it wasn't meant to be repeated, and it was definitely not meant to be mean. The fact that Karen apologized isn't going to be enough to make everyone forgive her. They think she was making up something about two nice people to make others think less of them, and that she was doing it on purpose. Yet, we all know now that it truly was just a silly thought she said out loud, just to share her imagined fantasy."

Sheila said, "But she did apologize, and that's hard to do. So, if everyone knows that, shouldn't that be enough to make them forgive her?"

Mrs. Kaufmann continued explaining. "Well, girls tend to withhold their friendship as a punishment for mean behavior, or to protect themselves. Sometimes they say that they're fine with that person and they forgive her, but then they just store that incident away in their memories to protect themselves from that girl later on. In other words, they watch their backs or they stay guarded. They never really, really forgive, and they never really, really trust that girl again unless a lot of time has gone by."

Karen exclaimed, "That's so true! I still remember there was this one mean girl when we were in first grade. She made everyone laugh at me until I cried, and just because I got a short haircut. Then she laughed even harder when I cried. I knew I never wanted to be friends with after that, but I acted nice around her so she wouldn't get mad at me and do something like that again. I was actually afraid of her, so I pretended to like her."

"I remember her!" Sheila jumped in. "I was so scared of her, and I was nice to her, too. When my mother told me that she moved away that summer, I was so excited that I ran and hugged my mom!" Karen and Janet both laughed.

Mrs. Kaufmann said, "See? You can't always tell what's going on in people's minds. Just because people say they forgive you, it doesn't mean they will forget what you did--or especially how you made them feel. That's one of the best reasons to always talk about a misunderstanding with your friends, so you can set the record straight. It's too easy to believe you know what that other person was thinking or intending. Look at Karen, for example. She thought she just threw out a crazy image of something to be entertaining to people around her. She never intended to suggest Sheila and Greg actually did that at Janet's party. In fact, she chose Sheila and Greg especially *because* they're both shy, which is why it made it even more of a ridiculous image."

"Mrs. Kaufmann?" Karen interrupted. "Can I apologize to Claudia here with you? I don't think she'll let me if I try later, even if Janet tells her I didn't mean it. Everyone knows Janet is really nice, but Claudia will do that thing that you said. She will never trust me again, so she won't believe me."

"Sure, Karen. Let me get Janet and Sheila back to class first, and then I'll ask your teacher to allow Claudia come down if it's okay. Then I'll have to get you back to class, too," Mrs. Kaufmann said, as she then wrote out a hall pass to allow Janet and Sheila back to Mr. Jackson's class. She also wrote a note out for Mrs. Keiland, so the girls could drop it off to her on their way back to class. It read: Dear Mrs. Keiland, I'm almost done working through a "rumor event" and appreciate your patience as I keep interrupting your class. I only need to see one more student, Claudia Hammerer, for just a few minutes. If all goes well, I will send both girls back together. Please give me a call and let me know if this is okay to do right now. Thanks, Mrs. K.

Sheila and Janet stood up and took their pass and Mrs. Keiland's note. Karen jumped up to hug them both, and they hugged back with only good feelings left to share. Janet and Sheila gave a quick thanks to Mrs. Kaufmann and left the office, walking closely together to talk all the way back.

Mrs. Kaufmann asked Karen if she was nervous about talking with Claudia. "Yes, a lot!" Karen answered. "We've been best friends for a long time, and I get really upset whenever she's mad at me."

"Does she get upset with you often? And why is that?" Mrs. Kaufmann continued.

"Sometimes I say silly things, and she doesn't think they're so funny. Like when I say things about her and I'm just joking," Karen admitted.

"Sounds like you have to be careful with your words, do you think? Maybe your imaginings said out loud make people feel uncomfortable?" Mrs. Kaufmann suggested, hoping this would be an "aha moment" for Karen, considering the recent trouble she just got into with her last "silly comment."

"I guess so. I don't mean anything bad by them, but I guess everybody else doesn't get what I think is funny," Karen admitted.

The phone rang, and Mrs. Kaufmann felt it break the flow of this self-discovery time for Karen, but she had to answer it. "Hello?" she said while Karen sat listening. "Okay, great. We won't take long, I don't think. As soon as we're done, I'll send Claudia and Karen right back to class. Thanks for your help." Mrs. Kaufmann could see Karen sit up straight and began fidgeting. It was going to happen and she was scared.

"Are you ready, my dear? I will pave the way for Claudia to listen to you tell her what really happened. I also think it might be a good chance for you both to talk about how Claudia feels about your sense of humor. It might make things better between you two and help keep you out of trouble in general." Mrs. Kaufmann winked at her as she got up out of her chair to go out through the waiting room and into the hall to meet Claudia. She needed to make sure Claudia Hammerer was even willing to speak to Karen.

Karen had a few minutes to wait alone and think about the history she and Claudia had had. Then she heard Mrs. Kaufmann talking out in the hallway. "Hi. Claudia. Thanks for coming, my dear, and no, you're not in any trouble. I just thought I might be able to help you today, because I know you're upset with your friend Karen. She's in my office right now, and she was very upset by the misunderstanding that happened yesterday with the rumor about Sheila and Greg. It got her into so much trouble with everyone, and she's most upset about *you* not knowing what happened. She's hoping that if she is able to explain what she actually did, you won't be angry anymore. You certainly do not have to talk with her or even come into the office if you don't want to. I just thought if I could offer this quiet opportunity for you to hear Karen out, you would know more than you do now, and then your decision to keep or end your friendship would be based on what happened, and not what everyone's saying happened. What do you think?"

"Okay," Claudia answered reluctantly. Mrs. Kaufmann could see she was uncomfortable with all of this attention on her now, so she continued talking as they turned to walk into her office. "Karen just spoke to Janet and Sheila too and really wanted to explain it all to you." As they entered the office and the girls looked at each other, Mrs. Kaufmann quickly said, "Have a seat, Claudia. Karen, would you like to start telling what happened?" Mrs. Kaufmann looked at Karen, who was almost falling off her chair getting ready to talk.

Claudia looked at Karen a little sideways, since straight on, eyes to eyes, would have been too uncomfortable. Karen started talking, immediately explaining everything exactly as she had before. As she did, Claudia's body language softened, and she began to look directly at her. When Karen was done talking, Claudia looked at her and said, "Karen, you do this all the time! You always picture people doing things you think are funny, but it's embarrassing to them. I can understand now that you didn't *mean* to hurt Sheila, but I would have died if you said that about Greg and me. It just means everybody's picturing it…picturing it! That's so embarrassing! That makes it almost real, and then sometimes people even forget if it was real or they just imagined it!"

Mrs. Kaufmann was very attentive now. It certainly wasn't what she and Karen expected, but letting it unfold was perfect. This was working out to be the best chance for Claudia to teach Karen the lesson she needed. And it might work to help their friendship, if Karen could see that changing her ways would be necessary to make that happen.

Karen was still for a minute, and then she dropped her head and said, "I know, I'm sorry. I guess I didn't think about how it wasn't funny, since I've always laughed at those things."

Claudia was on a roll, so she continued making her point rather firmly. "Remember the time a bunch of us were at the movies, and in front of the ticket collector, you said something about picturing all the candy I was sneaking in in my bag? The ticket collector looked at me like I was bad or sneaky, and you just laughed. I almost got in trouble and you thought it was funny. What if everyone did that to you? Would you like it?"

"I'm sorry, Claudia. I won't do that anymore, I promise. I feel really bad now. You never said anything, so I thought you were laughing with everyone else. I just thought I was making people laugh. I'm sorry," Karen said sincerely.

Mrs. Kaufmann interrupted to help move things along. "Claudia, I'm really glad you got to tell Karen how you felt. And I know from experience that when people make fun of you in front of others, you feel like you have to look like you can take it, even if you feel embarrassed. That's why it always seems like everything's okay to the person *using you* to entertain everyone around you. The worst part is it makes the 'clown person' believe they really are a funny person. And no one can tell you're embarrassed, because you laugh along to avoid looking like a bad sport."

Then she turned to Karen, "Karen, can you see why a person would not want to be your friend if they always had to risk being uncomfortable whenever they were with you?"

Karen nodded and said, "I'm sorry, Claudia. I really won't do that to you ever again. I'm not trying to be mean--just silly, really."

"I know, Karen, that's why we're still friends. I like that you like to be happy and make jokes, and most times you are really funny. I just knew how Sheila felt yesterday, and I wasn't sure I wanted that for me from now on. If you're sure you won't do that anymore, then we're okay," Claudia offered.

"Yes! I'm sure. Thanks, Claudia. And if I start to say anything that makes you uncomfortable, will you tell me? I really didn't know you were feeling this way, and I never knew for sure why you'd be so mad at me."

Claudia firmly answered, "Oh, I will!" she said, with a little satisfied smile. She looked quite relieved that it was over, and they agreed to a new and better deal between them.

Mrs. Kaufmann quickly suggested, "I think you two have made your friendship so much better here today. It's like a new friendship. You've cleared the air and each made a promise that will help you in all your relationships. Karen, you've learned to have more empathy for what others may be feeling. And Claudia, you've learned to speak up, so your friend knows how you really feel now. She knows you don't want to feel disrespected. And now I have to get you two back to class. I just love it when things work out better than I expected!" Mrs. Kaufmann declared, smiling from ear to ear. It broke the seriousness among them all, and both girls looked immediately relaxed.

"Thanks," Karen said to Claudia, as they both stood up to go back to class.

Claudia said, "I'll tell everyone your silly sense of humor got you in trouble again, and that you're not mean. Thanks, Mrs. Kaufmann."

Mrs. Kaufmann wrote out a hall pass and handed it to Karen. She thanked Mrs. Kaufmann as she walked out into the hallway side by side with her "new" best friend, both talking at the same time and laughing.

Rumor fire put out! Mrs. Kaufmann thought as she pulled up her e-mail to let the teachers know, too. *I really do love it when I get a two-for-one special. Today's friendship repair was a bonus!*

Discussion Points:

- Rumors spread faster than forest fires, leaving the victim truly burnt. Stopping them with the truth is almost impossible, and the damage doesn't always even get repaired.

- Once a visual image is created in people's minds, it gets "remembered."

- When you tell people you appreciate them for something they did, it does a world of good for their self-esteem.

- When you apologize with an explanation and your sincere feelings about *how* you made your mistake, others will hear how it seemed human and will forgive you more easily. They will identify with you.

Reflection Questions:

1. Have you ever told someone something you heard but didn't know if it was true? How can you tell what's true and what's not? Can you even know what is really going on in someone else's mind? Do you know what you'll be thinking next?

2. What can you do to "undo" a rumor that has already spread? How hard is it to keep something you heard to yourself? How do you know what to believe when you hear something from a friend?

3. Have you ever seen someone do something that seemed so mean that you knew you'd never forget it? How have you thought about that person afterwards? How long does distrust last? Was it mean, really, when you think back now?

4. When someone has done something that hurt another person, what helps you forgive them when they apologize?

CHAPTER 13:
He Puts Me Down Because I'm a Girl

When Meanness Begins

"Hey, Mrs. Kaufmann, wait up! I have a favor to ask of you today, if you're not too busy." Mr. Baron called to the school counselor when he saw her going down the hall. She stopped and turned around quickly, just as he caught up to her. He continued, "Boy, do we have a problem with our kids at the whole grade level, and we could really use your help."

Mrs. Kaufmann immediately answered, "Sure, what's going on, and how can I help?"

"Our whole team has noticed a lot of fighting, hurt feelings and general meanness. Is there any way you would be able to join us for our team meeting today? We were hoping we all might be able to schedule you to come and do your lesson on friendship for each of our health classes next week. That topic actually goes right along with our lessons in health right now on stress, and we each have our homerooms for health class, which is perfect for follow-up. We could also use some insight as to what's going on with some specific students who seemed to be at the heart of all the problems. How does your calendar look for third period today?"

Mrs. Kaufmann answered enthusiastically, "Sure, I can wiggle some appointments around and be there right when you start. This doesn't surprise me. This group has some really strong characters that are way behind their peers in social skills. In fact, they have a reputation for this pattern every fall. Once the new school year starts with its shuffling of friendships into groups, and the novelty and fun of the new grade has worn off, some of these kids become quite persnickety because they feel left out…again. I'll bring my calendar, and we'll set up one class a day for five days next week. That should cover all five classes. Sound good?"

"That would be great! Thanks so much for clearing your appointments to fit us in. And I have to laugh at your description as persnickety!" Mr. Baron laughed. "You know, everything seemed fine a few weeks ago when the school year started, but their social problems have really begun to take up a lot of classroom time recently, especially first thing in the morning, after special classes, and mostly after lunch and playground. It is happening almost every day now."

"I'm not surprised," Mrs. Kaufmann responded as they both continued on their way. "See you at your meeting," she said, turning the corner and heading for the office.

"Thanks again," he replied.

As Mrs. Kaufmann hung up the phone in her office, she heard the hustle and bustle in the hallway of students changing classes from second to third period. She quickly grabbed her keys and calendar, locked her office door, and headed for Mr. Baron's classroom. When she got there, he and the other four teachers on the team were pulling up chairs to a big round table for their meeting. They all greeted each other and got right to reporting to Mrs. Kaufmann about the bigger incidents that had recently occurred among the students and how the teachers handled them. They each had several stories about how they lost time from their lessons because they had to stop and take care of someone crying or reporting some kind of mean behavior.

The teachers then listened quietly. Mrs. Kaufmann began to fill them in on some of the more troubled students whose past behaviors created similar problems in previous grades. Her goal was to help the teachers to become aware of the backgrounds of those students by understanding their home environments. She felt they needed to see how there was a gap in their social growth, due to a lack of appropriate learning opportunities throughout their life experiences. She reminded the teachers to see them as young people who needed their guidance and patience, in order for them to learn how to get along with their peers.

She went on to explain to the teachers that many of those students' role models and parents did not teach them the importance of respecting others either, from whatever was lacking in their own emotional development. "These little guys can only know what they've been taught," she said. "I'm afraid we have to fill in the gaps with lessons on what we think is common sense. And I know you all feel like you're not here to teach behavior as if you were their parents, but I honestly can't think of a better place to learn good character and good virtues than here. Here is where we have so much opportunity to show them how it really works. This is their truest field experience, if you will."

Mr. Baron immediately led the response. "You make good sense, but we'd need to lead off with some common definitions and basic expectations. That's why we'd each like to package that up in a health lesson for our own homerooms. It would give us a starting place that is the same for all students in the grade level."

"Absolutely, I love doing those classes! They set the stage for the follow-up character-building classes I can offer you throughout the year, too, whenever the behavior patterns scream the need." Mrs. Kaufmann laughed. "The longer I do this and the older I get, the more I can predict the patterns. I figure the students will rally after this first lesson, as the awareness just magnifies any meanness. Most of them will be on good behavior until the holidays come around, and then everything starts to change. That's when we'll have another wave of misbehavior, as the holidays test their maturity. Their egos will be calling to them with a resounding, 'I want this and that…me, me, me…mine, mine, mine.'

"We adults do it to them around the holidays every year. We want to make our kids happy by giving them things and promising them pleasures, until they feel they deserve it all, and shouldn't have to deny themselves anything. Of course that leads to a sense of entitlement. Then, having to do without anything, in this school setting of taking turns and sharing things, makes those who are less mature rather cranky. Of course, it's in school where many students learn delayed gratification…a hard lesson, but ours to teach. Aren't we lucky?" she said with a wink and a smile.

With that, she opened her calendar to the next week and scheduled each teacher with a "Friendship Class," one a day for five days. "I'll also create a follow-up sheet with the highlights of this lesson for all of you to post in your classrooms. And, just so you know, I'll also give a copy of these expected grade-level behaviors to each of the specials teachers to post in their art, music, library, and computer classes. Of course the cafeteria and playground supervisors will get one, as well as the bus drivers." She felt it had to be universal if it was to become the new standard for the rest of the school year. "I will also ask the principal if I can put the summary of those behaviors in our school's parent newsletter in my little 'Guidance Corner', so the parents can learn what we expect from our children. Maybe it will be the first time some of them were exposed to these clearly defined expectations themselves."

"That will be perfect!" Mr. Baron jumped in. "Thanks for all your help with this." The other teachers also thanked Mrs. Kaufmann as she stood up to get back to her office for an appointment. She was hoping to meet with a particularly sad student she had seen coming in to the school that morning. She guessed the reason was exactly what the team had been talking about.

"You are so welcome! I can't wait for next week. I love teaching this lesson every October!"

The Lesson on Friendship

From left to right on the big whiteboard in front of the classroom, Mrs. Kaufmann wrote the various categories of behaviors that students exhibit with one another. On the far left, as she explained to the class, was teasing *with* a friend, during which time both students enjoyed the laughter and were even complimented by the feeling of closeness and acceptance. "The teasing brings you even closer, as you feel safe and mutually accepting and with no bad feelings," she said, as the students sat silently focused on her explanation. This was a hot topic for these students, and you could tell they listened with a lot of thought as to their own friends' behaviors.

Mrs. Kaufmann then moved to the right of the "Good Teasing" category on the whiteboard and wrote "Not-Good Teasing." She explained, "Not-good teasing is when the teasing is done in any other way than as fun between friends. It is simply wrong, because it comes from a mean-spirited place. It's done with the intent to embarrass someone and make them feel uncomfortable or bad," she continued with no hesitation. This silenced the room.

"Students who like to put down other students, or make fun of their shortcomings or problems, are being either self-centered at best, or simply mean, at worst." She went on, "Any student who makes fun of someone else in front of others to either make himself look cool or witty for an audience is mean-spirited. Those kind of teasers have shown they have little compassion for the students they are embarrassing, just so they can feel better about themselves, even at the other person's expense." She further explained, "If a student makes fun of others, the people standing around will have a tendency to laugh along. However, make no mistake about this," she warned the class, "that insincere laughter is prompted by fear or discomfort. If you don't laugh along with the mean behavior to indicate to the mean teaser that you understand his or her joke, you fear being the next target. Some people laugh to try to bring some comic relief to such an uncomfortable moment. After all, public embarrassment causes most people to feel compassion for the victim, but they are too frightened to stand up to the person being mean."

Again, the class remained almost motionless, and the air was thick with thought. Each student was running through the memories of their experiences that felt all too similar to the descriptions they were now hearing. They were also doing self-inventories, trying to remember if they were guilty of making themselves look bad by making fun of others, which was exactly what Mrs. Kaufmann had hoped.

The third category that she wrote on the board was "Bullying." Mrs. Kaufmann began to describe the difference between mean teasing and bullying, which she warned would get you in a whole heap of trouble there at Hillstown Middle School and any other school for that matter. "Bullying," she explained, "is an act of using power over another person, to control him or her. It could be physical, verbal or emotional, but it is always about power. When any stronger student controls another student through intimidation or power, it's against the law. The school had to officially adopt what they call their Zero-Tolerance Policy to deal with that kind of behavior. No student should ever be afraid to come to school for fear of another student, so the school policy now has official steps for punishing those who bully others. These behaviors require the principal, by law, to make sure the parents are called in, and there is a suspension or other major punishment. It's big, believe me," she emphasized.

"Let me give you some examples of what is referred to as bullying." With that, she gave several typical examples of each kind of bullying, pointing out that it was certainly not just the physical "take your lunch money" kind of act. She made sure they heard stories of how students would use repeated embarrassing comments or laughs to deliberately intimidate others. "Eye darting and snickering," she said, "counts as methods of communicating that kind of put-down, so please realize those simple acts are not hidden."

She discussed the effect they have when it happens more than once and becomes so unbearable over time to the targeted student, that he or she can't take it anymore and becomes hopeless. She continued, "And the worst kind of bullying is the kind that's done over the internet. 'Cyber-bullying,' as it's called, is the worst, because the bully hides behind his or her computer and causes enormous, widespread damage to another person. That feeling of helplessness on the part of the victim is the most cutting, and the most humiliating. The victim isn't even present to defend himself or explain. Of course, that's the goal of the bully, to do the cruel act without fear of retaliation or anyone defending his or her victim. None of us should tolerate witnessing that kind of torture. I know I certainly will not." It was rare for Mrs. Kaufmann to be so firm, and the students got the message loud and clear, to gauge by the looks on their very serious faces.

Mrs. Kaufmann then explained that each of them was now officially made aware of the consequences, so there was no more pretending they just didn't know. She continued with the fact that they were now all responsible for letting an adult know when anyone was suffering from being bullied. "It's the right thing to do for others, and bullying really is breaking the law," she emphasized. She explained that they all needed to work together to make sure they had none of that in their school. "We all need to be able to come here feeling safe every single day." This time she saw a lot of wiggling in their seats. She had placed the accountability squarely on their shoulders. The level of discomfort had risen to exactly what she expected…high!

Continuing on, Mrs. Kaufmann wrote "Harassment" as a fourth category. She explained that picking on a student because of his or her skin color, religion or nationality, or because of the fact that he or she is a girl or boy, is called "harassment," and is also against the law. She gave them examples of court cases in which the parents of the children who harassed others at school were found guilty and had to pay big fines. At this point she knew she still had their attention, completely.

"Why am I telling you all of this?" She finally put the marker down and moved into the middle of the students. "I'm telling you because the law says you are now old enough to be responsible for your behaviors. The law also says we are to make sure our society protects its members. It's what's right to do. And it isn't about tattletaling, which is trying to get someone in trouble when no one is getting hurt. It's about making sure no one does get hurt. The law tells me and all of the other teachers in the United States that we must teach you this and hold you accountable. It is about human rights. It is what you have to know to be a law-abiding adult in America. And, I teach you about this for yet another reason that may seem more important to you for your lifetime. Knowing the differences among all of these behaviors is the key to being a good person, and that is also the key to making and keeping friends.

"You already know this, but I'm going to put it into words today," she explained. "Good friends, I mean really good friends, are people with whom you can be happy and trust they wouldn't hurt you. These people laugh *with* you, not *at* you. On the other hand, people you can't trust are not good friends. They are just acquaintances, school mates, etc. They could have become good friends if enough time was spent establishing comfort and trust, but mean teasing or bullying won't do that, for sure. In fact, it will leave the teaser looking bad even if he or she doesn't get caught and punished. It will expose him or her as someone you definitely can't trust. Eventually, the mean-teasing person begins to feel left out of things."

Mrs. Kaufmann continued, "Over time, the person who likes to laugh at others starts finding himself or herself getting no calls to come hang out after school. None of his or her 'supposed friends' are extending invitations to go places on the weekends anymore. The people who used to seem like friends to the bullies, and who used to laugh along at the jokes, were really just trying to stay safe themselves. They only appeared supportive, but definitely were never confrontational. Bullies eventually notice they aren't invited to be partners on class trips or camp-outs. In fact, over the years--and it does take time for people to build up the nerve to move away from the bullies--the bullies will eventually find themselves totally without friends and alone. It won't be obvious at first, but I see you all thinking about those people who have been doing this to others, and how you really feel about them."

She stopped talking for a few minutes and allowed the silence to finish teaching that part of the lesson. It was powerful but dangerous to leave it right there where it was. Part two of this lesson was about to turn it all around for the good.

Part Two of "The Lesson"

Mrs. Kaufmann began to hand out a survey form to the students in the class, explaining what she was distributing. "Take one of these forms and pass them on. Put your name at the top and today's date. Make sure you have a book or another sheet of paper to cover your sheet as you fill it in, because this information is highly confidential. It will be between just us – no one else. I ask that you honor that privacy by not asking your friends what they wrote when the class is over, please. That would put them on the spot, making them feel uncomfortable, and you don't want to do that to your friends."

Mrs. Kaufmann then described why she was doing this. "I want to go over the virtues of good character so that you know what is admired in most people. Trying to be a better and more likeable person is a sure way of having more friends and better friendships. What we'll do is this. I'll describe each of twenty-one virtues or qualities, like being honest, or responsible, or dependable, etc. and how it improves your character. After each one, you mark on your sheet a number from one to ten as to how well you're doing developing that quality so far at this age. If you think you are perfect at it already, give yourself a ten. If you're about halfway to the best you could be, give yourself a five. And, of course, if it's one virtue you really don't seem to have much of, like patience, or being a good sport, and you struggle to improve it all the time, be honest, and give yourself a one.

"You can pick any number from one to ten that you feel describes about where you are in becoming a person of great character. It's about your growing up and becoming one. It's not about being perfect at everything, because that's not possible. You haven't finished sculpting yourself yet as the final product of who you will be in this world. That comes with time, so relax and enjoy today's part of your journey, okay? So this little sheet is your opportunity to do a private self-inventory. It's a great way to set goals for the school year, like a school-year resolution. No one else will know what you're working on, except me, and I only collect these and lock them up in a confidential drawer in my filing cabinet, so I can bring them out again for you to look at when we get to the end of the year. That way you can remember what you thought at the beginning of the year, and see how you did. Whatever you want to focus on for the year is up to you, and you will all probably get better at most of these qualities anyway, simply from the life experiences that make up your maturing process. Okay? Are we ready?" Mrs. Kaufmann looked out over a room full of excited-looking students with pencils ready, and many books and folders covering all the survey sheets on the desks.

She then proceeded to go through the twenty-one virtues, one at a time. Each quality was described with an example of how too little (or sometimes too much) of it became a problem in relationships, and the balance that's needed. The students sat silently and looked quite thoughtful as they were remembering events in their lives that made each example make sense. After each virtue, they all marked their papers, carefully covering their numbers as soon as they did.

When they completed the last one, Mrs. Kaufmann asked them three more questions. "Okay, now that you all have done a challenging rating of your own characters, I'm going to ask you to pick the qualities that you want to focus on this year…probably the ones with the lowest scores. These will be your weakest virtues right now, so I would think they would be the ones you'd want to improve."

Mrs. Kaufmann paused and then said she was ready to move to the second question. She asked the students to think for a minute about a person in their grade at school that they considered really had a lot of great character, and whom they admired because of it. "Please write down the name of anyone you most admire--without worrying about spelling, of course-- and then what virtues or character qualities they have. No one will know whose name you wrote, but I will be able to tally the names of those people who are admired by the most students. Then, when I see some people are chosen repeatedly, I will collect the descriptions of those most admired people and post those descriptions on the bulletin board in the front hall. I won't put any names on them, so no one is made to feel uncomfortable, but I will put the descriptions up there for the top five most admired girls and the top five most admired boys – just numbered – no names.

"No one will know who anyone wrote down, so this isn't about putting your friends' names down, and it's not a popularity contest. It's about people who stand out because they have a lot of great qualities, and why we admire them. I think the most fun part is later, because when you all read these descriptions, you all start guessing who they might be. Plus, you find out what a difference good character really does make. So let's do it right now, while the outstanding people are coming to your minds." She then gave them time to scribble down the names and descriptions.

Then, when all the pencils were back down on the desks, Mrs. Kaufmann asked the students to do one last thing for her. It was her third question. "And now I have to ask you all to do a favor for me, so I can do a favor for all of you. Here's the deal. I would love to know which students you think really need to work on making friends. These would be the students who have a lot of work to do on their behavior. These would be the people who didn't know not to tease or bully, or harass. My hope is that after today, there just won't be any more of that, so this isn't about turning anyone in. This is about me knowing who I should watch out for, to help make friends. Remember, this is highly confidential, no one else can ever see these sheets, and it is meant for only me to know who needs help.

"These students would be the ones who you actually saw doing mean teasing, or bullying, or harassing, like I talked about earlier, and now are losing friends because of their bad reputations. These are the students I worry about. I think of them as eventually becoming very unhappy and alone, because they have made so many people upset with them, or afraid of them. They are the students I truly hope I can help to show respect or more kindness to others. I can work on this quietly, behind the scenes, in my own way. Like when I go out on playground or to the cafeteria, I can casually observe their behavior. I can have quiet, private conversations with these students afterwards, to see if they are aware that others are laughing at their jokes only to *pretend* to be friends. So often, these students really need attention in life, and think they have found a way to get friends to like them. Or, as bullies, they feel powerless at home and think they are getting power over others at school, to feel better about themselves. The sad thing is, they may have no idea that they are gradually losing respect from their peers, and their so-called friends will pull away and avoid them one at a time.

"So, if you can let me know anyone who you think I can help, that will actually help you all. If we work together to support one another to become better people, then you all benefit every day you come to school. And don't we all learn better when we feel safe and our minds aren't thinking about being teased or laughed at? I can do this with your help every year, because it's what I do. I am here to cheer you all along your journeys to becoming wonderful people with great character. I want you all to be the grown-ups I would love to have as neighbors! And please," Mrs. Kaufmann really emphasized, "keep your papers covered when you write to me. Also, if you, yourselves, have been bullied or harassed, please let me know, so I can see how I can help you. If you do want to chat with me, tell me how you prefer we meet so that it can be absolutely private…like before school, or we could e-mail, or talk on the phone, or you can come to me for some other reason during the day. I know how uncomfortable it can be to begin that conversation, but this is your perfect opportunity to let me help you with complete confidence. And remember, this is not something I will share with anyone. It is just to help me to know where to look to find the people I need to help. You can fold these papers in half when you're done, and I will collect them as I see them getting folded. Remember, there can only be silence until we are *all* done, so please be patient after I pick up your survey."

Once again, the writing was the only sound except for the immediate folding of survey sheets. Mrs. Kaufmann scurried around the classroom taking them from the students' hands and thanking each one. Some students began to fold the sheets in half over and over again, until there was a small square of paper ready to pop open like an accordion. She smiled and assured those students especially that only she would read these results. She was excited to be able to read the results, but held off from unfolding any and peeking. The students, too, seemed lighter once they had handed over their private information.

"Okay, I have them all, and I want to thank you. I have one more reminder before you all get up and go out into the hall to your next class. Please come up with something else to talk about as you join each other right now. What you all wrote should remain completely private, so respect each other by not asking each other what they wrote. I suggest you talk about what you'll be for Halloween and who you'll be going out with for trick-or-treating, because that's coming up in just a couple of weeks. Or, what clubs and extracurricular activities you're signing up for on Friday this week. Okay, my friends, thank you for being so great today, and especially for any help you were able to give me. I love teaching this lesson, because I believe it helps you all to have many good friends and to mature into such great people!"

The students thanked Mrs. Kaufmann as they filed past her to get to their next class. There was a feeling of connection between her and the students now, as if they were partners in making a difference. And, even better, it was a wonderful feeling of trust.

Friday finally came, and all five classes on "Friendship" were completed. Each teacher thanked her for doing the class, and they all felt hopeful that Monday would bring a resulting change in behavior from this exposed awareness. All students went home for the weekend, and Mrs. Kaufmann went home with a briefcase full of interesting surveys to read and tally. It was a lot of work, but so worth it. Throughout the weekend she made her lists of "Most Challenging Virtues at This Grade Level" and "Most Admired Students' Qualities" for the bulletin board, for Monday morning. She also made her private lists of those students who were indicated to need some work on character, as well as a list of those students who wanted to come see her privately. It was to be a busy week coming up, but so valuable. These were the secrets that students usually kept from the adults in their lives that festered into such pain and unhappiness all school year. And now, Mrs. Kaufmann was tallying all that confidential information. It was a real treasure for a school counselor. It was a way to really help make a difference, and she couldn't wait for Monday morning to get started.

Monday Morning

Standing on a small footstool with her stapler in hand before school started on Monday morning, Mrs. Kaufmann was busy putting up the results of the survey on the newly covered bulletin board. It was bright and cheerful and quite attention-getting, especially with the big circles labeled "Most Admired Girl #1" or "Most Admired Boy #1." There were ten colorful circles altogether, five for the girls and five for the boys. Each circle had a printed sheet of quoted comments that had been used to describe just one most-admired person. There were observations such as "She is never mean to anyone," and "Always tries to make everything be fair." "She tries to include everyone all the time," and "She shares her stuff." Or, "He is a great sport whether he wins or loses and never puts anyone down or makes fun of anyone." "He always has respect for all people." She loved reporting this back to the students, and was even prouder of their ability to look beyond who dressed the best or ran the fastest in gym class. For her to be able to brag publicly to all teachers, parents, and students, just felt so great, since more often people look at what's wrong with kids rather than spotlight what's great about them.

"Mrs. Kaufmann, can I talk to you sometime today?" a little voice quietly spoke from behind her as she stood on the stool. Stepping down and turning around, Mrs. Kaufmann saw one of the students she had put on her list to see that day from a request on her survey form.

"Hi Shirley! Sure, my dear. Is now a good time to talk, since no one is here yet? We have about twenty minutes to get started before school starts. Just before the school bell rings, I can slip you right out of my office to get you to class, before everyone starts coming into the school. That way no one will see you. Sound okay?"

Shirley looked relieved. "Okay, thanks, Mrs. Kaufmann. My mom dropped me off early, hoping I would be able to talk to you. I'll just go down to your waiting room." She began to scurry down to the guidance office before Mrs. Kaufmann had even picked up her stool and papers. Shirley was trying to distance herself from the school counselor, in case anyone might be in the halls that morning who might figure out that she was going for help. Mrs. Kaufmann noticed that and honored that distance. She deliberately took her time and avoided any conversation with Shirley as they walked separately, one in front of the other in silence, back to Mrs. Kaufmann's office.

Once they both got into the room and closed the door, Mrs. Kaufmann said, "Shirley, I am so happy that we connected just now, because you were on my list to see today. I just didn't know how I was going to reach you without anyone noticing, so this is perfect. I read your note from the survey on Friday and saw you needed to talk. I believe you said it was about a boy that you weren't sure was doing mean teasing, or if he was harassing you. Can you tell me about it?"

Shirley blurted out immediately, withholding nothing. "It's Jett. He keeps making fun of me, being a girl and doing things like girls do. I am so tired of it, and he does it all the time."

"What kinds of things does he say, and where does he say these things?" Mrs. Kaufmann pursued.

"He makes fun of the way I throw the ball in gym class. He says that I throw like a girl. And when he shows me a worm, up close, he laughs when I pull away. He calls after me that I'm such a scaredy girl, and then he just keeps laughing. He does it mostly on playground. I wish he would just leave me alone and go play with the boys." Shirley's voice sounded like it was cracking, and she was holding back the tears.

"How often does he do this?" Mrs. Kaufmann questioned her, sliding the tissue box toward her, letting her know it was okay to cry if she needed to.

"Any time he goes by me. I play jump rope with some other girls, and I hear him do it to some of them, too," Shirley offered.

"Does he ever join in games with the boys? Does he play soccer or Wall Ball?"

"No, I don't think so. I just see him wandering around the playground and making comments wherever he goes. He is so annoying, and I can't make him stop."

"Well, the good news is I can help you right away without him even knowing you came in for help. It will be easy, because I can just go out on playground and observe his behavior. Remember how I said in my lesson on friendship, that I can use everyone's inside scoop to help me know where to look? Once I see, or hear, what's going on, I will chat with Jett at a time he won't be embarrassed either. I had planned to go into the cafeteria and out on playground today anyway, with the list of students I made over the weekend. So, today, if he starts to tease you about being a girl, I'll hear because I'll be right where the girls do their jump-roping, okay?"

Shirley's face and tense shoulders relaxed. "Thanks, Mrs. Kaufmann. But what do I say when he does it whether you're there or not? My mom keeps saying to just ignore him, but he gets worse when I do."

"Well, maybe the friendship lesson last week has him thinking about himself today. It sounds like Jett already doesn't have friends to hang out with on playground. It also seems that he just wants attention, and he's going about it all wrong. I could just picture you looking right at him and saying sincerely, 'People don't like to be around you when you make fun of them, Jett. Why don't you try to be nice so you can make friends?' That might surprise him if you speak up to him." Mrs. Kaufmann continued, "I'm just thinking that you are important to him, or he wouldn't be constantly trying to get your attention. If you say it without sounding mean, maybe he'll hear you. Would you be able to do that?"

"I don't know," Shirley answered reluctantly.

Mrs. Kaufmann explained further. "From what you and others have told me, Jett is so used to teasing as his primary playground activity, that he must also be used to getting back angry comments. It's probably what he expects. He wouldn't plan on anyone being nice back to him or saying anything that would help him, so that would maybe make him speechless for a minute. He most likely wouldn't be nice right away, but I'd bet he'd hear the echo of your words later. You would just be the reminder of what I taught last week…but only if you felt up to it."

"I guess I could try," Shirley answered, still giving it some thought.

"That's up to you, for sure. If you couldn't or don't want to, I would understand completely. The most important thing is that you let me know if he doesn't stop after today. Now that he knows what he's doing is called sexual harassment, which is to make fun of girls for being girls, he must realize this is going to get him into trouble. Hopefully, he already knows he has to stop. If he doesn't, please let me know. It means he didn't get the importance of what I was teaching after all. You can even slip a note in my 'comments box' in my waiting room to tell me, or you could call or e-mail me when you get home. Of course, he will not know it's you or any of the girls who might also want to report this, so not to worry. And we can always meet again if you like, but right now the bell is going to ring. If you feel like you're okay, then how 'bout you grab your things so you can get on your way to homeroom before the crowds come?" Mrs. Kaufmann stood up with Shirley to walk her to the door. "Thanks for coming to see me this morning. Like I said, you were on my list today, and you made it easy."

Shirley smiled and said, "I'm fine now, Mrs. Kaufmann. Thanks. It was actually my mom who brought me to you this morning. Yesterday I was telling her about your class on Friday, and about what Jett was doing, so she wanted me not to take it any longer. I'll try to say something to Jett today if he puts me down for being a girl. And saying it like I care about him probably would really shock him."

"One other thing, Shirley," Mrs. Kaufmann added. "There's nothing wrong with being a girl. There's nothing wrong with being tall or being a boy. There's nothing wrong with what Jett is teasing you about you, you know? It's like teasing him for being brunette. That doesn't even make sense. He just doesn't have anything else to tease you about. You and he are just different, and neither one of you is wrong. Just keep remembering that if he says something. You could also just look at him like you don't get it and you're questioning his sense of humor. That might stop him if he can't get the reaction from you he was going for."

"Oh, that's even better," Shirley said. "I know I can do that because it's simple, and I don't have to worry about what he'll say back. Okay, I better go. I hear kids coming down the hall. Thanks again, Mrs. Kaufmann."

"Bye, Shirley. Let me know how it goes after playground today, okay? Swing by and give me a thumbs-up or thumbs-down, and I'll know to take it from there, all right? Have a great day, my dear," she called after her.

"Okay, I will," Shirley answered happily.

Mrs. Kaufmann thought how perfect it was that Shirley was the first name on her "Wants to See Me" list and Jett was the first name on her "I Need to Observe Them" list for playground that day. Jett had had the highest number of students naming him as "needing help." *This will definitely be a great day to end a lot of misery!* she thought.

The "Talk"

Jett was already doing his thing on playground that day, running around the girls who were jump-roping and making annoying comments. Each girl who was teased made a face equal to the annoyance, and Mrs. Kaufmann's sudden presence near them made him move away from the girls to another place on playground. Mrs. Kaufmann's eyes connected to Shirley's, and she searched her face for a reaction. Surprisingly, Shirley said something to her best friend Raney, and then they both ran up to her without any hesitation.

"Mrs. K," Raney called to her. "Would you please make Jett leave us alone? He keeps laughing at us for playing girl games."

Mrs. Kaufmann said with a big smile, "Sure, but think about it. You are girls, and there's nothing wrong with that or the fun you're having. I've always been a girl and very proud of it. He doesn't seem to get why that's not really anything to tease half the world's population about!" she laughed as she answered. "If there are seven and a half billion people in the world, there must be between three and four billion females, give or take a few, so what's wrong with that? Did either of you say anything back to him?" She looked at both Raney and Shirley, hoping Shirley felt free to answer.

"I just said that I didn't get what he meant, and I just looked at him and waited," Shirley said proudly.

"Good for you," Mrs. Kaufmann complimented her, knowing that hadn't been an easy thing to do.

"I called him a jerk," Raney said proudly.

"What were his reactions to what each of you said?" Mrs. Kaufmann asked purposely that way. She expected to point out that Raney's further name-calling was not exactly the best way to handle Jett's name-calling.

Raney said, "He did the usual. He laughed like he was making fun of me and called me a dumb girl, and then he laughed at me for being mad at his teasing. But I have to admit, he looked kind of weird when Shirley said she didn't get it. He didn't say anything, and that's when you came near us."

Shirley jumped in, "He really did look surprised that I didn't react the way he expected. It actually worked."

Mrs. Kaufmann smiled and told the girls she was going to move around playground for a bit and see what Jett was up to. "It does seem like he really thinks it's all in fun or funny, and not like he wants to hurt you. It's as if he wants your attention, and he thinks it is okay to make fun of you for being girls. I definitely have to have a little talk with him. Let me know if he bothers you two again after recess is over, okay? If he doesn't stop with the girl jokes, I'm thinking that continuing to look at him like he's not making any sense is the best response from both of you, and it might teach him it isn't funny. That's when I'll have to report this and call his parents to come in to the school. Then he'll learn for sure, but that's the hard way."

As the girls said okay, they skipped back to the place where the other girls had formed the Double-Dutch line. Mrs. Kaufmann wandered over to the swings, where she saw Jett pretending to jump in the way of the girls trying to swing. He kept laughing at them while he teased them, and never saw Mrs. Kaufmann walking up behind him.

"Hi, Jett, I have a question for you," she said. She figured she surprised him because she caught him in the act of annoying the girls. She asked him if he would mind joining her for a little "walk and talk" back toward her office. She said quietly, "I think I might be able to help you with a problem you may not even know you have," and she smiled.

Jett became very curious, and felt relieved that he didn't seem to be in trouble for getting in the way of the girls on the swings. They both walked away from anyone who could hear them, and back toward the outside door near her office. "What help do I need?" he asked trying to seem very casual.

"Jett, I tallied the results of that survey, and it turned out your name came up over and over, as someone who teases others. It also came up as someone who does sexual harassment, because they say you keep putting down the girls for being girls. Were you aware that your peers thought of you that way?" she asked directly.

"No. I'm just joking, and girls like that. I'm teasing *with* them, like you said. How many people said that, and who were they?" Jett immediately answered defensively, showing sudden surprise and concern.

"Well, the good news is some of them feel sorry for you because they think you have no friends because of it. Others are just so annoyed that I think they wanted you to get into trouble. And you know I can't say who they are, because I promised confidentiality, but I can say you had nineteen different people who witnessed you doing that. You're not in trouble with me, yet. If you continue to harass the girls after this conversation, I will have to report this to the vice-principal, and he will require that your parents come in to the school. That would be really bad, but you are getting a warning here. I'm just making sure you know your girl-teasing is unwanted, it's repeated, it's against them for being female, and they do not like it. That's what makes it sexual harassment," she said clearly so Jett understood she was not treating it lightly.

"I'm sorry, Mrs. Kaufmann," Jett said very quickly with his face getting red. "I didn't think that's what I was doing at all! I like those girls I was teasing, well, not *like,* like," he qualified. "I just figured they thought it was fun, too."

Mrs. Kaufmann spoke now with more compassion. "Jett, as I watch you on playground, I notice you don't hang with friends, or play a sport, or even look like you are connecting with anyone. Do you have friends, or do you think maybe your teasing may have made the boys pull away?"

Jett dropped his head. There was quiet for a while, and Mrs. Kaufmann waited, in order for Jett to have time to think and decide how he wanted to answer. Finally, with very low energy, Jett admitted he didn't have any friends. When he looked up, his eyes were filled to the brim with tears.

"Jett, it's okay. It's a start, and we can fix this, I promise. I'm just glad that you can see what happens with too much teasing. I'd like to help you get some good attention back now. Let's work on changing your reputation as a teaser or harasser to a more considerate guy, and that will help you get some friends. Will you work on that with me? I know you would be a happier person if you did, and I know the girls would be relieved."

Mrs. Kaufmann tried to put Jett at ease by reminding him what "the deal" was….that she was there to help him learn how to be a great person, even if learning the lessons could sometimes be hard when you didn't learn them right away.

"I tried to join them in soccer, but they wouldn't let me," Jett offered.

"I'm sorry that you have to deal with being excluded, because I know it hurts. Remember though, if I tried to make them let you play, I think that would backfire, because they would resent it and they wouldn't really want you there. That would feel even worse. There's a reason they are not letting you play. Do you know what it is? We may have to fix that first," Mrs. Kaufmann suggested.

"I don't know. I just like to have a good time joking with people," Jett answered.

"What exactly do they say to you when you approach the game?" Mrs. Kaufmann asked.

"They just call me names, like I'm a jerk or a loser," he said, with tears filling up in his eyes again.

Mrs. Kaufmann suggested they go right inside to her office, seeing his tears and wanting to save him the embarrassment with so many students in the area. Jett slipped inside the building ahead of her and headed directly to her office, while Mrs. Kaufmann followed, allowing some distance between them. Once they both sat down in her office she said, "Okay, I have to ask something. Why do you tease girls about being girls?"

Jett smiled and said, "They are funny when they get all excited when I say things to them."

"Do you enjoy upsetting them?" she asked.

"Uh, no, I just want to see them get all stirred up. I don't mean to upset them. I just want to have fun and be funny."

"Do you remember what I talked about last week about friendships? Perhaps what you think is funny isn't what others think is funny. That's what is costing you your friends, my dear. If you know it feels bad when the boys call you names, how do you think the girls feel when you call them names?" Mrs. Kaufmann challenged him.

"Because the guys are trying to make me feel bad and go away, but I'm only calling girls, girls," he explained.

"But does that really feel like 'friendly' teasing? Do you hang out with these girls as friends? Do the girls like it and feel closer to you as a friend? If the teasing is playful, and back and forth, and makes you closer with a friend, then that's okay teasing. That's the kind that makes you laugh and feel really connected. Any other kind of teasing is not good, because it makes people feel bad, just the way you feel when they do it to you, you know?" Mrs. Kaufmann explained.

"I guess so," Jett admitted. "What do I do now if nobody likes me?"

"Well, a bad reputation takes some time to build, so it takes some time to make go away. The truth is, if you stop the teasing, and maybe even apologize to some of the students you teased a lot, that may begin to turn things around. I can help you with that if you decide to do it. I really want you to find something to do on playground, other than just wander around. Would you consider playing Wall Ball? There are a whole lot of boys playing that, and there are no teams or limited numbers like soccer. They couldn't reject you, and you would have the perfect chance to start practicing new behaviors, like put-ups instead of put-downs," she suggested.

"What if they make fun of me and call me names, too?" he challenged her.

"It's not as likely as with soccer. That's where there are only so many people on the field so they are more selective. With Wall Ball, it's the more the merrier. I have another idea, too. There's a new boy in your grade this year, Aaron, who just plays Wall Ball every day, but he doesn't appear to have any friends yet. Maybe you might make friends with him? But, you know, if you really want to have a friend, you have to be a friend. You have to be the kind of person you'd feel most comfortable with yourself. You need to show him the good side of you, the fun side of you, and the person that can be funny without public teasing or embarrassing comments. Would you be willing to work on that?" Mrs. Kaufmann asked encouragingly. "It's a trust that develops between people. It makes them feel relaxed and comfortable with you, knowing they can feel safe when they are with you and not fear you will humiliate them in front of others."

"Okay. I can do that. Who's the boy?" he asked hopefully.

"It's Aaron, the tall, dark-haired boy in Mrs. Gunther's class. I can bring you two together in my office tomorrow after I do my 'new student check-up' with Aaron, if you like. I'll need to see if he would like this as well. If he likes the idea, you could be his support person for now and help him become more comfortable here at the school. My idea is that he might need someone to go trick-or-treating with, since Halloween is just around the corner. What are your plans?"

"I didn't have any. I figured I'd just tag along with my younger sister and her friends like I always do." Jett boasted that her little friends all liked him and always giggled at what he said about girls.

"So they like the attention?" Mrs. Kaufmann asked. "Do you think maybe they just like the fact that you're an older brother who flatters them by spending time with them, even if it is teasing? That makes them feel important, I imagine. Girls your age are not flattered when you put them down. They think that *you* think you're better than them. You think?" She laughed and Jett did, too.

"Okay, I won't tease any more. And I do want to meet Aaron. Should I just come here for playground tomorrow?" Jett asked.

"Yes, I'll have him meet me here for the check-up right after lunch, and you'll be here in the waiting room then, too. In the meantime, let's get you to class right now, because the kids are just coming in from playground. If you have the opportunity to apologize to Shirley and Raney, I would do it. I did overhear what you were saying to them, and I think it would be smart to do. It may be hard, but we have to start cleaning up your reputation. I'll see you at playground time tomorrow. You are a good kid, Jett, and a kind person with just an inappropriate sense of humor. It's something you can learn to change easily. In fact, I think you just did. If you stick to your promise, you will get friends, but be patient. We just have to break old habits and make new ones, and then others will come to realize that over time. You'll see."

Jett gave a quick "Thanks," and was on his way.

I believe he will change now, but I doubt he'll apologize to the girls today. We'll see, Mrs. Kaufmann thought, and then she went back into her office to work on her "list."

The Hippo Birds

The next morning seemed to fly by, with Mrs. Kaufmann having "new-student check-up" appointments back to back. Mrs. Kaufmann's plan was to make sure all of the new kids in the school were absorbed by a group or had at least one friend by Halloween. She would ask each one about how the new classwork and homework matched up to what they had been doing at the old school, and then go right into the importance of them having fun, too. She stressed that she wanted them to feel like they fit in, even though that would take some time. She worked to make matches to help them all make new friends. The last new student for the morning came in with his pass. It was Aaron.

The school counselor greeted him, "Hi there, my new friend. How are you doing?"

Aaron smiled and came right in the door quite comfortably. This was the first place he had come when they visited in the summer, and Mrs. Kaufmann was the first adult he had met. She promised him she would watch out for him, and they had met every so often since then. He was quite relaxed with her now, and didn't even protest not being out on playground. "I'm doing okay," he answered.

"How are your grades looking?" she asked first.

"Oh, they're okay. Some of what I'm learning in math is brand-new, though, so it's hard, and my grades aren't the best," he admitted.

"Did you know your teacher comes in before school to give extra help? You just need to let him know when you can come in early, and he'll be happy to help you. I also run a Peer Tutoring Program. I can ask the volunteer math tutors on that list if any of them would like to tutor a new student with his homework. They love to volunteer, especially for new students who just need to fill in gaps from the old school. Some actually give their home phone numbers to be used like a hotline. Would you want to try either one of those options?" Mrs. Kaufmann offered Aaron.

"Both would be great. I'll talk to my teacher first to see what days he's coming in this week, and I think my mom wouldn't mind driving me to school those mornings. How do I meet the Peer Tutor?"

"Oh, I'll send a pass for you once I get one and make contact with him or her. Do you have a preference?" she checked.

"Not really if they are older, I guess."

"And friends? Have you made any new friends that have come to your house yet?" she continued.

"No, not yet. I really don't know what to say to anyone to invite them. It feels weird, you know?" Aaron leaned forward in his chair, showing this was an area of transition that was not working yet.

"Have you tried at all, or do you have anyone in mind that looks like he might be fun to get to know?"

"No," he answered with some embarrassment. "With other boys, if you say the wrong thing, they'll make fun of you. Also, the boys playing soccer play together every day, and are always in the same group, so I just play Wall Ball. I know almost everyone already has their old friends, and I don't want to try to separate them. It's just weird."

"Well, I know another boy that feels the same way and is willing to play Wall Ball. I thought maybe he could be your support person as a new kid for a while and explain how things work around here in general. Would you like to meet him?" she asked. "I even suggested the same thing to him yesterday, and he really liked the idea," she said reassuringly.

"Yes, for sure," Aaron answered, perking up.

"Well, his name is Jett, and he planned to come to my waiting room at playground time today to see if you were willing to have his help. He is very happy to do that."

Aaron said quickly, "Oh, is that the boy that teases everybody on playground?"

"He did," Mrs. Kaufmann admitted. "He has decided to stop, but the other students don't know that yet. He really misunderstood people's reactions, because he thought they were laughing *with* him and enjoying his silliness. I gave that lesson on friendship last week, and he won't be teasing anymore, so not to worry. He could use your help not to do that, too, if you would be willing to help him break his habit. It reminds me of how hippos and birds help each other out so perfectly. The bird eats the bugs that land on their backs, where they can't itch or shoo them away. The birds need food and protection which the hippos offer them. It's a perfect match. I can help set it up, you'll see. Let me go see if he's out there, and I can introduce you two right now," she said as she got up to open the door.

Jett was sitting right there and stood up, excited to meet the new boy.

"Should I come in there, Mrs. Kaufmann?" Jett asked.

"Absolutely. Jett, I'd like you to meet Aaron. He was new this September from Cleveland. And Aaron, this is Jett, who was new back in first grade. I'm sure you'll both have plenty to talk about, both having been the new guy for a while. I was hoping Jett could help you meet some of the other students. My goal for my new kids is to make sure they have a group or a friend to go trick-or-treating with by Halloween, so you two can talk about how that may work out for you both." Mrs. Kaufmann led them to all they needed, to get started talking.

"Oh, and one more thing I want to mention, guys. I see a wonderful way you can both help each other. Aaron, Jett loves to laugh and be funny, and he has always used teasing as a way to be playful with others. His intentions were never meant to embarrass anyone. Now the kids don't know he wants to stop. They don't trust he won't tease them in front of others, so he needs time to prove it, right Jett?"

"And Jett, here's a new friend, a clean slate. He can accept that you are working on that and can be a great friend to help you, too. I'm thinking Jett could use a little, unnoticeable nudge whenever he starts teasing people, just as a reminder. Would that help you at all, Jett?"

"Actually, yeah," Jett answered, "just not in front of everybody."

"And Jett, Aaron has been uncomfortable inviting kids over to get to know them, because he doesn't want to sound weird when he asks. Finding the right words is a hard thing to do around kids who already know each other well and seemed to have formed tight groups of friends. That could make them tease him, you know what I mean? He doesn't need that as a new kid. I'm hoping you can be the one to introduce him to people and let him know how things work around here. Maybe you can tell him about the clubs, sports, and extracurricular activities that you both can sign up for this week in homerooms. I know you can both play Wall Ball, so it's like the hippo and bird thing. You both can offer exactly what the other guy needs right now. Does it sound like a plan?" Mrs. Kaufmann asked.

Both boys chimed in at the same time with an energetic, "Yeah!" They both felt like they would value the relationship, as much as *be* valued in it. It was the perfect hippo and bird match.

"Okay then. You guys have about ten more minutes of playground time. Since you're not in the same classes, why don't you exchange phone numbers, e-mail addresses, and bus routes so you can connect after school? Then you guys go out and have some fun!" Mrs. Kaufmann exclaimed.

Within seconds the boys had each scribbled down their information, exchanged it, and taken off to play Wall Ball. Mrs. Kaufmann smiled as she opened her office door to the waiting room so the boys could go outside. "Don't run!" she called after them, since they took off like bullets toward the outside door.

"We won't," they called back, as they tried their hardest to slow down but still beat each other to the door. They both looked so happy that it just tickled her, too! *Let me zip outside to see how it all turns out*, she thought, and she grabbed her office door keys and went outside. Right there jumping rope were Shirley and Raney. They both stopped and ran up to Mrs. Kaufmann.

"Guess what?" they both said. "Jett just ran by us and yelled, 'Sorry!' We think he was apologizing!"

"Well, how about that!" Mrs. Kaufmann said with surprise. She couldn't help but try to give him some help. She told the girls, "I think Jett really has a good heart, and I think he really does feel badly now that he realizes his teasing wasn't fun for others. Maybe he's changed?"

"Maybe," the girls said as they ran back to their jump-roping friends, like it really didn't matter right now anyway.

Kids are amazingly resilient, Mrs. Kaufmann thought, *and they really do prefer to be considered good people. That seems to be what makes most of them feel happy. Thank goodness!*

Discussion Points:

- When people tease others, it is not the teasers who decide if what they are doing is good teasing or not. It's the people getting teased who need to let the teasers know whether they find it fun or not.

- We need to remember that people who make fun of others may not have learned the rules for making good friendships. Once we learn how to treat others, we need to be forgiving for those who don't know yet.

- Some friendships can be very good and supportive because of the differences between the people.

Reflection Questions:

1. Do you enjoy teasing with your good friends? Can you tell if you hit on something that they are sensitive about? What do you do to assure them you don't mean to upset them?

2. How do you let people know you don't like being made fun of in public? Should you make fun of them back? How do you help a friend who's getting teased?

3. Why did Jett think his teasing was just funny? What kind of teasing was Jett doing? (Friendly, unfriendly, bullying, or harassing?)

4. What suggestions would you give new students to help them join established groups of long-time friend groups? Have you ever reached out to get to know new students, or, at least, make them feel more comfortable?

CHAPTER 14:
When Does Being Special Go From Unique to Weird?

Charley's Tail

"Hi, Mrs. Kaufmann," Charley Bond called over to the school counselor as they were filing out of school for a fire drill. He was alongside her in a parallel line of people, hurrying to get outside and out from under the blaring fire bell. It was a warm, beautiful October day at Hillstown Middle School, and the principal needed to get another fire drill done. It was a gift for all but the teachers who had something time-limited going on in their classrooms. Most everyone else was loving the interruption and the sunshine.

"Hey there, my friend," Mrs. Kaufmann called back to Charley, without being able to say much more than that over the loud noise. As Mrs. Kaufmann reached the outside double doors, Charley jumped forward to hold them open for her and everyone else, which was not typical for a boy in a middle school. Most boys are "movement motivated" and not as likely to stop and look around to see what they could do for others, but Charley was special. He was quite a thoughtful person, with a kind, pleasant, and non-aggressive manner. He didn't seem to reach out to make friends, though, so his non-assertiveness in school caused others to just leave him alone.

What seemed wrong to Mrs. Kaufmann was that he seemed to have no friends at all, and he mostly walked head down, not expecting anyone to even talk to him. The only two things she had observed that made him different from the rest of the boys at his grade level was that he wore only black T-shirts and had long hair, with a really long narrow lock of hair that he allowed to grow down past his shoulder blades – a "tail," he called it proudly. It had been popular among some middle school boys quite a while back, but never in this school, and not in his grade. Because he was unlike all the other boys in his class, he was considered different. The common clothes for the other boys in his grade varied in color, and the hair cut for the boys was the buzz-cut or the clean-cut look. Mrs. Kaufmann guessed this might be the reason that Charley was avoided by the other boys. She figured they thought he didn't bother to cut his hair and just judged him as "weird."

Mrs. Kaufmann remembered that earlier in the year, Charley had come to her office bringing a note from his teacher so she was able to talk with him for a bit. She asked Charley how long he wanted his tail to grow, and Charley's face broke into a huge smile. He was very proud of his non-traditional haircut and bragged that his mom told him he could keep it, to stand out in a way others might think was "cool." Charley told the school counselor that his mom thought other boys would admire his courage to be different. Mrs. Kaufmann knew Charley needed friends and his mom was just trying to help him. His parents were divorced, and both had to work long hours. His older brother was away in college, so he spent a lot of his non-school time home alone. He was a good person, tried hard to get good grades in school, usually ending up with B's, and was almost over-willing to please everyone, just for the simple feedback of attention.

In order to make friends, Charley thought if he looked "cool" wearing black and having long hair, maybe others would find him interesting and reach out to him. He and his dad thought this haircut would do just that. But, the longer his tail grew, the more the other boys avoided him. He had no idea what his dressing in black every day, with his long shaggy hair and tail, was doing to his image. The other boys weren't mean, and they didn't tease him. They just didn't try to be friends with him...ever. To them, he was just too different.

"Thanks, Charley. What a gentleman!" she said, as she passed him through the doors to get outside and into the sunny, non-bell-ringing day.

Charley beamed from ear to ear. He just loved having anyone give him attention, no less kindness, and that concerned Mrs. Kaufmann even more. She wished he could just be happy with friends, like the other students who appeared so delighted by this free pass from class.

Of course Charley continued to hold the door for the endless line that followed them. It was his feel-good deed for the day, and he needed every one of the little repeated muffled thank-you's he was getting because of it.

"Hi, Mr. Bears," Mrs. Kaufmann said to Charley's teacher, as he was getting his line of students quiet to take attendance. "Just so you know, Charley Bond is still back there holding the door," she offered, so he knew where Charley was and didn't mark him absent.

"Oh, thanks, and I'm not surprised. He's such a nice kid with real manners," he answered, and continued to take attendance. Mrs. Kaufmann waited by him and his line while he finished. Charley ran up to him to let him know he was back, and then went to the end of the line, turning and facing the school.

Mrs. Kaufmann winked at Charley. She then leaned into Mr. Bears and quietly asked him if Charley seemed to have any friends this school year so far. "Not a one," Mr. Bears answered. "It's as if he just assumes he won't have a friend; like he's given up. He never goes up to any boy or group of boys and acts like he wants friendship, either. He's such a loner--it's sad. And yet he is the kindest and politest student I have. He often ends up sitting at a girls' table when it comes to free choice for group work. They just accept him, almost with a feel-sorry attitude. Yet, on a positive note, no one treats him like a loser. They just don't want or need to connect with him. He seems to have separated himself from the school culture here, by his choice of black clothes and that long hair. It's such a ragamuffin look that it keeps the rest at a distance."

"I've noticed that loneliness in the cafeteria and at recess," Mrs. Kaufmann added. "Are there ever any put-downs on the part of the others?" she asked.

"No. I have a pretty nice group of boys this year, and none of them seem to be rude or mean. Charley doesn't do anything to them, either," he added.

"It's always so sad when a student just appears different from the others, and they get rejected because of that alone. I'm wondering if I could see him after this fire drill for a few minutes? Just long enough to 'take the pulse' on his situation, and while all the others are settling back into their seats. I needed to give your class their attendance award certificates anyway, so why don't you send him down to my office-- randomly chosen, of course. You can ask him to pick them up for you," Mrs. Kaufmann suggested. "The last thing I would want is to make it look like something was wrong with him, and that he was being sent down to me with a problem."

"Good idea. And good luck. The puzzling part to me is that he seems to really like this 'uniqueness,' as he calls it. I think he thinks it's cool. He can't see that his unusual look is turning off the other boys."

"I know, and that's the problem. It would be fine if he were already a student that others looked up to, or saw as a leader. If they saw him as really cool, then coming to school with a totally different haircut, and a totally different dress style, could start a trend and others would follow. Charley's problem is that he hasn't established himself in this class as a leader, so instead, he is seen as weird or too different, and therefore avoided and left alone. I have to somehow make that point without hurting his self-esteem, or sounding like I don't agree with his parents' suggestions, either," Mrs. Kaufmann added, as the follow-up fire bell sounded for everyone to go back inside.

"I'll send him right along," Mr. Bears said, as he turned to the line of students and signaled to them to start back to class.

"Thanks," Mrs. Kaufmann answered, moving quickly to get back to her office and gather the attendance awards together to give to Charley.

Award-Worthiness

Sure enough, Charley suddenly appeared in her doorway with a big smile, and still feeling appreciated from the door-holding compliment from her. "You are such a gentleman," she said to him as she saw him appear. "Come on in, Charley Bond, how have you been?" she asked enthusiastically.

"Thanks," he answered with his face beaming and smiling from ear to ear. "I'm fine and my mom and dad both make sure I am polite. They remind me all the time!" he complained, but rather proudly.

"I'm glad, sir, because kindness and manners are life's lubricants, I always say. I believe they make other people feel comfortable to be with you, and you, my friend, certainly are a kind and thoughtful person! Okay, let me get those awards Mr. Bears is waiting for. Just have a seat and give me a minute. Besides, Mr. Bears knows I always chat with students for a little bit when they come to visit me."

Charley sat in one of the office chairs facing her big desk, as he was accustomed to whenever they met about grades or attendance or whatever. "Am I getting an attendance award for first marking period?" Charley asked.

"Well, let's see," Mrs. Kaufmann answered, somewhat absorbed in shuffling through the stack she finally found in a drawer. "I'm not sure, but let's take a look," she said as she looked slowly through the awards. She was taking her time because she wanted to chat about his lack of friends and how he felt about it.

"No, I don't see one. Maybe you had a sick day this year?" she asked, as she came to her desk to sit down and talk with him.

"No, I haven't been sick…oh, wait a minute." He stopped himself in the middle of his answer. "I did come in late one morning when my mom wasn't feeling well, and my dad had to pick me up at Mom's and drive me to school. Does that count against my perfect attendance?" he asked.

"Unfortunately, yes, unless it was an 'excused late' like they do for a doctor's appointment. Do you remember if your mom or dad wrote a note that day?" she asked.

"No, I don't think so, but it's okay. I didn't really have a reason. Mom just woke up late, so I couldn't be excused," Charley answered quickly.

"Maybe next marking period you can get one?" Mrs. Kaufmann suggested. "By the way, how's it going with your parents? Has the back-and-forth visitation become any easier?"

"Oh, yeah, it's okay. I'm used to it now. Every other weekend and Wednesday nights with my dad is fine," he answered comfortably.

"What about friends at your dad's place?" Mrs. Kaufmann slipped in, trying to get the discussion going in that direction. "Do you have any friends there where he lives?"

"No, but my dad and I hang out together mostly, so it's okay. I'm more alone when I'm home with Mom, because she's gone so much during the week. And Timmy's at college now, and I can't have friends over after school when I'm home alone."

"When do you invite friends over, Charley, just the weekends?" she asked directly. "And who do you consider your friends from school?"

"Well, I kinda don't," he said with a lowered voice. "I've asked Bruce Dowling if he wanted to ride bikes a couple of times, but he said he was busy. And I asked my neighbor, Davey, who goes to a different school, but he was busy, too," he admitted. "I'm not sure why no one wants to hang out with me. I've asked a few people, but they always just have a reason why they can't hang out on weekends," he added sadly.

"Have you ever done anything with them before? Is there any history of something going wrong between you and them, or do they just pull away for no reason?" she pursued.

"No reason that I know. My mom says to give it time. I will meet someone who will want to accept me as I am. My dad tells me I have to keep asking kids and not give up. I'm just getting embarrassed by being rejected, you know?"

"I don't blame you for feeling bad, but I agree with both your parents, actually. I know you are a really good, caring person who would be a great friend to a lot of people, but they just don't know you yet, that's all," she assured him. "We won't give up. I think there is a two-part solution here. The first one is to find out what it is that's causing your invitations to be turned down, and you can't be the one to demand they tell you. That's something we have to find out some other way," she suggested, "and I'm willing to help with that. Then, once we clear that up, we can get you involved in activities that would connect you to several boys through common interests. That's how you make friends. Do you want to work on that with me?" she offered.

"Sure," he answered. "But how will you find out what's wrong with me?" he asked.

"Oh, my dear, nothing is *wrong* with you. You are a great kid. They just don't know you yet. There might be something about you they think is different from them, so they aren't sure if they would be comfortable with those differences. There might be something you like to do or wear or say that they don't get, you know?"

"Okay, but how will you find that out?" Charley asked, showing some concern.

"Oh, it's just a matter of my having a group into my office to work on something for a school project, and I ask questions about their friends and the other kids in their class rather casually. It's always a nice conversation in which I'm basically asking them who I should be helping make friends. Now, since you do walk the halls alone, they may give me your name as a quiet person who needs to be with other boys. Typically when I ask them why they are recommending these people, they almost always tell me honestly and in a kind way, because the purpose is to be helpful. Are you okay with that?" she checked.

"Okay. But what if they don't mention my name?" he checked.

"Then I just get the information I'm supposed to get for that day, for whomever I'm supposed to help. It might take a while, but at least we're working on it, right?"

"Right," Charley answered, looking relieved.

"Okay, sir, here are the awards for Mr. Bears. Let's get you back to class before you miss any more social studies, okay?"

Charley jumped up, took the stack of awards from Mrs. Kaufmann's hand, and said, "Thank you so much for all your help, Mrs. Kaufmann!"

"Oh, you're so welcome, my dear. I just can't help but think we'll get you a friend who will thank me for giving *you* to *them* as a friend!" she said, making him feel better on his way out. "I'll let you know when I find something out, but I won't tell anyone else what we're working on, I promise. You can tell your parents, but that's up to you." Charley didn't answer, but his walk looked quite spirited as he left her office.

"Okay, now I have to think about what I can put together as an excuse for this meeting of boys," she quietly mumbled to herself. "It has to look legitimate, that's for sure."

The Boys' Meeting

"Come on in, guys!" Mrs. Kaufmann welcomed four boys from Charley's class into her office the next day at lunchtime. "Before I want to share with you why you were chosen to help me, I need to make sure you guys all have your lunches and drinks with you, and then we can get started."

Eager to eat, all four boys started ripping open their sandwiches and pushing straws into the little openings of their milk cartons. Realizing no one had answered her in their rush to eat, they then all assured her that they were ready to find out why they were chosen.

"Okay, then. Here's what I need from you while you have lunch today. And if we can brainstorm a working plan quickly enough, you might get to recess faster than normal!" she baited them. "What I need to know from you four, and I have a couple of other small groups I'm surveying as well, is an idea for how we can put a suggestion box in my waiting room. I have to make sure students don't use it to tell on each other or write ridiculous things. Any ideas for what I should write on the box so it can help me help students?"

"How 'bout you say something like that…'Let me help you,' and print it right on the side of the box?" Eric asked.

"Or what if you just write the word 'Suggestions,' but then go out to classes and tell everyone what you want?" JB chimed in.

Mrs. Kaufmann jumped in, saying, "I like both ideas, but I have to tell you. Last year I put one out there like that and told everyone it was to help people, and I got one tattletale with no signature, one complaint about the vice-principal being too strict, asking me to fire him, and a candy wrapper."

All four boys burst out laughing, and Mrs. Kaufmann joined them. "Okay, maybe it's not a suggestion box that I want. How would you boys suggest I reach out to determine which kids are lonely and need friends? I can't just ask everyone; they wouldn't tell me, because they'd feel embarrassed. I worry about the lonely ones, because school can't be much fun when you don't connect with people you like. Maybe I should just sit and have lunch with small groups of students like the four of you?" she probed.

She saw a full round of positive reactions, and then one spoke. "We can tell you who walks alone in the halls and doesn't seem to hang out with anyone, if you want."

"That would really be helpful, Jack!" Mrs. Kaufmann quickly responded. So who do I need to help, as far as you can tell?"

The boys named a couple of new boys, Arden and Wyatt, and then they named Charley Bond. Jack said, "We just don't know the new guys, but Charley is just, uh, different." He looked uncomfortable when he said it, because he didn't know how to put his thinking into words that would be acceptable to an adult. The other three boys nodded in agreement.

Mrs. Kaufmann jumped in, so their discomfort would not silence them now that she was on a roll. "What is it about Charley, let's say, that makes him *different*?"

JB looked at the other three for support, and then answered Mrs. Kaufmann. "If he cut his hair some, especially that long tail down his back, maybe he wouldn't look so weird. And he always wears black. Maybe if he dressed normally, he'd fit in."

Eric added, "Even my mom asked about him, as if he had a problem. She wanted to know if he hung out in the streets after school, or got into trouble at school. I don't think she'd say yes if I asked to have him over, because he's just so different. I think she thinks I'd get into trouble if I hung with him."

"And he's always walking with his head down, like he doesn't want friends, or doesn't want to talk to anyone anyway," Jack added.

Mrs. Kaufmann continued to be very interested in what they were all telling her. "So, if you were

Charley, and I were to let you know that some of the boys in your class think your hair is just too long, do you think you would cut your tail? Or do you think you'd ask your mom to buy you new shirts?" she asked sincerely.

There was a pause. Jack answered first, "I think I would if I were lonely and wanted friends."

Eric said he'd have to think about it, but he probably would after a while.

Mrs. Kaufmann asked, "Do you think his long hair and black shirts are his way of trying to be a little different, so he could get noticed? He seems to be a really nice person, isn't he? Sometimes students feel as if they have nothing interesting about themselves to offer others. They think they don't attract anyone, or that others will think they might be too boring, and they think that's why they have no friends. Some of these students try to come up with something unique about themselves, so they can stand out in the crowd as interesting, you know? Do any of you feel like that sometimes?"

JB nodded his head and said, "I remember when I first moved to this school and I didn't dress like everyone else here. I wore a lot of my old T-shirts with dumb sayings on them and I think people stayed away from me because of that. I just stayed quiet, hoping I could make a friend, and I never reached out to try and make one. After a while, my mom got me some new clothes, more like the ones everyone else was wearing. Then I felt more like I belonged here, and that was good. It was being different that was causing the other kids to keep their distance. As soon as I blended in with what everyone thought was 'the in thing' to wear, I began to make friends."

"I remember that. Didn't we have a new-student get-together at lunch one Friday, where you and Bruce planned to go see a movie that weekend?" Mrs. Kaufmann asked.

"Yeah, and then the two of us joined in the soccer game at recess that next Monday. After that, we just sat with those soccer guys at lunchtime."

"And JB, did that work out okay? Did you think you had to give up something about you in order to blend in with what the other guys thought was normal in our school?" Mrs. Kaufmann asked. "I wouldn't want students to have to be someone they are not. And I would hope students would not have to give up being who they are for the sake of pleasing others."

"My mom got me a few new sports jerseys, since that was what everyone else was wearing here. That was cool for the time being, and then it was up to me to start talking to other boys to get to know them," JB answered.

"I know. Students who have their regular friends or their groups established, don't think to reach out and bring the new students into their groups. My new student-assigned buddies only seem to make that effort on the first couple of days, I've noticed. They mostly just show their assigned new students around, so they don't get lost. After that, the new kids are on their own. By the way, do any of these three boys you mentioned play in the big soccer game at recess?" she asked.

"No, but the two new kids play Wall Ball. As for Charley, I think he just talks with the playground aide a lot, and offers to help teachers and the librarian at lunchtime. I'm not sure he even comes out most days."

Having received enough insight from her "guests" that day, she figured she needed to wrap it up. "Okay, so, getting back to the suggestion box idea, I gather I should cancel it?"

The boys all laughed and agreed. "So, I should just ask the students themselves who I should help? It's obvious that all I have to do is trust the kind and helpful students in my school, right? I also know you would keep this conversation between us, too." She loved giving the message to students that she trusted them and valued their opinions. She knew there was goodwill intended by their sharing, and maybe they might be more willing to give Charley a chance after that session…or not.

"Right," they all answered in harmony, smiling really big, while grabbing their garbage and shooting their crumbled paper bags toward the garbage can, with high-fives for the ones that scored.

"Well, I thank you for your help today," Mrs. Kaufmann said, as she stood up to wrap up the boys' session, "and if you have any other ideas for how I can help your classmates, feel free to let me know anytime, okay? We don't need a suggestion box, but we do need to get you all outside right now. I can hear the students in the cafeteria lining up to go out now. You guys get to be first ones on the playground today!" she smiled, and the four of them shot right out of her office without looking back. "I'll get the soccer ball," Eric called to the others.

She hoped she had helped them become a little bit more open-minded and less judgmental. Most importantly, she realized she needed to find a way to share this with Charley, in a positive way and with a simple shift of thinking.

Charley's Choice

"Good morning, Mr. Bears," Mrs. Kaufmann spoke into her phone, leaving a message for when Charley's teacher arrived at school. "If you're getting this message first thing this morning, would you be able to send Charley Bond to me during homeroom so it won't be noticed? Maybe if he brings the lunch money envelope down to the main office for you, you can let him know to stop by my office on the way back. And if you don't get this message until later today, just give me a call to let me know when he can miss a little class time today, okay? Thanks, Mr. Bears." She hung up and began to get all her messages that collected from after-school, the previous day and evening. In between the voice-mails, the phone rang in her hand. "Hello, this is Mrs. Kaufmann," she said immediately.

"Mrs. Kaufmann? This is Mr. Bears. I can send him right now if it's still good for you."

"Yes, please. Thanks. I'll try not to take too long, but I have to be very tactful, and that sometimes takes a little longer than when I can get right to it."

"Take your time," he said, "I'd like to see that little guy have some friends, too. He's going to his music lesson after homeroom, so I'll let his music teacher know he'll be a few minutes late."

"Thanks, that would be really helpful," she said, as she went out into the hall saying good morning to the last of the students still straggling into school late. She only waited for Charley a couple of minutes before he appeared coming from around the corner on his way to the office.

"Good morning, Charley," she said as she spotted him. "Got a minute?"

"Good morning. Yes, Mr. Bears said I could talk with you. I just have to get this envelope to the office, and I will come right back," Charley answered.

"Great, I'll be waiting for you. Just come on in," she answered.

In just a couple of minutes, Charley came walking right into her office and plopped down on one of the chairs in front of her desk. He knew she might have some answers for him. "Did you find out anything? Like what's going on with me?"

"As a matter of fact, I did. I met with a group of boys, and we were talking about suggestion boxes. I told them I wanted to be able to put one in my waiting room, so maybe I could find out which students seem to walk alone in the halls, or don't join in any activities on playground. I told them I wanted to help those students find friends, and that I thought students would share names using a suggestion box. After we talked a bit, we all agreed it wouldn't work, but then they just mentioned three boys, and your name was one. They seemed quite sincere in helping me, or I should say helping the three boys," she said.

She continued, "They seem to care about you and explained why they thought the other boys might be keeping their distance from you. I am so happy to tell you that it only has to do with a haircut and your choice of shirt color you wear. They don't understand your tail, and they don't get why you wear black all the time. I suggested maybe you were just trying something different, just to be unique. But they thought it was too different and made them uncomfortable. I was so relieved to hear it was simply long hair and black shirts. How simple is that?" she said happily, hoping Charley would take it as no big deal, too.

"Really, that's all? The only thing is, I kind of like the 'tail.' It took me a long time to grow it. The shirts I don't care about, and I have other ones I can wear. I just thought black was cool," he answered.

"Okay, so now we have to decide whether you want to be unique and keep your long hair and 'tail,' knowing it causes the other guys to keep their distance, or not. It's your choice, and it's a matter of comfort. It's about your comfort in choosing to be who you want to be. And it's about the comfort of the other boys, with how your looks affect them. Remember, middle-school students do think that who they hang out with affects what others think of them. It tells me that their self-esteem is not what it should be yet. Confident grown-ups aren't always judgmental that way, but insecure ones are. In middle school, most students are struggling to figure out how they want to express themselves, and create a personality. And the biggest fear is being alone. That's why so many students worry how others will think of them, by the choices they make. That's what students react to, even when they have no other reason to judge one another. Does all this make sense? It doesn't appear that they don't like you, and it doesn't appear that they are being mean. They are just not comfortable with your choices, because they don't match what everyone else thinks is the way to go…short hair and colored shirts," Mrs. Kaufmann explained.

"Now, you have the choice, and you will have to weigh both sides to see how each decision feels. Cut the hair or leave it long…or maybe just cut it shorter? Also, remember that you can decide to stand out in other ways, too, not just hair and shirts. There are so many ways that you can show your strength, your personality, and your maturity, that are appealing to others, and don't cause the other boys to feel uncomfortable. So, what do you think?" she asked. "Do you want to talk about it with your mom tonight, or would you like me to explain all this to her to get that conversation started? I really wouldn't mind at all, and it might make it easier for you."

"Okay," Charley said quickly. "I'd like that. She doesn't get home until 5:30. Is that too late?"

"Oh, heavens no. That's not too late at all. How about I call between 6:00 and 6:30? That way you can talk with her if you want to before I call, or you can just wait and see what she suggests after she and I talk about your options," she offered.

"That would be good," Charley answered, sounding satisfied with the plan. Should I be getting to my music lesson?" he asked, worried about being late.

"Good idea, but not to worry. Your music teacher was told you would be a few minutes late because of an errand you were doing for Mr. Bears. You have a great day, and don't worry about making that decision in a hurry, either. There is no rush on that one. I'm just happy you now have a choice, and you know that it's your decision," she added, hoping the echo of her words would stay with him, as he walked out of her office in a hurry to get to his music lesson, looking thoughtful.

That night, Charley heard his mother's car pull up in the garage after work. When she came inside the door, he immediately blurted out, "I have something to ask you, Mom."

"Sure, my Charley Boy, what's wrong? You look so serious," she said, as she put her purse and keys down on the dining room table.

"Should I cut my hair short?" he asked, not knowing what to expect.

"Your tail? I thought you really liked having that tail, and you've been growing it forever. Didn't you think it would make the other kids think you were cool?" Charley's mom asked in surprise.

"Yes, but they don't think it's cool. Mrs. Kaufmann was talking with some boys today, and they told her they didn't get why I'm not cutting my hair. She told me later. Yesterday I was telling her I didn't have any friends, and she was trying to help me. The boys she talked to were talking with her about kids who walk down the hall alone. When she asked them why, that's what they said about me. The tail they didn't get and my black shirts."

"Have you been wearing just the black ones every day again? I thought you were mixing them up with the white ones I find in the hamper," his mom asked quickly. "Actually that doesn't surprise me. You look nice in them, but not every single day, Charley, really. That would make you seem different to me, too, if I were a kid. Black clothes nowadays are a sign that a student is angry, and it leaves other kids and their parents suspicious. Do you need me to get you more shirts? We can go out tomorrow night and pick up a couple if you like. How about those nice T-shirts I got you when school started? Can you start wearing them?" she suggested.

"Yeah, I will, but some of them are so not cool with the crazy things they say. The guys at school wear baseball and football jerseys mostly. Can I get a couple of them?" he asked excitedly.

"Sure, honey. I didn't know what you wanted before. We'll go tomorrow after dinner, okay?" she offered. Now, what about the hair? Do you really want to cut your tail? I'm all for making friends, but I'd hate to think you have to look like everyone else and give up being you, in order to have friends. I'd like you to want to stand out in the crowd, be different and be proud. However, if you really want to cut it off, we can do that tomorrow night, too."

"I think I'd rather have friends than the tail. Mrs. Kaufmann suggested I could stand out in a way the kids would admire, rather than in a way that would make them uncomfortable. If my long hair makes them think I'm angry, then I don't want it. I'm not angry, I'm just lonely. The tail just doesn't work at this school. Besides, I guess I wasn't being me anyway, if I used growing my hair just to get friends. I think I do want to cut it. Can I think about it a little more tonight? It's going to be so weird." Charley added just as the phone rang. "Oh, and she's supposed to call you tonight to tell you all about this," he said quickly, as his mom picked up the phone.

"Mrs. Bond?" Mrs. Kaufmann asked when she heard a woman's voice.

"Yes, is this Mrs. Kaufmann?"

"Yes, it is. I hope Charley told you I was calling, and I hope I'm not disturbing your dinner," she told his mom.

"Yes, he just told me as the phone rang. We were just talking about his tail and black shirts. I had no idea it was costing him friends. I should have remembered from when I went to school how much kids judge other kids for however they are different. I think he wants to cut his hair now, but he wants to give it a little more thought, and we're getting him some different-colored shirts and jerseys tomorrow after work."

"Oh good. I always encourage students to work at being individuals, but in middle school, your style and clothes can make or break you. I told him he can stand out in ways others will admire, and that will get him positive attention. Or, he can just relax, be himself, and make friends without trying so hard. I felt that he grew his hair and wore black shirts to impress them by appearing to be cool, and it backfired, because they ended up feeling uncomfortable with his look," Mrs. Kaufmann explained.

"I understand and agree with you," Charley's mom said. "He was working at it, for sure, and his dad and I both supported him in his choices. We'll take care of his look, but how do we help him make friends now?"

Mrs. Kaufmann answered her with some questions. "Why don't you and Charley look over our extracurricular activities list in his school handbook tonight, to see if he wants to sign up for any of them? That, to me, is the perfect way that students have to talk to one another and build relationships. Then, you will need to see what can be done to get him rides home, before or after school, on those days. We can figure this out, I'm sure, and I'll be happy to help," Mrs. Kaufmann said with positive energy, to make Mrs. Bond feel positive, too.

"You're right, we'll be fine. Charley and I will certainly discuss some of this a little more tonight. Thanks so much for doing this for Charley, and I know he appreciates your help, too."

"You two have a great evening making plans, Mrs. Bond, and I hope to meet with him tomorrow to get it all started at my end," Mrs. Kaufmann offered. "By the way, feel free to e-mail me at school or use my voice mail anytime. Busy people need a way to connect that fits into busy schedules. You and Charley can even e-mail me with any thoughts or decisions you have tonight, and I can write back tomorrow when I get to my office. And please let me know when Charley would like to chat again, or how I can help, or whatever. I would love to get this going."

"Thanks so much, we will," Mrs. Bond said, as they both hung up feeling good about their plans.

Mrs. Kaufmann was looking forward to getting her e-mail and voice mail the next morning. She was quite curious as to whether the haircut would be happening.

Becoming Himself

As usual, the red message light was blinking on her phone as Mrs. Kaufmann came into her office the next morning. She put away her things and turned on her computer, where she also had several messages waiting. The first voice mail was a reminder from the principal to join her in a parent meeting that afternoon. The second was a person moving to the area who needed to know more about the school system. The third was Mrs. Bond. "Yay, I get to hear the verdict!" Mrs. Kaufmann laughed to herself as she hit the button to play the recording.

"Mrs. Kaufmann, this is Mrs. Bond, Charley's mom. I wanted to thank you again for taking the time from your evening to call me. It really helped, because Charley and I truly focused on the person he is, and what he enjoys, and how he wants to stand out in general. He also realized tonight how hard he was trying to be cool and impress people with the person he is not. So… **he's** definitely decided to cut the tail, wear all his clothes, not just the black ones, and join the Chess Club! Isn't that great news? And the Chess Club is in the morning before school, so I can just drop him off on my way to work. It has all worked out, and he said he's looking forward to telling you his decisions today. I called to give you the heads-up that he plans to stop in to see you on his way to recess, so he doesn't miss any classes this morning. Okay, have a great day, and thanks again for all your help."

Mrs. Kaufmann was smiling during the whole message. It was music to her ears. And now that she heard the news, she hoped she could look as happy when Charley told her at recess. It was a great solution, but she felt there still needed to be a little more of an intervention if Charley was to make friends more quickly. She had to think about what else needed to be done. As she started to write out passes for the students she needed to see that day, she had a thought. *I wonder who in the Chess Club would make a possible match for Charley*. Then it occurred to her. She wrote out two more passes for the other two new boys. Arden and Wyatt, whose names she got from the lunch group she had spoken with before. "Maybe the two new boys in Charley's class, who also walk alone in the hallways, would want to join the Chess Club. That might be a perfect opportunity for all three of them to meet and share a mutual interest. Good idea," she complimented herself.

Later that morning, Arden and Wyatt came to see Mrs. Kaufmann at the appointment time written on their hall passes. She called the ten-minute appointments her "new-student check-ups." As they walked into her waiting room, she was in the office doorway waiting for them. "Hi, gentlemen!" she said enthusiastically. "I called you down for your new-student check-ups at the same time. I wanted you to be able to walk together, but we will meet separately so I can give you each your privacy. Which one of you wants to come in first and chat for a couple of minutes?" she asked.

Wyatt answered quickly, "I will!" He then came into the office and sat right down at the big desk. Arden smiled and sat down on one of the chairs in the waiting room. He casually picked up a pamphlet describing the middle school extracurricular activities, which Mrs. Kaufmann had deliberately placed on the table next to the chairs.

Mrs. Kaufmann quickly said, "Oh, good, you can look through that pamphlet to see what activities are being offered this year. See what you might like to join while Wyatt and I chat, and then Wyatt will have some time to do that also. I hope you two will find some interesting activities that we offer here at this school. It's the perfect way to make friends." With that, she turned to go join Wyatt, closing the door behind her.

"So, my friend, tell me how it's all going for you," she started.

"It's good. The work is the same as at my old school, and I don't feel lost anymore," Wyatt answered. "I just don't know too many people yet, but I'm working on it."

"That's great. I really believe that joining an activity or two will help you do that. In fact, there's one starting this week called the Chess Club. I believe there are a lot of boys from your grade level who have already signed up. Does that interest you at all?" she said encouragingly.

"Yes, that sounds cool! How do I do that?" Wyatt asked.

"You just need to sign up in the media center, which is our library. There's a sign-up sheet on the counter there, and that's also right where they hold the Chess Club on Friday mornings for an hour before school."

"How do we get there in the morning? I have a baby brother and I'm not sure if my mom can drive me."

"Well, typically kids look over the sign-up list to see if there's anyone they know from around where they live. Then, they talk to each other to see if their parents can take turns driving them in the morning. We can see who you know on the list. I also know one boy whose mom intends to drop him off on her way to work. There might be several possibilities, but let's first see if even signing up is okay with your mom," Mrs. Kaufmann answered.

"Okay," Wyatt said as they both stood up, and he walked into the waiting room to swap places with Arden.

"Your turn, Arden. Let's see how things are going are for you now," Mrs. Kaufmann said as the boys switched places. Wyatt sat down in the waiting room, picking up the very brochure Arden had just put down. Mrs. Kaufmann then went into her office, following Arden, and closed the door. "So, how's it going, Arden? Any problems?" she asked.

"No...not really. I still miss my old school, but I'm beginning to like it here, too. My classes are fine and I think I want to sign up for the play, I don't know," Arden told Mrs. Kaufmann.

"That sounds really great. And what do you do when you go out for recess?" she continued.

"Oh, I mostly shoot the basketball with a couple of kids. One of them is Rudy something, and the other one isn't in my class, so I don't know his name. Once in a while, if they aren't there, I'll play Wall Ball," he added.

"Sounds good. Do you and Wyatt hang out at all?" she asked.

"No. We're not in the same class, and we don't take the same bus, so it's hard to make that happen," Arden answered.

"Do you want to get to know him better, and do you think Wyatt might want to become better acquainted with you, too? I know he just said he wants to join the Chess Club, and so does Charley Bond and a few other boys from your classes. It might be a good way to have time to talk and come up with things you could do together, on the playground or on the weekends. Just a thought," she added.

"Maybe I could if my mom says it's okay, because I just read that it meets before school. She wanted me to join things, so I think I could get her to bring me, but we're all so slow in the mornings," he admitted.

Mrs. Kaufmann quickly told him about the carpooling idea, so the ride would not seem like it would stop him from joining. "If you want to sign up for the play, Chess Club, or anything else, make sure you go to the media center before Friday, so you get on the lists, and you can do that before or after school, or even today during recess," she reminded him. "In fact, I can write a pass for you two to go the media center right now on your way back to class. You can always e-mail the librarian to remove your name if your mom doesn't want you to join, but you can't always get down there to sign up before Friday," she suggested.

"Oh, good, I was trying to figure out how I would get there, because I take a bus, which doesn't give me time before or after school. And we're not missing anything from class today, because we're taking turns doing book reports. That would be perfect, thanks!" Arden answered excitedly.

Mrs. Kaufmann looked at her watch and quickly changed the pace. "Okay, so I think we've used up all our time. Let's get you and Wyatt on your way. I think if you talk about these activities with Wyatt, you and he might have the same interests, and that would give you two a good opportunity to get to know one another," she suggested, as she stood up and headed for her office door.

Arden followed her to the door and joined Wyatt in the waiting room. Mrs. Kaufmann said to Wyatt, "I had an idea while Arden and I were talking. I offered to sign your passes to give you a chance to get to the media center on the way back to your classes. That way you can get your names on the lists for whatever you want to join. You can always let the librarian know later if it won't work out for rides before and after school, but, like I told Arden, at least you will have signed up in time. This is such a great chance for my new guys to get to know their classmates, so they can start to feel comfortable here and make new friends. Sound okay?" she asked Wyatt.

"Sure! Thanks." He, too, was quite happy with that opportunity.

Mrs. Kaufmann wished them luck with the activities and reminded them, "If you need any help with contacting anyone to get rides with parents, just let me know. I definitely can help," she offered.

Both boys gave quick thank yous as they left the waiting room holding on to their passes and brochures, and then went out into the hallway to get to the media center. Mrs. Kaufmann watched them as they were talking excitedly all the way down the hall.

"I hope we've jump-started that friendship today for those two. Now I have to see if I can get Charley Bond going to the same activities. Maybe there's a friendship or two in there somewhere."

Two appointments later, it was recess, which was usually the busy time for Mrs. Kaufmann. Charley came straight from the cafeteria to Mrs. Kaufmann's waiting room and sat down. The school counselor's door opened, Mrs. Kaufmann appeared, and her eyes lit up as she saw Charley, who was wearing a bright-red

T-shirt. "Come on in. You look great today. Your shirt is very bright and very sharp. I really like it. And I'm dying to hear what you and your mom decided last night," she exclaimed as she and Charley went into the office and closed the door behind them.

Charley was beaming as he sat down, almost as if he loved pausing in order to hold the suspense before he spoke. "Well, I'm going for a haircut after school today so I can get a buzz cut. I am so excited!" he shared with Mrs. Kaufmann. "And…I'm going to join the Chess Club, and maybe try out for the school play, I don't know," he proudly told her, as if he gave her a gift.

"That is absolutely wonderful! Do you feel okay with the decision to cut off the tail? I know you look great in red."

"Thanks, yes, I'm actually happy to be cutting it off. It was getting old and was a lot of work. It was always so wet after my shower in the morning. Then when I would come to school, my shirt was always soaked. I kept thinking I needed it as my 'who I am' thing. I think I was trying to look a little tough with the tail and the black clothes. I was thinking that's the way I needed to be for the other boys to respect me. Now I feel like I can change that and do my hair the way I really want – a style that needs no work at all!" Charley declared.

"Wow. It feels like you've decided to be yourself…no more trying to impress anyone. Do you feel lighter and freer?" she asked encouragingly.

"I do!" he answered. "I was getting tired of my three black shirts, too. Plus, I had so many people tell me I looked good today and that my shirt was nice. I didn't realize so many people were even noticing, so that was really nice!"

"It's great, isn't it? Now you get to be you, and you can stand out as unique, for whatever you want to focus on. You could be really good at a sport, or acting, or even chess. Those are the places people notice you in a good way. If they admire you or want to be like you, then that's a 'good different.' If you're difference is in a way they don't admire and aren't comfortable with, then that's a 'bad different,' if you know what I mean," Mrs. Kaufmann summed it up with a smile, knowing that he had made the right choice for now.

"Cool," Charley simply said, getting it.

"Oh, and I almost forgot, the two new boys in your grade just went down to the media center a little while ago to sign up for some extracurricular activities, maybe even including the Chess Club. It may end up being the best opportunity to get to know them. If you all exchange phone numbers, maybe the three of you can have your moms help each other, by taking turns doing the drive on Friday mornings. Then that would make it easy to connect for other out-of-school get-togethers," she told him. "Plus there might be other students you will get to know there, too. You'll have so many people to walk with in the halls once that gets going. And the school play, well now, there's a whole other batch of possible friendships.

"Look at you! A whole new, *real* Charley! I am so impressed watching you become yourself!" she congratulated him. "Now, it's time for you to get out to recess so you can join in a game and have fun! Run around and get that great oxygen into your brain and muscles, so you can be your sharpest in your classes this afternoon. See if you can say hi to the two new boys if you join them playing Wall Ball, and let them know you're signing up for chess. That might make them feel better about going, since they are new and don't have any friends yet. Oh, and I *have* to see that buzz tomorrow! You'd better give me a knock on my door, even if I'm in here with someone. You can give me a thumbs up, a thumbs sideways, or a thumbs down, to let me know how you're feeling, okay?" Mrs. Kaufmann said with great enthusiasm.

Charley jumped up out of his chair saying, "Okay!" and went right out her door to head for the playground. He couldn't look happier or more excited, and Mrs. Kaufmann was, too.

Breaking the Ice

Mrs. Kaufmann made three more phone calls after the playground flurry of students, before she went to lunch. She made one to each of the three moms, leaving voice mails for all three – Charley's, Arden's, and Wyatt's. She let Arden's and Wyatt's mothers both know that she had had a good new-student checkup with the boys, and felt that their academics were going well, but welcomed their input if they felt the adjustment was difficult in any way. She also told both of the moms that she really encouraged their sons to sign up for extracurricular activities, as a way to break the ice in this new school and create opportunities to make friends. She explained how friends not only make so much of a difference in the happiness of a student, but also in his academic performance. And lastly, she told them both about the activities including the Chess Club, and the idea of carpooling before and after school to make it possible.

For Mrs. Bond, she left a different message. She told her how excited Charley was that so many students complimented him on his red shirt. She also told her how much happier he looked without the burden of that effort to impress others as a tough-looking kid. She shared her enthusiasm for his choice to present himself in a positive way that was so much more comfortable for his peers. Then she told Charley's mom all about the new boys signing up for activities that might include the Chess Club, and how the carpooling might really break the ice between Charley and them. Then lastly, she asked Mrs. Bond to make sure to remind Charley to come see her with his new haircut tomorrow, and to enjoy this transformation as a great lesson in life learned so smoothly. She hung up the phone, grabbed her keys, and went to lunch feeling very pleased with her morning.

The next morning when Mrs. Kaufmann came into her office, there was already a student waiting for her in her waiting room. She took a second look at the student, because she didn't recognize him at first. "Oh my goodness, is that Charley Bond my eyes are beholding? You look so different that I almost didn't recognize you! I can't believe it. You look like a whole new person! I love the haircut." She was so surprised that, besides removing his tail, he had also cut back all the hair over his eyes and over his ears that had hidden his face. Now she could see this young man's full face for the first time.

Charley laughed right out loud. He was so happy with his haircut. He asked, "Do you think that the other kids will make fun of me?"

"They will be too shocked at first, but then yes, they will say certainly things like 'Who scalped you?' and other reactions to the new you," she assured him. "Don't take it as bad at all. Try to accept it as them expressing their surprise and wanting to connect with you. Just smile and act proud. After all, they are noticing the new, authentic Charley!"

"Okay. And I kept my tail in a plastic bag. My mom suggested I donate it to the American Cancer Society's for them to use for wigs and stuff, for when people with cancer lose their hair. That made me feel really, really good, too," he shared with her.

"I love that royal blue shirt today. Aren't you glad you can express whatever mood you feel each day by your choice of colors? You must be so happy your black days are over," she giggled.

Charley giggled back. "My mom got out the new school directory and called Arden's and Wyatt's moms to offer to drive them with me to our first meeting of the Chess Club next Friday morning. We might even have a play date this Sunday afternoon if it works out."

"Well, that just made my day!" she blurted out. "I still can't believe you, you look so different and so sharp! Why don't you go wait outside until the bell rings, so you can show off your buzz?" she suggested.

"All right, I will!" Charley grabbed his backpack and rolled out of his seat in one smooth move toward the door in a blink of an eye.

"I love happy endings," she smiled to herself, as she gathered up the new-student check-up passes to hand out for that afternoon and headed down to the office to put them in the teacher's mailboxes.

On her way to the main office, she couldn't help going to the big front doors where the students were all gathered. They collected there to wait for the morning bell that would allow them to come into the building. Some busses had dropped off their students early, so they were waiting with the walkers. Mrs. Kaufmann saw Charley, Arden, and Wyatt together, somewhat in the middle of a small group of students. It appeared the students were all talking to or about Charley's new haircut. She was thrilled that the three of them were interacting together and definitely doing a lot of laughing. Her favorite part was the beaming pride on Charley's face. How happy he appeared now that he allowed himself to be who he was most comfortable being – himself.

Discussion Points:

- Some people hate to stand out and be different. Some people hate to blend in so much that they feel they aren't even noticed.

- Students in middle school may have a hard time joining comfortable groups of established friends.

- Being too different in appearance or behavior makes students feel uncomfortable. It could make it harder for them to be friends.

- Standing out among your peers in areas of skill, talent, or accomplishment will cause them to admire you.

Reflection Questions:

1. Would you prefer to stand out or blend in, and in what ways?

2. How comfortable are you with people who look different from the rest of your friends? Does it make you feel like others will judge you if you hang out with them?

3. What kinds of things can you do to be admired by your peers? Will those things make them like you or make them keep away?

4. What is it that makes a student "cool"? What makes a student definitely "not cool"?

CHAPTER 15:
Everything at Home Feels Bad and Wrong

Letters to Parents in Transition

Mid to late October was always one of the times in the school year when the students with problems at home began to show the stress at school. Mrs. Kaufmann, the school counselor, began to get requests from teachers to help students who were not doing their homework, not studying for tests, not bringing their lunches, and coming late for school. It was always apparent that there was less structure or support from home, which often meant there wasn't consistent parenting going on there. Her request to the teaching staff was to give her the names of the parents who had indicated changes at home on any returned new school year forms. She was especially interested in any parent restraining orders, changes in marital status, or changes of addresses for parents or other custodial care. She would then take the list and compare it to the office records to see which parents had reported being newly separated or divorced over the summer, and what the new parenting status and living and visitation arrangements were most current for those students. This was the time of year she knew she should offer group support to the students and parents of those families in transition. Her letter to them would read:

Dear Parent,

Every school year it has been my tradition to assemble students into grade-level support groups for families going through transitions. I call them my "Changing Families Groups." This letter is an invitation for your child, _____, to join us in one of those groups. My goal is to remind the children that they hold no responsibility for the decisions their parents make in the best interest of the family; that they didn't cause their parents to separate or divorce; that their parents will always be their parents and will take care of them; and that they need to accept the changes and move forward, finding the positives that come from the new living circumstances. The groups traditionally show the children that they are not alone. They learn that their new transitional schedules may feel uncomfortable at first, but a new normal will get established. The group offers a safe, confidential place to share their fears, problems, and concerns. The group can also offer a sense of comfort and a place to share strategies about going back and forth between their parents' homes, as well as suggestions for being successful at school.

These groups, of approximately six children of the same age group, run once a week for six weeks from mid-November to the December holiday vacation. I have been told repeatedly by parents that the group experience made a big difference in the lives of their children, in terms of comfort and speed of adjustment. Teachers also have reported back an increase in academic performance.

If you are willing to allow your child to participate in this group experience, please sign below. Also, please indicate if you and your child prefer to have your child meet during his or her forty- minute lunch and playground period, or if you and your child prefer a group that meets forty minutes before school starts.

Thank you for your prompt attention. Feel free to call my office if you have any questions or just want to know more about it.

Sincerely,
Mrs. Kaufmann, District School Counselor

This particular year, Mrs. Kaufmann had received enough responses from parents for four such groups. Three groups were to meet at lunchtimes. These were the children of the younger grades, by grade level, who thought having lunch with an adult made them feel important. They couldn't wait to eat during a special meeting, play games, make presents for their parents, and have discussions, instead of having to go outside for recess. These children felt chosen, and they really looked forward to their group experiences. They even had to be reminded when the meetings were about to end as they got closer to the last one, because of the disappointment of it all being over.

On the other hand, only one group from the middle school was established, and it was to meet before school. She knew these students wanted to be with their friends during their lunchtimes. And, more importantly, they didn't want to have to explain to their friends why they were in the school counselor's office. Being dropped off early was no problem, and that's what they needed…no more problems, as it was hard enough to deal with what was happening to them in the first place. To make sure the group members would feel comfortable and safe, Mrs. Kaufmann knew she needed to meet with each student in advance to explain how she would make it fun. She also needed to make sure they understood why it was so important to keep what they discussed confidential. And lastly, once she knew the students wanted to be there, she would disclose the names of the other students that were to be in their group. She might even bring them together in brief meetings of two to three students at a time to let them get comfortable with the other members of their group. The morning group was told there would be breakfast snacks and juice, in case it was so early that they didn't have time for breakfast at home. They always liked hearing that.

It's time to start calling the students down to talk to each of them about the Changing Families Group that will start in two weeks, Mrs. Kaufmann was thinking, after she had almost all of the signed parent permission slips returned. *Besides, it's almost Halloween. Maybe I can also check to make sure the students' Halloween plans are not forgotten about because of the family's new schedules. I can just chat with each of them about how their changing parent visitation schedule was working out with this year's homework and school activities for them. Then, I'll ask them what kind of juice and breakfast food they prefer and how they feel about drawing cartoons*, she laughed to herself. It was her art therapy approach that gave the students something to be working on while they talked. It lessened the discomfort of sharing difficult feelings in a face-to-face setting. She laughed only because they were always so surprised when she told them that they'd be drawing cartoons.

Mrs. Kaufmann thought about the first year she ran the older student group, when she had asked the students to draw cartoon pictures of faces, showing the emotions of what they'd gone through. She told them that their cartoons would be given to the younger children in her other groups so that they, too, could discuss their feelings more easily. Once the morning Changing Families Group students realized they were being helpful for younger children, she knew they would begin to draw up a storm and have great conversation-starters before, during, and after group time. It was an amazing hit, and they loved it. She also knew, more importantly, that these troubled students used these cartoons to get in touch with their own feelings. They usually weren't able to express their fears, their guilt, or their sadness, before this drawing experience, so this sharing drew it out of them.

This was one of Mrs. Kaufmann's most satisfying activities of her job, though it wasn't always smooth in the beginning. This year, according to a parent's note on her permission slip, there was one student who was begging his mom not to have to go. Her most reluctant student was John Alexander. It was important she meet with him right away so the stress didn't build. She needed to ask his mom if she could bring him to school early the next day to meet with him briefly, and talk about what he had been experiencing. She thought it might help him get in touch with his feelings so that he could enter into the group process more comfortably. And, if he, or any other student, still objected to meeting in a group, Mrs. Kaufmann would just meet with each one on an individual basis throughout the school year until the transition was over.

"Hello, may I please speak with Mrs. Alexander?" Mrs. Kaufmann asked after a woman answered the phone at John's mother's office.

"This is she," Mrs. Alexander replied.

"This is Mrs. Kaufmann, John's school counselor at Hillstown Middle School," she said.

"Oh, yes. I'm glad you called. Did you get my signed permission for John to attend your group sessions? I wasn't sure if he would bring it to you, being that he is really resisting it," Mrs. Alexander shared with her quite honestly.

"I did, and I also read your note. This resistance happens more when the children get older and don't like what they feel, or they feel guilty about even having those feelings, and they've buried them deeply in order to get on with each day. Most times it becomes easier to function at school as if the feelings aren't there. They just suppress them and don't want to share those uncomfortable feelings with anyone, no less an unknown group of peers from school. At home, sometimes they feel so much tension, or outright blaming between their parents, that they don't want to fuel any arguments by sharing feelings there either. They think the easiest way to keep peace and avoid flare-ups is to keep their emotions to themselves. And sometimes, they simply fear the other group members at school will use their fears against them later, outside of the group sessions. They just feel overwhelmingly vulnerable everywhere. I need to find out what John's particular resistance is all about with a brief meeting, but I don't want to embarrass him by having him come see me during the school day. Do you think he'd prefer to come to school early so that no one could see him going into my office?"

"Absolutely!" John's mom responded quickly. "I know he won't want to get up early, but I will take care of that. I will remind him he needs to give it a chance. I've always taught him that. Just to keep an open mind and give it a chance," she repeated.

"I believe he won't be sorry," Mrs. Kaufmann assured her. "Does he like to draw? I use that as a distractor from the discussion discomfort and to give them a goal of helping younger children."

"John loves to draw. He doodles all the time, so that may be a great selling point for you. And his younger brother is in one of your lunch groups, so he may really like helping the younger kids going through this divorce stuff," Mrs. Alexander said with a new enthusiasm.

"That's great news!" Mrs. Kaufmann exclaimed. "What day does an early drop-off work for you and John? I have conference on Friday, but all the other days will work for me this week."

"How about I bring him tomorrow morning? I'd like to put John out of his misery. He just keeps saying that this is stupid, just so you know. Sorry, but I want you to know what you're up against, to be fair. It may not be as easy as you think," Mrs. Alexander admitted. "My son is a lot like his father, in that respect, very stubborn."

"I expected that could be the case for John, and it's perfectly okay. He's a private kind of guy and not very talkative. After he's given it a chance, if group work turns out to be too uncomfortable, I will let him know that he and I can meet in the morning, whenever we need to. I don't push, especially if students think of it as torture. Also, if you ever need referrals for private outside counseling, I can provide them to you as well," Mrs. Kaufmann offered.

"Thanks, but I'd like him to work with you to get comfortable learning to express his feelings. I would actually feel relief myself, knowing he has support any day he needs it, right there with you. If we can make this group thing happen, I would be grateful. Besides, the cost of private counseling may be out of reach for me right now."

"I understand. Going from one home to two can put a real strain on the budget, but keep in mind, some employee benefits allow for some free counseling sessions per person, per event, so don't discount that too soon. Anyway, I will do my best tomorrow morning with John. Thanks for your help," Mrs. Kaufmann added.

"No, thank you! I really appreciate all that you're doing for my boys. Will you be able to share with me what he tells you in group, or is that kept confidential?" she checked.

"If ever there is a reason to be concerned about his safety, I would tell you immediately. Everything else I encourage them to share with their parents so that you don't feel left out. They can, however, share the emotions with me that they don't want to share with you at this time. I'd rather they express them privately so I can help them process them, than to keep them bottled up or suppressed. Usually, over the period of six weeks, they work through so much that they can talk about those emotions as having been in the past. Then, as for their continuing concerns, I have a lot of success with them letting me tell their parents how they feel. It takes the pressure off of them, but still communicates their needs. Not to worry. My goal is to have all parties get through this transition smoothly and as a growing experience. My personal goal is to get them in touch with their feelings and then learn how to safely express them to their parents," Mrs. Kaufmann assured her.

"Okay, that's really comforting. I have to go now, but I'll be there with John first thing tomorrow."

"Yes, I have to get going, too. I will let you know John's decision tomorrow after we meet, and I will tell him I'll be calling you with that decision," Mrs. Kaufmann promised.

Breaking Down the Walls

Mrs. Kaufmann was meeting with the boys, like John Alexander, who were permitted to join her morning Changing Families Group. She knew that many middle school boys whose parents were going through a divorce tended to get quiet and become more distant to one or both of their parents, especially the one being blamed for the separation or divorce. They often went through a whole array of emotions after they found out what was happening to their family. They would first feel surprised, then sad and hurt, and embarrassed, sometimes guilty, then angry. They didn't always acknowledge these emotions, but when their parents became emotionally absent, dealing with their own stresses of that transition, they just stayed behind a wall of silence. These were the students Mrs. Kaufmann needed to convince that verbalizing these feelings was going to help…no easy task.

Mason Copeland came to Mrs. Kaufmann's door and knocked softly. "Mrs. Kaufmann, can I talk to you for a minute?" he asked shyly with his little French accent. Mason was new to the school from France a few years before. He had just settled in by making friends when his home life was changed dramatically because his father moved out of the house.

"Sure, my dear, what class are you coming from, and does your teacher know you're here?" she checked.

"No, he doesn't," he admitted. "I just went to the nurse's office, and I'm on my way back to class. I only need a minute."

"Okay, what's up? You look worried about something. May I help?"

"Yes. My mom told me she gave me permission to go to that morning group you're having for kids whose parents are getting a divorce, but my dad doesn't want me to go. He said that no one should know our dirty laundry, and he was even mad. Now I don't know what to do," Mason said, with his voice cracking.

"I hear you, and I can help you. I will call your dad to see if I can explain why it would be a good thing for you. Maybe I can change his mind. Would that help?" she offered.

"Yes, thank you," Mason said, looking relieved.

"I'll try to reach him today. How about you come to see me from morning homeroom tomorrow, and I'll let you know how I made out?"

"I will. Do I need a pass?" he asked.

"Yes, and I'll give you one right now, so it won't be a problem in the morning. Now, you can put that problem right out of your mind for today. No sense wasting perfectly good thinking space in your brain on that!" she said with a little laugh. "How about we get you back to class before you miss too much more class time?" she suggested.

"Thanks, Mrs. Kaufmann. See you in the morning," Mason said, as he took the pass and left quickly.

That makes two walls to break down, so far, she thought, as she walked to a PTA meeting to tell the parents about this support group. *I sure hope Mason's dad isn't as stubborn as John*, she laughed to herself.

After her meeting, Mrs. Kaufmann decided to call Mr. Copeland. She mentally put herself into her most patient and understanding mindset, knowing Mason's father felt strongly about not exposing their family problems. She found his work number from the student data file and hoped he would not mind being disturbed during his work day. "Mr. Copeland?" she asked as a man answered who had a French accent like Mason's, but with a very deep booming voice.

"Yes, it is. And who is calling?" he responded briskly.

"This is Mrs. Kaufmann. I'm Mason's school counselor, and I'm the one who sent home the invitation for my Changing Families Group. I wanted to make sure I called all of the parents of my morning group, since I know I'm possibly imposing on already hectic Tuesday-morning schedules. I know Mason is looking forward to the morning snacks and the cartooning and other playful activities. More importantly, I'm interested in helping the students to learn new coping skills and how to find the positives in all the changes going on in their lives. I also like to have them learn from others who have gone through the same transition. They often share strategies for staying organized as they go to and from school from different homes. It can be tricky, but the students really help one another," she said encouragingly. "And, probably the biggest benefit of the group is to have their feelings validated so they don't feel so alone."

"And what feelings would they be?" Mr. Copeland interrupted her challengingly.

Mrs. Kaufmann continued explaining what the students expressed. "They often feel like they caused the divorce, and they believe deep down inside of them that it's their job to put their parents back together. It's a heavy burden, but one they get to get rid of after six sessions. They hear how adult relationships work, so they understand the kids' role in a family is not to repair them. I'm really looking forward to helping them, and I hope you are as well," she finished up. It was all she could do to set it up as valuable for Mason.

"Do the kids share stuff that's happened between the parents if they heard them fighting?" It was the only other question Mr. Copeland had after the whole explanation.

"Well, the ground rules include keeping the conversation on their own feelings, their own worries, and their own ability to deal with the changes. I usually start off the group letting them know that I will assume, as a premise of the group, that they all just experienced watching their parents' struggle some before their decision to separate or divorce. I validate for them that they witnessed their parents deal with a very challenging and possibly extremely sad or hurtful experience. I tell them that their parents married with dreams it would last forever, and it didn't. Of course their reactions to that disappointment were hard on them. They may have argued, yelled, cried, and showed their kids all of their pain, and that alone had to be hard to observe. After that introduction, we don't need to describe what happened between the parents at all, only how they, the students themselves, felt about it," Mrs. Kaufmann replied.

"Oh, good, so basically you keep the subject on the kids?" he checked one more time.

"That's the idea. The group is for understanding and insight, validation, and information and strategies…for them. The part where you benefit is that I give them a release valve to let out the built-up, negative emotions they don't feel free to express with you yet. I give them permission to forgive their parents' extreme behaviors and to share their feelings with you. They pick up tips and ways to make life easier as they have to become more responsible in their constant travels between homes, and I show them how to be happy again, by seeing how they benefit from what life gave them. I do hope you can see the value of this group for Mason. I know he would like your blessing."

Mrs. Kaufmann then remained quiet for the minute it took Mr. Copeland to answer. She knew she had given it her best, and now she had to be okay with however Mason's father felt. She also knew that the primary custodial parent was the mom with whom Mason lived all the time except visitations, and that she had the last say. The primary parent could say yes and outvote the parent that the child just visited. However, creating more friction between the parents, and more guilt on the part of the child, was to no one's benefit. If he refused to allow Mason to attend, she would suggest to his mom that they do individual counseling instead, in order to keep the peace.

"Oh, one more thing," Mrs. Kaufmann had forgotten to say. "If Mason goes to the first meeting and feels uncomfortable, or you and his mom are not happy, just let me know and he just stops attending. Any of the students can drop out at any time, and I can meet with them individually as needed." It was important Mr. Copeland did not feel backed into a corner, since he seemed to be feeling so vulnerable.

"Well, that's fair," he said immediately after that last offer. "Then let's give it a go," he said decisively.

"That's great," Mrs. Kaufmann replied. "I'm hoping you will be pleased with Mason's shift of thinking as a result. And please don't ever hesitate to call me if you have any doubts, questions, or comments. I'll let you go now, so you can get on with your day. Thanks again," she said, thinking they both felt the conversation had been a success.

One wall taken down and one wall to go with John tomorrow morning, she thought, as she looked up the next parent's phone number to call.

John's Turn

The next morning, Mrs. Kaufmann got to work a little earlier. She wanted to be there in case Mrs. Alexander needed to drop John off at an earlier time in order for her to catch her train. She didn't want to leave John standing there feeling exposed when he was supposed to slip into her office unnoticed. As she turned around to put her briefcase on her desk, John was already standing in the doorway. "Oh, you startled me! Good morning, John Alexander. I do love your name. It sounds so strong in character," she told him. John immediately smiled and came right into her room more comfortably as a result.

"Just put your backpack anywhere and join me at my desk. I wanted to have a chance to explain the way my morning Changing Families Group works. After I do, you can decide if you're willing to give it a chance." She spoke quickly, so the silence wouldn't cause time for any uneasiness.

"Okay," John replied, not knowing what else to say.

"First of all, I call it a Changing Families Group for the grownups, but for the students I name it the Cartooning Club. I do that because that's what we'll be doing after we have a little breakfast snack when you all first come in. The cartooning will allow everyone in the group to express some feelings in a safe way. Then, when we share our 'art' with the younger groups, they feel okay about what they have experienced. It ends up really helping the little guys who are pretty confused. Does that sound good so far?" she dared to ask.

"Yeah, I like to draw," he said positively.

"Okay then, so far you're on board! Now, the part I think you're worried about is the sharing, right?"

"Right," John answered assertively. He made it perfectly clear he wasn't ready to say much at all.

"That's fine, because at the first session, I do most of the talking. I first explain what we're doing with the cartooning. Then, as you all do your free doodling, I give you background on adult reactions to divorce in general, and children's reactions to what they perceive as a family breakup, and what happens during the aftermath as a 'new normal' gets established. I share this with everyone so that it just gets said and understood as typical. No one has to share their feelings or reactions to any of what I say at the first session, unless they are dying to. So, you have one free breakfast and a chance to better your artistic talents just by attending the first session. I have plenty of how-to cartooning books for everyone to look through or borrow. And, you know, John, no one ever really *has* to talk. You can speak whenever you're ready, or not at all. I think you will gradually get more comfortable once others have shared, because you'll see you're all in similar circumstances. Does that sound like you can do it?" she asked him again.

"I could do that. Who else is going to be in my group?" John asked. That seemed to be one piece of importance.

"Well, we have two boys and three girls who have accepted, and you will make number six. The two boys and two of the girls are in the grade below you. You and the other girl are in the same grade," she explained.

"Who's the girl from my grade?" was the last concern John seemed to have.

"Allison Beeker is coming, the new girl this year. She's the one with the really long black hair, from Mr. Donato's homeroom. Her parents divorced over the summer and her mom moved here, so she had to change schools. Now that is hard. I hope you can make her feel comfortable, because she was very shy about coming to the Changing Families Group, also. That's one reason why I was really hoping you would join us. She needs to know there is someone in her grade coming, too."

Mrs. Kaufmann seemed to have found a reason that appealed to John, by the relief in his face.

"So are you feeling okay with coming to the group now?" she asked John directly.

"I'm good with it," he answered with a smile.

Mrs. Kaufmann added, "I'm really glad Allison Beeker will have someone there from her grade so she doesn't feel new and out of place. Thanks, John. I promise you I will make it as much fun and as good for everyone as I can," she said heartily. "Now how about you go outside through the back door and walk around to the front. No one will be any wiser as to where you came from, and you'll have a few minutes to hang with your friends before the bell rings. I will call your mom right now to let her know you're in."

"Okay," John answered and left right away.

Mrs. Kaufmann picked up the phone and called Mrs. Alexander's cell number. There was no answer, so she left a voice mail. "Hi, Mrs. Alexander, you're probably on the train on your way to work, so I'll just leave you a message. John is now willing to join the group without too much arm-twisting. Call me if you need to; otherwise, please have him here for the first session at the same time you dropped him off this morning. And, just a suggestion, why don't you ask him about our conversation, so he can get used to the two of you having dialogue about it? That may pave the way for further discussions down the road."

Mrs. Kaufmann hung up the phone and mumbled to herself, "Well all right then. The second wall came down, and the groups are a go!"

First Group Session

Mrs. Kaufmann was busy setting up the tray of banana bread, granola bars, and cantaloupe squares for the mini-breakfast. Her morning Changing Families Group students would be there any time, and she wanted everything to almost look like a party. The napkins and plates and cups were brightly colored and were all laid out on the table with the orange juice and chocolate milk. She turned on the radio to happy music, and put the clipboards loaded with fresh, new drawing paper on the seats in the discussion circle of chairs. No sooner had she finished setting it all up, than she heard some students walking down the hall toward her door.

"Oh, wow, this is so cool!" Miranda exclaimed, as she and Claire came through the office door with Allison following right behind them. All three girls were smiling huge smiles as they put their backpacks down in the corner. The others were coming in one at a time. Each student looked positive and interested.

"This is exactly what I hoped for this morning," Mrs. Kaufmann said. "Everyone has made it. I have six happy students who have come to eat and draw and enjoy one another. Help yourselves to breakfast, and take any seat in our circle where there is a clipboard of drawing paper."

As the students immediately piled food on their plates and poured drinks, the chatting began among most of them. John and Allison were the quiet ones so far, exactly as Mrs. Kaufmann had predicted. She waited until they were all seated, turned down the music, and then she began. "Good morning, everyone; I am so glad you could all make it. Now the rule here is you can get up to get more food or toss your plates in the garbage, or whatever you need, as long as you are able to keep up with whatever's going on in the group. We also will need to remember how important it is to just listen to one another when they are talking. We'll all try not to interrupt or talk too long. You don't have to share if the topic doesn't make you feel like it, and we need to speak only about ourselves. Our parents have been through a rough time emotionally, so you all have seen a variety of their worst behavior. I'm sure you will keep the details about them to yourself. What you do tell about is what has changed in your life, and that still needs to be kept confidential. Your feelings about things, your stories, and your fears, everything you hear here should never be repeated. Do I have your word on that?" Mrs. Kaufmann looked into each student's eyes and waited for a "yes" from each one. "This room has to be a safe space for all of us, or the group will need to end. You may tell your parents what you shared about you, but not what others have told us."

Allison raised her hand, and Mrs. Kaufmann smiled and said, "Go ahead."

"Will you be telling our parents what we say in group?" she asked.

"Not unless someone's safety is at stake. Your conversation must be safe here, okay? Is everyone clear on that?" she repeated.

All six students nodded happily as they enjoyed mouthfuls of food. Mrs. Kaufmann got right down to it.

"Here's what you need to know for our next six Tuesday mornings. You can ask me anything at any time, but let's be good listeners for one another," she reminded them one more time, "and you can eat when you come in, clean up, and then grab a clipboard. That clipboard will be yours every time you come in, and your cartoons will still be there.

"To begin with, I want you to think about the process of your mom and dad meeting, dating, marrying, and planning a life together. We can assume they loved each other and must have truly believed it was forever. When problems came up, and feelings were hurt, there might have been a lot of arguing, and it might have been upsetting to you. That's how it is when your friends argue too, except with your friends, you often take sides. With your parents, you don't want to take sides. Some parents want their children to understand why they feel what they feel, but to you it sounds like they want you to be upset with the other parent. That may make you think they want you to take sides, but remember that they are just hurting, and they often believe the other parent has done something wrong. You just need to let them work things out. It isn't something you can fix. You also can't change any of their negative feelings. They may have fear, hurt, sadness, anger, shame, disappointment, or guilt, but you can't make either parent not feel them. You only need to own your own.

"Remember, too, their decision to be apart is between them, and it is definitely not something you or anyone else has the power to change. It's probably one of the hardest things they ever had to do, so you need to be patient. It will get better as they work through it. Always remember, they certainly don't mean to be ignoring your needs, even if they seem very busy with all the changes from the divorce or separation. They still love you, both of them. You have not lost a mother and you have not lost a father. You will always have them. They just don't want to be married to each other, but they always want to be with you," she assured them.

"They may not choose to live in the same house, so you won't have them together when you hang out with them. However, if you look at the positive, you may now have two homes, two places to hang out, two places to sleep, and two neighborhoods to play in. You actually have more than you had before. You are fine and safe and loved in both places.

"Let's clean up our plates while I tell you about the cartooning we will get to do for the younger students," Mrs. Kaufmann suggested, as the six students all hustled around the trash can, tossing out their plates, cups and napkins. She continued as they went back to their seats, picking up their clipboards and pencils.

"What I'd like to do is offer your little pictures of children, or just faces with emotions, for the younger students to use when they write their stories about what they are going through. In the past, I've asked them to tell me about their feelings as the changes in their family were happening. I've helped them illustrate their stories by allowing them to use the older students' drawings. They've pasted the cut-out faces on the pages of their booklets that matched the new emotions as they would write about them. So, what the students of my younger groups will want this year will be the faces you draw or doodle showing the emotions that they will need to tell their stories. So let's see, what emotions will they need? What did all of you remember feeling?" she asked the group, to get them in touch with their own feelings.

"I didn't know what was going to happen or where I was going to live," Ted offered.

Mrs. Kaufmann asked the others, "Thanks, Ted. Did anybody else feel that way?"

Allison agreed. "When my parents told me they were getting a divorce and that my dad was moving out, I was scared I wasn't going to be able to see him anymore. When I cried, they cried, and that made me cry harder, because I didn't want to see them sad. I wasn't sure if I was sadder for them or more scared for me."

"That is really well said, Allison. I'm sure you all felt a real mix of a lot of different emotions, sometimes several at once. Does anyone else remember surprise or fear?" she asked.

Ted started to speak quietly. "I do remember being scared, but then I felt embarrassed when I thought what other kids would be thinking about me and my family. I used to feel bad for other kids whose parents split up, and I couldn't believe it was happening to me."

Mrs. Kaufmann suggested they try to sketch out some faces that looked sad, or scared, or embarrassed. "What other emotions do you remember?"

John looked up, and he simply said, "I was really mad."

"What made you angry?" Mrs. Kaufmann was thrilled he spoke and wanted to draw more out of him if he was willing.

"I dunno. I think I was just mad that they shouldn't have done that to us. That it was going to be hard on all of us, and because they weren't thinking about me, I guess," he said, as if he was thinking it through for the first time. "Now, I realize I didn't get how much they didn't want to be together. In fact, now I feel I was being selfish," John said, looking embarrassed.

"Oh, no, you didn't do anything wrong. Children have all of these feelings, because they are part of the normal reaction. After all, you were interpreting what you were hearing as your whole life turning upside down. Of course you all would be surprised, then scared, and embarrassed and angry. Did anyone feel guilty?"

Claire immediately raised her hand and called out, "I still do. My brother and I used to fight a lot, and I thought we drove my parents to it."

"That's not unusual, either. Many, if not most, children have had the thought that if only they had been better behaved, their parents would've been happier. But the truth is, grown-ups know whether they like each other, love each other, and whether they can make each other happy. Their children are innocent like puppies. Sometimes a puppy wets on the carpet, and there might even be an argument over who has to clean it up, but that could never cause them to get a divorce. You are little to them. They love you and know you have to make choices and mistakes and do kid things in order to grow up."

She looked at all six of the students and repeated her point. "What you do as you grow and learn could never be the reason your moms and dads would love each other or not love each other. You and your brothers and sisters, and all the puppies in the world, could not affect their decisions to stay married. So, may you all have no more guilt, okay? You're just like lovable puppies getting trained."

Claire smiled really big and sighed. "That's a relief." She then continued, "I also like what you said about us not having the power to bring our parents back together. They really are too upset anyway, and they aren't even listening to me."

"That's normal, too," Mrs. Kaufmann told them all. "They are just so wrapped up in so many emotions and new concerns that they just can't be as attentive as they used to be. Don't take it personally, please. By the way, how are your drawings coming along?" she asked. "Can we show each other our sketches?"

They all started talking and laughing as they showed each other their not-so-great artistic talent, except for John. They all complimented John on how great his cartoon faces looked, and he thanked them. He didn't even have to label the expressions by what emotion he was trying to draw, because they were drawn so well.

"John, you really do have quite a talent in art. Would you consider helping me illustrate a brochure I'm working on for the guidance office waiting room? That's if you're interested," she suggested.

John lit up. "Sure!" he answered.

"I might be able to use many of these drawings if the rest of you are willing to share your sketches with the younger students and me. They are all really good, and I'm impressed!" She complimented all six happy students.

"Okay, I wanted to chat a little more about your emotions about your new living arrangements, but I think that will have to wait for next Tuesday morning, because we're running out of time right now. I would like to wrap it up by asking you all to tell your parents what we talked about today in general. We won't tell exactly who said what, but you can tell them about the emotions that members of our group had at the beginning of all these changes. It will be so helpful for you if you tell your parents what *you* felt especially. It's the perfect opportunity to share your feelings. That will remind them to pay attention to your reactions as the changes continue, just in case they get wrapped up in their separating process again," Mrs. Kaufmann suggested.

"Keep in mind that you can always repeat everything I said to you all. I would even appreciate it if you did tell them. Let them know I told you that you didn't cause the divorce, you can't change it back, and you need to understand how hard it is on your parents, too. Your parents also need to know that what you felt was normal. The best thing they can do for you is to love you, to make sure you know they will always take care of you, and to make sure you have enough time with both of them. I will give you each a parents' guide to take home for your parents so they can help you through these changing times. In fact, I'm giving each of you two of them, one for each parent. The guide reminds them not to argue in front of you, not to tell bad stories about the other parent, and not to share all their worries with you," Mrs. Kaufmann described to them.

"My goal is to remind them to let you be happy. You will have a new 'normal way' of life you will gradually get used to. Your 'new deals' might even seem better in some respects than it was before the divorce, because of new neighborhoods or new privileges."

Mrs. Kaufmann stood up to end the session and asked them to put their clipboard of drawings into a plastic bin on the counter for the next Tuesday's meeting. "Next Monday I will have a reminder put in the announcements for the Cartooning Club for the next morning…that's us!" she announced.

All six students busily put away their clipboards and picked up their backpacks. Mrs. Kaufmann said, "If anyone asks what you're doing in my office, let them know you are helping me with my guidance brochure, and helping the younger children from the other school."

They filed out quickly, with John being last. He turned back as he was going through the doorway, paused, and quietly said, "Thanks, Mrs. Kaufmann," and walked out of the office.

It gave Mrs. Kaufmann a really great feeling. She figured he would be back next Tuesday after all.

And Then the Next Tuesday

The second group meeting was so much easier. After Mrs. Kaufmann said good morning to each one as they came in, she suggested they grab something to eat. She gave them a little extra time to talk among themselves. She hoped it would help them break the ice a little more. Since the rules were understood and they knew the routine, they were able to start drawing quickly, enjoying their attempts to make their sketches look like the samples in the "How to Draw" books available around the room.

"Okay, let's get going." Mrs. Kaufmann called the group meeting to a start as she joined the circle and looked around at all the drawings. "What are the emotions we're cartooning this morning? Anything new?" she checked.

Allison was the first to share. "I'm trying to draw frustration, but I don't know how, and I'm frustrated," she laughed.

"Now that's a good one to talk about. Is there anyone here who can identify with that one?" Mrs. Kaufmann asked.

Claire immediately answered, "Oh, I know that one! When I'm at my dad's and I'm finally feeling comfortable, I have to pack up and go back to my mom's. And sometimes, I leave things at the other place, and then I have to do without it for days. That is so frustrating."

Miranda chimed in, "Me, too. I just can't think of everything I'm going to need for the next couple of days when I'm packing. And I'm leaving stuff at home that I need for school, and my parents are both working, so they can't bring it in for me. Then, the really bad thing is, the next school day I still don't have it, because I'm not going back to that other house yet where I left it. Sometimes the teacher is upset but tries not to yell at me, because it's my parents' fault, not really all my fault. It really is very frustrating, but I don't know how to draw frustration, either," she giggled to Claire. "Maybe I should draw your face right now, and you could draw mine!" Everyone in the group laughed, and the bonding had truly begun.

Mason had been really quiet up to this point, but, after the laughter, he broke his silence finally. "I feel really sad, a lot. When I'm with my mom, I miss my dad. Then when I'm with my dad, I really miss my mom. It feels like an ache in my chest that just won't go away."

"That is a perfect description of sad, Mason, and my guess is everyone else understands what you're describing, right?" Mrs. Kaufmann asked, as she looked around at the others.

"My mom said it will get better," Allison jumped in, "and it is starting to bother me a little less now since I've been doing the back-and-forth thing for about six months already."

"Thanks," Mrs. Kaufmann said to Allison. Then she looked at Mason and said, "You know, Mason, the way I think of this transitioning is a little like when you first started in kindergarten. Do you remember how much you missed your mom when you first started school? You were so used to being with her all during the day that it was hard at first to get used to not being with her. And yet, after a few weeks of school, you didn't even think about your mom during the school day, because that was your 'new normal.' You got used to being with your teacher and your friends each day during the week. Then, later in the school year, when you'd get up one morning on a vacation week, you'd miss some really good friends from school. It's all a matter of what you're used to, and that takes time," Mrs. Kaufmann assured him and a couple of other group members who were still new to the one-parent-at-a-time schedule.

John agreed. "It was hard for me at first, too, but now I have a routine, and I know I can call my mom anytime when I'm at my dad's, and in reverse, too. The good thing for me is that my parents will take me back to the other house in an emergency, if I've left something important for school. They don't like it, and I don't do it too much anymore, but they don't want my grades to go down because of that."

"You're lucky," Ted jumped in. "My parents figure that I will learn to remember my stuff if I get punishments when I don't."

"It's true. For the most part, that is how we learn," Mrs. Kaufmann offered Ted. "What we can share at our next session can be what memory tricks or systems you have developed for remembering what you'll need when packing. I have some tips I've learned from other students in my other groups, too.

"Before I do that, do you mind if I go back to how you all made out last Tuesday after our first session? Did any of you tell your parents what went on in group? I hope you gave both of them my guidelines. Anyone want to share?"

Mason said, "I gave my mom the sheet when I got home, and she read it. Then she began to ask me a lot of questions about how I felt before and how I'm feeling now, so I told her. Then she apologized and cried. Then she apologized *because* she cried. I told her it was okay, and then I cried and she hugged me. Then, the next morning, we both had a laugh about how we cried. It was weird."

"What was your dad's reaction, if you don't mind sharing?" Mrs. Kaufmann pursued, seeing he was comfortable talking about it.

"He didn't say anything about it. I gave him the paper Friday night when I got to his apartment, he looked at it, and he put it on the kitchen counter. Then he asked me what I wanted to do that weekend, which, by the way, I hate because I have no idea."

Ted jumped in, "Yeah, isn't that a pain? Why do they think we know what they even mean?"

"I always think of things, now," John told them. "I didn't know at first, but then my dad kept taking me out to eat. I figured that's how I can get to go places that my mom doesn't have time to take me to. I always wanted to go to the movies, and she never had the time. So now, I get to see a lot of movies by telling my dad that's what I want to do," he said, almost giggling, like he was taking advantage of the situation. "My dad doesn't like to talk much at the apartment, so he just keeps us busy, I guess. Anyway, it works for me."

Mason looked like he'd just discovered a great idea for himself. "Cool!"

Mrs. Kaufmann saw this was an excellent opportunity for them to give each other ideas, so she went with it. "Any other suggestions for what you do when you visit your dad's place?"

Ted said, "My dad and I like sports, so sometimes we go fishing, or hiking, or swimming at the YMCA, or we shoot hoops behind the school. We've been riding our bikes on the park trails recently, too. We only go to movies if it rains or something."

Claire said, "My dad doesn't ask me. He usually just tells me what we're doing, and I just go along. I don't mind too much, because it feels like the way it used to be. I think I would feel guilty if I thought he was spending a lot of money on me to keep me happy. Sometimes, we go shopping for food, and he lets me pick dinner. He even lets me cook some easy stuff sometimes. It's like I get to play the mom, and it makes me feel important."

Allison told the group that her dad had a girlfriend, Belinda, and she seemed to be there all the time. She told them, "I get upset that I have to share him with her. I miss him at home, and then when I get to be with him, he and Belinda are always talking."

"Have you ever asked to do something with just him for just a short time during your visit, or would he feel like you wanted to cut Belinda out?" Mrs. Kaufmann asked.

"I asked why Belinda was always there once, and he didn't like it. He said she was his guest, and I needed to be polite," Allison answered. "I like Belinda and everything, but sometimes I want to have him to myself," she complained. "When I told my mom, she just went ballistic. She never speaks to Belinda, so I know I can't talk about it with her anymore, either."

"What if you asked your dad if he would take you somewhere to get something you need for school? You and he could get in the car and talk for a little bit alone that way. Or, if he announces he's going out to a store or whatever, and you see he's going alone, why don't you just stop what you're doing and tell him you'll go with him? Watch for those opportunities and jump on them. That would give you a little alone time with him, but you wouldn't be actually excluding his friend, Belinda. Right now, she makes him happy. It's a new relationship, so it's taking his attention at this time, and you do want him to be happy, so this one requires some patience.

"After a while, especially when the newness of his relationship with Belinda wears off a bit, your dad may come to value those opportunities to talk with you alone. He may discover that you tell him more about what's going on in your life when it's just the two of you. He may even try to carve out more of that special time down the road. The big thing is to accept Belinda as his friend, the same way you would hope he'd accept the friends that make you happy. Like I said, this process may require some patience, Allison, and I know that's hard. Patience is hard for me, too!"

"Okay, I'll try some of those ideas this weekend," Allison said. "I do need some poster board for my project. I might even ask if he could help me work on it."

"Now that's using your noggin!" Mrs. Kaufmann laughed. "I'm thinking since our time is running out this morning, maybe next week when we meet, we can focus on things that are bothering us and maybe come up with more strategies to deal with these situations, like we just did. I think it's really important to figure out what we should make an effort to change for the better, through win-win-solutions. We also need to be smart enough to know what part of the new arrangements we should just get used to as part of our 'new normal.' Acceptance with adjustments can make a big difference in our sense of peace versus stress, if you know what I mean."

John said, as they were all putting away their clipboards and getting their backpacks, "You know, I think I'm going to use that idea about having my dad help me with my science project this weekend. Sometimes I just don't want to stay busy doing things and going places to fill up our time. When it isn't really fun, it makes it seem more like an uncomfortable visit with a friend, and not like I'm at just at home with my dad. I think he doesn't know what to do, and he figures he has to make it special every weekend. Working together would be nice, too."

"Good plan, John. Remember to please keep communicating your feelings, your ideas, and your needs to your parents. They are new at this too, you know. Next week we'll talk about that as well. Have a great week, my dears!" she called out after them, as she watched them file out of her office, satisfied that they were much more upbeat than when they came in.

Hitting the Nitty-Gritty

The announcements were playing over the intercom at the end of the school day on a Monday in late November. "This is a reminder from Mrs. Kaufmann for the members of the Cartooning Club. We will meet tomorrow morning at the usual time."

Mrs. Kaufmann was glad for the reminder about her Changing Families Group. She needed stop at the store to pick up some juice and to come extra early that next day. She put down on her agenda for that week the need to discuss their families' Thanksgiving plans. She also wanted to talk about the students' communication practice with their parents, and any reactions from the guide that was sent home the week before that. She definitely had to focus on opening up comfortable dialogue for the families, if the students were going to get the feeling of having some control back in their lives. She looked at the calendar and knew this was the Tuesday before Thanksgiving, and the students would most likely have some disruption to their already disrupted routines in life. Hopefully, it would be a good day for the family or friends with whom they'd spend the day. Her other hope was that the other parent would not make them feel any guilt about having been left alone on this holiday. *I pray the grown-ups will be grown-ups*, she thought.

Holiday times can be the worst if the children are not prepared for the end of some of their favorite family traditions. They need to be braced for the increased emotions on the part of their parents, because of their sense of loss, too. The children need coping skills to deal with the strain or pull on them to meet their parents' needs to be happy, given this tough time in their lives, she thought.

Of course, I'll need to show them how to give both of their parents a present for Christmas or Hanukkah, or at least a special card, without having to ask the other parent to do it for them. Mrs. Kaufmann then got out some of examples of ideas of what the students could make for them during their group time, over the next three sessions. She also made a note to herself to take pictures of the children. Cards with their own pictures on them were always the top choice for the students to use as presents. That way she could have two photos printed for each group member, for the week after Thanksgiving when they would start making their cards. Once her list was made, she wrapped up her calls and headed home.

The next morning, Mrs. Kaufmann came into the school and headed down to her office with her customary two big bags of food and juice to start off the group session. She had her clipboards on the seats in a circle as usual, but on her big desk, she had many "make-it" ideas for presents, along with some sample cards with magazine cut-out faces for pictures. She also put her note on her desk so she wouldn't forget to take pictures of each of the students in group that day. This morning, as she greeted them and gave them some time to talk among themselves while they ate, she also spoke to each student about how it was going.

"Good morning, Allison!" Mrs. Kaufmann greeted her. "How did it go at Dad's this weekend? Did you have any success having some alone time with him?"

"Yes." She lit up. "In fact, we bought the poster board, and then Daddy really got into the project with me. The two of us worked on the lettering for over an hour. Belinda wasn't interested at all, so she went off and did her thing. It was a really good visit. Then we had dinner, Daddy brought me home, and I finished my homework," Allison told Mrs. Kaufmann.

By then, John, Claire, Ted, Mason, and Miranda had all arrived and were already putting their backpacks aside and filling their plates. Mrs. Kaufmann turned to Mason. "How was your weekend with your dad? Did you have a good time?"

"Yes, on Saturday it was good, but not really good at all on Sunday. Saturday I asked if we could go to the new movie that I wanted to see, and we did. After that, he wanted to go to the hardware store to pick up some supplies for a project he wanted to work on the next day. He thought I would want to help him, but I really didn't want to, and I think I disappointed him. I wanted to get my science project done, but he didn't want to work on that. He told me to get my mom to do that with me that night, and was a little angry that I had let it go to that last weekend. Then my mom was mad at my dad for not helping me with it, so that she had to when I got home," Mason admitted, in more of a tattletaling way than usual.

"Oh, boy, that must've been a surprise for you. First of all, I'm glad you spoke up for yourself as far as what you wanted. I'm just sorry both you and your dad had different ideas on how to fill your day. I can see where both of you were coming from, too. Now here's what I think about avoiding that conflict in the future. My guess is your dad sees your homework as your responsibility and/or he may feel strongly about not waiting to the last minute for big projects. Either way, that lesson about him is learned, right? Did you get it done?" she asked.

"Yes, I worked on it till late last night, and my mom ended up not helping me very much either. She said she had her own homework to do, and if I needed someone's help I should have told her before Sunday night," Mason answered.

"Okay, let's all use this as a good lesson here. One of the great advantages of being a child from a two-home family is that you'll need to become more responsible and more dependable, faster than you normally would have. That's how you'll survive. You'll learn not to let anything go, especially big homework projects, because you won't be able to predict your life as easily as you could before. Now that, my friends, is a gift. You may not see it that way, but when you plan well, your grades go up, because a well-done project gets a higher grade than a thrown-together, last-minute one. That way, there's no stress, and you have no disagreements with parents, and you don't have a miserably tired day after the late night. Those are all presents. You were only given your own responsibilities, not any big burden, so it really is a good thing, you know?" Mrs. Kaufmann said convincingly.

"Remember I said on my Changing Families Group letter that I would help you shift your thinking to see the positives of the divorce? This is one of the biggest ones. You get to be a better person because of it!" she said enthusiastically.

"You get to be more mature, too. Look at how many times you've been asked to think about what your parents are going through. I've said you'll need to be patient, allowing them to attend to what hurts them.

I've asked you to not take it personally when they are preoccupied with the divorce-related problems and they aren't thinking about you. These are all maturing thoughts. Now you have to own your own job – schoolwork. You have to learn to communicate your needs, and plan ahead. My goodness, it's like you're becoming so mature so fast…so self-reliant! You can do it, too. That's why we meet. Hopefully, you are learning how to do all this by practicing and reporting back, then practicing some more. It's all a learning process, and you've come so far already. I am really proud of you all!" she praised them.

John commented right away. "Sometimes I feel like I'm the father, and my dad acts like an angry boy. I'm feeling more in control all the time."

"That's why kids whose parents get divorced become so much stronger. They end up with more insight and maturity while the only other choice would be to stay angry, or get lost in the sadness and go the other way."

"Like what's the other way?" Allison interrupted.

"Well, I've seen children just pout, and get angry that they can't get what they want, and then act out. When they get into trouble, they blame it on their divorced parents. Then their parents take the responsibility off of their children by blaming the other parent for what happened, or getting depressed that they aren't any good at parenting," Mrs. Kaufmann continued. "All they really need to do is to continue to set their priorities to include talking with their children, to know their needs on a regular basis, and then to role-model problem-solving in a positive way.

"Children whose parents don't ask them what they have to say, learn how to creatively express their needs. Sometimes children say they want to work on a science project together, and they get bonus talk-time like Allison did. Some, like Mason, have their parents do the deciding as to how they will structure their talk time, like working on a construction project together. Sometimes you have to take what's offered and, as John's mom says, just give it a try," Mrs. Kaufmann suggested. "Your whole goal is to feel peace in your life, not start problems. That's what gives us happiness," she concluded.

Miranda then opened up a new discussion by asking a question. "May I tell you about my dad's reaction to that guide you sent home?"

"Sure. We just go from topic to topic as you all need to. That's what our group is for. Go ahead, Miranda."

"Okay. My dad finally read the paper you sent home on the facts about helping the children, and he called my mom up and hollered at her for putting him down in front of me. The bad thing was that I had to hear it. I know my mom gets really mad at him about not giving her the money she needs, and she lets him know she's mad when he calls to tell her he's on his way to come get me. So now, when he picks me up, he's already mad. I hate hearing them fight, and I know my dad is broke and doesn't have the money she needs. I just wish I didn't have to listen to them fight any more. Sometimes I wish I were old enough to get a job and help them earn money, and sometimes I wish I weren't there to cost them anything. What do I say to them if I'm supposed to tell them how I feel? This would just upset them both. I can't win," Miranda described her predicament, sounding like she was going to cry.

"Oh, good, I was hoping we could touch on that… what to do when your parents continue to argue? One thing I always suggest is for you to take care of yourselves. One of the best devices you can get is music for your ears, so you can't hear them when they are fighting on the phone or in person. When your dad comes to pick you up, just be ready, and get right into the car with your bag and shut the door so you can't hear them argue. Or, if it's too hot or cold to sit in the car, stay in your bedroom with the music on and the door shut until they are done and you're ready to leave. At other times, when you are present and can't go to a quiet place, remind yourselves that for the time being, *you* don't have a conflict, so *you* are fine and actually acting more like the grown-up. Then, like John said, picture them like you see your friends when they argue. Imagine them as children, smile to yourself, don't let it bother you, and stay in your mature mode.

"Lastly, I will tell your parents that I suggested these strategies to all of you to reduce stress. What will happen is the next time they see you get right into the car and shut the door, or go behind your bedroom door, or put your headphones on, they'll see it as a flag to remind them to stop arguing in front of you. They will need reminders without you having to say it to them with words. Signs and behaviors communicate just as well, and it all counts as communication. Does that help, Miranda?" Mrs. Kaufmann asked.

With a big grin, she laughed and enthusiastically said, "Oh, yeah!"

"Now don't any of you take these strategies as permission to be rude and get yourself into trouble. None of your parents should allow you to disrespect them or do something that will upset them. You have to remember that your parents have to be treated as parents, even if they may be acting like children temporarily. It's just human emotion along with their egos and tough times that push them to their limits. You need to be a little more forgiving while you go through this transition, okay?" Mrs. Kaufmann checked with the group just to make sure she hadn't filled them all with too much entitlement, making them disrespectful.

"No, I wouldn't be." Miranda said. "I really like your idea about getting right into the car. That should work. I'm thinking I could even be ready and at the door to meet him outside to avoid my mom talking to him at the front door completely."

"See? You get to be a great problem-solver from this whole experience. Good thinking, my dear!" Mrs. Kaufmann applauded her for visually pre-planning her solution. "Anyone else want to talk about the guide I sent home? Did any parent have a reaction that surprised or upset any of you?" Mrs. Kaufmann waited a minute or so to see if anyone wanted to share.

Ted broke the silence. "My mom has asked me every single day since I gave it to her how my day was, or if I wanted to talk about anything. She doesn't talk about my dad in front of me anymore. I think it worked for her. I don't think my dad has read it yet, but he doesn't usually read anything I bring home from school."

"Oh, okay, so we have one more parent being careful not to make you feel involved in their issues. That's good! Thanks for sharing." Mrs. Kaufmann continued, "Well, if no one else has anything else to talk about today, I do. I want to know where you'll be eating Thanksgiving dinner on Thursday, and with which parent. Let's just go around the circle, and let's start with Claire."

Each student relayed where they'd be for the weekend, or just Thanksgiving Day itself, and how their parents had worked it out. In five out of the six cases, the Thanksgiving dinner was swapped in some way for their December holiday dinner, or for travel arrangements to another family member's house. All six were looking forward to the upcoming vacation weekend with friends and family. The good news was that all parents seemed to have worked it all out rather fairly.

"I do have one more thing to do with you all before this group session will be over. I need to take two pictures of each of you so you can use them, if you want, to make a holiday card for each parent," Mrs. Kaufmann informed them. "Let's keep this a secret so you can surprise them with it, if you'd like. While you're waiting for that, why don't the rest of you draw some possible sketches for your card?"

This activity stirred them all up. There was a lot of chatting while each student took turns posing for the picture standing by something they liked in her office. When it was all done, the group quickly cleared up their clipboards, grabbed their backpacks, and thanked Mrs. Kaufmann just in time for homeroom attendance.

Mrs. Kaufmann turned on the computer. This week she decided to e-mail all twelve parents to let them know the topics that were discussed, and the advice she gave the students. She bragged about them all learning how to be more mature, more responsible, and hopefully, more patient with the changing family process. She deliberately left out the picture and card plan, but was very clear on how she was helping them to be polite, and yet extract themselves from times when their parents might "disagree" out loud in front of them. That was the best support she could give them this week.

She then began the process of calling some other students down to see her who were not in any group. These were students whose families seemed to always stay in one transition or another. She wanted to check on them for how the holidays were getting planned for them. *Busy time of year*, she thought, *busy time of year*.

The Final Weeks

The Tuesday after Thanksgiving proved interesting. Mason was not there, but his mom had called and left a voice mail. She said his dad took him on a week's vacation to his grandmother's house. She was sorry he wouldn't make group that week, because it had really been helping them all. She also thanked Mrs. Kaufmann for the e-mails keeping her informed in general. She said it helped her open up conversations with Mason that he might have otherwise kept bottled up.

Mrs. Kaufmann was pleased to hear that. She never knew if her attempts to inform the adults of about the Changing Families Group's activities would be seen as an intrusion or not. She just knew that good concerns and suggestions were coming up, and she was the advocate for the students, so she shared.

Miranda was the first one to bring up a problem that had happened on Thanksgiving. "I heard my mom crying in the bedroom with my grandma. She was really crying, and it made me want to cry, too. I tried to just understand, but that didn't work. I went to the family room by myself for a little bit, and I just cried some, too. I think my eyes were red when I came back out, and my grandma hugged me. My mom came out of the bedroom a little while after that, and my uncle said something about her red eyes. I was so glad he didn't notice mine."

Mrs. Kaufmann addressed Miranda, but intended a message to the whole group. "Here's another little tip I can give you about the value of having lots of people in your life. You can reach out to them when your parents are emotionally preoccupied, like Miranda getting a hug from her grandmother. Miranda, you have an older sister in college who will talk with you on Skype or e-mail or the phone, whenever you need to connect with someone you know cares about you. We all need to stay connected with our loved ones and feel the soothing it gives us. We can always reach out to feel the comforting of another close person when our parents are upset and unavailable. Learning to take care of yourselves is another very important skill for the rest of your life," she assured them all.

"Remember, sometimes journaling works, during which time you just free write and get your emotions out on paper. That's a great technique for coping, plus you'll be able to read it later and realize how much progress you have made since this time of transition."

While the students were gluing their photos on the card stock they had folded for cards, they began to share how they e-mailed people back and forth all the time, and how good it did feel. Some of them would call the other parent to just say hello if they missed them. After a simple call, they would then feel better. They gave each other some great ways to keep that feeling of connection, even if it was just texting.

The last two sessions ran quite smoothly. Each week they made cards and little presents while they munched and chatted. They shared the highs and lows of their weeks, only to find out how much wiser they were about dealing with change and relationships. They learned that even though their birth families didn't all live together, there was nothing wrong with the new families they were creating. In fact, they began to celebrate how having two places was beginning to be cool. The best part of their growth, the way Mrs. Kaufmann measured it, was the way they spoke of the "inconveniences" now rather than the end of the world. They were adjusting, and learning how to cope with whatever came up. They had more insight into their parents' emotions and allowed room for them while doing some self-soothing, too.

On the last day of their group meetings, they had a little holiday party. This time the food was sweeter and more colorful. They wrapped their completed presents, two from each, and handed over their cartooned drawings for the younger children. Just before the end of that last session, Mrs. Kaufmann asked if any of them would like to exchange e-mail addresses to keep in touch with each other for support. If so, this would be a good time. She then gave them her card with her office phone and e-mail address. She reminded them that she would check her e-mail every day and would love to hear how they were doing from time to time. She also said if they wanted a mini-reunion of their Cartooning Club, she would have one a couple of weeks after they came back from the holiday break. She promised to tell them at that meeting how the younger students ended up using their drawings, too. They just had to listen for announcement of the meeting of the Cartooning Club Alumni. She wished them all very happy holidays, and they left with that wonderful, joyful energy that children can feel without the burdens of life. It was the group's best report card ever.

Discussion Points:

- When parents go through separation or divorce, children feel such emotions as shock, sadness, fear, frustration, and anger. Often they feel more than one at a time.

- Children who have to bring things to and from school while they go to and from two different homes could really use help setting up a schedule or system. Teachers need to be informed when they have an "out-of-control" living arrangement.

- When children are missing a parent, the one they are with should allow them to make contact with the other through phone, e-mail, Skype, or some method of connection to help relieve the sadness.

- Children should be encouraged to tell their parents, or a trusted older close adult, what they are feeling. Bottling up sad, fearful, frustrating, or angry emotions is not good.

Reflection Questions:

1. If your parents are going or have gone through a divorce, have you been able to tell a trusted adult about the concerns or emotions you have felt? Can you now?

2. Are you able to understand that adults make decisions about being in love and living together without it having anything to do with you or what you may have done?

3. When your friends argue, are you able to stay out of it, not pick sides, and let them figure out what they want? What do you say when they ask you to take sides? How do you handle your parents when they tell bad stories about the other parent?

4. What do you do when others argue or cry, it's not about you, but you have to be there?

5. Where can you go and what can you do to make sure you don't own the problem?

CHAPTER 16:
I Will Suddenly Want to Cry Some More-- When Will It Stop?

See Me When You Get In

Mrs. Kaufmann came to work at the Hillstown Middle School early one Monday morning and found a note in her mailbox telling her to see the principal as soon as she arrived. *Something tells me my plans for the day are about to change*, the school counselor thought, knowing these kind of notes typically involved something of a serious or urgent nature. She knocked on Mr. Gonzalez's open door and saw him sitting at his desk. He looked up and motioned her into the room as he got up to close the door behind her. It was obvious that he was about to share some sensitive information that he didn't want overheard by anyone walking by the door.

"Did you want to see me?" she asked.

"Yes, I did. I've also called Mrs. White and Mrs. Cain to help. We're going to need to offer you, the school psychologist, and the school nurse to the students and staff today, in order to provide both classroom and individual counseling with an additional place for those students whose concerns are more physical."

"Uh-oh," she said, as she sat down across from him at his desk. "What's going on?"

"Mr. Powers, one of our parents, passed away over the weekend. Mrs. Powers called me last night and informed me of all of his involvements in the community and this school. He was the girls' community soccer coach last fall, which means we may have several of our students coming for counseling with you or Mrs. White today. We may also have some who will want to see Mrs. Cain, because they are more comfortable going to the nurse's office. Many of our students have had no experience with death in their lives, and this may set off a chain reaction, as it often does, especially with middle-school girls. Mrs. Powers told me that their daughter, Marilyn, wants to see you when she returns to school next week. Losing her father will be hard on her and her mom. They were an extremely close-knit family."

"Oh, I'm so sorry. He was a really good man, a great dad, and was so involved in this whole community, including working as a volunteer fireman. His loss will be felt by so many, that's for sure. I will let Marilyn's teachers know when I leave here, and I will also notify the teachers of the other seventh-grade girls who knew him from soccer, the neighborhood, or other school functions. I'll plan to attend the service, too," Mrs. Kaufmann assured Mr. Gonzalez. "By the way, do you know what caused his death? He was such a young father and so involved in marathon running that it seems unusual."

"It turns out that he actually had been suffering with cancer for the last few weeks, so it was not a total surprise. Mrs. Powers said he was in a lot of pain and seemed to go downhill very fast just this week. This was just sooner than the doctors thought," he answered.

"Knowing it's going to happen doesn't make it any less sad. I would imagine they could feel some sense of relief for him, though, especially if he was suffering so much. That had to be hard to witness. I will definitely see Marilyn at the service and let her know she can talk to me anytime – not just when she comes back next week."

"That will relieve her mom. Anyway, thanks for letting the teachers know. If any of Marilyn's teachers also want to go to the memorial service, have them come see me so I can get coverage for their classes," Mr. Gonzalez offered.

"I will, and thanks for letting me know," Mrs. Kaufmann answered, as she turned to leave. She was certain now that she'd have a red blinking light on her phone when she got into her office. There always seemed to be voice mail accumulated from the weekends anyway, but now, with the passing of Mr. Powers, there were possibly several. She also had to get to all the teachers that she needed to speak to before students came in the building. On her way to her office, she ran into two of the teachers coming in to work.

"Good morning, Mrs. Tatum and Mrs. Franko. Do you have a minute? I need to share some information with you before the students come in this morning."

"Sure," they both answered, stopping in their tracks and looking very curious from the tone in Mrs. Kaufmann's voice.

"One of our students, Marilyn Powers, lost her dad over the weekend, and he had been a soccer coach for several of your students. If any of those students have a tough time dealing with the news, please allow them to come to my office. Also, there may be other individuals for whom it could bring up a lot of sadness, since this can trigger unfinished grieving from other personal losses of people or pets. So, even if you don't know the connection to Mr. Powers, you may allow them to come to me also," she offered.

"What if it gets to be more than just a couple?" Mrs. Franko asked. "Do I send them all?"

"No, not if you think it's becoming a contagious reaction. If that happens, call me or Mrs. White, and one of us will come to your classroom to talk with the whole class, while the other will stay back in an office to receive individuals. A class discussion usually allows them a chance to process the information if they're just hearing it, or if it's just sinking in. That way, we can spot the ones who can't really get past the feeling of grief in that short time period, and we will allow them to come back to our office for some more time to process it. Many of these students have never had someone die that they knew, much less a significant caring figure in their lives," she explained. "And some may even feel suddenly anxious about the vulnerability of their parents, especially those who have been, or are now dealing with, a serious disease such as cancer."

Mrs. Tatum jumped in, "I was planning to give a quiz this morning first period, but I don't really think it would be appropriate now, do you?"

"I wouldn't give it, considering you have several girls from the soccer team in your class who might be hearing about this for the first time. Activity is good, but expecting their full attention for a graded quiz wouldn't be fair to them. In fact, if you find you aren't even able to teach the lessons you planned and you need an idea, maybe you could allow the class some time to make cards for Marilyn. People like to feel like they can help by *doing* something, and that would be perfect," she suggested.

"What if some students don't want to make a card?" Mrs. Tatum asked.

"You don't have to force it. They could quietly read, since they are always supposed to have their outside reading books with them. If you think there's an unusual discomfort with that for anyone, and they ask to go to the library or the bathroom, they may need some distance to be alone for a few minutes, so I would allow it. This is one of those times your intuitive sense will serve you well," Mrs. Kaufmann assured them. "Just use your common sense about your students since you know them very well, but don't hesitate to call me if you need anything."

Mrs. Franko quickly said, "Thank you. Would you like us to help you pass on this information to the other teachers in our hallway? I could call for a quick meeting to assemble our team in my room for you.

How about we collect five minutes before the school bell? Would that work for your schedule?"

"Oh, that really would be so helpful, and it would save me a lot of time trying to get to everyone in the next few minutes. I will be there then. Thank you!" she said gratefully.

The two teachers then parted and headed for their classrooms to open up and get ready for the day. Mrs. Kaufmann also went right to her office to make two calls. She wanted to notify the school psychologist, Mrs. White, as well as the school nurse, Mrs. Cain, that teachers would be informed by the time their students came in for homeroom. She let them know about the meeting in Mrs. Franko's room as well, in case they wanted to attend. As she completed those voice mails, she started checking all of the incoming voice mails and e-mails she received over the weekend. Most messages were people calling in to let her know about Marilyn Powers' dad.

One call was from Mrs. Clark, the mother of Marilyn's best friend. "Mrs. Kaufmann, this is Mrs. Clark, Sandy's mom. I just wanted you to know that Mr. Powers died this weekend, if you haven't already heard. My daughter Sandy is having a really tough time with it. We have been close friends with the Powers family for years, and, as you probably know, Marilyn and Sandy are inseparable. For Sandy, it feels like she just lost her second father. We are all so broken up by the whole thing. I'm going to be with Marilyn's mom, Debbie, all day today, and I'm sending Sandy to school because I need to help the Powers family with the arrangements. She seems okay this morning, but I wanted to give you a heads-up. She might need to come see you today, if she can't keep it together. Please use my cell phone if you need to call me. I just think it would be better for her to get her mind off of it for a little bit, since she's cried so much over the weekend. You don't need to call me back unless you need me. And I just want to thank you for being there for all of us." Mrs. Clark's voice began to break with her last words, as she was beginning to cry and barely made it to the end of her message.

Mrs. Kaufmann grabbed a tissue for herself to dry her eyes. She knew it would be so sad for so many today, and, sure enough, her next message was from a student in Marilyn's class. "Mrs. Kaufmann, can I see you today? It's Jonah, and I need to talk with you."

She knew Jonah had recently lost his grandmother and was a sensitive boy as well. She figured he would be having a tough day today, too, as he had not yet finished grieving for the loss of his grandmother, and he hated crying at school. It was early enough that he might not have left for school yet, so she called him back immediately. She knew he would be building up anxiety about crying in front of the other boys if something didn't help him slow that momentum down.

"Jonah, this is Mrs. Kaufmann. I got your message and will be happy to see you this morning," she said as she heard his weakened little voice answer.

"Oh, thank you, Mrs. K. Did you hear about Marilyn's father? I picture her crying in school all day today," he said getting choked up.

"Yes, Jonah, I've heard. You don't have to worry about Marilyn. She's home with her mom and some friends today. They are sad, but they are helping each other get through this together. In fact, she won't be back to school for a few days, so you don't have to worry about her at all. How are you doing?" she asked him, knowing his answer.

"Okay, I guess, but I still cry sometimes, and I never know when it's going to happen. I miss my Grandma so much. When is it going to stop?" Jonah asked.

"Are you crying less often, and maybe not as long now when you do cry?" Mrs. Kaufmann checked.

"Yeah, I guess I am, but I know the sadness today about Marilyn's father is going to set me off, and I don't know how to make sure it doesn't," he said, sounding almost desperate.

"I know you can't always stop it, but you can find ways to allow it without embarrassment. I know we'll talk later, but here are a few thoughts for you to hold on to for this morning, while I'll be helping the students who knew Mr. Powers. First of all, there will be a whole lot of people who will have tears in their eyes today, or who will actually be crying. You will not be alone if it does just happen to you, too. Plus, students who are having a difficult time will be allowed to come to my office or take a quick walk to the bathroom. That will already be set up with the teachers, so it won't be hard to get excused. Does that help at all? It's really okay to feel your sadness today, since you will fit right into the crowd," she consoled Jonah.

"That does help, thanks Mrs. K. I have to leave for school now," he said quickly.

"Okay, yes, don't be late. Stop by to give me a quick hi, if you can. I'd like to know you're doing all right."

"I will. Bye!" The phone call instantly ended. Jonah sounded better. She also knew there would be more students asking for help with their almost overwhelming sadness as the day unfolded. Mrs. Kaufmann looked at the clock and saw she only had a few more minutes to check the rest of her messages before she needed to head down to the meeting of teachers that had been called together for her.

Reactions Begin

As Mrs. Kaufmann was going down the hall toward the classroom where the teachers were all heading, she could hear the chatter. They were all talking at once as they were hearing the news. Mr. Powers had been such a helpful parent to the school, and several of the teachers had benefitted from his time and efforts throughout Marilyn's school activities. She was glad the teachers had a couple of minutes to deal with the loss themselves before they had to be braced for the students' reactions. When they saw Mrs. Kaufmann come into the room, they began asking her questions about how Mr. Powers passed. She started off by thanking them for coming to meet her so unexpectedly on a Monday morning, and then started sharing what she had just learned from Mr. Gonzalez.

"Mrs. Powers said that he passed away over the weekend from cancer, and it was sooner than expected. She also said that Marilyn wouldn't be back to school this whole week. And Mr. Gonzalez asked anyone who wants to go to the service, to let him know so he can get coverage."

There were soft mumblings within the group of teachers. One even had tears in her eyes, as she had spent a good deal of time working with him on a large classroom project. Mrs. Kaufmann continued, "He was a well-respected and well-liked man in this community and was the girls' soccer coach. Today might be challenging for you depending on the size of the reaction you get. If you find you have just an individual student or two who need a little time away from the classroom, you can send them to me or Mrs. White. If you have students who say they aren't feeling well, as usual, they can absolutely go to the nurse's office. If Mrs. Cain determines that they are not sick and just sad, wanting comfort from her, she'll decide if she should bring them to me on a case-by-case basis. When students say they need to go to the bathroom, you can certainly give them that personal time, but please make sure you send for them, or call me, if they're gone too long. We don't want them to go there just to hang out, meet up with friends, or simply take advantage of our relaxing of the rules. And if you do have several students upset, including those who fear losing parents or who have recently lost someone or lost a pet, call for one of us to come in to talk with the whole class," she offered.

"I don't suggest you try to push to accomplish any lesson or test that will require concentration today if you see it would be an unfair expectation." Mrs. Kaufmann continued. "Feel free to postpone some or all of your plans for the day's lesson to allow them to make cards for Marilyn. Learning to be actively supportive for people you care about is really quite therapeutic for the givers as well. This is a lesson in life, after all, and a discussion about how to cope with sadness can be helpful for all of them. Trust that you'll all know exactly what to do as it unfolds. Today, the grieving will have to be the priority if their emotions are in the way of academics. After you give them a chance to discuss it briefly and 'be with it,' you may even find they are not that affected as a group. If that's the case, they may actually look to the change of focus and will *want* to get back to work.

"Most times, students do better if they're just given the chance to deal with it. When or if they choose to make a card first, that may make them feel better. But then don't be surprised if halfway through your class time, you can tell they need to get back into some school-related activity or lesson. They may want that as a diversion from the sadness that feels so uncomfortable. Today will be the day your compassion, intuition, and creativity will really pay off," she assured them.

"What if the discussion goes sour?" Mr. McDuffy asked. He was known to be the oldest and most structured teacher on that seventh-grade team of middle school teachers, and with a very abrupt and matter-of-fact style. "I'm not one of those sensitive kind of guys, you know?" he admitted a bit uncomfortably, with some humor to lighten the moment. There were some compassionate giggles among the other teachers on his team who knew him to be a bit gruff on the outside. However, after years of working with him, they also knew he could draw on a deep understanding from his heart when called upon to do so.

"I know this is not one of our usual roles in a school setting, so no one can judge you, but your instincts will serve you today," Mrs. Kaufmann assured him. "These young people just typically don't have the advantage of our life experiences. They haven't learned how to just *be* with sadness, and accept it as a process that is part of life. The human psyche or ego doesn't deal well with the extreme sadness of loss, nor does it deal well with our own mortality. This may be a first time for many of them. And to make it more challenging, when we want to give them our comforting strategies from our own religious or spiritual belief systems, we can't, because we can't give our belief systems to them. We can only remind them that they may have one, or that we use ours when we cope. By the same token, we can't cause them to feel bad, if they've not been raised with one. We are there, however, to remind them that this sadness, fear, or discomfort is not permanent."

Mrs. Kaufmann continued, "I often tell them it's like a stormy day at a beach when the ocean's strong, high tide comes in, and we are standing at the water's edge. It will consume our attention at first, and it may even knock us for a loop and spin us around under water until we get back on our feet. The waves will keep coming for a while, because the storm is bringing in the high tide. However, we do know that eventually the storm will be over, the tide will go out, the waves will become calmer and lower, and we will be able to go swimming in calm waters once again. We will never forget the discomfort we felt from being knocked around by the waves, but we do go into the ocean again to swim happily once the tide is out." She offered Mr. McDuffy this analogy so he had a metaphor he could quote to console the students, should a discussion take place. "Trust that you have all the experience you need to help them learn from this life lesson today," she encouraged him.

"Okay, we've got to roll, everyone--the bell is about to ring, and I have a student stopping by on his way to homeroom. Oh, yes, be conscious of students, particularly boys, who simply fear crying in front of the other boys. They may need to be allowed to go see the school nurse for something sounding made-up. Just allow it today. Like I said, the nurse will send them to me if she sees the need to. If you have any other questions and want to just e-mail me, I will get back to you as soon as I can." She got up quickly, as did the others. There wasn't a lot of chatter from the teachers on the way out. Instead, the chair legs grinding against the wood floors filled the room with harsh noise. It appeared as if they were all deep in thought as to how they would be teaching this new and unexpected lesson today.

Mrs. Kaufmann walked briskly down the hall toward her office and saw Jonah coming out of her waiting room. "Hi, Jonah!" she called to him to get his attention. He turned around and smiled.

"I just left you a message," he said with a sense of urgency. "Can I see you right now? Do you have the time?" he asked, showing anxiety all over his face.

"Sure," she said as she approached him and saw the message on the little white board she had hanging on her inner office door.

It read, "Help – I need to talk with you, Jonah."

Mrs. Kaufmann matter-of-factly erased the message, and then looked squarely at Jonah and said, "I want you to know that I just talked to all of your teachers about Mr. Powers passing and our situation today. They now know there may be students who need to leave the classroom to go to my office, Mrs. White's office, the bathroom, or the nurse because of their need to cry. The teachers will surely allow students some time to deal with their sadness."

"Phew," Jonah exhaled, and the tightened muscles in his face relaxed.

Mrs. Kaufmann continued, "To be honest, my friend, today may be the easiest day you can have here because you share it with so many people. All your teachers have been alerted to the possible range of emotional needs of all the students as they connect with Marilyn's dad's passing. Even some of your teachers had tears in their eyes. You won't feel so alone today with your own fear about becoming overwhelmed with the memories of your grandmother. The way is paved for you to ask to leave the classroom for a chance to deal with it without being challenged. If you only need a couple of minutes, just ask to go to the boys' room. Go into a stall and take a couple of minutes to release that 'need-to-cry' flood of tears. It's so hard to hold it back when it burns in your throat and floods your eyes. You will actually feel better once the dam breaks and the tears have been emptied, and there's some science to the brain chemistry that backs that up, too. So, today you get to do some grieving without worry," she encouraged him.

"Thank you, Mrs. K," he said immediately.

"Your day will be good after all, no matter what needs to happen. Now, you can relax and maybe you will be fine all day long!"

Jonah beamed, grabbed his backpack, thanked her, and took off to get to homeroom before the late bell rang.

Mrs. Kaufmann went into her office, walked to her desk, and saw the red light flashing again, so she listened to her first new voice mail. "Mrs. Kaufmann, this is Mr. Petrovich. Our class ended up having a discussion, and then they decided to write sympathy letters for Marilyn. That's when Sandy Clark came up to my desk and said she wanted to go home. She asked me to call her mother. What do I do? The class had a discussion, and her eyes filled up. I've asked her to see if she could start a card or letter for Marilyn, and I said I would call you to see if she could come down to see you. Give me a call please?"

Mrs. Kaufmann heard the urgency in Mr. Petrovich's voice. She called his extension immediately. "Mr. Petrovich, you can send Sandy down now to see me, and thanks," she said as she scanned her e-mail to see if there was any other urgent message there that might've just come in.

"Thank *you*! I appreciate your calling so fast." Mr. Petrovich responded. "She is just holding back those tears with all she's got. I'll send her right down," he said as he hung up.

The phone rang almost in her hand as she was putting it down, so she hit the talk button. It was Mrs. White. "Mrs. Kaufmann, can you talk right now, or do you have students with you?" she checked.

Mrs. Kaufmann answered, "I have one on the way, how about you?"

"I'm going out to talk to a class right now and wanted to let you know, just in case you were planning to send anyone to my office."

"Thanks, I'll notify the office so they know you're doing a class, and I'll stay in my office collecting the individual students sent to either of us. Would you put a sign on your door for students to go to the guidance office in case they don't go to the office first? Also, I just got a non-urgent e-mail from the librarian asking if one of us could stop in. She had a student taking out a book on dealing with the death of a loved one. She wasn't sure if she should recommend that student to see one of us. Do you want to take that if you're down that way near your class talk?" Mrs. Kaufmann asked her.

"Sure, and if I get anyone who's having difficulty keeping it together during my class talk, how about I send them to you?" she suggested.

"Sounds good," Mrs. Kaufmann replied, just as the sound of sobbing came through her door from the hallway. "Gotta run, thanks," she said to Mrs. White as they both quickly hung up.

Sandy Clark walked right into her office and dropped into a big chair across from Mrs. Kaufmann, letting the tears pour down her cheeks. She sobbed, "I'm so sorry to be crying like this, but I can't help it. I tried to hold it in in class, but I just couldn't. Mr. Powers was like my father, and even more. My own father is never home, and I was always at Marilyn's house. He was so much fun, and I'm going to miss him so much." Her head fell into her hands, and she bent over with her shoulders heaving up and down. Mrs. Kaufmann brought the tissue box over to her and handed her a few tissues, and sat near her silently.

"I'm so sorry. I know this hurts," she said softly, making no attempt to try to stop her. This was her safe place to cry, and that was what Sandy needed to do. There was nothing but the sound of sobbing in the room for a little while, and then Mrs. Kaufmann spoke compassionately again. "You are so not alone in this sadness, and you don't need to apologize at all, Sandy. People all around you understand that you had a special relationship with the family and Mr. Powers. You don't need to hide your tears if they need to come out today. I'm thinking of all the people whose lives he touched. He was a loved man and he will be missed. Don't feel bad that you are so sad. Of course you are, and everyone around you understands. In fact, the whole school grieving is quite a tribute to Mr. Powers, showing that he was so loved, and it's proof that he made a positive difference in so many lives."

Sandy looked up with her red, watery eyes and grabbed a few more tissues. She blew her nose and thanked Mrs. Kaufmann. "Can I go home?" she asked.

Mrs. Kaufmann dreaded that question. She had so much sympathy for Sandy and would have liked to let her go home. She knew, however, the rule of thumb was that she and Mrs. White try to help students stick it out if possible, especially if their parents had sent them to school knowing what they were going through. She then said to Sandy, "Well, your mom knows you can spend time with me if it turned out to be too hard to be in the classroom. She is with Marilyn and her mom today, helping them make all the funeral and service arrangements, so I believe she wanted you to try to stick it out here. Do you think you can do that for them?" Mrs. Kaufmann asked Sandy, hoping to encourage her willingness to help them.

"I am so grateful that you and Marilyn have one another right now. The two of you can share your special memories after school today when you go home. Marilyn will need you then, and she'll be done with the exhausting planning with her mom. You can talk with her about all the good times you had with her and her dad as you do that special laughing and crying together in complete comfort and close friendship. That will truly help you both in your grief."

Sandy was quiet while listening to Mrs. Kaufmann. She stopped crying and was wiping her eyes. She finally spoke thoughtfully. "I guess if I went home now, there would be no one there if they are all out at the funeral home or wherever."

Mrs. Kaufmann jumped in, "That's what I'm saying. Your place is to be here today. You will be able to tell Marilyn all that went on, all the good things people said about her dad, and you will bring home any assignments for her today so she doesn't feel like she was missing something and got behind. It will be so helpful to her, and I know she'll be grateful. You'll be able to go to the memorial service so you'll miss that day, but, in the meantime, you are here for Marilyn. Can you do that?"

"Yeah, I can. I actually feel better now that I cried so hard. I guess I needed that," she admitted.

"Oh, I know. I was expecting you." Mrs. Kaufmann smiled. "I'm happy to be able to give you a safe place to go. If it happens again and you don't feel comfortable letting the tears out during a class, come back here for a break. Also, just as a practice for when you're not in school or home, try telling yourself that it's okay to be sad. You don't have to put on a big smile all the time. Allow yourself to feel your feelings. They are real, and you are being genuine. They will pass, too. Later, if you need this room or me, just ask to come back. Today, your teachers all know what's going on, so you won't have to explain yourself, okay?"

"I think I'll be okay. Thanks, Mrs. Kaufmann. Do I need a pass back to class?" Sandy checked.

"Not today, my dear. I'll call Mr. Petrovich so he knows what you're dealing with, if that's okay with you. I'll let him know you may need to come back, but you're on a mission to get through all your classes today," Mrs. Kaufmann offered. "My guess is you'll be fine. When you see Marilyn after school, please tell her my heart is with her, and she can e-mail me or call me, at any time, if she wants or needs to. Let her know she doesn't have to worry about her schoolwork. She'll be given time to catch up once she gets back to school, I promise." Mrs. Kaufmann knew if Sandy could have a purpose and feel useful, it would help her not feel so helpless in her sadness.

"You can call Mr. Petrovich, and I think I'll be okay now, too. I'll tell Marilyn everything you said. Thanks again." Sandy picked up the mound of wet tissues from Mrs. Kaufmann's desk and tossed them in the trash as she went out the door. She heard Mrs. Kaufmann speak into the phone to her teacher just as she said she would. She started back to class with a new resolve – to help her best friend.

Mrs. Kaufmann felt relieved for Sandy. She also saw there were three girls sitting in the waiting room, crying, as Sandy opened the door to leave. They all nodded to each other sympathetically, and Mrs. Kaufmann recognized them as Mr. Powers' soccer players. They were hurting, too.

The Group Cry

The three girls stood up immediately from their chairs in the waiting room and filed into the office. Each one sat on a chair at the big desk and grabbed some tissues. They appeared uncomfortable at first, probably thinking how sad Sandy must've been because of her closeness with Marilyn's dad compared to them, but their tears were streaming, and they couldn't be in the classroom.

"Hi, ladies," Mrs. Kaufmann said. "This is a hard day, isn't it? It's so very sad." She then allowed them to lead her with their feelings. "Did you want a little break from the classroom to be able to get some of the sadness out?" she asked.

Serena answered first. "I feel *so* bad for Marilyn, and I keep starting to cry. If my father died, I don't think I could stand it," she said, as she started to cry again.

Anna spoke up next. "We had to put our sick cat down last weekend, and I keep thinking how much worse it must be for Marilyn losing a dad, compared to just losing a pet – and even that is still so sad for me," she said, breaking down into more tears. She got her voice back and continued, "I also feel like it's unfair. Like, there are really mean people in this world, you know? Why did it have to be Mr. Powers? He was so nice, and everyone everywhere really loved him, especially as a coach." The three girls began to cry together and hug one another even more.

Mrs. Kaufmann spoke respectfully. "I know what you feel. It's pure sadness, and it's real. I am so sorry for you. As for losing a pet, Anna, I must say we feel as close to them as we do to people, and the sadness is just as sad. They often play a role in our families, and we accept them as family members, so don't feel like that wasn't big for you," she assured Anna. "It's so hard for us to even understand death, and even more to wrap our heads around the thought that we won't have that person or that pet anymore. We often feel a huge hole in our lives and our hearts for a while. Some people have their religion or spiritual beliefs to help them with that. When my dad passed away, I started to pray, as if I was talking to him. It helped me feel like he was with me in my heart. That's what helped me. I remember one student, who lost his grandfather, began writing about him and his special memories of all the times they had spent together. He did it so he would never forget him, but it did something else. He said he felt like his Grampy was with him in spirit as he wrote in his special journal. Feeling connected with him really made him feel better. All people do their own thing, to give themselves comfort and peace. Each of you will, too."

Donna, the third girl, and the shyest, finally spoke. "My grandfather has cancer right now, and this makes me think of him, too. Then, when I see Sandy, Serena, and Anna crying, that makes me want to cry some more. I've cried so much, and I just want to go home. I'm really beginning to feel like I'm going to throw up."

"You know what, Donna? I think it might be a good idea if you went across the hall to the nurse. She might have something to help settle your stomach, and it also might give you a break from watching others cry. That just adds to all the sadness. Our brain needs a break from this – like changing the channel on a sad television show." Mrs. Kaufmann knew three girls crying could keep each other crying for quite a while, almost as if it was catching. They usually felt so connected with strong emotion that it was hard for them to let go without risking the feeling of disloyalty, too. The separation of the girls would definitely help them end their crying.

"Let me give the nurse a call to see if you can hop over there, okay Donna? Serena and Anna, we have to let you both get to your next class anyway in a little while. I know that going to gym class will really help you both, because your mind will be on your exercise, and that will help 'change the channel' in your thinking, too. The brain will also get some endorphins, or brain chemicals, from all that exercise, to help work out the sadness, so you really need that class today."

Mrs. Kaufmann saw the reluctance in the looks and body language of the three girls. They were feeling somewhat privileged to be out of class and together, so she needed to get everyone moving before the crying began again. She spoke to the nurse on the phone very quietly, letting her know about the girls and Donna in particular, while the three girls talked to one another. As she hung up the phone, she turned around to Donna and said, "We're all set. The nurse said you can come right over. Go on in and have a seat. She's giving a hearing test at the moment, so don't knock." With that she stood up and opened the door for Donna to leave. "I hope your stomach feels better, my dear, and don't forget to get your books from your last class."

"Thanks, Mrs. Kaufmann," Donna said, as she walked across the hall to the nurse's office.

"Okay, Serena and Anna, you two need to get back to your last class, too, so you can get your homework before you go to gym." Mrs. Kaufmann spoke matter-of-factly to avoid making the moment too soft. She didn't want to encourage the crying to start up again. She then quickly asked, "Would you both be so kind as to make sure Donna gets the homework, in case she doesn't make it back from the nurse in time? That would be a really kind favor."

Both girls agreed and got up to get back to class, thanking Mrs. Kaufmann on their way to the door. The plan was working until the waiting room door opened and two other girls from Mr. Powers' soccer team were arriving in tears– Gradyn and Colinda. Once Serena and Anna saw the two of them, all four began sobbing and hugging each other. Mrs. Kaufmann had them all come in, closed the door behind them, and just gave them time to talk and cry together. After all, they were a team, and they had lost their beloved coach. They needed to feel understood and connected, so she gave them their time.

After a while, once the crying came to an end, she told them they needed to get back to class because she had to go to a meeting. "Gradyn and Colinda, are you two okay now? I know this was hard for you today, as it was for Serena and Anna and all the girls on your team."

"I'm feeling better now. Thanks, Mrs. Kaufmann," Gradyn answered.

"I am, too," Colinda chimed in.

"I'm glad," Mrs. Kaufmann answered. "You know, I had a chance to talk with some of the other girls on your soccer team today, and I'm thinking that you all may feel better if you are able to do something for Marilyn. Being helpful or making a difference for someone usually makes everyone feel better. Maybe you could talk together about writing something or making something for Marilyn and her mom from the team, like maybe a collection of good memories? It's just a thought." Mrs. Kaufmann hoped that giving them a direction with a purpose would help them all guide their thinking into a constructive project instead of into their sadness.

"Maybe we could meet at my house tomorrow after school, if my mom lets us," Colinda offered. "My mom was feeling like she wanted to do something for Mrs. Powers, so maybe she can help our team do this."

The other girls agreed and began to talk all at once. Mrs. Kaufmann interrupted them to suggest they talk about it on their way to the next class. She told them she needed to get them moving, and she needed to get to a meeting herself. This time, the girls seemed energized by their new plan, and they willingly left her office, walking slowly as if in a huddle, talking excitedly all the way down the hall.

Mrs. Kaufmann checked her e-mail and voice mail. There was nothing that needed her attention right away, so she grabbed her keys and headed for the team meeting of the teachers she had spoken to that morning. They had e-mailed her asking if she might have some free time to come back and talk about where to go from here after today. As she was leaving her guidance office, Donna ran into her as she came out of the nurse's health office with a smile.

"Are you feeling better?" the school counselor asked her.

"Yes, I am. Am I late for gym?" she asked.

"Just a little, but you're not far behind Serena, Anna, Gradyn, and Colinda. They were all in my office talking about what the girls' soccer team can do for Marilyn. In fact, Colinda was going to ask her mom if the team could meet at her house tomorrow after school to talk about what to do," she told Donna. "Anyway, they left just a few minutes before you. If you hurry, you might catch up to them."

"Oh, okay. Thanks," Donna said as she scurried away ahead of her. "I have an idea for them, too."

"That's terrific!" Mrs. Kaufmann called after her.

"Hey guys, wait up," were the last words she heard, as Donna turned the corner and saw the other girls.

I know anything they do for Marilyn will be appreciated and comforting. I'm so glad she has such a team of caring friends, Mrs. Kaufmann thought.

The Debriefing

She arrived at the meeting just as the others did, too. "How did it go this morning?" Mrs. Kaufmann asked right away.

"Not as bad as I thought it might," Mr. McDuffy answered. I told them that Marilyn's father had died over the weekend, and she would probably need to know we were thinking about her. They pretty much all knew that anyway. Then, once I told them the quiz would be postponed till tomorrow so they could make cards or write letters, they were pretty happy. While they were working, they were talking about it and no one asked me for anything. I just collected what they did and said I would give it to you to give to Marilyn and Mrs. Powers. I hope that's all right with you," he said, as he handed her a large envelope filled with letters and cards.

"That's perfect. I'm glad no one seemed upset, including you," she smiled as she answered him.

"Oh, I did have to let Jonah be excused to the boys' room after they all started writing, but he wasn't gone too long, and no one else even noticed."

"Yes, I figured he might have to take a time out, since his sensitivities are heightened right now. His family just lost his grandmother, and he was very close to her, so he's not done grieving yet," she explained. "New deaths trigger memories of other deaths quite easily."

"How were the soccer players, Donna, Anna, and Serena?" another teacher asked. "They started to cry almost in unison, so I wasn't sure if they just wanted to be together. I sent them down anyway, and I hope that was okay that I sent all three at once."

"My two soccer girls did the same thing," another teacher jumped in. "You must've had your hands full in there!"

"Oh, that's fine. They all needed to cry, and they shared the 'group cry' because they are a tight group. It actually worked out well because their energy is now redirected to doing something for Marilyn, so they aren't feeling so helpless. They should be fine this afternoon," Mrs. Kaufmann assured them. "In fact, you all really did a great job allowing the students to deal with their emotions. They wrote some great letters to Marilyn for support, too. Thank you for doing that. You may be able to get on with the rest of your day now as planned."

Mr. Petrovich added, "Thank you, too. Yeah, after I sent Sandy out of the room, the tension in the air was gone, and they all just chatted quietly. One of my boys, though, began acting out, trying to be funny, but I sat on that right away! He was so inappropriate, I couldn't believe it."

"Was that Antonio?" Mrs. Kaufmann asked.

"Yes, of course! He always needs to be the clown. It's always all about him. You'd think with all the problems in his home life with his dad's drinking and all, he'd be more sensitive."

"Actually, that's why he appears to be the inappropriate clown," Mrs. Kaufmann reacted quickly in Antonio's defense. "That's his learned role at home, to take the tension out of the air and divert it to him as the comic-relief person. My guess is that he does that in any uncomfortable group experience. He must have that 'elephant in the living room' discomfort at home probably every night, and that's how he copes. He changes the focused attention over to him through his clown act."

"That makes sense, but what about his sidekick, Benji? He started right up with Antonio, and I had to nip that whole thing in the bud. Benji's family is a serious, hard-working, no-nonsense family. He was ready to join in, and I told them both to knock it off and be respectful," Mr. Petrovich admitted.

"Well, Benji's family is exactly that – serious and no-nonsense. They aren't a very touchy-feely group, so they don't get into feelings very often. So today, with that much emotional tension and talk about sadness, it must've been extremely uncomfortable for Benji. He would naturally look to join any way out of that, and Antonio offered him that way out. I think that neither Antonio nor Benji would want to be acting disrespectfully. They just needed to escape the discomfort. It was good for both of them to learn a little about dealing directly with emotions."

"That's good, then?" he checked.

"It's all good. It's all life, and isn't that why we're here anyway? We're just getting them ready for the rest of their lives," Mrs. Kaufmann assured them all.

Mr. Petrovich forewarned Mrs. Kaufmann, "You may have one more this morning. Andy seems to be just barely holding it together. I decided not to ask him if he wanted to go see you. I was afraid he'd burst into tears and then be embarrassed. I'm hoping gym class will help him shake it off."

"See? Your instincts were right on! That's exactly what would've happened. The girls on the team had no problem crying publicly together, almost as if it would be expected. Sensitive boys often feel embarrassed when they cry, especially if the other boys don't. What a pressure and a shame. My guess is after gym class, math, and then lunch and recess, he will have worked it away. He may be fine for the rest of the day. He is totally in touch with his emotions, but he's also worked very hard to learn how to manage them." Then Mrs. Kaufmann asked Mr. McDuffy what he had planned for math for the next period.

"I was going to have them practice their division and work in groups, but I think I'll do a simple competitive division game as a lighter alternative," he suggested.

"Perfect," Mrs. Kaufmann reacted. "His 'thinking channel' will be redirected long enough to reset the emotions, and he should be fine if the conversation at lunch doesn't go back there. Even if it does, he would be comfortable stopping in to see me after that, maybe during recess. If you want to send him down for an 'emotional time-out' later this afternoon, just give me a call. I only have one other appointment this afternoon, right after lunch, and a short class at the end of the day. Mrs. White might be available too, if I'm not there. The big thing is for you to send him on a mission as a courier and not as if he needs to go."

"Sounds good, thanks," Mr. McDuffy answered.

Mr. Petrovich asked, "What about the memorial service on Wednesday afternoon? I have Marilyn in my homeroom, so I feel I should go. Will Mr. Gonzalez get some coverage for me?

"Absolutely. Let him know. I will be there, too. Does anyone else want to attend?" she asked.

Two other teachers said they would want to attend, and they'd make the arrangements. They also asked about Marilyn's return to school, as far as what to expect and how to help her from being behind.

"I have asked Sandy Clark to collect her books and her work today, so she'll have them for whenever she's ready to concentrate again. Sandy's family is so close to the Powers family that she is more than willing and able to do that for Marilyn. They are both good students, but I would still write down what you want done. There's too much going on in their lives to expect either one will remember verbal instructions. I would also guess Marilyn will want to have at least one place in her life that gets back to normal. She should be back Monday of next week and I will see her first. I also figure you'll need to give her at least a week to catch up. Use your instincts again. You'll know what feels like a push, and definitely allow her to schedule make-up tests or quizzes before or after school to everyone's convenience, including her mom. Also, if you need someone to just monitor a quiz or test, I can do that if her mom can't drop her off early."

Mr. McDuffy asked uncomfortably, "What do we say to the students or Marilyn on the day she comes back?"

"I will hope she and I will be done talking before school starts that day, so she can just slip into homeroom without too much attention. I will also recommend to her mom that she talks with her friends before she returns, so they will all have had their chance to show their sympathies. If you want to do the same, you might make sure you give her your sympathies at the service, or at least put your thoughts into a card. You only need to make sure she knows you will be sensitive to her needs when she does return. That will be very reassuring. Once all that is processed, she'll be comfortable returning to your classrooms. At that point, you'll only need to say 'welcome back.' You can let her know you will help her catch up throughout the week, once she catches her breath, and especially if she looks overwhelmed. If she looks anxious to be caught up, which Marilyn might, take her lead for how fast. My guess is she'll hear your compassionate treatment and be totally relieved, and that's what we want," Mrs. Kaufmann suggested.

"Okay then, if you need me, you know how to reach me," she said, as she stood up from the meeting.

"By the way," she added, "thank you all for your help this morning. I really appreciated it."

The teachers all nodded and accepted the appreciation as Mrs. Kaufmann left to get started back to the appointments she anticipated that day. Her list now was so very different from the one she had when she first came into the building that morning.

Helping Marilyn

Mrs. Kaufmann left the building to drive over to Mr. Powers' memorial service. When she got there, she promptly parked, went into the building, and got into the reception line to give Mrs. Powers and Marilyn her sincerest sympathies. As she approached them, they were open-armed and genuinely appreciative for all the messages, cards, and offers to help that she had sent or delivered. "You have my deepest sympathy, and my sincerest wish to be available to help you any time you need it," Mrs. Kaufmann said as she hugged them both.

"Marilyn and I are so grateful for you being there for us, and we will call you when this week is over. Would you have time to come back to the house for some cake when the service is over?" Mrs. Powers asked. "I know Marilyn and the girls on the team would really be honored if you could."

"That's very kind of you, thanks. I'll see you there," Mrs. Kaufmann said to them both, as she moved forward to take a seat for the service. She thought it would be helpful to talk with them a bit more at the house, so there was more of a shared experience to talk about later. It would help eliminate the need to explain things when Marilyn had to get back to the daily routine, too. As she moved through the crowd, she saw Mr. Petrovich seated, so she went over to sit beside him.

"This place is absolutely packed!" Mr. Petrovich said as she sat down.

"I know. He was so active and so well-liked that it doesn't surprise me," she responded. "Did you have any trouble getting coverage?"

"No. As a matter of fact, my substitute teacher was willing to cover me for the whole afternoon, so I don't have to get back. I was invited back to the Powers' house, and I'd like to go. That way I can talk with Marilyn for a bit and put her mind at ease," Mr. Petrovich said.

"That's what I want to do, too," Mrs. Kaufmann admitted. Then, the organ music started, the people left standing took their seats, and the service began.

Back at the Powers' house, Mrs. Kaufmann approached Mrs. Powers in the kitchen. "Thank you so much for having me back here. That was one of the most beautiful services I have ever attended. The readings were incredibly sincere and really described what an amazing man he was," Mrs. Kaufmann said to her with great respect and compassion.

"Oh, I know. I never realized how deeply he touched the lives of so many people. Did you see the awesome book the girls' soccer team made us?" she asked.

"No, I haven't, but I'd love to," Mrs. Kaufmann answered.

Mrs. Powers went to the mantel over the fireplace and pulled down a giant red and white scrapbook with pictures of roses and hearts all over the front. She opened it to show Mrs. Kaufmann the letters written by each and every single member of his team. "Marilyn and I just sobbed our heads off as we read them," she said. "We will cherish it forever. Here, you have to read these. The girls are such support for Marilyn right now. Actually they make Marilyn want to go back to school, but I told her Monday would be fine. The whole team came over last night to give it to us while Sandy and her mom were here. What a memorable evening." Mrs. Powers spoke with tears in her eyes, but a huge smile of gratitude on her face.

"Oh, I would just love to!" Mrs. Kaufmann exclaimed, as she carefully took the prized possession from her hands. Mrs. Powers then moved away to greet some of her other guests with equal graciousness. Mrs. Kaufmann sat in a nearby chair and began to read the entries. There was one long, group letter from Colinda, and Anna, and Serena, and Gradyn, right in the front followed by all the rest. Each one brought tears to Mrs. Kaufmann's eyes because of the sincere gratitude they had for the difference he had made in their lives. It spoke so highly of the character of all the girls as well.

"Hi, Mrs. Kaufmann," came a small voice right near her. Mrs. Kaufmann looked up and saw Marilyn standing near her and Sandy right behind her.

"Well, hi, ladies!" Mrs. Kaufmann lit up when she saw them. "I love your home, and I absolutely love this scrapbook!"

"Isn't that really nice?" Marilyn answered. "My mom and I cried a lot when we read it. I had forgotten a lot of the things my friends mentioned."

"That was a really thoughtful set of letters. They showed you how much they care about you and want to help you through this, any way they can. If you need them, don't be afraid to ask for help. And ask me for help, too. When you come back to school on Monday, you can stop by my office before school so you don't have to wait outside for the bell. Maybe we can get you to your homeroom before the bell and the crowds come. It will give you a minute to gather your thoughts, talk to your teacher, and get situated."

"Oh, good, I was worried about all the attention outside that morning," Marilyn admitted. "All these people here keep saying they're sorry, and I must be so sad, and I have their sympathies. That's making me uncomfortable, and I'm not even back in school yet. I never know what to say, either. Sometimes I feel guilty when I stop crying and feel normal for a while, or even laugh."

"I always just say 'thank you.' I remind myself not to have any guilt when my brain needs to take a break from the sadness. Laughter is actually healing. I know they are trying to make you feel better, but they don't know how, so they say things to tell you they care," Mrs. Kaufmann offered.

"If I don't come back until Monday, I am going to have so much work to catch up on. I've been trying to do a little every night, at least the stuff Sandy brings me. My mom says not to worry about it, but I can't help it."

Mrs. Kaufmann replied right away. "Your mom is so right. You do what you can do if you feel like it--especially if that helps you actually feel better. After that, don't worry about the rest of it. None of your teachers expect that you'd be doing anything this week, anyway, except dealing with all of this, so you can really relax. After you come back, each teacher will let you catch your breath and then see what you owe them. Then you can make arrangements for what works for you. There is no rush, okay, my dear?" Mrs. Kaufmann assured her.

"Oh, phew," Marilyn said, as Sandy gave her the old I-told-you-so poke in the back. Marilyn turned around and laughed at Sandy. "I know, I know, that's what you said, too." And as fast as Marilyn and Sandy appeared, they took off again in the direction of the little ones playing in the family room. They seemed to be so good with the younger children, and the younger ones really looked up to them.

Mrs. Kaufmann took that opportunity to return the precious scrapbook back to the fireplace mantel where it had been sitting before Mrs. Powers had removed it. She then signaled to Mrs. Powers with a thank you, so as not to bother her from the crowd that surrounded her right then, and she made her way out the door, to her car and back to the school. Once inside her office, she shut the door and just sat down in her big chair for a few minutes before catching up on all her messages. She simply wanted to remember some of the beautiful and important messages that the memorial service speakers had shared, especially the one about taking some time to be grateful for all we have. Mrs. Kaufmann decided to do exactly that, right then.

Monday morning, when Mrs. Kaufmann came in, the red light on the phone was blinking, as usual. As she heard the first voice mail, she knew it was Mrs. Powers and hoped everything was still on for that morning. "Mrs. Kaufmann, this is Mrs. Powers. I'm so sorry I didn't get to call you before the weekend, but I would like to bring Marilyn in this morning. She said she can come in before school, and that you'd all figure out how she can catch up with the work. And thank you again for putting Marilyn at ease back at our house. She said you had tears in your eyes when you were reading the soccer team's scrapbook, so I'm happy I showed it to you. All of her teachers have just been so supportive and kind, too. We are so blessed, for sure. As a result, she isn't too nervous at all about coming back this morning. Please call me and let me know what time and if you want me there, too. Bye."

Mrs. Kaufmann immediately picked up the phone and called her back. "Good morning, Mrs. Powers. You can come over any time you'd like. I'm here in my office, and there aren't many students at the front door of the school yet. You don't need to come in unless you want to or Marilyn needs you to. I know you need to get to work, so you can drop her off, and she can come right on in. I'll let the main office know, so she won't have to sign in."

"That's great. I think we're ready to leave in a few minutes, so she'll be right there."

Mrs. Kaufmann hung up and then called Mr. Petrovich's extension to let him know she might be bringing Marilyn to his homeroom a few minutes before school started, so she could get organized and comfortable. Just as she was about to hang up, Mr. Petrovich appeared in her doorway. "Oh, good morning, Mr. Petrovich," she said to him. "I just left you a message that Marilyn Powers is coming here in a few minutes, and then she would like to go to your classroom before the bell. Is that okay with you?" she asked him.

"Sure, and that's what I was coming here to ask. I'll go get my mail and head back to my classroom to be there for her. Thanks, and I'll talk to you later."

A couple of minutes after Mr. Petrovich left her office, Mrs. Kaufmann heard his voice from down the hallway. "Good morning, Marilyn! Welcome back! I should be back from the main office in a flash so you and Mrs. Kaufmann can go on in and put your things away." Mrs. Kaufmann couldn't hear Marilyn, but within a minute, she appeared in her office doorway, standing there with a smile.

"Hey, Marilyn, come on in. How are you feeling this morning, my dear?" she checked.

"I'm okay, just feeling like it's been forever since I've been here. I'll be glad when I'm all caught up and it doesn't feel weird anymore," Marilyn said with some anxiousness.

"I totally understand, but remember, that's the good student in you who doesn't like to feel behind, not the teachers putting any pressure on you," Mrs. Kaufmann reminded her. "All you have to remember today, for all the friends who remind you how sorry they feel for you, is that they just want to see you happy. Would you prefer if your homeroom teacher said something on behalf of everyone to get it over with, or would you prefer to keep it low key and just try to get through the day without a lot of reminders?"

"The second choice, please," she requested. "I'm so tired of all the attention. I just wish it could all go back to the way it was."

"We'll try to make it go as smoothly as we can today. Let's get you going to your homeroom. How have you done catching up with the work Sandy brought home for you?" she asked as they started walking to Mr. Petrovich's classroom.

"I did everything I could do. Some things I didn't know how to do, so I will need some help. My mom said she could bring me early any day on her way to work, if the teachers are here and can help me," Marilyn told her.

"That's really great. I'm so happy you were able to do that much, so now, you should be caught up and comfortable in no time. If at any point today you want to see me or ask me anything, just have your teacher give me a call. You are always welcome," the school counselor reminded her. As they reached Mr. Petrovich's door, they saw he had already returned to his room and was writing on the board. "Oh, good, you're back," she said to him, as they went into the room.

"Come on in, Marilyn, and notice the new sign-up sheet we have for students who want to be interviewed to be a Peer Leader. The interviews are in two weeks, and you would be a perfect candidate if you're interested. Okay, I'll let you settle in," he said, as he turned to Mrs. Kaufmann. "How are the sign-ups going?"

"We have so many students signed up already, and I can't wait to get that group going." She spoke loudly enough for Marilyn to hear. "We have so many students with really great character and a lot of interest. One of the big points is whether they will be willing to make up the work they miss when they are out. That's key, along with the ability to be kind with younger children when they work with them. They've heard how much fun we have at our training retreat, and the older students have bragged about how cool it was to get out of classes to do the outreaches with the younger children. Our Peer Leadership Program's reputation as being really great definitely encourages students to sign up. I really can't wait. Okay, I have to get back to my office. If Marilyn needs anything today, just give me a call."

"I will," he answered.

"See you later, Marilyn. Enjoy your day back with your friends!" Mrs. Kaufmann spoke encouragingly.

"I will," Marilyn answered, with enthusiastic energy back in her voice.

Mrs. Kaufmann left the classroom hoping she had planted the seed well enough to have Marilyn sign up for the Peer Leadership interviews. *That would be so perfect for her right now*, she thought. *Her 'new normal' needed something positive, and this could be it. She is certainly a very special student because she's so caring and capable. I believe she could bring a lot of happiness to young children if she was chosen.*

Then she remembered the words of one of those memorial speakers. He said, "Mr. Powers made everyone and everything around him feel special. It was his wish to bring happiness to this planet, and he certainly did more than his part. We should all take a lesson from the example he set in his life." Mrs. Kaufmann knew Marilyn had that same potential, and she knew it was now her goal to help her do just that. Marilyn might have some high tides come in and out for a while, but she would be fine. In fact, she would be better than fine.

Discussion Points:

- Grieving is not something anyone needs to hide or feel bad about. It is a normal process, and it would be unhealthy to try not to grieve.

- When a new sad situation happens, it sometimes reminds us of the other sad events of our lives. When we see friends cry over a death of someone they didn't know well, it's sometimes a collection of emotions connected to others who have passed.

- Some people spend very little time feeling their emotions. That means, when there is a very emotional experience to be processed, they may find it very uncomfortable.

Reflection Questions:

1. When you know someone is sad because of the death of a loved one, do you feel bad for them and then feel their sadness? When someone is deeply saddened, does it remind you of times you were, too?

2. Are you someone who is comfortable feeling your emotions? Or, are you someone who is not? How do you know this? What do you do when it is hard to feel all of your emotions at once, or it seems overwhelming?

3. When you know someone who seems insensitive, do you think he doesn't feel strong emotions the way you can? What do you think makes a person seem insensitive?

4. What advice would you give a friend if they wanted to do something for someone whose parent just passed?

CHAPTER 17:
My Friends Are Smoking, and I Can't "Just Say No"

The Basketball Game

As Mrs. Kaufmann passed by a group of girls decorating for the school dance in the gym, Jed Tindall's name came up in whispers and giggles. The school counselor thought nothing of the giggles whenever the girls talked about the cute star basketball player, but the whispering in a huddle always caught her attention--especially with the concerned looks across all of their faces. "Hi, ladies!" she said to them as she passed by. "You must all be so excited about this weekend with the dance tonight and the big basketball game tomorrow!" She wanted to see their reaction to her presence within hearing range.

Julianna called right back, standing up straight and stepping back from the pack. "It's going to be the best weekend ever!" she exclaimed, as the rest of the girls followed her lead and quickly stepped back from the huddle to resume making the crêpe paper streamers. There were lots of smiles, and there was lively agreement, with Darcy Lei breaking into loud giggles.

"I can't wait to hear all about it Monday morning," Mrs. Kaufmann replied. "This place looks great! By the way, I was looking for Mrs. Gillow. Have any of you seen her recently?"

Darcy answered, "I just saw her in her office in the locker room."

"Thanks, Darcy," Mrs. Kaufmann answered, as she went in through the locker room door to talk with the gym teacher. Have fun this weekend!"

The girls all gave her their happy comments, while Mrs. Kaufmann saw that they immediately drew right back into their whispering huddle, like a spider draws its legs into a ball.

"Hi, there, Mrs. Gillow," she said as she approached the gym teacher's office door and saw her at her desk. "I just talked with the girls decorating out there and having such a good time. They are so excited about this weekend, and I overheard Jed Tindall's name in whispers. Is he the new heartthrob this week?"

"Oh, he is, absolutely. You should see the girls showing off for his attention in gym class. They get so silly right before the dances anyway, but also having our Hillstown Middle School make it to the big play-off game with Linton Hall Middle School tomorrow adds to the crazies. By Monday we should be back to normal," Mrs. Gillow said with her noticeable calm, from experience.

"Maybe for you, but my guess is that I will have a good number of calls by then. These busy middle school social weekends definitely stir the pot! I'm anticipating a busy Monday anyway, since grades are going home that day, and some students will be given their grades in their classes," she replied. "In fact, that Tuesday should be even busier, with all the parent calls in response to the lower-than-expected grades. Speaking of which, that's actually why I came to see you. It's about report card grades and students who are doing poorly. I have two of your basketball players on my list. I have Eddie Grimms, who is failing

English, and Jed Tindall, who is failing social studies. Both of their teachers have said they have recently stopped turning in major assignments, and their report cards will officially hit their homes on Monday. Both teachers asked me to notify you and Mr. Gonzalez that the two boys will need to be pulled off the team and put on probation effective next Tuesday until their grades improve significantly."

"Oh, no, there goes the title. Those two boys are first string, and Jed is our best player. The team is going to feel so let down, too," the gym teacher said with disappointment.

"Well, they can still participate in the play-offs tomorrow, but if our team wins that game and makes it to the championships in two weeks, those boys won't be able to play in that. I'm really sorry to have to deliver this bad news. I just found out now, and it's practically the end of the day. I have to notify the boys and their parents on Monday. It always seems like they are all so surprised when I tell them. They are either surprised by the grade their child is getting, or that the school policy requires that they have a C or better to participate in extracurricular activities, or both. I know they sign all the papers that tell them about the minimum grade when the season starts. Plus, we tell all the parents about our policies and make sure it's all in the school handbook given out on the first day of the school year, but it's still such a shock. I'm not even sure who takes it harder, the parents or the students," Mrs. Kaufmann commented.

"Oh, boy, that could really spell disaster for the team. Is there anything that can be done?" Mrs. Gillow asked, hoping there might be one last effort that could save the day.

"Actually, there is one possibility for a small miracle. If both boys' averages really dropped *mostly* because of recent assignments not turned in, and, if they both really worked all weekend to get them done, there could be a miracle after all. It can't change their grades in the system by Monday, or their probation on Tuesday, but it would show their teachers the beginning of the 'significant improvement' that is required to get off of probation. The trick will be to let the boys know how important this weekend is for their academics. They have to really work hard to catch up over the weekend now, and that may even mean not going to the dance tonight, to work for their grades and their team. I just need to see if the boys can make that happen. Wish me luck, and I'd better hurry with only ten minutes left of school," Mrs. Kaufmann said, as she turned to go out of the locker room office in a rush, to try to give both boys a chance to literally save the day.

"Good luck, and thank you!" the gym teacher called to her.

"Good luck at the game tomorrow! Oh, and you might want to let them both know when you see them that you know about the failing grades, the impending probation, and what needs to be done this weekend. Suggest they do the right thing if they want to be considered good team players and not let the team down. That might add a reminder and a little pressure," Mrs. Kaufmann said with a smile. She then moved quickly toward the main office around the corner. She knew if she could just make a call to the boys' classrooms to have them sent down to the main office immediately, she might be able to at least let them both know what was at stake and what they both needed to do. Then it would be up to them.

Mrs. Kaufmann looked down the hallway and saw Eddie and Jed both emerge from their classrooms. They were hustling as they entered into the hall, saw one another, and started walking fast toward the main office. They definitely looked worried, because it was the end of the day and they had no clue as to why they were being called down.

Mrs. Kaufmann started walking toward them in a hurry as well. "Hi, Eddie and Jed. I was the one who wanted to see you, and this isn't an emergency. I just had to give you a heads-up before the weekend." She spoke quickly and in a rather business-like manner, which was not her style. It did make the boys listen more carefully, though, and that's what their school counselor wanted – complete and undivided attention.

"I will speak to each of you a little more on Monday, but you both need to know that you have less than a C average in one of your subjects. In fact, you both have a failing grade for your report cards on Monday. Eddie, yours is English, and Jed, yours is social studies. The reason I feel it is so important for you to know this today, before you go home, is because it will get you both off the basketball team and on probation by Tuesday, as you potentially face the final championship game. If you owed work that you never turned in this marking period, you might want to spend your weekend getting that done and turned in on Monday morning. Your grades will still be the grades you earned, but doing the work to learn the material, and showing responsibility to your teachers may cause them to see you as trying. If that translates into the beginning of the 'significant improvement' you need to get back to active status, you will have turned the tide away from a major disappointment to your team. Remember, you must be on probation until you have proven to your teachers that you can make at least a C average. You two must perform a miracle this weekend," she pressed.

"Take whatever books home you need to make this happen, and you may have to give up the dance tonight if you're serious about saving yourselves. I will see you both on Monday morning, but remember, I have to call your parents on Tuesday unless I hear otherwise from your teachers. Do you two understand the seriousness of the impact of all of this?"

Both boys looked shocked. Jed went white. Their eyes went into a glassy stare as they both said yes in a low harmonized tone. "Okay, then, I'm positive you can both do the work that you owed your teachers, and I sincerely wish you the best of luck getting yourselves all caught up by Monday morning. If you need to ask your teachers for anything to help you do that, don't hesitate to go to them before you leave school today. At least they will know you're planning to try, okay?" she said affectionately, knowing they were looking ahead at some tough consequences. She also knew that they were still somewhat in control of the worst outcome…losing the championship.

"Okay, thanks," Jed said, as he and Eddie turned away to get back to class.

"Yeah, thanks," Eddie echoed.

The two boys didn't appear to be talking on their way back, Mrs. Kaufmann noticed. She felt good about moving quickly enough to help them possibly turn things around. The miracle was no longer in her hands.

By Monday Morning

Mrs. Kaufmann came into the building Monday morning to see a big hand-painted sign that read, "Congratulations to the Boys' Basketball Team for Saturday night's win and qualifying for the Championship Game for this season's Tournament Finals in two weeks!"

Okay, she thought, *That means Eddie and Jed knew by Saturday night that the team still needed them to play, so the pressure to get the work done was squarely on their shoulders on Sunday. I will be so curious to see how they handled the pressure, the make-up work, and the weekend in general.* She let herself into her office and went right over to the phone's blinking light. She hit the button to play the recordings as she was putting away her belongings. She ran through her e-mail, and the only significant one was the last one, which was from Eddie's language arts teacher. His message was short and to the point. He told her that Eddie Grimm had just stopped in and gave him all the work he owed, so he was caught up.

Good for Eddie, she thought. Then she played the first voice mail. It was Mrs. Tindall. It soon became obvious, from how upset his mom sounded in her message, that Jed had shared his dilemma with her.

"Mrs. Kaufmann, I need you to call me as soon as you get in. This is extremely important. I will have my cell phone on and with me all day," Mrs. Tindall said quite sternly.

Mrs. Kaufmann decided to do that return call immediately so her anger didn't build any more. A woman answered the phone. "Mrs. Tindall?" she asked, recognizing that same voice from the message.

"Yes?" she answered curtly.

"It's Mrs. Kaufmann returning your call. I actually wanted to call you also, but I'll let you go first, in case your reason for calling was the same as mine," Mrs. Kaufmann answered.

"I have to tell you that I am just so upset," Mrs. Tindall started right in. "Jed told me this morning to brace myself for possibly a really bad grade in social studies today when his report card comes home. He said you told him that he might be thrown off the basketball team on Tuesday, and not be able to play in for the championship. Is that true? Really? He thought it might be because last weekend he was supposed to have finished his research paper, which was due last Monday and was worth a third of his grade. It wasn't done then, so he figured he'd get to it during the week and just never did. He thinks that's the only reason his grade dropped, because he got C's on his two big tests and did most of his homework. Is that possible?" she asked challengingly.

"Yes, and yes," Mrs. Kaufmann answered her. "That is why I wanted to call you. Last Friday, just before the end of the school day, Jed's teacher had just finished his averages for the report cards and saw that Jed was failing his social studies…."

"Failing???" Mrs. Tindall interrupted. "He's *failing* social studies? That can't be right. How could I not know it? There was no warning notice!"

"Yes, his average was lowered because of work not turned in right at the end of the marking period. If he was at a C level all along, and then lost all of the thirty-three percentage points that the research paper was worth, then that easily averaged out to below a D for the marking period, especially if his homework grade was not 100% to help the average. If any student in this middle school, who is participating in extracurricular activities or sports, has a grade that falls below a C in any subject, they go on probation until their grades go back up. That is the district policy. What terrible timing this year's calendar had, with the report cards coming out right before what would have been the basketball team's end-of-season opportunity to be the regional champions."

"This is crazy. You're telling me that a late paper will cost my son a passing grade and the school the basketball championship? That he wasn't given a chance to make it up?" She continued to challenge the facts with disbelief, exactly as Mrs. Kaufmann had predicted.

"I don't know that he was not allowed to make it up, but I did reach him within a couple of minutes of the end of the day on Friday to suggest he do it anyway and to turn it in today. I hope it will show his teacher that he can be responsible and is willing to do the work. I'm also hoping that it will make a difference in what he's supposed to learn by doing it. All of this may add into whether the teacher thinks he's made 'significant improvement,' which is required in order to be actively playing on the team."

"Well, that won't matter if the season has ended by then. I just can't believe this is happening to Jed," she insisted.

"May I ask a question about Jed's homework these last few weeks?" Mrs. Kaufmann interjected politely. "I'm curious about what he's been doing in the evening other than working on that research paper," Mrs. Kaufmann spoke directly. "I also know he's the only student that failed social studies this marking period. I know his teacher would not likely tell him he couldn't hand it in. There was something to be learned by doing that research and by writing a paper that Jed needed to learn. I just wonder what he is doing in the evening instead."

Mrs. Tindall seem to drop the sharpness in her voice when she said, "Well, to be quite frank with you, he hasn't appeared to be doing much of anything at all in the evenings, other than chatting with people on his computer when he gets home from what he calls 'hanging out with his friends.' I've asked him about it, but he always says it's all done. I can see now that he's been less than honest with me," she admitted.

"Do you know if he worked on the paper this weekend? And do you think he finished it to turn in today?" Mrs. Kaufmann followed up.

"I certainly hope so," Mrs. Tindall said with less anger, as she began to see that her son had actually caused and deserved his failure, as well as being on probation. "Come to think of it, Jed did stay in his room all day yesterday and didn't want much dinner. I thought he was just tired from the game on Saturday. There seems to be a lot of peer pressure on these kids today, so I think winning that game for the school has been on his mind. Plus the girls call non-stop. They drive me crazy. I even have to cut it off at night so he can get some sleep," she said now with open frustration.

Mrs. Kaufmann spoke sympathetically. "I do understand how hard it is for these young boys to balance sports, being popular, and their schoolwork. I know that being organized has always been a particular challenge for Jed. All the various homework assignments, projects, and tests, etc., are hard to manage as it is, no less the basketball schedule, the popularity with the girls, the pressure to be cool, and then add a research paper."

"I know, but what can I do? He doesn't listen to me anymore, and his dad is either not home or goes ballistic if he messes up," she said, sounding even more frustrated.

Mrs. Kaufmann continued, "Okay, here's the reality. We have our jobs, and, on a smaller scale, schoolwork is his job. All that the teachers assign is not over their heads, but it does teach them how to balance it all. The goal of education, after all, is to prepare them for when they are adults juggling everything the way we do every day. What he needs to be learning right now is how to prioritize his activities and manage his time. His job should be his primary focus right after his health and well-being, just like it is for us. These assignments are within his developmental and academic ability. He just needs to learn that his social activities have to come last, even though his ego is so pumped up and feeling good enjoying being the cute star basketball player. That's why it's so difficult for him. What he wants least is most important, and what he wants most is least important," Mrs. Kaufmann explained.

Mrs. Tindall now seemed noticeably quieter. "How can I help him do that?" she questioned.

Mrs. Kaufmann said, "You and I have learned delayed gratification, nose to the grindstone, and all those lessons as we grew up, but Jed has not learned the value or rewards of a good work ethic, yet. That is what we'll need to talk about with him. I'll show him how grade averages work and the impact of any missing assignment. You can show him how his homework will need to take priority over the hanging out and chatting. You'll need to help him develop a new after-school schedule. It should be one he'll need to keep from now on, and not just until his grades improve. Just trust that if he has to be on probation and not play in the tournament, or even if he *thinks* he can't for a while, that will end up being his best teacher. It will actually have more power than all our words or lectures combined. What we need to do is to allow the lesson, and show him what will need to be done from now on."

"Do you think he'll be able to play in the game in two weeks?" she asked.

Mrs. Kaufmann had to answer honestly. "I have no idea. If he needs enough time to show what's called a 'significant improvement' in grades, then that will be up to Jed's effort, the opportunities to show it, and his teachers' grading system within the next two weeks. We will just have to allow the lesson to come to Jed as it will. This isn't the end of the world, really, but very hard for you to have to watch, I understand. We so badly want to save our kids from the pain, but the pain is what teaches them. Each time we postpone their lesson, they have to learn it later, and then it is usually harder, because the stakes are bigger." Mrs. Kaufmann spoke kindly, hoping Mrs. Tindall learned her lesson, too. She knew it was very common for parents to come to the rescue of their children from upsetting consequences. Being the child advocate meant helping parents learn how to parent their children as well.

"Okay, I will have a sit-down with him tonight. His report card today will definitely give us that cause to talk anyway. We will make 'new arrangements' for his evenings, shall we say?" Ms. Tindall laughed. "And I will wait to hear from you about whether he will be playing basketball after tomorrow. Wow, this is going to be really tough on Jed. The whole team--no, the whole school--sees the championship riding on him. He is definitely going to feel he let them down," she said, realizing how big of a lesson this one was going to be.

"Yes, and I actually used that point to try to convince Jed to get that paper done this weekend. I am really curious as to whether he did it or not, and whether he turned it in or not," Mrs. Kaufmann confided in his mom. "I'm just glad we're working together to help him. Jed is a really good person, and I hope this will be the last time he lets something go like this. I will be talking with him today, and he knows I'll be calling you tomorrow, so you'll find out more as the story unfolds."

"That's good. I know he doesn't tell me much, so I will be glad to know what's going on," Mrs. Tindall said, sounding relieved.

Mrs. Kaufmann said in response, "I have an idea. Why don't you call his social studies teacher today, so you can know how much time and direction the students were given for this research paper? You can also ask for his grades and what dates his homework was not turned in. Being an informed parent will give you so much more leverage when you have your 'new arrangement' talk with Jed tonight. There won't be any gray area that gets in the way of making a clear, workable schedule that way."

"Good idea, thanks. I will do that," she said, with a total 180-degree change in her voice from when she had first called.

"I will, too. I think if we both remove Jed's excuses and rationalizations, we can strip it all right down to honesty and move forward with a plan based on good decision-making. I'll see if I can get him to come up with a better evening schedule on his own. Then, he'll have something to offer you when he hands you his report card tonight. And if you have to take away his time using social media or the phone for a while, that will actually help him. He won't want to tell everyone he would rather do his homework than talk to them, so blaming his parents will take the pressure off of him."

"This is a good plan. I feel so much better now that we've talked. Thank you so much," Mrs. Tindall answered her.

"You're so welcome. I will look forward to finding out how your night went when we talk tomorrow. Have a good day," Mrs. Kaufmann said, ending the call and feeling positive about it. She then e-mailed Jed's social studies teacher to ask him for Jed's grades for the marking period. She said she hoped he did the research paper after all and would like him to send Jed down to her from social studies that morning, for his failing grade academic conference. Mrs. Kaufmann said she had spoken with his mom, who also might be calling to get the scoop on how he had failed, so that she and her husband could talk with Jed tonight. She added that she hoped things would now be changed for the better.

Her next voice mail was from Julianna Adamson's father. He asked that she call him when she got this message and said it was about the basketball game Saturday night. He sounded very business-like. She picked up the phone and called his cell number right away. She knew his cell phone would be private, and she didn't want him to have to explain her phone call to his receptionist if he was at his office already.

"Mr. Adamson?" she said, as she heard a man's voice answer.

"This is he," he answered. "Is this Mrs. Kaufmann?"

"Yes, it is. How can I help you?"

"Well, I'll come right to the point. I don't want my daughter Julianna to know I called. She would never trust me again, because she likes this young basketball player a lot. Can we keep this between us?" he checked.

"Sure, if no one's safety is at stake," she assured him.

"Well, I don't know about that. There's this kid, a player from her class that was apparently smoking out behind the high school where they played their play-off game Saturday night. Julianna was talking about it with her friends. She said there was a whole group of boys that were supposed to have gone to a party down the street after the game to celebrate. The thing was, two of them snuck out of the party and went to have a smoke. She found out when one of the boys wrote to one of her friends that he or his friend, I'm not sure which, got grounded when he got picked up early by his father, who smelled the smoke and found his cigarettes in his pocket. Julianna was so afraid that Jed was the other boy, and was going to get caught and grounded, too."

He continued, "I didn't want to call his parents, because I'm not even sure it was him and, you know, parents tend to defend their kids anyway. I didn't want my daughter to hate me for snitching, either. I just think if it's one of our basketball players, he is too young to start that stuff. My bigger concern, of course, is the influence it would have on her, because she likes him so much. Anyway, I thought I would just help you keep informed, in case you have a way of handling this through the school, and you can help this young man."

"I understand," Mrs. Kaufmann replied. "Do you happen to know who the other boy was that got grounded?"

"I don't know his name. He actually goes to the other school that they played against, Linton Hall Middle School, and he's friends with the kids in our school. I really have to go now. I'm at work and getting another call. Thanks for not letting Julianna know I called, and I hope I've helped," Mr. Adamson said quickly, as he hung up.

Mrs. Kaufmann was getting a better picture on why Jed's grades had recently dropped, and what he might be doing when he was just "hanging out" with his friends. This changed her entire strategy for her "academic conference" with Jed that day. In the meantime, she needed to go see the principal and let him know about the smoking issue.

Getting Down to the Truth

"Mr. Gonzalez, would you have a minute?" Mrs. Kaufmann asked, as she caught him coming out of his office in a hurry.

"If you can walk and talk. I'm late for a meeting, so I have to keep moving," he answered.

"I'll be happy to, and I only need to inform you of something," she answered.

"Uh-oh. That sounds like a problem. Go ahead."

She spoke quickly, as she also kept the brisk pace with the principal. "I got a call from a student's father telling me he overheard his daughter say a boy from Linton Hall Middle School was grounded for smoking behind the high school after the game Saturday night. One of her friends said that the other student smoking was one of our basketball players, and that it might be Jed Tindall. The father wanted to remain anonymous, but called because he didn't want his daughter affected by this boy's possible behavior. I don't know if this counts as a reportable incident, considering it is all so cloudy, hearsay, and rumor-like. If you have to report this as a substance abuse incident, I would be surprised, but I wanted you to be aware of it. I will bring this up with Jed when I meet with him today. He was coming in to talk about his failing grade in social studies, so that goes hand-in-hand with that kind of behavior. I'll be curious what Jed says when

I mention it. I will also share this very loose rumor with his mother, who is trying to be on top of his new 'hanging-out' behavior. This may give her another reason to tighten up on his free time. I'd like her to be aware of what she might be up against as far as his possibly new risk-taking friends. That's all I needed to tell you," she said as she smiled.

"Thank you for keeping me informed. I really do appreciate it. I would like to talk with you after you meet with him, okay?" he said, as he turned into a classroom for his meeting.

Mrs. Kaufmann turned around to get back to her office. She hadn't finished listening to her morning messages yet, and she needed to get to her academic appointments for the day. Besides, Jed was going to be there shortly, and she was hoping she had an e-mail from his social studies teacher with information about his grades.

Jed Tindall appeared in her doorway saying, "Mrs. Kaufmann, did you want to see me? My teacher sent me down with this note for you."

"Yes, Jed, I was wondering what you ended up accomplishing over the weekend with that research paper," she said, as she took the paper from his hand. As she looked at it, she saw all the grades his teacher had recorded, including a note that Jed had just turned in a belated research paper that he had not had a chance to grade.

"I did it!" Jed announced proudly. It took me all day Sunday, and I gave it to my teacher when I came in this morning. He said he was proud of me for doing it after the term ended, and that he would grade it tonight and let me know how I did tomorrow. He also said the report card grades are already in the system, so I have to bring home the failure that I earned, but I warned my mom this morning that my grade would be low," he admitted.

"I am really proud of you, too," Mrs. Kaufmann told him. "I figured it couldn't change your grade, but I hoped it would change your teacher's opinion of you and your opinion of you," she told him. "You really need to have done a research paper in order to learn the form and all the footnoting rules. It's something that will help your grades as long as you go to school, and I wanted you to know you can do it so you don't postpone it ever again."

Jed smiled, and then he asked the big question. "Will this put me back on the team?"

"You're not off the team, just on probation. You need to prove to your teacher that you are back into the 'C or better' range in his class. Do you know what assignments or tests you have coming up to show him your new quality of work?"

"Well, we'll be at the end of a chapter on Wednesday, the review on Thursday and then the big test is this Friday. If I get a C, would that do it?"

"It might, but I don't know. I'll bet your teacher will at least be feeling better about your change of attitude from your efforts yesterday. It looks like we'll have to wait and see. Sorry. I do want to talk to you about your grades last marking period to see if you understood how this failing was happening. Let's do a little math together right now. I want to show you the power each missing grade has on your average. I have all the assignments, what percent each was worth, and which ones you turned in." She paused and then said slowly, "and which ones you didn't."

Jed smiled sheepishly. He admitted, "I think I was going good at the beginning of the marking period, but I forgot a couple at the end."

Mrs. Kaufmann asked him, "What percent of the assignments do you think you did, and what effect do you think that had on your grade?"

"Uh, I think I probably got about a B for the homework part of my grade."

"It says here that you turned in 5 of the 10 assignments. That is a fifty percent grade because it is one-half of the homework, and that has the power of being a third of your grade. Then you had a 76 average on your tests, which is another third of your grade. The last third of your grade was a zero, because you didn't turn in a research paper. Your teacher had no score to put down for you. Now, if you average together the 50, the 76, and the 0, you get 126 divided by 3. That's 42. If you turned in a research paper which, let's say, was a B, or an 84, then your 3 scores would have been a 50, 76, and 84. You would have had a grade of 70, or C-. Now if you had turned in all 10 of your homework assignments, you could have had a 100, a 76, and an 84 which would have given you a grade of 87. And all you had to do was your homework!"

"Oh, wow, I didn't know that. I didn't think a homework assignment here and there could add up like that," Jed said, looking honestly surprised.

"Yes, the little things really do add up. So what have you been doing at night when everyone else is doing their homework?" she asked directly, but with a smile. "I'm sure it seems like the other kids are chatting online with you and not doing their homework, either, but they are. No one else failed social studies, so they must be getting their work done first and then getting online. Maybe they get it done earlier?" she suggested.

"But I have basketball practice after school, so I can't do it then," he protested.

"I'd love to help you create a better evening schedule for doing your homework this next marking period. I think it would be especially good if you go home with one today to go with that report card. I'm hoping your mom will like your new schedule and she won't have to give you her own," she hinted at Jed, to encourage him to work cooperatively with her.

"Okay. I guess I used to come home from practice, eat dinner, and then ask to go to my friend's house to hang out a little before I did my homework. Then, when I got home, I wouldn't feel like doing it anymore," he admitted.

"I'm proud of you for being honest with me. I know it's hard to admit, but I have one more question for you that will be hard to admit to, too. I had a call today from a man who believes you might have been smoking behind the high school after the big game on Saturday night. Jed, was that you, and are you doing some 'hanging out' that you can't share with your parents?" Mrs. Kaufmann asked sincerely.

Jed's face went pure white, and he stumbled over his words. He stuttered about what party he went to that night, but he knew she could tell he was lying. His denial was making it hard for her to talk about it, so she went another way to get to the issue. "Jed, how about I just ask you this. If you were a student who loved basketball, what would make you try smoking, knowing how bad it is for your lungs?"

Jed's eyes filled up, and he looked down for a minute. Mrs. Kaufmann waited quietly, too. Then, she finally spoke again. "I'm just saying *if*. What would make it so easy to do, or so hard to resist *if* it was a student like you?"

Jed's shoulders dropped and he finally spoke. "The health teacher always says to 'just say no,' but when your friends are all smoking and they expect you to be a part of the group, you can't 'just say no.' They would make fun of you, and you wouldn't be able to hang out with them anymore. They'd think you'd be a snitch, and then you'd have no friends," he admitted.

"I totally understand," she told him. Then she asked, "How do you think it must feel for that person, *if* it was you, to have to hide it, keep the secrets from his parents, lying and doing something that causes lung diseases?" She continued with the "what if" discussion. "Do you think that person would like it to stop? Do you think that boy would want to change friends so the pressure would end?"

"I know it wouldn't feel good." Jed played along, too. He was so resistant to admitting anything, and yet he wanted to actually talk about it.

"Okay, Jed, let me just tell you that I have to let your mom know about that call. I would suggest you tell her the truth and allow all the bad news to hit at once today and get it over with." Mrs. Kaufmann saw Jed's eyes get wider than ever, and she continued. "I think your new schedule for homework could easily eliminate that 'hanging-out' time after dinner, which will help you be done with the whole problem. No one will expect you anywhere because of the 'new deal' that you and your parents agree to. I know you know that smoking is really bad for you, and you can decide if you will be smart and won't be doing it anymore. Your parents will be happy to help you, once they get over their disappointment, of course. Can you brave through that? Your life will be so much better, I promise. All that dishonesty separates you from your parents, and then you're angry with them and they are with you. Dishonesty always backfires. What do you say, Jed?"

Jed paused again and said quietly, "I'd like to be honest with my parents a lot of the time, but my dad always gets so angry."

Mrs. Kaufmann immediately asked, "What does he do when he gets that angry?"

"He yells a lot and takes away my computer and phone."

"What will happen today when he finds out about the failure in social studies and you being on probation?" she continued.

"He's really gonna lose it! I will definitely lose the computer, the phone, and be grounded," he answered her with tears in his eyes again.

"And if you were to also confess you've tried smoking? What would he do then?" she pushed.

"Uh, I don't know. There isn't anything else to lose. I really don't know."

"So, may I suggest that you have a 'coming clean' night? It's a night when all the old routines and bad habits are done, and all new routines and habits can begin. A fresh start, a renewal of an honest relationship, all to make your life totally better. Would you like to make things better?"

"I guess so, but I wouldn't know how to begin. I don't know if I can do this," he admitted.

"I will be happy to help. Who can you talk to more easily--your mom, I gather?" Mrs. Kaufmann needed to help Jed move forward now. "I have to call your mom anyway, as I told you. I can invite her into my office right now to get this over with. I can help you start the dialogue. You'll definitely get some points for owning up rather than waiting for the news to hit her from some other source. And you do know she'll be disappointed with the news. That's because she loves you, and she wants everything you do to be good for you. Smoking isn't good for you, to say the least, and neither is failing at school. This is just a bump in the road, Jed, and it's something that can be cleaned out, fixed, and then we all move on. Remember, she only wants you to be healthy, happy, and successful in life. She's your mom; she loves you."

"I guess so," Jed quietly mumbled, "but right now?" he checked desperately.

"Sure, let's get this over with and move on," Mrs. Kaufmann said, as she picked up the phone to call his mother. Jed faced her, frozen in his seat.

"Mrs. Tindall? It's Mrs. Kaufmann. Would you be willing to come over to my office to talk with Jed and me? Jed said that he told you this morning about his social studies grade and the probation. I'm thinking we could put together a better homework system for him with your input. We can also talk about his priorities academically and socially and get a good system working. I know this will help his grades and may help him make that 'significant improvement' this week, which is what he needs right now." Mrs. Kaufmann kept looking at Jed and nodding as if to say "It will be all right." She then said, "I'll see you in a little bit. Thanks!" and she hung up. Turning to Jed, she said, "How was that? So far so good?"

He smiled weakly. "I guess so, so far."

"Okay, let's make that plan for your homework routine so we'll have it to show your mom when she gets here. Let's make it so you can follow it from now on, not just while you're on probation with the team, or on probation with your parents. Remember, you don't have basketball practice after school for a while, so that will give you all the time you need. And let's not build computer or phone time in your schedule, to start out. That way, if you lose them, you won't be so disappointed. We can talk about how you'll add them gradually as your grades improve."

The phone rang from the main office, and Mrs. Kaufmann picked up. She and Jed had just finished creating a rough draft of a typical school-night schedule. "Hello?" she answered. "Okay, good. Thanks for letting me know," she said and looked at Jed. "Your mom is on her way here, and I think we are ready. How do you feel about this plan? Do you think she'll like it?"

"Yes, I think so," he answered her.

"Knock, knock!" Jed's mom's voice was at the door already. "Hi, Jeddy," she said, and then, "Hi, Mrs. Kaufmann. Thanks for inviting me in. I'd like to find out how today went."

Jed was quiet, so Mrs. Kaufmann jumped in and began to prompt him. "Jed, tell your mom about that research paper you did this past weekend," she started.

Jed sat up and began to chatter about how proud the teacher was that he did it, even though it wouldn't change the average from the last marking period.

Mrs. Kaufmann tried to move it along by adding, "So we know he'll be bringing the failing grade home today on his report card, and we also have talked about how this happened. Jed was rather surprised to see how just missing a few assignments made all the difference. He also has designed a homework schedule for school nights that he'd like to show you. His intention is to get those grades up, and quickly. There's a lot at stake here, and he knows it."

She continued, "The probation period has to stick until he has proven to that teacher that he can make a C average or better, and he has a big chapter test this Friday. We also think that turning in that research paper may have shown his teacher a change of attitude immediately," Mrs. Kaufmann told Jed's mom.

"This is good news," Mrs. Tindall said with reservations. "I must admit, though, that his dad and I will still need to give Jed some restrictions as a result of his being dishonest with us." She then turned to Jed. "Jed, do you understand how upset we are with this failure and this probation, and even more importantly, with this dishonesty?" she asked him.

He looked down and simply said, "Sorry."

Mrs. Kaufmann then felt the timing was right to finish the "cleaning-out" part. "Mrs. Tindall, I must share something else with you that will also be upsetting, but Jed is prepared to talk about it with you, so that the dishonesty is all out and on the table, and you can move forward from there. You see, I received a phone call this morning from someone who thought Jed might have been seen smoking. Now that's a lot of hearsay, but I feel we needed to address that. Jed has been 'hanging out' at night, and I believe that needs to end, don't you, Jed?"

Mrs. Tindall sat back in her chair looking shocked. Jed spoke quickly. "I'm sorry, Mom, I only tried it that one time, and I won't do it anymore, I promise. I know it's bad for me and everything, but I didn't know how to say no."

Mrs. Kaufmann jumped in to help keep the conversation constructive and to ward off Jed's mom from losing it in response. "Mrs. Tindall, I know you must be very upset with this news, and Jed knows you will have a good discussion about it tonight, but I am very pleased with Jed's willingness to make it right. He didn't have to own up, but he wanted to have an honest relationship with you and his dad again."

"I don't even know what to say," Mrs. Tindall admitted. "Smoking?" she said to Jed in complete disappointment.

Jed's eyes filled up, and he began to cry. He simply said, "I'm so sorry, Mom." Mrs. Kaufmann sat quietly to allow the moment, the one that would teach Jed what he needed to learn, and the one that would show his mom he was learning it.

"Mrs. Kaufmann, all I can say is thank you for helping us through this. I can see Jed feels bad about all of this, and he will lose some privileges and get on a better homework schedule, to be sure. His father will be quite upset, but I will let him know that we already met and what some of the good news is, too. In fact, I will call him when I get home. I just feel so strongly that Jed should talk more to you about what made him smoke in the first place, and what he'll have to do to be able to say no next time. Is that something you can help us with?" Jed's mother looked tired, and so did Jed.

"I would be very happy to. Peer pressure is a really big problem for middle-school students. There is so much pressure to be accepted and 'belong to a tribe' or group, so you don't look like nobody likes you and you're alone. The students will go along with whatever their group thinks is cool just to belong somewhere. Jed and I will talk more about this, and I will be in touch with his social studies teacher to keep up with his average," she offered.

"And Jed," she continued, "This is really an important week to do all your work as best you can. "Be thorough and do it all. Make sure your assignment pad has everything you need in it every day, and remember to bring your books home with you in the evening, okay?" Mrs. Kaufmann asked.

"I will, I promise," he answered her. Then he turned to his mother and said once again, "Mom, I am so sorry."

His mother put her arm around him and said, "It will be okay, Jeddy. We'll get through this. Your father and I just want what's best for you because we love you."

Jed looked at Mrs. Kaufmann as she said that, and Mrs. Kaufmann gave him a knowing wink.

Jed gave her a little smile back.

"Well," Mrs. Kaufmann said as she stood up. "I think this meeting was very good. We have a plan, and we all know what we can do to help Jed. Everything is a lesson, after all, so there's nothing bad, just a discovery as to what he has to do and what wasn't working. It's all good."

Mrs. Tindall and Jed both stood up also, and Mrs. Kaufmann wrote a pass for Jed to get to his next class. He took the pass, gave his mother a kiss, and left the office looking relieved but a little heavy with worry about his father's response. Mrs. Tindall then turned to Mrs. Kaufmann and thanked her for her time and effort to get to this point today.

"I love it when we have a big clearing, so it was my pleasure," Mrs. Kaufmann said sincerely. "It took quite a while for Jed to admit to that smoking, though. He was so afraid to tell you and especially his father, but he didn't want to live that lie, and he feared getting caught. He is a really good boy who made a bad choice. I'd like to show him that his parents will work with him whenever he has to confess to a problem.

"My suggestion is that his dad let him know he's disappointed with his decision to smoke, his dishonesty, and his failed grade. That needs to go on record, and Jed needs to know what that feels like. Then, you both need to let him know what he will lose and for how long, and then move on to the positive. Look at his plan, and let him tell you how he designed it. Work with him and praise his efforts to change and do better in school. Let him know you are proud of his willingness to make things right. That's important, because that part of his character can really use some positive reinforcement right now."

"That makes sense. I will definitely call his dad and have a talk with him before he gets home tonight. What a day! I do find it interesting, though, that I'm not that upset with it anymore. I guess I do tend to overreact. Thank you again for putting perspective to it all. I'd better get back to work now. Please keep in touch."

Mrs. Kaufmann shook her hand and said, "Yes, I will keep in touch. I want to see Jed feel better about his ability to make his own decisions, too. I will meet with him next Monday, and I will give you a call if I hear anything sooner. Have a good afternoon."

Mrs. Tindall left in a hurry, and Mrs. Kaufmann made a quick phone call to Mr. Gonzalez's voice mail. "Mr. Gonzalez, I just wanted you to know that the smoking issue has been discussed with the mother of that student, as well as his failure and the probationary status on the basketball team. It was a good discussion all around, and I believe we'll see his grades start improving right away. Call me if you need to know any more. Right now I need to meet with all the other students who didn't do so well on their report cards. Enjoy your day!"

The Verdict Is In

The next Monday rolled around, and Mrs. Kaufmann wrote an e-mail to Jed's social studies teacher, asking for the status of his grades. She also put a pass into his homeroom teacher's mailbox for him to give to Jed. She wrote that he was to come see her during gym class that morning. She didn't want to pull him from any of the time he needed to be in his academic classes. She figured he would be okay this one time, sacrificing a little time from that third-period class.

She made a quick call to follow up on Eddie Grimm's progress with his language arts teacher. He told Mrs. Kaufmann that Eddie had actually turned in a book report due that day, which was a first. He never usually even read the books that were assigned. Plus he had already received an 87 on a vocabulary test last week. "It's amazing what a great motivator sports can be, isn't it?" he said jokingly. "I wish we had a 'carrot' to put before all the students who don't do well."

"I know. For the students that aren't involved in anything, that's the kicker. We have to find or create that motivator. That's great about Eddie. And how's Jed Tindall doing, just out of curiosity?" Mrs. Kaufmann checked. "Has his average gone up at all?"

"Oh, he's doing better already, too. He got an 85 this morning. Like I said, probation is a great motivator. I will know about Eddie after this Friday's English test. I just want to make sure it wasn't a one-shot effort before he gets reinstated on the team."

"That's fine. It will keep the pressure on a little longer, but it will let Eddie get to practice a few times before the championship game, too. Thanks for the update," Mrs. Kaufmann said.

She then checked her e-mail again and saw the response from Jed's teacher. "I want you to know what a changed student Jed is. I just hope it lasts after basketball season. He got an 89 on his unit test, which is his best grade this year. Also, he hasn't missed an assignment. I have to tell you that his father called a week ago and asked me to let him know the instant an assignment was missed, until he was off probation. I believe Jed was right there when he called, too, so I don't think he has any room for error now. Also, his research paper would have earned him an 82, which is not bad considering he did almost all of it in one day! I think we can safely say his average has 'significantly improved,' and he'd better not let any of us down now."

She wrote back, "Music to my ears. I knew he could do it! Thanks. I'll share the good news with Mrs. Gillow and Mr. Gonzalez, as well as Jed and his parents. Thanks!"

Mrs. Kaufmann grabbed her keys, locked her office door, and headed off to the main office. She left a message with the principal's secretary to tell him Jed's probation was over, and he would be allowed to play again. She then went directly to the gym and saw Mrs. Gillow in front of her class, watching the students doing their stretching exercises. Mrs. Kaufmann slipped into the gym, walking around the sides of the room to reach her with a big smile. She shared the good news: "We just got a thumbs-up for reinstating Jed Tindall back on the team, and we should have Eddie Grimm back on the team just in time before the big game. Both boys pulled it off. You got your miracle!" Mrs. Kaufmann grinned.

"That is wonderful news! Do the parents know yet? Both fathers called me last week to let me know their boys were going to improve their grades, and they've asked me to call them if I heard anything about the probation. Will you be letting them know?" Mrs. Gillow asked.

"Oh, yes, that was my next question. Do you mind if I borrow Ted from gym today? I'd like him to make the call to his father from my office and give him the good news. I'll do the same for Eddie as soon as it's official. If you can call their moms to give the official word, and let them know when the next practice is, we can cover them both," she suggested.

"That would be really helpful. I don't get much free time today, with the team meeting during my prep period. Thanks for doing that--and hey, thanks again for the great news! Our team will be back!"

"My pleasure," Mrs. Kaufmann answered, as she turned to head back to her office.

—⊙—

The sudden increase in the hallway noise reminded Mrs. Kaufmann that class was over and Jed should be headed her way. She finished off writing the last pass for the academic conferences for the next day just as Jed appeared in her doorway. His face was not the troubled face she had seen before. He was smiling and came into the office with a bounce in his step. "Did you want to see me? Is everything okay?" he asked with the expectation that it should be good news this time.

Mrs. Kaufmann smiled right back and didn't wait a second more. "I just got back from telling Mr. Gonzalez and Mrs. Gillow that the probation is over, and you're free to play basketball again! Congratulations, my friend. You did it, Jed. I knew you could. You just got on the wrong track for a little while, but you're back on the right one again."

Jed grinned from ear to ear. "Awesome! Thanks! And now maybe I can get my computer or phone back. My father said I had to earn his trust first, so I'm not sure how long that takes," Jed said, with some restraint on his excitement.

"Want to call him right now and give him the good news?" Mrs. Kaufmann offered.

"Yeah, man. Can I?" Jed jumped at the chance to end the feeling of disappointment he had over all of his recent mess-ups. "Should I make the call myself?" he asked.

"Actually, I'll make the call to make sure we reach him, and then I'll put you on to tell him." She then called his cell phone, thinking the connection would be less invasive to his place of work.

"Hello? John Tindall here," he answered.

"Mr. Tindall, this is Mrs. Kaufmann, Jed's school counselor. I hope we're not disturbing you, but I'd like to put Jed on to share some news with you, if that's okay."

"Sure, and I sure hope it is good news this time," he said, with some optimism in his voice.

"All right then, here's Jed," she said, as she passed the phone over to him.

"Dad?" Jed started. "I'm off probation. I can play with the team again," he boasted.

"Son, that's great news. Congratulations! Did you tell your mother yet?" he checked.

"Not yet, but Dad? Can I have my computer or my phone back?" he asked coyly.

"We'll see, son. Your mother and I will talk about that tonight. Good job. I'm proud of you. Will you put Mrs. Kaufmann back on the phone please, and I'll see you tonight."

Jed handed the phone over to Mrs. Kaufmann. "Good news, right?" she said to Jed's father.

"Yes! Definitely! Jed and I needed this. The pressure was mounting at home, but I'm not inclined to give him back his equipment just yet. That dishonesty with the smoking put us over the edge, so that may have to wait. I think being allowed to play in the school championship game is the reward for doing his work. Getting his gadgets back from us will be the reward for gaining our trust at home. That will take a little longer."

"I totally understand. Trust is big, so the lesson has to be big. That one doesn't happen in a week. However, working hard to gain it back may need some positive reinforcement of some kind so the effort continues, if you know what I mean. Maybe one at a time? Just a thought," she suggested.

"It is certainly worth discussing with his mother tonight. Thanks for the call and your time," Jed's father said. "I do have to go. Thanks again for the good news."

"Well, your father was certainly happy with your efforts. You may have to go a little longer to prove your trustworthiness, you know? How are you feeling?" she asked Jed.

"I am so excited that I can play with the team now! I was feeling so bad about letting my team down, and now I can play. Woohoo! Oh, and my dad and I had a long talk about smoking. I told him I knew it was bad for me, but I just didn't know how to tell them I didn't want to join the others. At the time, I thought if I said 'no thanks' they would see it as if I wouldn't join them, or that I thought I was better than them, or that I was a goody-goody. It's as if you can't be friends with the other guys if you aren't willing to be a little bad with them. I'm still not sure what to say if I hang with them again. Right now I don't go out after dinner, but I will be with my friends when it happens again somewhere. How do I 'just say no' and yet keep the friends?" Jed asked very sincerely.

"I know that's a tough spot to be in, but here's what I have learned by talking with students who have pulled that off successfully. It's all in *their way of being* in general. Think about it. Pretend you are one of those friends that you are worried about pleasing right now, and there's a kid who seems needy or working at getting you to like him. Do you really like him or do you see him as trying too hard? It's difficult to respect him for who he is when you don't really know what that is. He just seems phony. And since he isn't being himself, you just expect him to continue on trying to please you. That's when you think he *should* be doing what you say or what you do. He *should* be smoking with you and not turning you down. That's your ego.

"After a while, you feel surprised if he does say no. So, when he says no, your ego is telling you that he isn't joining you for a smoke for a reason. Then, your ego thinks that might suggest *you* are doing something wrong. That's when you put the pressure on him. It's your inner voice trying to make yourself feel secure in your power, feel right about what you're doing, and get that comfortable position of power and control over that boy to say yes. Can you see the thinking in the minds of this group of 'friends,' as you call them?" she asked him.

"I can see what you mean, I think. It's just hard to think of them as worried about their power. It seems like they have it all over me. And I don't see what you mean when you say it has to be all in my *way of being*," Jed admitted.

"Actually, those boys have convinced you by *their* way of being that they are cool. You look at them and can't believe they could worry about what you think. That's because they look confident, don't they? It looks like they do what they do because they just want to. Actually they are not confident, and smoking is the evidence of that. Their smoking is the common ritual that those boys use to feel connected. They are connected by their secret. It's like a club. People love the feeling of being connected, because they don't like to feel alone. That's how a group of boys can get another one to join them, for exactly the very reason you did. They decide if you want to be with them by what you're willing to risk for their friendship, or for a group, or to be able to hang out with friends. That's what feeds their confidence," Mrs. Kaufmann explained.

"You were attracted to that connection. Does that make sense? The first two boys that originally decided to try the risk of smoking in the first place, did it together the first time for the risk-taking thrill. The rest of the boys were later added into the group depending on if they would 'pay' to join with the health risk, the legal risk, the addiction risk, the parental trust, etc. Now, just think about what you were attracted to. Think about what you risked. I will say that if your coach knew you did that, you would be off the team permanently. As it is, you paid the price using the trust of your parents, which cost you your computer and your phone. That was a big cost, because you lost your connection with real friends who don't expect you to pay to be with them. How about that?" she challenged.

"Wow," Jed said. "I never thought of it that way. I don't like thinking I have to pay to be with them, and none of them lost their computer and phone!" Jed began to be angry that he appeared so needy to them.

"Now, let's talk about real confidence, not the one that just *appeared* to be in control. Real confidence means you're fine with yourself, and you don't need to control anyone. You don't keep worrying about who does what, or who thinks what, because you know you'll be okay, that you can and will handle whatever comes along. That's real confidence. It's like being at peace. That's what I mean when I say it's just how you are. You can watch the boys who smoke and observe smoking as a sign of neediness. It's the risk that allows them to stay in their club of neediness. A confident person would decide to be friends by the comfort and fun they have together. A confident person enjoys the respect of others but doesn't depend on it to feel good. An insecure person would pay a price to get approval by joining in on the group's vulnerability. Which would you rather have for friendships?"

"So what should I say when I'm at a party and the smoking starts?" he asked, still unsure.

Mrs. Kaufmann said, "The confident person would simply say, quite confidently, 'No thanks,' and allow all who heard it to decide what it means to them. The confident person wouldn't care, because he knows who he is. He knows the price to his lungs isn't worth it. He knows the price to an athletic career isn't worth it, not to mention the daily life of dishonesty and secrecy to keep the addiction. The confident person makes every decision based on what's right for him, not what's good for a needy person. That is what I mean by 'your way of being.' You are Jed, and Jed is perfectly Jed. He puts out no put-downs. He makes fun of no one, and he goes through his life knowing he's making the best choices for himself that he knows how to make. That's all. A casual but firm, 'No, thanks.' And if you try to come up with excuses, I can assure you that any excuse you use will end up being used against you. Any reason you give them could backfire or be used to manipulate you," Mrs. Kaufmann continued.

"What do you mean?" Jed asked. "My dad said to tell them my parents would kill me."

"Ah, but they would say that *they* were brave enough to pay that price for their friendship. And if you said it will hurt my lungs, they would say but *they* were brave enough to risk that health problem in order to have their friendship. You won't win at any excuse. Your excuses force them to defend themselves and their habit. So, just be confident enough not to have to please them."

"Okay," Jed said, "but I don't think it will go well, I'm just sayin'."

"Here's another question for you," Mrs. Kaufmann posed. "What kids do you hang out with that don't make you 'pay' to be in their company?"

"I have my team members that I have over a lot, and we practice shooting hoops in my driveway. We have fun no matter what we're doing," he replied.

"Is there a price to pay for their friendship?" she asked.

"No, we're just ourselves. We don't pressure each other at all to do anything, except maybe what sport we most want to do when we hang out," Jed said.

"Why is that?" she asked.

"Uh, I guess we just like to be with each other," he answered matter-of-factly.

"Bingo!" she said, laughing. You just respect each other because you like each other's company. That's exactly right. Real friendship is about respect, not control. The boys who are hiding and smoking at night need a group, and they work at not getting caught, and they have to keep controlling those people in the group for their own safety. There isn't a mutual respect. In fact, there isn't even any self-respect. They definitely don't respect their bodies or respect their parents or respect the law. Can you see which friends are the most fun, the most respectful, and the easiest? Could there really be any choice?"

"No, there couldn't be. Besides, I really don't have to show up at night anymore with those old friends that smoke, because they all know I got caught and got grounded. Once my homework is done and my mom has checked it off, I'm allowed to play basketball in the driveway, so I can have my real friends over after basketball season," Jed explained to her.

"Sounds like your parents were really fair, considering the white hair you gave them," she said with a laugh.

"Yeah, they were. That smoking thing had them really upset. I don't think my dad said much because he was so mad. He was really trying to help me and my mom get through it. I still feel bad that I disappointed so many people," Jed admitted, with his eyes filling up.

Mrs. Kaufmann said, "Look, Jed. Everyone makes mistakes, even the grown-ups, and no one is perfect. You are human. We all travel our own learning journey for our whole lifetime, and we use every experience we have to get wiser and more mature. Then, when you're really old like me, you are, hopefully, wise enough to reach out and help others learn from their experiences. All these lessons you just learned are tucked away in your memory to use now. You just got smarter and wiser and more mature. Congratulations! No easy task and no going back, because you can never 'unknow' what you now know," she said with a smile.

Mrs. Kaufmann continued, "What you also got from all of this is respect for how well you handled yourself, and how you were willing to make things right. You were willing to face the consequences head on and make up the work, and earn back the trust, and win the respect of others. All that great character should earn you your own self-respect, and that will give you more confidence. I am really glad to know you, Jed. You are a truly special person!"

Jed looked quite pleased as he mulled over Mrs. Kaufmann's praise. He really did do all those things she said. "Plus, I can play in the tournament!" he added, with a twinkle in his eyes.

"Speaking of which, let's get you back to the gym. There's just a little time left for you to give Mrs. Gillow the high-five. She already knows. Oh, wait, did you want to call your mom and give her the good news, too?" Mrs. Kaufmann offered.

"I can't, she's on her flight this morning. I'll talk with her when I call her after school. I know she'll want to talk about it a lot then." Jed jumped up out of his seat to head for the door.

"Wait, wait. I have to sign your pass and put the time on it. We don't want anyone even questioning your integrity anymore!" she laughed as she signed his hall pass. "Now, keep those grades up, and make us proud at the tournament. Just give it all you've got, and that's all you can do!" she said as Jed turned to walk out the door.

"Then we're gonna *win*!" he declared in response, and began to run down the hall.

"Walk, please!" she called after him.

"Talk about confidence!" Mrs. Kaufmann laughed to herself.

Discussion Points:

- What is good for us may not be what we want most. Pleasing friends may be about getting their approval and shouldn't be more important than doing what is right, healthy, or safe.

- Sometimes the struggle of learning a lesson is the part that helps us remember the lesson.

- Dishonesty causes children to feel separated from their parents. "Coming clean" brings them closer. Honesty with parents rewards children with trust.

Reflection Questions:

1. When your parents trust you, are you allowed to do more things than when they don't trust you? Once you've lost your parents' trust, how long does it take to get it back?

2. Have you ever had a friendship in which the friend controls you, or you control your friend? How do you make sure your friendships are based on respect and taking turns?

3. How do you say "no thank you" when others try to pressure you into doing something you know you shouldn't do? If you ever have gone along with others who did force you, why did you? Why do you think they pressured you in the first place?

4. How have you felt holding a secret that you have done something wrong?

CHAPTER 18:
They'll Like Me More if I'm Thinner

The Referral

The fast, quick series of knocks at her door told the school counselor something urgent had just arrived. Mrs. Kaufmann quickly got up from her chair to see who was at her office door. It was Janie Rappaport, an honor student who loved life, participated in sports and the Junior Key Club, appeared to enjoy her many good friends, and was not a regular visitor at the school counselor's door. "Janie, what a nice surprise this is! It's so good to see you, but you look upset and out of breath. What's troubling you, my dear?" Mrs. Kaufmann stepped back so Janie could come into the office as quickly as possible, and then closed the door right behind her for her privacy. "Have a seat and catch your breath," Mrs. Kaufmann suggested.

"I can't stay long or everyone will ask where I went, so I have to talk fast," she said, sitting at the edge of her seat and rather winded from almost racing down the hall. "I was at lunch, and I asked the lunch aide if I could use the bathroom to wash my hands. Just as I went into the bathroom, I overheard Lin Soo throwing up. I knew it was her, because I could see the backs of her shoes under the stall door. She isn't sick at all, and I know she's trying to lose weight, so I started to think about what the health teacher told us. I also remembered Lin Soo mentioned to a group of us when we went shopping a couple of weekends ago that she feels so fat, but she sometimes gets so hungry that she just eats like crazy. Today she ate everything on her tray in huge gulps as usual and even asked me for my cookies. After that she waited a few minutes, and then got up to go to the bathroom.

"She does that almost every day, so I started to think about that bulimia thing Mrs. Hildago told us about. She said bulimia is not so uncommon for kids our age. What do I say to her?" Janie asked. "I've always noticed before this that she'd either eat nothing, or she'd just pick and then go to the bathroom. How do I make her stop? I'm scared she's going to end up in trouble like the real, real skinny kids whose pictures we saw. They looked like skeletons!"

"Okay, first of all, that doesn't happen overnight, so you can relax. I'm so glad you've come here to help her. This is really thoughtful of you. We really need a little more time to talk than just a fast minute or two, so what if we make an appointment for after recess? I know how girls pay attention to where all their friends are going, so let's do something different so they don't have to ask where you're going. I can have one of your teachers pretend to send you somewhere to deliver something, so you can come here without anyone knowing or asking you anything. As for right now, I think your class finished lunch and has already gone out for recess, so you'll need to get going, too. What class is the best one to leave from this afternoon?" Mrs. Kaufmann asked. She only gave that choice to good students, knowing they don't like to miss anything.

"How about I come from science sixth period? We had a quiz yesterday, and Mr. Conklin was going to go over it with us today. I already know I got a hundred because he congratulated me this morning, so I don't need to be there," Janie offered.

"That will work perfectly for me," the school counselor said, as she checked her appointment schedule. "I'll give him a call now and tell him our plan. Then, sixth period I'll call and ask that he send a runner, which will be you, to deliver something made-up to someone made-up so that you can come to me." Mrs. Kaufmann laughed at what she thought was one of her best ideas to help students have privacy. "This will work really well this time, because your grades are so good you would naturally be the one he'd pick to run an errand for him."

Janie laughed. "That's pretty tricky, Mrs. Kaufmann!"

"I know, and it works. I wouldn't say anything to Lin right now. These problems can be complicated, so it wouldn't be worth the risk letting her know you heard her in the bathroom today," Mrs. Kaufmann suggested.

"I know. I never tell on my friends, but we were told in health class that if it's dangerous for someone's health or safety, we really owe it to them to help them. That's why I came to ask you how I do that," Janie confided.

"I'm really proud of you for being willing to help her, and knowing when it was important to do that. Keep in mind, too, that helping her may simply mean getting the right help *for* her. We'll see what she needs, and what you can do from this point on," Mrs. Kaufmann suggested.

"I feel so much better now. I got so scared that I wouldn't say the right thing. Thanks, Mrs. Kaufmann. See you sixth period." With that, Janie slipped out of the school counselor's door as unnoticeably as possible and went down the hall and right out the playground door.

Mrs. Kaufmann immediately left her office and went across the hall to the nurse's health office door. Of course the room was full, as it always was during the lunch and recess times in the middle of the day. She saw that the school nurse was able to come to the door to see what she needed.

"Mrs. Cain, I'm so sorry to interrupt you in the middle of all you have going on here. Do you have a minute?"

"Sure," Mrs. Cain stepped just outside her door and replied, "none of these students has an emergency right now – mostly meds and minor problems. What's up?"

Mrs. Kaufmann lowered her voice so the students would not hear her and asked, "I just need to know if you've done the heights and weights for Lin Soo's class yet this year. I'll be curious what the change is from last year to this year for Lin. I heard from a friend of hers that she's trying to lose weight, so I figured we need to start with a baseline weight measurement and move forward from there, especially if we end up having to call home down the road."

"Do you suspect an eating disorder?" the nurse asked her.

"I have a reliable student who suspects it, so I need to follow up. The student is coming back sixth period after all the lunch and recess cycles. If you're free, and she's okay with having you there, you can join us. I think we make a good team for these cases, and it always helps when working with parents from the health angle rather than from just the psychological angle," Mrs. Kaufmann replied.

"Yes, I'll check her chart and I'll just come to your office at the beginning of sixth period. It may be easier to start with the three-person conversation, than to start with two and have to add a third and then start all over," Mrs. Cain offered.

"That would be smart. Thanks for your help," she replied.

Mrs. Kaufmann left the office and went back to her computer to check on Lin Soo's grades and attendance record. Her grades were straight A's, and she had never missed a day of school this year, except for an "excused late" one morning due to a dentist appointment.

Then Mrs. Kaufmann went to the cafeteria to check the sign-out sheet by the cafeteria door. She looked at the whole week and saw that Lin went out to the bathroom every day, just before going outside. That really didn't prove anything either, since that's when a good student naturally would prefer to use the bathroom rather than leave a class lesson. Some students also had to brush their teeth because of braces, and some simply wanted to wash their hands after eating. All of this could be true for Lin also. So far, her detective work wasn't giving her any new information.

She saw one of the cafeteria aides leaving for the day, so Mrs. Kaufmann went up to her to ask about Lin without divulging her name. "Hi, Mrs. Green, may I ask you a quick question?"

"Any time, Mrs. Kaufman. I hope I'll have an answer," she said, smiling.

"Are there any students who you would suspect as having a problem eating their lunches? Or is there any one throwing his or her entire lunch away?"

"Sure. As a matter of fact, most students pull what they like out of their lunch sacks, eat that, and then throw the rest out. It's really disgraceful the amount of food we throw out every day, and it's mostly the healthy foods. We could feed a small, starving village every day! Don't get me started!" she said, getting upset with the wastefulness.

"Here and there you get someone who doesn't like what their mom gave them at all. I do have a young man who really only picks. He acts like his food is the enemy. I also have a few older girls dieting, and they are the hardest to talk into eating their lunches. In fact, I basically leave the older kids alone. They already feel nagged enough by their parents."

Mrs. Kaufmann thanked Mrs. Green and agreed with her about the older children. "I remember when my daughters hit their filling-out age and didn't like their thighs. They were used to their skinny legs and thought having more of a woman's body with more of a body-fat ratio meant they were getting fat in general. They were pretty picky then, too, so we were heavy into salads in those days!" she laughed with Mrs. Green.

"Okay, thanks, I won't keep you. Have a good afternoon," she said, and they parted.

Fifth period ended and the last of the students who had wanted to talk to Mrs. Kaufmann left for class. Mrs. Cain arrived at the waiting room door and said, "Am I too early?"

"No, this is perfect. As soon as the noise settles down and the students have all changed classes, I'll call Janie's science classroom to get her. I know she'll be ready and she's fast, so we only have a couple of minutes. I must tell you that Lin's grades and attendance are perfect. We both know that's no surprise if it is an eating disorder, because they tend to be perfectionists or they just need to feel in control…or both. I did talk with the lunch aide, and there is only one young boy who stands out, along with all the older girls who are dieting. Besides, it sounds like Lin Soo may not eat, just pick, or binge and purge, so she doesn't have a pattern. That wouldn't show anything alarming about her to the aide either, so we are back to square one."

"Well, I do have something. I actually recorded a drop in her weight from last year. Her height has increased, but her weight went down, so we have something to question there. It wasn't significant enough for me to have worried about back when I was doing the screening at the beginning of the year, but I would like to get another weight on her now to see if she has lost even more. She's healthy otherwise and doesn't have any record of going home sick from school," Mrs. Cain offered.

"Well, it's not like I wanted to find a problem, but if we are dealing with an eating disorder, I'd like to think we could act on it quickly, with something substantial to use. We both know, having something other than hearsay evidence to get the parents involved really helps. All right then, let me make that call."

Mrs. Kaufmann picked up the phone and hit the intercom numbers for Janie's science classroom.

"Mr. Tatum, will you randomly select Janie now to run an errand for you as we spoke about?" she asked with some laughter because of this pretend selection act.

Mr. Tatum answered in the rehearsed form and rather loudly. "I will be happy to send it to you. Let me select a student to bring it to you right now. Glad to help," and then he hung up.

She turned to the nurse, laughed, and shared what she did to get students to come to her in order to keep their confidence. She said some students would otherwise not want to come see her if they had to explain where they were going to their classmates.

Just then, Janie appeared in the doorway, but paused because she saw the two grown-ups talking instead of just the school counselor. "Come on in, Janie. I hope it's okay if we include Mrs. Cain in our conversation," Mrs. Kaufmann explained. "She doesn't have to stay if you would like this to be just between us, but I know she will be able to help us with health information if we should need it. Would that be okay with you?"

"That's fine. I just don't want Lin Soo to know I came to talk about her. Just so you know, I asked her if she was feeling okay today when we were outside, and she said she felt fine. She looked curious as to why I asked, so I just told her that she looked pale, that's all. It looked like she didn't think about it anymore. I really like Lin Soo, and I want to help her."

"All right then, let's sit down and share our conversation with Mrs. Cain, so we can catch her up with your concern." Mrs. Kaufmann then pulled out two chairs near her desk and they all sat down facing each other. "Janie, how about you start and fill her in on what you heard and what you know."

"Well, I went to the bathroom today, and I could hear Lin Soo throwing up," Janie began. "The back of her new shoes under the stall door caught my eye because usually you only see the front of girls' shoes. I left right away and came here so she wouldn't know I heard her. I know she keeps complaining about being fat and telling everyone she's on a diet. The thing is she's so skinny. Plus last year she usually ate her whole lunch and then some, too. This year, because she would sometimes eat a huge amount, I didn't think she was dieting. Anyway, I wasn't worried about it until today, when I thought back to the other days she always went to the bathroom right after eating. I also remembered the talk we had about eating disorders in health class. That woman that came in showed us pictures of herself when she looked like a skeleton and almost died. That scared me. That's why I came down to find out what to do to make Lin stop."

Mrs. Kaufmann immediately answered her with the assurance that she only needed to continue to be her friend. "We need to take it from here, Janie, but we will promise not to let her know what made us pay attention to her behaviors. She will not know it was you unless you want to tell her. As I'm sure you learned in health, Mrs. Cain will recheck her weight and, if her weight tells us to act on our concern, we will. That's when the concern goes home to the parents for them to take on the health responsibility. You could never make a friend just stop, especially if she is that focused and driven. It isn't that easy. If she is convinced she is fat with her tiny body, there's something going on with her thinking that needs to be adjusted also. All of this must be handled by the grownups that do that. It really is quite an individual and complex problem. That means, my dear, you are now officially off the hook. Just be her friend," Mrs. Kaufmann assured her.

"Oh, thank you! Phew. I was so scared that I was supposed to be the person who would help her," Janie said with relief.

Mrs. Cain reacted right away. "Janie you *were* the person who helped her. You let us know so we can. That was perfect. You are such a good friend and a wise young lady."

Mrs. Kaufmann agreed. "You paid attention to your health lesson, about how serious this can get to be after a while, so doing something right away may have made all the difference. I am very proud of you, too. Do you feel better now?" Mrs. Kaufmann asked her.

"Yes, I do. So I don't need to do anything, really?" she asked one more time.

Mrs. Kaufmann smiled really big and said, "You've already done your part. You were alert, cared enough, and acted on your knowledge, observations, and intuition. That wasn't easy, either, slipping away, since everyone around here is always asking questions! Now, you just have to be supportive if she chooses to share with you. Be available; be her friend. Let go of the problem, and give it to me to worry about. This is when it's time for Mrs. Cain to do her part, and then I will do my part. We are a family here, and we all do our part!"

Janie finally smiled. She was undoubtedly relieved from the fears she had stirred in herself by owning the full responsibility. "Thank you, again!" she said with enthusiasm.

"Thank *you*," Mrs. Kaufmann replied enthusiastically. "So you can go back to class, feel proud of the good deed you did for a friend, and know what terrific character you have. Now let me give you a note to hand to your teacher so our 'little performance' looks complete." She scribbled "Thank you!" on a piece of paper that she folded and handed to Janie. "There you go, my dear."

Janie took the note, thanked her again, and left for class.

Mrs. Cain said, "Okay, I'm up next. I'll call for Lin and another student to get new weights on them as a follow-up. I have a younger student I wrote down on my notes for a recheck, too. I'll do that now and get back to you," she told Mrs. Kaufmann and stood up to go back to her health office.

"Sounds good, and thanks for meeting with us," Mrs. Kaufmann said to her. "It makes a referral so much easier when we team up, especially when confidentiality isn't a critical issue at this point. I figured Janie would be okay with you knowing, because she knows you keep the confidence of students, too."

Mrs. Kaufmann went to her filing cabinet to pull out some information packets on eating disorders. She wanted to be prepared to help Lin Soo and her parents if it became necessary. The hard part was to have patience while waiting for the nurse's phone call.

The Confrontation

The phone rang, and Mrs. Kaufmann saw the school nurse's extension number come up on the caller ID screen. She answered it quickly. "Hello. What did you find out?"

Mrs. Cain answered, "Well, she's lost enough for us to be concerned. I have her with me now, and I told her I did not like the increased loss of weight and that I wanted her to talk with you. Is this a good time for me to send her over to you?"

"Yes, it's the perfect time because I have no student appointments scheduled, and I can easily postpone the teacher contacts I was planning for the afternoon. Please let her know you've shared with me what you're worried about, so she and I can start from there," Mrs. Kaufmann replied.

"Lin Soo, I would like you to meet with Mrs. Kaufmann right now about your recent loss of weight. I've shared my concern with her, and she's waiting for you," Mrs. Kaufmann heard Mrs. Cain say as she was hanging up the phone.

The school counselor went to her doorway and saw Lin come out of the health office and walk toward her. "Hi, Lin Soo. Come on in so we can chat a bit."

Lin walked over to her office and went by her in the doorway to go in and sit down. She didn't say anything, and her body language showed she was very uncomfortable. "Lin, I spoke with the nurse about you losing a good amount of weight recently. I'm assuming you are *trying* to lose weight, since you don't have an illness or any other reason for it, am I right?"

"Yes, but I'm only dieting a little. I always eat my lunch and then have a salad for dinner," Lin defended herself.

"How is your body losing weight so quickly if you only cut back a little bit? I do know there are many ways students lose weight besides not eating, like extreme exercise or purging after meals. Lin, my concern is not what you look like. My concern is for your health, both physical and emotional. Why do you want to lose weight?"

Lin paused before she answered. She hadn't put it into words before and now she was expected to explain herself. "Well," she began slowly and with her eyes lowered, "all the thin girls get boyfriends. And girls admire thin girls more. They all look so cute, and they are more popular. I just thought that everyone would like me more if I was thinner."

"I am looking at a thin girl, now. How much thinner did you think you needed to be?" Mrs. Kaufmann followed up.

"I don't know, just thinner than I am now," Lin answered.

"Lin, can you describe what you see and what you feel when you look in the mirror?"

"I see a fat girl with fat legs and I feel disgusted," Lin admitted as tears began to roll down her cheeks.

"I don't. I see a girl who is thin and beautiful. Her body is maturing exactly as it should be as it's leaving the skin-and-bones skinniness of childhood, and beginning to grow into young womanhood. Your legs are actually taking on more shape to become more feminine. That's what your hormones do at this age. It's healthy for them to decide where to store some body fat to make you into a woman. Those hormones naturally allow more fat cells to go to the thighs and breasts, transitioning into the female form. You, as a person, are not fat, but you are maturing. You are becoming a young lady, not getting fat," Mrs. Kaufmann assured her.

"That's what my mother said, too, but I can't help it. She is always on my case to eat more, eat more, all the time." Lin spoke with a great deal of emotion. "I just don't want to be fat, but she keeps making me eat!"

"Is that why you sometimes throw up, to get rid of the food you just ate?" Mrs. Kaufmann asked her directly.

Lin Soo was startled. "Throw up? What do you mean?" Lin asked defensively.

"When you throw up in the girls' room, you can be overheard, you know," Mrs. Kaufmann was clear, but evasive enough not to invite Lin to challenge it anymore.

"I've only done it a few times," she quickly defended herself.

"Do you remember the speaker in your health class? She lost a lot of weight and had several health issues as a result. Do you see this happening to you?" Mrs. Kaufmann was clear in her concern.

"No, I'm fine. I said I just did it a few times, and that was when I ate too much," Lin continued to deny the problem.

"I worry it has already become an acceptable way of dealing with your weight, my dear. I also worry that your body self-image isn't healthy. You look wonderful, but you can't see it. Now…my thinking is that you would probably prefer to work with a counselor than with your mom. Am I right?"

Mrs. Kaufmann knew she needed to bring her mother in and to have her mother get some outside counseling help for her to uncover the underlying issues. She was trying to have Lin find that as acceptable before her mother was called. Just sending her home from school to the push-pull contest with her mother wasn't going to correct Lin Soo's need to be more in control, and to be thinner. It didn't matter what Mrs. Kaufmann said to her right then. Lin was obviously committed to her goal and thought she was still in control.

Mrs. Kaufmann continued, "Your mom cares about you. My guess is she's worried you're getting too thin, or that you are making yourself unhealthy."

"My mom is always on my case about something. She's either worried I'm not going to get all A's, or that I won't make the basketball team, or all the other things she's pushing on me for," Lin said, breaking into tears.

Mrs. Kaufmann slid the box of tissues over to her and asked, "What if your mom was to know you felt this way? What if she was to stop the pushing that you described? Would you be willing to eat a healthy diet that put you in a healthy weight range if your doctor worked with you instead of your mom?"

"My mom will never stop. It's too important to her that I am perfect," Lin insisted. "I'll be fine. I'll just stop throwing up," Lin offered quickly, so that Mrs. Kaufmann would not call her mother. "My mother will get all upset if you tell her," Lin reacted strongly.

"Remember at the beginning of each school year, I always promise to your whole class that I will be here for all of you if you need me? That I am your advocate? That I will look out for all of you, and if I ever knew of anything that could harm any one of you, I would help you myself or I would get you help? Well, this is one of those times. I think you are harming yourself right now. I feel I need to get you help. And I know you feel you don't need it, but it's my job to make that decision. I'm so sorry if you don't agree with me right now and you feel upset, but I am on your side. I am on the side of your good health, and I need to enlist the support of your parents to get you that help. I need to call your mom in to let her know about your throwing up and your weight loss."

"No! Please, Mrs. Kaufmann, please don't?" Lin Soo begged.

"What will happen, do you think?" Mrs. Kaufmann became concerned with how dramatic her protest was. She wondered if her mother might become too angry, or if Lin just didn't want to lose control.

"She'll just lecture me on how important it is to be healthy and all that. I already know that."

"Okay, then I will let her know she needs to seek professional advice, someone whose experience and reputation she respects and trusts. You want your freedom to make decisions for your body, and she has her right to take care of your body. You are her child and she loves you. An outside professional is the perfect solution if you don't want to hear it anymore from your mom. That expert will give you both the most responsible course of action, and you won't have to worry about a power struggle between the two of you. What do you say?" Mrs. Kaufmann hoped she had led her to the best compromise she could offer.

"I guess that would get my mom off my back," Lin admitted. "Are you calling her in right now?" she asked.

"I think it's time, don't you? We could spend days talking about what-ifs, but eventually I need to ask her to come in and chat. I will explain to her why going to a doctor or counselor would be the best solution," Mrs. Kaufmann promised. "Your mom needs to know you can use some help from someone who understands what you feel about losing weight."

"Okay," Lin finally agreed, seeing Mrs. Kaufmann was not giving up. Lin's shoulders dropped. She slumped back into the chair heavily, having to give up the resistance, and she began biting her nails and swinging her foot. She was definitely not feeling in control and getting very anxious about it.

Mrs. Kaufmann picked up the phone and called Mrs. Soo at work. She was worried that Lin's mom wouldn't be able to leave work right then, but also knew she couldn't send Lin home at the end of the day after confronting her with a serious concern. She knew to never predict how an upset student would react, especially when faced with a parent's potential anger.

The Hand-Over

"Hello?" Lin's mother answered.

"Hi, Mrs. Soo?" Mrs. Kaufmann checked.

"Yes?" Lin's mom answered.

"This is Mrs. Kaufmann from Hillstown Middle School. I'm Lin's school counselor and I have her here with me in my office. We've been talking about her weight loss this school year. The school nurse's height and weight measurements, when compared to last year, gave her reason to be concerned. Lin admitted you have been concerned as well, and I was hoping you might be able to come over to join us? I have some suggestions to make, and I would like the three of us to have this conversation together," Mrs. Kaufmann saw Lin squirming in her seat.

"Oh my goodness, yes, I will come right over. I just need to close up my office and let someone know I have to leave. I should be there in less than a half an hour," she answered, sounding concerned but cooperative.

"That's excellent. Lin and I will continue talking in my office until you come. We are fine," Mrs. Kaufmann said, trying to assure Mrs. Soo not to rush. She saw that Lin Soo appeared to be very anxious.

Mrs. Kaufmann hung up and looked at Lin. "This is good," she said in an upbeat way. "We need to have all of us here to clear the air and make a plan. Lin, I think it will be a good idea to let your mom know how you feel about her pressure to make you eat. How does it make you feel?"

"I hate it--that nagging, but I don't want to tell her that," Lin answered. "That would hurt her feelings, and then she'd take it all personally and get mad at me, or give me a long lecture about how it's for my own good. I think I hate that more!"

"What if I suggest that resentment often happens between moms and daughters when their girls want to lose weight? I will be happy to start by supporting your mom; the natural desire of a parent is to love her children and to make them healthy. I will also explain that the natural reaction of a child is to resist the push of a parent, and that they grow to resent anything that feels overdone."

"That would be okay," Lin Soo said with some reluctance. Then she asked Mrs. Kaufmann, "But are you going to tell her about the throwing up?"

"Yes, I'm afraid I have to tell her that, because that is what concerns me," Mrs. Kaufmann said in a strong, positive voice. "Just being on a diet would not have raised a flag for the nurse or me if that's all we were dealing with here. That's why she needs to know that it's important for you talk to an outside counselor who can spend some time helping you. Besides, there's a chance that your counselor will suggest to your mom that she doesn't nag you. That way, you can cut all the deals with just your counselor. Your mom's role would be to help you report back to the counselor as to how the follow-up went. Then that counselor will let you both know if and when there is nothing more to worry about. Now, you have to admit, that would be a good deal!" Mrs. Kaufmann said with convincing enthusiasm.

Lin Soo looked relieved for the first time. She didn't like heading right into the problem and having to answer to her mom, but there could be a person who could help them both. Lin Soo secretively liked knowing she had some power back, away from her mom's control. "I guess that could work…" Lin stopped in the middle of her sentence as she saw her mom's face peek into the office.

"Hi! Can I come in?" Mrs. Soo asked, putting her head in the doorway.

"Hi, Mom," Lin said.

"Hi, sweetie," Mrs. Soo answered her daughter. "Are you okay?" she asked with concern in her voice.

"I'm okay. Mrs. Kaufmann is just worried about my weight like you are, that's all."

"Come on in, Mrs. Soo. Lin and I have been chatting about her weight for a while now, and it's a little more than that. As I said on the phone, her weight and height measurements showed her weight is below what it should be for her height, and the loss has been intentional on her part, because Lin still feels like she's overweight. The problem for her has been people pushing on her to eat because she's thin. So, what she has started to do is to eat and then to throw it up. It's called bulimia," Mrs. Kaufmann explained.

"Oh dear," Mrs. Soo started to react, when Lin cut in.

"Mom, I don't do it all the time, and I can stop it anytime," Lin assured her mother.

Mrs. Soo looked back at Mrs. Kaufmann, "If she stops this bulimia, will she gain some weight?"

Mrs. Kaufmann answered, "I believe Lin could use some counseling just to get to the root of her negative feelings about her body. The emotions related to her weight control are complex and have caused her to develop this negative way of coping. I have seen students struggle with their parents. It usually turns out that each side tries to control the other, and so much resentment results because the problem is not really about eating. It goes deeper, and a professional can help her with that."

"Are you saying she needs to go to the pediatrician or a psychologist?" Mrs. Soo asked.

"Meeting with both is needed to help her deal with the whole picture. I'd like to see if you can get an appointment with a psychologist right away, so Lin can understand how her emotions affect her body self-image. I will e-mail you some referrals for psychologists with whom I've had success and have had satisfied families. You can check them out online. In fact, one of these three psychologists specializes in eating disorders for adolescents, so that might be a good choice. He has been extremely successful helping students get to an understanding of what drives them. She needs to make changes in her thinking."

"I will do that as soon as I get home," Mrs. Soo promised.

"Would you call me and let me know how you made out once you get the appointment?" Mrs. Kaufmann asked her.

"Sure. I will e-mail you right away. What about the doctor? Should I make an appointment with the pediatrician right away, too? I want Lin to have all the help I can get her."

"That would be really helpful. The doctor will need to give both of you information on her developmental needs right now, and about her correct weight for her height. Lin will also need to learn how to eat correctly. The binging and purging to a fast and dramatic weight loss has some serious health consequences, so she'll need her doctor to give you information on that as well," Mrs. Kaufmann explained.

"Like what kind of health consequences are you talking about?" Mrs. Soo asked quickly, catching that phrase from Mrs. Kaufmann's words. Lin looked at Mrs. Kaufmann as well. She remembered some of the problems the bulimics had from her health class, but she had never related that lesson with herself until this minute.

Mrs. Kaufmann spoke directly to Lin. "Well, Lin, when you throw up, what has to come back up from your stomach, through your esophagus, and across your teeth includes a damaging stomach acid that is hard on your esophagus lining and your tooth enamel. Your hormones are also affected by weight loss, which can have impact on your systems. Serious weight loss tells your body that you are starving, and the body will alter normal system behavior and drop to a starvation mode. When you lose weight too fast, it's muscle tissue you're losing too, with your heart being a muscle. So we don't want that to happen, either. Plus, it can even result in hair thinning. So, understanding these consequences will be helpful in making some new wise choices. Lin, do you believe it's time we get your life back in balance?"

"Yes, I do," she admitted. "It's getting harder to hide my throwing up, anyway."

"I'd like to see you happy again and see food as a pleasure and not the enemy. I'd also like you to accept becoming the beautiful young lady that your body is trying to give you," Mrs. Kaufmann said to Lin with a big smile.

"Me, too," Lin answered her.

"Okay, then. I have to get back to work, but I will make those appointments right away. Thanks so much for your time and for alerting me," Mrs. Soo said to Mrs. Kaufmann, as she stood up and shook her hand. The two of them walked out of the office and into the outer waiting room.

"My pleasure, really, and remember, Mrs. Soo," Mrs. Kaufmann spoke in a lowered voice, "when you reach out for the help from the experienced professionals, they will give you great advice, too. They will guide you with direction for your involvement as well as what they tell Lin. I believe that should relieve you of that need for the exhausting constant surveillance, you know? It will be up to Lin to honor the deals she will be making with them. Lin will then think of them as the heavies, not you. That will make things easier and more comfortable for both of you," she said to Mrs. Soo with another big smile.

Mrs. Soo and Mrs. Kaufmann said their goodbyes, and Mrs. Soo called a quick goodbye to Lin and left to go back to work.

Mrs. Kaufmann then turned to Lin and said, "Lin, your mom is now your cheerleader and no longer the nagging mom. She is on your side and supporting whatever plan your doctors work out with you. You, my dear, are in the driver's seat now. And, I have to let you get back to class before the class is over."

"My books are in my last class. I'd rather not have to go back in there to get them. Maybe I should just go to my next class and then grab them when that class is over?" she suggested.

"I don't want everyone asking questions either, but going to your next class where the other students all went, too, without your books would raise even more questions. For all they know, you've been waiting at the nurse's office this whole time," Mrs. Kaufmann suggested. "In fact, how about I send you back to the nurse's office, you fill her in on what we've done and what we've decided, and then she can give you a pass back to class from there. How does that work for you? That way you can swing by the last class, grab your books, and then get to the class you're supposed to be in now."

"I like that," Lin said. "Thanks for making the meeting with my mom work out okay. I am a little nervous now about seeing a shrink, though," she admitted. "Does that mean I'm crazy?" she asked, as she was getting up to leave.

"Oh, heavens, no!" she assured her with great emphasis. "See, we all have egos that want us to be safe and loved, but the thoughts that come from our egos sometime interpret things incorrectly. So, from time to time, we need to take a good look at what drives our thinking. If the thoughts come from fear, then it's helpful to have someone else point that out to us. That helps us shift our thinking and see our thoughts more clearly. You are quite lucky that your mom will take you to that clear-thinking professional to help you understand yourself as you really are. That, my dear, has nothing to do with crazy, just a shift of thinking."

"Oh," Lin simply said. She seemed satisfied by the logic explained and started to go out the door to the nurse's office.

"Don't forget to stop back after you meet your counselor to let me know how you like him or her, okay?" Mrs. Kaufmann called after her.

"I will," Lin answered and disappeared into the nurse's office.

Mrs. Kaufmann immediately sat down at her computer and wrote a quick e-mail to the school nurse. "Thanks again for your help with Lin Soo. All went well. Mrs. Soo came in and agreed to get outside help for Lin, who seems to be okay with it all now. I'll look forward to hearing how Lin sums it all up for you!" Mrs. Kaufmann laughed to herself as she hit "send."

Eddie's Turn

As Mrs. Kaufmann was leaving school that day, she ran into Mrs. Cain at the staff mailboxes in the main office. Mrs. Cain smiled really big and said, "I have to tell you about Lin's version. She announced that her mom will no longer nag her about eating, and that she gets to decide how she'll diet with her doctors."

Mrs. Kaufmann laughed. "Well, at least she's feeling empowered. Her counselor should be skilled enough to engage her into helping create the plan. I assume that power and insecurity are involved here, so that her sense of control is making her feel good right now."

"She did look happier than I've seen her look in quite a while," the nurse said.

Mrs. Kaufmann added, "Maybe there was also some relief that she doesn't have a secret to keep from her mom anymore. She also may have felt validated. She now knows that what has been feeling wrong has become important enough for us all to be willing to help."

The nurse then told Mrs. Kaufmann she had another student to refer to her with a potential eating disorder. "Remember that other weight recheck I did? It was for Eddie Bisset. He is only eleven and already very worried about becoming fat. His weight is too low for his height, so I asked him if he knew why he had lost weight since the first measurement this year. He was really happy he did, and he admitted it's because he's been trying to eat as little as possible. I told him he was actually underweight, so he needed to get back to normal eating, and he was not happy about that! I think it's time for you to meet with this young man, too," she suggested. "Okay, I have to get going. Let's talk more about this tomorrow, okay?" she asked, as she gathered her belongings to leave for the day.

"Yes. We'll talk in the morning. Have a great evening, and I will see you and Eddie tomorrow."

The next morning when Mrs. Kaufmann came in to her office, the red light on her phone was blinking. She put away her purse, lunch, and briefcase, turned on her computer, and listened to her first message. It was from Mrs. Bisset.

"Mrs. Kaufmann, this is Eddie Bisset's mother. I would like to talk with you today if you have a minute. Eddie came home yesterday quite upset about a visit to the nurse's office, and I'd like to share some of what's going on with him recently. I'll be home until ten this morning and back from work early evening, but I would prefer to talk with you when Eddie is in school. Thanks."

Mrs. Kaufmann saved the message and went out of her office and across the hall to the health office to see if the school nurse was in yet. She had just arrived also, and they greeted each other with happy "Good mornings." "I wanted to let you know that I'm about to return a phone call to Mrs. Bisset, who left a message for me this morning. She said Eddie was upset by his visit with you yesterday, so I can imagine we will be discussing his weight. I plan on referring her to you for more details of the weight history you have on file, unless you prefer I didn't. Any thoughts on that?"

"That's fine, and I will be happy to talk with her as well. Just let me know what she needs," she answered.

"Great, thanks," Mrs. Kaufmann said, as she turned to go back to her office to call Eddie's mom. "Good morning, Mrs. Bisset. Is this a good time to call? It's Mrs. Kaufmann."

"Yes, perfect. Eddie left a few minutes ago. I wanted you to know he has recently become more and more focused on food and eating healthy to the point he has become resistant to eating anything that he thinks will make him fat. Then, yesterday, he was called to the nurse's office to have his weight redone for some reason, and she suggested he put on a little weight. He was very disturbed by that, and didn't want to have to gain any more weight. I'm not sure what's going on with him, but he seems obsessed with this. How do I know if he's starting an eating disorder, and what can I do to have him put on a little weight now that he's so emotional about it all?" Mrs. Bisset asked sounding emotional herself.

"I have spoken to the nurse about the students who appear underweight. Feel free to call her as well for her height and weight information. The interesting thing is that I had spoken to the cafeteria aides a few days ago to see if the older girl I was worried about appeared to be not eating. When I asked them if they noticed anyone tossing out their lunches, they had noticed an unusual pickiness on Eddie's part. He was referred to as 'the young, thin boy.' That means they are aware of his not eating as well," Mrs. Kaufmann replied.

"Yes, my husband and I are really healthy eaters, so we don't have sugary foods in the house, but Eddie has even been leaving food on his plate that is healthy and we know he likes," she admitted. "He's noticeably trying to not eat. I wanted to ask him about it, but we always heard parents shouldn't get on the case of an anorexic child. I think that's because we aren't supposed to make an issue of it, or they may resist eating even more. That's why I'm calling. I just need to know what to say or what not to say."

Mrs. Kaufmann asked, "Has he been to his pediatrician recently? That is usually the best way to start the dialogue. Ask the doctor in front of him if he's the right weight for his height because of *his* concerns about that. Let the doctor talk with him, because he will believe the doctor. And if you would like me to chat with him to see why he's into this thinking, I can call him down very discreetly and see what he tells me. What I would like to do first is observe him in the cafeteria at lunchtime today. I'd like to see for myself what the other observers are describing," Mrs. Kaufmann offered.

"Yes, that would be great. His lunch is a small sandwich with a peach and a milk box, and he likes it all, so this should be interesting. He's actually due for his annual physical, so I can make that appointment today. Would you let me know if I have any reason to be concerned after you talk with him? You can use my cell phone when I'm at work."

"I'd be happy to call later, and I'll make sure it's before he gets home from school. I have one other question to ask. Do you know about when his attention went to his weight or what could have been a trigger?" Mrs. Kaufmann pursued.

"Not really. I think I started noticing his being very picky with his food over the summer. I think our whole family got very active after dinner with the later evenings, and his dad and sister went on a diet. For a while, there was a lot of discussion about sugar and fat and calories, so I don't know if that could've started anything. I am a nurse practitioner, I go to the gym and do yoga, and I talk about healthy eating a lot anyway. I just don't know of anything other than that," Mrs. Bisset admitted.

Mrs. Kaufmann answered, "It does sound like a lot of recent emphasis on weight loss, but we really can't always predict triggers or reactions to everyday experiences with our children. Who knows what he thought when he experienced something, and who knows what that something was. I do know that when children reach the level of an eating disorder, there's more to it than just a desire to lose weight. Once they focus on controlling their weight to the extent that a normal life is no longer possible because of abnormal eating and sleeping patterns, then we may need to seek some counseling to get to the real cause. Let's not go there just yet, in case this is simply a new temporary focus that hasn't reached that level of conviction or seriousness. I will chat with Eddie this afternoon, and then I will call you back."

"Thanks, I really appreciate being kept informed. I will call the school nurse to see what she can share with me also," she replied.

After the two hung up, Mrs. Kaufmann looked up Eddie's schedule on her computer. She had to be sure to be there ahead of time, so she could watch him as he came into the cafeteria. She'd want to see if he bought any snacks on the way in, or if he threw anything out. She decided to just be standing and talking with one of the cafeteria aides near his usual table when he arrived, so she could have a clear view of his every move as well as his gestures. And when he was done, she would select him to help her with some kind of errand, which would turn into a chat in her office.

At the end of the morning, the students' lunch time was fast approaching. Mrs. Kaufmann finished up her last phone call, grabbed her office keys, and headed to the cafeteria just ahead of the students. She got into place and explained what she was doing there to the cafeteria aide who always positioned herself by the table by the door. It worked out that it was right near where Eddie sat. She saw Eddie's grade level of classes come through the doorway within minutes after she got there. She laughed to herself as she saw the students entering like a bunch of ping-pong balls being shot out of a gun, with each one going into a different direction. Eddie came through the door with much less enthusiasm than the other boys and quietly sat down at the very end of his usual table of boys in front of Mrs. Kaufmann and the cafeteria aide. He appeared to be totally not engaged in any conversation with the others.

"That thin little boy was the one I told you about," the aide told Mrs. Kaufmann in a lowered voice and nodding toward Eddie. "Watch how he dumps his food on the table, maybe takes a bite of each item, and then gets up to throw it all out. What a waste," she added. "No wonder he's so skinny. He actually looks sickly, but I know he's here every day, so he can't have a serious illness."

"Does he do this every day?" Mrs. Kaufmann asked.

"Yup, every single day since this school year started," she answered with certainty.

Mrs. Kaufmann watched as Eddie did exactly that. He opened his sandwich, took a bite with just his teeth and without letting his lips touch the bread, and then folded the rest up to put aside. He did the same with the peach, and then took a couple sips of the milk. He rolled it all up, stood up, and threw it all in the garbage can. He sat back down and opened a book to read, with no effort to socialize with the other boys. She also noticed that the other boys made no attempt to talk with Eddie or include him in their conversations. He just appeared separated from everyone in the middle of the noisy crowd.

She had seen enough and preferred to remove him than to leave him there being so clearly disconnected. She walked over to the table and tapped on Eddie's shoulder. He turned around and smiled. Mrs. Kaufmann said quietly, "Eddie, may I ask you a question?"

He lit up, feeling important, and said, "Sure!"

Mrs. Kaufmann motioned to him to follow her, saying, "It is so loud in here I can't hear myself think. Let's go out in the hallway. In fact, grab your things and we can go into my office." Eddie immediately grabbed his jacket and hurriedly jumped up to follow her out of the cafeteria like a puppy. Mrs. Kaufmann noticed the other boys weren't even paying attention, so she slowed down. The two walked side by side, with Mrs. Kaufmann asking Eddie how his classes were this year and what book he was reading at the lunch table. Eddie was chatty and seemed to like the attention, not acting as if there was anything wrong.

When they got into her office, Mrs. Kaufmann asked him to sit down and eased into the sensitive subject area with a general question about the cafeteria food. "Okay, what I wanted to ask you about was our lunch period. I've been observing the lunches students bring, the seating arrangements, the amount of time it takes for the students to eat, and the way they clean up and go out to recess. I noticed you weren't eating very much and you weren't talking to the other boys at your table, so I had some questions. First, did you sit at a table of boys that aren't your friends?"

Eddie immediately answered that he wasn't with his friends. He said, "The others at the table play sports together and I don't, but I was assigned to sit there."

"Who assigns the seating, the cafeteria aide?" she asked.

"Yes. On the first day of school I went to sit down at a table with my friends, but there were already eight people. The other table only had seven, so she put me there. That became my spot. It's okay. I have a good book and I like to read." He seemed quite comfortable with his solution. "As for my lunch, I wasn't hungry. I just didn't want to eat it all."

"I noticed you only took a couple of bites. Why is that?" she pursued.

"I just don't need all that food," he answered.

"Eddie, I have to be honest with you. The amount of calories you ate is not enough fuel for your body and brain for the rest of the afternoon. It simply wasn't enough to nourish you. I even asked the aide, and she told me you do that every day, not just today. Are you trying to lose weight?" she asked directly.

"Everyone keeps asking me about why I'm not eating. I just don't want to get fat," he said, with a noticeable defensiveness.

"With your activity level, you use up what you eat in no time if you just eat the regular amount, so you couldn't get fat if you ate your whole lunch. And what made you think you might get fat?" she asked calmly, so he wouldn't feel challenged.

"Well, my father and older sister have both been on diets and it's hard for them to lose weight even though they aren't eating very much. My mom keeps telling them that they eat bad foods, but those are the foods they like. I just don't want to get fat like them," he explained.

"What would it be like if you were fat? What would happen to you?" she asked knowing there was more to it than that.

"My mom likes that I'm not fat. I know my father and sister say they wish they were more like me. I just really don't want to get fat," he insisted.

"I can understand that. You feel like you have something special that they wish they had? And being the youngest in the family, that must feel good," she said encouragingly. "But I have to ask you, why are you still trying to lose even more than you need to? I think that when you go out onto the playground, your body, your muscles, your organs inside need fuel. How does your body grow up to be strong and healthy if you starve it?"

"I just don't want to get fat, that's all," he repeated.

"Well, then, what do you want to look like, or what weight are you aiming for? Or do you even have a specific goal?" Mrs. Kaufmann continued.

"I don't have a size or whatever."

Mrs. Kaufmann said, "Eddie, are you trying to get thinner and thinner just so you can be absolutely positive you can't get fat?"

"I guess. When I see myself, I always think I'm getting bigger, and I don't want that."

"When I was your age, I couldn't wait to be older and eventually be a grown-up woman. Do you not want to grow up healthy and strong into a man?" she asked him.

"I just want to be a little boy…and not a fat one. My mom likes me that way. She says I'm thin, trim, and healthy, too. Besides, Danny Longo gained weight last year, and everyone laughed at how slow he ran in gym class one day. Then, last summer he was teased at his pool party. He even cried and went inside the house. I can't let that happen to me," Eddie said, as his eyes filled up. Mrs. Kaufmann always knew when she hit the underlying sore spot or the trigger to the increased fear. When the student's eyes filled up, she knew she had arrived. She could also see that Eddie wanted to stay his mother's little boy for the approval it gave him. And it certainly caused some envy on the part of his older sister and dad, which afforded him a small position of power in their family.

"I understand what you're worried about, but I don't know if you are aware of the health risks of being *too* thin," she warned him. "There is a healthy, happy middle of the road that you need to shoot for. I think that if a doctor told us you were healthy and a good weight, then I wouldn't worry about you. Would you like to know for sure that what you're doing is healthy, or find out if it isn't?" Mrs. Kaufmann asked him.

"Okay," he agreed almost challengingly. He appeared to believe that if he felt fine, he wasn't doing anything wrong. He also seemed to be saying that he was confident his doctor would tell everyone his weight was just fine, because that was the image of himself that he saw in his mirror.

"Then how about I mention it to your mom to see if you two can talk about this with your doctor when you have your next check-up?"

"That would be okay," he answered. "Are we done? Can I go outside?"

"Sure, Eddie. We're done, my dear. While you're out on playground, I'll call your mom, so she knows what we talked about," she said, as he grabbed his book and jacket and was out the door in a flash.

Mrs. Kaufmann made the call to Mrs. Bisset right away. "Evelyn Bisset, here," Eddie's mom answered.

"This is Mrs. Kaufmann. Do you have a minute? I wanted to share what I observed at lunch today and about our talk afterwards," she said.

"Oh, yes, I do! Please, go ahead," Mrs. Bisset answered enthusiastically.

"Well, the cafeteria aide was right. I saw Eddie take one bite of his sandwich, one bite of his peach, and a few swallows of milk and then throw it all out. He then opened up a book and read. All of the other students in the cafeteria were talking and laughing, and he just withdrew into his book. Later he told me he wasn't part of that athletic group of boys with whom he was assigned to sit, so he made the best of it."

"Yes, he told me he wasn't able to be by his friends at lunchtime. I had suggested he just eat quickly. We figured it's probably only about fifteen minutes or so before he would be able to go out to recess and be with his friends. I didn't mean he shouldn't try to join into the conversation. And what did he say about his not eating?" she asked with concern.

"He kept saying he just didn't want to get fat. I felt as if there's a need to please you with thinness, because he equates thin with being healthy and being your little boy. He also has something that he can be better at than his father and sister, since they are really working at their diets. Children find it hard to have power in the family when their place as the youngest doesn't give them any advantage. Plus, he has witnessed a friend teased into tears because of being too heavy and therefore slow physically. That brought him to tears himself, which to me, is the sign of a very real fear," Mrs. Kaufmann explained.

"Oh, dear. I think our family has really focused a lot on weight recently, and I am guilty of drawing his attention to it, too. I tried to not bring it up, as I saw his recent pickiness at mealtimes, but I couldn't help it. It was always such a stand-off, with him having the power. I knew if I wouldn't let him up from the table until he finished a certain amount, he'd just sit there all night, or worse…he'd eat it all and then throw it up. That really scared me, so that's when I backed down and he won. He is looking so frail that it's been worrying my husband and me. So what else can we do now?" she asked.

"I spoke to him about finding the middle of the road with this. I suggested his getting the official opinion of his doctor, so he would know what weight he should have to be healthy. He agreed, but I honestly think he did it to get everyone off his back," Mrs. Kaufmann laughed.

"That's great, because I got an appointment for the end of the week. He'll miss school, though, is that okay?" she checked.

"Yes, because it makes a statement that his health is more important than school. That's what we want right now. It also allows the discussion to take place naturally with the doctor. If Eddie continues to lose weight anyway, disregarding his suggested meal minimums, then the doctor will let you know what he wants for him. If Eddie continues to not eat enough, he most likely will give you a referral or two for him to get counseling. And, if his pediatrician doesn't give you names and numbers, I have three therapists who have worked with children and adolescents with eating disorders in this area and have had a lot of success," she offered.

"Thank you. Should I have a conversation with Eddie tonight, or will that push him further into his resolve not to eat?" Mrs. Bisset asked.

"I already told Eddie I would call you today to get an appointment with his doctor, who will decide what he needs to do. Eddie agreed to that, like I said, and that lets you off the hook for having to exert any more pressure to make him eat. You should let him know that my call today was one of concern, based on the school nurse's concern, so that this isn't something that you and your husband can just ignore. A call from the school makes it official. That way Eddie will know it is serious enough to make a doctor's appointment with or without his consent. If he knows that, he'll know he should take the doctor's advice seriously, too. Hopefully, that will start to turn this determined little guy's thinking around."

Mrs. Kaufmann continued, "It would also be good if Eddie was given an opportunity to express some of the emotions he has attached to this need for power he has shown you. There may be issues of insecurity or a need for control in your family or in his life in general. He needs a safe place to share his thoughts, and that would be best done with a neutral person like a counselor, whether the doctor recommends one or not. It would be a smart move right now. Eating disorders can be very complex, and he may like having a place to work out his concerns so that food is no longer his control device. I'd like to see him happy and enjoying food in his lunchroom with friends instead of working on only eating enough to survive. That's no way to be the happy little boy that he should be." Mrs. Kaufmann smiled, knowing she had made it clear that he needed some outside counseling.

"You said you knew some therapists who specialize in these kinds of problems? I'd like the name and number of the one who you think would be best for Eddie," Mrs. Bisset replied. "I know when I need help, and this is one of those times."

"In all honesty, it's hard to predict how a student will relate to an adult, but there is one who I have seen relate to some of the most challenging, strong-willed, angry students we've had, as well as the most easily intimidated, shy ones. He is a kind, soft-spoken older gentleman who is just so easy to be with that he feels trustworthy. Any time a therapist can cut through weeks of trying to get a child to open up, that really saves a lot of time and money," Mrs. Kaufmann answered.

"That's the one!" Mrs. Bisset instantly replied, almost like calling out "Bingo" in the middle of the game.

Mrs. Kaufmann laughed. "I will e-mail you all three names and numbers, but I will put this referral first, so you know which one you've chosen. If he's not taking any new patients because he is so established and so popular, the other two are very qualified and capable as well. One is a woman who has a friendly, comfortable, matter-of-fact style, and the other is a man who likes to be funny. You'll need to go by Eddie and what he responds to best, then your taste, your convenience, and your insurance coverage," she concluded.

Mrs. Bisset gave Mrs. Kaufmann her e-mail address followed by a huge thank you. She said, "You were a gift today. I never expected the school would call about his eating pickiness, but I am so grateful. I was really getting scared. I will look forward to that information, and then I'll call for an appointment. I just thought of something. Do you think that getting a therapist appointment will upset Eddie?" she asked. "He is such a little control freak, as my husband describes him privately to me."

"It just might, if that's the case. An interesting way to approach it is this. You might tell him that *you* need suggestions for how *you* can help him right now, and you made an appointment with this counselor for *you*. Tell Eddie that when you go, you'd like him to go with you to explain his concerns about his weight first, so that the counselor will understand the situation. That way, Eddie will feel as if the counselor is helping you be the better parent, and that he's not the patient," Mrs. Kaufmann suggested. "Check with the counselor to see if he agrees with this strategy and how to divide up the time. Reversing the patients can reduce the resistance at first."

"I like that idea, and it really isn't far from true!" Mrs. Bisset laughed. She sounded relieved, and thanked Mrs. Kaufmann again. "I will look forward to hearing what Eddie says about your talk today. He probably will be annoyed again, like he was with the school nurse," she laughed.

"And I would like you to call me to let me know how you make out with his doctor and counselor. I know we'll see the results if it's working!"

They both hung up in a better place. Mrs. Bisset had her professional resources to turn to now, and Mrs. Kaufmann felt better knowing Mrs. Bisset intended to follow through and get Eddie the help he needed.

She then grabbed her keys, locked her door, and headed to the cafeteria to talk with the aides who assigned the seating. She had remembered that there was an empty table that could be used to redistribute the boys involved. She figured they could make two tables of eight boys become three tables of five or six, just so Eddie would finally be able to sit by some friends. She thought to herself, "This little guy certainly deserves our help to make that happen!"

The Journey

Two weeks after Mrs. Soo had been called into the school, Mrs. Kaufmann e-mailed her to follow up on their discussion. She asked how the first appointments went, and if she and Lin were still having open dialogue. Mrs. Soo sent a brief e-mail back. "This is going to take a long time and a lot of work on both our parts! I will call you tomorrow."

Mrs. Kaufmann was not surprised. Bulimia had always been quite a complex eating disorder to control. Those teenagers who had used that for losing weight, figured they'd be alone when they went to the bathroom, so it was easy for them to eliminate the food they had just consumed. It was a private and fast solution for them whenever anyone pressured them to eat. They would then have no problem going on with their day on an empty stomach either, because once the hunger message in the brain discontinued its signal, they would no longer even feel hungry. She knew that it was the therapy that was going to make all the difference.

Once she read her messages and returned her calls, she headed down to the main office to check her mailbox. She passed Lin in the hallway and gave her a quick wink, not wanting to draw attention to their connection. Mrs. Kaufmann saw Lin look happy, but then drop her eyes so she wouldn't encourage any further efforts to communicate. Lin didn't know how aware a school counselor must be not to reveal their counselor/counselee relationship where others would notice. Mrs. Kaufmann made sure there was always another, more acceptable, reason to approach students in the hall, like questions about the Honor Roll, volunteers for Peer Tutoring, Community Service Projects, Peer Mentoring, or Peer Leadership. That day she had no reason to fake a conversation about any of those topics, so she just kept moving after the wink as if she barely noticed her at all. Mrs. Kaufmann did notice, however, that Lin was still the same Lin. She was thin as a rail, but then again, it was too early in the treatment to expect her to look much healthier.

The next morning, the phone rang just as Mrs. Kaufmann came into her office. "Hello, this is Mrs. Kaufmann," she answered.

"Mrs. Kaufmann, this is Mrs. Soo. I just wanted to let you know that we did go to Lin's doctor, and he agreed she was quite underweight. He also recommended a target weight for her to work on, with some suggestions about more frequent smaller meals now that her stomach is so small, but Lin is having a tough time with that. We then started her counseling, but her therapist warned us that eating disorders don't just go away overnight. She has gone twice but seems rather upset when she comes home. She and the therapist made a new goal for her, and it isn't easy, so she is finding it a challenge. Then, her bad mood makes her take it out on me – the easy target. The therapist said she won't like giving up the power at first, but her thinness is serious enough now that she has to compromise. Lin knows being hospitalized and losing total control would be even worse. This is definitely a challenge for us all!" Mrs. Soo's voice sounded tired and frustrated.

"I know it is. Like I said, these eating disorders can be quite complex and quite difficult to resolve, but there is no other choice. We all want Lin Soo to enjoy a healthy body and a healthy and happy life, so it will be so worth it," Mrs. Kaufmann assured her.

"I know. That is my goal for sure. I just never felt so powerless in controlling a problem before. And Lin can be so stubborn sometimes, especially about the way she looks. She is convinced we all want her to be fat right now, so the resistance is ever- present. Her father has no patience with it either, because he, too, feels powerless," Mrs. Soo admitted. "What else can I be doing right now?" she asked, rather desperate for something that would make it easy.

"Just follow the treatment plan so that Lin trusts you, and be very careful not to keep reminding her about eating, or she'll turn a deaf ear to you, thinking you're just a nagging mother. That tends to fix their resolve to keep their control. The doctor and she have their commitments and deals between them. They will let you know how you can make changes that will support them, and you need to follow those suggestions. Maybe you can find foods for her that are calorie-dense but very healthy. That way Lin doesn't have to eat so much. Other than that, that's all you can do. Honor their relationship, their plan, and their appointments. After that, you need to make peace with it. At some point, parents do all they can do and allow their children to experience what is being given to them as life lessons. Lin Soo will learn from this. She will learn a lot about herself. Keep in mind, you are learning about yourself as well, and this isn't an easy lesson."

"I guess you're right. That's all I can do. I can't help but think of the last line of that Serenity Prayer… 'and the wisdom to know the difference.' I guess I'm having to become wise whether I like it or not," she added.

"Aren't we all?" Mrs. Kaufmann replied. We each have our own journey with our joys and our own set of lessons along the way. Well, I have a student at my door for an appointment, so I have to get going. Thanks so much for calling, and give me a call if there is anything I can do to help you from this end," Mrs. Kaufmann offered.

"I will," Mrs. Soo said, "and thank you for helping me help Lin."

Mrs. Kaufmann replied, "Actually, helping our children *is* one of the joys of my journey!"

As Mrs. Kaufmann got up to see who was next, she reminded herself of what she had told Janie…that helping others may really mean just getting the right help *for* others. After all, when you're a team player, you have to know when to pass the ball and when to hold on to it. These two students required her to make the pass. She now knew they were in very good hands, and she could expect to watch them gain weight as they began to get back to a healthy perspective.

Discussion Points:

- Eating disorders are very complex problems for the people living with them. Solving them should involve different professionals and are not to be solved by friends at school. The best help you can give a friend with a suspected eating disorder is to tell a trusted adult that you are worried.

- If you have an eating disorder, you need to recognize that you see a problem that may not be there. Keep in mind that the thinking that made you see your weight as a problem, is not the clear thinking you'll need to get you out of it. Trust the professionals working with you.

- Parents sometimes feel that pushing their children to do more, do better, try harder is the right way to parent, but that can also sometimes be too much pressure for some children. People have different amounts of frustration that they can tolerate, and some children try too hard to please their parents.

Reflection Questions:

1. Have you ever looked in the mirror and thought you were too fat? How have you handled it?

2. If you have ever had a friend who is not eating, or throwing up after he or she eats, what have you done about it? Did you try to talk to them first? Would you be willing to let a parent, teacher, school nurse, or school counselor know when you do worry?

3. What situations do you know you have to turn over to a trusted adult?

CHAPTER 19:
My Little Sister Is a Pain, and My Older Brother Beats Me Up!

The Middle Child's Dilemma

The list of students scheduled to be discussed at the Intervention and Referral Services meeting at Hillstown Middle School that month arrived in the mailboxes of those professionals who were to be in attendance. There would be one teacher representing each grade level, the school nurse, the school counselor, and the school psychologist. There was to be a teacher from the team of special subjects, the school vice-principal, the principal, and the school secretary who would take the official minutes. Mrs. Kaufmann pulled her list from her mailbox and knew she needed to prepare for that meeting. She needed to bring all the records of those students including their end-of-year state test scores, their recent grades and attendance records, their permanent folders, and any other guidance information that she could offer as the school counselor. She read through all the names on the list and was not surprised by any of them. She had actually counseled them all for one reason or another. That I&RS meeting, as it was called, was the next morning, so she needed to get started gathering that information right away, before this day made its own agenda.

Nick Armanti's name was first. He was in danger of failing language arts and math for the marking period, so an intervention was clearly needed. Mrs. Kaufmann pulled her notes from her file drawer, which, to anyone else reading them, would be sketchy abbreviations that read like code. She always took notes from her confidential conversations in a way to protect them if the information was ever read by anyone other than her. As she looked them over, the conversations all came back to her immediately. She then remembered his parents were recently divorced, and his mom found it really hard to pay the bills. She and her four children ended up having to move in with her ailing mother, and then she took on two jobs to get by. The husband had a lawyer who managed to give the wife as little financial support as he could, and he fought her for anything she needed for the children thereafter. Her life would be hard, but she had felt emotionally abused in her marriage, and it was a more self-respectful life to live. The problem was the lack of supervision after school and into the evening for the children, especially on the nights when she was out working her long hours.

Nick's oldest brother had had a horrible fight with his father when he heard how little he had given his mom for living expenses. He had planned to go to college, but that had to be postponed after his father used the savings to buy his new townhouse, new sports car, which only seated two, and expensive golf clubs. That was the last straw for Nick's brother. He left the house, got an apartment with a friend, and got a job at the local warehouse.

Then there was Anthony, the second-oldest son, who was in high school. He was failing several subjects, resulting in being cut from the football team, not to mention he was caught smoking and drinking. He was very angry because of his parents' divorce, and he stayed out of the house as much as he could. Whenever he came home, he would argue with everyone and talk back to his mother, if she was there. Then he would storm out again for several hours, only to come home and lock himself in his room. He was somewhat respectful to his grandmother, but she had no ability to control him, and he knew it. He would always leave to go out with his friends after school, finding relief from his pain through his risk-taking behavior with them. For him, as he spiraled down the failure chain, it just kept getting worse.

Nick had a younger sister, Sarah, a kindergartener who also was acting out from the recent loss of the attention from her absentee father and her emotionally and physically absent mother. She felt the constant tension in the house, but stayed close to her grandmother and ended up being her favorite. She was the spoiled one and usually got what she wanted through her little tantrums and attention-getting behaviors. She was the relatively happy one, though, and did provide some comic relief with her antics around what was left of the family.

Then there was Nicholas. He was a bit of a lost child. He didn't demand attention and therefore didn't get it. Everyone else was hurting and surviving, so, if it didn't squeak, it was assumed to be okay. He was, however, sad and therefore unmotivated to read the assigned books or do the homework at night, which was costing him dearly. He always felt guilty and behind, and then he found he didn't know enough to even start his homework. It all eventually became one big burden that he worked to avoid completely. He needed help from the school, and Mrs. Kaufmann was glad his name had made the referral list this month. The individual counseling she had had with him was not enough. And he never showed up on the mornings when the Changing Families Group met, since his grandmother couldn't drive him to school and his mother had left much earlier for work.

As she prepared his file and his grades, she was interrupted by a light little knock at her door. It was Anya Yotranka. She peered into the office shyly and asked if the school counselor had a little extra time to talk to her.

"How wonderful to see you, Miss Yotranka! Please come in. I have all the time in the world for you, my dear," she spoke invitingly, to assure Anya she was welcome.

Anya's face lit up with a smile that made her little face beautiful. She came right into the office from the waiting room without hesitation now. Then, as she started to speak, her eyes filled up and overflowed with tears almost immediately. She quickly sat in the big chair facing Mrs. Kaufmann's desk and said, "It's my sister, Veli. She picks on me after school every day, and I can't stop her. If I call a friend, she gets on the other line and interrupts or listens until I hang up so she can use the phone. She has a cell phone, but our parents gave her a limit on how much she can use it, so she takes the house phone away from me. And we have to share the computer, too, but she doesn't. She just takes whatever she wants, whenever she wants it, telling her friends that I'm her annoying little sister." Anya started to sob as she poured it all out. Mrs. Kaufmann slid the tissue box in front of her and she pulled several tissues out immediately.

"What do your parents say when this is going on?" Mrs. Kaufmann asked, looking concerned. She knew these parents to be loving and caring and very involved in school-related activities, so she wondered if they just didn't know about the older sister taking advantage of Anya when they weren't there.

Anya answered, "They both work late. Our babysitter is supposed to just be watching the baby, not taking care of us. So when Veli and I get off the bus, we are supposed to get our snacks and relax a little before starting our homework. My mom gets home at dinnertime, and my dad gets home from work later than that, usually after we eat dinner," she answered, sniffling and drying her eyes, but not sobbing anymore.

"Then what do your parents say when they get home?" Mrs. Kaufmann pursued.

"My dad always just says that he had to work things out with his brother when he was growing up, and now it's my turn to work things out with my sister. That will make us feel closer for life. My mom agrees and says if we continue to bother them with these little arguments, we will both be punished. She says that it's hard enough working all day and coming home to make dinner and take care of the new baby."

"Well, it looks like that means we have to work things out. I'm glad to see you've decided not to be the 'sister-victim.' You have been smart enough to use your own resources – like coming to see me," Mrs. Kaufmann assured her. "Okay, let's roll up our sleeves and see what sort of options you have, or what kind of compromises you can offer your sister. Let me hear what your thoughts have been so far," Mrs. Kaufmann suggested.

"I did tell on her a couple of times, and we both got sent to our rooms, so neither of us could use phones or our computers. Veli got so mad at me that she took it out on me the next day after school. She kept talking about me to her friends and told me she was going to text my friends about me if I ever told on her again," Anya said, with her eyes filling up and her voice cracking.

"Sounds like bully behavior to me. She has out-powered you, and I don't like her taking advantage of being older. I have to ask you, though, if there is anything that you can admit you do to her. Is there anything you do that upsets her so she thinks she has to get even in such a controlling and uncaring way? Please be honest with me so I can help you, okay?" Mrs. Kaufmann asked in her kindest voice.

"She says I annoy her when her friends are over on the weekends. All I do is just come into the room to watch television where they're hanging out, and she tells me to leave. I don't, because it's my house, too, and I want to watch television. She doesn't want me in there so she can tell secrets and talk about boys with her friends. That's when she calls me a pain, and they get up all mad and go to our bedroom. Then, if I go in our bedroom to get anything, they get up again, tell me to quit following them, and call me a pest."

"That can be a problem when you have to share your space. What does she do when you have your friends over?"

"My friends like it when she's around, because she's older and they think she's cool, but she calls us annoying and usually leaves the room anyway."

"I have an idea!" Mrs. Kaufmann said almost interrupting "Anya, would you be okay with a 'sister mediation meeting' with Veli, you, and me? I'm just thinking that there might be a whole lot of little annoyances that you two have built up over time that need to be talked out in a neutral place. Just a wild idea, if you're willing."

"But Veli would get mad that I told on her to you," she reacted instantly.

"Oh, I would never let on that you came in. I would just need a different reason to talk with her so that it could lead into her complaints about you. Then I would suggest this meeting as a way to help her. I think it's brilliant!" Mrs. Kaufman laughed. "What do you think?"

Anya smiled at Mrs. Kaufmann's confidence. "But what would be the reason you'd call her down to talk with you?" she checked, knowing her sister was really smart and might guess something was up.

"At her grade, there are so many volunteer programs she could sign up for that I use them as excuses to talk with students to invite them to get involved. I've been noticing her good grades and thinking she might want to be a Peer Tutor for younger children. That could lead to all kinds of related discussion, don't you think?" she asked Anya.

"When would you do this, and what should I do in the meantime?"

"I could see if she could talk to me today, or tomorrow afternoon, but our little mediation will probably not happen until next week. Would you be willing to try to go into whatever room she's not in with her friends, just for this weekend? Let her know you're trying to get along. That may warm her up to you a little, to be less bullying for now. Most times it just takes one person to start the turn-around from a bad place to a more cooperative place. And sometimes, that can be started by the little sister. Try it, okay? Just see if it works, and let her know you're trying."

"Like, what do I say?" Anya asked.

"In your own words say something like this. 'Veli, I know we always fight when you have friends over because I'm hanging around you. Will you let me know where you and your friends want to talk, and I'll get my stuff and leave the room to give you some private time, okay? I'd like to try not to fight in front of our friends anymore.' You might even want to write it all down before you decide to say it to her."

"She'll think I've gone out of my mind, but I know she'll like being left alone." Anya giggled at the thought of being so out of character, mature-sounding, and shocking her sister.

"She will be surprised and may not even believe it, but try to make good on your word. Don't go back into the 'thinking that you deserve to be there.' You do have your rights, but being all mad and acting out about not getting what you deserve, only sets your sister off. One thing you have learned is that her reactions can lead to some tough-to-take consequences," Mrs. Kaufmann said bluntly. "So let's see how you, being the bigger person, will start to turn things around. It will certainly help me with the mediation next week."

Mrs. Kaufmann figured Anya would actually make the first move for their mediation session. Certainly Veli, as her older sister, would like to be considered the more mature sister when they would talk later. This action on Anya's part might be the perfect motivation for her to want to work on a compromise plan next week.

Anya liked the idea, thinking it could lead to something better for her. She also liked knowing Mrs. Kaufmann understood her side of things and was willing to help her sister stop bullying her. "I can do that," she said, looking actually excited by their plan.

"Well, all right then. I'll give you a pass to get to your next class, since morning homeroom is over, and I'll see about meeting with Veli today. I'll give you a pass to your teacher for our meeting next week once it gets set up. Be patient until then and, Anya, try to be as compromising, fair, and mature as you can, all right? It will really work in your favor down the road," Mrs. Kaufmann advised her.

"I will. Thanks, Mrs. Kaufmann!" she said, as she left her office.

I have to think about whether calling their parents in advance will work in favor of this meeting or against it. It's important never to keep anything from parents, but reporting every non-significant visit from the students isn't necessary either. In fact, I owe Anya confidentiality on this one. I have to think about how I will approach this, she thought, as she went back to getting the other I&RS preparations done for the next day.

The I&RS Meeting

First thing the next morning, Mrs. Kaufmann brought her files and binders into the big conference room so she would be ready for the meeting. As she went back to her guidance office, she saw Veli coming into the building for band practice before school. *Perfect opportunity*, she thought. *Let me ask her about meeting me this afternoon.*

"Good morning, Veli," she said casually.

"Good morning, Mrs. K!" she answered enthusiastically.

"Hey, Veli, I meant to ask you about being a Peer Tutor this year. Would you want to do that?"

"Sure. How does that work?" she asked.

"I can tell you all about it this afternoon, once I get out of this morning's meeting. Can you come see me at lunchtime? You can bring your lunch, and I can tell you all about it. Or, if you want to be with your friends at lunchtime, we could maybe find a class that you could leave from without losing anything," Mrs. Kaufmann offered.

"Lunch would be fine. I really can't miss any of my classes this afternoon. As for lunch today, I need to go buy my milk first. Should I just come into your office or wait in the waiting room?" Veli asked.

"Just come right in if the door is open, since I'll be expecting you. If the office door is shut, please knock first in case I have an emergency, and I'll come to the door to let you know what we'll do then," Mrs. Kaufmann answered her. "I just know you will make a great peer tutor! It only takes patience with younger children, since you already know all you need to teach them," Mrs. Kaufmann assured her, but planted it in her mind as the key ingredient. She knew it would also help them when they got into the sister discussion later.

"See you at lunch!" Veli said cheerfully, as she turned into the music room door.

Mrs. Kaufmann felt lucky that she had run into Veli. She didn't want to miss meeting with her before the weekend came. After all, Anya needed some help for the weekend if she was to reach out to Veli successfully. The least Mrs. Kaufmann could do was to make Veli receptive to her attempts by having her focus on practicing being patient with her younger sister.

It was time for the meeting to begin and each of the staff members was settling into his or her seat around the huge oval conference table. There was a lot of friendly chatter among them until the principal, Mr. Gonzalez, called the meeting to order and the secretary began typing on her computer. "Our list is a little long today, so I'd like to get started discussing these students right away. The first name on the list is Nicholas Armanti. Will his grade level teacher please read the referring request from his language arts teacher?" he asked.

The teacher for his grade level read Nick's teacher's I&RS referral form with the description of the problem for which she needed help. "Nicholas Armanti is currently failing language arts, due primarily to a failure to do any homework. His parents divorced last spring, and he lives with his mother, his grandmother, and older brother in high school, and a sister who just started kindergarten. His home life is such that there is no follow-through there, and his self-confidence is going downhill." She read more specifics about Nick's test and quiz grades, averaging a C, and then proceeded to report her own attempts to help him, including all the calls to the mom and lunchtime detentions. She was now reaching out to the I&RS Committee to help her.

Mr. Gonzalez then called on Mrs. Kaufmann to report on his state test scores, past grades, and his attendance record, as well as any other insight or previous contacts she had had with the family.

"Last year, first marking period before his mother filed for a divorce, he was a B student all around, including language arts. He's not fond of reading, and that began to pull his grade down at the end of last year as the home life became more turbulent. His parents were too busy to make him read, and I understand it was a difficult divorce with a lot of arguing in the evening. He told me then that he wasn't able to concentrate on the books assigned. His grade dropped to a C- by the end of the last marking period, and I think that was a gift through extra credit opportunities."

Mrs. Kaufmann continued, "His attendance is always good, and he used to be a generally happy, laid-back kind of boy, but this year he appears to be sad and disengaged. I've tried to encourage his parents to get him to come to my Changing Families Group that I run on Thursday mornings, but she said it's too hard to get him there in the morning. She then said she would try, but he never made it to one," she concluded.

Then the nurse spoke up. "I've also called his mother about his overdue health forms. Mrs. Armanti explained she has to get him to the doctor first for his physical, but works two jobs now and doesn't have the time. She explained that his father works too far away to help with that, and her mother's vision is too bad to drive. She said she was working on getting a friend to take him and she'd get back to me."

The school nurse continued, "I also want to add that Nick came to see me quite often last spring for little things like paper cuts and cough drops. That was at the end of the school year, when the arguing and divorce proceedings were at the highest. He just needed some kindness and a safe place. This year, I've not seen that so much, and yet he seems to be even unhappier. I don't know if he feels embarrassed to leave his friends from playground, or if he just can't get the comfort he needs from that little visit anymore, compared to what he gets being with friends. He is a sad little boy."

Mr. Gonzalez then asked if the "specials team" representative had any feedback from those teachers about Nick's performance in his gym, art, music, or computer classes.

The music teacher spoke next. "I know he has a guitar and wanted to join my morning guitar club, but he didn't have a ride to school that early. His mom leaves early and his grandmother doesn't drive. He hasn't shown much enthusiasm this year in my class, either. I have to agree that he isn't the same student as he was at the beginning of last year, at all. The good news is, the other students just accept him, and he gets along well with everyone. He is a considerate student, and I feel bad for him. As for the other teachers, all of them say about the same thing when I asked for input yesterday. They all see an unhappy little boy."

Mr. Gonzalez then opened it up to the whole committee to help him brainstorm ideas for how the school could intervene and help this student.

The school psychologist, Mrs. White, suggested that the principal ask the head of the After-School Program if he would accept Nick into the program to do his homework after school. If he could just go to the library every day and get started doing his homework and his readings, the habit could be formed. At least this would allow him a quiet place to read and do his homework, away from the distractions at the house. Plus, he could get help with his homework, because there would be a staff member who would be there after school to help all the students.

"That's a good idea. I will contact him today," Mr. Gonzalez said. "There may even be some money in my budget to pay a stipend to the After-School Program, instead of asking for him to be taken in for free. And I certainly don't want to put a bigger financial burden on his mother now. After we get Nick out of this emotional slump, maybe he'll have developed the habit of doing his homework and will assume the responsibility at home on his own. I think our goal is to help him with his sadness. Then, maybe, he'll have his motivation back."

Mrs. Kaufmann spoke right up, "I'd like to begin meeting with Nick for counseling once a week for a while, to help him keep a check on his own grades. I also want to make a call to his mother to talk about their morning schedule, just to see if we could wiggle things around to get him into those guitar lessons and into my Changing Families Group. Mr. Gonzalez, would it be okay if Mrs. Armanti is allowed to drop Nick off to the main office, to sit for the ten minutes until guitar club begins? I'd really like to try to make this work. It's only two mornings a week and would give him some positives in his life. He needs that extra attention with the counseling. If we could get him caught up with his academics, too, then that could turn this little guy's head around. I figure it's worth a try."

The music teacher jumped in, "Actually, I get here at least fifteen to twenty minutes early that morning to get set up, so he can just come to my room whenever his mother drops him off. Besides, he might like the extra attention from me before the others come."

The principal then said, "I will call Mrs. Armanti after you do, Mrs. Kaufmann, to officially give her the results of this committee's plan. I also feel like it would be wise to invite her to attend the next monthly I&RS meeting, if Nick continues to maintain a failing average in spite of these efforts. Let's get that into the minutes, unless anyone disagrees."

The committee members were in agreement, and the principal then suggested they move on to the next student on the list. Mrs. Kaufmann finished writing her notes about Nick Armanti, and then looked at the name of the next student up for discussion.

The Phone Calls Begin

The I&RS committee finished up discussing all of the students on the agenda right at the start of lunchtime, so Mrs. Kaufmann had to get back to her office to meet with Veli. She walked into her office, and no sooner had she put her binders on the shelf than Veli walked right in. "Hi, Mrs. Kaufmann," she said excitedly, as she sat down, opened up her lunch, and put the straw in her milk carton. "I've been thinking about the Peer Tutoring Program all morning, and I think I'd really like to do it. Pat Steinberg, her friend, explained how it worked for her last year, and she liked it. Can I just sign up for one subject? I like math, and I feel comfortable with it."

"I'm so glad to hear you're interested. I assume you will be able to make some time after school for students who sign up? We often have our tutors and the students that need help meet together in the library after school, where the After-School Program meets," Mrs. Kaufmann explained.

Veli was quick to agree to any day or every day, because she became quite excited to be in this program and able to help someone. Mrs. Kaufmann then said to her, "I actually have a younger student right now who is a little behind in math. He also hates to read, so we need someone with whom he can discuss his assigned readings and take an interest in his progress. Would you be able to do that?"

"That doesn't sound hard. And my mom can pick me up on the way home from work," Veli offered.

"Like I said before, you just need to have a lot of patience with him, and I'm assuming that with two younger sisters, you have learned that by now," Mrs. Kaufmann said to her, expecting a reaction.

"Well, I'm not as patient with my sister Anya, because she is such a pain, but I would be okay with someone else," she admitted.

"Why?" Mrs. Kaufmann asked. "What does Anya do that annoys you, that wouldn't annoy you if it was another young child?" Mrs. Kaufmann knew she was now heading into the discussion she wanted to have in the first place.

"Everything, I swear! Everywhere I go, she follows my friends and me. And when I tell my parents, they just tell me to work it out, or else both of us will be punished," Veli complained, with a lot of sudden emotion.

"Do you want to change things? I can help if you want."

"How? Anya doesn't ever listen to me," Veli challenged her.

"What if the three of us had a talk, and Anya was to learn the art of compromise?" Mrs. Kaufmann suggested with a big smile, as if she was up to something. "We could call it a 'sister mediation session' and we could cut some deals, if you are willing. Besides, she may think you are the one who doesn't try or doesn't hear her, you think? It usually does take two people to have an argument. I believe it will take two people to understand the problem in order to fix it. It would be a good practice in patience, I'll bet." Now Mrs. Kaufmann threw the challenge back at Veli.

Veli paused for a minute. She felt like she needed to accept her school counselor's suggestion. She also knew any attempt to stop the fighting with her sister must be better than not trying at all. "Okay, I'll do it. But when do we meet? We don't have the same lunch times."

"I believe you have lunch when students at her grade level are having specials right after their lunchtime, and I know those teachers will be okay if she misses a part of their classes. How about next Tuesday? I believe that's when Anya's class has music. Do you think that would work for you, if I invited her to come then?" Mrs. Kaufmann suggested. "Maybe then I can have that student who needs tutoring to come to my office at the end of that period to meet you, right before you leave. I just have to call his mom to make sure she's fine with his staying after school for tutoring, and that he is willing also."

"Okay, I'd like to try that with Anya, and I do want to meet that boy. I hope he wants to work with me," she said a little nervously.

Mrs. Kaufmann then asked, "Veli, do you want to tell your parents that you and Anya will be having this 'sister mediation session' next week"?

"No, just in case it doesn't work," she smiled. "Besides, my mother and father want us to work it out on our own anyway. So we'll use you! Mom's so busy with the new baby and work that she'll just be happy if our fighting stops," Veli admitted.

"Sounds good, and I love to be used," Mrs. Kaufmann said jokingly. "Your mom will be happy you are learning to use your resources, and I am considered a resource here at the school. Okay, I have a lot of calls to make. And when the boy comes to meet you, we'll set up how it will work best. I'd like to make sure he's part of the planning, so he feels more committed to making it work. We'll need to have you both swap your phone numbers too, so you can call each other the day before every tutoring appointment, if ever either of you won't be able to make it. I also have to remember to get you an extra math textbook and extra required reading book. You've already read that story when you were in his grade, but I'd like you to have one of your own so you can brush up. I want him to know you are on top of what he's working on with you. Right now, let's get you back to lunch."

"So I just need to get my milk and pizza and then come here next Tuesday?" she checked.

"Yes, and try to practice patience this weekend. See how you do, and we'll talk on Tuesday. Have a great weekend!" Mrs. Kaufmann said, as Veli left for the cafeteria.

Her next move was to write out a pass to Anya, to let her know she was to have her "sister mediation session" next Tuesday during her music class. She wrote on the top of the pass, "Don't forget to be the bigger person this weekend. Maybe Veli's patience will surprise you. Remember, it takes one to start the change, so you go first, and feel proud of yourself. Good luck!"

Mrs. Kaufmann then brought the pass to her homeroom teacher's desk, so she would give it to Anya before she left school that day. She had started back toward her office when she ran into Nick Armanti's class, all clamoring in from playground. She followed the line to the classroom, and went into the room with the students immersed in all the excited post-playground noise and chatter. She quickly asked his teacher if she would quietly send Nick to see her right away. The teacher just nodded, and then Mrs. Kaufmann went out of the room into the hallway, to draw less attention to her presence.

The Next Deal

In less than a minute, Nick popped out of the room into the hallway and was surprised to see Mrs. Kaufmann standing right there. "Hi, Nick." She spoke quickly, so he wouldn't think he had done something wrong, "Let's go to my office so I can ask you about that guitar club your music teacher has started for 8:00 in the morning." Mrs. Kaufmann kept walking and talking, because she knew to limit time with students in the hallway. She needed to keep her contact with them not that obvious, so that other students did not notice and ask what was up.

"I understand you usually walk to school in the morning just a short while after your mom leaves for work. What time does she leave?" she asked him.

Nick said, "Around 7:40, unless she's running late."

They got into her office and closed the door. Mrs. Kaufmann continued, "I was just thinking, maybe she could drop you off here at the school for morning clubs and activities on her way out of town. You might get here at ten of eight, but your music teacher is here by then, so you could just come in and get settled, like he does. Wouldn't that be cool to learn guitar?" she said excitedly.

Nick paused for a moment, almost afraid to embrace this possible happiness. "Do you think my mom would want to do that? I could ask, but she's always so crazy busy in the morning and in such a rush to get out the door. Plus, my older brother has been sleeping so late and won't get up until she screams at him, and she really wants him up before she leaves for work. She's afraid he'll stay home and play hooky."

"I don't think she'd mind. I'd like to call her and chat with her. The big thing is you have to be ready to get in the car the second she's ready to leave…the very second. Since mornings are so crazy in your house, you don't want to add to the craziness anyway. But that would have to be your deal in this. Maybe two mornings a week would give you something to look forward to," she suggested.

"Two mornings a week? I thought guitar club was only one?" Nick asked.

"Oh, yes, I forgot to mention," Mrs. Kaufmann gave him a huge smile. "That's the other part of the deal. If we can get you here on Tuesday mornings for guitar club, then we can get you here on Thursday mornings for my Changing Families Group. We really have a good time on those mornings, too. I bring breakfast, and we draw and do art projects, which I know you love. What do you think?" she asked. "Is it a deal?"

Nick then allowed the thought to make him happy. "Really, do you think she will drive me?" he said as if he was still trying to believe it all.

"I do think so. And I also have another offer for you if things work out. Boy, this is your lucky day, my friend. I have a possible peer tutor for you, if her mom is okay with letting her stay after school, and if your mom is okay with you staying after school. The tutor is older, very nice, good at math, and she will help you read those extra books you have been assigned. That would be after school, until your mom picks you up on her way home from work. This can be for a while, until you get your grades up. It could also get you into the habit of reading on your own. She will definitely help you get caught up in math. Think this is a good idea?" she asked.

"Wow," he said. "I'm going to be here all day, if my mom wants to do all that. Could you just ask her for the mornings?" he offered, obviously not interested in doing all his homework there after school, too.

"No. Sorry, dear. I'm asking for the whole package. I know you wouldn't be allowed to participate in any clubs if your grades weren't high enough, so the after-school part has to take priority. And, actually, it should come first. Are you willing to get your homework done in order to take the guitar lessons?"

"Yes, I've really wanted to do that for a long time now. My dad gave me my guitar for my birthday last year," he said enthusiastically.

"But what about the homework part?" she smiled. "That has to come first. Is that a deal or no deal?" she continued.

"Okay. I already did tell my mom I would try really hard to keep my grades up this marking period," he told her.

"Well, all right then. We have our deal," Mrs. Kaufmann said with conviction. "I'll call your mom and see if we can make some magic happen early next week. Your job will be to get ready early on Tuesday and Thursday mornings, and get your homework done after school every day. Maybe, by next Tuesday, I can put a pass in your music teacher's mailbox for you to come here and meet your new peer tutor. We could make that the last ten minutes of class. That's when we can go over where you'll meet each other and what help you would like. Sound good?"

"Sounds good," Nick said with equal enthusiasm. "I kinda like not being in the house when my mom isn't there. My older brother always pushes me around and wrestles me to the floor really hard whenever he just feels mad about something else. Now he's started punching me in the shoulder or back so that I leave our bedroom. He does that so he can be alone on our computer after school. And my sister screams when she doesn't get her way. She is so spoiled, and she's always throwing a fit about something. My grandmother sometimes can make Sarah stop by giving her her way, but she really can't stop Anthony. Besides, he punches me when she's not looking, so he gets away with it," he complained.

"Nick, I do need to let your mom know about this when I call her. It troubles me that Anthony is getting away with that, and you shouldn't have to be getting hurt in your own home."

"As long as she doesn't tell Anthony that I told on him, that's all. The only thing is she's not there to stop him, so I don't think he'll change. He's so mad all the time as it is now," Nick admitted.

"Well, that's why we have these Changing Families Group meetings. That's the kind of thing we can work on there. I have seen a lot of students get some really great strategies for dealing with their sisters and brothers through those tough times. Anthony is angry, and he needs help, too. Maybe that's how your mom will stop him, by getting him some help, or getting him to talk about it with her or his counselor. You'll be surprised what changes we can make to help you."

Nick looked at her, deep in thought. He was obviously trying to imagine the strategy that would work on Anthony. Mrs. Kaufmann quickly said, "Okay, let's get you back to class before you miss any lessons. We have to get those grades up, so you can become famous playing some of that wild guitar music some day!" she laughed. She noticed him giggling to himself as she sent him out the door to go back to class. *That happy giggle is such a refreshing sound,* she thought. *And now to make those phone calls.*

Mrs. Kaufmann called Veli's mom first so she could check off Veli becoming a Peer Tutor. "Hi Mrs. Yotranka, how are you?"

"I'm doing just fine. Is there anything wrong? I hope my girls are behaving themselves. They have been arguing so much at home that I think school is the only place they can't get to each other, and we all get a break!" Mrs. Yotranka answered.

"I actually called for a different reason, a good one. I was talking with Veli today about becoming a Peer Tutor. I have a young boy who needs a little help getting back on track in the homework department. He's having a little trouble with math and doesn't like to read. I have asked if he could be allowed to go to the cafeteria after school, where the After-School Program is held every day. I also know that Veli would like to be a Peer Tutor and go there to help students after school. She said she would be very comfortable helping this student with his work, if his mom would allow him to stay and then bring him home afterwards. And if Veli stays, would you be able to pick her up on your way home from work? Does this work for your schedule?" Mrs. Kaufmann checked with her.

Mrs. Yotranka answered happily, "That would be no problem at all. I would just need to know what days. That would be really good for Veli. She doesn't have any patience, and I know she'll have to get some to do that tutoring. I also like to think she's off the phone and off the computer after school, for a little while at least. She's on them so much, now."

"I liked the idea too, because I think she can help this young boy turn his grades around. I think it's a win-win, as long as I'm not really inconveniencing you or his mom. I'm thinking Veli can get some of her homework done while that boy does some of his. She can just sit with him to keep him on track, to answer questions, and to check to see if he's understanding what he's reading a couple of times. They would only need to do this Monday through Thursday, with Friday being her early day if the other four went well. I'd like to see if this young man will carry his responsibility on his own over the weekend. And maybe they only need to do this up to the end of this marking period. By then, the habits would be established. They will both get used to feeling ahead of the game, by the time they get home for dinner." Mrs. Kaufmann spoke very enthusiastically.

"I think it's a great idea for her and him. Yes, I'll be happy to swing by there on my way home. I'll come in the first time to meet the After-School Program supervisor and the student she's tutoring. I'll just tell her to be at the door waiting for me at a specific time after that. Great plan!" Mrs. Yotranka said enthusiastically. "I think this will really make Veli feel proud, too."

"It always does. I've noticed that volunteerism provides more self-confidence to students than almost anything else they can do. They can witness that they have value, and that resulting self-worth has incredible power!" Mrs. Kaufmann replied. "I just have to call the mother of that young boy next. Then I'll call you back with a start date."

Before she could look up Mrs. Armanti's work number, the phone rang in Mrs. Kaufmann's hand. Mr. Gonzalez was calling to discuss Nick. "Perfect timing, Mr. Gonzalez," Mrs. Kaufmann laughed as she answered the phone, seeing it was him. "I was just about to call Nick's mom, and I needed to know if it was okay that Nick stay after school in that program."

Mr. Gonzalez also laughed. "We are usually on the same track, aren't we! Yes, the After-School Program supervisor has agreed to allow Nick to join the After-School Program. He was full, but Nick is a well-behaved student who doesn't require much attention at all, so he will take him. I told him I had some money in my budget to cover his fees until the end of the marking period, but he told me to keep the money in my budget for another student that might need some help. He's a good man."

"That's great, and he certainly is kind and generous. I have some good news, too. I have an older girl who is an excellent student, who has agreed to sit with Nick as his personal tutor after school. Her mother will be delighted to have her stay and be a Peer Tutor. I just have to make sure Mrs. Avanti will be willing and able to pick Nick up after school, on her way home from work. This could give Nick a break from his older brother and little sister, and a chance to catch up academically," Mrs. Kaufmann added.

"That won't be a problem because I already called Mrs. Avanti to let her know we were looking into placing Nick in the After-School Program. She sounded so relieved. She said she was so grateful for all the school is doing for her and Nick. She called him her 'lost' child. She also felt helpless because of having to work long hours. This was such a gift to her. So this means we're all good to go," Mr. Gonzalez said with confidence.

"I will need to call her anyway, because I'm cuttin' a deal!" Mrs. Kaufmann laughed again. "I spoke to Nick, and we did some talking about him getting a ride from his mother in the morning, on her way to work. He so badly wants to take guitar, and I so badly want to get him into my Changing Families Group. He knows he has to get his grades up, and that I have a tutor to help him. He also knows I will be calling his mom for the ride two mornings a week. She might have to drop him off before the morning activities officially begin, but the music teacher and I are always here early, so we're okay with that."

"Good idea, and good work!" Mr. Gonzalez complimented Mrs. Kaufmann.

"Thanks. I also want to talk with his mom about getting Anthony, the older brother, some help at the high school, too. Wish me luck. We can't do much about that at this point, except let her know the impact his anger is having on Nick," she explained.

"Good luck. I've gotta run," he replied, and hung up quickly.

Mrs. Kaufmann then looked up Mrs. Armanti's cell phone number. She didn't want to disturb her at work, but would give her the option of picking up or checking her voice mail later. She rang until it went to voice mail and then she left a message. "Mrs. Armanti, this is Mrs. Kaufmann. I wanted to talk to you about the possibility of dropping Nick off at school on Tuesday and Thursday mornings on your way to work. I can get him into the Guitar Club and give him some support with the Changing Families Group, if you can."

Mrs. Kaufmann continued, "And I understand you have heard the good news from the principal about the After-School Program taking Nick in. I have more good news, too. I have a really good older student who is a Peer Tutor, and she is willing to work with Nick after school. I'd like to talk about the arrangements, if you could give me a call back at your convenience."

She then heard a little knock at her outer waiting room door. She hung up the phone and went to her door to see who was there. It was Anya. She looked at Mrs. Kaufmann and said, "I was on my way to the nurse's office and just wanted to ask about this weekend again. What was it I was supposed to do again?"

"You were going to try really hard to let Veli be alone with her friends and not come into the room they are in when she wants her privacy. And if she makes fun of you when she gets impatient, you are to ask her to have a little patience with you, because you're really trying not to argue in front of your friends anymore. This weekend, you're going to be the bigger person to start the turn-around to a better relationship. Can you use my words or say it in your own way, so it doesn't make her upset?" Mrs. Kaufmann asked Anya.

"Oh, that's right. I forgot. Okay, I can do that," Anya said happily.

Mrs. Kaufmann said, "I have a feeling things are going to get better for you really soon, if you can be more mature like that on the weekends, and if Veli gets more involved in after-school activities. That should just about do it. Just remember that there is no winning if you irritate her, not for you or her. You go first, and she may follow. And we have our 'sister mediation session' scheduled for Tuesday, during your music class. Don't forget. I'll put a hall pass in your homeroom teacher's mailbox Tuesday morning."

"Awesome," Anya said, as she turned around and went back to class.

Mrs. Kaufmann wrote the passes out. One for Anya, for Tuesday from music, one for Veli for Tuesday from lunch, and one for Nick for Tuesday from the last ten minutes from music, also. She then sent an e-mail to the music teacher, Mr. Morris, to let him know she was contacting Mrs. Armanti, to see if Nick could come to Guitar Club, and she just wanted to give him the heads-up in case it meant Nick would arrive early.

As she finished the e-mail, the phone rang. It was Mrs. Armanti. "Hi Mrs. Kaufmann, I got all your wonderful news. Wow, this is great. I would be delighted to bring him in for guitar lessons and the support group. I thought I left too early so it wouldn't work. He really needs both of these right now. And the after-school help is such a gift for us. You have no idea. I am so grateful. Thank you!" she spoke excitedly.

"I can't wait to tell him. Just so you know, he promised to be ready to leave whenever you need to go, so you won't be late. He is such a good boy. His tutor will be Veli Yotranka. She is an excellent student and is so excited about helping him. The one thing I have to ask you is about Nick's older brother. I have to ask you not to disclose this to him, but Nick has described the way Anthony treats him when you're gone. He knows your mother can't stop him, and that he has so much anger that Nick doesn't like taking the punches. Is there any way he could get some counseling and some academic help at the high school? I think that would make quite a difference for Nick and the general climate in your home," Mrs. Kaufmann suggested.

"Yes, my mother told me that Anthony has really been acting out. I have to see what my insurance can cover for counseling, though. We don't have the extra money, and I can't drive him anywhere after school," Mrs. Avanti explained.

"What about calling the high school? I know they have great counselors there who could direct you to their substance abuse counselor. Their SAC works with students who have abused substances, or simply are at risk and need counseling to help prevent them from using. They also have academic support after school and during certain study halls. His school counselor should be able to send you in the right direction for

285

that. I just believe Anthony is hurting and taking it out on his younger brother. It is really important we protect Nick. It would anger Anthony even more if he thought Nick got him into trouble. Let's use this information to get him help," Mrs. Kaufmann advised her.

"I would never tell Anthony that Nick told on him, and I agree he definitely needs help, too. I don't want him to end up like his older brother who recently moved out instead of going to college. What a disaster that was. I will definitely call the high school right now and start getting some help. And thank you for all you've done." Mrs. Armanti was very grateful, and Mrs. Kaufmann knew it.

"You are very welcome. I'm hoping we can turn Nick's sadness around and get him motivated into doing homework now. And the guitar lessons won't be available to him if he doesn't keep his grades up, so that will be a motivation. Your part will be to work on getting Anthony the help he needs. And I will make a call to the guidance office at the high school, to let them know you will be calling. I'll let them know that here at the middle school, we have his younger brother, who is putting up with his older brother's angry outbursts."

"I will call them now," she said, as they both said goodbye.

Mrs. Kaufmann put the phone down and smiled to herself. *Now if everyone just does their part, we will have made a lot of people much happier!* she thought.

Tuesday Finally Comes

Monday afternoon, Mrs. Kaufmann put the hall passes in the mailboxes of the homeroom teachers for Anya, Veli, and Nick. She was rather excited thinking of the "set-up" she had put together, and hoped everyone did their part. She decided to make a call to Mrs. Armanti to see if she followed up for Anthony, and what the start date would be for Nick at the After-School Program.

"Mrs. Armanti?" she asked, as she heard her answer her cell phone. "I wanted to call to see when you planned for Nick to start in the After-School Program."

"Hi, Mrs. Kaufmann. I called the supervisor first thing this morning and arranged for him to start today. I will come by to meet him and thank him for his generosity when I pick Nick up afterwards. I also called the high school. I spoke with Anthony's school counselor and she is going to contact the SAC to have him called in for an appointment. She said the SAC already knew him, and I'm not surprised. The SAC told Anthony's counselor he would be happy to meet with him individually, right away, and maybe in a group later. His school counselor said she would also call him down today to get him set up after school for academic help by the end of the week. Anthony is not happy, but my mother and I are. I hope he is willing to work with them. His attitude has been horrible lately, and his dad hasn't helped at all," she admitted.

"How is Nick feeling about everything?" Mrs. Kaufmann asked.

"Oh, he is so happy about the Guitar Club tomorrow, I can't tell you. It is a real pleasure to see him smile again. What a different boy. He played on his guitar all weekend. I also made sure he knew that I wouldn't bring him for that club if his grades dropped again. He promised he would keep them up. We'll see," Mrs. Armanti said with enthusiasm.

Mrs. Kaufman then said, "I will have him meet his Peer Tutor tomorrow, and we will set up how they will meet and work. The important thing is this: You will have to remember to call Veli and her mom any morning, or even the night before, when you know he won't be there after school. If he is too sick to come to school, we don't want Veli staying after to help him, only to find out he's not there. Then she would have to stay there until her mother came to get her. Plus, her mom should know that she doesn't have to pick Veli up at the school on her way home from work. I will tell Veli that she must also let you know when she won't be there to help him after school. Otherwise, she is planning to be there Mondays through Thursdays for the remainder of the marking period. I think this will give Nick his chance to get his homework done and his grades up."

"I am so grateful. I will encourage Nick to give his best, and thank her for giving up her free time to help him. I know he's looking forward to it, but he is just a little bit nervous," Mrs. Armanti shared.

"He'll feel better once we all meet today and talk a little. Tomorrow they will start, and then he will be fine," Mrs. Kaufmann assured her.

After the women hung up, Mrs. Kaufmann called the After-School Program supervisor to notify him of all the arrangements. Then she thanked him once again for his compassion and generosity. She was quite happy that it all was moving along so well.

It was Tuesday, and Mrs. Kaufmann was listening for Anya and Veli to arrive at her office door. When she heard them laughing together, she was relieved that the mediation had a good chance of going well.

"Hi, Mrs. Kaufmann," Veli said. "Is my student coming to meet me right now?"

"Not till the end of the period. I gave him a pass for ten minutes before the end, so you and Anya and I will have enough time to have our little sister session," she said with a big smile. "So how did the weekend go?"

Anya spoke up first. "I had a friend come over on Saturday, and Veli wouldn't get out of our bedroom when we were in there. On Sunday, when Veli had her friend over, I got out of the bedroom to let them have their privacy. I tried really hard, Mrs. Kaufmann, and Veli didn't."

Veli had a weak smile on her face that faded as soon as the mediation began to open up. Mrs. Kaufmann just looked at Veli and waited for her defense. "Her friend doesn't mind, and she says so. Her friend likes me."

Anya reacted quickly, "Yeah, but I don't want you there, and I asked you to leave and you wouldn't," she said, on the verge of tears, remembering the powerless feelings she had had.

Mrs. Kaufmann jumped in. "Okay, let me lay down the ground rules for our mediation before this turns into just another argument. Our goal today will be to find a solution you can both agree to for each problem. It's called a compromise. Each side gives something up, in order to get something she wants more. And the second rule is we treat each other with complete respect. You are sisters, and life will be so much more peaceful and happier when your deals run smoothly at home. You'll always be making deals, but doing it in a mature way will make all the difference. So let's begin. The first issue is privacy with friends in your shared space at home, right?"

Veli was still feeling embarrassed by her younger sister's willingness to cooperate when she didn't. "My friends and I talk about things that Anya shouldn't hear, anyway," Veli protested.

"Okay, then whose responsibility is it to leave the room when friends come over? That's the real question." Mrs. Kaufmann spoke from her experience. "I, personally, think it depends on the room. I'm thinking that the sister who has no friend over, should be able to stay in her own bedroom, agreed?"

The school counselor saw acceptance in their nods and continued. "I also think if I had a friend over, with whom I wanted to share secrets or private conversations, then it would be up to me to find another place in the house where my friend and I could hang out alone. I don't think, though, that it would be fair that the family would not be allowed to watch TV in their own living room or family room, or wherever they usually go to relax. Certainly any guest should be able to join the family and share that common space, but the family shouldn't be asked to leave so I could have it all to myself. And, once I moved, I would expect that my sister would be mature and courteous and not follow me on purpose. Respecting each other's needs should be the last rule."

Anya quietly said, "So I can stay in my bedroom if she has a friend over?"

Veli answered, "Yes, you can stay in the bedroom, and that means if we go in the TV room to get away from you, you can't follow us," she laughed.

"Actually, it doesn't mean that at all." Mrs. Kaufmann interrupted. "I see the bedroom as the really private place. The girl without the friend should not be kicked out of her own bedroom. But the TV room is the room you both want to be in to watch TV when you come out of the bedroom. That's the community room that your whole family and all your guests should be able to hang out in. So that eliminates the right for either of you to throw the other sister out of those two rooms. So where does that leave you for your privacy, when the other sister is home?" she asked.

Veli sat thinking for a minute. She wasn't that thrilled with feeling like she was losing her rights. Anya spoke up. "What's wrong with the kitchen? You have Mom's little television and DVD player, and the counter, the table, and all the food right there. I wouldn't mind having my friends there if I needed to talk secrets," she offered. "Besides, we're still allowed to be in the TV room with our friends, if we want to, right?" she asked as she looked at Mrs. Kaufmann.

"Sure, as long as you don't try to chase any family member out of a room so you can take over. They live there. To me, the responsibility of finding a private place goes to the person with the friend visiting. No one should be sent out of a room in his or her own home. And the person having the company is having a good time anyway, so why not have them go find a place to talk privately? Doesn't that sound reasonable?" Mrs. Kaufmann asked them both. "However, like I said, following a sister around after she has already changed rooms isn't fair either. After you try out this plan, you may discover that showing respect for one another will make you both feel more cooperative in the future."

Anya was delighted and gave an enthusiastic yes. Veli thought about it and then agreed. It did seem like a reasonable plan. "But what about the phone?" Veli came back with a challenging tone. "Anya hangs on it forever."

Mrs. Kaufmann looked at Anya and waited. Anya knew she did stay on the phone for a long time. She finally said, "Well, what if we took turns and didn't stay on for more than thirty minutes at a time?"

Veli replied, "That might actually work, unless I have an emergency."

"You always say that," Anya protested. "It's not fair that she can call things an emergency and then take the phone away from me."

"Wait, Veli, don't you have a cell phone? And can't you put aside some minutes for those emergencies so you can keep your deal?"

"Uh, I guess I can," she admitted reluctatntly. "But what about when we share the computer, and Anya always says it takes her longer to type things out, because she's slower at typing, so I have to give up the computer more?"

Mrs. Kaufmann looked at Anya, who then quickly suggested that they each only work on the computer when the other one was on the phone, or not home. "Excellent," Mrs. Kaufmann said, and looked at Veli.

"Okay," she admitted. "But what if I have to stay after school, do I get all that time back on the computer to do my homework, when I get home?" Veli asked, knowing she would be with Nick four days a week, starting the next day.

"Anya, does that sound fair?" Mrs. Kaufmann asked. "That would mean you'd need to get your homework done on the computer after school on the days Veli comes home later and will need it."

Anya agreed. She and Veli both looked pleased. "See how cooperation works? Both of you have agreed to limit the use of space, and the computer, and the phone, to make it work. And you both get plenty of time everywhere to meet your needs. Now the important thing will be for you both to honor your agreement. Can you do that?"

Both girls smiled and agreed. It was a good mediation, and there seemed to be a settled feeling between them. "Anya, why don't we get you back to music class so your sister can have a chance to eat lunch before her student arrives?" Then the school counselor filled out a pass and handed it to Anya.

As Anya hurried out the door, she called out, "Thanks, Veli and Mrs. Kaufmann!"

The Deal Completed

Veli was devouring her sandwich, as Mrs. Kaufmann explained how the Peer Tutoring process worked. "You need to be on time, and help him get his homework organized. Then see if he brought everything he needed to do the work. I have a copy of his math text and his outside reading novel for you to borrow. You will need to start with the math first, because that's his weakest subject. Be patient. Listen to him explain to you what he believes he's supposed to be doing. That way, you can check for understanding, and you can hear his mental calculations to see if they are right. Whatever you do, make sure you congratulate him when he succeeds, and support him with compliments for trying when he doesn't succeed. He won't want to work with you if he feels like a failure. He really needs positive reinforcement, every baby step, until he has caught up. Does that make sense?" Mrs. Kaufmann asked.

"Yes, I can do that. I teach the kids I babysit how to play their board games, and I am very patient with them."

"That's great! Then, the next thing you'll want to do is get him started with his chapter of reading each day. That's where he really falls behind, and I think he'll feel good if he can get that done. At first, ask him to tell you what he read, every couple of pages, just to make sure he has paid attention. Then, let him go longer periods. Or, if he's finding it hard to concentrate, you might even want to go sit in the corner of the library, on the floor, and take turns reading softly out loud. He might really like that, but only in the beginning of the chapter to get him hooked into the story. Then he has to learn the self-discipline that reading requires."

Veli finished her sandwich and drank her milk as Mrs. Kaufmann finished the briefing. They both turned to see who knocked at the door, as Nick appeared.

"Hi, Nick! We were just talking about the tutoring. Come on in. Veli, this is Nick Armanti. And Nick, this is your Peer Tutor, Veli Yotranka. She is very comfortable with math and reading, so she will be able to help you with anything you are assigned for homework," Mrs. Kaufmann said, knowing she needed to get them talking. The two students both seemed a little shy, so she started them off.

"So Veli, where do you think you and Nick would have the most privacy in the library, to talk softly, and yet not disturb the others?" she asked.

Veli looked at Nick and said to him, "Do you think we should sit all the way over by the water fountain near the door?" she suggested.

Nick looked pleased to be consulted. "Okay," he said very cooperatively.

Mrs. Kaufmann then asked Nick to show her where in the text they were working right then in math class, and what he had just done for homework. Veli was looking on while he flipped through the pages. He came to the multiplication page and showed them. "This was hard last night, and I got a few wrong," he said, a little embarrassed.

"That's not a problem. In fact, it's a good thing," Mrs. Kaufmann said, very matter-of-factly. "Veli can look over the ones you got wrong first to see if you're having trouble with your multiplication facts, or with the multiplication process. This is good. She can help you troubleshoot and get you back on track—right, Veli?" Mrs. Kaufmann asked.

"Oh, yes, I had trouble with these big problems, too, when I was in your grade. We can even do some flash cards if you want, Nick," Veli offered.

Nick lit up, and not because he liked memorizing his multiplication facts. He was feeling important to this girl. It was nice to have someone pay attention to him and want to help him. *This is going to work*, Mrs. Kaufmann thought.

"Okay, then, we're all set. Tomorrow morning, Nick, you'll be coming to Guitar Club, and tomorrow afternoon, you and Veli will meet in the library, after school, to get homework done. Great plan!" Mrs. Kaufmann said energetically.

Nick and Veli looked happy, too. "Let's get you back to music class, Nick. And don't forget to get your weekend homework done on Fridays, when Veli won't be there, okay? Your guitar lessons depend on it!" She smiled, and so did Nick.

He took off down the hall with an extra skip in his step every now and then. Veli threw out her lunch trash and started to get her books together to go outside for recess for the last few minutes. "How do you feel it all went?" Mrs. Kaufmann asked.

"With my sister or Nick?"

"Both," Mrs. Kaufmann answered.

"I like our deal for home, and I'm really excited about the tutoring. I think I'm really going to like it."

"Excellent! You've done a wonderful job today, I might add. I'm very proud of you. You will be a patient tutor and a patient big sister!"

"Thanks!" Veli said, as she left the office. "That's me, Miss Patience!"

Mrs. Kaufmann couldn't wait to do a quick check back with them all on Wednesday. She had a good feeling about it all.

That Wednesday morning, Mrs. Kaufmann went to the front door of the school where the students collected to wait for the bell. She mingled with some of the students in her Peer Leader group, which was a good reason to be talking with them. As Veli and Anya arrived, she went over to them to talk about the Peer Tutoring session Veli had had the day before.

"How did it go?" Mrs. Kaufmann asked Veli.

Anya misunderstood and blurted out, "We didn't have one fight. Veli didn't even come home, so I got all my work done before Mom and Veli got home for dinner. It was awesome!"

Veli laughed. "Mrs. Kaufmann was talking to me about the tutoring, Anya!"

"Oops. Sorry," Anya said, embarrassed.

Mrs. Kaufmann immediately made her feel better about it. "Oh, that was happy news. Don't feel bad about that!" she said supportively.

Veli continued talking to Mrs. Kaufmann. "Yeah, that actually worked out really well. I had all the computer time I needed after dinner and didn't get on the phone much after that. I really liked helping Nick a lot. He doesn't know his facts at all, so we made flash cards and practiced after his homework was done. He has trouble reading, too, so I can see why he doesn't like it. I tried to make it fun, and I even read to him a little. He liked that, and I can't wait to go back today."

"This all sounds terrific. Did you or Nick have any trouble with your mothers picking you up?"

"Actually, our moms came about the same time, so that was good, too, because they met each other when they met the teacher," Veli explained.

"We certainly made some good deals yesterday, didn't we?" Mrs. Kaufmann asked.

The Yotranka sisters smiled the same way at the same time.

Mrs. Kaufmann wished them a great day and went back inside to go to Nick's math teacher's classroom. She saw him in the front of the room writing the day's homework on the board. "Hi, Mr. Damon, how are you this morning?"

"Just fine, Mrs. Kaufmann. What's up?"

"I just want to stay on top of Nick Armanti's math grade this marking period. I also want you to know he is going to the After-School Program every day and has a Peer Tutor helping him Monday through Thursday. It started yesterday, so I will be interested in how his first week goes, especially Monday morning, when he will have been on his own."

"That's great news. That little guy really needed some support. He was falling further and further behind as the year was going, and lunchtime detentions had no effect at all. Do you think it will last?"

"Well, he has guitar lessons at stake, so that will be motivation to get him started. I hope he can feel caught up and successful after a while, so it can then become habit and feel good. I also think if his older brother gets some help, there will be less chaos in the house. At least Nick gets to stay out of that chaos a couple of mornings a week, and every day after school. That's my plan, anyway. Let's hope it works."

"Sounds like a good plan," Mr. Damon agreed.

"Have a great day, and keep me informed, okay?" Mrs. Kaufmann asked.

"Sure will," he answered.

I really do have a good feeling about Nick now, Mrs. Kaufmann thought, as she went back to her office to get the messages that would start her new day.

Discussion Points:

- When children have to deal with tough problems at home, sisters and brothers can become the bigger problem. Older children can take out their anger and frustration too easily on their younger siblings. And younger children can become very annoying and uncooperative to the older ones.

- Once a student gets behind in his or her work at school, the gap itself makes it seem too hard to catch up. Then, just being willing to get the work done may not be enough. Losing information can sometimes make it too hard to understand what needs to be done.

- Looking for something positive in your life can sometimes be just the right incentive to turn around a feeling of sadness or depression.

Reflection Questions:

1. When you get behind in your work, what do you do to make it up? If you have missed what you need to know to do the make-up work, how do you tell your parent or teacher what you need?

2. What person would you tell if you asked an older brother or sister to stop treating you badly and he or she didn't stop? If they continue anyway, how do you handle it? What can you stop doing to them that might be causing their bad behavior to you?

3. When a younger sister or brother is really bothering you, how do you handle him or her, tactfully or aggressively? What else can you do if they still won't stop? What are some ways you can remove yourself from them to end the problem?

CHAPTER 20:
I Want to Run Away From Home!

Larry's Suspension

Hillstown Middle School's principal, Mr. Gonzalez, stopped in to see the school counselor. He knocked on her door, and, as he saw her alone and reading her e-mail, he came in and sat down in front of her desk.

"Mrs. Kaufmann, I need you to see Larry Feinberg tomorrow morning, if you are free. He is on out-of-school suspension today for talking back and running away from one of the crossing guards, Mrs. Stiles, this morning. The problem is that he still thinks he was right, because she spoke quite sternly to him, and that set him off. His mother was forced to take a day off from work today, which she really can't afford, and his father said he'll bring him in tomorrow morning, for my re-entry meeting with Larry. It took a few back-and-forth phone calls between the parents just to arrange that much. I can't imagine how they handle their three children's daily activities. Anyway, I'd also like you there at that meeting."

"Sure. I can be available first thing. I've met his father at an Open House a couple of years ago when his older brother, Kyle, first started school here. His father is a big, stern kind of guy. I think he's a policeman. I'm sure he's not happy about the time off, either," Mrs. Kaufmann replied.

"No, he's not happy, but not because he's missing work. He works the late-night shift and will be just getting home, tired and ready for bed. He sounded like he had absolutely no patience for Larry's nonsense, yet again," Mr. Gonzalez explained.

"Oh, boy, that doesn't sound good. I've been in contact with his mother and his father separately over the years and know they have quite opposite parenting styles. They had a nasty divorce a couple of years ago and are still have difficulty communicating, so there was a lot of blame to go around, especially from the father. It's an interesting dynamic, but I can see how Larry would have a tough time with all of this, on top of his ADHD and special classes. He has a lot of anger for his father, too, so that isn't good. Plus his teacher told me just last week that she has been noticing him getting into a lot of arguments with the other kids in his class recently," Mrs. Kaufmann added.

"That's interesting, because Mrs. Tanner, the playground aide, brought him in the other day from the playground, saying Larry needed to cool down and sit out for the rest of recess. She thought he had been teased into pushing another boy to the ground. She knew with Larry's hot-headed reactions a fight could start, so she broke them up. The other boy said his required apology and went away, but Larry still wanted to punch him. She said he remained so fired-up that she had to keep talking him down from his anger. She finally decided he was his own worst enemy and brought him in to the office to sit out for the rest of his playground time and cool off. That's when he became angrier. He thought he was getting punished, but the other kid got to stay out on the playground. I heard he was sitting out in the office area, but I decided not to give him a suspension for fighting on the playground. I gave him a break instead. I told my secretary

I wasn't calling him into my office to see him. She was to just tell him he got lucky today, to let it go and get back to class when the recess bell rang. She has a soft spot in her heart for our special kids. She knows they seem to keep getting themselves into trouble, so she was happy to do that."

"I know. I like Larry, too. He hasn't had it easy with his immature and loud behavior that turns the other students off, the learning disabilities, and his parents' situation. Plus, his older brother is so opposite him. Kyle is a quiet little gentleman and a bit of a worrier. His reputation has always been so glowing from all the students and teachers that Larry feels like the complete loser in the family, mostly for causing all kinds of trouble at school. Then there's the older sister in high school now, who is extremely quiet and still getting perfect grades. I understand she is also perfectly behaved, and still as shy as when she was here in the middle school. Larry's role is the entertaining baby of the family, and he is somewhat excused by his mom because of his disabilities. His brother and sister also have compassion for their baby brother, so he seems to have been given some extra rope at home. Of course, that doesn't fly with his father's ego and strict parenting style. Anyway, Larry really is likeable for his honesty, gullibility, and for wearing his heart on his sleeve. I will be happy to help out tomorrow," Mrs. Kaufmann assured him.

"Great, thanks. I'll let you know if anything changes with the meeting time," Mr. Gonzalez said, as he got up, looked at his watch, and left the office in hurry.

Mrs. Kaufmann went back to the computer to check on Larry's performance record. She found his last state test scores were in the "unacceptable" categories. His grades were almost all C's, even though all of his work was modified to fall within his ability level, so he should have been able to get an A on everything. His attendance record was perfect. He had a write-up in his permanent file from last year, after he was officially discussed at the Intervention and Referral Services meeting. The issue was his behavior on the bus and playground. The decision of the committee was to take away those two privileges for a while, putting pressure on the parents to drive him to and from school. This enraged his father, stressed his mother who also had a new job, and increased the tension in the home. There was also a recommendation that the family go to counseling, which wasn't affordable at that time. Mrs. Kaufmann wondered if they had ever ended up going. She decided to call Larry's mom, knowing she was home today with Larry. Besides, it would help brace her for the meeting the next morning with the angry father.

"Mrs. Feinberg?" Mrs. Kaufmann asked when a woman's voice answered.

"Yes, and who's calling?" she replied.

"It's Mrs. Kaufmann. How's it going with Larry home today? I just heard."

"Oh, hi Mrs. Kaufmann, I'm so happy you called. You know my Larry. He has a strong sense of justice or fairness, mixed with his immaturity and ADHD and you get…Larry!" she said with a frustrated laugh.

"I know. He's a real special little guy," Mrs. Kaufmann said compassionately.

"Not everyone thinks that's so special. Today his father has had it with him, and I'm afraid that won't come to anything good tomorrow. I'm just picturing how angry his dad will be when he comes to get him to bring him in to see Mr. Gonzalez. Larry is already so mad at his father for grounding him for saying something flip when he visited the other weekend. You know how he has a hard time not saying what comes into his head."

"I do. And it's so hard to teach impulse control. His attention deficit hyperactivity disorder makes it really difficult for him all around. Has his father ever understood what ADHD is? I know Larry still has to stay within the expected social rules, but having both parents understand him would make it a whole lot easier," Mrs. Kaufmann replied.

"I tried. When he was first diagnosed, his father believed it was just a made-up name for a condition that he himself has, and no one ever named or excused it. He knows he had to overcome it, so he doesn't have a lot of patience for Larry. And, one of the reasons we never got along was the way we see things, and therefore the way we parent. He always said I was too soft on Larry, and that I was making a soft boy out of him, and he wouldn't have that," Mrs. Feinberg shared.

"I remember you telling me that before. That is too bad. Larry will certainly have to adapt to the two different reactions as to how he ticks. I guess that will be one of the lessons he will learn in life. Not all people think alike. He will get to be comfortable with his mother and his siblings, but he will have to be more on guard when he's with his father, and out in the world. Two different places, with two different expectations," she concluded.

"Thank you for that," Mrs. Feinberg responded. "That actually makes it easier for me to let go of my need to control his father's behavior. I can't, anyway. I keep thinking I need to come to Larry's defense, so his father will back off. Your words make me realize it will be just that for Larry…a lesson in life. Thanks."

"Well, that's how I've come to see the world. I just accept all people as fellow travelers moving along their own road of experiences, good and bad, and learning from them all. At every point in the road, we can stop and see how we are turning out as a result of what we've been given along our pathway. We then can decide what we want to do with that information. I know now to appreciate my whole past, because it gave me such great gifts of understanding, or wisdom if you will. I can choose to use it all to help others. Then they can see they are empowered by free will, to give back to the world their gifts of insights. Larry will do that someday, too. His will be his own special package of insights he gets from being your son, as well as from being his father's, too," Mrs. Kaufmann shared.

"Wow, that really gives me peace. I guess all I have to do is be myself, then, and let him do the same," Mrs. Feinberg concluded.

Mrs. Kaufmann laughed and said, "Who else could we be, anyway?"

"So true. Well, today my little guy is trying to get all of the work done that he thinks was piled on him as punishment. He only has to do the classwork he's missing, and the homework, plus one paragraph. He was told by Mr. Gonzalez that he has to write a letter of apology to the crossing guard. I'm treating the punishment seriously, but he won't. He still thinks she was wrong, so he shouldn't have to say he was sorry. It's almost funny, though, to hear his protesting to the mirror in his room. Plus, he hates to write, just to add insult to the whole thing. Poor Larry," Mrs. Feinberg said sympathetically.

"That is the lesson this time. Sometimes we have to do things we don't want to do, like it or not. I can just picture him pacing and talking out loud, angry as a hornet. Do you think he will be humble at all tomorrow morning, when he has to speak to the crossing guard in Mr. Gonzalez's office? I'm a little worried that he hasn't learned the respect that is expected for authorities, whether they seem to deserve it or not," Mrs. Kaufmann commented.

"I was hoping this time would be it, but I can't promise anything. He said the crossing guard said something about him riding his bike recklessly in the middle of the road, like a crazy person. He didn't like being called a crazy person, so he decided not to listen to her. Then, when she told him to get off his bike and come over to her, he refused and pedaled away as fast as he could. Talk about mad! That guard went wild in the office, I understand from the secretary," Mrs. Feinberg told Mrs. Kaufmann.

"Oh, dear, does Larry have to ride his bike by her to get to school every day?" Mrs. Kaufmann asked.

"I'm afraid so, because he lost his bus privileges last week for the whole month for talking back to the bus driver. That's why I was hoping he would get past his self-righteous anger and see he had been disrespectful to authority. The guard was not professional, but she was in charge, and Larry has to follow her safety orders. She did have a right to report him."

"Okay, then, this will be one time his father's toughness may be exactly what he'll need for that meeting. Larry needs to think he doesn't have any wiggle room for further disrespect in that serious, formal meeting. It's actually a good thing for Larry, not a bad one. The law is the law, the school rules are the rules.

And truly, I can picture him showing off, riding dangerously on his bike, down the center line. He loves to be the clown, and this kind of performance could get him hurt in the future. It's a good lesson after all… just a hard one," Mrs. Kaufmann assured her.

"That's so true. Thanks for that. He's in there now protesting out loud that he got suspended, and the crossing guard got to be mean and didn't lose her job. That's where Larry is at the moment. Just like last week, another boy on the playground teased him for his buzz haircut until Larry couldn't take it anymore. Then, when Larry pushed him to get him out of his face, he thinks he lost his recess time just for that, and not all the threats he actually was making. He thinks the other kid just got to say he was sorry and walk away free. Larry doesn't get that all of his protesting and angry reactions are what is getting him into trouble, and he won't listen to me today. But, as you suggested, I'm letting go and allowing his lesson," Mrs. Feinberg said with a little amusement. "I just have to keep working today from home, so I don't lose my job."

"Okay, I'll let you get back to work, and I'll get back to mine. It was really good to talk to you again, and good luck with Larry. Hopefully he'll be subdued by morning. I can't wait to read his apology, too. Talk to you soon," Mrs. Kaufmann added.

"Yes, it is always a pleasure. And I'm looking forward to reading it as well. Take care," Mrs. Feinberg said, as the two women hung up.

The next morning was cloudy and dark, and just beginning to rain as she got to school. Mrs. Kaufmann noticed that those pre-storm mornings with low barometric pressure seemed to make people sleepy, run late, and feel sluggish throughout the mornings. They also made people cranky as the day went on. The morning slowness would work for Larry if it would reduce the energy typically aroused in him by his sense of injustice. The meeting might just go smoothly after all.

Mrs. Kaufmann was coming from her office toward the main office, just as Mr. Feinberg and Larry were coming into the front door of the school. They ran right into each other and said their good mornings. Larry looked tired and unhappy, and walked obediently behind his father. Mr. Feinberg looked annoyed and very business-like. They all entered the main office to sit in the waiting area together. They were asked to wait for Mr. Gonzalez to come out to invite them into his office. The secretary said he had just texted Mrs. Stiles, the crossing guard, asking her to join them after her duty was over.

Mrs. Kaufmann felt the tension between father and son very strongly. She made some small talk about the impending storm, and Larry didn't speak at all. Mr. Feinberg made a comment about going home and going to bed, figuring the storm would all be over by the time he went back out for his midnight shift.

Mr. Gonzalez then came out of his office, extending his hand to Mr. Feinberg and saying good morning to him and Larry and Mrs. Kaufmann. "I'm glad we are all here together to discuss what happened yesterday morning, and the seriousness of this infraction. Larry, did you write your apology?" he asked immediately.

Larry sat up straight and said, "Yes, I did. Do you want it now?" He started to fish around in his totally messy backpack, with crumpled papers all falling out. As Larry pulled his hand back out, he was clutching the letter.

"Yes. I'd like to read it before we give it to the crossing guard. She will be here once all the students are off the street," Mr. Gonzalez said very sternly.

"Here," Larry said, handing the letter to the principal and looking respectful but tired.

Mr. Feinberg interrupted, "Larry, what do you have to say to Mr. Gonzalez?"

"I'm sorry, sir," Larry said, sounding obviously rehearsed with his father, since the word "sir" was not one he normally used.

Mr. Feinberg then looked at Mr. Gonzalez and Mrs. Kaufmann and said, "I'm sorry to have inconvenienced you both, too. This will not happen again, right, Larry?"

Larry dropped his eyes and nodded his head yes.

"Look at us when you speak to us, and please answer so you can be heard." Larry's father spoke with no patience at all.

"Yes, I mean, no, it won't happen again," Larry spoke up, responding quickly to his father's command.

"Well, that's good to hear, Larry," Mr. Gonzalez said, in a tone that was lightening up somewhat. "Let's see what you wrote to the crossing guard." He read out loud: 'Dear Mrs. Crossing Guard. I am sorry for not listening to you and riding my bike to get away from you. Larry.' Mr. Gonzalez smiled, and handing it back to Larry, said, "This will do. It's short and to the point, and I'm giving it back to you so you can hand it to her yourself."

"Thank you," Larry said, not knowing what else to say at that point.

Mr. Gonzalez continued, "Larry, do you understand why this was such a serious thing you did? Why breaking rules or laws on the roadways can be dangerous? It's also important that you understand that you have to obey the guards and policemen that are hired to enforce the laws and keep us all safe. Do you get that now?"

Larry just said, "Yes, sir."

Mr. Gonzalez then directed his next comment to Mrs. Kaufmann. "I have to ask you, Mrs. Kaufmann, if you will meet with Larry when we're done here, so you can help him with some anger management. I understand Larry has reacted with anger recently in a way that has received attention from his teachers, the playground aides, and now the crossing guard. I believe he could learn some strategies from you that will help him stay out of trouble around here."

"I'll be happy to," Mrs. Kaufmann said, and then she gave Larry a smile. "We will meet today, and then maybe a couple more times to follow that up. Sometimes we just need to practice, and I'll be glad to share his progress with both of you and his mom."

Just as she finished speaking, the secretary appeared in the doorway to say Mrs. Stiles had arrived. Mr. Gonzalez told her to bring her in and got up from his chair. "Larry, please stand up," he said as he went to the door to greet her. "Come on in, please," he said to her and then introduced everyone to one another. "Larry, do you have something for her?"

Larry looked at her with respect, and, while handing her his letter, he said, "I'm sorry."

The crossing guard nodded, but didn't say anything except "thank you." She looked uncomfortable having walked into a meeting already in session and appeared to want to leave the room. She looked at the crumpled piece of paper, read it quickly, and then looked back up at Larry with a nod and a smile. Larry smiled nervously back.

Mr. Feinberg immediately assured her that it wouldn't happen again, and she nodded and left the office.

Mr. Gonzalez then put an end to the meeting by asking Larry if he had done all the classwork and homework and had it all with him to turn in. Larry told him he had, and began to go into his backpack to show him. "Larry, there is one more thing. I want that backpack cleaned out by tomorrow. Now, let's put this incident behind us. You have learned an important lesson, and that's what school is all about. Let's have a good day today."

Mrs. Kaufmann and Mr. Feinberg both stood up and shook hands. She turned to Mr. Gonzalez and said, "Is it all right if Larry and I go to my office now?"

"Yes, and Mr. Feinberg, thank you for coming in. I know it was hard for you to make this appointment.

I believe we give a strong message to our children when they see we take these suspensions quite seriously and go out of our way to make that clear."

Mrs. Kaufmann looked at Larry and said, "Okay, my friend, let me give you some tips on controlling that anger of yours," and she motioned him to follow her. He picked up his backpack and scurried out the door behind her, through the main office and out into the hall. She noticed that neither Larry nor his father made any effort to say goodbye, or wish each other a good day, much less a father-son hug. Their relationship was not in its best place right now.

"Have a good day, Mr. Feinberg--or should I say a good day's sleep?"

He answered, "Yeah, I am beat." He shook Mr. Gonzalez's hand and went out the office doors, passing Larry and not looking back. It bothered Mrs. Kaufmann, and she knew it had to bother Larry.

She and Larry both started walking briskly down the hall toward her office, with Larry's disposition looking happy and relieved, like an escaped convict. "How was yesterday?" Mrs. Kaufmann asked, knowing he would complain, but that's where she had to start with him. Larry moaned and started talking a hundred miles an hour.

Larry's Story

"Yesterday was no fun at all. I thought a day out of school would be okay once my work was done, but my mom was so upset having to lose a day of work because of my suspension, that I wasn't allowed to watch TV or play on the computer. It was an awful day!" Larry freely complained to Mrs. Kaufmann, as he was used to doing.

"I usually tell you that I feel bad for you when you've had a hard time or are unhappy, but this time it feels like that was what it was supposed to be…you know, no pain, no gain?" she said, smiling, so he didn't feel like she had ganged up against him, too.

"I know, but it was so bad. Then this morning when my mom dropped me off at my dad's house, my stepmother was annoyed because I woke the baby up ringing the doorbell. And my dad was so angry anyway because he had just gotten home from work and had to go to the principal's office. He's always angry, but this time he really yelled at me louder than usual. He said I can't use his computer when I go there this weekend. That's going to be horrible, since there isn't anything else to do there, especially now that they have a new baby."

"I thought your dad signed you up to play in a community baseball league around his house on Saturdays."

"He did, and then he took me off when he said I wasn't doing what he told me to do. He used to yell at me during the games, to focus, and stand still, and stuff like that while I was standing in the outfield. It was so embarrassing. Then if I had strikes when I was up at bat, he yelled at me from the bleachers some more. I'm really glad I don't have to do that anymore," he shared.

"What do your brother and sister do when you all go to your dad's together on his weekends? I didn't think your brother liked sports," Mrs. Kaufmann said.

"He doesn't, and I think it's because of what Dad did to him when he first tried. Now he just says he doesn't want to, and he works on projects he brings with him. Once he brought a model of a ship to build, but it fell apart while we were gone. When we came back two weeks later, he found it broken on the card table. Our stepmom said the cat jumped on the table, and she felt bad."

"How about your sister, what does she do there?" Mrs. Kaufmann asked again.

"My sister plays with the baby now, and she likes it. She even wants to go there. I usually play computer games, and now that I can't, I don't want to go. Last weekend I told my mom I didn't want to go, and she said I had to. It was his turn to have us, and the court said so. I hate that. My dad puts me down all the time, and I can't talk back."

"What else does your dad like to do on weekends when he isn't working or sleeping? Does he ever go fishing, or does he play card games?" she pursued.

"Maybe fishing, but the weather has to be really good, and he says he doesn't play games," Larry added. "He usually just watches television and says he's tired."

"I'd like to think about this and see if we can come up with something for this coming weekend. I think you both might be able to enjoy something together. I'll try to think of activities that will help relax the tension or anger you feel when you're there. What else gets you angry these days?" she asked him.

"The kids know they can make me mad just by teasing me about anything, so they do that, just to laugh. That makes me so mad, because they think it's funny that they can do that," he answered, with tears filling his eyes.

"I'm sure that hurts. I think they are feeling power, power to control another person. Remember your sister's dolls that had a pull string? You'd pull the string to make it talk? Well, these kids pull your string to make you mad. You've become their predictable toy. I think they only pick on you because you react the same way every time. If you were to shrug them off, like an annoying mosquito, they couldn't affect you, and it wouldn't be their game anymore. It would be as if your string or talking tape broke. So, I think we need you to practice not letting them control you. We need *you* to control you. Let's start with that today, since we still have a couple of days before the weekend to research common interests for you and your dad. All right then, what are the things they tease you about?" she asked.

"I just got a buzz cut, and they teased me about it, and that made them all laugh at me."

"What is wrong with a buzz cut? I guess I don't get it. Do any of them have one?" Mrs. Kaufmann challenged him. "It's like laughing at you for having brown eyes. So what? What's wrong with a buzz, and what's wrong with brown?" she pointed out.

"Nothing, but when they point and say it over and over, it makes me crazy," he said, with the tears coming again.

"That would really get to me, too, especially because of the chanting. Okay, just picture this...what if you stood there and looked right at the one doing the teasing, and shook your head like they sounded ridiculous, and continued on your way. Continue walking to play wall ball and strike up a conversation with another friend, as if the teasing kids were not even there. Totally ignore them by treating them as if they had absolutely no power whatsoever and were making themselves look silly. We may have to make sure you are near a real friend when you go outside, so you have someone to talk to as you're ignoring them. That way you will have reduced them to powerlessness. Teasing you would feel like a waste of time for them after a while. Would you like to do that?" she asked.

"I don't know if I can. Sometimes I just suddenly feel so mad I want to explode, and I do something faster than I can think to stop myself. How do I control my temper, if I can't control '*the me*' that's supposed to control it?" he asked sincerely.

"Here's what works for a lot of students. First, you change the way you see them. Think about how your brother looks at things. Picture him out on playground, and some of these kids are teasing him about his haircut. He's older, so he would see them as goofy and laugh a little inside his head. He wouldn't even think the boys were trying to make him feel embarrassed. That way he wouldn't give them power. He'd just look at them somewhat entertained and feeling completely comfortable with himself," she pointed out.

"I've discovered that when I look at people's behaviors and think about *why* they do what they do, I don't take it personally. It's like I'm making an observation in a study of human behavior. I almost always see that people do unpleasant things to others when they aren't happy with themselves. Notice your brother doesn't do mean things to you or anyone else. He doesn't have any reason to do that. Somehow he just sees people as needy, and feels bad for them. The amazing thing is your brother gets so much respect for being above the nonsense and for being mature. Now, there isn't anyone who would dare to make fun of him without risking looking foolish. Quiet and above it, that's what works."

Mrs. Kaufmann kept driving her point home. "Let's talk about the time it happened recently. How many boys actually said anything? Usually there's only one, and the others laugh along. Is it always the same one when it happens?" she asked.

"Yeah, usually, it's Davey Shallice. He does it to me on the bus, too, and whenever he's with his friends and no adult is around," Larry told her.

Mrs. Kaufmann said, "I generally call in the bully and tell him to stop it, but that would only stop that one person, maybe, or just make him so angry with you that he tries to hide it better. The best thing I can do is to teach you how to think about it. If you can treat teasers as if *they* have problems, and act like you are above it, then they will eventually stop. Truly ignoring them is a tool that removes their power. It's mature and effective, and then you don't get that anger from feeling helpless."

Mrs. Kaufmann continued, "And if you see them as not in control and see them as *needing to look cool*, like little five-year-olds sometimes are, it helps you to feel *in control*. Think you can try it?" she asked. "Can you see Davey as a real little boy looking for attention, because he can't find it by doing something good? Think of his friends as other younger boys pretending they agree with their 'cool-looking' little leader by laughing along with him. They may be afraid Davey will turn around and laugh at them, so they have to stay loyal and laugh at his jokes. That's the right thing to do, in their minds, because they are more worried about themselves than you. So, they are needy, too. Remember you just said that they all laughed at you? Actually they all laughed at Davey's joke, not at you. There isn't anything to laugh at with a buzz cut. Would you laugh at all our Marines with their buzz cuts? Of course not. That's what I mean about Davey. He's just looking to have some power somewhere, and he predicted he could have it over you. He pulled your string and got you to react. It made him feel powerful and got a few laughs, which made him feel like he was funny, too."

Larry sat quietly for a minute while it began to sink in. "Okay, I need to see them all as not okay with themselves and needy and little. Then I just don't say or do anything at all while they laugh? I act like those real little kids look like they are playing all cool and look silly, and I totally ignore them?" Larry summarized.

"Yes!" Mrs. Kaufmann declared. "Treat them the way your brother treats people that aren't okay or very young. He's doing what parents and teachers tell you to do, just ignore them. I know that isn't easy, so that's why changing your thinking about them has to come first, so that you *can* ignore them. Let's take Davey, for example. Does he always talk real loud and put people down and make fun of everyone?" she asked.

"Yes, he does. Everyone laughs at him, and he loves that!" he replied.

"That tells me he's looking for an audience to get approval… to make sure everyone thinks he's funny or witty. He *needs* to check to make sure that *they* think he's okay. That tells me *he* doesn't believe it. Notice your brother doesn't have to throw comments at other kids, like darts, to see if he can draw a crowd and entertain them. He just doesn't need it. Notice the word 'need'? That's why the teasers love it when they can get power over someone. They 'need' to have that power or response from others to assure *themselves* they are in control. That's how they can convince themselves they are important or special, or whatever it is that they need. We just have to remember not to react. Then their jokes go out having no power to make you do anything. Their attempts go flat and aren't funny. How embarrassing is that to them? They'll have to stop, if they're made to feel like their jokes failed. They will look powerless, and that will feel awful inside of them. That's when you have succeeded. You looked cool, and they looked ridiculous!"

"That would be so awesome! I have to try that next time. I almost want someone to tease me now, so I can look cool!" he laughed, and then Mrs. Kaufmann laughed with him. It was great to see Larry "get it" and more importantly "like it."

"All right, that's enough for today. I better get you off to class so you can turn in all that work you did yesterday. Please don't forget, my dear. Your teacher will be reporting back to the principal whether you did it or not. And he will call your parents, if he thinks you didn't. Oh, and don't forget to clean out that backpack tonight. You might want to write that down in your assignment pad, so you don't forget. Mr. Gonzalez might check on that tomorrow, too. Do you feel any better about things in general now?" she checked, as she wrote out a hall pass for him.

"I feel better about school. I'm still in trouble at both houses, though. And I'm really not happy about going to my dad's this weekend," he admitted.

"We'll do one thing at a time. Changing the way you think about things requires small steps and practice. Each time you succeed, you feel better about yourself and your power, and it all becomes easier and easier with time. You have a great new tool to use at school, and we'll work on more the next time you come."

"Okay, thanks. Can I come again before I go to my dad's?" he asked.

"Sure. How about the end of the week? Just bring your lunch on Friday, and then you can go out on recess. I don't think you should miss any more classes after yesterday. Maybe by then I will have a brainstorm about some common interests for you and your dad. You think about that, too."

Larry was happy with that plan. He took the pass and scurried out of the office and down the hall to his classroom. Mrs. Kaufmann now needed to think about how to advise him to respond to grown-ups who didn't treat him with respect. That would be more of a challenge, for sure.

A Crisis Hits

Just as Mrs. Kaufmann went to check her voice mail and e-mail that morning after Larry left her office, Stacey Edgar suddenly arrived in her waiting room, late for school and hysterical.

"I hate my mother, and I'm never going home again! I want to run away from home!" she sobbed.

Mrs. Kaufmann jumped up out of her chair, invited her into her office, and shut the door behind her. "Stacey, I'm so sorry this has happened again. I can feel how hurt you are. Sit down, my dear, and tell me how it all started. I want to hear everything."

Mrs. Kaufmann then interrupted herself. "Oh, wait, I must know if you have checked in to your homeroom yet. You know how the attendance officer will see you're absent, and she'll know your mom didn't call to say you'd be absent? That is the flag for her to call home to let your mom know you haven't arrived yet. That will set off a whole chain of events with the principal, and the police, if I don't let the office know you're in school and with me."

"No, I didn't check in. I ran away this morning after my mom and I had a horrible fight. I threw on some clothes and just grabbed my backpack and ran out of the house. I yelled that I would never go back there. I told her that I'd rather live anywhere else, and my mom said, 'Good, I'd rather you live anywhere else, too!' and she went into the bathroom and slammed the door. That's when I took off. I won't go back there, I swear, Mrs. Kaufmann. I don't know where to go, but I think I can stay with a friend for a while." Stacey then broke into heavy sobs again.

"Okay, my dear. I will be happy to help you work through this one. First, like I said, I have to make a call to the office, just to let them know you're here and safe, so they don't send the police to look for you. That would get your mom even more upset, and she would come here. Let me do that first. You can take your jacket off and get comfortable so we can talk. If you didn't have a breakfast, there are some breakfast bars and a couple of juice boxes in that cabinet over the sink. Help yourself. And you might want to wash your face and comb your hair, and take a few deep breaths while I make this call to the main office."

Stacey blew her nose and sniffled while she took her jacket off and went to get something to eat. Her face and her eyes were all red from her crying, and her hair wasn't even combed yet that morning. Mrs. Kaufmann had no doubt in her mind that if she didn't fix things, Stacey would run away by that evening. The relationship she had with her mother was like gasoline and matches, with explosions going off about every other day. And since Stacey got grounded after each one, she seldom got her freedom back anymore at all. She no doubt had reached her limit.

"Hi, Mrs. Tanner, I'm sure you must be ready to make your calls to the moms that forgot to call in to tell you their child is home sick. Let me save you one call. I have Stacey Edgar with me in my office. She and I are talking, and she hasn't made it to her homeroom to check in yet. She isn't absent."

"Thanks, I did have her on my list, so you saved me. Is she okay?" Mrs. Tanner asked out of concern, and then realized it might have been confidential and she shouldn't have asked.

"She will be," Mrs. Kaufmann answered, and then said she needed to get going. They both hung up, and Mrs. Kaufmann saw Stacey eating a breakfast bar, after having combed her hair. "There, you look much better now. I am so sorry you and your mom had another flare-up this morning. That makes it so hard on both of you, and your little brother. What was it about this time?" she asked.

"It just was the same old thing. I asked her if I could stay after school for the basketball game today, because my grounded week was finally up, and she said that I had to come home and watch my brother. I got mad because I can't ever do anything with my friends. I always have to take care of him. That is so not fair. I told her she should be taking care of her own children, or at least paying for a babysitter, so I could have a life. That's when she told me I was such a selfish baby, and that she didn't have a life either, or any money for a sitter. She said I should be glad I had a roof over my head and food on the table and not be such a spoiled brat. That's when I lost it. None of my other friends have to take care of their sisters and brothers after school or on the weekends, and none of them have mothers that call them names. I am not going back there ever, I swear," Stacey said loudly, and then she started sobbing again. "I just hate her!"

"Where does your mom think you are now? Does she think you ran away? I don't want her to call the police to look for you," Mrs. Kaufmann explained.

"I don't know, but she would do that, I'm sure. She would do that just to show me who's boss. She always says that she's the parent and I'm the child, and I'm to do what I'm told without backtalk."

"Okay then. I need to let her know you are in school and safe. I will let her know you are upset and we are talking," Mrs. Kaufmann told Stacey.

"Oh, God, don't do that! She'll come right over to punish me," Stacey begged and cried.

"Listen," Mrs. Kaufmann said. "I will call the school psychologist and the principal to come here with us, if we need to, but I will invite her to come in to talk separately…later. Does your mom ever hit you?" Mrs. Kaufmann needed to be direct.

"No, but she did say her mother used to smack her across the face when she talked back to her. She said that I needed to learn some respect, too. I figured she was going to hit me one of these days, because I always talk back," Stacey admitted.

"I need to call your mom now, and I want you to trust that I will help you, or get help for you, to change this relationship. I do understand you are afraid of the consequences of talking back and taking off this morning, but it will be so much worse if the police are called, believe me. We have a whole day to make this better, and my promise to you is that I will help you," Mrs. Kaufmann assured her as she picked up the phone.

"Mrs. Edgar?" she asked, while Stacey sat stiff in her chair, almost ready to bolt.

"Yes?" Stacey's mom answered.

"This is Mrs. Kaufmann. I'm Stacey's school counselor, and I wanted you to know she's here with me in school and okay. She is upset from the argument she had with you this morning, so I'd like to talk with her a while before I send her to class. I'd also like to talk with you today, too. Is there a time you can come over and see me?" Mrs. Kaufmann asked, as Stacey's eyes grew wide. Mrs. Kaufmann wrote on a piece of paper "Not with you!" and showed it to Stacey. Stacey then relaxed back in her seat, but she stayed attentive to every word.

Mrs. Edgar sounded like she had been crying. "Is she okay? I was so scared and just prayed she'd gone to school. I knew if I didn't hear back from the attendance lady, she was there, and I didn't want to call the school and embarrass her. Then she'd never speak to me again. We had such mean words again. This time I totally lost my temper. It's so hard when you have a strong-willed teenager. Her father is a dead-beat dad, and no one knows where he is. I know that's a source of her anger, and definitely a source of mine. And she is so stubborn, just like me. We are truly bad for each other. Maybe I can apologize to her today when I come?" she asked.

"I'm planning on it. Right now I need to go and talk with her. Can you come at 11:00?" Mrs. Kaufmann asked.

"Yes, that would be great. Thank you," Mrs. Edgar replied.

Mrs. Kaufmann then got off the phone quickly. She needed to make sure Stacey didn't think she was taking her mother's side with too much friendly chatting.

"Okay, now, Stacey, let's talk. I think we have to look into what your buttons are with your mom, and what sets her off with you. I can tell you this, my dear, she loves you. She may not be perfect at parenting, and none of us really are, but she does love you," Mrs. Kaufmann assured Stacey, so she could at least get her wanting to talk. Mrs. Kaufmann continued, "It sounded like she has been crying since you left the house, and that is a long time to be that upset. She told me she was scared to death you didn't make it to school, but she didn't want to call the school and embarrass you. She wants to apologize, too. She obviously loves you but has a lot of anger about your dad. My belief is you do, too. You and your mom have similar strong personalities, and are maybe a little bit stubborn?" Mrs. Kaufmann smiled as she suggested that. Stacey smiled back, knowing Mrs. Kaufmann knew her very well.

Mrs. Kaufmann continued, "If you two are both strong-willed and stubborn, then I am not surprised that the two of you would have a relationship that is tested all the time by the frustrations and difficulties of life. When you both are feeling challenged, then those times have the potential of a big flare-up, like this morning. It was a volcanic eruption, but not a reason to run away. Not really," Mrs. Kaufmann said quite convincingly.

Stacey sat quietly listening to her. She wanted to be right, and she wanted to be justified to run away, but what she was hearing crumbled her case. She knew, though, she still felt so hurt that her mother had said the word "good" when she threatened to live somewhere else. That hurt so badly. "Why did she say that then?" she asked, challenging what Mrs. Kaufmann said.

"For the same reason you said you would never come back…same exact reason. You both raised the stakes to make your point and be right and be strong. That's why she's crying now. She's hurt by you, and ashamed of her lack of self-control. Being a mother doesn't make you have complete control when you're emotional. Mothers just try really hard. You lost it, and your mom lost it. I'd say it's a tie in this battle, except that everybody lost, you know?"

Stacey's eyes filled up again. This time, though, she was crying because she was giving up the battle, and giving in to what she knew she needed to do…make up with her mother. She felt sad and defeated, and lost her sense of self-righteousness. She also began to think clearly and realized there was no place else to go live. She knew she had to go back home. She just felt drained and needed to cry. Mrs. Kaufmann slid the tissue box a little closer to her.

"I know this is a hard morning, but I believe from every big bad situation, comes a big, good lesson. This is the perfect push for both of you to learn how your dynamic works, how you work, what sets you off, and how to contain it. There is a lot of information you will get from this experience, and the same for your mom," Mrs. Kaufmann explained.

"How do we do that?" Stacey asked. "We can't even talk together without eventually exploding."

"We definitely have a challenge here. But remember, it's only a challenge, not an impossibility. You will have to face your fears, that's all. Your mom does, too. You both need to learn to think differently. You also both feel you have your rights, and you are entitled to certain things. That's what increases your need to fight to win, no matter what it costs. It's about what you believe is right and fair. That thinking won't always work for you in this world. It will cost you one relationship after another if you'd always rather be right than get along. You may win arguments, but lose your loved ones. So, your job will be to control that strength of will, and the impulse to explode. You'll need to stop pushing to out-power your opponent when making your point," she explained. "After all, your goal is to get along and live harmoniously together, so that you both have peace and happiness," Mrs. Kaufmann reminded her.

"Stacey, I think you've felt that what you're fighting for is just so important. I understand why you feel strongly about freedom and friends at this age, but the thing is, having a relationship with your mom is even more important. Having time to socialize, or not to have to babysit, should not be a reason to run away and give up on your mom. To declare you want to leave her forever was not in balance with the problem you're both having. Problem-solving is a much better way to go," Mrs. Kaufmann explained.

"Believe me, even an argument and a careless comment is no reason to believe that she would ever give up on you, either," Mrs. Kaufmann assured her. "Those are things people say only when they are fighting, and I think your mom slipped back into her emotional, out-of-control place, like you did. The funny thing is, you both probably understand each other better than anyone else does, because you think and react with a lot of emotion, am I right? You both love each other, or you wouldn't have been able to hurt each other so deeply. Keep that in mind. We can fix this," Mrs. Kaufmann said quietly and then stopped.

"So what do I do now?" Stacey finally spoke after being silent for a while.

"What would you like to do?" Mrs. Kaufmann asked. "Would you like to talk more about this now, or are you tired of the emotional drain and would like to get to some classes as a break? I can assure you that you will have the opportunity later for you and your mom to patch things up."

"Okay, I think I need a break," Stacey admitted. "I definitely need to get to math next period, because we're having a big test. What do my eyes look like from the crying? Are they really red?" she asked.

"No, just a little pinkish. Use that mirror on the back of my door to see for yourself. They do look much better now than they did when you first got here. You and your mom have both done too much crying today," Mrs. Kaufmann said, as Stacey looked in the mirror. "See? They're only a little pink. I call it 'allergy pink' and a lot of people have allergies."

"What about when my mom comes in at 11:00? Do you want me to come back and talk to her?" Stacey offered.

"Yes, but let's not plan it for right at 11:00. Let your mom have some time with me so she can see what you both have to work on, okay? I can call for you after she's had a chance to talk it through. You will both be fine. Nothing is stronger than love, and that is something you both have and can depend on. I told you, we can always fix things."

"Okay, thanks, Mrs. Kaufmann, thanks for your help," Stacey said, as she took the hall pass and grabbed her backpack. "May I leave my jacket here so no one will see that I'm just coming in to school? I don't have the energy to explain. I can get it later when I go to lunch or something."

"Sure, and I'll see you later. Good luck on your math test, and don't worry about a thing. Two good apologies, a good understanding of each other's thinking, and a big hug usually make the bad feelings all dissolve very quickly, you'll see," Mrs. Kaufmann said, as Stacey left her office.

Eleven o'clock came, and Mrs. Kaufmann got a call from the main office. Mrs. Edgar had arrived and she was on her way there. "Okay, yes, thanks, I was expecting her."

Mrs. Edgar appeared in her doorway. "Mrs. Kaufmann, thank you so much for helping Stacey today." Mrs. Edgar came right in and sat down in a hurry, talking the whole time. "She can be so emotional and so stubborn, just like me, that it's scary. I only worry because she goes to all extremes to get her way. I think one of these days she really is going to run away. Her drama really scares me." Mrs. Edgar had tears in her eyes again. "Ever since her father left us, I have been struggling to make ends meet. So, like I said, we both have anger issues, and we react whenever we get frustrated."

"I'm sure she is a handful, as strong-willed as she is. And I also believe she could make good on her word to run away if you two don't change the way you both handle stress together. Sorry to be so blunt, but I just witnessed her will power."

Mrs. Edgar replied, "Don't I know it! She's always been that way, from the time she was a baby. And now that she's a teenager, her demands are constant and so self-centered. She doesn't care what I'm going through. It's all about her, and I've lost my patience."

"I hear you describing a teenager, and a strong-willed one at that. Teenagers don't have a lot of empathy for adults, since they figure we're the grown-ups and we should be able to handle our own problems, you know? And since they have no life experience as an adult, they don't know how we can feel as scared and tired and angry as little kids inside, too. I'm sure it can't be easy being the only grown-up in your home. You must need an outlet yourself, someone you can bounce things off of, or with whom you can problem-solve. You need friends, too, especially moms of other teenage girls who get it," Mrs. Kaufmann suggested. "Our friends remind us we're not alone and sometimes help us laugh at the situation. That can be the best therapy ever!"

"I wish I did have an outlet. I don't have the time to have friends," Mrs. Edgar complained, tearing up again.

"I used to think that, too, until I had a friend who would come over for coffee on Saturday mornings while I did my laundry. She'd stop by on her way to get groceries and we'd talk a while. I would always feel renewed, because someone understood me. That fresh perspective made me see my teenage girls differently, and with more patience. I saw them as just that--teens. It became obvious that their hormones had them in a tailspin, and they lived to be with their friends. We used to laugh that our girls acted possessed, and we were grateful we weren't there anymore ourselves," Mrs. Kaufmann shared.

"I guess I could have this one neighbor over for tea. She keeps asking, and I have brushed her off," Mrs. Edgar offered. "It sure would feel good to laugh again."

Mrs. Kaufmann explained further, "I see Stacey as thinking of her friends as her whole world, so having to stay home is setting her off. Maybe she could babysit her younger brother one night so you can go out to the movies with your friend, and she could earn a night out with her friends," Mrs. Kaufmann suggested.

She continued, "Again, there is a whole lot of old anger about her dad that you both have buried and is festering. I think it's time to clean out that anger and hurt, and start fresh. It's an excellent way to learn about yourself, and a way Stacey can learn about herself, and how to communicate under stress. That's not impossible, you know. People learn how to discuss emotional issues all the time to avoid built-up, violent eruptions. Have you ever thought about counseling? I know it may sound expensive, but if you have insurance, you might discover it's not that bad, especially for the discussion strategies and peace of mind it could give you. There are often programs that are free, like Employee Assistance Programs for employees in some places. You might want to check to see if your company offers one," Mrs. Kaufmann told her.

"I will. That actually sounds familiar. Thanks for the suggestion, I didn't think of that. I'm not sure Stacey will go for that, and I don't need to start yet another battle!" Mrs. Edgar exclaimed.

Mrs. Kaufmann replied, "I believe I can convince her, if you are willing to go. I also think you need this now, whether she goes or not. You have issues to resolve to be at peace yourself. And if you do have an EAP benefit where you work, they often give each person in your family six free sessions for each presenting issue. You could discuss your husband walking out on you, and you could discuss handling an angry teenager, and your teenager can discuss controlling her anger. We're up to eighteen right there!" she responded.

"I personally think you'd both really benefit from even a couple of sessions together. Just think of the gift you would be giving your daughter for a lifetime of relationships! Do you think you could check into that? Otherwise, you're going to continue to co-exist from one explosion to the next, and Stacey will learn only how to blow up and run away from every hurtful person or experience. We really have more options than flight or fight nowadays." Mrs. Kaufmann laughed to lighten the moment.

Mrs. Edgar said, "You certainly are a good saleswoman. I will check on that today. And if you think you can talk Stacey into going too, I'd like to see this!"

"You will," Mrs. Kaufmann smiled. "Are you ready to see her? I know she felt tremendously hurt when you led her to believe you were happy she wanted to leave, not to make you feel bad, but to let you know what her tipping point was. She believed you." Mrs. Kaufmann was reminding Mrs. Edgar she needed to apologize as the grown-up that lost control and said something inappropriate as a mother.

"Oh, I will let her know how sorry I was that I acted so out of control. Now I think I was more like an angry teenager, instead of an in-control mother."

"How about I call her down now? I know she wants to see you and fix this, too," Mrs. Kaufmann said, as she picked up the phone to call Stacey's classroom teacher.

"Mr. Lambert? I need to see Stacey Edgar. Her mother is here and I need to get them together. Would you please slip her a note to come to my office so that no one notices? This is confidential and we need to be discreet," she added.

"No problem. I'll do that right now," he answered.

"Thanks," she said as she hung up the phone and turned to Mrs. Edgar. "She should be here in just a minute."

The Fix

Stacey became visible in the outer waiting room, but her body language said she was reluctant to come in. She said nothing as she stood there staring directly at Mrs. Kaufmann. Mrs. Kaufmann spotted her and got right up to greet her, and to talk to her first. "Hi, my dear, your mom is here, and we are already past the morning argument and into making sure it won't happen again. So come on in and help us find some really workable solutions. Your input is very important here, because you both need to be on the same page. From what I've heard from you both, you are. So come on in, and let's get to work, okay?" Mrs. Kaufmann knew they would need to back up briefly to put their emotional closure to their early morning words and actions. Her intention, though, was to take away that hurdle in order to get Stacey comfortable enough to come into the room with a good attitude. She also needed to know that the issue at hand was one of growth, not a debate as to who was more right.

Stacey came in as her mother stood up and walked right toward her to hug her. She said in her ear how sorry she was for saying what she did. "Sweetheart, I love you, and I would never ever want you to move out, ever. I lost my cool and acted badly – like a little kid. I'm so sorry." She hugged her tightly.

Stacey started to cry, wrapped her arms tightly around her mother, and said, "I'm sorry too, Mom. I know I mouthed off and pushed you again. I ran away because I was hurt, not mad. I thought you didn't want me anymore, and you didn't love me because I was being so selfish."

Her mother said, "You are my little girl, and I'll always love you no matter how unlikeably you behave! Remember the time you threw your soup at me when you were little because I wouldn't give you dessert first? I loved you then, I love you now, and I'll love you forever – soup or no soup." Stacey and her mom both laughed through their tears.

Mrs. Kaufmann had been quiet to allow the closure. She now had two people willing to go forward. "How about we look at what we can do before these old, hot issues come up again and set off that complex mother-daughter spark?" she suggested.

"I think we need to clear out the old issues with some discussion today, and then I believe each of you really needs to look at what's going on inside your hearts…the stuff that's really framing your thinking and motivating your actions. Give yourself the gift of dealing with and cleaning out your stored resentments or hurt feelings. Truly let them go with understanding and forgiveness. The past is so done and doesn't have to be lugged around like heavy baggage that only hurts you again and again. It's the negative thoughts and fears that fuel your anger. That will happen to you both, whether you're together or not. It will happen with bosses, and co-workers, and friends, and boyfriends, and neighbors. Letting go is the perfect purge, and it will give you such peace. A few sessions of learning and discovering for each of you alone, with a counselor, and then a couple sessions together, might turn everything around for you two. Sound good?" she asked them both.

"How could we say no to that--right, Stacey?" Mrs. Edgar quickly jumped in to add to the momentum.

Mrs. Kaufmann knew Stacey wasn't sold yet. "Stacey, I can see your wheels spinning and assume you may have some reluctance. What's your concern?" Mrs. Kaufmann said directly.

"Who would I be talking to, and will she tell people what I say?" she asked.

"Whatever counselor you get is sworn to secrecy, unless of course you are about to hurt yourself or someone else. He or she will listen skillfully for ways to help show you how your thinking affects your behavior. You will learn so much about the way you tick that it will actually be interesting. I love to remind myself of my made-up limitations and motivations when I'm stressed. Being out of my ego feels so genuine and is so freeing. You will feel lighter, less angry, and you won't need to engage in any drama. It will, however, take a little practice. The best part is that it will diffuse that volcanic build-up you've been getting recently."

Mrs. Kaufmann continued, "You will still have feelings about things, but you will be aware of why, and your extreme reactions will begin to change. Once you see the bigger picture, you'll be able to understand where your real emotional energy is coming from. It will become clear that it really isn't about some smaller issue at hand. The best part is that your mom will be able to do this, too. That should really make a difference if you both become aware, don't you think? What a gift!" Mrs. Kaufmann explained.

Mrs. Edgar just sat back and watched Mrs. Kaufmann frame it into a safe, positive package for her daughter, and remained quiet and hopeful.

Stacey sat thoughtfully and calmly. She finally responded, "That would be such a relief. It would be so nice to get ungrounded for a change, too," she said, looking at her mother a little sheepishly. She didn't want to jinx the positive flow of the conversation, but she just had to say that.

Mrs. Kaufmann knew she spoke honestly but wasn't sure if that was going to fire her mother back up. She immediately laughed and added, "Spoken like a true teenager!"

Mrs. Edgar had paused at first, but then laughed at Mrs. Kaufmann's comment, too. She witnessed her own feelings of defensiveness react first, and then she saw how Mrs. Kaufmann's comment helped lighten the moment with a little humor. She saw how she de-personalized it from what felt like a personal attack of her as a bad parent, to just one of those normal things that every teenager does. "I know counseling will help us both, so I will make our appointments when I get home. Did you say you thought we should both start out with our own private sessions?" she checked.

Stacey interjected immediately, "That's definitely what I want!"

"Good, you will both be happy you did this. A good clearing every now and then is important in life. We too often believe what we think is right, just because we think it," she pointed out, laughing. "So, are we good?" Mrs. Kaufmann brought the meeting to an end.

Mrs. Edgar immediately said, "I'm great—how 'bout you, Stace?"

Stacey smiled really big. "I am too. Thanks, Mrs. Kaufmann."

They all stood as Mrs. Kaufmann said to them both, "I just love the moments when I get to see children and their parents reconnect and remember how much they do love each other. You two gave me my gift for the day! Thank you!"

Stacey asked, "Do I need a pass to go back to class?"

"Probably not, but I'd rather do what's right and give you one. Mr. Lambert shouldn't even acknowledge you when you slip into class."

"Oh, Stace, wait a minute, I brought you your favorite lunch. Here."

"A meatball sandwich?" Stacey lit up, took the bag, and opened it for a smell. She then hugged her mom before she took the pass.

"That hug should make the rest of your day, right?" Mrs. Kaufmann asked.

"No kidding--and thanks again," Stacey said, as she walked out the office door.

Mrs. Edgar then walked toward Mrs. Kaufmann with her eyes filling up again and her arms opened up for a hug. "Thank you," she said softly.

Mrs. Kaufmann smiled, hugged her back, and said, "From one mom to another...you are so welcome. Now, make a plan with a friend for a 'mom play date' after you make those appointments," Mrs. Kaufmann added, "And please let me know how it works out with the counselor you choose, okay? I always like to know the names of good counselors so I can refer them to others in the future."

"I sure will. Have a great day!" Mrs. Edgar said as she left the office.

Mrs. Kaufmann knew her e-mails and voice mails were backed up, but she knew the way triage worked in her office. The most critical always came first. That last crisis for Stacey and her mom needed immediate attention regardless of how long it took, and catch-up would come later. She turned on her computer while she hit the "play message" button on her phone and got back to work.

Finding Common Ground

Driving home from work was usually the first opportunity Mrs. Kaufmann had each day to do her postponed problem-solving. Today's unfinished business was the brainstorming she needed to do for Larry and his father. She wished she could get them to counseling, but his father rejected that outright every time it had been suggested so far. His need for control was so strong that it made sense he wouldn't want to submit to talking about his inner fears. The only problem was he truly didn't understand Larry, and he believed he could whip him into shape by demanding what he wanted. He had no idea how he was impacting his relationship with his son. She realized there were several parts to fixing this puzzle. Mr. Feinberg had his own issues tied to his ego, and keeping control was tiring because he couldn't control Larry. In all reality, Larry couldn't control Larry, but his dad didn't understand that. So she had to deal with the dad's issues, Larry's issues, and their relationship issues.

Mrs. Kaufmann decided to focus on the last one, their relationship. She needed to find some common ground through activities that did not require perfect focus for a young boy with attention deficits, as well as hyperactivity. She thought, *The hobby, sport, or pastime I suggest has to be something that allows physical movement for Larry's activity level without expecting him to stay focused. On the other hand, it can't require a lot of exertion from his dad if he has just worked long hours. It also has to be something that his dad wouldn't feel upset about if Larry didn't learn fast enough, or do well enough. This will be a challenge.*

There simply couldn't be any reason to attach Larry's success to that of his own ego or need for control. Board games had been a bad suggestion for the required focus and lack of activity, but fishing might be good, even though it was only for good-weather days. She needed a few more ideas before Friday came. She also decided she would call Mrs. Feinberg the next day to see how Larry described his new way of thinking to his mom. She would also ask Larry's mother if she had any ideas for her ex-husband's hobbies or interests from the past.

As she drove home, Mrs. Kaufmann thought about Stacey and her mom, as well as other teenage girls she had worked with, who also had complex, argumentative relationships with their mothers. She witnessed these girls completely transform as they moved into adolescence, replacing adoration, love, and respect of their mothers with judgment, criticism, and anger. Suddenly, the daughters had a strong pull away from their family in order to be approved by and connected to their group of girlfriends.

She remembered the exhausting struggle the mothers had endured, imposing limits to keep their daughters safe, in spite of the daughters' resentment, new raging hormones, and intense desire to impress their friends. These girls came to her guidance office regularly to express the anger and frustration they had with their mothers. The girls truly saw them as annoying barricades to their happiness, as if their own mothers were their enemies.

She thought, *If only those moms could have looked at their teenage daughters' resistant behavior as normal for their age. If they didn't take their acts of defiance as painful, personal challenges to their authority, they would have had so much more peace. They formed who they would become into adulthood by this critical look at their parents, putting down the parts they criticized, as a statement of what they would not be, and assimilating the parts they accepted. It was a growing experience, nothing personal.*

The sad part for mothers was that, in spite of this seeming rejection after so much love and sacrifice, the moms felt they had to get tougher in order to enforce the rules that kept their daughters healthy and safe. They felt trapped between their responsibility and their daughters' resistance. The push-pulls usually got worse before they got better unless they sought some form of counseling or intervention to break the pattern.

Mrs. Kaufmann continued her thoughts, comparing this with the father-son relationship, which she knew to be equally complex. She related this to Larry and some of the other students she had helped. Most of the time, the boys' fathers attached their sense of who they were by how their sons performed, feeling a sense of personal achievement through their sons' athletic ability, respectful behavior, or good academic performance. When these sons hit adolescence, they started measuring themselves against their male role models, namely their fathers, assimilating qualities that they liked, and rejecting the ones they didn't. In order to grow up strong, each boy measured his power and strength against his father's. These teenage boys were simply focused on becoming strong and independent adults, but the constant and competitive power struggle with their fathers created hard feelings. In spite of this power struggle and perceived disrespect, the fathers knew they still had to set and enforce limits, even as their push-pulls exhausted them both. Sadly, in many of the cases she remembered, the fathers and sons gradually separated emotionally.

She knew that if these parents could have just removed their egos and stepped back to see the broader picture objectively, they might have been able to see what was motivating them and what their children truly needed. The school counselor had always suggested patience, understanding, and a sense of humor, but there were always those parents who either refused to give an inch or others who simply gave up.

Before she knew it, she was home. She put her purse and briefcase down, let the dog out, and decided to call Mrs. Feinberg right then. Larry's mom answered. Mrs. Kaufmann said, "Hi Mrs. Feinberg, I know this is a terrible time of day to call, I'm sorry. I just had one quick question. Because I think it would be helpful for Larry and his dad to bond this weekend, can you think of anything his dad would enjoy doing with him? I think they need some positive pastimes to share as common ground to rebuild their relationship, don't you?"

"I'm so glad you called, and it's no bother at all. Larry has been talking my ear off about how he's going to be so cool with these boys in his class, but how he just doesn't want to go to his dad's on Friday night. You hit the nail on the head. They do need something positive, because this whole struggle to get him there is draining," Larry's mom confessed. "He has started saying he hates his father and gets mad at me if I try to talk him out of it."

"I could feel that the other day," Mrs. Kaufmann admitted. "I gather baseball ended up being a failure, because Larry couldn't be good enough, and they both came home embarrassed and upset. Can you think of anything else that your ex-husband enjoyed in the past and might want to share with Larry? It needs to be something that would have no pressure or expectations. Building things and construction, fishing and aquariums, music, movies, visits to old fortes, towns, lighthouses? I have thought of a lot of ideas, but they have to click with these two people and fit all the conditions. Are there any that you remember?" Mrs. Kaufmann asked.

"My ex has such a short temper with Larry that I always stayed away from anything he really cared about, so it didn't set him off. We almost have to stick to things he doesn't have any invested interest in, if you know what I mean," Larry's mom explained. "Even fishing didn't work. You'd think Larry couldn't mess it up. But he never baited the hook right or cast it off far enough. John kept saying that Larry made so much noise that he scared all the fish away."

"That makes sense. What about passive-type activities, like going to the movies or collecting baseball cards?" she continued.

"My ex hated going to the movies in general, so anything for kids would drive him up the wall. He's just not a patient man. Larry's older brother and sister don't even try to engage with him anymore. Sadly enough, Larry kept trying, so he kept getting criticized or rejected. I'm sorry I can't help you more," Mrs. Feinberg added.

"You've actually been really helpful, because I see the problem, and I understand Larry so much better now. I'm not going to encourage him to keep trying. I think he needs to bring something to do when he goes to his father's, that's all. That's too bad that his dad is so angry that he can't develop a relationship with his own children. How about his wife, their stepmom?"

"She's really very nice. She just had a baby and works full time. She's very quiet and shy. I even feel sorry for her, but she married him!" Mrs. Feinberg laughed.

"Maybe Larry can do something to help her when he's there, though I don't picture him volunteering to work," Mrs. Kaufmann said with a chuckle. "Well, I have to get going. Thanks so much for giving me your time and the insight I needed. It will help me help Larry. Have a good evening," Mrs. Kaufmann said, as they both hung up.

The next day at school, Mrs. Kaufmann was going into her office and saw Larry coming down the hall toward her. It was between classes, so no one else was in the hall, and he called out to her loudly, "Mrs. Kaufmann, can I please talk to you? Please? I already checked with my teacher and he said it was okay. Please?"

The urgency was apparent, and she quickly motioned to him to come on in. "Sure, what's the matter, Larry?" she asked with concern.

Larry burst into tears as soon as he got into the waiting room. "I was talking to my mom last night about my dad. I told her I didn't want to go there this weekend, because he was just going to punish me all weekend. She told me I had to go because the judge said so. I started crying and I said I'd rather run away than go there. Dad picks on me all the time and I hate him!" he said as he began to sob.

"I'm sorry, Larry. You must've had a bad night. I understand about your dad, and I think we can get through this weekend if we prepare for it. Maybe we can make it better than you think," she offered.

Larry continued, "Well, I got my mom so upset that she decided to call my dad and tell him what I said about not wanting to go there because he always picks on me. Now my dad is even madder than before. He hung up on her, and I really don't want to go there tomorrow night. I'm scared, and I really do want to run away!"

"Well, first of all, you can't run away, because there's no place for you to go, and it would be too dangerous. Your dad would never actually hurt you. He may still be upset about having to come to school, and you may still have to give up the video games, but you will be fine. You've only expressed your feelings, not broken a rule or a law or done anything to him. He's mad about other things in his life, and you're an easy target, that's all," Mrs. Kaufmann assured him.

"Should I do that cool thing like I do to the mean kids who tease me?" he suggested.

"No, that looks disrespectful to adults and especially to your father. He needs to feel respected and in control, so you have to show him that he is, if you are to get along with him. I think that you just need to bring projects, puzzles, or some interesting activities to keep you busy and happy. You pick it, you bring it, and you can make your weekend as interesting as you want to. You really don't have to play video games all weekend at all," Mrs. Kaufmann suggested.

"Like what would I do?" he asked, as his crying stopped and he began to look interested and hopeful.

"How about learning magic tricks? You could download and print some ideas from the computer before you go, like such things as tricks with cards, or cups and coins, or scarves or whatever you have around the house, and you can practice them this weekend. And what about that science project you're supposed to be working on? Don't you have to set up an experiment? Perhaps you can ask your mom or stepmom for ideas and start to plan it out. Find something that you'd really like to do. You also love to draw. Why don't you take one of my 'How to Cartoon' books and 'How to Make Comic Strips' books and try your hand at that? I can even give you drawing paper and a clipboard. Doesn't the weekend sound better already? Maybe you're learning that you don't need to get everyone's approval. Sometimes you just need to be okay being yourself and taking care of yourself. You can make yourself happy. You're a pretty special guy, and I always enjoy your company," she said with a big smile.

Larry smiled back really big, too. "Thank you! I'm going to tell my mom you said so. And I'd really like to borrow those books and paper and clipboard. I'm beginning to get excited about doing all that stuff!" he said, talking very loudly.

"See? You can make yourself happy. You know, if you can go to the library this afternoon, you might be able to check out a book or two on magic tricks or drawing. Just don't leave them at your dad's, so they don't end up overdue," she suggested. "Are you okay now? Are you ready to get back to class?"

"Yup, thanks! I don't need my dad's computer this weekend. I've got better things to do." With that, Mrs. Kaufmann pulled a couple of books off her shelf, put a stack of plain white drawing paper in a clipboard, and handed it all over to Larry. Larry took it from her hands carefully, as if it was the most special gift he'd ever been given. "Thank you so, so, so, so much!" he said, with a huge smile on his face.

"You're so, so, so, so welcome! I hope you give yourself a really happy weekend, my friend. You deserve it."

Larry left the office happy. Mrs. Kaufmann knew it was doubtful that he would get the approval of his father, so she decided that teaching him not to seek it would be the best gift she could give him.

Discussion Points:

- People who like to tease others usually pick on an easy target so they can get a laugh. Others laugh along because they aren't strong enough to defend the victim, or because they are afraid of the one who is teasing. Truly kind people consider the feelings of others and don't hurt them in order to impress others.

- People turn out to be products of all of their past – both the good, and the part they thought was not so good. In the end, it all taught them to be unique.

- We can't control another person's behaviors, but we do need to be responsible for our own.

- We will find the most peace when we stop trying to get approval from others and just learn to find ways to be happy with ourselves.

Reflection Questions:

1. Do your parents and teachers all think differently about what should and shouldn't be done? Is it hard for you to follow different rules in different places? Do you believe everything you think is true because you think it?

2. Can you think of anyone who can't teach you at least something?

3. How hard is it to obey authority figures when you find it hard to respect them?

4. Do you ever think of your parents as just people with the same feelings as you have?

5. What do you tell yourself when you have to do something you really don't want to do? Have you ever tried to be creative and think of a way to be happy even in an unpleasant situation?

About the Author

Bobbi Rise started out at Ohio University with a dual major of Elementary Education and Special Education, and ended up earning a Master's of Science Degree along with other various certifications throughout her career including Elementary Education (K-8), School Personnel Services (K to College), Substance Abuse Counseling, Mathematics, Computer Science, and Gifted and Talented Education. Additionally, she coordinated a local adult community education program as well as three summer schools. She was the first recipient of the NJ Governor's Teacher of the Year Award, and was also awarded The Bellcorp Teacher Grant along with other educational grants.

Bobbi's first career lasted thirty-four years throughout a full spectrum of educational experiences. She taught every grade level from kindergarten through eighth grade, working with students in basic skills, regular education, and the gifted and talented. She developed and implemented innovative G&T programs, summer school study skills and enrichment programs, and Saturday life-skill programs. She tutored at the high school and college levels as well as for adult literacy. She was the curricular chairperson for both the K-3 and 4-8 schools helping to infuse and coordinate all areas of the district curriculum. She was the only school counselor for a two-school district of approximately 1000 kindergarten to eighth-grade students for thirteen of those thirty-four years, counseling parents, teachers and students through life problems. She was the district's testing coordinator, the district's substance abuse contact person, the character education contact person, and ran various support programs to include peer leadership, peer tutoring, peer mentorship, and group counseling.

Throughout this career, Bobbi spoke before various forums and an array of organizations including a county-wide Convention on Anti-Bullying Best Programs, college forums presenting G&T Programming, as well as various round-tables, parent groups and parent workshops. She was an active member of several professional organizations including the local Consortium of the Gifted and Talented and several local, school, and state counselor consortiums. Her broad educational background, her full range of skilled counseling experiences, and her sincerity and enthusiasm have collectively provided her as a gift to children and adults for over four decades. Her inherent insightfulness and experiential wisdom have been instrumental in helping thousands of people shift their thinking to find their joy in life and their sense of peace and balance.

Bobbi runs a business as a Nationally Certified Life Purpose and Career Coach, which continues to be fueled by her love, passion, and commitment to help others self-actualize. She also became a Certified Clinical Hypnotherapist through a state licensed school to help her help others find their peace. This additional career has afforded her with insight into the conscious and subconscious minds, explaining behavioral motivation to its widest range. She has two highly successful adult daughters and six grandchildren. She lives with her husband in Florida where she runs her business and is active in various organizations, clubs, and volunteer work.